COMMENTARIES FOR BIBLICAL EXPOSITORS

An Annotated Bibliography
of Selected Works

Revised and Enlarged
1993 and 2004

by
Dr. Jim Rosscup
Adjunct Faculty
The Master's Seminary

Kress Christian
PUBLICATIONS

Kress Christian
PUBLICATIONS

P.O. Box 132228
The Woodlands, TX 77393
www.KressChristianPublications.com

Library of Congress Cataloging-in-Publication Data

Rosscup, James E.

Commentaries for Biblical expositors: an annotated bibliography of selected works / by James E. Rosscup. – Rev. and enl.

Originally published in 1966 and later revised in 1983, 1993, and 2004

ISBN 0-9772262-3-9

1. Bible—Commentaries—Bibliography.
2. Bibliography—Best books—Bible. I. title.

Z7770.R67   1993   [BS491.2]   016.2207

ACKNOWLEDGMENTS

I would like to express my deep appreciation to God for His strength and to others who make this book possible.

First my immeasurable gratitude to my wife, Mildred, who graciously supported me in the many hours of study.

Thanks also to the scholars who wrote supporting words— John MacArthur, Jr., Dick Mayhue, Cyril Barber, Harold Hoehner, and Walter Kaiser, Jr.

Thanks to those who spent many hours typing the manuscript—Nancy Martin, Amy Brandenstein, Carole Milam, Christine Dixon and a former student of mine, John Metcalf.

Thanks to Floyd Votaw for his capable assistance as librarian and to Joshua Lee and Lauren Garber for making books available at The Master's Seminary Library.

Gratitude is also due to Stephen Wheeler, former Director of Grace Bookshack, who cheerfully carried out the many phases of production to bring the first edition of this book to fulfillment.

Much appreciation goes to Doug Downer, Director of Grace Books International, who did yeoman work to put the entire expanded new edition into a new type, correct proofs and arrange for publication.

—Jim Rosscup

CONTENTS

FOREWORD

By John MacArthur
Pastor, Grace Community Church
President, The Master's Seminary

Anyone who is committed to the exposition of Scripture knows the tremendous challenge of the study that faces him: the need to reconstruct the historic setting, deal with the language, maintain a consistent theological relationship with the rest of Scripture, unravel the difficult and obscure portions and make all of that study produce a work that is both profound and practical.

I'm convinced that trying to do all of that alone is nothing short of foolish. You need some friends; men who have more insight than you in their various areas of expertise, men whom the Holy Spirit has illuminated, men whom time has proven to be gifted, excellent interpreters of Scripture. Where can one find such a group to work with, such an enlightened, insightful, wise group of friends? I have found such a group of friends with whom I meet every week on the pages of their commentaries. In fact, I probably spend more time with them than I do with any other group. They are my teachers providing the benefit of past illumination and all the Holy Spirit-directed insights of centuries and decades past and present.

I have found commentaries are vital for several reasons. They interpret a given passage in the larger book framework so that there is always recognition of the compelling matter of context. Secondly, they give me the benefit of seeing how each text fits into the author's theological frame of reference; that is, how Calvinists, Arminians, Lutherans, etc. interpret passages. This helps me work through all the arguments that might be made in each given interpretation. Thirdly, commentaries help with the difficult sections. And fourthly, they speed up the process of cross-referencing by suggesting related passages. Time saved, scholarship tapped, illumination shared, problems solved, these and more are the benefits of having such friends. Who wouldn't want to be able to access the best of Christian biblical interpretation throughout the centuries and up to the present in a short time?

Having said all that, there are more commentaries in print than one could or should read. Since time and money is of the essence and there is little benefit to

be gained from collecting or muddling through inept discussions, every expositor is in desperate need of help in selecting the right commentaries. Dr. Jim
Rosscup becomes for us the friend who helps us choose our other friends. This
annotated bibliography of commentaries is so foundational and so necessary
that no student of Scripture who intends to exposit it accurately and effectively
should begin to select his commentary friends until he has spent time first with
my friend, Jim Rosscup, and come through his careful evaluation of the available commentaries on all the books of the Bible.

No man could ever accumulate this information without unrelenting diligence lasting over four decades. This is a treasure and you need to learn to first
make friends with it and it will introduce you to the other friends who will
enrich your life and the lives of those who hear you.

PREFACE

By Dr. Cyril J. Barber
Author, The Minister's Library

When George Barna conducted his poll to determine American attitudes and mores - a poll that was later published in What Americans Believe (Ventura, CA: Regal, 1991) - he uncovered some startling facts. Barna also learned that only 36% of those calling themselves Christians read a single Christian book during the previous year.

When seeking to determine what Americans deemed to be important, family and health topped the list, with leisure time and friends coming second. Church attendance and reading the Bible did not come in third, for only about 50% of those calling themselves Christian found them to be necessary to support their beliefs.

The conclusion reached after interpreting the results of his survey led Barna to make the following comment: While the Bible may be the book most frequently bought (and nearly all homes had at least one copy), it continues to be the least read of any book available today.

These troubling facts recall to mind the situation of the northern tribes of Israel after the division of the kingdom. The Lord, speaking through one of His prophets, said:

"My people perish for lack of knowledge ..." (Hosea 4:6).

Jeroboam 1 (931-910 B.C.) had consecrated as priests any who wanted to buy their way into this office, and as a result there arose a body of individuals who were untaught in the Scriptures and the history of their people. They were blind leaders of the blind. That is why God, speaking this time through Amos, said:

"Behold the days are coming when I will send a famine on the land, not a famine for bread or a thirst for water, but rather for hearing the words of the Lord" (Amos 8:11).

And that seems to sum up the way things are in our land today. History has repeated itself. The example set for all who minister the Word of God faithfully is to declare to the Lord's people "the whole counsel of God" (Acts 20:27 AV).

But how is this to be achieved?

Those in the ministry, as well as those preparing for it, need to become people of "the Book." And this is where Professor Jim Rosscup's annotated bibliography is so helpful. For as long as I have known him (i.e., for the past 40 years) he has been a diligent student of the Scriptures. His knowledge of Bible, and of Bible commentaries and related works, is exemplary in evangelical circles. Those students fortunate enough to study under him should make the most of every opportunity and learn from him.

And they, together with those not as fortunate, should avail themselves of this bibliography and attempt whenever possible to acquire the books Dr. Rosscup has recommended.

Dr. Rosscup has condensed a lifetime of personal research into these pages. His comments are judicious and his recommendations reliable. Happy, therefore, are those who will emulate his example and become students of "the Book"!

Obviously a small library of several hundred commentaries cannot be acquired overnight. Those entering the ministry would do well to plan their preaching and secure in advance those books that they will need to use as a part of their sermon preparation. In this way, and over time, their library can grow.

One of the greatest problems facing us in this "information intensive age" is the need to bring people and resources together. I trust that, in the providence of God, what Dr. Rosscup has incorporated into this bibliography will be a means of achieving this goal. To that end I commend this work to the present generation of pastors, as well as to those who are "ministers-in-the-making."

RECOGNIZED LIMITATIONS
OF THE BIBLIOGRAPHY

I. It is selective.

    A. Not all helpful works relating to Bible exposition are included. For example, the bibliography contains few and in some cases no books on such areas as Bible geography, archeology, manners and customs, history, chronology, apochrypha and pseudepigrapha, versions, alleged discrepancies or problem texts, etc. Scores of specialized works in systematic and biblical theology are of immeasurable help in Bible exposition, but these are not noted here. Then there are the invaluable helps in dictionaries, encyclopedias, works on certain limited portions of Scripture (i.e., like Marcus Rainsford on John 17, *Our Lord Prays for His Own*; Erich Sauer, exposition of Hebrews 12 in his work *In the Arena of Faith*, etc.), books on specialized subjects like Bible miracles, parables, types, humor, plants, birds, women, promises, the Flood, the Law, the tabernacle, characters like Abraham, Moses, Elijah, Paul, Peter, the speeches (as in Acts), the cities of the New Testament (William Ramsay's, Merrill Unger's and Colin Hemer's works, etc.). Only a few of such books are included.

    B. Not even all helpful commentaries are included. The list is very selective in this sense and could be greatly expanded. There are various reasons for omitting works which may be deemed important by some who may read the list. First, the compiler of the bibliography was not seeking to be absolutely exhaustive but to serve the practical purpose of suggesting helpful works for expositors who are seeking to build their libraries. The demand has been so incessant that it was the arranger's opinion that a reasonable list could be made available. Second, some works are not included because, while helpful in themselves, they make no special contribution beyond the commentaries which are listed. Third, it is readily acknowledged that the field is so vast that the compiler may nor be aware of some works which *should* be included. Fourth, some works of great value have undoubtedly been left out inadvertently. Fifth, there has been no attempt to include a large number of Puritan or other reprints. Many are expositions of books and have been recommended highly in lists by such men as Cyril Barber and Charles Spurgeon.

C. Not any work later than 2002 is included with an annotation.

D. Not all editions have been indicated. For example, a foreign edition may be listed although there may be also an American edition. Further, the date, place, and publisher indicated do not necessarily represent the latest or current publication. New editions of some works are continually appearing.

II. It is succinct.

Though an annotation is given for each work, comments are brief in varying degrees. Some books do not receive the fuller entries of which they are worthy. And it is expected that in any such list there will be disagreement among readers as to the relative helpfulness of any given work.

III. Responsible Convictions in the Bibliography

Those who agree that loyalty to God's Word is more than just a claim, as this reviewer is convinced, will appreciate the stand taken in comments about works that deal with Scripture. This author believes that he should tell his readers what they truly can expect in commentaries, that is, let them know if writings genuinely show belief in the reliability of biblical statements, or not. God takes a stand, and those who profess to serve Him ought also to take a firm stand. Being candid about the nature of works, however, can be carried out in a good even is firm spirit.

Another conviction behind this effort is that those who study the Bible are served most responsible and wisely if a list reflects writings *both* recent and old. Some of the best things writers of commentaries have said are in works *before* the present decades, yet some of the most help is in works of very *recent* production. It seems the better choice to include even older writings, in reprint or out of print, for even if out of print many users can find them in theological libraries, or may locate them via used book dealers. To withhold these under the idea that only recent works are of "scholarly" contribution is to withhold much wealth, where a better service can be given to readers. Let us learn from *both* old and new, and give thanks for what is of benefit in *both*.

New Ratings of Commentaries on the 66 Books

The rating is in three categories: (1) detailed exegetical works which may include much technical material; (2) competent expositional surveys, and (3) more predominantly devotional efforts which can include some exposition and, at times, handling of interpretative problems. The rating is based on the reviewer's estimate of how well writers explain the text we have. Works which go aside into speculative theories rather often negative toward a real explanation of the text that is before most readers here, however painstaking their scholarship is in technical matters, may be left out on occasion.

Detailed Exegetical	Expositional Survey	Devotional Flavor

Pentateuch

	Expositional Survey	
	1. J. Sailhamer	
	2. H. Wolf	
	3. C. H. Bullock	
	4. H. Livingston	

Genesis

Detailed Exegetical	Expositional Survey	Devotional Flavor
1. V. Hamilton	1. J. J. Davis	1. W. H. Griffith-
2. G. Wenham	2. A. P. Ross	Thomas
3. K. Matthews	3. J. Sailhamer	2. J. Phillips
4. B. Waltke etc.	4. R. Youngblood	3. D. Barnhouse
5. H. C. Leupold	5. D. Kidner	4. A. W. Pink
6. R. Harbach	6. H. Morris	
7. H. Stigers	7. J. Boice or T. Epp	
8. G. Aalders	8. L. Wood	

Exodus

Detailed Exegetical	Expositional Survey	Devotional Flavor
1. F. Bush	1. J. J. Davis	1. J. Currid
2. W. Kaiser	2. J. Mackay	2. B. Ramm
3. N. Sarna (Lib)	3. R. Youngblood	3. A. W. Pink
4. B. Childs (Lib)	4. R. A. Cole	4. Peter Enns
5. C. Houtman	5. J. Hanna	5. M. Bentley
6. C. Keil/F. Delitzsch		6. F. B. Meyer

Detailed Exegetical	Expositional Survey	Devotional Flavor

Leviticus

1. M. Rooker	1. R. L. Harris	1. A. Bonar
2. R. K. Harrison	2. F. Lindsey (BKC)	2. S. Schultz
3. G. Wenham	3. D. Kidner	
4. Milgrom (Lib)	4. L. Goldberg	

Numbers

1. G. Wenham	1. S. Maarsingh	1. J. Philip
2. R. K. Harrison	2. D. Kidner	
3. J. Milgrom (Lib)	3. R. Allen	
4. G. Gary (Lib)	4. T. R. Ashley	
	5. R. A. Cole	

Deuteronomy

1. P. Craigie	1. R. K. Harrison	1. S. Schultz
2. E. Merrill	2. J. S. Deere	
3. J. A. Thompson		
4. C. Wright		
5. S. Driver (Lib)		
6. J. Ridderbos		

Joshua

1. M. Woudstra	1. J. D. Davis	1. Dale Davis
2. R. Boling/	2. C. Goslinga	2. R. K. Hughes
G. Wright (Lib)	3. Paul Enns	3. F. Schaeffer
3. J. Bright	4. A. Cohen	4. A. Johnson
	5. D. Campbell	5. W. G. Scroggie
	6. A. W. Pink	6. F. B. Meyer

Judges

1. D. Block	1. Paul Enns	1. C. Barber
2. L. Wood	2. C. Goslinga	2. Dale Davis
3. A. Cundall/	3. F. Lindsey	3. F. B. Meyer
L. Morris		

Detailed Exegetical	Expositional Survey	Devotional Flavor
Ruth		1. C. Barber
1. F. Bush	1. Paul Enns	2. J. V. McGee
2. D. Block	2. J. J. Davis	
3. E. Campbell	3. E. J. Hamlin	
(Lib)	4. R. Hubbard, Jr.	
4. A. Cundall/	5. A. B. Luter	
L. Morris	6. C. Goslinga	
5. D. Atkinson	7. J. Reed (BKC)	
I, II Samuel		
1. R. D. Bergen	1. J. C. Laney	1. C. Barber
2. M. J. Evans	2. E. Merrill (BKC)	2. F. B. Meyer
3. R. P. Gordis	3. L. Wood	
4. C. F. Keil	4. J. J. Davis/	
	J. Whitcomb	
	(Hist. of Israel)	
	5. J. C. Baldwin	
I, II Kings		
1. R. Patterson/	1. D. J. Wiseman	1. R. Dilday
H. Austel	2. L. Wood	2. F. B. Meyer
2, P. R. House	3. T. Constable (BKC)	3. L. Wood (Elijah)
3. S. DeVries (Lib)	4. I. Provain	
4. J. Montgomery	5. J. J. Davis	
5. C. F. Keil		
I, II Chronicles		
1. J. B. Payne	1. E. Merrill (BKC)	1. M. Wilcock
2. J. Thompson	2. A. Stewart	2. C Barber
3. M. J. Selman	3. J. Sailhamer (brief)	
4. R. Pratt		
5. J. Myers (Lib)		
6. C. F. Keil		

Detailed Exegetical	Expositional Survey	Devotional Flavor

Ezra/Nehemiah

1. F. Fensham	1. J. C. Laney	1. J. Boice
M. Breneman	2. D. Kidner	2. S. K. Evers
2. E. Yamauchi	3. J. C. Whitcomb	3. D. K. Campbell
3. J. Blenkinsopp	4. J. McConville	(Neh)
4. H. Williamson	5. J. Martin (Ez),	4. C. Barber (Neh)
(Lib)	G. Getz (Neh),	5. H. A. Ironside
5. J. Myers (Lib)	both BKC	6. C. Swindoll (Neh)
	6. A. E. Cundall	7. J. I. Packer (Neh)

Esther

1. M. Breneman	1. J. Baldwin	1. C. Swindoll
2. D. J. A. Clines	2. J. McConville	2. H. A. Ironside
3. C. A. Moore	3. J. Whitcomb (1979)	3. M. Hess
4. A. Cohen	4. F. B. Huey	4. J. V. McGee
5. L. B. Patton	5. J. Martin (Est. BKC)	5. D. Prime

Job

1. F. Andersen	1. E. Smick	1. A. Blackwood, Jr.
2. J. E. Hartley	2. R. B. Zuck	2. D. Thomas
3. R. Alden	(BKC, EvBC)	3. R. Stedman
4. N. Habel	3. D. Garland	4. D. Atkinson
5. E. Dhorme	4. E. Gibson	
6. R. Gordis	5. G. Archer, Jr	
7. A. B. Davidson	6. H. L. Ellisen	
8. F. Delitzsch		

Psalms

1. J. van Gemeren	1. G. Wilson	1. C. Spurgeon
2. D. Kidner	2. A. P. Ross	(1 or 6 vol.)
3. H. C. Leupold	3. R. Davidson	2. J. Phillips
4. J. J. S. Perowne	4. W. G. Scroggie	3. R. Alden
5. P. Craigie, etc.		

Proverbs

1. D. Kidner	1. R. Harris (WBC)	1. J. Draper, Jr.
2. A. P. Ross	2. S. Buzzell	2. E. Woodcock
3. F. Delitzsch	3. R. Alden	3. J. Phillips
4. W. McKane (Lib)	4. D. Garrett	4. W. Mouser
5. M. Fox		

Detailed Exegetical	Expositional Survey	Devotional Flavor

Ecclesiastes
1. J. S. Wright	1. W. Kaiser	1. D. Kidner
2. H. C. Leupold	2. M. Eaton	2. C. Swindoll
3. T. Longman	3. R. Zuck	
4. G. A. Barton	4. D. Glenn	
5. E. Hengstenberg	5. W. Brown	
	6. L. Goldberg	

Song of Songs
1. G. L. Carr	1. J. S. Deere	1. H. A. Ironside
2. R. Gordis	2. P. Patterson	
3. T. Longman	3. C. Glickman	
4. M. Pope (Lib)		
5. D. Kinlaw		

Isaiah
1. J. A. Motyer (Amill)	1. J. Martin (Premill)	1. H. A. Ironside
2. G. Grogan (Premill)	2. J. A. Motyer (Amill)	2. D. Thomas
3. J. Oswalt (Amill)	3. W. E. Vine (Premill)	
4. E. J. Young (Amill)	4. G. C. Morgan	
5. H. Leupold (Amill)	(Premill)	

Jeremiah
1. C. Feinberg (Premill)	1. C. Dyer (Premill, BKC)	1. P. G. Ryken
J. Thompson (Amill)	2. R. K. Harrison (Amill)	2. J. Guest
2. W. Holladay (Lib)		3. D. Kidner
3. F. B. Huey, Jr. (1993)	3. I. Jensen (Premill)	
4. T. Laetsch (Amill)	4. F. B. Huey, Jr. (1991)	
5. P. Craigie (Amill)		
6. S. R. Driver (Amill)		

Detailed Exegetical	Expositional Survey	Devotional Flavor

Lamentations

Detailed Exegetical	Expositional Survey	Devotional Flavor
1. F. B. Huey, Jr.	1. R. K. Harrison	1. P. G. Ryken
2. H. L. Ellison	2. I. Jensen (1974)	2. W. Kaiser
3. D. R. Hillers	3. C. Dyer	3. J. Guest
	4. D. Kent	4. F. Schaeffer
	4. A. W. Streane	
	5. J. Calvin	

Ezekiel

Detailed Exegetical	Expositional Survey	Devotional Flavor
1. C. Feinberg (Premill)	1. R. Alexander (Premill)	1. I. Duguid
2. D. Block (Amill)	2. C. Dyer (Premill, BKC)	
3. L. Cooper (Premill)		
4. W. Zimmerli (Lib)	3. Paul Enns (Premill)	
5. W. Eichrodt (Lib)	4. J. Taylor (Amill)	
6. L. Allen (Lib)		

Daniel

Detailed Exegetical	Expositional Survey	Devotional Flavor
1. S. Miller (Premill)	1. J. Pentecost (Premill)	1. J. Phillips, J. Vines (Premill)
2. L. Wood (Premill) E. J. Young (Amill)	2. R. Culver (Premill)	2. K. Gangel (Premill)
3. J. Walvoord (Premill)	3. J. Whitcomb (Premill)	3. S. Olyott
4. J. Montgomery (Lib)	4. J. Baldwin (Amill)	
5. H. C. Leupold (Amill)	5. L. Wood (Premill)	

Minor Prophets Overall

Detailed Exegetical	Expositional Survey	Devotional Flavor
1. T. Laetsch (Amill)	1. BKC entries	1. H. A. Ironside
2. R. Chisholm (Premill)	2. C. Feinberg	2. J. Phillips
3. C. Bullock (Premill)	3. J. Boice (Premill)	
4. C. F. Keil/ F. Delitzsch (Amill)	4. P. Fink (Premill)	

Detailed Exegetical	**Expositional Survey**	**Devotional Flavor**

Hosea

1. F. Andersen/D. Freedman (Amill)	1. J. Riggs (Premill)	1. D. Kidner (Amill)
2. D. Garrett (Amill)	2. C. Feinberg (Premill)	2. G. V. Smith
3. T. McComiskey (Premill)	3. R. Chisholm (Premill)	3. D. Hubbard (With Bands)
4. H. Wolff (Lib)	4. D. Garland (Amill)	4. J. M. Boice (Premill)
5. D. Stuart (Amill)	5. D. Hubbard (Premill)	5. J. Phillips (Premill)
	6. P. Fink (Premill)	6. H. A. Ironside (Premill)

Joel

1. R. Patterson (Premill)	1. R. Allen (Premill)	1. J. M. Boice
2. I. Busenitz	2. C. Feinberg (Premill)	2. H. A. Ironside
3. T. Finley (Premill)	3. R. Chisholm (Premill)	3. J. Phillips
4. D. Garrett	4. P. Fink (Premill)	
5. T. McComiskey (Premill)	5. D. Hubbard (Premill)	
6. H. Wolff (Lib)	6. A. Gaebelein (Premill)	
7. D. Stuart (Amill)		

Amos

1. S. Paul (moderate)	1. C. Feinberg (Premill)	1. J. A. Motyer (Amill)
2. T. Finley (Premill)	2. H. Veldkamp (Amill)	2. J. M. Boice (Premill)
3. G. V. Smith (Amill)	3. D. Garland (Amill)	3. J. Phillips (Premill)
4. D. Stuart (Amill)	4. D. Sunukian (Premill)	4. H. A. Ironside (Premill)
5. T. McComiskey (Premill)	5. J. L. Mays (Lib)	
6. B. Smith	6. G. Hasel (Lib)	
7. F. Andersen/ D. Freedman (Lib)		
8. H. Wolff (Lib)		

Detailed Exegetical	Expositional Survey	Devotional Flavor

Obadiah

1. I. Busenitz (Premill)	1. C. Feinberg	1. J. M. Boice
2. T. Finley (Premill)	(Premill)	2. J. Phillips
3. P. R. Raabe	2. D. W. Baker	3. H. A. Ironside
4. J. H. Eaton	3. P. Beyer (Premill)	
	4. W. L. Baker	
	(Premill, BKC)	
	6. H. Wolf (Lib)	
	7. D. Stuart (Amill)	
	8. R. Chisholm	
	(Premill)	

Jonah

1. F. S. Page	1. J. Hannah (BKC)	1. J. M. Boice
2. J. R. Kohlenberger	2. C. Feinberg	2. T. Epp
3. J. Simon	3. R. Chisholm	3. J. Phillips
4. J. H. Kennedy	4. P. Fink	4. H. A. Ironside

Micah

1. F. Andersen/	1. B. Waltke (Amill)	1. J. M. Boice
D. Freedman (Lib)	2. J. Martin (Premill)	2. J. Phillips
2. K. Barker (Premill)	3. J. R. Riggs (Premill)	3. H. A. Ironside
3. T. McComiskey	4. C. Feinberg	
(Premill)	(Premill)	
4. J. L. Mays (Lib)	5. R. Chisholm	
	(Premill)	

Nahum

1. R. Patterson	1. J. N. Heflin	1. J. M. Boice
2. O. P. Robertson	2. E. Johnson (BKC)	2. J. B. Phillips
3. W. Bailey	3. C. Feinberg	3. H. A. Ironside
4. W. Maier	(WycBC)	
5. J. R. Kohlenberger	4. R. Chisholm	

Habakkuk

1. R. Patterson	1. J. N., Heflin	1. D. M. Lloyd-Jones
2. O. P. Robertson	2. C. Feinberg	2. J. M. Boice
3. W. Bailey	3. J. R. Blue (BKC)	3. J. Phillips
	4. C. Barber	4. H. A. Ironside
	5. R. Chisholm	

Detailed Exegetical	Expositional Survey	Devotional Flavor

Zephaniah

1. R. Patterson (Premill)	1. J. N. Heflin	1. R. Allen (Premill)
2. O. P. Robertson	2. C. Feinberg (Premill)	2. J. M. Boice (Premill)
3. W. Bailey	3. C. Barber (Premill)	3. J. Phillips (Premill)
4. J. A. Motyer (Amill)	4. J. Hannah (Premill, BKC)	4. H. A. Ironside (Premill)
	5. R. Chisholm (Premill)	
	6. P. Fink (Premill)	

Haggai

1. E. Merrill (Premill)	1. J. N. Heflin	1. J. M. Boice
2. P. A. Verhoef	2. F. Lindsey (Premill, BKC)	2. J. Phillips
3. J. A. Motyer (Amill)	3. C. Feinberg (Premill, WycBC)	3. H. A. Ironside
4. T. Laetsch (Amill)	4. H. Wolf (Premill)	
5. J. Baldwin (Amill)	5. R. Wolff (Premill)	
6. D. L. Petersen (Lib)	6. R. Chisholm (Premill)	
7. R. Coggins		

Zechariah

1. K. Barker (Premill)	1. C. Feinberg (WycBC)	1. J. M. Boice
2. C. Feinberg (Premill, God Remembers)	2. F. Lindsey (Premill)	2. H. A. Ironside
3. H. C. Leupold (Amill)	3. J. C. Laney (Premill)	
4. M. F. Unger (Premill)	4. H. Heater (Premill)	
5. J. Baldwin (Amill)	5. J. N. Heflin	

Malachi

1. A. Hill	1. C. Blaising	1. J. M. Boice
2. W. Kaiser, Jr.	2. C. Feinberg	2. G. C. Morgan
3. P. A. Verhoef	3. H. Wolf	3. H. A. Ironside
4. B. Glazier-McDonald	4. G. P. Hulenberger (2:10-16)	
5. J. Baldwin	5. R. Chisholm	
6. R. J. Coggins		

Detailed Exegetical	Expositional Survey	Devotional Flavor

Matthew

1. W. Davies/	1. L. Morris	1. W. H. Griffith-
D. Allison (Lib)	2. W. Hendriksen	Thomas
2. J. Broadus	3. C. Blomberg	2. H. A. Ironside
3. D. A. Carson	4. H. Kent	
4. D. Hagner	or E. Glasscock	
5. C. Keener	5. R. Mounce	
	6. S. Toussaint	
	7. R. France	
	8. L. Barbieri (BKC)	

Mark

1. W. Lane	1. D. E. Hiebert	1. R. K. Hughes
2. J. Edwards	2. R. A. Cole	
3. H. Anderson (Lib)	3. J. Grassmick	
or R. Guelich (Lib)	4. D. Burdick	
4. C. E. B. Cranfield	5. R. Wolff	
5. W. Hendriksen	6. W. G. Scroggie	
6. R. Gundry		
7. H. B. Swete		
or V. Taylor		

Luke

1. I. H. Marshall	1. C. M. Pate	1. R. K. Hughes
2. D. Bock	2. L. Morris	2. M. Wilcock
(longer work)	3. D. Bock (IVP)	3. D. Bock
3. W. Hendriksen	4. J. Martin (BKC)	(NIV Applic.)
4. A. Plummer	5. W. Liefeld	4. W. H. Griffith-
5. R. Stein	6. M. C. Tenney	Thomas
6. J. Green	7. D. Gooding	
7. W. Arndt		
8. J. Fitzmyer		

Detailed Exegetical	Expositional Survey	Devotional Flavor

John

1. D. A. Carson	1. J. C. Laney	1. J. Phillips
2. R. E. Brown	2. H. Kent	2. J. M. Boice
3. W. Hendriksen	3. E. Blum	3. R. K. Hughes
4. F. F. Bruce	4. M. C. Tenney	4. F. B. Meyer
5. L. Morris	5. A. W. Pink	5. J. Mitchell
6. B. F. Westcott	6. W. G. Scroggie	6. J. C. Macauley
7. R. Schnackenburg	7. G. Burge	
9. F. Godet	8. G. Borchert	

Acts

1. F. F. Bruce (NICNT)	1. S. Toussaint	1. J. Stott
2. R. N. Longenecker	2. H. Kent	2. A. Fernando
3. J. Polhill	3. J. MacArthur	3. R. K. Hughes
4. I. H. Marshall	4. G. E. Ladd	4. T. Walker
5. S. Kistemaker	5. W. Larkin	5. J. Phillips
6. C. K. Barrett	6. J. Boice	6. H. A. Ironside
7. E. Haenchen (Lib)	7. W. H. Griffith-	
8. J. D. G. Dunn	Thomas	
9. B. Witherington III	8. C. C. Ryrie	
10. R. Rackham	9. D. J. Williams	

Romans

1. C. E. B. Cranfield	1. R. Mounce	1. R. K. Hughes
(ICC)	2. A. J. McClain	2. A. Johnson
2. D. Moo	3. L. Morris	3. D. M. Lloyd-Jones
3. T. Schreiner	4. J. MacArthur	4. W. H. Griffith-
4. W. Sanday/	5. F. F. Bruce	Thomas
A. Headlam	6. J. Witmer (BKC)	5. D. Barnhouse
(old ICC)	7. J. Stifler	
5. W. Hendriksen	8. J. Stott	
6. J. Murray	9. W. Newell	
7. J. Fitzmyer	10. J. M. Boice	
8. J. D. G. Dunn		
9. E. Harrison		

Detailed Exegetical	Expositional Survey	Devotional Flavor

I Corinthians

1. G. Fee	1. S. L. Johnson	1. C. Blomberg
2. A. Robertson/	(WycBC)	(NIV Applic.)
A. Plummer	2. W. H. Mare	2. D. Prior
3. C. K. Barrett	3. L. Morris or	3. H. A. Ironside
4. R. C. H. Lenski	R. Gromacki	4. G. C. Luck
5. H. Conzelmann	4. J. MacArthur	
(Lib)	5. D. Lowery (BKC)	
6. B. Witherington III	6. R. B. Hughes	
	7. C. Hodge	

II Corinthians

1. R. Martin	1. H. Kent	1. S. Hafemann
2. C. K. Barrett	2. R. G. Gromacki	(NIV Applic.)
3. P. Barnett (NICNT)	3. L. Belleville	2. P. Barnett (BST)
4. P. E. Hughes	4. C. Kruse	3. A. T. Robertson
(old NICNT)	5. D. Lowery (BKC)	4. A. B. Spencer,
5. D. Garland	6. R. V. G. Tasker	W. D. Spence
6. V. P. Furnish	7. C. Hodge	
7. S. Kistemaker	8. J. W. McCant	
8. F. W. Danker		
9. M. Harris		

Galatians

1. E. D. Burton	1. L. Morris	1. S. McKnight
2. F. F. Bruce	2. J. Stott	2. D. Hubbard
3. J. B. Lightfoot	3. H. Kent	3. L. Strauss
4. T. George	4. R. Gromacki	4. H. A. Ironside
5. R. Fung	5. J. MacArthur	
6. R. Longenecker	6. R. A. Cole	
7. W. Hendriksen	7. E. F. Harrison	
8. J. D. G. Dunn	(WycBC)	
	8. D. Campbell (BKC)	

Detailed Exegetical	Expositional Survey	Devotional Flavor

Ephesians

Detailed Exegetical	Expositional Survey	Devotional Flavor
1. H. W. Hoehner (large work)	1. H. Hoehner (BKC)	1. R. K. Hughes
2. P. T. O'Brien	2. J. MacArthur	2. K. Snodgrass
3. A. Lincoln	3. J. Stott	3. H. A. Ironside
4. F. F. Bruce	4. H. Kent	4. L. Strauss
5. W. Hendriksen	5. D. M. Lloyd-Jones	
6. M. Barth (Lib)	6. A. Martin	
7. T. K. Abbott		
8. B. F. Westcott		

Philippians

Detailed Exegetical	Expositional Survey	Devotional Flavor
1. P. T. O'Brien	1. R. Mounce	1. P. S. Rees
2. G. Hawthorne	2. R. Martin	2. F. Thielman
3. G. Fee	3. H. Kent	3. S. Ferguson
4. J. B. Lightfoot	4. J. MacArthur	4. F. B. Meyer
5. R. Martin	5. D. M. Lloyd-Jones	
6. W. Hendriksen	6. J. M. Boice or J. D. Pentecost	
7. F. F. Bruce		
8. M. Silva	7. R. G. Gromacki	
9. B. Witherington III	8. R. Lightner (BKC)	
10. R. Melick	9. L. Strauss	
	10. J. A. Motyer or D. A. Carson	

Colossians

Detailed Exegetical	Expositional Survey	Devotional Flavor
1. P. T. O'Brien	1. R. G. Gromacki or J. MacArthur	1. D. Garland
2. F. F. Bruce or S. L. Johnson (articles)	2. R. K. Hughes	2. P. S. Rees
	3. H. Kent	3. A. Gannett
3. T. K. Abbott	4. R. C. Lucas	
4. R. Martin (NCB)	5. N. T. Wright	
5. W. Hendriksen	6. N. Geisler (BKC)	
6. J. B. Lightfoot		
7. E. Lohse		
8. M. Harris		

Detailed Exegetical	Expositional Survey	Devotional Flavor

I and II Thessalonians

1. R. L. Thomas	1. J. Stott	1. M. V. Holmes
2. F. F. Bruce	2. R. Mayhue	2. H. A. Ironside
3. I. H. Marshall	3. T. Constable (BKC)	
4. C. A. Wanamaker	4. J. Walvoord	
5. D. E. Hiebert	5. C. C. Ryrie	
6. L. Morris		
7. A. Malherbe		
8. E. Best		
9. W. Hendriksen		

Pastoral Epistles

1. I. H. Marshall	1. H. Kent	1. G. King
2. W. Mounce	2. T. Lea	2. B. Chapell (Titus)
3. G. Knight III	3. R. K. Hughes	
4. J. Quinn and	4. J. Stott (2 Tim.)	
W. Wacker	5. G. Getz (2 Tim.)	
(I, II Tim.;		
Quinn on Titus)		
5. J. N. D. Kelly		
6. C. K. Barrett		
7. W. Hendriksen		
8. G. Fee		

Philemon

1. M. Barth/H. Blanke	1. J. MacArthur	1. R. K. Hughes
2. P. T. O'Brien	(cf. Col.)	(cf. Col.)
(cf. Col.)	2. N. T. Wright	2. P. Rees (cf. Phil.)
3. J. A. Fitzmyer	(cf. Col.)	3. D. Garland
4. J. B. Lightfoot	3. H. Kent (cf. Col.)	4. R. C. Lucas
5. F. F. Bruce (cf. Col.)	4. E. Deibler (BKC)	(cf. Col.)
6. W. Hendriksen		5. H. A. Ironside
(cf. Col.)		
7. R. Martin (cf. Col.)		
8. M. Harris (cf. Col.)		

Detailed Exegetical	Expositional Survey	Devotional Flavor

Hebrews

1. F. F. Bruce	1. L. Morris (EBC)	1. G. Guthrie
2. H. Altridge	2. J. MacArthur	2. A. Murray
3. W. Lane (WBC)	3. R. K. Hughes	3. W. H. Griffith-
4. P. Ellingworth	4. R. Gromacki	Thomas
5. D. Hagner	5. R. E. Brown	
6. B. F. Westcott	6. S. Kistemaker	
7. P. E. Hughes	7. W. Lane (NIBC)	
8. C. Koester	8. L. Morris	
9. H. Greenlee	9. J. D. Pentecost	
	10. J. Owen	
	11. Neil Lightfoot	

James

1. R. Martin	1. D. Moo (Tyndale)	1. D. P. Nystrom
2. P. Davids	2. S. Kistemaker	2. G. King
3. J. B. Mayor	3. H. Kent	3. J. Motyer
4. C. L. Mitton	4. J. MacArthur	
5. J. Adamson	5. R. V. G. Tasker	
6. L. T. Johnson	6. L. Strauss	
7. D. E. Hiebert (revis.)	7. R. Wolff	
8. D. Moo (Pillar)	8. G. M. Stulac	
9. K. Richardson		
10. S. Laws (Lib)		

I Peter

1. E. G. Selwyn	1. C. E. B. Cranfield	1. R. Leighton
2. J. N. D. Kelly	2. R. Mounce	2. F. B. Meyer
3. P. Davids	3. I. H. Marshall	3. K. S. Wuest
4. J. Elliott	4. E. Blum	
5. P. J. Achtemeier	5. A. M. Stibbs	
6. W. Grudem	6. R. Raymer (BKC)	
7. D. E. Hiebert or	7. L. Barbieri	
S. Kistemaker		
8. J. R. Michaels		
9. B. Reicke		
10. C. Bigg		

Detailed Exegetical	Expositional Survey	Devotional Flavor

II Peter

1. J. N. D. Kelly	1. R. Mounce	1. D. M. Lloyd-Jones
2. J. B. Mayor	2. M. E. Green	2. K. S. Wuest
3. R. J. Bauckham	3. C. E. B. Cranfield	3. P. Gardner
4. C. Bigg	4. E. Blum	
5. D. E. Hiebert	5. C. Green/R. Lucas	
6. S. Kistemaker	6. G. H. Clark	
7. B. Reicke		

1, 2, 3 John

1. R. E. Brown	1. J. Stott	1. G. Burge
2. D. Burdick (1985)	2. C. C. Ryrie	2. R. E O. White
3. S. Smalley	3. F. F. Bruce	3. G. King
4. I. H. Marshall	4. M. Thompson	4. K. S. Wuest
5. S. Kistemaker	5. D. Burdick (EBC)	
6. B. F. Westcott or A. E. Brooke	6. W. E. Vine	
7. D. E. Hiebert		
8. D. Akin		
9. C. Kruse		
10. T. F. Johnson		

Jude

1. J. N. D. Kelly	1. M. E. Green	1. J. MacArthur
2. J. B. Mayor	2. C. E. B. Cranfield	
3. S. Kistemaker	3. E. Blum	
4. W. Jenkyns	4. R. Wolff	
5. D. E. Hiebert	6. C. Green	
6. R. Bauckham	7. T. Manton	
7. G. Lawlor		
8. B. Reicke		
9. C. Bigg		

Detailed Exegetical	Expositional Survey	Devotional Flavor

Revelation

Detailed Exegetical	Expositional Survey	Devotional Flavor
1. R. L. Thomas (Premill)	1. J. F. Walvoord (Premill)	1. C. Keener (NIV Applic.)
2. G. Beale (Amill)	2. J. MacArthur (Premill)	2. J. Stott (Rev. 2-3)
3. S. Kistemaker (Amill)	3. G. Ladd (Premill)	3. R. Mayhue (Rev. 2-3)
4. I. T. Beckwith (Amill)	4. J. B. Smith (Premill)	4. T. Epp
5. D. Aune (Amill)	5. A. Johnson (Premill)	5. J. Phillips
6. R. Mounce (Amill)	6. L. Morris (Amill)	
7. G. R. Beasley-Murray (Amill)	7. W. Newell (Premill)	
8. P. E. Hughes (Postmill)		

COMMENTARIES ON THE WHOLE BIBLE

I. SYNTHETICAL

This section relates to commentaries of a more general, synthetical, survey-type treatment.

Baxter, J. Sidlow. *Explore the Book*. 6 volumes. Grand Rapids: Zondervan, 1960. Also available unabridged in I volume, 1966.

Here is one of the best syntheses in lucid exposition by an outstanding and beloved Bible conference teacher of England who has had a wide ministry in the United States. There is a helpful overall view of each book in the Bible. The 1,600 page work is the result of more than 30 years of preaching. His treatment of Zechariah is very fine, and he is exceptionally good on Ephesians also.

The Beacon Bible Commentary. 10 volumes. Kansas City, MO: Beacon Hill, 1964-1968.

This major work of the Nazarene Church offers its readers a paragraph by paragraph (but not always verse by verse) study of Scripture with the King James Version text printed in bold face type. Though there is considerable use of the Hebrew and Greek, the commentary is primarily calculated to be an aid to the average layman. Among the top scholars in the Nazarene Church who contributed to the commentary are Drs. Ross Price (Isaiah) and Paul Gray (Jeremiah) of the Point Loma College (Nazarene).

Believers Church Bible Commentary. Various Vols. Scottsdale, PA: Herald Press.

One finds a series geared more for lay readers and pastors wanting simple and broad explanation with some principles made plain. Vols. are helpful at times, not consistently, through a Bible book, and sometimes with material that does not reflect broad investigation. Frequently problem texts are passed over, and writers often do not show awareness of prophetic possibilities beyond their own amillennial perspectives, or problems premillennialists would raise hermeneutically. This reviewer would go to many other works, expecting more frequent help. But for more elemental survey and practical issues (at times) products in this series offer some help.

The Bible Speaks Today. Downers Grove, IL: IVP, 1986ff.

Here are volumes attempting to give survey expositions of Bible books in a lucid way that explains passages concisely, deals with some problems, and seeks to show the practical import of principles. Writers often draw on considerable scholarly help for a competent evangelical product. Joyce Baldwin does The Message of Genesis 12-50 (1986).

Derek Kidner contributes Love to the Loveless (Hosea) and A Time to Mourn and a Time to Dance (Ecclesiastes). Michael Wilcock is fairly helpful on Chronicles, John Stott very good on Galatians and Ephesians, R. C. Lucas vital on Colossians and Philemon, etc. For lay readers and pastor-teachers desiring a readable tracing of the chain of thought, the volumes often offer much that refreshes.

Bible Study Commentary. **Grand Rapids: Baker, 1969.**

This is a popular, usually brief set of evangelical commentaries designed for lay people but offering simple, quick surveys even for preachers, leaders of Bible groups, etc. The authors are well-known scholars, for the most part: Leon Wood (Daniel), Alan F. Johnson (Revelation), Leon Morris (Hebrews), Howard F. Vos (1, 2 Samuel), etc. Competence in aware scholarship is wedded with simplicity in synthesis, with comments of worth on some of the main problem texts.

Brown, Raymond, et al, editors. *The New Jerome Biblical Commentary.* **Englewood Cliffs, NJ: Prentice Hall, 1990. 1,475 pp.**

After 22 years this update of the Jerome Biblical Commentary has appeared to account for recent learning. It offers some of the cream of Roman Catholic scholarship on commentary and special articles on topics such as the Pentateuch, wisdom literature, prophetic scripture, apocalyptic, Hebrew poetry, apocryphal sources, Dead Sea scrolls, other Jewish literature, text and versions, modern Old Testament criticism, biblical archaeology, and religious institutions of Israel. It is about 60 per cent a replacement.

Bruce, F. F., General Editor, *The International Bible Commentary.* **1 volume. Revised edition. Grand Rapids: Zondervan, 1986. 1st published in 1979 as The New Layman's Commentary.**

The old edition of this evangelical work used the RSV, the new version the NIV. Some of the writers on books are: Genesis (H. L. Ellisen), Psalms (Leslie Allen and John W. Baigent), Jeremiah (Donald Wiseman), Ezekiel (F. F. Bruce), Matthew (Ellisen again), Romans (Allen again), Hebrews (Gerald Hawthorne), Revelation (Bruce again). The book has introductory articles on the Old Testament and the New Testament and updates each 1979 article's bibliography. The product is aimed at lay people. It skips some verses and often is too thin. There is some focus on leading problem verses, as Isaiah 7:14.

Carter, Charles W. (Ed.). *The Wesleyan Bible Commentary.* **6 volumes. Grand Rapids: Baker.**

Wesleyan scholars highly respected in nine evangelical denominations contributed to this attempt to make relevant in the 20th century scene the traditions of John Wesley and Adam Clarke. It is done with spiritual flavor and aware scholarship. Three volumes deal with Old Testament, three with the New Testament.

Crossway Classical Commentary. **Wheaton, IL: Crossway Books.**

The purpose is to reprint certain classic, old-time commentaries such as Thomas Manton's work on Jude. One gets quite an amount of good comment in using such works along with more recent and usually far better all-around commentaries on exegesis and application, minus some of the wandering.

Darby, John N. *Synopsis of the Books of the Bible.* **2nd edition. NY: Loizeaux, 1950.**

Brief surveys of all 66 books (Genesis, pp. 20-83; Exodus, 84-143, etc.). Darby seeks only to give a short synopsis of the main subjects in each book, often so cursory it is of little use except as the most elemental summary for a beginner. The conviction is pre-millennial, as in Isaiah 64-65, Jeremiah 31-32, 33, Ezekiel 45-47, Daniel 2, 7, Rev. 3:10, chapter 20, etc.

Eason, Lawrence. *The New Bible Survey.* **Grand Rapids: Zondervan, 1963.**

A 544-pp. popular-level evangelical work written as a survey for beginning students of Scripture which provides much helpful material for teachers. It is very useful.

Elwell, Walter, editor. *Evangelical Commentary on the Bible.* **Grand Rapids: Baker, 1989. 1,229 pp.**

The one-volume work is designed to help those without technical training understand, an aim already fulfilled by several commentaries which also were not done for scholars. Writers from many viewpoints are included, with no aim at unity (p. viii). Some of the better writers are: Genesis and Ezekiel (Victor Hamilton), Leviticus and Ezra/Nehemiah (Louis Goldberg), Joshua and Judges (Andrew Bowling), Ruth (R. K. Harrison), I and II Samuel (Herbert Wolf), Proverbs (R. K. Harrison), James (Douglas Moo), and Johannine Epistles (James B. DeYoung).

Focus on the Bible Commentaries. **Geanies House, Fearn, Ross-shire, Scotland: Christian Focus Publications.**

All of the vols. are of a survey type, usually well-organized to provide fairly good expo-sition to pastors wanting simple material, students seeking lighter discussion, or lay read-ers looking for refreshment in principles dealt out lucidly and quickly. One encounters very debatable opinions such as allegorizing by Brooks on the Song of Songs. In some cases very profitable, contributing exposition is consistent, as by R. Mayhue on the Thessalonian Epistles. On prophecy, such treatments as Fyall's on Daniel can really steer one afield into guesswork about the time or form of fulfillment the words convey, show-ing no grasp of a good natural hermeneutic to support in any solid way claims of what details mean.

Halley, H. *Halley's Bible Handbook.* **Revised edition. Grand Rapids: Zondervan, 1992. 860 pp.**

A much-used older evangelical handbook bringing together a brief commentary on Bible books, some key archaeological findings, historical background, maps, quotes, etc. It is helpful to a lay Bible teacher, Sunday School leader, or pastor looking for quick, perti-nent information on a Bible book. This is the 72nd printing somewhat revised. Halley packed in much information. Unger's is better overall, but that is not to say that Halley's will not provide much help on basic information.

Henry, Carl F. H. *The Biblical Expositor.* **3 volumes. Philadelphia: Holman, 1960.**

Sixty-five conservative scholars teamed up to produce this work which has brief outlines and gen-eral surveys of the Bible books. Authors are men like H. C. Leupold, Edward J. Young, Merrill C. Tenney and Merrill F. Unger. It is a good, broad synthesis, authored by outstanding men.

Holman Commentary. **Nashville: Broadman & Holman.**

A number of Bible books are represented now. Readers get a very well-packaged assortment of survey charts, main principles, panels, and cursory remarks on passages running through a Bible book. Generally comments offer help in a broad treatment, not elucidating a lot, and skipping much. Other series will provide more substance to those wanting material that addresses issues more fully and frequently. Those desiring simple survey attractively presented in a readable flow will get benefit here, but would draw more from the NIV Application Commentary, or any number of other reasonably simple expositions, old and new.

Interpretation. **Louisville, KY: John Knox Press.**

The emphasis is on literary and theological points, offering help for the more academically minded, as Brown does on Ecclesiastes. Candidly, the reviewer did not find nearly as much help overall as in many other works, and realizes that this series at times will not enhance a high view of Scripture reliability that many believe is right. One often gets a scholar's theorizing in place of substantial explaining of what is in a text as it is, and respecting this so that light breaks forth in some way that can be defended as reasonable, while upholding Scripture's veracity.

Ironside, Henry A. *The Ironside Collection* **(Joshua to Revelation). Neptune, NJ: Loizeaux, 1987-89.**

A famous Bible teacher much sought after a few decades back continues to minister after his departure, as A. C. Gaebelein, A. W. Pink, W. H. Griffith-Thomas and others. He is staunchly evangelical, showing good broad surveys based on diligent study, practical turns, even choice illustrations. In prophecy he is premillennial dispensational. The series now reprinted offers Joshua, Ezra, Nehemiah, Esther, Psalms, Proverbs, Song of Solomon, Isaiah through Malachi (various volumes), Matthew-Revelation (again different volumes). Many preachers have found that Ironside works, read along with heavier books on details of exegesis, help them see the sweep of the message and prime their spirits for practical relevance.

John Phillips Expository Commentary. **Grand Rapids: Kregel.**

This expositor's writings have been a simple, often illustrated practical help to many lay people as well as pastors and students. One can find surveys giving highlights in the flow of Genesis, Proverbs, the Minor Prophets, John, Revelation, etc. These serve in lighter study, and accomplish edifying work, while those wanting more meat can find simple panoramas and illustrations, but go elsewhere for more substantial help, as in exegesis and fuller exposition. In some cases, Phillips' material will be too scanty on really unfolding the text, though his illustrations are plenteous (and may be the only attraction that draws those who have access to the substantial works).

Liberty Bible Commentary, **edited by Jerry Falwell et al. Nashville: Thomas Nelson, 1983. 2,721 pp.**

Liberty Baptist issued this evangelical work on the whole Bible. Some contributors are: S. R. Schroder (Genesis), James Borland (Exodus), Paul Fink (Minor Prophets) and Charles Feinberg, visiting lecturer (Revelation). It is frequently cursory but does have good surveys, handles some problems well, and offers a premillennial perspective on long-range prophecy as in the Major Prophets, Minor Prophets, Matthew 24-25, the Thessalonian Epistles, and Revelation.

Luck, G. Coleman. *The Bible Book by Book.* **Chicago: Moody, 1991.**

A brief, simple but capable lay person's look at the historical outline and synthesis of each book by a long-time Moody Bible Institute professor. It is evangelical and premillennial. Sometimes it is fairly good, although overall J. Sidlow Baxter's Explore the Book offers more survey help.

MacDonald, William. *Believer's Bible Commentary.* **Revised edition. Edited by Arthur Farstad. 2 volumes. Nashville: Thomas Nelson, 1990.**

This work, originally issued in 1983, is conservative and premillennial, written to help teachers, preachers and people in every walk of life with different views, explanation and application. The 2-column format runs verse by verse for the most part, usually in a helpfully knowledgeable manner, and there are several special sections such as "Prayer" in Acts and "Legalism" in Galatians. The premillennial view is evident on Acts 1:6, 3:20, Romans 11:26, Galatians 6:16, Revelation 20, etc.

Mays, James L. editor, *Harper's Bible Commentary.* **San Francisco: Harper & Row, 1988. 1,326 pp.**

Eighty-two scholars of the Society of Biblical Literature provide introductory essays and commentaries, The work's essays deal with such topics as reading and interpreting the Bible, Old Testament context, context of Apocrypha and New Testament, how the Bible relates to literature of the ancient near east and the Greco-Roman era, Jewish interpretation, and introductions to sections of the Bible such as Psalms and Wisdom, with a bibliography ending each. The work is shot through with leanings to a JEDP theory on some Old Testament books, Canaanite religious ideas, the view that Genesis 1-2 give conflicting creation accounts, etc.

Morgan, G. Campbell. *An Exposition of the Whole Bible.* **Westwood, NJ: Revell, 1959.**

Morgan deals with the Bible chapter by chapter, with nearly 300 words on each. He devotes 400 pages to the Old Testament, 150 to the New Testament. It is a stimulating broad evangelical coverage of Scripture, if the reader is looking for synthesis rather than detail. Morgan was a master expositor in the early part of this century. Some of the effort is so general it is of little help except to those looking for sketchy treatment. It is evangelical and premillennial. Morgan is better in such works as The Crises of the Christ.

A New Catholic Commentary on Holy Scripture. **Edited by Reginald Fuller et al. Camden, NJ: Thomas Nelson and Sons, 1969. 1,363 pp.**

The work includes more than 30 introductory essays to Old Testament, New Testament and main sections, and surveys of all Bible books by Catholic scholars. Readers can see how Catholics explain passages, especially those where they often differ from Protestant writers on certain doctrines.

New American Commentary. **Nashville: Broadman & Holman.**

This series, employing commentators committed to inerrancy and careful scholarship written (usually) in quite lucid fashion, has flourished in the past decade. It features works on both the OT and NT. Contributors uphold a good standard in explaining passages, grappling with the Hebrew (OT) or Greek (NT) as in word studies and grammar, showing the relevance of customs and background, and resolving problem texts. They strike a good balance between giving synopses on each set of verses and then delving into details verse by verse. In most passages they seriously shed light on meaning, based on diligent study, as Rooker in Lev., Block on Judges, Bergen on 1 and 2 Samuel, Breneman on Ezra, Nehemiah and Esther, and C. Blomberg on Matthew.

NIV Application Commentary. Grand Rapids: Zondervan.

Works vary in this series, according to contributors, but often users gain well-studied synopses on sections of verses within a biblical book, comments on some of the main issues within a set of verses, and later copious suggestions of principles for applying main truths. Some of the better works are by S. Hafeman (2 Cor.), D. Bock (Luke), C. Blomberg (I Cor.), and A. Fernando (Acts). On prophetical books with passages about a blessed future for Israel, or in such a case as the Book of Revelation, one generally encounters blurred, generalized amillennial views that do not handle in any natural sense many of the details in the actual wording, if taken in the most obvious sense that the predictions seem to convey, and the biblical prophetical picture overall anticipates.

Phillips, John. *Bible Explorer's Guide*. Neptune, NJ: Loizeaux, 1987. 274 pp.

This general introductory work, evangelical in nature, has two sections, Hermeneutics and Helps. Under the first are 22 divisions such as studying Words, Figures of Speech, Culture, Context, Types, Parables, Prophecy, Devotional Rule, Application, Christ the Ultimate Key, etc. The section deals with a quick survey of the Bible, summary of Bible history, symbols, helpful books, etc. Phillips is well-known for his Exploring the New Testament series of clear, practical expositions of key books such as John and Romans. He is premillennial.

Preaching the Word. Wheaton: Crossway Books.

The editor of this series is R. Kent Hughes, pastor of the Wheaton College Church and contributor of many vols. that launched and sustained the effort. Some of Hughes' products deal with Mark, Ephesians, Colossians, and Hebrews. Recently Ryken has done Jeremiah and Lamentations. The vols. blend survey exposition with frequent illustrations that will help pastors, students, and lay people who use the treatments as catalysts for growth. The writing is stimulating, and shows messages preached through Bible books.

Richards, Lawrence 0. *The Teacher's Commentary*. Wheaton: Victor Books, 1987. 1,110 pp.

This is an evangelical effort by a Dallas Seminary graduate to survey each book of the Bible and provide special material to help teachers of Sunday Schools, Bible study groups, and pastors teach on different sections. The special features are material to illustrate and apply, definitions of biblical and doctrinal terms, background, maps and charts, and teaching suggestions. Coverage of sections is very broad synthesis, picking out some key points and skipping a lot. Psalms 74-150 are given five and a half pages, Proverbs 10-31 and Ecclesiastes dealt with similarly, etc. Readers can be deeply agitated at how much is by passed. The work is set up in 2 columns with very readable type.

Scroggie, Graham, *Know Your Bible.* **2 volumes. Old Tappan, NJ: Revell.**

The evangelical volumes are divided between the Old Testament and New Testament and include introductions and outlines for each book of the canon. The comments are pithy in the Scroggie tradition.

Smith, F. LeGard. *The Narrated Bible in Chronological Order* **(NIV). Eugene, OR: Harvest House, 1984.**

An evangelical professor at Pepperdine University in Los Angeles sought to arrange the Bible in sequence. He uses black print for Bible verses, red for frequent explanatory synopses, very frequent headings that pin-point concisely the subject of a paragraph, etc. Smith is also known for Out on a Broken Limb (Harvest House, 1986), answering Shirley MacLaine's New Age books *Out on a Limb* and *Crystal Lies* (Vine Books, 1989).

Unger, Merrill F. *The New Unger's Bible Handbook.* **Revised by Gary N. Larson. Chicago: Moody, 1984. 720 pp.**

A former Professor of Old testament at Dallas Seminary, evangelical writer of many scholarly books, did this in his late years. He has sections on each Bible book, archaeology, Major Prophets, Minor Prophets, between the testaments, the four gospels, epistles of Paul, how the Bible came to us, Bible statistics, outline of church history, creation stories, Ur of Abram's day, Egypt, Assyria, the Chaldean empire, demonism, miracles, Bethlehem, Dead Sea scrolls, Corinth, Ephesus, Rome, etc. The work includes more than 20 charts and 30 maps and has color sections. Unger has good material at some points in surveying passages, dealing with certain problems, etc., and handles the long-range prophecies in a premillennial way. Often he is very cursory.

Walvoord, John F. and Roy Zuck (eds.). *Bible Knowledge Commentary.* **2 volumes. Wheaton: Victor Books, 1983-1985.**

A work entirely by Dallas Seminary faculty aiming at a consistent theology, conservative and premillennial. Contributors write on every verse or group of verses, use Hebrew and Greek expertise, deal with problem passages, and provide historical settings. The work varies in quality from book to book as some of the contributors are from departments of biblical expertise and some not. Most books are done well in a concise yet well-informed manner. Notable exceptions at many points are the treatments of Hebrews and John's Epistles, which have strange, different twists on verses, advocating a "non-Lordship salvation."

Welwyn Commentary. **Auburn, WA: Evangelical Press.**

The series serves the purpose of providing readable surveys of Bible books, giving frequent principles and illustrations. It seems primarily useful for those wanting a simple, broad flow through a book, without spending much time on problem verses or giving views (generally). In treatment, it is hit or miss, sometimes up, sometimes down. Writers tend not to be much informed, or informed at all about premillennial interpretations of key biblical passages, as explanations are amillennial and issues blurred. This reviewer does not consider the vols. nearly as helpful in really explaining passages as many other commentaries do. One can compare D. Thomas on Isaiah with J. Alec Motyer in either of his two works on Isa., even with the shorter, less technical effort, and he will see the vast difference in what is explained and what is left out.

Wesley, John. *John Wesley's Commentary on the Bible.* **Grand Rapids: Francis Asbury Press of Zondervan Publishing House, 1990. 612 pp.**

Wesley (1703-1791) originally published Explanatory Notes on the New Testament (1755) and had 3 volumes on the Old Testament (1765-66), 3,682 pp., all told. Here now is a one-volume condensation by G. R. Schoenhals, who for ten years had been editorial director of the Free Methodist Publishing House. Wesley drew a lot of help from works of his day such as Matthew Henry, Matthew Poole, and John Bengel (New Testament). Wesley adds much from his pastoral concern. He felt that Henry's work (6 large volumes) was too long, heavy and expensive for the common person (p. 8). The editor, seeing that Wesley's own work would today cost more than $100, did the abridgement! He left out the Bible text, some of the technical material, and other things to trim the work to about one-sixth.

Westminster Bible Companion. **Louisville, KY: John Knox Press.**

Here is a series which claims to be readable for lay people. When one seriously considers the heavy level of content that comes at times, he can question that. Bruegemann on Isaiah is more for scholarly intake, dealing with setting, exegesis, and theology. Some denials of things many conservatives accept will disturb them. For example, Bruegemann denies that NT authority in Matt. 1 can be part of validly explaining Isaiah 7:14. Clements on Ezekiel and Long on Matthew are other examples of skeptical opinion given in place of explanation that enhances parts of God's Word. In contrast to all those who think they profit from such efforts, many will turn to what they regard as sources that uphold the Scripture more consistently.

II. ANALYTICAL

Commentaries here are of a more detailed, specific nature in discussing the text of Scripture.

The Anchor Bible. **ed. by W. F. Albright and D. N. Freedman. NY: Doubleday, 1964.**

Several volumes are out in this basically liberal work, The format includes an introduction, original translation, notes and commentary. Speiser's work on Genesis (1964) is an example. Though rejecting the unity of Genesis, he has a lucid translation and notes which abound in rich grammatical, philological and historical value. However, the work sometimes lacks spiritual illumination. The series was conceived with a plan to include Catholic, Jewish, and Protestant authors. There is a wealth of information and fine documentation of rich sources. Some of the work is outstanding, e.g. Jacob Myers (1, 11 Chronicles and Ezra-Nehemiah), Raymond Brown (John), etc.

Barnes, Albert. *Barnes' Commentary on the Bible.* **Grand Rapids: Baker, 1975rp.**

This includes 16 volumes on the Old Testament, 11 on the New Testament. The New Testament part of this old work was first published in 1832-1851. Various authors contributed. It is evangelical and amillennial. Also see the Kregel reprint (1966) in I volume of 1,776 pages on the New Testament. Often the explanations of verses are very worthwhile.

Bewer, Julius A. (Ed.). *Annotated Bible Series.* **NY: Harper, 1949.**

This is a critical approach by liberal men who use the King James Version throughout.

Bible Student's Commentary. **Grand Rapids: Baker, 1981.**

This is an effort of Baker to offer a translation of the Korte Verklaring, a well-respected conservative commentary among the Dutch in various parts of the globe as early as the 1930's with an updating in some instances in the 50's and 60's. The set is prepared for lay readers without knowledge of Hebrew and Greek, and little grasp of critical issues. Baker has edited the NIV text into the commentary. Even scholars have a healthy respect for the usually solid explanation and exegetical insights reflected here. Some of the contributors are G. Charles Aalders (Genesis, 2 volumes) and A. Noordtzij (Leviticus; Numbers).

Black, M. and H. H. Rowley (eds.). *Peake's Commentary on the Bible.* **New York: Thomas Nelson, 1962.**

The new Peake's has some contributions by good scholars (usually liberal) that are especially helpful at points, e. g. Krister Stendahl (Matthew), C. F. D. Moule (Colossians) and C. E. B. Cranfield (I Peter), as examples. One has to remember the theological perspective that shows up in certain critical presuppositions, as in Matthew, but finds much good comment informed by careful study and wide reading. The old Peake's was edited by Arthur S. Peake (NY. Thomas Nelson and Sons Ltd., 1919, new addition 1937).

The Broadman Bible Commentary. **Edited by Clifton J. Allen et al. 12 volumes. Nashville: Broadman Press, 1969.**

Evangelical work from a Southern Baptist press, for ministers and lay people, using the RSV. It holds the high reliability of Scripture but sometimes buys into "priestly" material theory etc. in the pentateuch (1, 109, 120 etc.). It says "there is no way that the days of Genesis I can be held to 24 hours" (1, 121). But it upholds the trustworthiness of the material as tradition that is true, as Genesis 2:4bff. The work favors an amillennial view (volume 12, p. 350).

Bullinger, E. W. *The Companion Bible.* **6 volumes. London: Lamp. One-volume edition became available in the United States, 1964.**

By a church of England clergyman who produced the famous Critical Lexicon and Concordance to the Greek New Testament. When Bullinger died in 1913, the companion Bible was completed only up to the middle of John. His followers finished the work with comments from his prolific writings elsewhere. The name comes from the fact that a wide margin is left to be a companion to the text, and the work is intended to be the Bible reader's companion. Bullinger was an ultra-dispensationalist, but his system does not usually shine through noticeably in the work. The C.B. is not especially helpful today because so many other works are better.

Calvin, John. *Calvin's Commentaries.* **22 volumes. Grand Rapids: Zondervan, 1979rp.**

Calvin was not only a great theologian but also a great expositor, and his insight into Scripture contributed to his grasp of doctrinal truth. His commentaries are deep in spiritual understanding, usually helpful on problem passages, and refreshing in a devotional sense to the really interested reader. He usually offers good help on a passage. The present work skips Judges, Ruth, Samuel, Kings, Chronicles, Ezra, Nehemiah, Esther, Job, Ecclesiastes, Song of Solomon, II and III John and Revelation. Calvin is amillennial on long-range prophecy, but in other respects usually has very contributive perception on passages and doctrinal values edifying to the believer. He also can be very wordy, but the serious and patient glean much.

The Cambridge Bible Commentary. **Cambridge: University Press, 1965.**

Several volumes are now out in this set which follows the New English Bible translation. The Cambridge Bible Commentary is aimed more at the general reader, with comments which are exegetical but brief. The brevity renders it less valuable to the student who wants a more thorough study which he can obtain elsewhere. There is little original contribution.

Clarke, Adam, 1760-1832. *A Commentary and Critical Notes*. 6 volumes. NY: Eaton and Mains (n.d.).

This old, conservative Wesleyan Methodist work is good devotionally and aggressive for righteous living. Laypeople can find it still valuable today. It is Arminian in viewpoint and thus helpful, for example, in showing the reader how this approach deals with texts involving the eternal security question. The work contains much background material from many sources on all books of the Bible.

Ellicott, Charles J., 1819-1905. *Commentary on the Whole Bible*. 8 volumes. Now published in 4 volumes. Grand Rapids: Zondervan, 1959.

Though often scanty, the work edited by a brilliant scholar is sometimes very helpful. Ellicott was an Anglican bishop. The New Testament part is more valuable. The work dates back to 1897 and is verse by verse, consisting of 2,292 pp. Ellicott was an outstanding Anglican conservative scholar of the 19th century in England. He also wrote critical commentaries on Galatians, Ephesians, Philippians, Colossians, Thessalonians and Philemon. Different scholars here contributed on different scripture books, Famous names included are George Rawlinson (Exodus), H. D. M. Spence (I Samuel), E. H. Plumptre (Isaiah, Jeremiah, Lamentations, Acts, 2 Corinthians), W. Sanday (Romans, Galatians), Alfred Plummer (2 Peter, Jude), etc. A one-volume condensation edited by John Bowdle is available (Zondervan, 1971, 1,242 pages).

Everyman's Bible Commentary. **Chicago: Moody Paperback, 1960ff.**

These are less expensive, concise evangelical expositions by such men as Hiebert on I Timothy, Pfeiffer on Hebrews, Coder on Jude, and Ryrie on Revelation. In prophecy it follows a premillennial pattern.

Exegetical and Expository Commentary. **Grand Rapids: Baker.**

As its name claims, this series provides careful exegetical details by scholars with expertise and also meaningful exposition that assists on passages. One example is J. Alec Motyer et al on Zephaniah, Haggai and Zechariah. On long-range prophecy, the tendency is to explain details for Israel's eventual blessing in amillennial fashion, generalized in the future and not in a millennial regathering of Israel to enjoy such a boon after Christ's Second Advent.

Gaebelein, Arno C., 1861-1945. *The Annotated Bible.* **9 volumes. NY: Our Hope Magazine, 1913-1921. Also published by Loizeaux.**

This dispensationally oriented work is not verse-by-verse, but deals with the exposition on a broader scale, treating blocks of thought within the chapters. Cf. also Arno C. Gaebelein, Gaebelein's Concise Commentary on the Whole Bible (I Volume, Neptune, NJ: Loizeaux, 1985), the Annotated Bible revised. The author was a popular evangelical Bible teacher of the first part of the century, much like H. A. Ironside in his diligent but broad, practical expositions of Bible books. Gaebelein was premillennial and dispensational, and editor for many years of Our Hope Magazine.

Gaebelein, Frank E., ed. *The Expositor's Bible Commentary.* **12 volumes. Grand Rapids: Zondervan, 1979-1992.**

The top general work of scholarly evangelicalism by 72 writers from several countries who hold to divine inspiration and premillennialism (for the most part). They use the NIV. The associate ed. is J. D. Douglas, and consulting eds. are Walter C. Kaiser, Jr., Bruce K. Waltke, James Boice and Merrill C. Tenney. The work represents study abreast of recent literature, issues and views in exposition. Some very skilled, established scholars are among the contributors, men on introductory matters such as Gleason Archer, Jr., G. W. Bromiley, Donald Guthrie, R. K. Harrison, Carl Henry, Harold Hoehner, Walter Kaiser, Bruce Metzger, Roger Nicole, Robert L. Saucy, Bruce Waltke, Andrew Walls, Donald Wiseman, and Edwin Yamauchi. Scholars on New Testament books are such men as M. C. Tenney (John), R. N. Longenecker (Acts), James Boice (Galatians), Homer Kent, Jr. (Philippians), Robert L. Thomas (Thessalonians), D. E. Hiebert (Titus), Leon Morris (Hebrews), Edwin Blum (1, 11 Peter, Jude), and Alan Johnson (Revelation).

Gill, John. *Gill's Commentary.* **6 volumes. Grand Rapids: Baker, 1980 from 1852-1854 edition (London: William Hull).**

Gill (1697-1771), a pastor of England, wrote these which are two-column pages, ca. 900-1,000 pages per volume, Originally they were 9 volumes, folio. He also wrote Body of Divinity, 3 volumes, and several other volumes. His commentary is evangelical, wrestles with texts, is often wordy and not to the point but with worthy things for the patient who follow the ponderous detail and fish out slowly what his interpretation of a text is. He feels the thousand years in Revelation 20 cannot begin until after the conversion of the Jews and the bringing in of the fullness of the Gentiles and destruction of all antiChristian powers (volume 6, p. 1063) but in an amillennial sense of new heavens and new earth coming right after Christ's second advent (1064-65), and the literal thousand years of binding at the same time. He feels the group that gathers against the holy city at the end of the thousand years is the resurrected wicked dead from the four quarters of the earth (i.e. from all the earth, etc. (1067)).

Grant, F. W., 1834-1902. *The Numerical Bible.* **5 volumes. NY: Loizeaux, 1894-1903.**

This premillennial-dispensational work gives good expository notes, but they are irregular. It omits several poetic books of the Old Testament. There is a stress upon the significance of numbers in Scripture. Grant also authored a book called The Numerical Structure of Scripture (Loizeaux, 1899).

Guthrie, D. et al. *The Eerdman's Bible Commentary*, **i.e. New Bible Commentary Revised. 3rd edition. 1 volume. Grand Rapids: Eerdmans, 1970. 1,310 pp.**

An evangelical updating (since the 1st edition, 1953, 1,119 pages) of the New Bible Commentary edited by F. Davidson et al. Some of the best known commentators are: 0. T. Allis (Leviticus), Gleason Archer, Jr. (Micah), Joyce Baldwin (Ruth, Esther), G. R. Beasley-Murray (Ezekiel, Revelation, etc.), F. F. Bruce (Judges, Acts, Thessalonians Epistles, etc.), R. K. Harrison (Deuteronomy), Derek Kidner (Isaiah, amillennial), Meredith Kline (Genesis), 1. H. Marshall (Luke), R. P. Martin (Romans, Ephesians), Leon Morris (John's Epistles), etc. In the revision, 37 commentaries on books are by different scholars, and five articles are new. Extensive revision occurs in other respects, and the work uses the RSV rather than the KJV.

Henry, Matthew, 1662-1714. *Commentary on the Whole Bible.* **6 volumes. Revell. Now out in one-volume abbreviated form edited by Leslie F. Church, Zondervan, 1961, and other more recent one-volume editions.**

This evangelical work, devotional in character, has been in constant demand for about 280 years. Its insight into human problems is great, but it often does not deal adequately with problems in the text. The one-volume form eliminates the Biblical text and is thus less bulky. It has sold very well. The late Wilbur M. Smith, internationally noted Bible teacher, seminary professor and lover of books, tabbed this "The greatest devotional commentary ever written" (cover, I volume edition). Henry was born in a Welch farmhouse, studied law, and became a Presbyterian minister near London. He wrote this commentary in the last 13 years before he died at 52 in 1714. The first of six volumes was published in 1708. He completed through Acts, and the rest of the New Testament was done by 14 clergymen (p. ix, I volume edition), Another I volume edition, unabridged but in 3 columns and small but clear print, is Matthew Henry's Commentary on the Whole Bible (Peabody, MA: Hendrickson, 1991, 2,248 pages).

Hermeneia. **Philadelphia: Fortress Press.**

Technical exegetical detail and strong acquaintance with a plethora of scholarly learning over the centuries, and today, are features. The series is for scholars, and leans to the liberal perspective. Some examples of helpfulness at times to advanced students are Achtemeier on I Peter and Altridge on Hebrews. Due to the complex academic nature of contents, it serves the more trained and advanced in some details, but is not as serviceable for most expositors as many other works are. One will learn not to be surprised to find statements that call scriptural reliability into serious question, and can substitute scholarly leanings in place of really explaining the text in straight-forward ways that recognize connections some regard as sensible in passages. The patient, advanced inquirers will glean out much from the wealth of details presented, and gain a wider perception on scholarly thought on verses, whether they agree with conclusions or not.

Hubbard, David A. and Glenn W. Barber, gen. eds. *Word Biblical Commentary.* **Waco, Texas: Word Books, Publisher, 1982.**

This recent, sometimes liberal, sometimes evangelical work, with many volumes already out, projects 52 volumes and an imposing list of around 50 scholars, many of them internationally known. The Old Testament editor is John D. W. Watts, the New Testament editor Ralph P. Martin. Each contributor prepares his own translation of the biblical text and fits his exegesis to this, yet makes the technical, scholarly matter understandable and relevant for seminary students (in some places more advanced ones) and pastors as well as professional scholars and teachers. The introductions and commentaries on individual books are done in fairly good detail, even with well-organized excursuses on larger problems and lengthy bibliographies of books and journal literature. For the verse by verse comment, Hebrew or Greek words or phrases are printed and the explanation of their sense follows. Often, good detail is devoted to different views on the sense of a passage, e.g. F. F. Bruce on I Thessalonians 4:4, whether skeuos ("vessel") means a man's wife or his body. Other contributors are such names as Gordon Wenham (Genesis, 2 volumes); Peter C. Craigie (Psalms 1-50; Marvin Tate, Psalms 51-100, and Leslie Allen, 101-150); G. R. Beasley-Murray (John); James D. G. Dunn (Romans); Ralph Martin (2 Corinthians, James); Richard Longenecker (Galatians); Robert Mounce (Pastoral Epistles.); Wm. Lane (Hebrews), etc. The venture varies on different books as is true of any set of such breadth.

The International Critical Commentary (ICC). Edinburgh: T. & T. Clark, 1885-1964.

This usually liberal work was begun in 1885 under the editorial supervision of C. A. Briggs, S. R. Driver and Alfred Plummer. The intention was to provide for English readers a Bible commentary equal in scholarship to the critical German productions of that day. The emphasis is critical and philological. Volumes have now been produced on all Old Testament books, and among better ones available are: Kings (Montgomery); Ezekiel (Cooke); Judges (Moore) and Daniel (Montgomery). In the New Testament, the better works are: Luke (Plummer); Romans (Sanday and Headlam; later replaced by Cranfield's 2 volumes); Galatians (Burton); First Corinthians (Robertson and Plummer); St. Peter and St. Jude (Bigg). The technical nature of the work renders it quite helpful to the trained expositor, especially in detailed problems. In quality it varies. Recently Davies and Allison have three often highly helpful volumes out on Matthew and I. H. Marshall has made a fine contribution on the Pastoral Epistles.

International Theological Commentary. Grand Rapids: Eerdmans.

Hamlin on Ruth is an example of how this series can do fairly well in giving substantial light on passages. Scholars vary in convictions about biblical matters, sometimes offering a worthy view of these, sometimes discounting them. Used as one among several sources, the vols. can furnish frequent help, even if they do not rate high for consistent contribution when compared with several other works.

The Interpreter's Bible. 12 volumes, ed. George Arthur Buttrick, et al. NY: Abingdon, 1952-57.

A great amount of money was poured into this series which is beautifully printed and has elaborate, often very informative introductions. The work has more than 11,000 pages. It is very liberal. Actually much good material that is presented can be equaled in other commentaries such as the Expositor's Bible Commentary with more done in a satisfying way. But the set has exercised a wide influence over ministers in the United States. Cf. also Layman, Charles M., Editor of The Interpreter's One-Volume Commentary on the

Bible (1-volume, Nashville: Abingdon Press, 1971. 1,386 pp.). This too is a liberal work of brevity by seventy scholars who are Protestant, Roman Catholic, and Jewish, compared with the multi-volume Interpreter's Bible that takes up passages more at length. One also finds articles on historical, literary, linguistic, geographical, archeological and theological areas as related to biblical interpretation, from liberal perspectives.

Jamieson, Robert, A. R. Fausset, and David Brown. *A Commentary on the Old and New Testaments.* **6 volumes. Grand Rapids: Eerdmans, 1961. 1,591 pp.**

This is a helpful old set of 1863 for laypeople and pastors to have because it usually comments at least to some degree on problems. Though terse, it provides something good on almost any passage, phrase by phrase and is to some degree critical in nature. It is evangelical. There is also a 1-volume edition, briefer at some points (Grand Rapids: Zondervan, 1961). Especially in its multi-volume form this is one of the old evangelical works that offers fairly solid though brief help on many verses. Spurgeon said, "It contains so great a variety of information that if a man had no other exposition he would find himself at no great loss if he possessed this and used it diligently" (Commenting and Commentaries, p. 3). Things have changed greatly since this assessment! It is primarily of help to pastors and lay people looking for quick, though usually somewhat knowledgeable treatments on verses.

Lange, John Peter, 1802-1884. *Commentary on the Holy Scriptures.* **12 volumes. Grand Rapids: Zondervan, 1871-1874.**

The treatments of books within this evangelical set vary in importance. Generally, one finds a wealth of detailed commentary, background, and some critical and exegetical notes. Often, however, there is much excess verbiage that does not help particularly. On the other hand, it usually has something to assist the expositor on problems and is a good general set for pastors and serious lay people though it is old.

Maclaren, Alexander, 1826-1910. *Expositions of Holy Scripture.* **25 volumes but now in 11 volumes without abridgement. Grand Rapids: Eerdmans, 1959.**

This evangelical work is both homiletical and expository and is often very good homiletically but weaker otherwise. Helpful in discussing Bible characters, it is weak in prophecy at times because of allegorization. It is not really as valuable today as many other sets for the serious Bible student. The expositions are in the form of sermons.

Morgan, G. Campbell, 1863-1948. *The Analyzed Bible.* **10 volumes. NY: Revell, 1907-1911.**

Morgan was an evangelical master at surveying a book and giving its message within a brief compass. He introduces each book with a chart giving an analysis and synthesis. Revell put it out in a one-volume form in 1959 (see Synthetical), and it is adequate to have the one-volume work, since Morgan is broad in his treatment anyway.

The New Clarendon Bible. **Oxford: Oxford University Press, 1963.**

This commentary uses the NEB as its translation like the Cambridge BC, but is aimed at a higher intellectual level. Thus it is more technical than the CBC.

Nicoll, W. Robertson (Ed.). *The Expositors Bible.* **26 volumes. NY: A. C. Armstrong, 1903.**

Though this work is generally helpful on historical background, it is often not of great assistance on the original text or problem passages. It skips over these many times. It is generally conservative, but not always. The value is greater on some books because the authors have done an excellent work: Kellogg on Leviticus; Blaikie on Joshua and I, II Samuel; Plummer on the pastorals, James and Jude. Some sections are by radical liberals, for example George A. Smith on Isaiah and the Minor Prophets. By and large, the student will do better to use a detailed set like The Expositor's Bible Commentary plus individual best works on the different Bible books or sections of Scripture.

Parker, Joseph, 1830-1902. *The Peoples Bible.* **28 volumes. NY: Funk and Wagnalls, 1888.**

This work, later called Preaching Through the Bible (Baker Book House), is rich in its applications and exhortations, though often not particularly helpful for the reader who is looking for exposition that stays right with the text. Treatment of the texts is sermonic.

Pfeiffer, Charles and Everett Harrison (Eds.). *The Wycliffe Bible Commentary.* **1 volume. Chicago: Moody, 1990rp of 1962 edition. 1,525 pp.**

Conservative and premillennial scholars here have been experts in their fields. The work contains brief introductions and attempts to give a verse-by-verse exposition, though it does skip over some verses. The treatments vary with the authors, but as a whole it is a fine one-volume commentary for pastors and students to use or give to a layman. Outstanding sections include, for example: Whitcomb on Ezra-Nehemiah-Esther; Culver on Daniel; Ladd on Acts; Harrison on Galatians; Johnson on I Corinthians; and Ryrie on the Johannine Epistles.

The Pulpit Commentary. **Edited by H. D. M. Spence and Joseph S. Exell. 23 volumes. Grand Rapids: Eerdmans reprinted at various dates, 1950's -1970's.**

Many authors contributed to this work that had the aim of giving preachers material on introduction, verse by verse exposition, a section on homiletics, and a section of collected homilies (outlines, etc.) by various preachers, which can stimulate thought. It moves through one small section of Bible verses after another.

The Seventh-day Adventist Bible Commentary. **Edited by Francis D. Nichol et al. 7 volumes. Washington, D. C.: Review and Herald Publishing Association, 1953-76.**

These are large volumes by 34 writers (Volume 1, on Genesis-Deuteronomy is 1,120 pages, 2 columns). General essays appear on such topics as the languages, manuscripts and canon of the Old Testament, science and a literal creation, evidences of a global flood, archeology, daily life in the Patriarchal Age, chronology, etc. The commentaries are extensive. Genesis is pp. 201-487, Exodus 491-689, etc. Ellen G. White's comments are sprinkled in sections throughout as supplements.

The Twentieth Century Bible Commentary. Edited by G. Henton Davies et al. Revised edition. 1 volume. NY: Harper and Brothers, 1932, 1955. 571 pp.

Designed for ministers, Sunday school leaders, Bible teachers and lay people, this sometimes liberal, sometimes evangelical work (cf. contributors, pp. vii-viii) has general articles and extremely brief commentaries such as Genesis (24 pp. 2 columns). Parts of the Pentateuch are assigned to the "priestly" or some other alleged strand of writing centuries later. It is not of solid value.

The Wesleyan Bible Commentary. Edited by Charles W. Carter, et al. 6 volumes. Grand Rapids: Eerdmans, 1967.

Devotes 3 volumes to Old Testament and 3 to New Testament, upholding views within the Wesleyan theological frame of reference, as of John Wesley and Adam Clarke. It is evangelical, expositional, Arminian, practical, homiletical and devotional. More than 20 scholars of the United States wrote it, coming from the Church of God, Church of the Nazarene, Evangelical United Brethren, Free Methodist, Friends, Methodist, Missionary Church Association, Pilgrim Holiness and Wesleyan Methodist. It is written for the average minister, Sunday School leader and teacher, Bible teacher, college professor, student and Christians in general. The commentary is 2 columns in format. It deals with some problems but not others, as the supposed high totals in Numbers 2. It has much good summary and upholds a high view of Scripture's reliability. Sometimes one writer was asked to do too much, as on Joshua-Job.

COMMENTARIES ON THE OLD TESTAMENT

I. SYNTHETICAL

Benware, Paul N. *Survey of the Old Testament* **(Everyman's Bible Commentary). Chicago: Moody, 1988. 267 pp.**

A Professor of Bible and Theology at Moody Bible Institute and more recently Trinity Evangelical Divinity School gives brief, sweeping surveys. For a quick lay person's glimpse it is helpful, and well-done, but it does not deal with as much or provide nearly the help of the works by Baxter, Scroggie, Unger or Wood, to name a few.

The Daily Study Bible (OT). **Philadelphia: Westminster Press, 1981ff.**

Various scholars join efforts to cover the Old Testament for the general public in a way similar to William Barclay's 17-volume Daily Study Bible on the New Testament. Portions of the Old Testament are divided off for daily readings and comments. The work is liberal, and also amillennial on prophecy. Evangelicals who for briefer expositional treatments use the Bible Study Commentary (Zondervan) or Everyman's Bible Commentary (Moody) will not find a lot here that adds to the picture.

Jensen, Irving L. *Jensen's Survey of the Old Testament*. **Chicago: Moody, 1991.**

A broad evangelical look at key things about each Old Testament book - background, outline, theme and synthesis with reading lists and charts. Cf. also Jensen's New Testament survey.

Merrill, Eugene A. *Historical Survey of the Old Testament*. **Nutley, NJ: The Craig Press, 1966.**

A good brief evangelical survey to give a person quick perspective, especially helpful for introductory, beginning study. Merrill stops on some problem areas to state his view and reasons. For example, he believes that Melchizedek in Genesis 14 is the preincarnate Christ.

Schultz, Samuel. *The Old Testament Speaks*. **NY: Harper and Row, 1960.**

This is an excellent general survey of Old Testament backgrounds and arguments of books. The evangelical author was then abreast of illuminating archaeological discoveries and shows that he has read broadly to devote to this work an exacting type of scholarship. Though brief, he is helpful on some problem passages like Joshua 10, the account of the long day, and Judges 11, the problem of whether or not Jephthah actually offered his daughter as a sacrifice. It is a good general work to possess.

Scroggie, W. Graham, 1877-1958. *The Unfolding Drama of Redemption.* **3 volumes. London: Pickering and Inglis Ltd., 1957.**

This evangelical master of synthesis has produced a well-organized survey of Bible books which is valuable to the student who is seeking to work his way through for his own knowledge of the Bible or for a series of messages or lessons covering the sweep of the Old Testament. His survey stops at the end of Acts.

Unger, Merrill C. *Unger's Commentary on the Old Testament.* **2 volumes. Chicago: Moody Press, 1981.**

The former head of the Department of Old Testament and Semitics at Dallas Seminary wrote this work of 2,090 pp. shortly before his death. Volume one covers Genesis-Song of Solomon, volume two the rest of the Old Testament. A somewhat detailed introduction is given for each book, looking at the title, author, date, canonicity, problems modern critics discuss, the basic theme, and a detailed outline. In the commentary, Unger writes section by section, commenting on what he regards as the key expositional issues, using Hebrew words at times, historical background, and context. We see the view of a well-known conservative and premillennial dispensational scholar on many a text, sometimes very helpful and other times cursory and general by the nature of the broad range of the study.

Wood, Leon J. *Survey of Israel's History.* **Grand Rapids: Zondervan, 1970. Revised 1986 by David O'Brien.**

This is one of the most rewarding surveys available from the standpoint of giving a survey and yet pausing on key problem areas to state a well-considered view and specific supports marshalled briefly. It is firmly evangelical.

II. ANALYTICAL

Cohen, A. Soncino *Books of the Bible.* **14 volumes. Bournemouth, Harts, England: Soncino, 1945-61.**

These volumes represent the best in popular, orthodox Jewish scholarship, though the editors come from all three schools of Judaism. The Hebrew text is printed and a commentary is given, though actual Hebrew exegesis is sparse. The order of pages naturally accords with the Hebrew text, running from right to left. A good brief introduction is presented for each book, and these are generally conservative in outlook (see Slotki on Isaiah for a notable exception). Tradition plays a large role, hence the use of views by Rashi, Kimchi and other former Jewish scholars. Since it is Judaism's best, concise work, it is valuable to have if the student can afford it. Much of the historical background information is somewhat helpful. One of the better works is Ezekiel, written by Fisch, even though it will be far from satisfying in some of its views, for example on prophecies in Ezekiel 40-48.

Keil, C. F. and Franz Delitzsch. *Commentary on the Old Testament.* **25 volumes. Grand Rapids: Eerdmans, 1950.**

This is the best older, overall treatment of a critical nature on the Old Testament Hebrew text verse by verse and is a good standard work to buy. The student can buy parts or the whole of this series. Sometimes it is evangelical, at other times liberal ideas enter.

Old Testament Library. Philadelphia: Westminster Press, 1985ff.

A scholarly series steeped in critical issues, views and reasoning that does not please firm evangelicals with its aspects of liberalism. It can be helpful on verses but too often is not. Some volumes are more profitable in explaining passages along lines conservatives can value, as Joseph Blenkinsopp frequently on Ezra-Nehemiah. But many of the entries will have their greatest usefulness among quite liberal readers. Examples are G. von Rad on Genesis and Deuteronomy, and Robert P. Carroll on Jeremiah.

COMMENTARIES ON THE PENTATEUCH

Hamilton, Victor P. *Handbook on the Pentateuch.* **Grand Rapids: Baker, 1982. 496 pp.**

Hamilton was at the time Professor of Religion at Asbury College with an M. A. and Ph. D. from Brandeis University. This is a one-volume exposition that can serve as a text for an English Bible college survey course. He has done his survey with a good grasp of what is vital for comment, an awareness of different main views on certain problems, and a very readable style. He is evangelical in his conclusions, as on the unity of Genesis 1-2, and follows many evangelicals on the Messianic thrust of Genesis 3:15. His lists for further reading at the ends of chapters provide many sources from a wide knowledge of commentaries and journals but focus on only the last ten years before his book, include mostly liberal works, and at times overlook key evangelical sources,

JPS Torah Commentary. **New York: Jewish Publication Society, 1989-1993.**

These recent commentaries are surveys as Nahum Sarna's on Genesis and Exodus and Baruch Levine's on Leviticus or massive as Jacob Milgrom's on Numbers (520 pp.). Thorough study in a wide range of sources is poured into the effort, especially in Milgrom's work, and one sees how scholarly Jews explain passages. There is more depth of detail than in the Soncino Series and use of recent writings. Jeffrey Tigay's work on Deuteronomy has also appeared. The commentaries are liberal but on many points the explanations contribute, viewing what is said in a helpful light. One learns much about Jewish background and customs.

Livingston, G. H. *The Pentateuch in Its Cultural Environment.* **Grand Rapids: Baker, 1987. 2nd edition. 322 pp.**

A readable, comprehensive, well-respected evangelical work by a professor of Old Testament at Asbury Theological Seminary since 1953. Livingston discusses peoples of the ancient near east (Sumerians, Assyrians, Amorites, Egyptians, Hyksos, Hittites, Philistines, Canaanites and others). He also writes of relevant ancient scripts, literature (compared with the Pentateuch), concepts, practices, schools of thought on Pentateuchal studies, Mosaic authorship, Dead Sea scroll relevance, the JEDP theory, literary criticism, form criticism, canonical criticism,etc. The final chapter (10) deals with canonization of the Pentateuch and factors related to this. Indices of subjects and scripture verses help readers locate specific discussions.

Mackintosh, C. H. *Genesis to Deuteronomy, Notes on the Pentateuch.* **Neptune, NJ: Loizeaux, 1989. 912 pp.**

This is a one-volume edition of an old evangelical devotional work. It has some value at times, especially for lay readers, yet is not to the point as much with pertinent material as W. H. Griffith-Thomas on the Pentateuch (also old) and John Sailhamer's recent introductory survey.

Sailhamer, John H. *The Pentateuch as Narrative. A Biblical-Theological Commentary*. Grand Rapids: Zondervan, 1992. 522 pp.

An associate professor of Old Testament, Trinity Evangelical Divinity School, offers an introduction to the Pentateuch (1-79) looking at background, authorship, sources, literary form, structure, purpose, theology, basic principles, etc. Later he provides a fairly detailed, well-outlined survey of each book section by section, for example Genesis (81-240), and Exodus (241-322). He is concerned with style and structure so as to relate details to their context. He not only connects parts and surveys what is said but deals with leading problems such as Genesis 1: 1-2, 6:2, 4 (sons of God), etc. He handles the Hebrew skillfully, is usually lucid and has a high evangelical view of the integrity and unity of accounts. He is steeped in awareness of literature on issues as reflected in footnotes, some of which are quite substantial. If one does not agree with Sailhamer on everything, this still is, overall, one of the most adept, informative books on the Pentateuch and has proved very helpful for teachers, pastors and students. Sailhamer in an appendix lists together all the commands of the law in various categories and gives examples where Jesus and New Testament writers adduce the principles (482-516). He is insightful on many verses, for example the validity of a Messianic reference in Deuteronomy 18:18 (456). For further Sailhamer detail on Genesis, one can go to Sailhamer's commentary in The Expositor's Bible Commentary.

Wolf, Herbert. *An Introduction to the Old Testament Pentateuch*. Chicago: Moody Press, 1991. 276 pp.

Wolf was then associate professor of Old Testament, Wheaton Graduate School. He provides an evangelical discussion on introductory aspects such as the fivefold division of the Pentateuch, unity, impact on other Old Testament and New Testament books, theology (God, man, salvation, the Messiah, faith, atonement, covenants), the Samaritan Pentateuch, literary characteristics, and Moses' significance. He argues for Moses as the main author and for the unity of the Pentateuch. Then he deals with each of the five books. In Genesis, he discusses key problems in 1:1-2:3, sons of God in 6:2, 4, the extent of the flood and other issues. Wolf sometimes gives various views, as on the length of "day" in Genesis 1, but it is not easy to find where he states a definite preference (84-88). The same is true in lengthy comments on sons of God (97-100). He would often be more helpful if, when he introduces a question, he finally concludes with some clear preference. An example where he does do this is his decision that the exodus occurred early (148). There are fine discussions of several problems, such as the much-attacked numbers for Israel as in Numbers 2 (148-51). Overall the book is well worth the reading, though surveys of Pentateuchal books are briefer than Sailhamer's. A good bibliography appears (223-61). Indices of subjects, authors and scriptures also offer help.

COMMENTARIES ON INDIVIDUAL
OLD TESTAMENT BOOKS

I. GENESIS

In any case where commentaries on a book of the Pentateuch are sparse, the notes by W. H. Griffith-Thomas, Through the Pentateuch Chapter By Chapter (Eerdmans) will be a warm devotional help. Cf also Barnhouse, Boice, Calvin, etc. One may use the ICC work here by Skinner for a liberal treatment. Speiser's volume in the Anchor Bible series is also liberal but at times helpful in exegesis and background. Better commentaries old and recent from the conservative and other standpoints are:

Aalders, G. Charles. *Genesis (Bible Students Commentary)*. 2 volumes. Grand Rapids: Zondervan, 1981. 311 + 298 pp.

Zondervan has issued English translations of the top evangelical commentary in Dutch dating from the 1930's and 40's, a 62-volume set called *Korte Verklaring der Heilige Schrift*. It is designed for lay readers but is so well done in detail that it is of substantial benefit to teachers up to the seminary level too. It is Reformed, and in the English effort uses the NIV. Aalders is clear, deals with problems usually well, explains most verses quite adequately, and defends at length Mosaic authorship and the infallible truth in the Pentateuch (pp. 1-41, cf. p. 40). He sees 1:1 as an absolute statement of original creation, sees no gap in 1:2, is non-committal about the length of the days except to say these are not twenty-four-hour days. "Sons of God" in 6:2, 4 are humans, and Aalders devotes a detailed look at views. He views the flood as universal. The work is well worth the time.

Baldwin, Joyce G. *The Message of Genesis 12-50* (The Bible Speaks Today). Downers Grove, IL: 1VP, 1986. 224 pp.

This is not a commentary per se but a well-organized, popularly readable exposition in a devotional vein, with refreshingly conceived lessons applied to life today. Using the RSV, Baldwin deals with faith, patience, etc., stimulating readers in rich paths. She provides helps on geography, customs, and other areas, and shows, for example, how Abraham's responses are like Christians' today. The book shows a considerable use of scholarly literature in the footnotes.

Barnhouse, Donald G. Genesis, *A Devotional Commentary*. 2 volumes in 1. Grand Rapids: Zondervan, 1973. 208 + 250 pp.

Provocative principles drawn by a famous Bible teacher and radio voice a few decades back. As to devotional lessons in Genesis, this book rates just behind W. H.

Griffith-Thomas. It is suggestive of points for preachers, and rewarding for laypeople. Boice is a tie with it or third, though more recent.

Boice, James M. Genesis, *An Expositional Commentary*. 3 volumes. Grand Rapids: Zondervan, 1982-87.

Broad exposition here is not verse by verse. The long-time pastor of 10th St. Presbyterian, Philadelphia chooses doctrinal and practical emphases, which can help a Christian grow by seeing how to apply truths. Boice can be very helpful or can read in meanings that some will doubt are in Genesis, such as seeing the pact between Abraham and Abimelech as teaching on church and state matters (pp. 206-11).

Brueggemann, Walter. *Genesis* (Interpretation). Atlanta: John Knox Press, 1982. 384 pp.

This is by the Professor of Old Testament, Columbia Theological Seminary, Decatur, GA. Using the RSV, he does an exposition with the belief that Genesis arose from diverse narratives from many times and places (p. 2). He leans a lot on commentaries in critical areas. He subjectively assigns some material to J and P and follows von Rad in placing Joseph material in the tenth century (pp. 6-7) and some portions in exilic days. While there is a lot of insight at times, the work is often an exercise in speculation which gets in the way of seeing what the text itself says without Brueggemann's encrusted theory. He assumes, for instance, that 1:1-2:4 uses older creation stories and cosmologies from Egypt and Mesopotamia composed in the sixth century to address exiles (p. 24). Claims of Genesis 1-2 are not to be taken as literal to say what happened but only to witness to us of God's lordly intent (p. 26). Historic or literal reality disappears beneath disclaimers that leave one mystified as to why the text says what it says about a fall of humans or gives an account of how evil came into the world or death entered (41-42). He feels that Paul in Romans 5 draws conclusions not founded in the Genesis text (42). The book is an exercise in how a liberal mind construes things quite differently.

Calvin, John. *Genesis* (Geneva series). 2 volumes in 1. Carlisle, PA: Banner of Truth Trust, 1975rp. 523 pp.

This was first issued in Latin in 1554 and in English in 1578. It has no outline but is verse by verse. Much space is used printing English and Latin translations side by side before the comments. Calvin usually has something quite helpful, so this is profitable reading. He sees 1:1 as summing up original creation, *ex nihilo*; 1:2 is the initial, shapeless and empty or incomplete state that is formed and filled in 1:3ff. Days are twenty-four hours. The Trinity is reflected upon in 1:26; 4:1 does not state it so, but Calvin thinks Cain and Abel were twins; sons of God in Chapter 6 were men of the godly line; the flood was universal; 49:10 refers to the Messiah, etc.

Candlish, Robert S. *Exposition of Genesis*. Wilmington, DE: Sovereign Grace, 1972. Reprint, two volumes in one.

This was rated by Spurgeon, *Commenting and Commentaries* (past century) as then "the work on Genesis". There are 72 chapters in lecture form. Candlish believes in a young earth but alas, the universal fatherhood of God. His work is often helpful in spite of some peculiarities, but not nearly as beneficial as many works since.

Cassuto, Umberto. *From Adam to Noah* **(I) and** *From Noah to Abraham* **(II). 2 volumes. Jerusalem: Magnes Press, 1961.**

This Jewish scholar covers thirteen chapters only, fluctuating between good and weak in his helpfulness explaining salient points. He is sometimes good, but not consistently enough to rank with the top commentaries.

Cummings, Vera. *Noah's Ark: Fact or Fable?* **San Diego: Creation Science Research Society, 1971.**

This book traces various trips to the Mt. Ararat region in search of an ark; gives intriguing accounts of some who have allegedly either seen an ark or traces of it in that area; and stirs the reader with the question of whether or not Noah's ark might yet be discovered. A more recent work on this same subject is John W. Montgomery's *The Quest For Noah's Ark*, It examines the attempts in history to find the ark, tells of his own experiences in the quest, and discusses biblical matters relating to the ark.

Custance, Arthur. *Without Form and Void.* **Brockville, Canada. Privately published, 1970.**

The author published this book after nearly thirty years of special study. He presents evidence favoring the gap view in Genesis 1:2 correlated from many sources. In recent times this is the most detailed effort arguing for a gap. Fields' work below answers it in detail from a no-gap view.

Davis, John J. *Paradise to Prison.* **Grand Rapids: Baker, 1976.**

This is an excellent, well-documented and readable survey on some of the key passages and problems in Genesis. It does not discuss verse by verse but does hit crucial areas such as views on the time of creation, whether there was a gap in Genesis 1:1, 2, what the days of Genesis I mean, key problems of Genesis 3, whether the flood was local or universal, who were the "sons of God" in Genesis 6, and so on throughout. Davis is helpful in that he usually comments on main issues and reflects careful thinking as well as reading awareness of scholarship on the areas. He is a staunch evangelical Old Testament scholar, teaching at Grace College, Winona Lake, Indiana. This work, the one by Allen Ross (*Creation and Blessing*), and a more recent work on the narrative of Genesis by John Sailhamer are the best three broad scholarly surveys of Genesis.

Delitzsch, Franz, 1813-1890. *A New Commentary on Genesis.* **2 volumes. Edinburgh: T. & T. Clark, 1899.**

The author holds to the documentary hypothesis but does not deny the uniqueness of Genesis or minimize the significance and authority of its message. He is careful in the Hebrew and deals with the problems, providing much to aid the expositor.

Fields, Weston W. *Unformed and Unfilled.* **Nutley, NJ: Presbyterian and Reformed, 1976.**

A detailed evaluation and critique of Arthur C. Custance's *Without Form and Void*, based on Fields' Th. D. dissertation in Old Testament at Grace Theological Seminary, Winona Lake, Indiana. He argues at length against a gap in relation to Genesis 1:2 and favors a recent creation of the earth, with twenty-four-hour days and with 1:1-5 speaking of the creative work during the first day. He holds to a universal flood geology. He has brought into a systematic presentation a wealth of details from rather wide research that enter into a competent discussion of the issues.

Filby, F. A. *The Flood Reconsidered*. Grand Rapids: Zondervan, 1970.

He lucidly argues that the Flood was local but destroyed all mankind, those not aboard the Ark.

Garrett, Duane. *Rethinking Genesis*. Grand Rapids: Baker, 1991. 273 pp.

This is a conservative array of evidence vs. the documentary hypothesis and critical theories seeing Genesis as late dated and disunified. The author concludes the book was written during the Exodus period (cf. p. 237).

Hamilton, Victor P. *The Book of Genesis, Chapters 1-17; Vol. 2, 18-50,* (NICOT). Grand Rapids: Eerdmans, 1990. 522 pp.

This first of 2 volumes has a very informative introduction of around a hundred pages surveying the history of critical theories and not arriving at a firm view of authorship. He gives twenty-five pages of bibliography. On some problems he is detailed, as in examining interpretive issues such as days in Genesis 1. He is thorough on the meaning of verses in view of biblical usage of words, context, and Near Eastern literature in which he is steeped. Overall it is a standout commentary along conservative lines, even covering many subjects relevant to Genesis. Some of what he writes in the introduction will be readily grasped only by scholars; others will be guessing and re-reading to figure things out, if patient and capable. The author is not able to decide on which view about "sons of God" (6:2, 4). One will have to search to decide where he explains if the Flood was local or universal. The explanation at times is very good, at other times falls short of really illumining a passage, as on the ritual ceremony in Genesis 15. But so much data is given that the reader is bound to receive much to think about.

Vol. 2 continues to reflect broad reading in both commentary and copious footnotes. Both throw much light on the text. In Gen. 22 rather full explanation appears, yet Hamilton has a questionable view that Abraham's expecting Isaac to return (22:5) is resorting to deception (he did not really expect it). But Jacob in his cattle deal is ingenious, not deceiving (284), and his peeled rods were not the reason for the success, rather in spite of his superstition God increased his flocks. Hamilton explains well Joseph's purity before the temptress. Occasionally, no explanation is offered on a problem, as in Joseph's having a divining cup.

Harbach, Robert C. *Studies in the Book of Genesis*. Grandville, MI: Grandville Reformed Church Publication Committee, 1986. 938 pp.

A long-time Reformed pastor gives a conservative, thorough explanation of verses, interacting knowledgeably with scientific disciplines but in cases of tensions favoring Scripture (he has a high view of it). He opts for original creation in 1:1-2, no gap in 1:2, twenty-four-hour days, a creation date of Adam around 6,000 B. C., and is opposed to evolutionary theory. He defends Mosaic authorship. Very often he is helpful on normal questions readers have passage by passage, and is clear. He is non-dispensational (p. 45).

Hartley, John E. *Genesis* (New International Biblical Commentary). Peabody, MA: Hendrickson Publishers, 2000.

The author reasons in his introduction for reliability of the Genesis accounts. In his commentary he is often right to the mark, but sometimes does not grasp fairly or explain clearly the views (as on 1:1-2, though he favors the view that 1:1 is a summary heading for all of the creation and 1:2 the circumstances before God had gone on to stages of bringing order in 1:3ff. (41)). Some verses are treated too briefly, with silence about problems until later in special notes, as in saying God produced light in 1:3 without need of sun, moon or stars, then created sun, moon and stars on day four (52). He lacks support for his view of an ordinary day in Gen. 1 (52), and seems to ride the fence between two views on the woman's "desire" (3:16). In his view "sons of God" (6:2) are human, but he is sparse on discussion. In 12:1-3 he says so little about "nation," "land," or "seed" that one does not know his view. He does view Abraham as having faith in 22:5, 8 that God would allow Isaac to survive. He is vague on Jacob's colors to influence the color of animals born (269-70). A commentary that is only fairly good results, not a standout.

Jacob, Benno. *The First Book of the Bible, Genesis*. New York: KTAV Publishing-House, 1974.

Translated but reduced in length by about 2/3 from the 1932 German edition, *Das Erste Buch der Tora, Genesis ubersetzt und eklaert* (Berlin: Schocken verlag). The English product is 357 pp. Jacob was a Jewish scholar, often helpful on seeing things from the standpoint of what the text itself means. In the abbreviated English work, much valuable philological explanation was cut out, as well as details that argued against a documentary approach to Genesis.

Keil, C. F. and Franz Delitzsch. *The Pentateuch*, Cf. Commentaries on the Old Testament, Analytical.

Kidner, Derek. *Genesis*. Wheaton: Tyndale House, 1968.

It is evident that much study lies behind this concisely stated commentary in the Tyndale series. Kidner has packed in a lot of understanding of word meanings, movements of thought in different parts of Genesis, customs, God's purposes, and relationship to other parts of Scripture. It is a solid but brief work. Cf. his works also on Psalms and Proverbs.

Kikawada, Isaac M. and Arthur Quinn. *Before Abraham Was*. Nashville: Abingdon Press, 1985. 144 pp.

Two who before believed in the documentary hypothesis show how patterns of. structure in Genesis 1-11 convinced them of the unity of these chapters and writing by one person. They argue that the same phenomena run through all of Genesis and the Pentateuch.

Kline, Meredith G. "Genesis," *New Bible Commentary Revised*, ed. D. Guthrie, et al. Grand Rapids: Eerdmans, 1970, pp. 70-114.

Famous professor of Old Testament, Gordon-Conwell Theological Seminary, favors Mosaic authorship, defends historical reliability of events (cf. p. 80) and the unity of the material in opposition to the documentary hypothesis. He is conservative in views. He takes the days of Genesis 1 as figurative for ages, 49:10 as looking on to the Messiah, etc.

Lawson, George. *The History of Joseph*. Carlisle, PA. Banner of Truth Trust, n. d. Reprint of 1807. 12 volumes. Cf. 1972 edition, Edinburgh, Banner of Truth.

Here are many stimulating lessons for the spiritual life, some of them dated. If one is preaching in a series of Joseph, the book can be very helpful in priming the pump. Lawson expounds each verse in Genesis 37-50 with vital truths for Christian life. A person looking for a very detailed discussion here will appreciate the book as well as Martin Luther's 2 volumes (of eight on Genesis) that deal with' 37-50. Cf. also on Joseph sources listed under Theodore Epp, plus John Hercus (*Pages From God's Case Book.* Downers Grove, IL: IVP, 1962).

Leupold, H. C. *Exposition of Genesis*. 2 volumes. Grand Rapids: Baker, 1990 reprint.

In this very thorough, monumental work on Genesis, the author is conservative and uses the original Hebrew constantly. He considers carefully most major truths of the book and uses the grammatical-historical method. This is one of the most valuable works to have on Genesis. It came out originally in 1942.

Luther, Martin. *Luther's Commentary on Genesis*. A New Translation by J. Theodore Mueller. 2 volumes. Grand Rapids: Zondervan, 1958. Also cf. *Lectures on Genesis*, 8 volumes. Ed. J. Pelikan. Saint Louis: Concordia, 1965.

A great Lutheran scholar and man active in missionary writing did this translation (he authored *John G. Paton, Great Missionary to Africa*, etc.). At the beginning of the first day God created a shapeless mass or lump of earth with fog and water (1:1, 2). This He later fashioned and adorned and also put into it the light, which was an as yet imperfect light that He completed on the fourth day. One has to plod amidst much detail to search out what kind of "day" Luther means, but on p. 34 (citations are from Zondervan publication), he says the six were natural days. The serpent is a literal animal the Devil used as an agent (65). Luther is refreshing in saying of things God has not revealed, concerning which men ask questions, that we ought not judge God or ask an account of what He does or permits, but accept His will and be clay in the Potter's hands (65). Luther defends the estate of marriage in Genesis 4:1 against papists who he says condemn the marital communion of husband and wife as unclean. Eve in 4:1 believed "I have the Man, the Lord," meaning the Redeemer of 3:15. The "sons of God" in Genesis 6 are male descendants of the godly line, who lapsed from the true religion into sin with unions with the daughters of the wicked. Luther's compassion shows as in chapter 7 where the flood caught away men and other creatures, and Moses perhaps "could not describe these things without tears in his eyes" as he saw them "without hope and help, only to be destroyed." There is a great amount of material that explains pertinent questions very relevantly to the serious reader. Two volumes deal with the fourteen chapters on Joseph in great detail (in the 8 volume set).

Matthews, Kenneth A. *Genesis 1—11:26* (New American Commentary). Broadman and Holman, 1996.

The first volume of 528 pages is helpful in many cases, vague on others despite lengthy discussion (as on "seed" and "land" in 12:1-3, 7 and how these relate to Israel and to the nations, pp. 56-60). Matthews sees Moses as compiler of Genesis (81). Some introductory remarks say much but do not usher readers to clear points to draw matters together. The work views the creation narrative as historical (111). It seems to explain Gen. 1 and deal with problem phrases, its footnotes reflecting awareness of views and other pertinent data. However, Matthews regards the days as nonliteral and is vague about the length (149). "Sons of God" (6:2) are Sethites, the flood was universal, and good indices appear for subjects, persons and Scripture. On most matters, this is one of the best studies on these chapters. Matthews offers a wealth of awareness about ancient culture and writings helpful to background. Some of his well-argued views are for godly humans as "sons of God" in Gen. 6, and gaps allowing more time in Gen. 5.

Morris, Henry M.. *The Genesis Record*. Grand Rapids: Baker, with Creation Life Publishers, 1976.

A verse by verse work of over 700 pp. by a strongly committed evangelical scholar, Morris deals with many of the difficulties in normal exposition views of creation, whether 2:19 and other details in chapter 2 contradict the sequence in chapter 1, the "sons of God" in chapter 6, the extent of the flood, the prophecy of Noah, etc. He makes a special attempt to deal with scientific questions in chapters 1-11, since that has been the area of his life-long primary focus, and has a heavy emphasis on universal flood geology and a recent creation perspective. He was a coauthor with John Whitcomb of *The Genesis Flood*. Many laymen have regarded this as one of the most helpful and readable works. Cf. also *The Revelation Record* on the Apocalypse, by the same author.

Phillips, John. *Exploring Genesis*. Chicago: Moody Press, 1980.

A good expositor from the Moody Bible Institute Extension Department gives a well-organized, often provocative survey of the meaning, with principles made evident for application. Phillips' works on many of the Bible books in recent years have been a help to preachers and laypeople. He is conservative, clear, and often has a very good outline of a passage.

Pink, Arthur W. *Gleanings in Genesis*. Chicago: Moody (n. d.)

This conservative, premillennial work has good application and devotional spirit. It is often of help in tracing out prophecies fulfilled and unfulfilled, but many feel that Pink sees too many types. A weak element is that it does not deal so exhaustively with most passages as does Leupold. It is not based on the Hebrew text.

Ramm, Bernard. *The Christian View of Science and Scripture*. Grand Rapids: Eerdmans, 1971 paperback reprint of 1954 work.

This is not actually a commentary, but a work dealing with supposed tensions between Scripture and science. Ramm was well-read and penetrating in his discussions so that the reader is deeply stimulated. However, some of Ramm's conclusions are not tenable in the opinion of many conservatives, for example, his pictorial revelatory day view in Genesis 1, his view of progressive creationism, and his local flood idea. But he has discussions of these areas which at least seek to deal with the problems as he sees them. He is helpful on many other areas like Joshua's so-called long day (Joshua 10) and Jonah and the great fish.

Ross, Allen P. *Creation and Blessing*. Grand Rapids: Baker, 1988. 744 pp.

This is a major contribution, growing out of immense study in relevant literature of recent times dealing with ancient literature. Ross does a broad exposition section by section, not verse by verse, and handles major problems with adept awareness of views and discussion of arguments. It is a valuable scholarly work in surveying issues and literature that deals with them. Also cf. his "Genesis," *Bible Knowledge Commentary*, Volume 1, eds. J. F. Walvoord and Roy B. Zuck. (Wheaton, IL: Victor Books, 1983).

Sailhamer, John. "Genesis," *The Expositor's Bible Commentary*, **Volume 2, ed. Frank Gaebelein and R. P. Polcyn. Grand Rapids: Zondervan, 1980.**

This Genesis contribution to the commentary is by the then Associate Professor of Old Testament and Semitic Languages, Trinity Evangelical Divinity School, Deerfield, IL. It is a very good conservative work verse by verse, with insights from a wealth of literature from the ancient Near East that throws light on details and their relevance in their connections. Sailhamer shows much on competency, conciseness, clarity, and is frequently perceptive on the applicational relevancy.

Schaeffer, Francis A. *Genesis in Space and Time.* **Downers Grove, IL: Inter-Varsity Press, 1972.**

These chapters give a survey (not verse by verse study) of Genesis 1-11 with particular attention devoted to such matters as: showing the literal historicity of the events and persons in answer to many modern theologians, commenting with conviction on the meaning of without form and void (1:2), the alleged contradiction of chapter 1 by chapter 2, the chronology of chapters 5 and 11, the sons of God in 6:2, whether the flood was universal or only local (he feels universal), etc. He relates the truths here solidly to other Scripture and has helpful discussions of such areas as the image of God, marriage, sin, redemption, the genealogies, and the confusion of tongues at Babel.

Stigers, Harold G. A *Commentary on Genesis.* **Grand Rapids: Zondervan, 1976.**

A detailed work by an evangelical which moves verse by verse and is thorough on many of the problem passages. It is geared more for the rather serious student and is a good contribution. Laymen might consider it tedious reading because of its length on many of the verses.

Thomas, W. H. Griffith. *Genesis.* **Grand Rapids: Eerdmans, 1960. 507 pp.**

This work is good in tracing the argument and showing connections between chapters. It is usually quite good devotionally and gives suggestions for meditation at the ends of the chapters. Applications are often usable. It is an excellent book to put into the hands of a layman who is not ready to grapple with the minutia of exegesis, but who is serious about his Bible study. It is also good for the preacher and teacher. Since it is out of print, readers must search in other places for it. Since the work is out of print, those desiring to find it will need to check at some biblical libraries.

Vos, Howard. *Genesis* **(Everyman's Bible Commentary). Chicago: Moody, 1982. 174 pp.**

A simple, broad survey by a conservative who tends to give some good comments but at times not nail down his view to explain a matter (cf. his survey of four views on days in Genesis 1, then leaving the matter hanging, and not commenting on how long God rested in 2:1-3; or his not choosing a preference on "sons of God" on Genesis 6 after a shallow consideration of issues). However, in a concise treatment he does touch on many of the problems.

Waltke, Bruce K. with C. J. Fredricks. *Genesis, A Commentary.* Grand Rapids: Baler. 2001.

The 656 pp. frequently have outstanding work. One sees amillennial commitment on the Abrahamic Covenant (12:1-3, 7, etc.). One can see this also in Waltke's *Looking into the Future: Evangelical Studies in Eschatology, ed. D. W. Baker* (Grand Rapids: Baker, 2001). The spiritual seed in Gen. 12 is taken in the OT to be mostly Abraham's physical offspring and in the NT mostly Gentiles (48). The land and seed undergo in the NT a paradigm shift, with the physical meaning mostly dropped in favor of the spiritual. "Neither Christ nor His apostles ever teach that dispersed ethnic Israel will again return to Canaan" (49). Waltke offers a view of creation in Gen. 1 with judgment on a creation earlier than 1:1 and a gap before 1:2, a view that James Jordan critiques in his *Creation in Six Days*. The commentary shows extensive research in Hebrew exegesis, word meaning, context, literary analysis and theology, and early backgrounds thought to be relevant. Careful inquiry into many problems is evident. Strands of literary material (J, E, D, P) are apparently assumed (24-28), and the authors posit some contradictions in the strands (26, 28), and even for example in Gen. 1 if their view is not taken. Moses, they feel, used document sources (27), and an unknown final author edited the material (28). They favor a universal flood but comment briefly on this (132-33). The work is often helpful on problem verses even if at times briefly, as on Jacob's method for influencing the color of animals born (Gen. 30) and Joseph's divining cup (Gen. 44). In many cases the commentary statements and wording are superb, but in some many readers will get lost in the literary analysis and wish to cut through to comments verse by verse.

Waltke, Bruce K. *Creation to Chaos: An Exegetical Study of Biblical Cosmology.* Portland: Western Conservative Baptist Seminary, 1974.

Lectures on Genesis 1-2 compared with Mesopotamian creation accounts. Waltke argues a gap before 1:1, not between 1:1 and 1:2.

Walton, John H. *Genesis* (NIV Application Commentary). Grand Rapids: Zondervan, 2001.

This is a combination of mediocre survey explanation, helpful in places for quite patient readers, with some application and frequent parts that seem to wander afield from a direct bearing. The wandering in the introduction alone can almost cause one to put the book aside and use another. Once in Gen. 1, the further lack of reasonably quick clarity in bringing things together, and enabling a user to find comments on particular verses consistently, plus a lack of synthesis giving a perspective on the movement can be frustrating. The obtuse nature of some discussions make the task tedious, with spotty results in getting at concrete help. One can gather some basic material, but it is not as profitably done as in many Genesis commentaries. Sections on application do furnish some relevance.

A simple, broad survey by a conservative who tends to give some good comments but at times not nail down his view to explain a matter (cf. his survey of four views on days in Genesis 1, then leaving the matter hanging, and not commenting on how long God rested in 2:1-3; or his not choosing a preference on "sons of God" in Genesis 6 after a shallow consideration of issues). However, in a concise treatment he does touch on some of the problems.

Wenham, G. J. *Genesis 1-15* and *Genesis 16-50* (Word Biblical Commentary). Dallas, TX. Word Books, 1987, 1994.

Wenham gives much readable and good information on the Hebrew text, word study, exegesis and insightful exposition. He is somewhat freed from traditional critical views and holds to historicity of events and persons. He does not deny theories that different strands of literary composition have led to the Genesis we know, but is skeptical toward this. He places his stress on the canonical text as a unity. Despite this, many conservatives wonder what kind of evangelical he is when he uses J and P, not clearly explaining how his usage departs from the intent usually involved in these designations. His claims that certain P material, so-called, was earlier or later than J material will be regarded as arbitrary and speculative.

In volume 2, beneficial introductory sections discuss the patriarchs' historical setting, chronology and religion, and Egytian background for Joseph. Wenham handles well Abraham's intercession for Sodom, and has a mixture of good and unnecessary reading into the offering of Isaac (cf. waffling on 22:5), as well as dubious suggestions (32:30; 37:4 among others). But usually remarks are very profitable. In 44:5 more data could help in regard to Joseph's using of a divining cup (424). As is typical of the WBC, a reader finds a very fine listing of serious literature on each biblical section.

Westermann, Claus. *Genesis: A Commentary*. Translated from German. 3 volumes. Minneapolis: Augsburg Publishing House, 1984-86.

The 3 volumes came out covering Chapters 1-11, 12-36 and 37-50. In more than 1,500 pages, a form critical scholar discusses critical matters on the text and also word meaning, history, theology, all in immense detail. Cf. his one-volume condensation in *Genesis, A Practical Commentary* (Eerdmans, 1987. 338 pp.). The latter, for about one-seventh the cost, focuses on Westermann's own convictions in much briefer, simpler form, without the technical comments. While one can by careful discrimination glean out much that is profound and helpful in the 3 volumes, some statements will puzzle many. One is his idea that the God of the fathers is not the same as the God of Israel (p. 107). Often the work is of help to the scholar, whether often in the commentary or considerably in the bibliography (though most entries are German works and few are evangelical). Textual comments and summaries on the history of interpretation of some parts (Genesis 14, 15, 16, etc.) are informative. Westermann thinks Genesis 37-50 was from a separate, independent writing that later was composed during the era of David and Solomon and assembled into a unity with Genesis. The work is often disconcerting to the conservative in its low view of the authority of the text, and often opposes conservative views. It has a large amount of material arbitrarily theorizing how the text came into the form we now have. It rejects original sin in Genesis 3.

Whitcomb, John C. and Henry Morris. *The Genesis Flood*. Grand Rapids: Baker, 1971 paperback reprint of 1961 work 518 pp.

A theologian formerly from Grace Seminary (Whitcomb) and a civil engineer at Christian Heritage College near San Diego (Morris) combined their efforts to produce this carefully documented work in defense of a world-wide flood. They have assembled the evidences in a masterful fashion, dealing seriously with both Scriptural and scientific data. The book represents the results of years of research in areas relating to the flood and careful study of hundreds of books, journals and papers available in many libraries. They integrate the basic scientific factors, as they see them, into the flood account in Genesis. It is the most impressive book on the flood problem by the conservative side. See also the well-documented book, *The Biblical Flood and the Ice Epoch*, by Donald Wesley Patten (Seattle: Pacific Meridian Publishing Co., 1966).

Wood, Leon J. *A Shorter Commentary on Genesis.* **Eugene, OR: Wipf and Stock Publishers, 1998.**

This is a republication of the 1975 study guide of 152 pp. below.

A staunch conservative offers a quick survey in basic information, often resolving main problems briefly. He leaves open the length of the days in Genesis 1, employs a detailed outline, and primarily assists lay readers and students looking for a terse review. A fine, brief evangelical survey of the main flow of the book, with a number of quite helpful comments on problem areas most readers want to see discussed. Among the briefer works this is one of the best.

Young, Davis A. *Creation and Flood: An Alternative to Flood Geology and Theistic Evolution.* **Grand Rapids: Baker, 1977. 217 pp.**

A good statement by an evangelical who believes in age days in Genesis 1 and an old earth. The son of Edward J. Young, Davis has his Ph. D. in geology from Brown University, B. S. E. in Geological Engineering from Princeton University, and M. S. in Minerology and Petrology from Pennsylvania State University. He argues against the flood geology in such a work as Henry M. Morris and John C. Whitcomb, *The Genesis Flood*, believing that a study of the rocks shows a much older earth than the fairly recent creation they champion. He holds an age-day view of the "day" concept in Genesis 1, arguing that the Genesis account only focuses on the chief or climactic events that were finished on each of the days. The days overlap. In appraising Young's position, one might find help from some of his critics' reviews (cf. Charles A. Clough and Louis E. Fredericks, "Creationist Science: A Challenge from Professor Young," 20 pp., Clough, Lubbock Bible Church, 3202 34th St., Lubbock, TX, 79410; Henry M. Morris, "*The Day-Age Theory Revisited*," Institute of Creation Research Impact Series, No. 55, 2716 Madison Avenue, San Diego, California 92116).

Young, Edward J. *Studies in Genesis One.* **Philadelphia: Presbyterian and Reformed Publishing Co., 1964; also** *In The Beginning, Genesis 1-3 and the Authority of Scripture.* **Carlisle, PA: Banner of Truth Trust, 1976; and** *Genesis 3, A Devotional and Expository Study.* **Carlisle, PA: Banner of Truth Trust, 1966.**

All three books present careful discussion of issues within the passages they treat, grappling with views and reasons and offering much to conservative readers. The work on Genesis 3 deals with the matter verse by verse.

Youngblood, Ronald. *The Book of Genesis.* **An Introductory Commentary. Grand Rapids: Baker, 1991. 2nd edition.**

This is extensively revised from the first edition in 2 volumes (chapters 12-50 in 1976 and 1-11 in 1980). It is a broad exposition by the Professor of Old Testament, Bethel

Theological Seminary, West. A brief introduction (pp. 9-18) upholds Mosaic authorship and a date between 1445-1405 B. C. Youngblood sees no gap in 1:2, days of chapter I partly in literary order and partly in chronological, and favors science's claim that man-like creatures were on earth five million years ago (p. 46) but man in the Adamic race in a covenant relation with God at a more recent date. He favors the human view of "sons of God" in Genesis 6 and concludes the flood was local. He offers a fairly good, very readable survey of Genesis, but it is not as valuable overall as the work by John Davis or the ones by Ross and Sailhamer.

II. EXODUS

Bentley, Michael. *Travelling Homeward. Exodus Simply Explained.* Auburn, MA: Evangelical Press, 1999.

The pastor of the Great Hollands Free Church in Bracknell, Eng., writes lucidly after his sermon series. Moses, in his view, wrote Exodus. The pharaoh in chap. 1 was a foreigner who gained power. The midwives lied as Rahab did, but God could not bless a lie itself. Bentley gives frequent practical lessons as well as a quick exposition, making many comments that become suggestive for pastors and lay readers.

Bimson, J. J. *Redating the Exodus and Conquest.* Sheffield, England: University of Sheffield, 1978.

A case reasoning that archaeological data points better to a 15th century B. C. invasion of Canaan than a 13th century date. He shows a competent grasp of information.

Binz, Stephen J. *The God of Freedom and Life. A Commentary on the Book of Exodus.* Collegeville, MN: The Liturgical Press, 1993.

This 147-pp. pb by a Catholic assumes a documentary hypothesis with Exodus put in final form ca. the 6th/5th cent. B. C. and an exodus ca. 1250 B. C. (8). No clarification occurs on whether native Egyptians or Hyksos ruled Egypt after Joseph's day. Binz passes over whether the midwives told the truth or lied to the Pharaoh. Nothing is done on the route of the exodus (57) and what "Red Sea" means is so generalized that readers see no view (58). Binz misleads in writing that whether the plagues were miracles or natural phenomena was foreign to the Israelites' minds (36). He holds to inconsistencies in Exodus (37), due to his view that a compiler at a late date juggled different sources rather frequently.

Bush, Frederic W. *Ruth, Esther* (Word Biblical Commentary). Dallas: Word, 1996.

Bush's evangelical stance is wedded with thorough scholarly attention to detail in the Hebrew. Professors, pastors who study deeply in scholarly works, and somewhat advanced students can find stimulation in probing issues with Bush, even if they will not agree at every point. In exegesis and background, with a wealth of reading in pertinent investigative literature, Bush has one of the more respected fairly recent commentaries.

Calvin, John. *Harmony of the Last Four Books of the Pentateuch.* Grand Rapids: Eerdmans, n. d.

The Geneva theologian/expositor is richly profitable on the many laws he believes cor-relate with the ten commandments (he felt that the many are facets of the ten at the core). Drawing from here and there, he has much to say. The index at the close helps the one who keeps using it. Still, particular developments in sections and chapters of the Pentateuch are not always drawn in to show how things fit together.

Childs, Brevard S. *The Book of Exodus: A Critical, Theological Commentary* (Old Testament Library). Philadelphia: Westminster, 1974. 659 pp.

Childs was Professor of Old Testament, Yale University. He has a mere four-page intro-duction, and is committed to a subjective form-critical, tradition-historical idea of strands of compositions going through a redaction process. He says he intends to explain the final, canonical text for the church's good, yet assumes and frequently brings in much on redactional strands from literary critics, and appears subjective and questionable. Each section begins with a bibliography. The textual and philological notes can be quite help-ful. But Childs calls in question the historical veracity of details as Exodus relates them (cf. p. 11). Still, the immense learning provides detailed discussions that aid the reader to look at matters from various angles and see what others regard as problems and possi-bilities. The work is more suitable for scholars or intense, advanced students who have discernment to weigh what is good and what is subjective theory pressed in. Though often liberal in its critical decisions, this work is frequently perceptive theologically to a discerning student who is maturely capable of gleaning the good and leaving the bad without being misled. In some ways its good points make it a serious example of an attempt at theological exegesis.

Clements, Ronald E. *Exodus* (Cambridge Bible Commentary). Cambridge: University Press, 1972.

He comments on the NEB text for pastors, students in schools and laypeople. He takes them often to speculative theories of strands of material, J, E, D, P. All the materials in this construction are supposedly from centuries after events they purport to describe. Clements has many references to them, assuming mere theory as fact. Typical of many works, he dates the exodus late (p. 7). He skips some verses; the commentary often is piecemeal and does not actually explain much (cf. 1:15 and its context, p. 14). At 3:2 he feels fire in the bush is a sign of God's presence, but does not discount natural explana-tions (p. 20). In 4:24-25, Clements is unable to represent to readers that the Lord really met Moses, as the text witnesses, for he supposes that this has to be out of harmony with the context. His own idea is in his judgment better: some evil power of the desert attacked Moses (p. 31). Much comment, however, is beneficial if one weighs things with discern-ment and is on guard wisely about Clements' liberal perspective; he sifts the good from the misleading opinion.

Cole, R. Alan. *Exodus*. Downers: Grove, IL: IVP, 1973. 239 pp.

A good commentary reflecting a breadth of reading and awareness of good scholarship, in the Tyndale Old Testament Commentary series. It is one of the better brief works.

Currid, John D. *A Study Commentary on Exodus*. Auburn, MA: Evangelical Press, 2000.

Simplicity and application mark this 415-pp. help for lay people, young Christians and pastors needing suggestions on how to show the relevancy. The book is by a faculty member at Reformed Theological Seminary, Jackson, Miss. He covers Exod. 1-18. Though he dates the exodus in the 13th century when it ought to be ca. 1447 B. C., he deals at times with expositional problems such as whether the midwives (Exod. 1) lied or spoke truthfully to the Pharaoh (he says the latter as God' blessing allowed Israelites to increase). In each section, Curris shows how to apply a point today. The book is good, but not near being among the top works.

Davies, G. Henton. *Exodus: Introduction and Commentary* **(Torch Bible Commentary). London: SCM, 1967. 253 pp.**

A preface and lengthy introduction (11-55) concludes that not all material in Exodus is from Moses' day. It gives a survey of scholarly opinion, and thinks much bare fact does appear in the account (p. 29). The plagues were historical, the exodus was late, the two and a half million in the exodus is too high a figure (p. 41), and he endorses J, E, P documents in a redactional process (48, 53-55). The commentary is frequently fairly good, frequently explains little (1:1-6; 1:1522), intersperses subjective theory about which redactional strand is involved (this interrupts the flow of thought, cf. p. 75) and pulls in highly unnecessary suggestions at times (the firstborn theme in Exodus 4 does not occur again until after 11:4, so the sequence is from 4:22f. to ch. 11, and chs. 5-10 are a series of parentheses (p. 76)). Overall, this work ranks far down the line in getting at what Exodus itself is saying, even if it has good material at many spots.

Davis, John J. *Moses and the Gods of Egypt.* **Grand Rapids: Baker, 1972. 331 pp.**

Here is a series of chapters on highlights of Exodus, reflecting a good grasp of historical backgrounds, customs, the divine message in Exodus, and the like. Davis has established himself solidly as a very competent and widely studied writer on various parts of the Old Testament. He is on the faculty of Grace College, Winona Lake, IN.

Driver, S. R. *The Book of Exodus.* **Cambridge: University Press, 1911.**

This work in the Cambridge Bible series is another careful work in Hebrew exegesis with helpful comments on matters of historical background and word meanings. It helps on problems, though Driver was liberal.

Durham, John I. *Exodus,* **(Word Biblical Commentary). Waco, TX: Word Book, 1987. 516 pp.**

He furnishes much help on textual and exegetical details, customs, etc., and often has good comments in explaining verses as they stand. However, he uses higher critical assumptions in such a way that he casts doubt on or denies reliability of details. He recognizes that the final form of the text which we have is what needs to be explained, but does not think that such matters as chronological references of when things happened are accurate. He provides lengthy lists of sources but gives little attention to conservative studies. No doubt his work will be primarily of assistance to liberal readers, despite the WBC being billed as an evangelical work.

Ellison, H. L. *Exodus* **(Daily Bible Study Series). Philadelphia: Westminster, 1982.**

Surprisingly, barely over a page of introduction precedes a commentary on the RSV set up under brief captions such as "The Burning Bush." He dates the exodus late. Much space is used just printing the RSV, and it breaks up continuity. He assumes the midwives lied, and says apart from the last plague "there is nothing supernatural in the plagues on Egypt" (p. 40). He deems it probable that when Moses thrust a piece of wood into Marah's waters, "nothing miraculous was intended" (85). Yet to him the manna and the water out of the rock were supernatural (90, 92). Quite a bit of the survey is helpful, even if one is perplexed here and there by Ellison's unnecessary conclusions.

Enns, Peter. *Exodus* (The NIV Application Commentary). Grand Rapids: Zondervan, 2000.

The series aim is to state three things, the original idea, comments making a bridge from then to now, and the application today. One partially misleading idea is that the original point is not vital unless somebody now points it out, whereas for interpretation or application the Holy Spirit is able to do this when the factors are right. Enns does shed light by lucid writing pursuing a clear outline, but the value varies. On 1:8, he seems unaware that the pharaoh who did not know Joseph may have been a Hyksos king from outside (42). At several points ponderous detail on bridging from the past to the present leaves more emphasis on application than really explaining the text. What takes several pp. might be stated in a couple of paragraphs. Sometimes so many Exodus chapters are explained in one section before giving application that much of the original import of details can be lost with no specific connections made. One can find a list of writers on Bible books in this series on p. 8, and the contribution will vary depending on factors in each case. Some writers are notable (Daniel Block, Deut.; Douglas Moo, Romans, also 2 Peter and Jude; Craig Blomberg, I Cor.).

Erdman, Charles R. *Exodus*. Grand Rapids: Eerdmans (n. d.).

This is only a brief, survey work. Its value to the expositor lies in its helpfulness in giving the sweep and movement of Exodus. It is not of help down in the trenches of exegesis.

Feinberg, C. L. "Tabernacle," *Zondervan Pictorial Encyclopedia of the Bible*, Volume 5, pp. 572-83. Grand Rapids: Zondervan, 1975.

Excellent well-organized survey of main facets of information about the Tabernacle, showing awareness of views and cogent reasons for conservative perspectives.

Getz, Gene. Moses: *Moments of Glory...Feet of Clay*. Glendale, CA: G/L Publications/Regal, 1976.

Simple character portraits with principles for ministers and laypeople today. Refreshing, stimulating.

Gooding, D. W. *The Account of the Tabernacle*. Cambridge: University Press, 1959.

A well-regarded work using the LXX text as a basis and exercising perception.

Houtman, Cornelis. *Exodus*. 3 vols. Kampen: Kok, 1993-1999. Only 2 vols. have been rendered into English so far.

Houtman provides a bonanza of detailed explanation using grammar, word study, and comments on views, as well as the significance theologically.

Hyatt, J. P. *Commentary on Exodus* **(New Century Bible). Greenwood, SC: Attic Press, 1971.**

A thorough-going liberal belief in J, E, P, R [the latter, he says, is a Deuteronomic redactor] pervades the introduction and commentary. So Exodus is not primarily a historical record but a deposit of traditions, he says (p. 37). Yet the narrative, professing to be history, "rests upon a solid core of historical happening" (38). "It is not possible, however, for us now to disentangle all the historical and legendary elements in this book" (38). He rejects an early date for Israel's exodus, favoring a 13th century exit (43). The comments verse by verse are often good, though the reader has to be prepared to read of inconsistencies, contradictions, etc. in Hyatt's opinion. The narrative of Moses' birth (2:1-10) is, he says, legend, not history, and compares with myths and legends as of stories about Hercules, Romulus, Cyrus, etc. (62). He cites as striking the similarity between Moses being put in an ark on the water and Sargon in the mid 3rd century B. C. whose mother placed him in a basket of rushes on a river where he was rescued by royalty (62). Hyatt here, as in other places, mentions helpful detail, e.g. Josephus' account of Moses' father having a vision of how Moses would deliver his people, and Philo's details of Moses' lavish education (63). In Exodus 12, no attempt is made to see aspects of the Passover as typical of Jesus Christ. He rejects the 600,000 figure for men in 12:37, Numbers 11:21 and the similar 603,550 in Numbers 1:46 as not credible and he supposes the correct number is a few thousand, exaggerated by Israelite tradition (139). Hyatt has many such ideas, often put forth by liberals, but also frequently good information helpful to those who take a more approving view of the text. As a liberal work, it is a good commentary and shows good use of recent scholarly literature.

Janzen, Waldemar. *Exodus* **(Believers Church Bible Commentary). Scottsdale, PA: Herald Press, 2000.**

This is for Bible study teachers, students, and pastors wanting a simple exposition. Janzen is out of an Anabaptist/Mennonite background. His discussion on passages varies from exposition that explains the biblical flow itself to taking general ideas and elaborating on their modern relevancy. At times claims are dubious, for instance Janzen's view that words taken to mean that Zapphora touches Moses' feet are a euphemism for touching his genitals; proof-texts offered for this are questionable (Isa. 6:2; 7:20; Ruth 3:4-14). (p. 85). A book such as John Davis's *Moses and the Gods of Egypt* gets to crucial points with accuracy more often. Janzen on occasion wanders about for a while, seeking to show modern relevancy, helpfully only in some of them, at other times distracting from the flow

Kaiser, Walter C., Jr. "Exodus" (*Expositor's Bible Commentary*), **ed. Frank Gaebelein and R. P. Polcyn. Volume 2. Grand Rapids: Zondervan, 1990.**

Conservative, Kaiser has fine verse by verse elucidation that shows keen awareness of and help on problems as well as the flow of the book. He is profitable in matters of context, word study, exegesis, background, customs, etc., and uses a wealth of scholarly literature to furnish further benefit. It is a firm evangelical effort.

Keil, C. F. and Franz Delitzsch. *The Pentateuch.* **Cf. his Commentaries on the Old Testament, Analytical (earlier in this work).**

Kidner, Derek. *Hard Sayings*. Grand Rapids: Eerdmans, 1972.

Concise comments on Old Testament moral teaching, often as related to the ten commandments. Sometimes provocative for Christian nourishment and growth, and a stimulant for expositors, done by a keen scholar.

Lockshin, Martin, ed. *Rashbam's Commentary on Exodus, An Annotated Translation*. Atlanta: Scholars Press, 1997.

Lockshin has edited, translated and furnished copious notes to help Rabbi ben Muir's (Rashbam's) commentary. The commentator lived ca. 1085—1174 in N. France, and was a scholar of the Jewish law and grandson of the eminent Rashi. Rashbam is devoted to getting the "plain" contextual and grammatical meaning, rather than midrashic additions of rabbinic belief; he wants the text to speak its own message. But his anti-Christian polemicist drive enters in. He reads into some verses, for example Moses was born after six months (Exod. 2), so was Samuel (I Sam. 1:20) (pp. 20-21). Still, on some verses he gives provocative possibilities (cf. 4:25). One learns much about Jewish interpretation, and scholars find stimulation at times. The work is for these, and does not seem to offer many expositors much extra help that other works do not cover.

Mackay, John L. *Exodus* (A Mentor Commentary). Fearn, Ross-shire: Great Britain, 2001.

Much good is here for pastors and diligent lay readers in an evangelical effort at interpretation and application. Mackay achieves one of the best expositions on the biblical book. He dates the exodus ca. 1447 B. C., and supplies detail on the early and late dating of the exodus (13-20); he concludes that evidence, especially the authority of the NT, supports Moses as the author (22-23). His remarks seem to be balanced as he does not dodge problem texts or become vague. An example is on seeing the plagues as miracles or natural phenomena, where he favors the former.

McCarthy, Dennis. *Old Testament Covenant*. Nashville: John Knox Press, 1972.

The reader will find much here in discussion of Old Testament laws and the ten commandments, with a lot pulled together.

Meyer, F. B. *Devotional Commentary on Exodus*. Grand Rapids: Kregel, 1978. 476 pp.

This is a reprint of an old classic, 2 volumes in 1. Meyer, who did the refreshing books on characters in Genesis and other Bible books, was a great English expositor known for his close walk with God, his stimulating spiritual life works, and preaching; he takes Christians through Exodus passage by passage. He organizes lessons to point out timeless principles which frequently are insightful and gripping. Many paragraphs are headed by boldface statements showing the subject.

Moorehead, W. G. *Studies in the Mosaic Institutions*. New York: Revell, 1893.

Excellent evangelical studies especially on the tabernacle.

Murphy, James G. *A Critical and Exegetical Commentary on the Book of Exodus*. Eugene, OR: Wipf & Stock, 1998 reprint.

This old evangelical work of 591 pp. has some value at times for pastors, but so many works are superior. Murphy gives only his own comments, and only now and then any special help. The old writing style slows reading and takes longer to get to a point. Comments often point in a good direction but brevity hampers. In 6:6, an attempt to explain "it repented the Lord" offers no direct resolution. In 12:1-3 one finds no explanation of what nation from Abraham would be blessed, or any elaboration, though much on God blessing all nations. Jacob's color scheme (Gen. 30) would influence colors of animals' offspring, but on Gen. 30 the author acknowledges that these allegedly "legitimate" means would succeed only if God caused this (cp. 453, 459). Murphy leaves unresolved whether Joseph used divination (545).

Noth, Martin. *Exodus* (Old Testament Library). Philadelphia: Westminster, 1962. 283 pp.

A highly regarded work among scholars pursuing literary composition theories and late-dating. Noth holds that the Pentateuch cannot be by one writer, Moses, due to what he regards as the assured results of scholarly study (p. 12). He subscribes to subjective J, E, P strands (12-18), and says his commentary deals with the final form. Throughout, he has frequent recourse to aspects of his hypothesis. Comments sometimes offer real meat, at other times have scarcely anything beyond generality which one can already see in the verses. Noth says parts of the narrative may have been grafted on artificially in a later composition by a redactor. Much speculative opinion posits editorial strands that were not in the original telling. We often get more of Noth's theory than substantial explanation of the text. He supposes contradictions, such as Moses being presented as a firstborn child in Exodus 2, then presently having an older sister (p. 25). To him, similar rescue stories shaped Israelite minds to make up a Moses story like this (27) to intermingle with whatever in the passage may have historically happened. The "story of the plagues has no real purpose . . ." (68). One often feels that things which can be seen meaningfully are being manipulated to suit the commentator's opinion. Conservative readers with perception and maturity can alertly find much good help amidst all of this. The work is an example of a scholar presiding in judgment over the Scripture, often bringing into question the veracity.

Phillips, A. *Ancient Israel's Criminal Law*. New York: Schocken, 1970.

He devotes more detail to exegesis than Kidner's work. One can glean much here by patient study.

Pink, Arthur W. *Gleanings in Exodus*. Chicago: Moody (n. d.).

Like his work on Genesis, this book is devotional in thrust and quite voluminous (384 large two-column pages, well over 700 pages in an ordinary book). If one is doing a detailed study of Exodus to present messages to a congregation, this is a good book to consult for stimulating thoughts as well as applications and exhortations. Pink overdoes some types.

Propp, William H. C. *Exodus 1-18* (Anchor Bible). NY : Doubleday, 1999.

Here is a translation, then an introduction, finally a commentary. Propp sees the exodus story as unmistakably resembling the Canaanite myth of the storm God Balu, biblical Baal (34), but some will not agree that an adequate resemblance exists. Propp's attempts to show the theme of Exodus miss the mark, the aspect of redemption (36-37). He is against Mosaic authorship and committed to a view of J, P, JE and E documents (49, 52) and later writers/compilers who wound up with contradictory accounts and laws (53).

One meets massive detail but extremely labored reading, sometimes disjointed statements that require patience getting through the maze of references. A "redaction analysis" gives Propp's perspective as to sources he thinks were behind statements (this in virtually each section). Often a passage's problems find no explanation, for example did the midwives lie, and if so how does he react to this (1:19-20)? No date for the exodus appears in chapter 12.

Ramm, Bernard L. *God's Way Out. Finding the Road to Personal Freedom through Exodus*. Ventura, CA: Regal Books, 1984, 1987. 166 pp.

Simple, clear, running commentary, not verse by verse, centered on God's attributes and work, types of Christ and His church, New Testament truth related to Exodus, and application to life today. Ramm has intriguing chapter titles, sweeping surveys rich in connections to life now, notes on word meanings, and refreshment that warms the heart. Chapter 4 on Moses' excuses and God's answers is entitled, "God Can Use Even You." The popular-level survey is adept in simplifying a long book into three very manageable points, Divine Redemption, Divine Morality (The Law), and Divine Worship. Its contribution is in the synthesis, the perspective that copes with so much detail.

Sarna, Nahum M. *Exodus* (Jewish Publication Society Torah Commentary). New York: JPS, 1991. 278 pp.

A Jewish effort that quite often furnishes definite help in its straight-forward approach, Sarna uses the Massoretic Hebrew text side by side with the JPS rendering into English at the top and his commentary on the last half or three-quarters of the large pages. Footnotes come in sections at the end of the commentary. Sarna is cogent with word meanings, customs, resolution of problems and giving possibilities briefly. He favors a late exodus. He cites scholarly literature without the constant intrusion of theories of literary strands, At times fairly good detail sums up matters, as on "flowing with milk and honey" (3:8; p. 16). The commentary is excellent on some texts, such as 6:3, 7:11, and 11:5. Some miracles passages are given a natural explanation, as Moses using a piece of wood to render Marah's water drinkable, e.g., the water filtered through porous wood, straining impurities (p. 84). By contrast, the manna is said to have no naturalistic explanation (p. 89). Among excursuses at the end, No. 2 is a fine citation of different abandoned hero stories sometimes cited at Exodus 2, with an evaluation that the account of Moses is markedly different in several details (267-68).

Soltau, Henry W. *The Holy Vessels and Furniture of the Tabernacle*. Grand Rapids: Kregel, n. d. Also The Tabernacle, The Priesthood, and the Offerings. Christian Publications, 1965.

He is often helpful on typology, giving insightful attention to connections with the New Testament. Cf. also C. W. Slemming's books *These are the Garments*, and *Made According to Pattern*, which go into much detail on priestly clothing and tabernacle furniture.

Stamm, J. J. and M. E. Andrew. *The Ten Commandments in Recent Research*. London: SCM, 1967.

The authors provide considerable exegesis of the text and therefore help on details.

Watson, Thomas. *The Ten Commandments*. **Edinburgh: Banner of Truth Trust, 1976 rp (cf. also his works on** *The Beatitudes, The Lord's Prayer,* **and** *A Divine Cordial,* **the latter on Romans 8:28).**

A popular London preacher in Puritan times wrote this exploration of the commandments in depth. Many insights are helpful for preaching, also a section on the law and sin, and the way of salvation. In the latter discussion, Watson deals with faith, repentance, the word, baptism, the Lord's Supper, and prayer, relating each to salvation and Christian commitment. He also has a section on infant baptism. The portion on the Lord's Supper covers the subject from various angles.

Youngblood, Ronald, F. *Exodus*. **Chicago, IL: Moody Press, 1983.**

Youngblood of Bethel Theological Seminary (West) in San Diego has written this helpful 144-pp. paperback for the Everyman's Bible Commentary Series. He divides Exodus into twelve great theses: Persecution, Preparation, Confrontation, Plagues, Passover, Redemption, Journey, Covenant, Law, Tabernacle, Priesthood and Renewal. His introduction shows that he is well-versed in the "documentary hypothesis," and he argues forcibly for Mosaic authorship of Exodus. He does, however, appear to be significantly less conclusive about a Mosaic authorship of either Genesis/Pentateuch. He adopts the more traditional evangelical date of writing (1445 B.C.) and defends it admirably. Youngblood also shows familiarity with Egyptian culture and setting. The volume is practical enough for the preacher and "Hebrew" enough for the seminary student. Youngblood's treatment of the nine plagues as three threes, and his desire to couch these in some form of scientific credibility is one of his debatable points. Additionally, he views the Red Sea crossing as the lesser possibility, and opts for the common idea "sea of reeds" which he locates further to the north. Chapters 19-24 of Exodus are dealt with under the general theme of "Covenant." Youngblood's entries under "Temple" and "Priesthood" are also excellent. They are descriptive enough so that even the novice can grasp the full ramifications of Jewish temple culture. Conclusion: on the whole a fine work by a conservative scholar, but it does require critical reading. -Jan Sattem

III. LEVITICUS

Allis, Oswald T. "Leviticus," in *New Bible Commentary Revised,* **ed. D. Guthrie et al. Grand Rapids: Eerdmans, 1970, pp. 140-67.**

A good, brief commentary by a skilled conservative Old Testament scholar. He takes Mosaic authorship, and for this in the same volume cf. J. W. Wenham, "Moses and the Pentateuch," pp. 41-43, and E. J. Young, "History of the Literary Criticism of the Pentateuch," 38-40.

Bamberger, Bernard J. *Leviticus* **(The Torah, A Modem Commentary). New York: Union of Hebrew Congregations, 1979. 417 pp.**

A Jewish scholar has subscribed to liberal theories. He says that the first half of Leviticus "contains much that is not relevant to our times" (xv). He assumes multiple authorship, discrepancies that show the book is a composite from various sources (xviii-xix), writing as late as the exile and post-exilic days, though with redactors preserving without change much of what was earlier. He says that the central tabernacle with its highly organized sacrifice system must have been added later since it is, to him, "completely inappropriate to desert conditions" (xix). He uses the Jewish Publication Society translation into English, revised in 1967. Sections of commentary are prefaced with general introductions as chapter I has six pages on sacrifices in ancient times. Comments are often very helpful, but usually terse, and some verses are skipped. He gives only one view for why Nadab and Abihu were consumed in Leviticus 10, but in a section called "Gleanings" presents other views (p. 85). Often he sheds light by reviewing explanations in history, as on reasons for dietary laws in Chapter 11 (pp. 90-9 1). There also is a good section on dietary laws in Jewish history (91-92) and in Reformed Judaism (93-94). The work has a wealth of help at times on Jewish interpretation and also on views in general.

Bellinger, Jr., W. H. *Leviticus and Numbers* (New International Biblical Commentary). Peabody, MA: Hendrickson Publishers, Inc., 2001.

This work using the NIV allots 166 pp. to Lev. and pp. 169-321 to Num. Bellinger assigns different parts of Lev. to different periods of composition, for instance the Holiness Code (chs. 17-27) came together probably in the 6th cent. B. C. (p. 6). Many readers will not think that necessary. Comments on verses are often terse, but frequently offer some good help. Some explanations fall short of adequacy, as on "unauthorized fire" in 10:1. The writer relates the double length of time for cleansing after a female is born to male chauvenism of the culture, "a social preference for males in the Priestly ideology" (78). That seems questionable and lacking adequacy. Citations of other studies are not nearly as copious or full as in some works, such as by Milgrom and Rooker. The pages on Num. are of about the same quality, good but not outstanding.

Bonar, Andrew, 1810-92. *A Commentary on the Book of Leviticus*. Grand Rapids: Zondervan, 1959; now Grand Rapids: Baker, 1978.

This is a reprint of a work which Spurgeon described as "very precious." Bonar treats the text in an expository and practical way, with critical notes. He is thoroughly conservative, and rich in application. Many regard this as the best older work on Leviticus from a conservative writer.

Erdman, Charles R. *The Book of Leviticus*. NY: Revell, 1951.

This is a synthesis which helps the student find his way through the many details of Leviticus with an understanding of the flow of thought or argument.

Gerstenberger, S. *Leviticus, A Commentary* (OT Library). Louisville, KY: Westminster John Knox Press, 1996.

This uses the new RSV, gives a translation from Hebrew, and seeks to show the socio-theological import of the text (19), with some focus on application to today. The writer assumes composition in the 5th to 3rd centuries B. C., and theorizes various layers that a compiler used. Due to his own opinion on a late date, based on his skewed ideas, he imposes incongruity into Leviticus. An example is his theory that to bring an offering to the tent's entrance gate, one site, and for Aaronic priests to officiate "disregards the dispersal of the postexilic communities" (35). Readers can be bothered by the lack of consistency in the commentary, for instance in giving an analysis for some sections and not for others. In some parts a reader finds verse by verse comments, in others none. Scholars seeking detail on some probing questions in Leviticus will find usefulness here only at times.

Goldberg, Louis. *Leviticus: A Study Guide Commentary.* **Grand Rapids: Zondervan, 1980.**

Goldberg was Professor of Theology and Jewish Studies at Moody Bible Institute. His introduction is very evangelical, he supplies a detailed outline at the outset, and has clear, well-standardized syntheses of sections as well as helpful comments on each sub-section that help an expositor. Unlike such a commentator as Snaith, he shows a relation to typology and does it sanely. He also pauses to point out principles for believers today. At various points he provides lists of suggestions for further pertinent study or reflection on key areas or questions. This is a good, brief commentary that gives insight on the chief details and can stimulate an expositor.

Gorman, Frank H., Jr. *Divine Presence and Community, A Commentary on The Book of Leviticus.* **Grand Rapids: Eerdmans, 1997.**

This 163-pp. pb puts its main focus on God's presence dwelling with His people. and what it means to live in God's presence (xi). Gorman looks at ways to enact holiness. He assumes that Lev. was written during Israel's Babylonian exile, even as it reflects practices of an earlier time, yet Israel in reflecting on matters in changing scenes adapted traditions, practices, and ritual life shaped at later times, not the days of Moses (p. 2). In such a view, some continue to ask how readers today can decide which details to relate reliably to the time of Moses and which are artificially put in as if fitting there but actually referring to the time of later shapers of the account. Gorman does offer some good comments on the relevancy of holiness, but complicates things with claims to see parallels between the Genesis creation account and details in Lev. Some of the discussions are quite oblique and perplexing, and the need to follow the reasoning hard to follow or view as fair. An instance is on pp. 17-19 which make it appear wrong or suspect for Christians to see details in Lev. as having meaning then but also pointing on to a fuller picture in Christ's redeeming work. While many comments offer help, one can wonder if the explanation too often stirs further difficulty , for example in saying that leaven and honey were not to be used with altar offering because they were related to decay and death. If so, why do they not fit on an altar where dead animals are offered?

Harris, R. Laird. "Leviticus" (*Expositor's Bible Commentary*), **ed. Frank Gaebelein and R. P. Polcyn. Volume 2. Grand Rapids: Zondervan, 1990.**

The Professor of Old Testament, Covenant Theological Seminary, is conservative, contributing by the panorama the introductory sections give on scholarly discussion and views, as well as verse by verse detail fitted in its historical context of the wilderness era.

Harrison, R. K. *Leviticus. An Introduction and Commentary* **(Tyndale OTC). Downers Grove, IL: IVP, 1980. 252 pp.**

Highly-regarded among conservatives, the book upholds veracity of many matters. Harrison draws from his expertise in ancient studies, Some believe that he does not give dietary details their due in explaining much as hygienic. He argues for Mosaic authorship and usually is very helpful on how sections fit and how verses can be explained reasonably.

Jukes, Andrew. *The Law of the Offerings.* **London: James Nisbet, 1870.**

This famous work deals exclusively with Leviticus 1-7, explaining the offerings and the laws regulating them. Devotional in character.

Keil, C. F. and Franz Delitzsch. *The Pentateuch*. **Cf. Commentaries on the Old Testament, Analytical.**

Kellogg, S. H. *The Book of Leviticus*. **In the Expositors Bible. NY: A. C. Armstrong and Son, 1903; rp by Klock & Klock, 1978.**

This lucid broader work is one of the best theologically on Leviticus. It deals perceptively with some questions not touched upon by Bonar. However, it is weak on application.

Kidner, Derek. *Leviticus, Numbers, Deuteronomy* **(Scripture Union Bible Study Books). Grand Rapids: Eerdmans, 1971. 92 pp.**

This is a preparation for laypeople's daily segments of Bible reading. An outline of each book runs throughout, and comments on each chapter are about a half page or more. Brevity prevails, and he has done a fine job in this to get to the gist of things for those who desire a quick look and survey.

Kurtz, J. H. *Sacrificial Worship of the Old Testament*. **Grand Rapids: Baker, 1980. Reprint of a work first appearing in 1863.**

Kurtz has long been a help on details on sacrifice at the tabernacle and how this met needs of Israelites. Its usability led Baker to make it available again.

Levine, Baruch A. *Leviticus* **(Jewish Publication Society Torah Commentary). NY: JPS, 1989. 284 pp.**

Assumes stages of redaction and different segments from various times (xxx). An extended introduction (31 pp.) synthesizes the structure (1-16, manuals of practical address to priests; 17-27, priests' teachings to the other people). It also has a good survey on the critical method and problems scholars think they are resolving. Levine includes notes at the ends of the introduction, commentary, and a special section on "Leviticus in the Ongoing Jewish Tradition," and at the end excursuses such as "The Meaning of the Dietary Laws," "The Sabbath," "The Annual Festivals," etc. The commentary verse by verse is sometimes brief, sometimes detailed, beneath the Hebrew Massoretic text and JPS English translation set side by side. Levine is excellent on word meaning, helpful on exegesis and customs (such as salt used in sacrifices, p.13; honey used or not used, p. 12). He cites a plethora of scholarly literature for perception on some matters. Often he gives several views, as on the nature of the offense by Aaron's sons (chapter 10; p. 59).

Milgrom, Jacob. *Leviticus*. **3 vols. NY: Doubleday, 1991—2000.**

This work is very impressive in its command of the subjects and scholarly literature helpful on them. Often Milgrom takes views conservatives will appreciate. He argues at length for the ancient rooting of material called priestly, and the reasonableness of seeing Aaron and his line of priests as historical. His commentary often cites from medieval Jewish exegetes who have been much passed over by scholarship in general. He also draws from scholars of the past century and a half, such as Kalisch, Driver, Noth, Snaith, Wenham, Harrison and Levine (cf. his lengthy bibliography, pp. 69-128). A translation and broad introduction precedes sections, then Milgrom gives "Notes" which deal exhaustively with verses (9 pp. on 1:1, etc.). He explains problems, such as prohibiting leaven and honey and including salt (2:11-13) and the reason Nadab and Abihu were struck down in the midst of service in 10:1 (cf. p. 598 and pp. 633-35 where he cites twelve views of rabbis). He goes into much detail on why some foods, as pork, were prohibited (cf. his verse by verse commentary plus special sections, 691-742). Few stones are left unturned. At the end are indices of subjects, terms, authors, sources in Scripture, Apocrypha/Pseudepigrapha, Qumran, Versions, Targums, Rabbinics, etc. The 3 vols add up to 2714 pp., at ca. $150.00. The last 2 vols. are, as the first, massive in learned explanation. Milgrom often gives much insight on what the text means, more overall than any other commentary. One must be aware that nearly 1/3 of the work's pp. are devoted to issues other than verse by verse comments, much of this helpful to scholars, wordy, repetitious or on matters that most will not see as needed. As in using Aune's 3-vol. work on the Revelation, one may have to pass over much to get at what seems most pertinent.

Noordtzij, A. *Leviticus* (Bible Student's Commentary). Grand Rapids: Zondervan, 1982. 280 pp.

Cf. Aalders under Genesis. Though this is an evangelical series and Noordtzij is conservative on much, he posits the Mosaic origin of some material and much later origin of other material (pp. 12, 189). The publisher's note at the outset alerts readers to the mixed bag. But on many details the author writes against the Wellhausen school, and says it sees much of Leviticus as "deliberate deceit" (11). On many passages he is quite helpful and frequently has a high view of the integrity, a good study of problems, etc. Read with alertness and discernment, the work yields some benefit.

Noth, Martin. *Leviticus, A Commentary* (Old Testament Library). Philadelphia: Westminster, 1965. 208 pp.

As on Exodus, Noth offers much solid material explaining verses with basic information conservatives will find usable. But again he depends on a theory of literary compositions according to scholarly guesswork and subjective reasoning. He admits scholars vary. The commentary is often terse but usually has some help. Readers need to be alert to discern where Noth is delivering speculation from his sources agenda and not the text itself. He is often clear, but sometimes unclear and incomplete, as when he leaves vague why leaven, prohibited in 2:11-13, is permitted in 7:13 (p. 61). On 23:17 he is a bit more helpful on leaven's allowance.

Rooker, Mark F. *Leviticus* (New American Commentary). Nashville: Broadman & Holman, 2000.

A graduate of Dallas Seminary, Brandeis, and the Hebrew University of Jerusalem did this. Rooker details the documentary hypothesis, evidence against it, and biblical reasons for Moses as author (23-39). A good section looks at theological themes—holiness, sacrifice, atonement and blood, repentance, and sacrifice/atonement in the NT, the purpose of the law in the OT and for the Christian, law and grace, etc. The writer reflects awareness of the offerings, use of leaven and salt, views on offering strange fire (10:1), a woman's purification after childbirth, and reasons for the different lengths of time after a male or a female child. He is helpful on other details such as cleansing from skin infections (chs. 13-14), the two goats (ch. 16), etc. Rooker's footnotes show broad research and offer enrichment for readers in a notably good commentary.

Schultz, Samuel. *Leviticus: God Among His People* **(Everyman's Bible Commentary). Chicago: Moody, 1983. 141 pp.**

This teacher for forty-one years at Wheaton College says, "Leviticus may be the most neglected book in the Old Testament" (p. 7). He provides fairly good introductory remarks (pp. 7-32). Chapter 2, next, leaps on to 8:1-10:20, "God Among His People." Then Chapter 3 switches back to 1:1-7:38. Why not recognize God among His people in Exodus 40, then move right on to Leviticus 1:1? From 11:1 on, Schultz keeps to the Leviticus sequence. He writes clearly, simply, explaining main aspects in a conservative vein and showing how they relate to today in principle. Some things are left unclear, as a reference to G. J. Wenham explaining uncleanness laws on food (Leviticus 11) as symbolical, stemming from a social anthropologist's study, but not defining what the symbolical meaning in that view is (p. 72). However, much of the book is to the point, even if brief.

Snaith, Norman H. *Leviticus and Numbers* **(The Century Bible). Camden, New Jersey. Thomas Nelson and Sons, 1967.**

He works on a foundation of non-Mosaic authorship, rather groups of authors from different centuries a la Robert Pfeiffer, Otto Eissfeldt, etc. This is a foregone conclusion with him. So, writers of P read back details of the Ezra temple into the ancient tabernacle of the wilderness (p. 28), etc. Many contradictions are seen in the account which have been reconciled well by others. From this standpoint it is disconcerting to come expecting explanations of the text and be met by various theories (assumptions) of different, supposed inconsistencies according to radical ways of construing things. Yet Snaith does, of course, have many helpful details on word meanings. Many verses are skipped over in comments. The reader is plunged into detail verse by verse without introduction of a kind that synthesizes or gives the sweep of sections or compares the offerings in Leviticus for perspective. Often details are interspersed to tell readers of similar or comparable practices among other peoples. Typological reference to the New Testament is missing. Occasionally Snaith gives helpful illustrations, e.g. on Leviticus 4:2, sinning "unwittingly": like "a devout Jew of modern times involved in a breakdown of transport on the Eve of the Sabbath so far from home that he must break the Sabbath rule concerning making a journey" (p. 41; cf. also 12:1-8, p. 90). He is not afraid to sit in judgment, as in 4:7 where to his notion putting blood on horns of the altar is "a wholly animistic way of thinking" (p. 43). The story of Nadab and Abihu being rejected (Leviticus 10) has to be, in his scheme, a late story of post-exilic times to justify why these two and their descendants had no place in the priesthood, and show the rights of the accepted Aaronic priesthood (p. 75). He appears to accept the idea that the holy devouring fire on Nadab and Abihu in Leviticus 10 is a primitive idea that should be discounted today as in liberal, humanistic belief (p. 76). He often perceives the point of an episode, as the two goats on the Day of Atonement (p. 112). Things many regard as types are not related to possible antitypes in the New Testament, as the great offerings, the Day of Atonement, manna. Snaith cannot grasp how God showed Himself to be holy in Numbers 20:13 unless it be in "might and awesomeness" (p. 276).

Wenham., Gordon J. *The Book of Leviticus* **(NICOT). Grand Rapids: Eerdmans, 1979.**

Sparkling, inviting and generally convincing effort at showing the modern meaning and relevance of Leviticus, based on the legitimate and inherent meaning of the text. Displays a minimum of "reaching," and a real respect for the canonical text. Indispensable for preaching or teaching, and rewarding for personal (serious) study. -Dan Phillips

IV. NUMBERS

Allen, Ronald B. "Numbers" (*Expositor's Bible Commentary*) Volume 2, ed. Frank Gaebelein and R. P. Polcyn. Grand Rapids: Zondervan, 1990.

A then Professor of Old Testament at Western Conservative Baptist Seminary, Portland, OR (he later has taught at Dallas Theological Seminary) has provided this excellent conservative introduction, also a verse by verse commentary, usually handling problems adeptly. Many will find this theory on the numbers being too high as hard to accept realistically with a high view of Scripture.

Ashley, Timothy R. *The Book of Numbers* (NICOT). Grand Rapids: Eerdmans, 1993.

This favors a preexilic date for final composition with Moses a key in the first writing for some of the material (7). A 24-pp. bibliography precedes the commentary. Ashley favors a late exodus date (47). He gives six problems in the census counts being so many (60-61), plus scholars' views and evaluations of views (61-65), finally suggesting that the numbers were about a third of what Numbers says (65-66). Then he concludes that the ancient system of counting is unknown to people today, but he does not take the numbers as literal. Much of the time is spent commenting on elements of different documents he recognizes and whether they are feasible or not. Still he devotes much explanation to many of the verses. Apparently he favors priestly details being in Moses' day, not devised only centuries later (88). Sometimes discussions end with no leaning, for example in the suspected adulteress's thigh falling and belly swelling (133). All in all one receives much help on what verses mean or may mean, but a tangle of differences between taking some details as reliable and others as not.

Budd, Philip J. *Numbers* (Word Biblical Commentary). Waco: Word Books, 1984. 409 pp.

Budd accepts a J, E, D, P scheme of literary sources, regarding Genesis-Joshua as put together by priestly writers in the sixth to fifth centuries B. C., writing to enhance their own concerns and meet problems of their day. Budd takes very little in the various incidents to be trustworthy history (xxvi-xxxi, etc.); it rather is tradition on which scholars can pronounce. If one wants to read on past the fairly current critical judgment on Numbers, gain profit from extensive bibliography, and stick with sometimes ponderous discussions of scholars' opinions, he can learn much here. But Budd holds that much is relevant only to a time centuries later than the wilderness wanderings. For example, Korah's rebellion (Numbers 16), in Budd's imagination, addresses a power struggle in post-exilic days between Zadokite and Levite priests. Much of the commentary furnishes examples of the commentator's theories artificially forced upon Numbers, this being more pervasive than an illumination of the book in a wilderness setting in which conservatives believe it more naturally fits. The discerning student who is rightly oriented to the wilderness setting of the book can profit much from understanding fine word study, exegesis etc. to relate to that and not later times where Budd places things.

Cole, R. Dennis. *Numbers* **(New American Commentary). Nashville: Broadman & Holman, 2000.**

This is a good commentary on most parts, but Cole follows Ron Allen in seeing large numbers in census lists as hyperbole. Many cannot take seriously or honouring to God his claim that badly exaggerated numbering "was not for misrepresentation but for powerful demonstration of Yahweh's continuous blessing and a statement of confidence" in His multiplication (82). Does God need untruth, and do such purposes justify untruth (cf. 78-82)? On many verses, Cole gets to the point more helpfully than some, and where relevant shows awareness of various possibilities.

Gray, George G. *A Critical and Exegetical Commentary on Numbers* **(ICC). Edinburgh: T. & T. Clark, 1912.**

This is a detailed commentary relevant to the serious student who desires help on problem passages as well as general help throughout the book. See earlier comments on the I.C.C.

Harrison, R. K. *Numbers* **(Wycliffe Exegetical Commentary). Chicago: Moody, 1990. 452 pp.**

Harrison's introduction is well-done in surveying main areas of scholarly debate. Though he sees different literary sources compiled into our present book, among these Balaam's oracles (Numbers 22-24) from a non-Israelite source but valid, he does hold to the historicity of accounts as coming from eye-witnesses during the wilderness trek. Moses, he feels, exercised supervision over these and contributed some material himself (pp. 22-23). The commentary often shows a well read scholar who is skilled in bringing in material that throws light on texts exegetically, historically, culturally, etc. Harrison is not ready, as Gispen and some others, to assume that the numbers of Israelites are correct, but wants more information before making a judgment (45-47). By and large he is very accepting of the passages as they stand, and free of tendencies to explain them away.

Huey, F. B., Jr. *Numbers* **(Bible Study Commentary). Grand Rapids: Zondervan, 1981. 115 pp.**

The work on Exodus in this series is also a fairly good survey. Here, the Professor of Old Testament, Southwestern Baptist Theological Seminary, Fort Worth, has a detailed outline which he follows well. He gives a summation of seven views on the numbers being allegedly too high (pp. 9-11). One wishes Huey stated the theme of Numbers distinctly at the outset. Sometimes he lacks clarity. He calls Moses' striking the rock in Exodus 17 "the parallel experience" with his striking a rock in Numbers 20 (p. 72). These were at different times and places, not strictly parallel. In the same discussion he gives as different scholars' views six different aspects of Moses' sin, which are not views and which can all be true together. Still, this is for the most part a good brief look at Numbers.

Jensen, Irving L. *Numbers, Journey to God's Rest-land.* **Chicago: Moody, 1964. Paperback.**

This is a brief but good evangelical survey exposition.

Keil, C. F. and Franz Delitzsch. *The Pentateuch* **Cf. under Commentaries on the Old Testament, analytical.**

As in their other works in this Old Testament set, the authors are careful in the exegesis of the Hebrew text.

Kidner, Derek. Cf. on Leviticus.

Levine, Baruch. *Numbers* **(Anchor Bible). 2 vols. NY: Doubleday, 1993.**

A very detailed work (526 and 614 pp.) uses Levine's translation, then his commentary is based on documentary hypothesis sources, positing editing and elaboration in the seventh century B. C. (48-84). Priestly material, he feels, shows later development than other data in Numbers, and he does not regard some Numbers material as authentically related to Moses' day. The 29 topics he treats before getting to the commentary (Vol. 1) deal with theories of matters above, priests as poets, such peoples as the Edomites, laws of purity, etc. This reviewer found no comment where he expected it on the large census figures (chs. 1, 26) except a brief idea that the numbers arose from a "sexigesimal system" using multiples of 60 to get 600,000, and Levine sees the numbers as unrealistic (139). At times his detailed sections cite ancient extra-biblical help to explain a text, such as Jewish writings on the wife accused of infidelity in ch. 5, where Levine sees a mixture of prayer, magic and ordeal (200-212, espec. 212).

Maarsingh, B. *Numbers.* **Grand Rapids: Eerdmans, 1987. 221 pp.**

This is lucid, brief, vigorous in tackling and explaining words, phrases and many issues with a learned grasp of text, exegesis, ancient customs, etc. Yet the author remains practical and has a freshness to spark application and growth. Lay readers and even advanced students can profit from the survey.

MacRae, A. A. "Numbers," *The New Bible Commentary.* **Edited by F. Davidson, A. M. Stibbs and E. F. Kevan. Grand Rapids: Eerdmans, 1953.**

This is a more concise discussion of Numbers by a well-known conservative scholar of recent times who was president of Faith Theological Seminary and a member of the editorial committee for the revised Scofield Reference Bible of 1967.

Milgrom, Jacob. *Numbers* **(JPS Torah Commentary). NY: JPS, 1990. 520 pp.**

As on Leviticus, Milgrom delves into rich detail; there are 331 pages of commentary, and 77 excursuses (pp. 335-513) usually one to three pages long. Topics of the latter are such as "The Census and its Totals," "Adultery...," "Repentance in the Torah and the Prophets," and "The Copper Snake," etc. Each chapter of commentary is followed by copious, helpful notes, some lengthy and reflecting wide reading in relevant literature. Notes on excursuses also have notes at the end of the section. Frankly, notes would be more handy if placed on pages in the commentary or right with an excursus. Milgrom draws much from medieval exegetes and gives sketches on 17 of these (pp. xlii-xlv). The section on theological and anthropological matters has good summary comments about God, intercession, etc. While the commentary is concise it is often contributive on crucial points. At times Milgrom champions a high view of the unity and integrity of passages. Not all will agree when he sees the Dathan and Abiram story in Numbers 16 as from a separate story not originally a part of the Korah episode (Excursus 39).

Noordtzij, A. *Numbers* (Bible Student Commentary). Grand Rapids: Zondervan, 1983. 304 pp.

This translation from the Dutch is at most points a very able treatment of the text, word study, background, and relation to other Scripture. Sometimes it is too thin on a verse, at other times exegetical detail is rewarding. The writer brings enormous reading and awareness to his comments on issues, and often has special details on episodes (20:2-12; 21:4-9, etc.). Pastors and students as well as serious lay readers will appreciate much of it. The publishers warn readers that Noordtzij, while in most places sound, has strange ideas at times. For example, he writes of God's law keeping an Israelite "from inhaling through his mouth and nose further demonic influences" (p. viii), He also lacks a bibliography, footnotes, and an overall doctrinal orientation in his introduction. He loses the flow of the book in details. He claims that instructions for camp format and order of march in Numbers 2 could not possibly have been given originally in the present form. For the number of men and names of leaders are out of place in such initial instructions (p. 12). Many will wonder how this naturally follows. Yet he often defends traditional views against critical theories.

Noth, Martin. *Numbers, A Commentary*. (Old Testament Library). Philadelphia: Westminster, 1968. 258 pp.

Cf. his works on Exodus and Leviticus; much the same applies here. He holds to late composition from various traditions, seeing confusion and lack of order, varied styles and methods which rule out a single authorship. To him it is self-evident that Numbers has repeated factually contradictory ideas in passages, and he sees no need for exhaustive proof (p. 4). His assumptions on which source a given part was from frequently intrude on explanations of passages. If, however, one patiently stays with the book, he can sift out much that is of help and leave much that is unconvincing, arbitrary conjecture. Conservatives may feel, for example, that it is far more reasonable to see the bronze serpent idea as continued by Israelites to the time of 2 Kings 18:4 than to say, with Noth, that "the later existence of the 'bronze serpent' . . . was certainly the reason for the telling of the plague ... in the wilderness . . ." (p. 157). On the beneficial side, Noth often presents several views and a good discussion of how a problem can possibly be resolved, for example the high numbers of Chapter 1 (21-23). The work will offer help at times to the advanced student who has discernment and skill in weighing matters.

Philip, James. "Numbers" (The Communicators Commentary). Waco: Word Books, 1987. 364 pp.

Philip has long been a bright light for the evangelical faith in Scotland, pastoring the Holyrood Abbey Church in Edinburgh. Using good sources and explaining the text conservatively, he also shows practical applications to people today.

Plaut, W. Gunther. *Numbers* (The Torah, A Modern Commentary). New York: Union of American Hebrew Congregations, 1979. 366 pp.

He also did the commentary on Genesis in this series. There he says many things against the veracity of Genesis, for example Genesis gives Israel's history "not, perhaps, as it was but as it ought to have been" (xviii). Abram's experience of God promising him Canaan "will not pass as historic 'fact,' (yet) its reality was accepted by generations ... and, for them, validated their possession of the land" (xix). Many verses of Genesis are not really explained, or are given liberal comments, or are just skipped, as most of the verses in Genesis 3 are. The finest value of the commentary for those taking a high view of scriptural integrity is its frequent examples of how a liberal mind thinks on verses, and also the rabbinic comment brought in helpfully at times.

In Numbers again he is brief and skips verses (as 1:4, 16-46; 1:5-15 receive seven lines) or is too brief to take up issues in any adequate way. Special notes, usually one to a section, do go into some problems or define issues, as "The Census Figures" (pp.18-19). Plaut is not certain but favors viewing the word elef, "thousand," as a tribal contingent; so, he theorizes Reuben's 46,500 to be 46 elefs, = a total of 500 men (p. 18, cf. 272). Each section ends with "Gleanings," citations from rabbinic sources or modern scholars, explanations of points, etc. Sometimes really key points, such as the cruciality that one look if he would live in Numbers 21, are passed over. At many points this is fairly good Jewish commentary, but very spotty and not anything near the helpfulness of Milgrom's impressive work.

Snaith, Norman H. (cf. on Leviticus)

Wenham, Gordon J. *Numbers* (TOTC). Downers Grove: Inter Varsity Press, 1981.

For its brevity, a superb commentary in lifting out the legitimate meaning of the text and applying it to the contemporary reader in a crisp, thoughtful and reverent manner. Good, solid treatments of the significance of the rituals and dietary laws, fair (but not always satisfying) treatment of most problems. Indispensable for preaching or teaching, an excellent aid for understanding. -Dan Phillips

V. DEUTERONOMY

Christensen, D. L. *Deuteronomy 1:1—21:9* (Word Biblical Commentary). Dallas: Word Books, 2001.

This detailed liberal work (458 large pp.) has lists of scholarly specialist writings on each section, and sometimes ponderous comments on verses. It is geared to be mostly of use to OT experts and some more advanced students. For much pastoral benefit, it appears so focused on issues some scholars may be curious about that it will not be of steady profit to others. Help is available on many verses, and on other verses the author offers comments that seem limited in their real help, for example on boiling a kid, where much has been written that finds no mention (14:21).

Craigie, Peter C. *The Book of Deuteronomy* (NICOT). Grand Rapids: Eerdmans, 1976. 424 pp.

Scholarly study of the text, based on analysis of the Hebrew and cognate languages, written in an attitude of faith and aimed at a broad (but serious) audience. Craigie notes and capitalizes on the book's similarity in structure to second-millennium ancient Near East vassal treaties, and holds the authorship to be Mosaic, finished by Joshua. Includes an 86-page introductory section, with a nine-page section on the theology of the book. Craigie, Associate Professor of Religious Studies at the University of Calgary, is inclined toward a Mosaic date or shortly after, agreeing with M. Kline. He usually shows good awareness of views and recent books and articles (cf. his select bibliography, pp. 69-72). He even furnishes in

Appendix III a "Concordance of Principal Qumran Manuscripts Relating to Deuteronomy" (pp. 84-86). The comments verse by verse are quite good, but sometimes lacking in detail on views and arguments (e.g. on 18:15, the conviction that the passage is "prophetic in foreshadowing another Prophet ... namely, Jesus" (p. 39), but with little discussion). - Dan Phillips

Deere, Jack S. "Deuteronomy" (*Bible Knowledge Commentary*), Volume I, ed. John F. Walvoord and Roy B. Zuck. Wheaton: Victor Books, 1983, pp. 259-324.

Conservative work showing expertise in scholarly literature and handling of Hebrew exegesis, history, customs, etc. Deere provides help on synopses of sections and also the verse by verse explanation an expositor needs.

Harrison, R. K. "Deuteronomy," *New Bible Commentary Revised*, ed. D. Guthrie et al. Grand Rapids: Eerdmans, 1970, pp. 201-29.

This is a very good evangelical work by a skilled Old Testament scholar. He favors Mosaic authorship, but thinks Chapters 32-34 were added shortly after Moses' death, partly by Joshua (Moses' death) and partly by Eleazer (p. 203). Restricted by space, Harrison offers a helpful, concise commentary that contributes on most verses and problems.

Hillers, Delbert R. *Covenant: The History of a Biblical Idea.* Baltimore: Johns Hopkins, 1969.

This 188-pp. book is useful as an introductory survey of the covenant idea in the Old Testament and extra-biblical literature. Deuteronomy is dated *late*, whereas Kline (*Treaty of the Great King*) sees it as early. -Dan Phillips

Keil, C. F. and Franz Delitzsch. *The Pentateuch.*

See annotation under Old Testament sets, Analytical.

Kline, Meredith. *By Oath Consigned*. Grand Rapids: Eerdmans, 1968.

This is a kind of sequel to the idea of a covenant in *Treaty of the Great King* (1963). Kline believes there is a treaty idea all through the Bible with the ordeal or self-malediction occurring with the forming or the renewing of a covenant. He develops circumcision (Old Testament) and baptism (New Testament) as ordeal rituals. Circumcision pointed on to Christ's death, a cutting off of God Himself in Christ, as he sees it. -Dan Phillips.

Kline, Meredith. *Treaty of the Great King*. Grand Rapids: Eerdmans, 1963.

A competent scholar wrote this book which most reviews hailed as an epochal work. Also see Kline's commentary on Deuteronomy in *The Wycliffe Bible Commentary* (Moody Press, 1962). The author investigates the relevance of recently discovered treaties of great kings to understanding the nature of the Decalogue and the covenant in Deuteronomy. He wrestles with the statements of higher criticism. It is conservative.

Knight, George A. A. *The Song of Moses*. Grand Rapids: Eerdmans, 1995.

Here are 156 pp. arguing that Deuteronomy 32:1-43, originated in Moses' day and composed by Solomon's scribes, is much used in other OT and NT Scripture. Knight furnishes detail verse by verse, usually good, and at times not agreeing with conservative opinion. In a postscript, he discusses main themes in the passage such as God's nature and fidelity to His covenant people.

Mayes, A. D. H. *Deuteronomy* (New Century Bible Commentary). Grand Rapids: Eerdmans, 1981. 416 pp.

This is by a lecturer in Hebrew and Semitics, University of Dublin. He is liberal, and his work is highly regarded by many. His exegesis is thorough and he has much excellent data on word meaning, background, etc., plus a good bibliography (pp. 9-23) and a lengthy introduction with a 3-page outline (27-108). As many he is persuaded that Deuteronomy is part of a larger deuteronomic history of Israel running through 2 Kings, a history finalized during the exile. He theorizes that particular verses were written later, according to his opinion. He feels Levites of the Jerusalem temple (p. 107) give the distilled teaching, so the historical background is there, not in the wilderness (81-82). Still, much of the verse by verse commentary has basic, explanatory material which conservative users with discernment can fit where it belongs into the time of Moses and not in exilic days with Mayes. Mayes sees in 18:15 nothing of messianic connection, and has no reference to the New Testament use of it.

McCarthy, Dennis J. *Old Testament Covenant: A Survey of Current Opinions.* Richmond, VA: John Knox Press, 1972. 108 pp.

This little book (89 pp. plus a 19-pp. bibliography) gives a good survey of views and developments among scholars in this field up to the time of writing (cf. good review by Walter C. Kaiser, Jr., JETS, XV, Fall, 1962, 241-42).

McConville, J. G. *Deuteronomy* (Apollos Old Testament Commentary). Downers Grove, IL: IVP. 2002.

This and the work by E. Lucas (Dan.) are the first works in this new production, issued late in 2002. The series is plugged as "evangelical" (cf. back inside cover flap), but readers will differ on what kind of "evangelical" this is, given the theories of composition as on Deut., and several claims in the Daniel work (cf. Lucas, Dan.). McConville's 544-pp. writing shows much learning on grammar, word meaning, customs, ancient texts that may shed light, and interaction with critical theory. His work at times seems far more complex than the billing of the Apollos effort to be particularly relevant for preaching help. It appears to be in a different world of issues that some scholars debate, and many may choke on it and turn to works that offer simpler help. The commentary often casts much brief light on verses. Some examples are: returning a stray animal (22:4), a woman not wearing men's garb (22:5), protecting a mother bird (22:6-7), or giving sanctuary to a refugee slave (23:15-16). In some texts such as 24:1-4 (divorce), the writer could but does not offer help on how details may relate to NT divorce issues preachers need to discuss (Matt. 19:9, etc.). Scholars and more thoroughly studious and patient pastors and maturely scholarly students can draw good help; they will agree or disagree with many of the details, but will see many main, possible turns of thought.

Merrill, Eugene H. *Deuteronomy* (New American Commentary). Nashville: Broadman & Holman, 1994.

An OT specialist from evangelical Dallas Theological Seminary offers a very good 477-

pp. effort. He takes Moses as writer based on OT and NT data as well as pre-critical Jewish and Christian belief. The exodus, he holds, was in 1447/46 B. C. He argues versus a source critical placement of Deuteronomy as a literary composition in the seventh century B. C. (32-37). Comments usually are lucid and to the point without being too brief, gathering pertinent factors. Notable verses draw more comment (6:4-5, 5 pp.). On some texts, as boiling a kid (14:21), discussion falls far short of what would be substantial on views. A similar lack occurs in the verse forbidding transvestism (22:5), whereas leaving a mother bird seems to be explained reasonably in 22:6. Footnotes reflect wide awareness on many points. The work is quite beneficial.

Miller, Patrick D. *Deuteronomy* (Interpretation series). Louisville: John Knox Press, 1990. 253 pp.

This is a sweeping exposition with essays on structure, motifs and sections in the book and not a verse by verse discussion. Miller, Professor of Old Testament Theology at Princeton Theological Seminary, follows the line of many in thinking final redaction took place during Josiah's career. However, here he does not devote much time to this but has many helpful perceptions on the meaning of the text we have. His well-organized work aims to help teachers, preachers and students by commenting on the RSV translation. Synopses at the outset of chapters orientate readers to the setting and how the section of Deuteronomy fits in the book and what the structure of this unit is, in Miller's opinion. At times Miller serves up such arbitrary ideas as: "It is highly unlikely that we have here an accurate historical report of words and actions by Moses on the plains of Moab" (p. 25). However, the book draws spiritual life lessons which are quite worthwhile (cf. chs. 38-40, for example). It just will not set well with conservatives to be told that the concern for possession of the land in Deuteronomy is because the book was done centuries later than the wilderness era when Israel was in danger of being uprooted from the land (44). Even then, Miller has many helpful things summarized about the land (44-52).

Ridderbos, J. *Deuteronomy* (Bible Students Commentary). Grand Rapids: Zondervan, 1984. 318 pp.

This work is frequently quite helpful, sometimes valuable in dealing with verses in a concise, competent, direct exegesis based on obvious wide knowledge. Ridderbos is conservative, discussing but finding Wellhausian theory as to authorship and unity invalid; he argues that Moses was the author, with a few sections or parts by editorial work after Moses "under God's special providence" (p. 22). On many matters the commentary is satisfactory, getting at vital things fully enough for many teachers, preachers and diligent laypeople.

Schneider, Bernard N. *Deuteronomy: A Favored Book of Jesus*. Grand Rapids: Eerdmans, 1970. 163 pp.

This is an attempt to show the close tie between Jesus' teachings and Deuteronomy (a book quoted or alluded to ca. 90 times in the New Testament). Schneider says the emphasis in Deuteronomy is on God's love for His people. Moses poured out his heart telling the people of Israel the message of love God had given (p. 11). A reader looking not for a detailed commentary but for a book setting forth section by section the vital spiritual truths of Deuteronomy that are relevant today as in Moses' day will find many stimulating things here.

Schultz, Samuel J. *Deuteronomy, The Gospel of Love.* **Chicago: Moody Press, 1971.**

This is in The Everyman's Bible Commentary series. It provides a good, brief explanation with a clear outline. Like Schneider, Schultz shows that God's love is the heart of this book by Moses the lawgiver.

Thompson, J. A. *Deuteronomy: An Introduction and Commentary* **(Tyndale Old Testament Commentary). Downers Grove, IL: IVP, 1974.**

A helpful verse by verse work abreast of recent scholarship on many of the issues in Deuteronomy for the more serious reader. Thompson believes that the book is not authored by Moses, yet much of it goes back to the time of Moses. But "the present Deuteronomy represents the end-point of subsequent revisions both in language and in form," and is derived from "the re-application of the great principles of the covenant at Sinai to the changing conditions of a new age, be it that of Samuel, or Solomon, or Hezekiah, or Josiah" (pp. 46-47). The material is mostly from Moses' day and Israel's situation then. But it has been retouched to serve the needs of later generations in Israel. Cf. an evangelical evaluation of Thompson's concessions to critical scholarship along this line in Meredith G. Kline, review, *Westminster Theological Journal*, 39 (Fall, 1976), 168-70. Deuteronomy, to Thompson, shares in the pattern of the ancient form of a Near Eastern treaty (covenant). He does not interpret some things literally, e.g. the 40 days of Moses receiving the law could mean an indefinite time (p. 140). Though some conclusions run against the grain for one who holds to inerrancy, Thompson in general says things consistent with a rather high view of the Bible, and evinces a scholarship of depth and breadth.

von Rad, Gerhard. *Deuteronomy, A Commentary.* **(Old Testament Library). Philadelphia: Westminster, 1966.**

Well-regarded in much of the scholarly community, though among conservatives of occasional help only to more advanced students. The author holds to a complicated history of different compositions and, like many, subjectively picks and chooses as he will. Priestly and Levitical composers centuries after the wilderness period sought "to make the old cultic and legal traditions relevant for their time" (p. 23). These men fictionalized the idea that the sermons were spoken to Israel in Moab (28) when in actuality, as von Rad recasts things, they were directed to Israel's needs centuries later. One can sift out much good explanation of what certain details mean, but he is often met by an intermeshing of theory about which parts are from the early days and which from the exile. The commentary is not verse by verse; it broadly gathers sometimes many verses into a paragraph or two, and often with more comment on von Rad's personal construction of things than on the canonical text. He deals only glancingly with the messianic possibility of 18:15, and without referring to the New Testament text. Quite frankly, despite the stature of von Rad to many, this work does not adequately enough get down to the straight-forward business of explaining passages in a way conservatives will regard as probable from the evidence, at least not often enough.

Weinfeld, Moshe. *Deuteronomy 1-11* **(Anchor Bible). NY: Doubleday, 1991. 458 pp. 1st of 2 volumes.**

Serious, skilled students will find much help here on the details of text, meaning of words and phrases, history, etc., as well as bibliography. The introduction brings together much thought on literary, critical, legal, historical and theological matters. The list of journal articles runs nearly 36 pages, Much of the material is assigned to centuries later than Moses (p. 13). Many readers will feel that his reasons are arbitrary, yet may appreciate seeing how such a case may be built. While much benefit can be laboriously gleaned from individual verse notes, some will wish there could be better synthesizing orientation before the plunge into the many details. It is not easy to keep the book's movement in view due to the fragmented nature of the minute aspects, and so the work seems primarily of help to the very patient, advanced user. Often, Weinfeld furnishes very worthwhile comments on problems, such as whether to take as literal or figurative the binding of the words on the hand and on the forehead (6:8; pp. 341-42).

Wright, Christopher. *Deuteronomy* **(New International Biblical Commentary). Peabody, MA: Hendrickson Publishers, 1996.**

The author holds to the integrity of the Mosaic era as distinct from a seventh century B. C. setting (8). Verse by verse comments and added notes on details after each section are usually adequate, at least on many of the main issues. But on some verses what is offered is too general, and Wright could have supplied more help (cf. an example on 22:5, regarding transvestism and issues today).

VI. JOSHUA

Boling, Robert G. and Wright, G. Ernest. *Joshua: A New Translation with Notes and Commentary* **(Anchor Bible). NY: Doubleday, 1982. 580 pp.**

This is thorough and in many places good help for in-depth students who already have a background in Pentateuchal and conquest studies and want a laborious study. Much in the notes will not be meaningful for those without such preparation and a high motivation. Liberal assumptions are frequent and the introduction is wordy but highly informative (pp. 1-110). The bibliography is 19 pages, and there is considerable aid on philology, archeology, customs, and the text. Gleaning much from details, the student can lose the sweep of the book and not see the forest for the trees. At times the authors assume things where other explanations are possible. They say the two scouts went to Rahab's place and "Probably the narrator intends to titillate by reminding readers of an immediate symbiosis between military service and bawdy house" (p. 145). Sometimes one finds a different view from the norm: destroying Achan's family with him was probably not because of complicity or solidarity in guilt but due to peril of contamination that could spread to hurt others (225, 228).

Bright, John. *The Book of Joshua, Introduction and Exegesis* **(Interpreter's Bible), Volume 2. Nashville: Abingdon Press, 1953. Pages 540-673.**

Bright shows breadth in his introduction, surveying issues and scholarly discussion. He is concise and often provides good information on verses, and one will soon take note of his liberal approach. More advanced students will find a good amount of assistance here.

Butler, Trent C. *Joshua* **(Word Biblical Commentary). Waco: Word Books, 1983. 304 pp.**

The diligently prepared bibliography on each passage can be of much help, yet one sees infrequent awareness of conservative literature. Readers need to realize that Butler is not evangelical in the traditional sense of the word, despite the series' claim to be evangelical. He buys into a system that posits that material not historical fact is meshed with things that may be true, written during exilic times (pp. 99, 117, 125). The book is taken up with concerns burdening the believing community during the exile. Some things are concocted allegedly in order to further truth; Butler believes in an inspiration in which clashing traditions blend after the passage of time as God's Word. God's Word is reliable and unreliable. Still, his bibliographies can aid a serious researcher, and textual notes put forth considerable assistance.

Campbell, Donald. "Joshua," in *Bible Knowledge Commentary*, editors John F. Walvoord and Roy B. Zuck. Volume I. Wheaton: Victor Books, 1983, pp. 325-71.

A skilled Bible expositor for many years and for some years President of Dallas Theological Seminary gives a lucid, perceptive brief commentary drawn from careful study. He is helpful on synopsis that keeps the flow of the book in view and also in details of many verses, word meaning, customs, how problems may be resolved, and how things fit. Cf. also his book on Joshua, *No Time For Neutrality* (Wheaton: Victor Books, 1981, 143 pp.), with more application and illustration.

Cohen, A. *Joshua and Judges* (Soncino Series). London: Soncino Press, 1950. 333 pp.

The Hebrew text is given side by side with the Jewish Publication Society English translation in a 2-column format with the commentary below. The writer sees the writing as being by a contemporary eye-witness, Joshua, with a unity of purpose. Joshua wrote all but a few later additions. The comments are fairly good quite frequently, but most of the time are concise. Sensitivity of the writer to main things needing explanation makes the work rather helpful a good percentage of the time. To him, the sun standing still can be seen as a miracle or explained by natural phenomena.

Davis, Dale R. *No Falling Words. Expositions of the Book of Joshua*. Grand Rapids: Baker, 1988. 204 pp.

These 21 expositions are by a former Professor of Old Testament at Reformed Theological Seminary. Davis furnishes evangelical material to help preachers blend sound exegesis, theological substance, interesting exposition and practical application. Davis groups his chapters under Entering the Land (Joshua 1-4), Taking it (5-12), Possessing it (13-21), and Retaining it (22-24). He uses creative chapter titles. The book title comes from 21:45 (cf. 23:14). The studies are not on every verse but key portions out of each chapter, done in a very readable style. At times footnotes cite good sources and add important help. Overall the book is a good survey of Joshua that preachers or lay people can enjoy. It has many ideas to provoke sermons and point to application.

Davis, John J. Conquest and Crisis. Studies in Joshua, Judges, and Ruth. Grand Rapids: Baker, 1969. 176 pp.

These evangelical studies provide very helpful and pertinent background material as well as a survey of the main elements in the passages. He is particularly helpful on some of the main problem passages.

Enns, Paul. *Joshua* **(Bible Study Commentary). Grand Rapids: Zondervan, 1981. 145 pp.**

A very fine conservative survey, well-organized, summarizing sections well and explaining most verses awarely, making good suggestions on many of the problems expositors face. Often on problems, as the sun in Chapter 10, he discusses several views and documents well.

Goslinga, C. J. *Joshua, Judges, Ruth* **(Bible Students Commentary). Grand Rapids: Zondervan, 1986. 558 pp.**

This is substantial conservative commentary, Joshua running through page 195, Judges to 510, then Ruth. Goslinga gets down to business explaining in a straight-forward way. He argues in ten steps that the book is a unit by a contemporary of Joshua, possibly Phinehas (pp. 11-19). He sees no true contradictions (19-26) and favors an early exodus date. Judges, though recounting events of more than three hundred years, is drawn into a unity by a governing thread (198, 205, 214-17). Samuel or someone under his influence wrote Judges. Goslinga gives much space to chronological problems of Judges (223-35). He looks fairly at arguments for two views of what Jephthah did to his daughter and cautiously concludes that either is possible (391-96). Ruth, he decides, was written during Solomon's reign (cf. 4:7). Verses in the books are handled with deep reverence for the integrity, diligent work to offer help, and energy to set forth spiritual lessons.

Gray, John. *Joshua, Judges and Ruth* **(New Century Bible). Greenwood, SC: Attic Press, 1967. 435 pp.**

A liberal work from which one can carefully gather many helps on details of word meaning, customs, etc. But Gray follows many in assuming a composition centuries after alleged events, before 586 B. C., and a post-exilic redaction (p. 2). He often does not hold to historical accuracy but feels accounts were created later (19, 31, 37, 360-61, etc.). Subjectivity abounds in his preferences of what may be reliable and what may not. He imagines inconsistencies where many diligent students will not think his judgment reasonable or necessary (cf. p, 53), and often regards his own doubts as better than what the book says (cf. his comments on great hailstones in 10:11). Only more advanced students will be persevering to sift through his assessments of which supposed compositional tradition appears at a given point. In Judges 11 he takes the view that Jephthah offered his daughter in death but does not look at views. Likewise many other problem verses are not explained (14:4; 16:3, forty miles, etc.). At times, however, he mentions views (cf. Ruth 3:4, "uncovered his feet,") so that readers are made more aware of how a verse has been seen.

Hamilton, Victor P. *Handbook on the Historical Books.* **Grand Rapids: Baker, 2001.**

This hefty (557 pp.) book surveys Joshua through Esther, with charts and discussions of background or certain problems, ending in each case with a bibliography (commentaries, other books, and journal articles). He believes that Jephthah offered his daughter as a sacrifice in death (146). Some lists are of special help, for example 13 common emphases linking Ezra and Nehemiah (509-23). The reviewer does not know why giving section by section summaries does not continue in Chronicles through Esther. The work provides help, but those consulting regular expositions would tend to cover bases without it.

Hughes, R. Kent. *Living on the Cutting Edge: Joshua and the Challenge of Spiritual Leadership*. Westchester, IL: Crossway Books, 1987. 172 pp.

A warm, popular, broad exposition dealing with some chapters in Joshua. Hughes often has good insights on analogies from Israel's victories for growth and victory today, through God's strength. He shows traits for effective leadership. Most lessons are good. One that disappoints is, "Rahab's lie was a stupendous act of true faith" (p. 37). Well, yes, she lied, and yes, she did have faith. But who says it is necessary to make the lie a part of faith or faith a part of the lie? Cf. also page 38: Hughes conveys the idea that a Christian musters faith out of a glass. In actuality, when we wrongly persuade ourselves that we have to clutch at certain means to come by faith, true faith is not generated by human fallacy but by the Lord, using means He can endorse, His Word etc. He can use us even though we fail Him by leaning on false means and tracing our effectiveness to those means, wrongly. Overall, the book is usually quite helpful for preaching or just for devotional aims.

Johnson, Alan F. *Thirty Days to Spiritual Power*. Wheaton: Tyndale House, 1975.

In thirty brief sections Johnson of Wheaton College (a past national president of Evangelical Theological Society) competently seeks to capture the main spiritual lessons of Joshua and Judges. He moves usually but not always chapter by chapter. He seeks to point out the relevance for life today. The book triggers many profitable thoughts for the lay reader or for the Christian worker feeding his life and preparing messages.

Meyer, F. B. *Choice Notes on Joshua - 2 Kings*. Grand Rapids: Kregel, 1985. 221 pp.

Meyer (1847-1929) published this originally in 1895. He left a big witness as a Christian, husband and expositor on the spiritual life. Here he is clear, simple, to the point, and practical in application. The book is especially suited for pastors, Sunday School teachers and laypersons. Sometimes he overdoes things, as in seeing Hittites and confederates as depicting "The evil habits of the old past" (p. 12). Yet in many cases he is apt, as using Gideon to show the need to look to God for adequacy. He sees Saul as unsaved, having the Spirit on him but not in him (103).

Pink, Arthur W. *Gleanings in Joshua*. Chicago: Moody, 1964.

This is a good devotional work on Joshua, though his study of types is overdrawn.

Rawlinson, George. *Joshua: His Life and Times*. NY: Revell (n. d.).

Here is a valuable work to have because it is very good from the historical standpoint.

Schaeffer, Francis. *Joshua and the Flow of Biblical History*. Downers Grove: IVP, 1975.

The man who led the L'Abri Fellowship in the Swiss Alps shows that the book is a bridge between the Pentateuch and the rest of Scripture. The rest is in continuity with the first five books. Continuities that go on are the written book, God's power, and the supernatural leader. Schaeffer shows how "alive" the text is by drawing lessons that can apply now as well as in the time of Joshua's conquest. This is a conservative, refreshing, absorbing flow of comment through Joshua. It is a companion volume to his Genesis in

Space and Time. His style is somewhat sermonic at times in dealing with major characters and incidents. He highlights central truths in each chapter of Joshua. A good book to prime personal study and home Bible studies.

Scroggle, W. Graham. Joshua in the Light of the New Testament: The Land and Life of Rest. Grand Rapids: Kregel, 1981.

This reprint of the 1950 edition shows a life of faith that rests in an inner peace drawn from the sufficiency of God and lived out in a life of costly effort that triumphs. Scroggie (1877-1958) pastored in Halifax, Sunderland, Edinburgh and Spurgeon's Tabernacle in London. He also was a teacher and spiritual life speaker at Bible conferences, known for diligently-studied expositions. He is best remembered for his three volume *Unfolding Drama of Redemption* and his gold mine called *Guide to the Gospels*. Here he is profitable in organizing some key lessons based on Joshua. Originally a series of Bible readings at the English Keswick Conference, this is another warm devotional treatment of Joshua.

Soggin, J. A. *Joshua, A Commentary* (Old Testament Library). Philadelphia: Westminster Press, 1972. 245 pp.

This liberal book follows generally-accepted theory that late dates the Book of Joshua to a composition centuries after the conquest. Soggin casts much denial on Joshua having the place in leading Israel in a unified conquest as the book shows. To Soggin, this is "a fictional construction" (p. 17); for Joshua's exploits were read back into things so as to have a well-known representative in Israel's history (18). Often Soggin imposes contradictions on the text which many will not consider necessary. For example, he has 1:10-13 teach a peaceable conquest, then 1:4ff a military thrust (33). It seems to strain his credulity that a prostitute would put herself at such risk with her own people in Joshua 2 (40). The Ark, he feels, could not have been used so early in conquering Jericho (87). He is skeptical about the numbers of Israelites in 7:5 (104), and feels the address in Joshua 23 is derived from the one in Chapter 24 (227). Yet his massive scholarship often has really helpful explanation, as regarding the flat roof where the scouts hid (41). In Joshua 10 he refers to ancient accounts of a god helping warriors win by delaying the sun's setting, as well as further views, but favors a miracle in the biblical case (123). He has a commanding grasp of views on some of the passages, at least from liberal works such as Noth's, and shows the problems many find in all the passages.

Wood, Leon J. *A Survey of Israel's History*. Grand Rapids: Zondervan, 1986. Revised, enlarged by David O'Brien from 1970 ed.

Chapter 8 surveys the Joshua period succinctly but very helpfully in conservative style, dealing with main problems such as the long day and providing frequently good footnotes. Another fine survey of conservatives is by John J. Davis & John C. Whitcomb, *Israel, A Commentary on Joshua-2 Kings* (Grand Rapids: Baker, 1989, 542 pp.). The latter work combines three former books, *Conquest and Crisis*, *The Birth of a Kingdom* and *Solomon to the Exile*. Wood's section on Joshua, as the other parts, offers comments that pull together main truths and seek to assist on main problems even to the extent of giving views and reasons.

Woudstra, Marten H. *Joshua* **(New International Commentary of the Old Testament). Grand Rapids: Eerdmans, 1981. 396 pp.**

A conservative effort that may well be the best overall commentary on Joshua so far, this holds to a possible authorship in Joshua's day or that of the elders who outlived him (p. 13). He argues for unity of composition even if with sources and brings immense scholarly awareness and use of recent literature to his commentary verse by verse. He explains matters in a careful vein kept in key with a high view of the book's reliability, so he is quite helpful to conservatives while maintaining a readability that serves teachers, pastors, and laypeople.

VII. JUDGES (cf. also on Joshua)

Barber, Cyril J. *Judges, A Narrative of God's Power.* **Neptune, NJ: Loizeaux Brothers, 1990. 293 pp.**

A well-organized, conservative exposition arising out of much study and skill in showing how alive biblical passages are. The Dale Davis book is fairly good, but this one is even better overall, although Barber does not see impropriety in some of Samson's episodes with women as he interprets the texts differently. Barber uses captivating headlines for sections, a vivid flow, arousing descriptions, analogies, illustrations, and applications. He deals with many problems awarely, using notes that sometimes are rather lengthy and meaty. Like Davis, he is competent, thought-provoking, and often sharp in exposing the timeliness of the book for life today.

Blaikie, William. *Judges.* **In The Expositors Bible. NY: Loizeaux, Inc. (n. d.).**

This is not a verse by verse commentary but a work with helpful character studies, since Judges is predominantly a series of lives.

Block, Daniel I. *Judges, Ruth* **(New American Commentary). Nashville: Broadman & Holman, 1999.**

An evangelical contributes 586 pp. on Judges and 151 on Ruth. Introductory sections for both books survey the state of scholarly opinion and his belief in the integrity and reliability of the biblical books. Copious footnotes, often lengthy, reflect on others' views, verifications of points in the books and also in other scripture, etc. Verse by verse work offers detail on grammar, word meaning, background, customs, and interpretive problems. Block holds that Jephthah sacrificed his daughter in death. On passages overall, this is a standout commentary, yet at times it states convictions without a specific answer to other leading views. One instance is in not commenting on the view that Ruth acted indecently with Boaz at night. Some accounts, as episodes of Samson, seem for the most part to be explained in reasonable detail.

Boling, R. G. *Judges: Introduction, Translation and Notes* **(Anchor). Garden City, NY: Doubleday, 1975. 339 pp.**

The "Notes" sections have much help in textual, exegetical and philological areas to explain passages. The work is liberal, claiming that later priestly editors finalized it in exilic days (pp. 32, 34). Boling assumes strands of material as if established fact. Comments on which alleged strand a passage is assigned to must be weighed by conservatives (63, etc). Boling offers very thin help on some problems, as Jephthah's fulfilling of his vow, or how 14:4 or 15:4 can be resolved, etc. He has a long introduction acquainting readers with scholarly thought (3-45), a selective bibliography (43-45), and is quite helpful on some verses, more usable to the trained student who can discerningly choose what is good and leave what is misleading.

Bruce, F. F. "Judges" in *New Bible Commentary Revised,* ed. D. Guthrie et al. Grand Rapids: Eerdmans, 1970.

A brief, evangelical commentary by the renowned scholar who always has much that helps.

Cohen, A. Cf. on Joshua.

Cundall, Arthur and Leon Morris. *Judges and Ruth.* Wheaton: Tyndale House, 1968.

This is a competent Tyndale Old Testament commentary even though somewhat brief. It enables the student to get at the meaning of the books more readily than the more detailed works. The writers pack a lot of expertise into verses.

Davis, Dale R. *Such A Great Salvation.* Grand Rapids: Baker, 1990. 227 pp.

A flowing, popular conservative exposition that can be suggestive for pastors on individual messages or series. Davis deals with problems in footnotes. He keeps the vital message foremost and points out the relevance to today. The book is usually refreshing to help one grow in grace. Davis keeps spotlighting the beauty of God. Cf. also his book on Joshua.

Davis, John J. Cf. his book listed under Wood on Joshua, and cf. the Wood book as well.

Both have very good survey material from a conservative standpoint, helpful on synopsis and problem passages.

Enns, Paul. *Judges* (Bible Study Commentary). Grand Rapids: Zondervan, 1982. 148 pp.

If one wants down to business exposition, well-organized, with keen sensitivity to providing help on problem texts, this is a very good, brief conservative work by a clear, diligent student. It almost always goes right to the point, deals with pertinent questions, and always upholds a high view of the passages as being the Word of God.

Goslinga, C. J. Cf. on Joshua.

This, too, is a fine conservative commentary on Judges, usually quite solid and helpful.

Jordan, James B. *Judges: A Practical and Theological Commentary.* Eugene, OR: Wipf and Stock, 1999rp.

Jordan's 1985 work (Geneva Ministries) is a 334-pp. evangelical exposition. He assumes authorship by Samuel (xi). Pastors looking for surveys of sections and ideas for application today will find readable stimulation. Jephthah devoted his daughter to life service in the sanctuary, he concludes. But he says that she was the only person devoted to God in life that he knows (207) If she was, would not Samuel and Samson, for examples, be others?

Lewis, Arthur. *Judges and Ruth* **(Everyman's Bible Commentary). Chicago: Moody, 1979. 128 pp.**

Though not as contributive as the work by Enns, also concise, this will help pastors with a quick review and provide material for Bible class teachers and laypeople. At times, the generalizing such as on Jephthah's vow offers no real explanation, yet he is better on some hard verses as 14:4, even if always brief.

Lindsey, F. Duane. "Judges," in *Bible Knowledge Commentary***, ed. John F. Walvoord and Roy B. Zuck, Volume I. Wheaton: Victor Books, 1983.**

Dallas Seminary faculty member gives a knowledgeable survey providing assistance on many of the normal problems pastors and Bible class teachers encounter in the book.

Meyer, F. B. Cf. on Joshua.

Moore, George F. A *Critical and Exegetical Commentary on Judges* **(ICC). NY: Scribners, 1901.**

This is a thorough study of the text and is valuable from the historical and philological standpoint. It is among the better works in the I.C.C. series, though liberal in approach.

Soggin, J. Alberto. *Judges: A Commentary* **(Old Testament Library). Philadelphia: Westminster, 1981.**

This is part of the Westminster Old Testament Library series. Writing from the perspective of recent higher critical conviction, Soggin handles passages with awareness of a broad spectrum of views, even by conservative Christian scholars. In each section he offers a bibliography, translation, discussion of textual and philological points, and his commentary. This is a liberal work along similar lines to his book on Joshua (cf. on Joshua).

Wood, Leon J. *Distressing Days of the Judges***. Grand Rapids: Zondervan, 1975. 434 pp.**

This is an outstanding work by a firm evangelical scholar. The book discusses in detail many of the key problems expositors need help on in the book, It provides solid help in understanding the main aspects of most sections. It is one of the most valuable books on the period of the Judges and on character sketches of the main judges.

VIII. RUTH (cf. also Joshua and Judges)

Atkinson, David. *The Wings of Refuge; The Message of Ruth***. Downers Grove, IL: Intervarsity Press, 1983. 128 pp.**

Atkinson, Chaplain of Corpus Christi College at Oxford in England has written this paperback for the Bible Speaks Today series. The author has set out to acquaint the readers with the overpowering concept of "providence." He reflects an awareness of liberal criticisms of the book, but offers little defense in the areas of authorship, dating, or time and place of writing. He prefers a 12/11th century B. C. setting, making Ruth a contemporary of the period of the Judges. At the same time, however, Atkinson does entertain the thoughts that pre-Deuteronomic ideas are present within the book. Thus, critical matters are not the author's primary concern. Atkinson has written a volume which will aid the Bible student/pastor in his appreciation for the "providence" motif. -Jan Sattem

Barber, Cyril J. *Ruth, A Story of God's Grace*. Neptune, NJ: Loizeaux Brothers, 1989. 198 pp. Originally Ruth, An Expositional Commentary. Chicago: Moody, 1983.

As on Judges, this conservative is creatively lucid in a way many pastors, students and laypeople in general will value. This time he has nine chapters, furnished with footnotes placed at the end, some having substantial added help drawn from wide reading. A section on critical studies (pp. 131-47) takes up authorship, date, unity of the genealogy in Chapter 4 with the rest of the book, and themes. Good illustrations appear at times. Barber usually touches briefly on problems, such as in defending the chastity of Boaz and Ruth in lying near one another, and explains customs.

Bush, Frederic W. *Ruth, Esther* (Word Biblical Commentary). Dallas: Word Books, 1996.

Much detail explains verses from the Hebrew, dealing with context and customs. Bush interacts with other views, as when he defends Ruth's honor on the threshing floor (165). The work's technical nature and ponderous detail make it more inviting to scholarly users, but pastors and students willing to invest time will gather help. On both books this is one of the most informative works on matters as a whole.

Campbell, E. F. *Ruth: A New Translation with Introduction, Notes and Commentary* (Anchor Bible). NY: Doubleday, 1975. 189 pp.

A highly regarded work filled with knowledge on words, often discussed in detail. A long introduction informs the reader of issues, and the verse by verse commentary offers much on exegesis. One is provided with a wealth of information from many sides and can be steeped in the scenes. Campbell, however, will not meet with some conservatives' approval in some matters, such as feeling that the genealogy (4:18-22) was not a part of the original book but appended later (172-73).

Cox, Samuel. *The Book of Ruth*. London: The Religious Tract Society, 1922 revised edition.

A devotional work, this is also helpful in Hebrew word studies and in explaining difficult passages. It is conservative.

Cundall, Arthur E. and Leon Morris. *Judges and Ruth* (Tyndale Old Testament Commentary). Downers Grove, IL. IVP, 1968.

These are fine commentaries based on a great breadth of reading. Some views favored, however, do not reflect that proper weight has been given to evidence, e. g. they hold a late date of the exodus (28-29) and understand I Kings 6:1 (480 years) as representing twelve generations of 40 years, not a strictly accurate number (31). Cundall has a stimulating discussion of moral problems raised by the book of Judges (41-45), using Samson as an example. Both commentators provide a competent verse by verse explanation. Often they defend against attacks on the reasonableness of details. -Jan Sattem in part.

Davis, John J. Cf. Wood on Joshua.

Enns, Paul. *Ruth* **(Bible Study Commentary). Grand Rapids: Zondervan, 1982. 75 pp.**

He deals with Ruth as with Joshua and Judges (cf. those books). This is a fine conservative, concise commentary.

Goslinga, C. J. Cf. on Joshua.

Gray, John. Cf. on Joshua.

Hals, Ronald. *The Theology of the Book of Ruth.* **Philadelphia: Fortress Press, 1969.**

Here is an exhaustive work, mediating, sometimes good and sometimes weak where he imagines things in passages beyond the evidence. Overall it has many helps. A thorough, insightful discussion of theological aspects, though some will feel that Hals sees more than there is in some details. The book is not a commentary but is frequently of great help to expositors.

Hamlin, E. John. *Ruth: Surely There is a Future* **(International Theological Commentary). Grand Rapids: Eerdmans, 1996.**

One finds a concise summing up of each section in an engaging way, explaining the most vital points. Hamlin describes Ruth's lying down with Boaz in terms that convey decency, and Boaz as a worthy man who would not take advantage (43). He patiently explains customs   such   as   the   shoe ceremony (Ruth 4), and its implications, and also kinship obligations via marriage.

Hubbard, Robert L., Jr. *The Book of Ruth* **(New International Commentary on the Old Testament). Grand Rapids: Eerdmans, 1988. 317 pp.**

The Professor of Hebrew at Denver Theological Seminary holds that the book dates from Solomon's era, to which the genealogy of Ruth 4 brings matters, and is a unity including 4:18-22. In detail verse by verse Hubbard is thorough and knowledgeable, documents well, sizes up issues from several angles, is skilled as to customs, and is adept in literature relating to the book. He writes primarily for pastors and laypeople.

Leggett, Donald A. The Levirate and Goel Institutions in the Old Testament with Special Attention to the Book of Ruth. Cherry Hill, NJ: Mack Publishing Co., 1974.

A specialized investigation that the diligent student may wish to consult for depth on customs in the Book of Ruth and how they worked.

Lewis, Arthur. Cf. on Judges.

Luter, A. Boyd and Barry C. Davis. *God Behind the Scene: Expositions of the Books of Ruth & Esther.* **Grand Rapids: Baker, 1995.**

This very readable evangelical pb of 377 pp. on women of success devotes the first 95 pp. to expounding Ruth (Luter), the rest to Esther (Davis). Creative titles of sections lure readers. Luter, a Dallas Seminary graduate, taught Bible at Talbot School of Theology. He defends Ruth's purity, but with opinion, not vigorous reasons. Both expositions are lucid and offer intriguing suggestions that might elicit vivid preaching or teaching in a lay Bible study.

Meyer, F. B. Cf. on Joshua.

Moorhouse, Henry. *Ruth, the Moabitess*. Chicago: Revell, 1881.

Many times the old works have much value, as here. This work is devotional and practical, by a preacher Dwight L. Moody liked to hear.

Myers, J. M. The Linguistic and Literary Form of the Book of Ruth. Leiden: E. J. Brill, 1955.

Scholarly study, often with much help on the subject of the title. The advanced student, even many pastors who study much, can find substantial benefit here.

Nielsen, Kirsten. *Ruth, A Commentary*. Louisville: Westminister/John Knox Press, 1997.

A Danish authoress gives in 106 pp. a scholarly, even sometimes complicated reasoning difficult to follow. After reading twice her treatment of Ruth at night with Boaz, the writer was still unsure what she was concluding, but she conveys the impression that Ruth was indecent (68-70). Nielsen explains customs, and even has an excursus on Levirate marriage (84-89).

Wood, Leon J. Cf. on Joshua.

IX. I AND II SAMUEL

Ackroyd, Peter R. *The First Book of Samuel* (Cambridge Bible Commentary). Cambridge: U. P., 1971. 238 pp.

This is much the same as his work on the second book of Samuel (cf. that entry).

Ackroyd, Peter R. *The Second Book of Samuel* (Cambridge Bible Commentary). Cambridge: U. P., 1977. 247 pp.

An attempt to meet general readers' needs. The approach is mildly critical. Ackroyd has a clear writing style and often is of help on the reading of a given text, historical setting, customs and explanation of the passage. The work is cursory.

Anderson, A. A. *2 Samuel* (Word Biblical Commentary). Waco, TX. Word Books, 1989. 302 pp.

Conservatives will find much to aid them here in meticulous exegetical detail and giving of different views, all done quite readably. One is soon aware, however, of the nonconservative perspective, as in supposing errors as to historical fact, misstatements, and portions ineptly inserted by an exilic redactor (cf. pp. 118-19, 132, 161, 168 etc.). Users will have to use the work with much carefulness but can glean heavy profit from places where he contributes well. Anderson is Honorary Fellow in theology, University of Manchester, England. His introduction takes up theories of composition that specialized scholars can follow completely, even if they do not agree. Many things said in Samuel are attributed to the artistic skill of the author, and one gains the impression that to Anderson they are not historically reliable (xxxiv, etc.). The form/structure/setting sections have much that can help evangelicals and much that gives liberal slants biased on ideas of theoretical sources. Careful advanced students can sift out much and leave much. Like Klein's work on I Samuel, the flow is broken in many ways, so the use of the commentary for any but specialist students will be slow plodding and spotty in benefit.

Baldwin, Joyce C. *1 and 2 Samuel: An Introduction and Commentary* (Tyndale Old Testament Commentary). Grand Rapids: Eerdmans, 1988. 299 pp.

A concise, competent, clear evangelical work using various sources, elucidating most passages well and showing their theological and practical relevance then and now.

Barber, Cyril J. and Carter, John. *I Samuel, Always a Winner. A Bible Commentary for Laymen.* Glendale, CA: G/L Publications, 1977. 160 pp.

Sunday School or Bible class teachers and laypeople in general can gain good ideas on how to present material, how to explain some of the main customs and resolve certain problems. The book is simple, well-organized, refreshing for a series of Bible readings in devotional times, but also has frequent things that stimulate for preaching.

Barber, Cyril J. *The Book of Second Samuel.* Neptune, NJ: Loizeaux, 2000.

Barber, a keen student aggressive to explain passages, surveys each segment in its main flow, and offers relational application. He uses provocative titles, vivid writing, often careful reasons for views, and valuable leads for teachers and preachers. He articulates lessons such as David's making decisions as regarding the Amalekite claiming to have killed Saul, David covering up sin, and problems to which wrong choices can lead (2 Sam. 13ff). Overall the work is a good catalyst for speakers, surveying students, and lay readers.

Bergen, Robert D. *1, 2 Samuel* (New American Commentary). Nashville: Broadman & Holman, 1996.

The commentator is a professor at Hannibal-La Grange College, Hannibal, MO. He argues for the accurate, reliable, relevant Word of God. His excellent work reflects wide knowledge of biblical literature in the text and in footnotes. The writing flows with lucid vitality, and Bergen invests much from word study, grammar, customs, geographical details, etc. His appraisal of Eli is arresting (69), as are comments on Saul's excuses of I Sam. 15 and David's fight with Goliath. Bergen's careful weighing of views about how Saul died ends with his harmonizing view that Saul fell on his sword (I Sam. 31), but in his final moments the Amalekite hastened his death (2 Sam. 1). This is a fine grappling with main details in the two books.

Davis, John J. Cf. on Joshua, under Wood.

Evans, Mary J. *1 and 2 Samuel* (New International Critical Commentary). Peabody, MA: Hendrickson, 2000.

A lecturer in OT at London Bible College did well-studied, lucid comments on verses, with added notes on certain details after each section. She covers most bases, resolves many problems, and elucidates customs, word meanings, and the like. She has no firm solution on some verses, such as the number left out in I Sam. 13:1. She believes that the Amalekite found Saul dead, and took advantage, supposing that David would reward him

(2 Sam. 1). She shows richness from wide reading awareness on many points.

Faulstich, E. W. *Historical Harmony of the Hebrew Kings*. Spencer, IA: Chronology Books, 1986. 304 pp.

The author says he will defend the Bible text vs. rationalism (pp. 2-3). His plan is in using a computer printout of astronomical events and matching things up with these dates from ancient Near Eastern literature. He assumes that biblical numbers are reliable because scribes were under the auspices of God and exacting in writing such detail. Cf. also James D. Newsome, Jr., ed., *A Synoptic Harmony of Samuel, Kings, and Chronicles, with Related Passages from Psalms, Isaiah, and Ezra*. Grand Rapids: Baker, 1986. 275 pp. This is an English harmony setting texts side by side, using the RSV but basing work on the Missouri text from I Samuel 31 through 2 Chronicles 36 (cf. also Wm. D. Crockett, *A Harmony of the Books of Samuel, Kings and Chronicles*. Grand Rapids: Baker, 1985 rp of 1951 ed.). Newsome's layout is easier to use. In cases of tension Newsome suggests possibilities. Many will regard it as a weakness that the harmony is in texts as given in Scripture, not necessarily in actual chronology of events in the books. He does not take up the issue of problems as the chronology in these biblical chapters. Cf. also John H. Hayes and Paul K. Hooker, *A New Chronology for the Kings of Israel and Judah and its Implications for Biblical History and Literature*. Atlanta: John Knox, 1988. 112 pp. These writers from Emory University reject coregencies, antedating and emendations. They say that the regnal years for Israel and Judah were dated from the first Fall New Year festival when a king was on the throne (this switched from Tishri to Nisan in Josiah's reign), and they use only Massoretic Text numbers. They offer their own explanations for numbers being inconsistent. Big problems persist at several reigns (pp. 23, 28, 33, 74 and others). Work by Thiele (cf. under Kings) has long been regarded well by many conservatives.

Gordon, R. P. *1 and 2 Samuel: A Commentary*. Grand Rapids: Zondervan, 1986. 375 pp.

This generally highly-regarded work offers much assistance verse by verse, using the RSV. The author comments a lot on the Hebrew text as to exegesis, word study, dealing with problems, etc.

Klein, Ralph W. *I Samuel* (Word Bible Commentary). Waco, TX: Word, 1983. 307 pp.

A detailed work that often assumes liberal, hard-to-follow ideas positing literary strands from various sources in the book. Klein feels that some accounts cannot be harmonized (xxx). Theories of textual criticism will be a frequent problem for many evangelicals, and much is unclear except to specialists. Still, a lot in the general summary explanations of passages is helpful for the patient and shows how things fit. For more advanced scholarly use the many lists of literature on sections can offer aid, and notes on technical matters in verses specify word meanings, readings, etc. The reader, however, will meet with many liberal perspectives. For the most part the helpful flow of I Samuel bogs down even for serious students in the mixture of explanation and heavy material or theory from Klein's critical system.

Laney, J. Carl. *First and Second Samuel.* **Chicago, IL: Moody Press, 1982. 132 pp.**

Laney, an assistant professor of Biblical literature at Western Conservative Baptist Seminary and more widely known for his volume *The Divorce Myth*, traces the lives of Samuel, Saul and David. This 1982 update for Moody Press's Everyman's Bible Commentary Series is a surprisingly resourceful paperback. Laney argues tersely for a 722 B. C. date for the Fall of Samaria. Thus, he prefers a time of writing for I & II Samuel sometime during or immediately following David's lifetime. He dates the dividing of the kingdom as 931 B. C. Regarding textual matters, Laney does not overlook the lacuna of I Samuel 13:1 as he states that great benefit can be gleaned from the LXX in a study of these two books. One interesting sidelight is his citation of the "dynastic defense" motif evident in I Samuel 15 and II Samuel 8, a setting apparently not unlike 13th Century Hittite tradition. Laney's discussion of God's will in I Samuel 8:21, 22 is quite helpful. In I Samuel 28 the treatment of the Witch of Endor is thorough. He concludes that God caused Samuel himself to appear. In II Samuel 7, Laney sheds light on the covenant by picturing its threefold nature. Laney's maps and graphics are well-placed and worthwhile. His treatment in 11 Samuel 24 of the two-sided nature of David numbering God's people is also worthy of attention. This is a well researched and supported volume. There are few volumes on I and II Samuel which could rightly claim to be more helpful on expositional matters. -Jan Sattem

McCarter, P. Kyle Jr. *I Samuel: A New Translation with Introduction and Commentary* **(Anchor Bible). NY: Doubleday, 1980. 475 pp.**

McCarter writes this liberal work out of an immensely broad awareness of scholarly literature (cf. his 14-pp. bibliography, textual notes and informed way of handling many of the problem texts). He goes after the meaning of a passage, seeks to reach defensible conclusions, provides one of the best recent, up-to-date commentaries for more advanced students needing technical help on I Samuel, and is conversant with critical studies. Cf. also his work *II Samuel* in the Anchor Bible (553 pp.). He was at the time Professor of Religious Studies at the University of Virginia.

Merrill, Eugene. "I and II Samuel," *Bible Knowledge Commentary*, **ed. John F. Walvoord and Roy B. Zuck. Volume I. Wheaton: Victor Books, 1983.**

Professor of Old Testament at Dallas Theological Seminary surveys both books with conservative expertise, dealing with Hebrew meaning, problems, customs, etc. He has a high view of inspiration and a good use of literature relevant in the area.

Meyer, F. B. Cf. under Joshua.

Vos, Howard F. *1, 2 Samuel* **(Bible Study Commentary). Grand Rapids: Zondervan, 1983. 166 pp.**

Vos was Professor of History and Archaeology, King's College, Briarcliff Manor, New York, In this conservative work he gives a long outline at the outset, then incorporates this in his survey of I and 2 Samuel. For many Bible teachers, preachers, and lay people the exposition helpfully sums up what is said and some implications. It offers brief explanation of some main problems, such as the number judged at Beth Shemesh in I Samuel 6:19ff. and how to fill in the number of Saul's years in 13:1.

Wood, Leon J. Cf. under Joshua.

X. I AND II KINGS

Cogan, Mordachai. *1 Kings* (The Anchor Bible). NY: Doubleday, 2000.

Reading Cogan's beliefs about late composition using various documents will give more awareness of theories putting I Kings in the sixth century B. C. and even changing its message to fit later beliefs. Remarks verse by verse explain much on passages, where one can distinguish between real explanation and opinions about a late editor who recast things his own way centuries later (cf. 196, Solomon's prayer for wisdom and display of wisdom, I Kin. 3). It requires great patience to glean the helpful for teaching or preaching, so scholars, advance students and very persistent pastors who devote a lot of time will discover benefits.

Constable, Thomas. "I and 11 Kings," in *Bible Knowledge Commentary*, ed. John F. Walvoord and Roy B. Zuck. Volume 1. Wheaton: Victor Books, 1983.

Constable shows awareness of Hebrew word meanings, has much good exegesis and judicious comments on many of the verses, even if brief. On several problem areas he offers helpful data, and reflects awareness of literature. This is a contributive conservative effort.

Davis, John J. Cf. Joshua, under Wood.

DeVries, S. J. *I Kings* (Word Biblical Commentary). Waco: Word Books, 1985. 286 pp.

This is a rather well-studied work offering frequent help on word meaning, views on problems, background, customs, etc. Used by conservatives who exercise discernment and see better possibilities for a high view of biblical accuracy at some points, it can be of considerable help. Cf. on Chronicles.

Dilday, Russell H. "l, 2 Kings," in *The Communicator's Commentary*. Waco: Word Books, 1987. 512 pp.

The president of Southwestern Baptist Theological Seminary in Fort Worth, Texas has given a thoroughly studied, clear, well-illustrated and applied work that furnishes rich assistance to an expositor. Dilday frequently gives different views on an issue and includes many footnotes with further sources for added help.

Gray, John. *I & II Kings*. London: SCM Press, 1964.

This is an attempt to provide a fresher technical, liberal commentary than the work of Montgomery which preceded it by 13 years. It uses works of the German form critical approach.

Hendricks, Howard. *Elijah*. Chicago: Moody, 1972.

Here are expository messages by one of America's long-time noted spiritual life speakers, a professor at Dallas Theological Seminary. Hendricks developed these lessons in Bible conference ministry, making them practical to effect change. They are suggestive for preachers and devotionally stimulating for any readers.

Hobbs, T. R. *2 Kings* (Word Biblical Commentary). Waco: Word Books, 1985. 388 pp.

He places the writing in the early part of the captivity by one writer, and is thorough on literature pertaining to 2 Kings as well as on matters of text, exegesis and theology. Students can glean considerable material that is worthwhile.

House, Paul R. *1, 2 Kings* (New American Commentary). Nashville: Broadman & Holman, 1995.

This is one of the most helpful more concise evangelical studies. He opens each section with comments relating it with the wider biblical picture, often gives pertinent remarks on verses, and ends sections with apt principles to apply. The well-researched work benefits teachers and preachers and is lucid for lay people. The introduction (27-84) shows carefully informed conservative convictions, with some detail about a single author, chronology, the political context, miracles (which he believes did occur), literary issues, the structure and plot of the two books, theological issues (monotheism vs. idolatry, etc.), and other matters. House often supports comments with pertinent data from other Scripture or outside ancient sources. He deals with many of the problems. The verse by verse remarks at times could offer more, but other works can supplement him (cf. Patterson/Austel, for example).

Jones, G. H. *1 and 2 Kings*. 2 volumes (New Century Bible). Grand Rapids: Eerdmans, 1984. 666 pp.

This liberal work is steeped in ponderous scholarly literature (cf. a long bibliography) and has an introduction of around 85 pages which pulls readers abreast of discussion and views up to the early 1980's, heavily so in liberal circles. Jones sees discrepancies between the Greek tradition and the Massoretic Text. He does not accept co-regencies as E. Thiele does to harmonize kings' reigns. Rather he uses basically K. T. Anderson's system of taking MT figures, consulting the LXX at some points, concluding some contradictions, etc. His own opinion picks and chooses arbitrarily what he wishes to regard as historically accurate and what he thinks is fictionalized addition (cf. 2 Kings 18-20, pp. 556-95).

Knapp, Christopher. *The Kings of Judah and Israel*. NY: Loizeaux, 1956.

The author, who served as an evangelist in the Bahamas and a missionary to Honduras, Central America, has given here a biography of each king in Judah and Israel. He traces the characteristics and accomplishments of each reign. In each case, he draws together all of the Bible references to the king's reign, gives the names of prophets ministering in his day, and presents a key verse which summarizes that reign in a nutshell. He has good sketches of the kings.

Meyer, F. B. Cf. on Joshua.

Meyer, F. B. *Elijah and the Secret of His Power*. Chicago: Revell, n. d.

Perceptive on many of the devotional principles, and often refreshing.

Montgomery, J. A. *A Critical and Exegetical Commentary on the Book of Kings.* **NY: Scribners, 1951.**

In an area of Scripture not frequently studied by Christians or made the source of sermons, Montgomery has provided a detailed work of a critical nature. A part of the I.C.C., it is often noted by conservative scholars as among the best single volumes in the entire set. The archaeological material throwing light on the era of the monarchy and the divided kingdom, plus the philological study, make the book very helpful.

Patterson, R. D. and Hermann J. Austel. "1 and 2 Kings," *Expositor's Bible Commentary.* **Volume 4, ed. F. Gaebelein and R. P. Polcyn. Grand Rapids: Zondervan, 1988.**

Staunch conservative work very well done in detail verse by verse, handling problems, using a wide range of relevant literature, The reader finds both the regular commentary and the notes sections packed with pertinent information.

Pink, A. W. *The Life of Elijah.* **Grand Rapids: Zondervan, 1956; also Gleanings from Elisha. Chicago: Moody, 1972.**

Rich devotional thoughts, frequently, on the character and situation of each prophet.

Provan, Iain W. *1 and 2 Kings* **(New International Biblical Commentary). Peabody, MA: Hendrickson, 1995.**

Provan sees the books as one unified, trustworthy narrative as opposed to a patchwork of literary compositions with scholars picking and choosing what they accept. His verse-by-verse material explains details in a good flow and reflects careful research on words, contextual connections, customs, and other Scripture that relates. The useful benefit is fairly on a par with Wiseman's work among briefer, yet usually adequate recent works. Some verses receive much attention, others are so generalized that certain details draw little comment or none. An example of Elijah's posture in I Kings 18:42, or what might be meant in 19:11-12 by the Lord not being in the wind, quake, or fire.

Thiele, Edwin R. *The Mysterious Numbers of the Hebrew Kings.* **Grand Rapids: Zondervan, 1983, revision of 1951 and 1965 eds.**

This is not a commentary but is very important since it is an outstanding work on the problems of chronology during the kings period. It is not an easy book to read because of the involved and intricate nature of working through seeming discrepancies of dates in the Biblical record and because of the many citations the author must make from ancient sources. But, for the serious student, it is an indispensable work.

Wiseman, Donald J. *1 and 2 Kings* **(Tyndale OTC). Downers Grove, IL: IVP, 1993.**

In a fairly profitable work, a noted scholar supplies concise comments, skipping some verses but showing adeptness on most details. He treats the claims as reliable. Though he usually explains things, at times he does not, for instance the possible point in the Lord not being in the wind, quake or fire (I Kin. 19:11-14). He defends the actions of Elijah in the deaths of the king's soldiers in 2 Kin. 1.

Wood, Leon J. Cf. on Joshua.

Wood, Leon J. *Elijah, Prophet of God*. Des Plaines, IL: Regular Baptist Press, 1968.

A careful, informed evangelical scholar writes with great benefit on themes and applications, and helps on problem passages.

Wood, Leon J. *Israel's United Monarchy*. Grand Rapids: Baker, 1979.

Wood develops material surveying the kings, explaining difficult passages, and pointing out pertinent truths that are of value.

XI. I AND II CHRONICLES

Ackroyd, Peter R. *I and II Chronicles, Ezra and Nehemiah*. London: SCM Press, 1973.

Liberal, using redaction criticism quite a lot. Perceptive and advanced students can sift out much that is of worth on the meaning of verses or pericopes.

Barber, Cryil J. *The Faithfulness of God, Devotional Studies in I, II Chronicles*. 2 vols. Santa Ana, CA: Promise Publishing Co., 2002, 2003.

A master of careful study and vivid adeptness to show the relevance of passages wrote these in pb, both having the same cover design (cf. his books on Judges, Samuel, Ruth, Nehemiah, etc.). This work is a catalyst for pastors, Bible school teachers, and laity, drawing lessons from various parts of the biblical book, and illustrating them colorfully. Volume I has 17 chapters, each of 15-20 pp. Barber sees Ezra as the probable author, before 400 B.C. (cf. arguments, iv-viii). Many points set up easy applications, as on Jabez' prayer (8-14). Some ideas will be suspect as arbitrary, e.g. Jabez was possibly youngest in his family, and his father was possibly slain by raiding Amalekites (5,7). Barber cites good scholars, and often is perceptively rich on devotional lessons, making this stimulating for a series of readings in times with the Lord. Examples of themes are three chapters on David's mighty men (51-99), marks of friendship (I Chron. 11:15-19), the power within (11;20-21), success without compromise or regret (11:22-25), a friend's loyalty (11:26-27), etc. The vol. on II Chronicles is about 20% longer than that on I Chronicles, and along the same lines and of equal value to be very useful among leaders and the led.

Braun, R. L. *I Chronicles* (Word Biblical Commentary). Waco: Word Books, 1986. 312 pp.

As one becomes accustomed to this series, he knows he will find much usable detail on the text, aspects of exegesis, customs, geography, and theological focus. He also comes to realize the contrast, at some points, with conservative convictions about the historicity of matters, and wisely gleans out what is worthwhile.

DeVries, Simon J. *1 and 2 Chronicles* (Forms of the Old Testament Literature Series). Grand Rapids: Eerdmans, 1989. 439 pp.

Such a work will show serious readers advanced in theological training how a scholar has done a form-critical analysis. One also will see discussion on the history of such study.

The work probes the structure, genre, setting and aim of each section, according to the opinion of DeVries, which the conservative student may find of value or pass up for what he regards as a more defensible view. DeVries' study can be very insightful at times but also can be quite arbitrary and subjective.

Dillard, Raymond B. *2 Chronicles* (Word Biblical Commentary). Waco: Word Books, 1987. 323 pp.

Cf. Braun for I Chronicles. Much the same comment is fitting here. One can feel he has a gold mine on many details of verse meaning and on bibliography, yet be aware of a less than conservative way of handling many things.

Ellison, H. L. "1 and 2 Chronicles," in *New Bible Commentary Revised*, ed. D. Guthrie et al. Grand Rapids: Eerdmans, 1970.

Ellison is limited to pp. 369-94. Like Cundall on Ezra and Nehemiah, he argues unity with Ezra and Nehemiah and a date around 400-340 B. C. (p. 369). He assumes that many problems in numbers arose from textual corruption, poor transmission of the text of Chronicles, and other explanations. Overall his commentary is a fair, concise work that often provides some help of an evangelical nature.

McConville, J. Gordon. *Chronicles* (Daily Study Bible). Edinburgh: Saint Andrews Press, 1984. 270 pp.

Generally conservative in outlook, this displays a firm grip on the data, aiming at looking at things in their setting during the kings period and applying principles to life now. He does not sidestep problems, such as a million dead (2 Chr. 14:9ff.). The RSV is printed in space that, for those with Bibles, would be better used for even more comment.

Merrill, Eugene. "I and II Chronicles," in *Bible Knowledge Commentary*, ed. John F. Walvoord and Roy B. Zuck. Volume I. Wheaton: Victor Books, 1983.

Conservative scholar from Dallas Theological Seminary deals with the passages knowledgeably, showing good awareness of relevant literature and handling many of the problems at least with some help.

Myers, Jacob M. *I Chronicles. Introduction, Translation and Notes* (Anchor Bible). NY: Doubleday, 1965.

Myers argues that the Chronicler wrote in the Persian period (ca. 538-333 B. C.), more precisely ca. 400 B. C. (p. LXXXIX. Ezra is a possibility, as language, literary mannerisms and interests are like those in the Ezra memoirs (Ezra; Nehemiah), but Myers leaves the matter there. In the commentary section, he gives his own translation, then brief notes on problem words, finally his comments on the more crucial issues in a chapter or part of a chapter. Myers does not always explain differences between statements, as in II Samuel 21:19 where Elhanan killed Goliath and I Chronicles 20:5 where Elhanan slew the brother of Goliath. Myers briefly offers just enough to leave one somewhat puzzled (p. 136, on v. 5). But cf. Gleason Archer, *Encyclopedia of Bible Difficulties* pp. 178-79, for further possible resolution of the problem. Myers, though often willing to take accounts in Chronicles as reasonable, sometimes assumes "obvious legendary accretions and embellishments" even if in his opinion "the nucleus of the story may be taken as historical" (p. 147), as in the census episode of I Chronicles 21. The back inside jacket of the volume says, "I Chronicles is to be neither accepted as a faithful narrative of the Davidic period nor dismissed as a forceful, imaginative recreation of that history. It must be taken as an important clue to the biblical process" (cf. also his II Chronicles, xx, xxiv-xxxii). He says in *II Chronicles* (p. xxxii): "... within the limits of its purpose, the Chronicler's story is accurate wherever it can be checked, though the method of presentation is homiletical. The only valid objection to the foregoing statement could be the numbers which, by any interpretation, are impossibly high. This fact perhaps more than any other has made the chronicler's work suspect." Liberal but sometimes moderately so, Myers defends the genealogical lists at many points as trustworthy history, whereas such scholars as Wellhausen had viewed them as fabrications. Myers does, however, disconcertingly make some statements that negate his claims about reliability, leaving the reader wondering about consistency. He looks at the numbers (statistics) as exaggerated in some cases but upholds them on occasion. He tries to offer suggestions for what he regards as high numbers. In archeological confirmation of various points in the books, he is profitable sometimes. He dates Chronicles-Ezra-Nehemiah around 400 B. C., answering critics who place these books about 330 B. C. or later. In his opinion, the same Chronicler composed all three books at the same time. He has contributed the Ezra-Nehemiah commentary to The Anchor Bible series as well.

Myers, Jacob M. *II Chronicles* (Anchor Bible). NY: Doubleday, 1965.

This is done along the same lines as his work on I Chronicles.

Payne, J. Barton. "1 and 2 Chronicles," in *Expositor's Bible Commentary*, Volume 4, ed. F. Gaebelein and R. P. Polcyn. Grand Rapids: Zondervan, 1988.

Another competent conservative treatment of the text, its exegesis and problems. Payne and Merrill advocate a high view of the integrity of history in the books and offer plausible solutions where there are difficulties. Their outlook is quite different from many on the books.

Pratt, Richard L., Jr. *1 and 2 Chronicles*. Geanies House, Fearn, Ross-shire, Great Britain: Christian Focus Publications, 1998.

A Reformed work, this assumes divine inspiration and historical veracity. Pratt is Prof. of OT at Reformed Theological Seminary, Orlando. Vast study is evident, and Pratt is diligent to show relevancy on various themes today (cf. pp. 15-59). He explains sections to give perspective, and gives good, well-organized detail on verses, often showing a tie-in with NT development on ideas. Well-known passages are seen in much light, for example David's census (I Chron. 21), and Jehoshaphat's prayerful coping with an invader (2 Chron. 20), Uzziah's successes and prideful infidelity (2 Chron. 26), and Hezekiah's career (2 Chron. 29-32). The 512 pp. furnish much help for evangelicals.

Sailhamer, John. *First and Second Chronicles*. Chicago, IL: Moody Press, 1983.

Sailhamer, formerly of Biola College and Bethel Seminary and more recently of Trinity Evangelical Divinity School, has written this 116-pp. paperback for the Everyman's Bible Commentary. Historically, I and II Chronicles are often overlooked by biblical commentators. This volume will add little to knowledge in the field. Sailhamer has recounted the important events and persons in these books in a rather cursory and simplistic fashion. Little problem solution is even broached and citation of Hebrew for support or exegesis is quite scanty. This volume due to its brevity and simplicity will benefit the new believer and those unfamiliar with the historical position and flow of Chronicles. -Jan Sattern

Selman, Martin J. 1 Chronicles, and *2 Chronicles* (Tyndale OTC). Downers Grove, IL: IVP, 1992, 1994.

The vol. on 1 Chronicles gives the introduction for both vols. His evangelical works deal with sections compactly, being well-informed on words, grammar, and background both biblically and from ancient sources (cf. for example on Sennacherib's death in 32:20-23). He follows a clear outline, and his comments usually get to the point judiciously. Selman is Director of Postgraduate Studies and lecturer in OT at Spurgeon's College, London. One will find considerable assistance here. To return to the introduction, Selman if read carefully covers much on the chronicler's focus, one more of interpreting history while not casting doubt on historical details, and giving features that characterize these two books. Among the latter are prophecies and prayers. He discusses main emphases, e.g. covenant, Israel as the covenant people, the temple as the covenant worship center, and the Covenant as a basis for restoration despite great Israelite unfaithfulness; the covenant guarantees God's restoration some day by repentance and prayer as well as by divine promises (cf. 2 Chr. 7:12-16), in Selman's statement. He does not spell out when and how, or tie it in with other biblical passages, as a unified prophetic program for Israel.

Stewart, Andrew. *A Family Tree, 1 Chronicles Simply Explained*; also a 2nd vol., *A House of Prayer, The Message of 2 Chronicles* (Welwyn Commentary) Auburn, WA: Evangelical Press, 1997, 2001.

These works of 222 and 476 pp. are highly readable, survey expositions attentive to providing meanings and applications. Preachers can find assists in this broader study to avoid losing sight of the forest while looking at the trees, and getting suggestive ideas for sermons. Examples are on Jabez (I Chron. 4:9-10), or in lessons from various kings. Help on actual explanation of passages appears more usefully in other works, for instance those by Pratt and Thompson.

Thompson, J. A. *1, 2 Chronicles* (New American Commentary). Nashville: Broadman & Holman, 1994.

An Australian OT scholar of Baptist persuasion made this well-studied evangelical contribution based on firm convictions for Scripture's trustworthiness. The introduction surveys themes. Verse by verse remarks are concise, to the point, and address many of the pertinent questions. The work is suitable for professors, students, pastors and lay users. Thompson resolves seeming contradictions, as on whether God or Satan incited David to take a census (cf. I Chron. 21:1; I Sam. 24:1). This is one of the best all-around works of medium-range detail (411 pp.), and the writer's comments can easily suggest principles to apply.

Wilcock, Michael. *The Message of Chronicles* (The Bible Speaks Today). Downers Grove: IVP, 1987. 288 pp.

An evangelical approach that defends conservative views on a number of the problems, feeling there are no errors. Wilcock sometimes delightfully applies the meaning to life today, and writes with clarity. He assists readers to see why material is used where it is, how it fits a need there, etc. Wilcock is vicar of St. Nicholas Church, Durham, England. For principles and for the movement in Chronicles this is a worthwhile book.

Williamson, H. G. M. *1 and 2 Chronicles* **(New Century Bible Commentary). Grand Rapids: Eerdmans, 1982. 428 pp.**

Some regard this as the top work on textual, literary-critical discussion. Much help is here on meanings of verses at times, drawn carefully from a wealth of learning and various sources. However, Williamson sees historical inaccuracies at many points, and conservative users will wisely deal with it in a very watchful judgment.

Wood, Leon J. Cf. on Joshua.

XII. EZRA-NEHEMIAH-ESTHER

Baldwin, Joyce. C. *Esther: An Introduction and Commentary* **(Tyndale Old Testament Commentary). Downers Grove: IVP, 1984. 126 pp.**

A frequent, respected contributor to this series, she presents careful research on setting, text, exegesis and related matters such as customs, with good notes. The work is evangelical, but some will think it strange that Baldwin says some details "continue to seem improbable" (p. 24).

Barber, Cyril J. *Nehemiah.* **New York: Loizeaux Bros., 1976.**

This is a clear, practical evangelical effort to do exposition and at the same time point out principles from the life of Nehemiah to help Christians be more organized in handling their lives and business today. The work grew out of a 26-week laymen's Bible class series geared to shoe leather living, but shows much study.

Blenkinsopp, Joseph. *Ezra-Nehemiah, A Commentary* **(Old Testament Library). Philadelphia: Westminster, 1988. 366 pp.**

He upholds the view that Ezra-Nehemiah gives a continued account of 1 and 2 Chronicles and are authored by the chronicler, an individual or a school. He also holds traditional views such as Ezra coming in 458 B. C., Nehemiah in 445. Often he is good verse by verse, and he includes a bibliography for each section, his translation, textual notes and a fairly thorough commentary. "The chronicles of Nehemiah" (1:1) he takes as referring to Nehemiah as subject, not author. He is saturated with the literature about the era.

Boice, James M. *Nehemiah: Learning to Lead.* **NY: Revell, 1988, 219 pp.**

One of America's famous expository pastors (10th St. Presbyterian Church, Philadelphia) issues a call to pattern life after Nehemiah's style of leadership. He brings out traits and shows how they can be relevant today, writing lucidly and using illustrations at times. His work is suggestive for expositors, also provocative for spiritual growth in usefulness to God.

Breneman, Mervin. *Ezra, Nehemiah, Esther* **(New American Commentary).
Nashville: Broadman & Holman, 1993.**

This evangelical writing, even longer than Fensham's, ranks right with it and Yamauchi's.
Breneman argues five reasons (43-46) for the traditional view that places Ezra (458 B.
C.) earlier than Nehemiah (445). Good sections take up the theology of Ezra-Nehemiah
and the significance of both men, later the historicity of Esther and the trustworthiness of
the Book of Esther. Verse by verse comments shine much light, and footnotes draw help
from wide awareness of literature, while keeping a reasonable brevity. Still, at times,
more comment to grapple with matters would aid a reader, as on Nehemiah's rough
action toward violators in 13:25. The many copious remarks on verses, as on Ezra 7:10,
off-set occasional shortness. Conservatives will value defenses of reliability against
many who find fault with details, as in Esther.

Campbell, Donald K. *Nehemiah: Man In Charge.* **Wheaton: SP Publications,
Victor Books, 1979. 119 pp.**

A long-time Bible professor at Dallas Theological Seminary, and for some time president, weaves lucid explanation of the book with choice illustrations. As a highly readable
survey, it is helpful to both lay person and a pastor or Sunday School teacher seeking a
clear tracing of the flow of the book plus a focus on key traits that made Nehemiah a good
leader. Comments are well organized and truth applied relevantly to highlight many of
the main lessons of Nehemiah. Preachers can get good ideas here, and any readers be
built up.

Clines, D. J. A. *Ezra, Nehemiah and Esther* **(New Century Bible
Commentary). Grand Rapids: Eerdmans, 1984. 342 pp.**

A concise work of deep study, usually with a well-organized explanation having support
and references pointing to further help. Clines provides alert, well-researched comments
arguing for the historicity of Esther, contra views of some such as Jobes.

Cohen, A. "Esther," in *The Five Megilloth.* **London: Soncino, 1946.**

Concise commentary treats many of the salient points of Esther showing Jewish concern
to explain the text meaningfully. Much of the work is very helpful to conservative expositors.

Cundall, A. E. "Ezra and Nehemiah," in *New Bible Commentary Revised,* **ed.
D. Guthrie et al. Grand Rapids: Eerdmans, 1970.**

Restricted to pp. 395-411, Cundall uses his space well. He favors unity with Chronicles
as one composite history and advances a summary of the main points of controversy over
the relationship of Ezra and Nehemiah (395-97). He deals with the critical theory which
rejects the traditional position and does not concur that the Chronicler has confused the
order of the books (397). In some number problems, he assumes copyist errors, as in Ezra
1:9-11 (399). Overall it is a terse work offering help many a time.

Evers, Stan K. *Doing a Great Work. Ezra and Nehemiah Simply Explained*
(Welwyn Commentary). Auburn, WA: Evangelical Press, 1996.

Chapters receive surveys focusing on worship to a holy God, obeying with full loyalty,
and uniting with His people in fellowship. Preachers, students, and lay people will find

the broad exposition easy to follow, giving quick principles. The book is one further light work with some explanation and application for those who may not see applications that should spring obviously from better commentaries when they expose truth that is pertinent for life.

Fensham, F. C. *The Books of Ezra and Nehemiah* (New International Commentary on the Old Testament). Grand Rapids: Eerdmans, 1982. 288 pp.

An evangelical effort knowledgeably rich in exegesis with a firm grasp of Hebrew, matters of introduction, and solid explanation of many of the verses. He shows a more meaningful grip on the relationship of the material in Ezra and Nehemiah than Williamson, and is better overall.

Getz, Gene. *Nehemiah, A Man of Prayer and Perseverance.* Ventura, CA: G/L, Regal Books, 1981.

Author of several books of Bible characters (Abraham, Moses, etc.), Getz clearly elucidates principles on prayer and patience in a book with thirteen references to prayer. A good conservative effort that can fan fires of prayer in laypeople and stir pastors and Bible teachers to more faithfulness in this area.

Hess, Margaret. *Esther: Courage in Crisis.* Wheaton: Scripture Union/Victor Books, 1980.

The writer sketches a good character picture of Esther in a way that can be life changing for other women and Christians in general. She does this competently against the clarified background of the crisis.

Huey, F. B., Jr. "Esther" in *Expositor's Bible Commentary*, Volume 4, ed. F. Gaebelein and R. P. Polcyn. Grand Rapids: Zondervan, 1988.

Detailed conservative comment on verses, taking up views and reasons on problem verses. This has quite a bit to offer.

Ironside, H. A. *Notes on Ezra.* NY: Loizeaux, 1946.

***Notes on Nehemiah.* NY: Loizeaux (n.d.),**

Notes on the Book of Esther. NY: Loizeaux. 1921.

Though Ironside does not get into the detail of the text, he does give a practical exposition on a wider scale in popular fashion. He shows how the message is alive, and at times helps with good illustrations.

Jobes, Karen H. *Esther* (NIV Application Commentary). Grand Rapids: Zondervan, 1999.

Jobes will not be clear to some in her view that a biblical book can have legitimate errors in historical matters for the sake of poetic license, without distorting the truth (34). She does not give evidence here to make her point clear or show that it is valid in Esther. She says that Vashti, Ahasueras [Xerxes], Esther and Haman may not be the actual names of the people to whom the events happened (36-37). The authoress's explanation of verses in Esther offer studied help, and each section ends with worthwhile comments on ways main lessons are relevant today.

Kidner, Derek. *Ezra & Nehemiah* (Tyndale Old Testament Commentary). Downers Grove: 1VP, 1979.

A fairly brief but model exposition, very good for rich historical background and treatment of problems in chronology and harmony, as well as profiles of the major characters. Included are solid appendices treating the questions of sources, the identity of Sheshbazzar, chronology, the book of the law, and a superb if brief discussion of Ezra-Nehemiah as history, concluding that "there is no merit in putting up memorials to the prophets we dismember" (p. 174) (Dan Phillips). Kidner has frequent logical defenses against the way the documentary hypothesis links Ezra and "P." He defends the biblical order of Ezra, then Nehemiah and argues that a different order faces problems that are bigger. He shows a high view of the text and a firm grasp of how to defend it against skepticism.

Laney, J. Carl. *Ezra and Nehemiah* (Everyman's Bible Commentary). Chicago: Moody, 1982.

A keen conservative scholar has contributed a well-studied and clear work in concise form. Laney is adept in context, word study, synopsis, customs, etc. and knows how to get at the main points, deal with some of the problems, and explain things reasonably.

Martin, John. "Ezra," also "Esther," in *Bible Knowledge Commentary*, ed. John F. Walvoord and Roy B. Zuck. Volume I. Wheaton: Victor Books, 1983.

A diligent, lucid exposition of both books by a former expositor in the Bible Department at Dallas Theological Seminary. Works like these and the ones here by Huey, Fensham, Laney, McConville, Whitcomb and Yamauchi provide quite a lot for conservative expositors.

McConville, J. Gordon. *Ezra, Nehemiah and Esther* (Daily Study Bible). Philadelphia: Westminster, 1985. 198 pp.

Books in this series differ greatly in whether liberal or conservative. The present commentator as on Chronicles reaches views quite often that staunch evangelicals (in the way this has traditionally been understood) will appreciate. Ezra came to Jerusalem in 458 B. C., Nehemiah in 445, and both took part in Nehemiah 8-10, 12. McConville assumes that events in Esther are historically reliable. Though at so many points too brief, this is a refreshing, warm, and good commentary done clearly and using historical/archaeological help to shed light.

McGee, J. Vernon. *Exposition of the Book of Esther*. Wheaton: Van Kampen, 1951.

This is a good popular evangelical treatment of the book originating as a series of Sunday evening sermons.

Moore, C. A. *Esther: Introduction, Translation and Notes* (Anchor Bible). NY: Doubleday, 1971. 118 pp.

Highly thought of in many scholarly circles, this is competent on the text, exegesis, history, culture and matters of introduction (in regard to surveying views current in literature). It offers much help.

Myers, Jacob M. *Ezra-Nehemiah* **(Anchor Bible). Garden City, NY: Doubleday, 1965.**

A faculty member of the Lutheran Theological Seminary in Gettysburg, PA has written this highly respected work after years of study. He sets well the background of the captivity in Babylon, the situation in Judah, the returns to Jerusalem. On the period of Ezra, Myers inclines to Albright's proposal that Ezra came in the thirty-seventh year, even after Nehemiah began, ca. 428 B. C., not earlier in 458 B. C. as the *seventh* year in 7:7, 8 suggests (thirty-seventh year, not seventh) (p. xxxvii). He shows some opinion in rabbinic and other ancient sources for Ezra-Nehemiah being one book, other evidence to make it separate. He feels that Nehemiah's memoirs were placed as an appendix with the larger corpus of the Chronicler, even if Nehemiah's coming preceded Ezra's (xli). To him the possible preference is Pavlovsky's theory that Ezra came with Nehemiah unofficially on his second tour in Jerusalem and was a key man in reforms. Later when Nehemiah desired it, Ezra came again to Jerusalem with kingly authority, heading a group of exiles from Babylon. He dealt with the problem of mixed marriages, then wrote a history (Chronicles and Ezra 1-6). One of his followers later contributed material from the work of Ezra and Nehemiah from various preserved sources (xlviii). Myers' idea of sources for the books involves a commitment to a JEDP theory. He dates the completion of the main work by the Chronicler ca. 400 B. C. The list of high priests (Nehemiah 12) does not include later priests (page lxx.) The commentary is at times fairly sparse and hit or miss verse by verse with some verses passed over. Such a verse as Ezra 7:10 receives little comment. Not much is attempted on drawing out spiritual life lessons based on the comments. Yet there is a wealth of data that explains and shows a competent grasp of Jewish conditions, word meanings, etc. Myers provides a five and a half page list of commentaries, other books, and articles (lxviii-lxxxiii).

Packer, J. I. *A Passion for Faithfulness. Wisdom From the Book of Nehemiah.* **Wheaton: Crossway Books, 1995.**

Packer writes in the "Living Insights Bible Studies" series, which focuses on surveys (not complete commentary) to foster key themes and godly living (ix). This claim for uniqueness is a seller's misleading one, since many longer or shorter commentaries actually do this. Packer uses Nehemiah as a servant leader to write about church-building, and often rather than explaining the biblical book merely dips in to draw lessons. An instance is Nehemiah's character qualities, His God, his godliness, his call to serve, his management, his enduring of trials, and his times of refreshing. Packer forms parallels between issues of Nehemiah's time and situations God's servants face today.

Patton, L. B. *A Critical and Exegetical Commentary on the Book of Esther* **(ICC). Edinburgh: T. & T. Clark, 1908. 339 pp.**

Though old, this still is a rich larder of information on details of word meaning, exegesis, history, etc. It is liberal in perspective but contributes much help if gleaned wisely.

Prime, Derek. *Unspoken Lessons About the Unseen God* **(Welwyn Commentary). Auburn, WA: Evangelical Press, 2001.**

This pb by a long-time UK pastor simply explains Esther in ten chapters that give principles for preaching and living. It is a help for those ready only for a light, brief, popular discussion as a catalyst for nurture.

Swindoll, Charles R. *Hand Me Another Brick* **Nashville: Thomas Nelson, 1978.**

One of America's top Evangelical Free Church pastors (Fullerton, CA) and later a president at Dallas Theological Seminary gives challenging expositions of main lessons in Nehemiah, with illustrations and ways to apply the truth. Pastors, Bible teachers and laypeople in general will find pointed principles to refresh their spiritual lives and direct them in service.

Williamson, H. G. M. *Ezra, Nehemiah* **(Word Biblical Commentary). Waco, TX. Word Books, 1985. 417 pp.**

Highly respected in the general scholarly community, this indeed does furnish help, often detailed, on many matters like word study, background, customs, and views on problems. He treats the books as essentially from the fifth century B. C., brought together fully by 300 B. C., and a literary unit. He believes the composer may have been misled by a mistaken identification of Sheshbazzar and Zerubbabel. He dismays conservatives at times by subjectively seeing so much material in Ezra and Nehemiah as fragmented (cf., for instance, p. 309). Yet he is somewhat conservative at times, and fairly includes evangelicals in his bibliography, etc.

Whitcomb, John C. "Ezra," "Nehemiah," and "Esther" in The Wycliffe Bible Commentary. Chicago: Moody, 1962.

The author, for many years Professor of Old Testament at Grace Theological Seminary in Winona Lake, Indiana has distinguished himself by co-authoring *The Genesis Flood* with Henry Morris and by his own work *Darius the Mede*. His commentary here shows the same painstaking research into historical matters as well as Hebrew meanings. See also his bibliography at the end of each book.

Whitcomb, John C. Esther: Triumph of God's Sovereignty. Chicago, IL: Moody Press, 1979.

Whitcomb has written this fine 128-pp. paperback for the Everyman's Bible Commentary. He includes a helpful bibliography along with charts and time-line illustrations. The chronology of Esther is dealt with in detail. The author uses nine chapters to discuss ten chapters of Esther. He uses a verse by verse format. Whitcomb's introductory remarks are very good but regrettably brief. Throughout the volume he counters two major detractors to the historicity and canonicity of Esther (Patton, ICC, 1908; Moore, Anchor Bible, 1977). Whitcomb dates Esther prior to the palace destruction at Susa in 435 B. C. He, like others, hypothesizes that perhaps a Diasporan Jew authored this work. His comments on the difference between canonicity and theological understanding are worthy of note. Whitcomb's approach to historicity itself makes valuable reading. The author equates Ahasuerus (486-465 B. C.) with Xerxes aka. Khshayarsha. Whitcomb's work here is especially valuable for its concern for the interplay between secular and sacred history. Conclusion: Outstanding approach and treatment. -Jan Sattem

Wright, J. Stafford. The Date of Ezra's Coming to Jerusalem. London: Tyndale, 1958.

Not a commentary, this study is an assist in discussing the problem and views as background preparation for expositors and scholars.

Yamauchi, Edwin. "Ezra, Nehemiah," in Expositor's Bible Commentary, Volume 4, ed. F. Gaebelein and R. P. Polcyn. Grand Rapids: Zondervan, 1988.

A conservative investigation with plentiful help on text, word meaning, history, culture, etc. Yamauchi cites from a wide swing of scholarly literature. He is sometimes concisely helpful on differences in numbers between Ezra and Nehemiah (cf. also on the numbers Gleason Archer, *Encyclopedia of Bible Difficulties*. Grand Rapids: Zondervan, 1982, pp. 229-30).

XIII. Job

Alden, Robert. *Job* (New American Commentary). Nashville: Broadman & Holman, 1993.

This evangelical effort of 432 pp. has a knowledgeable introduction on many main points relevant in getting set for exposition. Job, Alden feels, was an actual historical person (25), possibly living in patriarchal days though Alden is not certain. In exposition, the writer is usually clear, explaining some vital details (as "perfect" in 1:1, even Heb. Words, grammar, etc.). Haziness in regard to who "the Satan" is will disturb some (53), also not going as far on the posssibility of a future life in Job 14 as can reasonably be done. Alden does have a bit more on such a hope in 19:27. All in all, one finds a fairly helpful work, and will probably want this as one of his books.

Andersen, Francis I. *Job* (TOTC). Downers Grove: Inter Varsity Press, 1976.

Andersen has provided one of the best modern and informed expositions of the text of Job, displaying intimate familiarity with the Hebrew and cognate languages and literature (as well as referring to a broad range of English literature). He utilizes a good, almost conversational style and closely analyzes the text. Not all evangelicals will be pleased with Andersen's cyclical theory of composition (which he sees as reaching completion by 750 B. C., although he allows that composition could have occurred any time between Moses and Ezra). This is a valuable aid to exposition. -Dan Phillips. He dates job during Solomon's reign. On problem texts he gives views, as on 19:23-27, where he believes Job refers to a real meeting with God after death, though does not feel there is a full statement of a faith in bodily resurrection here (this point has been much debated). The verse by verse commentary is good most of the time, and Andersen is quite abreast of modern research on the book. -J. E. Rosscup.

Archer, Gleason L., Jr. The Book of Job: God's Answer to the Problem of Undeserved Suffering. Grand Rapids: Baker, 1982.

Occasioned in part by the death of a pastor friend due to lymphoma, this study provides a very helpful blend of solidly-based exposition and relevant personal application. Archer often comments by way of re-phrasing the speeches interpretively, making use of the Hebrew in a rather odd system of transliteration. Archer holds to the early dating (between 1876-1445 B.C. of the book and historical background for the contents, his exposition is sober and helpful for preaching, personal study, or even for counseling. -Dan Phillips.

Ball, C. J. *The Book of Job*. Oxford, 1922.

Here is a liberal scholar's detailed discussion that sometimes tries to rewrite a text (cf. on 19:23-27). But it is one of the fine liberal works on Job.

Beuken, W. A. M., ed. *The Book of Job*. Leuven: Leuven University Press, 1994.

Here 28 specialist papers give selections from what seventy scholars presented at a 1993 colloquium. Teachers, more interested pastors, and advanced students in OT studies will encounter recent ideas on Job, even if they may take some with a grain of salt, or ten grains. Among topics are why a book such as Job exists and what it accomplishes, progression in Job's speeches, empty pious slogans of Job, and papers on Job 19:25-27 (Job's expectation of seeing his redeemer), etc.

Bullock, C. Hassell. *An Introduction to the Poetic Books of the Old Testament*. Chicago: Moody Press, 1979.

A well-organized general evangelical introduction to wisdom in the Old Testament, how the poetic books relate to wisdom, wisdom in the ancient near East and in the apocrypha; theology in the Old Testament wisdom books (God, man, emphases on retributive justice, universalism, and law), and immortality in wisdom and the Psalms; the Book of Job; the Psalms, Proverbs; Ecclesiastes; and the Song of Solomon. The book has a 14-page bibliography, also a subject index, author index, and Scripture index.

Clines, David J. A. *Job 1-20* (Word Biblical Commentary). Dallas, TX: Word Books, 1989. 501 pp.

In many texts this is careful in handling details of text, syntax, views and reasons. Clines' grasp and use of scholarly writings enriches his effort, which seems of a conservative nature in many passages. He sees the story set in patriarchal times, but a writer between the seventh and second centuries B. C. using compositions from centuries before (a view that many will feel problematic). While so often productive on many aspects, Clines is a big disappointment in concluding on a key text, 19:25, that Job's redeemer is not God but Job himself in a personified plea, however that can be, which is not altogether clear.

Davidson, A. B. *The Book of Job*. Cambridge Bible. Cambridge: University Press, 1903.

This is a detailed investigation of the text verse by verse and has much to offer.

Delitzsch, Franz. *The Book of Job*. 2 volumes. Grand Rapids: Eerdmans, 1949.

See earlier comments on Keil and Delitzsch.

Dhorme, E. A. *Commentary on the Book of Job*. Translated by Harold Knight. Nashville: Nelson, 1967.

The work, first published in 1926, is massively detailed in introduction (224 pp.), though often too scanty on exegesis of the Hebrew. No serious extended scholarly study should be done without including such a study. For Dhorme excels in setting forth the book's plan and movements so that the reader is made aware of the pattern, coherence, and development of the drama so as to grasp the unity and what is going on in different parts as relating to the overall sweep. Dhorme's references to Hebrew are for the technically trained.

Durham, James. *Lectures on Job*. Revised/New Ed. Dallas, TX: Naphtali Press, 1995.

This is by a famous 17th century Scottish Presbyterian pastor in Glasgow (d. 1658), whose original work issued in 1759 was entitled *An Exposition of the Whole Book of Job, With Practical Observations*. The new ed. updates spelling, inserts defnitions in brackets, and has a few footnotes. Exposition of each of Job's 42 chapters ends with several principles for life from the passage. The work is one example of a very old preaching series, but does not give nearly the overall help that many works of recent times provide.

Ellison, H. L. *From Tragedy to Triumph: The Message of the Book of Job*. London: Paternoster Press, 1958.

This is not a lengthy study nor a commentary verse by verse (only 127 pp. including R. V. text which is reproduced). But it is an interesting character description of the friends of Job and an effort to portray how they would appear in 19th century church life.

Garland, F. David. *Job* (Bible Study Commentary). Grand Rapids: Zondervan, 1971. 107 pp.

Garland has done a creditable work in putting together help summarizing sections and going into some details of verses. He gives conservatives a fairly quick-moving commentary that touches competently even though briefly (usually) on problems.

Gordis, Robert. *The Book of Job: Commentary, New Translation and Special Studies*. NY: KTAV, 1978.

A 602-pp, work of very fine caliber by a professor of Bible and religion at Jewish Theological Seminary, New York City and a well-known scholar in the wisdom literature. He gives a very detailed exegesis, reflecting wide awareness of ancient and recent studies. He presents the Hebrew text and an English rendering. Often he argues against emendations or subjective re-ordering of the text (but cf. his own re-arranging of 26:5-14 after chapter 25 etc.). He climaxes the work with 42 additional notes on relevant topics and problem texts in the book. This is one of the more helpful works of recent times.

Habel, Norman C. *The Book of Job: A Commentary* (Old Testament Library). Philadelphia: Westminster, 1985. 586 pp.

This is widely regarded as outstanding on many aspects, usually showing high respect for the text and also the unity of the book (i.e. the prologue, epilogue and material between these, in a narrative plot). He has a good grasp of the Hebrew and its poetic and literary details as well as theological motifs. He does think that some speech material in the third cycle has been misplaced (p. 37), and subjectively shuffles segments to suit his own ideas. To him, Job's redeemer in Chapter 19 is a celestial being (cf. 16:19) who will be his advocate before God after death. Habel takes a postexilic date of writing (42). He views the Elihu portion as fitting and even is persuaded that Elihu is the arbiter Job longed for in 31:35. Habel skillfully comments on literary devices such as parallelism, irony, word plays, etc. He was for some years Professor of Old Testament, Concordia Theological Seminary, Saint Louis. He does much to guide readers to the theological message of Job.

Hartley, John E. *Job* (New International Commentary on the Old Testament). Grand Rapids: Eerdmans, 1988. 591 pp.

It is good to see this firmly evangelical work. This is evident in many places. However, Hartley is subjective and without real necessity in shuffling Job 27:13-23 to Chapter 25, etc. Generally, his careful handling of the text, syntax, views and reasoning constitute this one of the best conservative works on Job.

Kent, H. H. *Job, Our Contemporary*. Grand Rapids: Eerdmans, 1957.

A fairly good and sometimes stimulating study, with much to suggest relevance to people today.

Morgan, G. Campbell. *The Analyzed Bible*. Volume V. NY: Revell, 1909.

This is a good synthesis which helps to trace the developing thought of the book of Job. A detailed outline is given.

Rowley, H. H. *Job* (New Century Bible). London: Oliphants, 1970.

This liberal work is helpful primarily for its evidence of Rowley's wide reading and various views on problems. It is not one of the better overall commentaries verse by verse. Cf. also Rowley's chapter on approaches to Job in *From Moses to Qumran* (London, 1963).

Smick, Elmer B. "Job," in *Expositor's Bible Commentary* (Volume 4), ed. Frank Gaebelein and R. P. Polcyn. Grand Rapids: Eerdmans, 1988.

Smick was Professor of Old Testament Language and Literature, Gordon-Conwell Theological Seminary. Steeped in his area's scholarship, he provides a good introduction showing that Job is superior to all other literature in philosophical and theological depth (p. 844). He argues the reasonableness of seeing one man as the author, inspired by God, in the 2,000-1,000 B. C. period, and events of the book in the patriarchal era (847, 853). His bibliography is extensive (871-75) and much reference appears throughout to scholarly literature. After careful exegesis he sees the possibility of Job's personal, bodily resurrection in 19:25-27 (cf. 943). The Elihu speeches of Chapters 32-37 are seen to be in unity with and to serve a valid role with the rest of the book (998). Overall this is a very insightful and competent commentary by a conservative.

Thomas, Derek. *The Storm Breaks. Job Simply Explained* (Welwyn Commentary). Auburn, WA: Evangelical Press, 1995.

A popular evangelical work, this has ideas that might stimulate messages. One must go elsewhere to have discussions that deal with most problems, at least in any studied depth. Thomas deals with some problems, such as whether Satan has power over death (31).

Zuck, Roy B. *Job*. Chicago, IL: Moody Press, 1978.

Zuck, a Biola University graduate, Associate Academic Dean and Associate Professor of

Bible Exposition at Dallas Theological Seminary, has written this 192-pp. paperback for the Everyman's Bible Commentary. Written in thirteen chapters for use in Sunday school, this volume assumes a thoroughly orthodox position with reference to all critical areas. In addition, Zuck reckons a patriarchal time setting (perhaps akin to Terah's time?). One helpful section is Zuck's treatment of chapters 20 and 21 and the repartee between Zophar and Job. Zuck views the grand purpose of the book as dealing with motives behind worship. He sees its solemn lesson in the futility of criticizing God's ways. This volume is recommended for home Bible studies and Sunday school. -Jan Sattem

Zuck, Roy B. "Job," in *Bible Knowledge Commentary*, ed. John F. Walvoord and Roy B. Zuck (Volume I). Wheaton: Victor Books, 1983.

A fine conservative survey with help on many key verses, help of a kind that reflects painstaking and competent study. Zuck also writes very clearly and summarizes well.

Zuck, Roy B. *Sitting with Job: Selected Studies on the Book of Job*. Grand Rapids: Baker, 1992.

Here are thirty-four chapters (sketches) by different scholars on key sections or topics in Job, men such as R. Laird Harris, Francis Andersen, Norman Habel, Don Carson, etc. Zuck himself writes on 19:23-29 and on Chapter 28. The book offers comments with high expertise on subjects that an expositor can find very instructive in the midst of preparing for an individual message or a series.

XIV. PSALMS

The commentary by Moll in the Lange series is one of the best in that 12-volume set. In addition:

Alden, Robert. *Psalms*. 3 volumes. Chicago: Moody, 1974-76.

This has some good comments as a conservative work but artificially assigns the psalms to three categories of Christian living, Songs of Devotion (1-50), Dedication (51-100) and Discipleship (101-150). Comments tend to be extremely brief to serve quick reading laypeople.

Alexander, J. A. *The Psalms*. 2 volumes. Philadelphia: Presbyterian Board of Education, 1850.

This is one of the more thorough older exegetical works on the Hebrew text. It represents a re-working of the famous commentary on Psalms by E. Hengstenberg.

Allen, Ronald B. *And I Will Praise Him. A Guide to Worship in the Psalms*. Grand Rapids: Kregel, 1999.

This work, a pb devotional in a popular vein by a Dallas Theological Seminary OT professor, has two sections. The first addresses such topics as what a psalm is, poetry, praise, and howthe psalms came to us. The second section surveys praise (Pss. 13, 19, 138, 142, 65, 146). One of two other chapters tells of Allen and his family coming to know God better through the Psalms and via the trial of their daughter's lymphoblastic leukemia. The testimony is provocative.

Anderson, A. A. *The Book of Psalms* (New Century Bible). 2 volumes. London: Oliphants, 1972.

An exegetical treatment which often is helpful, by a liberal. It is one of the better recent liberal works from the standpoint of detailed commentary.

Anderson, B. W. *Out of the Depths*. Philadelphia: Westminster, 1974.

He treats sample psalms from each of the types scholars generally recognize since works by H. Gunkel (as *The Psalms*, Philadelphia: Fortress Press, 1967) and Sigmund Mowinckel (*The Psalms in Israel's Worship*, New York: Abingdon, 1962). He looks at doctrinal aspects and makes applications, some of which are quite worthwhile.

Armerding, Carl. *Psalms in a Minor Key*. Chicago: Moody Press, 1973.

Here is a series of brief, rich, simple, practical and stimulating chapters by a great Bible teacher (he taught at Wheaton College) on selected psalms. Many of the psalms are not usually treated in books on selected psalms, such as Psalms 3, 4, 5, 6, 12, 13, etc. But some better-known psalms are also included, e. g. 51, 73, 90. Armerding touches on many of the spiritual highlights in a lucid manner that will help a growing Christian and be thought-provoking to a pastor-teacher or other speaker.

Barth, C. *Introduction to the Psalms*. London: Blackwell, 1966.

This little book by a liberal author provides a general survey of approaches to the Psalms by critical scholarship up to the mid-1960's.

Bonhoeffer, Dietrich. *Psalms: The Prayer Book of the Bible*. Translated by James Burtness. Minneapolis: Augsburg Publishing House, 1970.

Jesus' disciples asked Him, "Teach us to pray," and Psalms is the book that shows how to pray, how Jesus desires men to pray. His "Lord's prayer" (actually the disciples' prayer) summarizes all the prayers of the Bible. Bonhoeffer presents prayer as the heart's conversation with God in this small 86-page book. He discusses prayer in relation to such things as the Law, suffering, guilt, enemies, and daily victory.

Bridges, Charles. Exposition of Psalm CXIX: As Illustrative of the Character and Exercises of Christian Experience. London: Seeley, Jackson, and Halliday, 1859.

This is a classic of detail on the psalm, with much rich, solid and provocative discussion that deeply feeds the serious heart. It first appeared in 1827 and continues to be published. Bridges (1794-1869) has a way of relating the truth to other parts of Scripture and to the spiritual life that reflects a profound grasp of things. He is wordy, leaving few stones unturned, but there are many veins of gold beneath the stones. The famous interpretation of details in the longest psalm is mingled with suggestions for self-examination, prayer and other stimulating devotional material. An 8-pp. index of subjects at the end is helpful at times in locating a discussion.

Bridges, Charles. *Psalm 119, An Exposition* (Geneva series), Carlisle, Pa: Banner of Truth Trust, 1987rp of work first issued in 1827. 490 pp.

Bullock, C. Hassell. *Encountering the Book of Psalms. A Literary and Theological Introduction.* **Grand Rapids: Baker, 2001.**

One finds a 266-pp. mini-encyclopedia by an evangelical on many topics about the Psalms, such as names, place in the canon, David's role, titles, musical instruments, parallelism, Messianism, divisions, and others. Sections also discuss various facets about praise, lament, trust, kingship, wisdom, Torah, imprecations, etc. The Select Bibliography on 33 topics lists, for example, four writings that offer help on imprecations. Teachers, pastors, students and Christians in general will find well-organized orientational assists in this "gold mine."

Calvin, John. *Sermons on Psalm 119.* **Audubon, NJ: Old Paths Publications, 1996, from 1580 English ed.**

This study, helpful at times but not nearly as much as Zemek's work, includes 454 pp. from Calvin's sermons of 1553 (Jan. 8—July 2). James Boice contributes an interesting survey in the "Foreword" about Calvin's preaching practice (vii—xiii). The work joins other writings on 119 by Spurgeon (*Treasury of David*), Charles Bridges, Thomas Manton (3 vols.), and Zemek. Calvin's contribution, among other uses, can have value as a series of readings while reflecting successively on helpful lessons in the 22 sections of the psalm. This writer's frank estimation is that readers are more likely to find more detail and more consistent help, often even more to the point, in Bridges, Kidner, Leupold, Phillips, Plumer, Scroggie, Spurgeon, Zemek, and comments in *The Bible Knowledge Commentary*, for examples.

Cohen, A. *The Psalms.* **London: Soncino, 1945.**

A Jewish scholar gives brief comments, which often are quite good in capturing the essence.

Craigie, Peter, Marvin E. Tate and Leslie Allen. *Psalms* **(Word Biblical Commentary). 3 volumes. Waco, TX. Word Books, 1983ff.**

Craigie did 1-50, Tate 51-100 and Allen 101-150. In his part, Craigie also includes an introduction covering many aspects of discussion such as the literary and poetic form of individual psalms and the New Testament use of the psalms and pertinence to life today. He does not consider any psalm originally messianic, and of course many will disagree with this. Allen is good on the form, structure, setting, and problems of the psalms, even excellent on many matters, but believes in a Deuteronomistic tradition and is arbitrary for many users in his ideas, at times, of literary sources. On individual verses, the work is frequently a rich contribution on word meaning, text, basic exegesis, customs, etc. and one can learn or review much.

Crenshaw, James L. *The Psalms, An Introduction.* **Grand Rapids: Eerdmans, 2001.**

This OT scholar of Duke University Divinity School looks at collections within the Psalter, related psalms, prayer, classification of psalms, wisdom, history, the artistic and theological design of the psalms, and four psalms (73, 115, 71, 24) at some length. He even discusses psalms in the Apocrypha, the so-called Psalms of David (Pss. 151-155), Psalms of Solomon, Qumran thanksgiving hymns, and NT hymns. His section on psalms wishing curses (pp. 65-68) is not easy to follow and seems to provide little real help (but cf. on this articles in Bullock's classified list), and the book is rather general on other topics as it is here. For introductory matters one would be farther ahead by going to the introductions in many of the commentaries, or to Bullock.

Crim, Keith R. *The Royal Psalms*. Richmond: John Knox, 1962.

This 123-pp. study is a sometimes helpful exposition of psalms that pursue the theme of kingship. He treats 2, 18, 20, 21, 45, 72, 89, 101, 110, and 144. The work is of special interest when the student is seeking to grasp where detail relates to a past, historical king of the days in which the psalms were written, or refers on predictively to Jesus Christ. At the beginning, Crim devotes 54 pp. to "kingship in Ancient Israel", and at the end 3 pp. to "Messianic Psalms." Crim has been influenced considerably by writers before him of liberal persuasions, such as Hermann Gunkel ("Psalmen", in *Die Religion in Geschichte und Gegenwart*, Vol. 4, 1st edition 1913, 2nd edition 1927); Gunkel and J. Begrich, *Einleitun in die Psalmen* 1933, pp. 140-71, quite comprehensive in Old Testament aspects; A. R. Johnson, *Sacral Kingship in Ancient Israel* (Cardiff: University of Wales Press, 1955), H. J. Kraus, *Die Konigsherrschaft Gottes im Alten Testament*, Tubingen, J. C. Mohr, 1951; A. Bentzen, *King and Messiah*; Helmer Ringgren, *The Messiah in the Old Testament*; Sigmund Mowinckel, *He That Cometh*.

Dahood, Mitchell. *Psalms I, II, III* (Anchor Bible). Garden City, NY: Doubleday, 1966-71.

A major contribution of Dahood is his philological material based on recent discoveries in Ugaritic. Sometimes it is helpful in throwing light on word meanings according to ancient usage. Dahood believes, for example, that many texts in the Psalms show expectation of life after death, and uses philological arguments. A problem with his approach is that he carries the point to an extreme, and finds life after death in many texts where it is not clearly there, as even evangelical Old Testament scholars have said (cf., for example, the evaluation of Bruce K. Waltke, review of Dahood's Psalms I, in *Bib. Sac.*123 (1966), 176; for more detail Elmer Smick, "The Bearing of New Philological Data on the Subjects of Resurrection and Immortality in the Old Testament," *Westminster Theological Journal*, 31 (1968-69), 12-21). However, finding life after death in some of the Psalms can be defended and has been firmly believed by many in such texts as 16:9, 10; 49:15; 73:24f, etc.

Davidson, Robert. The Vitality of Worship. A Commentary on the Book of Psalms. Grand Rapids: Eerdmans, 1998.

Here is work by a professor emeritus of OT at the University of Glasgow. Davidson explains problem verses and moves from interpretation to devotional import. He deals with all 150 psalms by the five books (sections), with an introduction into each. Some comments look at a psalm with overall orientating synthesis, then details on verses follow. Davidson wrestles with meaning and surveys Scripture, as in discussing Ps. 1, the problem of blessing on the godly and the fact that the ungodly often prosper (cf. also Ps. 73). Sometimes even good comments do not bring out the Messianic reference, as on Ps. 2:6-8, and some comments hint at but do not develop this enough to shed much light, as on 16:9-10 in relation to Acts 2 and 13. Davidson is not sure that David's experience appears in Ps. 51. He offers a frequently helpful running commentary that gets to some of the main matters, but his work, while fairly good, is far down the line compared to many others in this list.

Davis, John J. *The Perfect Shepherd* **(Psalms 23). Grand Rapids: Baker, 1979.**

Superb treatment and good example of caring, responsible evangelical scholarship. Davis analyzes the Hebrew text, and draws on his own experiences with shepherds in the area of Palestine, and applies the text practically to the modern reader. - Dan Phillips. Davis is well-known for several works, for example his *Paradise to Prison, Moses and the Gods of Egypt*, and *Biblical Numerology*, all very helpful. He teaches in the Old Testament at Grace College, Winona Lake, IN. On Psalm 23, cf. under Keller.

Dickson, David. *Psalms.* **2 volumes in 1. Carlisle, PA: Banner of Truth Trust, n.d.**

Though this is a very old work, reprinted, it is heavily laden with richness that edifies in explaining the text and making truth clear. It is well worth the time, even if dated in parts.

Goldingay, John. *Songs From A Strange Land.* **Psalms 42-51 (The Bible Speaks Today). Downers Grove: IVP, 1978.**

The author was a lecturer in Old Testament at St. John's College, Nottingham. He offers a fresh rendering of each psalm, interprets it as showing man's response to God as helper, comforter, king and redeemer, and points out the relevance to spiritual life now. His outline is clearly stated in headings and covers many of the vital aspects of life in a captivating exposition. The main headings are: "God has forgotten me" (42, 43); "God helps us" (44); "If God is King" (45, 47); "If God is with us" (46, 48, 50); "But God will Ransom" (49); "Will God Forgive?" (51). The treatment on 51 is worth the price of the book: repentance faces up to sins, recognizes sin, appeals to God's love, pleads for forgiveness, longs for spiritual renewal, looks forward to testimony, and offers the sacrifices for which God looks.

Hay, D. M. *Glory at the Right Hand. Psalm 110 in Early Christianity.* **Society of Biblical Literature Monograph Series, No. 18. Nashville/New York: Abingdon Press, 1973.**

This grew out of a Yale doctoral dissertation (1965). It provides a survey of how Psalm 110 was interpreted by ancient Jews and early Christians up to the 4th century, also a discussion of Christian references to the psalm. For in-depth study of 110, this is quite enlightening and helpful.

Hubbard, David A. *Psalms for All Seasons.* **Grand Rapids: Eerdmans, 1971.**

Brief homiletically arranged studies of key psalms with good relevance to life today (Psalms 1, 2, 7, 8, 9, 14, 16, 23, 32, 40, 45, 49, 51).

Keller, Philip. *A Shepherd Looks at Psalm 23.* **Grand Rapids: Zondervan, 1970.**

Many are the books on Psalm 23. Cf., among many, John J. Davis, F. B. Meyer, and Haddon Robinson. Yet Keller has much to offer on insights into phrases in the shepherd imagery, as well as refreshing illustrations that can be provocative of interesting preaching or teaching.

Kidner, Derek. *Psalms 1-72 and Psalms 73-150* **(2 volumes) (Tyndale Old Testament Commentary). Grand Rapids: Eerdmans, 1973-75.**

A good study by a leading evangelical, providing a reasonably detailed commentary, though too brief in many cases as well. This is one of the better works in recent times and on many points shows an in-depth grasp of things (cf. also his fine work on Proverbs).

Leupold, H. C. *Exposition of the Psalms.* **Minneapolis: Augsburg, 1959. 1,010 pp.**

This Lutheran, amillennial commentary refers to the original text, gives attention to the background and has good introductions to the psalms. It is one of the better works on Psalms in regard to providing competent, pertinent material of a serious nature to the pastor, teacher, or layman.

Lloyd-Jones, D. Martyn. *Faith on Trial. Studies in Psalm 73.* **Grand Rapids: Eerdmans, 1965. 125 pp.**

The famous successor of G. Campbell Morgan in London's Westminster Chapel, also famous for many outstanding books, deals in deeply perceptive and practical ways with profound problems God treats here. Why do the ungodly prosper? Why does He allow suffering? He seeks to show that true joy is realized only in a person's conscious sense of God's presence. This is one of the finest books I have ever read on a psalm in the area of deep insight into life and how God's Word helpfully guides us in right attitudes of trust. Some of Lloyd-Jones' other great books are *Studies in the Sermon on the Mount*, *Spiritual Depression*, and commentaries on Romans and Ephesians.

Lockyer, Herbert, Sr. *Psalms, A Devotional Commentary.* **Grand Rapids: Kregel, 1993.**

Done in 1974, this 792-pp. work by the writer of the series on "All" (the miracles, parables, kings, promises, etc.) gives his lifelong notes. These turn out to be mostly illustrative entries, and actual comment to help on what psalms mean is very sparse. Speakers dipping in can find some richness to put into messages. This frankly appears to be the only real value, if one chooses to undergo the expense to borrow illustrations here and there, but must go elsewhere for help on actual exposition of God's Word itself.

Longman, Tremper III. *How to Read the Psalms.* **Downers Grove: IVP, 1988. 166 pp.**

An evangelical work showing the main types of psalms, aim of the psalm titles, Davidic authorship, lines of covenant thought, messianic themes, relevance of psalms in the ministry of Jesus, charm of the psalms for us, parallelism, etc. Longman looks in detail at Psalms 30, 69, and 98 as examples. This is a good recent general introduction on certain main issues about the psalms, and reads well.

Manton, Thomas. *Psalm 119.* **3 volumes. Edinburgh: Banner of Truth Trust, 1990. Originally in 1680. 1,685 pp.**

This reprint gives 190 sermons based on a verse by verse study. Though the old classic has much insight it does not get down to the text enough, It is highly devotional, sometimes with inductive control but frequently without any. Another devotional work is the famous classic on Psalm 119 by Charles Bridges, which is even better known to many.

Mays, James L. *Psalms* (Interpretation). Louisville: John Knox Press, 1994.

Mays, using the New RS, emphasizes literary and theological points and puts stock in the Psalms statements of trust. The series limitation to one vol. causes real brevity on some psalms, and not furnishing help on some vital points in verses. At other times one has to wade through much to get to the essence and put a picture together, as in Ps. 2, due to the way the commentary evelops. But the persevering can locate comments on verses here and there and draw a meaningful progression. The relation of such important verses as 16:9-10 to NT claims is very generalized as a sort of tack-on. Psalm 51 is seen as making sense only if composed during or after the exile (199). Psalm 110 is viewed generally, with verses not explained well in their flow to fit some clear perspective.

McGrath, Alister and J. I. Packer, eds. *Psalms by Charles Spurgeon*. 2 vols. Wheaton: Crossway Books, 1993.

One finds an edited condensation of Spurgeon's multi-vol. *Treasury of David*, the latter done over 21 years. These 740 pp. relate the Psalms verse by verse, cutting out Spurgeon's copious citations of what others said but retaining much of the essential richness.

Meyer, F. B. *The Shepherd Psalm*. Grand Rapids: Kregel, 1991. 139 pp.

A master of devotional writing gives many perceptive thoughts on the believer and the Shepherd.

Mowinckel, Sigmund. *The Psalms in Israel's Worship*. 2 volumes. Oxford: Blackwell, 1962.

Taking the "type-critical" approach in classifying the Psalms, Mowinckel follows in the train of Hermann Gunkel of Germany. There is much here for the more detailed and discerning conservative student because the two volumes offer an encyclopedia of information about the Psalms and the history of their interpretation at many points. However,, the higher critical viewpoint is assumed and many of his conclusions are unacceptable. This is not a commentary, but a discussion of various facets in the Psalms.

Olsen, Erling C. *Meditations in the Book of Psalms*. Neptune, NJ: Loizeaux Bros., 1941.

This work, here in its second printing (1975), devotes about 4-6 pp. to each psalm. There is much practical wealth and illustration in the author's comments (formerly broadcasted), which are richly suggestive for emphases in messages. For example, in Psalm 1, we are not to spend all our time just meditating on the Word, but become busily involved as Jesus was in the lives of others, p. 3. This, however, is not a book that helps in grappling with problem verses; it simply helps a preacher or teacher come down to earth.

Perowne, J. J. Stewart. *The Book of Psalms.* **2 volumes in 1. Grand Rapids: Zondervan, 1976. Rp of 1878 ed. Zondervan issued 1966 ed. also, 2 volumes; and cf.** *Commentary on the Psalms.* **2 volumes in 1. Grand Rapids: Kregel, 1989rp.**

Distinguished among 19th century works on Psalms, this model 1864 work by a competent Anglican Hebrew scholar has much that is detailed and discerning along evangelical lines. Perowne has a fine introduction though it lacks findings of the past century. He shows, among other things, that the psalmist often went far beyond himself in statements and projected his thought prophetically to Christ. In most cases the verse by verse commentary solidly explains the text. Perowne often shows the unity between a Psalms statement and New Testament truth.

Phillips, John. *Exploring the Psalms.* **5 vols. Neptune, NJ: Loizeaux, 1985— 1988. There is a 2-vol. ed. by the same title and publisher, 1988, with the same content.**

One of America's fine Bible expositors, from Moody Bible Institute's extension department, gives more of his lucid work (he has works on several books of the Bible). His outline for each psalm is intently alliterated, though it seems apt in many cases at least. The exposition is broad and sweeping, with many statements that seize the reader's mind and heart. Due to the clarity and flow, this would be suggestive for preachers and also refreshing for any Christian to use in daily worship times, reading his Bible and then the comments on given verses.

Robinson, Haddon. *Psalm Twenty-Three.* **Chicago: Moody, 1968.**

A scholar of Gordon-Conwell Theological Seminary has turned excellent expository preaching on Psalm 23 into this series of devotional chapters. The material reflects keen insight into shepherd customs behind the phrases and then crystal clear relating of the truth to the spiritual realm of believers today. Cf. his more recent publication, *Trusting the Shepherd: Insights from Psalm 23.* Discovery House, 2002.

Ross, Allen P. "Psalms," in *Bible Knowledge Commentary,* **ed. John F. Walvoord and Roy B. Zuck. Volume I. Wheaton: Victor Books, 1983.**

Outstanding grasp of things, explanation from many sides, conservative clarity and knowledge of the literature brought together. The reader gains much insight here, as in Ross's work on Proverbs in the *Expositor's Bible Commentary* or his survey on Genesis, *Creation and Blessing.* He helps users follow the structure, see word meanings, customs, parallelism, and other parts of the study, shedding a lot of light.

Scroggie, W. Graham. *The Psalms.* **Westwood, NJ: Revell, 1965.**

This is an excellent *synthesis* on each of the 150 psalms, with homiletical outlines, choice quotes and concise glimpses of the thought. A sentence title is given to each psalm.

Spurgeon, Charles H. *The Treasury of David.* **3 volumes. Grand Rapids: Zondervan, 1975. Rp of 7 volume 1889 work; there is also a 6-volume ed. from London: Marshall, Morgan & Scott, 1957.**

In this very detailed exposition, the London pulpit master dealt with each verse, giving a wealth of illustration, practical comment, and preaching hints. Spurgeon shows that he read widely in the best literature of his day, gleaning out rich quotes. On any given verse one can expect to find exposition or quotes looking at it from various angles. The devotional flavor is excellent. Here is a suggestive source for preacher or teacher and much wealth for general readers, though readers must go elsewhere for word studies and exegesis to supplement their own personal exegetical study. There is also a condensation of the Treasury which cuts out about two-thirds of it, leaving much of the richness (David Otis Fuller, *Psalms by Spurgeon.* Grand Rapids: Kregel, 1976. 703 pp.). The condensation is a help to the busy who want to get at the hub of things quickly. Also cf. McGrath (this section).

Stott, John R. W. *Selected Psalms and Canticles.* **London: Hodder & Stoughton, 1971. Chicago: Moody, 1988.**

Here is a brief but excellent exposition of several key psalms by one who has come to be known for his stimulating articulations of favorite Bible passages. The Moody edition of 127 pages has many color pictures to illustrate psalms. Stott deals lucidly with Psalms 1, 8, 15, 16, 19, 22-24, 27, 29, 32, 34, 40, 42-43, 46, 51, 67, 73, 84, 90-91, 95, 98, 100, 103, 104, 121-123, 125, 127, 130-31, 133, 139, 145 and 150.

van Gemeren, W. A. "Psalms," in *Expositor's Bible Commentary,* **Volume 5, ed. Frank Gaebelein and R. P. Polcyn. Grand Rapids: Zondervan, 1991.**

The writer provides a good introduction on key aspects of the study, also a good bibliography (pp. 39-47). His own list of titles gives the subjects of each of the 150 psalms (48-51), and he offers a detailed commentary in 880 pages. He gives an introduction for each psalm, discussing main aspects to orientate readers. He deals with problems in verse by verse study and in special appendices. In some psalms he copiously lists sources before moving on. The Hebrew word study and grammatical remarks are quite helpful. This is an outstanding commentary, showing some of the best of evangelical expertise.

Weiser, Artur. *The Psalms, A Commentary,* **Translated by H. Hartwell. London, 1962.**

A lucid, liberal commentary of some detail which sometimes reaches rather evangelical conclusions (cf. on 16:9-11; 49:15; 73:24 etc.). Weiser has a lot of stimulating insight.

Wilson, Gerald. *Psalms 1-72 (NIV Application Commentary).* **Gd. Rapids: Zondervan, 2002.**

Wilson's work is one of the finest scholarly, yet practical, detailed studies. It combines careful use of Hebrew for accuracy, fairly full explanations of verses, rich devotional comments on how to apply the points, and an easy, flowing style of writing. He is conservative, and usually perceptive in opening up passages.

Zemek, George J. *The Word of God in the Child of God: Exegetical, Theological, and Homiletical Reflections from the 119th Psalm.* **Believers Fellowship, 2000.**

A former Professor of OT at The Master's Seminary produced this as a study of many years penetrating into Ps. 119. Zemek's text and copious footnotes reflect just what his students remember of him, his very careful expertise and clarity, opening up this rich psalm. In addition to detailed commentary on each of the 176 verses showing the Hebrew meaning, he discusses at length matters such as attitudes toward the psalm, authorship and date, the literary features, an overview from analysis and from theology (for example descriptions of God's Word), and other subjects. The verse by verse analysis provides a very contributive exegetical elucidation on 119 (pp. 63-385), then Zemek lays out pp. 388-431 as a diagrammatical analysis for each of the 22 stanzas.

XV. PROVERBS

Aitken, Kenneth T. *Proverbs* **(Daily Bible Study). Philadelphia: Westminster, 1986. 264 pp.**

Though Aitken late-dates the present form of Proverbs to fifth/fourth century B. C., he furnishes many insights of value on possible renderings of phrases. He looks at Proverbs 1-9 in sequence, then in 10-31 switches to a topical method, dealing with the scoffer, drunkard, liar and other characters. He also devotes parts to honoring parents, old age, false witnesses, sadness vs. gladness, prayer, etc. All in all it is a very profitable work, and time will be spent well here.

Alden, Robert L. Proverbs. *A Commentary on an Ancient Book of Timeless Advice.* **Grand Rapids: Baker, 1983.**

Alden was Professor of Old Testament at Denver Conservative Baptist Seminary, and also author of a 3-volume commentary on the Psalms and a good work on Job. The present work is based on specialized study into canonical wisdom literature. The commentary deals in capsule style with each verse based on analysis of the Hebrew, but mentions the Hebrew words only occasionally. Alden seeks to relate the message to 20th century life.

Arnot, Wm. *Studies in Proverbs.* **Grand Rapids: Kregel, 1978, rp of 1878 work. 583 pp.**

These homilies were originally issued in 1857 as *Illustrations of the Book of Proverbs,* later as *Laws from Heaven for Life on Earth* (1878). There is much rich material, but Arnot skips Proverbs 7 and 21, and various verses in the other chapters. The work is famous for the grasp of spiritual truths and the easy-flowing style.

Bridges, Charles. *An Exposition of the Book of Proverbs.* **Grand Rapids: Zondervan, 1959. Reprint.**

Originally issued in 1850, this conservative work is still valuable. Spurgeon called it the best book on Proverbs in his day. About one page, sometimes more, is devoted to each proverb. There is some good exposition, and the emphasis of the work is mainly practical. Cf. Santa for one-volume edition. Bridges also did the famous work on Psalm 119.

Buzzell, Sid S. "Proverbs," in *Bible Knowledge Commentary*, ed. John F. Walvoord and Roy B. Zuck. Volume I. Wheaton: Victor Books, 1983.

A former teacher at the Dallas Theological Seminary has done this concise, clear, adept work. He shows a fine grasp of Hebrew exegesis and word meaning, use of context where it is pertinent, parallelism, customs, etc. The pastor, other church worker or layperson who uses this for preparation to speak or to live in God's values will benefit much.

Cohen, A. *Proverbs* (Soncino Series). London: Soncino, 1946.

Comments are very much the same as on the Psalms. It is a fairly good terse commentary, just not nearly one of the best.

Clifford, Richard J. *Proverbs, A Commentary* (OT Library). Louisville: Westminster John Knox Press, 1999.

In 286 pp., the writer supplements the 1970 work in the OT Library by William McKane, which was more than twice the length. This work's clarity is easier to follow. Clifford, Professor of OT at Weston Jesuit School of Theology, provides translation, notes on technical details, and concise commentary, at times needing more warrant such as from exegesis. He does advance some evidence to enhance certain views that differ from popular notions, such as seeing 22:6 as not about nurturing a child aright and the child proving steadfast as an adult, but the error of indulging a child's self-will, and the child's becoming set fast in that self-will. If so, v. 15 can offer some buttress, though several verses removed. Teachers will find the work at times stimulating.

Delitzsch, Franz. *The Proverbs of Solomon* (2 volumes). Grand Rapids: Eerdmans, 1950. Reprint.

From the standpoint of Hebrew exegesis and careful detailed scholarship this is very good.

Draper, James T., Jr. *Proverbs: The Secret of Beautiful Living*. Wheaton: Tyndale House, 1971.

A clear, concise, refreshing book at many points, offering some good help especially to laypersons and stimulation to expositors.

Fox, Michael V. *Proverbs 1-9* (Anchor Bible). NY: Doubleday, 2000.

Fox did this first of two expected vols. with exegesis requiring no knowledge of Hebrew or reference to more technical works (xiii). Despite this claim, sometimes the discussion is at a level only meaningful to scholars. Footnotes address more specialized matters such as word meaning, theories and views. A check shows that regularly many Heb. words, though transliterated, are not accompanied by their English meanings. Fox feels that "Historically, it is improbable that many—if any—of the proverbs were written by Solomon" (56; cf. problems he adduces against Solomon). One finds much learning and insight on how a critical skeptic about the reliability of many matters views them. Among many subjects are "The Redaction History of Proverbs 2" (127-28). This reviewer's appraisal is that the work will be mostly usable to Hebrew specialists, but in a limited way for readers patient to sift rich meaning in literal translation in verse by verse explanations.

Frydrych, Tomas. *Living Under the Sun. Examination of Proverbs and Qoheleth.* **Leiden. E. J. Brill, 2002.**

Teachers as in seminary and college will find, not a commentary but a supplementary help on what wisdom is, the proverbial worldview as in contrasts between the righteous prospering and the wicked failing, and allowance in Proverbs for things to work out differently from this paradigm. The godly may be poor, the ungodly prosper, and other matters. The author reasons that the perspective in both books, when fairly valued, simplifies things for a specific purpose, and the wisdom works validly under limited conditions (51-52).

Garrett, Duane A. *Proverbs, Ecclesiastes, Song of Songs* **(New American Commentary). Nashville: Broadman & Holman, 2001.**

A Professor of OT at Gordon-Conwell Theological Seminary did this evangelical survey. It gives 252 pp. to Prov., 253-345 to Eccles., and 347-432 to the Song. Garrett opts for Solomonic authorship of much in Prov., of Eccles., and of the Song. He sees the Song as fitting the last of 7 views he surveys, that of a love song, not on historical events, the "Solomon" being a poetic symbol for the splendor of the bridegroom (365). This will not commend itself to all as being necessary. He sees Eccles. as teaching readers to realize they are mortals who must put away illusions of self-importance, face death and life firmly, accept with humility their human limitations, rely on God, enjoy life as His gift, and revere Him (278). He explains some proverbs, skips some in generalizing summaries of several. But he brings well-informed perceptions to supply the main ideas, often syntheses, but often as well details on salient points in verses. Overall the work gives frequent and valuable helps, and is usable for scholars, pastoral workers, church teachers, students, and Christians in devotional times.

Harris, R. Laird. "Proverbs," in *Wycliffe Bible Commentary*, **ed. C. Pfeiffer and E. F. Harrison. Chicago: Moody, 1962.**

A competent, well-studied and often contributing treatment by a top Old Testament conservative scholar. One of the best brief commentaries, offering considerable insight.

Ironside, H. A. *Proverbs.* **NY: Loizeaux, 1952.**

Selected proverbs are expounded practically with the author's usual warmth, illustration, and insight into spiritual living.

Jensen, Irving. *Proverbs.* **Chicago: Moody Press, 1982.**

In the Everyman's Bible Commentary series, this is a 116-page simple layman's help geared to provoke application to life. Several charts and a detailed outline printed at the outset and followed in the sweeping survey help in this. Of course many verses are passed over, but the survey draws many things together in perspective and can be a catalyst used along with more detailed works in preparation to preach or teach or just to enjoy a brief sketch that can refresh.

Jones, Cody L. *The Complete Guide to the Book of Proverbs.* **Union Lake, MI: Quintan Publishing, 2000.**

Jones uses 566 large pp. to compile brief (a paragraph or page) synopses of what selected proverbs convey on dozens of topics. Some themes are: wisdom, kindness, violence, watching the heart, smooth talk, wrongs to shun, drinking from one's own well, etc. Often, entries reflect on customs (as substances for eye make-up, 6:25b, p. 59). One section gives six popular translations in six parallel cols. (328-545), another prints NT references to Proverbs. An index helps users find topics. As is clear, the work is not a complete guide but a partial one.

Jones, Edgar. *Proverbs and Ecclesiastes* **(Torch Bible Commentary). London: SCM Press Ltd., 1961.**

The Professor of Hebrew and Old Testament at the Northern Congregational College, Manchester, England did this. He feels that some parts of Proverbs linked with Solomon's name may be due to Solomon, but the majority of the material comes from later times (8th to 3rd centuries). In his theorizing Solomon did not write Ecclesiastes; rather more than one teacher in the wisdom school wrote parts of the book, taking the pseudonym of Solomon ca. 250 B. C. Verse by verse this is usually a fair, though quite concise commentary touching on some of the most crucial aspects and based on use of modern critical scholarship on the liberal side. The brevity results in passing over many verses with generalized comments too sparse to be of serious help (cf. Prov. 3:5, 6; 22:6). His lists of sources do not reflect use of evangelical works available when he wrote.

Kidner, Derek. *Proverbs.* **Downers Grove, IL: InterVarsity, 1972.**

Many reviews have been enthusiastic about this evangelical work. It offers a wealth of brief comments on the Proverbs and an especially helpful section on various key subjects and what the proverbs as a whole say about these themes. It is one of the most stimulating treatments of Proverbs from the standpoint of offering to-the-point relationships to our experience today.

Kidner, Derek. *The Wisdom of Proverbs, Job and Ecclesiastes.* **Downers Grove: IVP, 1985. 175 pp.**

An introduction to wisdom writings, touching on themes, and treating readers to recent thought on wisdom literature. He looks at the biblical material alongside apocryphal wisdom sources and parallels in ancient Near Eastern works. He often helps on proverbs that seem to clash, and has insights on how to view the ones that generalize and do not work in some cases. Chapters of this evangelical effort deal with Old Testament wisdom literature, Proverbs, Job, Ecclesiastes, recent thought and evaluation of higher critical studies, and the correlation of Proverbs, Job and Ecclesiastes in certain ways. Three appendices treat each Old Testament wisdom writing in relation to Near Eastern works. Kidner also shows comparisons and differences between Ecclesiasticus, Wisdom of Solomon and the Old Testament books. Cf. Bullock under Job for another outstanding study of the Old Testament poetic literature.

Lawson, George. *Exposition of Proverbs.* **Grand Rapids: Kregel, 1980 rp of 1829 ed.**

Lawson was a Scottish clergyman (1749-1820) who learned exegesis at the University of Edinburgh and later became Professor of Theology there for 33 years as the successor of John Brown. His 890 pages here are not of a critical nature but seek only to explain the verses with simple, practical, judicious comments flavored with pertinent quotes, illustrations or thoughts that suggest illustrations. His definition of the fear of the Lord in 1:7

is choice, and he gives good food for counsel in 3:5, 6; 4:18; 6:25, 26; 7:6-27; 8:14-32 applied to Christ; 22:6; 26:4, 5; 31:10 ff., and many others. This has to rate as one of the most helpful older works in reference to the main task of explaining the English sense of verses, often quite well.

McKane, William. *Proverbs. A New Approach*. Philadelphia: Westminster, 1970.

This liberal work provides a wealth of material on philological connections with Proverbs and can make the serious reader really think about the meaning of phrases. McKane is highly regarded, and his work well-respected as one of the better commentaries by a critical scholar for technical use.

Mouser, William E., Jr. *Walking in Wisdom*. Downers Grove: IVP, 1983.

A fairly lucid book that can prime the thought and set it running in productive paths as one prepares a message, or as any Christian seeks help from wise counsel.

Murphy, Roland E. and Elizabeth Huwiler. *Proverbs, Ecclesiastes, Song of Songs* (New International Biblical Commentary). Peabody, MA: Hendrickson, 1999.

This exegetical work is brief, giving some technical details, Murphy on Proverbs and Huwiler on the others with both using Hebrew and the NIV. Murphy's notable expertise on wisdom literature lends to awareness of issues needing comment, and his assists are often good, though some are misled or short-sighted, for example his deciding that no human has all the virtues of the woman in 31:10-31 (154). Huwiler sees Ecclesiastes as postexilic, not by Solomon (233). These furnish frequent insight, but are not the best on the books. Cf. also Murphy's *Proverbs* (WBC) (Nashville: Thomas-Nelson, 1998). In this, after an introduction discounting Solomon as writing any proverbs here, Murphy gives his translation and general comments on form/structure/setting, then verse by verse comments, some explaining the sense (16:3; 22:6), others not covering enough details (cf. 3:5-6). Some introductions to sections give debatable views, an example being in 31:10-31 (245-46). Murphy here also is hesitant to imagine a woman having all the virtues in a lifetime as this super woman (249), so he imagines the possibility that the woman is used simply to be symbolic of wisdom to furnish a climax to the book on wisdom. Cf. Whybray in this section.

Phillips, John. *Exploring Proverbs*. 2 vols. Neptune, NJ: Loizeaux, 1994, 1996.

A writer of popular exposition is profitable here to many due to sermonic points, outlines, and illustrations in a book of 1,230 pp. Preachers can find it a catalyst, so can church class teachers and lay readers looking for food given in an easy flow. Phillips has much about wise choices, trust (cf. 3:5-6), purity as in 4:23, dealing with temptation (7:5-21), and such themes. This is at least one of the best recent detailed devotional products on Proverbs. Verses are usually taken in their traditional sense, as 22:6 is on training a child, and 31:10-31 is in assuming godly women who live this way.

Ross, Allen P. "Proverbs," in *Expositor's Bible Commentary* (Volume 5). Ed. Frank Gaebelein and R. P. Polcyn. Grand Rapids: Zondervan, 1991.

This is an outstanding conservative effort (pp. 881-1134). Ross, who has written also well in Genesis and Psalms, has a good introduction concluding with a three-page list of key literature. He includes a very helpful index of topics (897-903) before the commentary to facilitate finding exact subjects discussed. He draws richly from wide reading in noted sources to pour much help into many of the verse comments, and is helpful on main views and aspects that are pertinent (cf. on the wife in 31:10-31).

Santa, George F. *A Modern Study of Proverbs*. Milford, MI: Mott Media, 1978. 752 pp.

Actually this is a revision of the famous commentary by Charles Bridges (1794-1869). It replaces the archaic English in a direct, clear vocabulary of today. Still, Santa clings fast to Bridges' meaning.

Whybray, R. N. *The Book of Proverbs*. *A Survey of Modern Study*. Leiden: E. J. Brill, 1995.

Whybray reviews for teachers and more advanced students how scholarly study has viewed various matters. Examples are: critical discussion in earlier years, proverbs and Israelite folk wisdom, theories of literary development, kinds of proverbs, the figure of wisdom in Prov. 1-9, units such as 31:1-9 and 31:10-31, speech and silence, etc. On 31:10-31 one finds a survey of what the description of a woman has variously been thought to express, even pessimism of some that details can fit a real woman, alleged contradictions that prompt some to take it as an allegory of wisdom (105-06), etc.

Wiersbe, Warren. *Be Skillful*. Wheaton, IL: Victor Books, 1995.

The "Be" series deals with Prov. 1-9, giving frequent illustrations and terse Wiersbe maxims, in chapters contrasting wisdom/folly, wealth/poverty, also dealing with speech, righteousness, guidance, besetting sins such as disrespect, greed, pride, etc. Preachers, students, and lay users will gain some enrichment.

Woodcock, Eldon. *Proverbs*. Grand Rapids: Zondervan, 1988. 237 pp.

A Dallas Theological Seminary graduate and Professor of Bible at Nyack College in New York deals with key topics such as wisdom (Hebrew words for this, folly, righteousness, and wickedness), fear, human relationships (adulterous woman, wife, family circle, speech), counsel for a work ethic, and other subjects. Rightly heeded, the principles Woodcock clearly sets forth can lead to true success. The book is of special benefit to laypeople in a series of devotional times but can prime the pump for preachers too.

XVI. ECCLESIASTES

Brown, William P. *Ecclesiastes* (Interpretation). Louisville: Westminster John Knox Press, 2000.

Among features that contribute to scholars, pastors, and students are clear details on contrasts of life in 3:1-8, and ideas about death, purpose, work, vocation, and knowing God (121-37). The source is helpful at times, but those also using more detailed tools will be glad they did.

Bullock, C. Hassell. Cf. on Job.

This is outstanding in giving a well-organized survey of main issues relating to interpreting the book. It also has a rich exposition of several of the sections. Teachers and church workers preparing to speak on Ecclesiastes would wisely acquaint themselves with this material before going ahead.

Crenshaw, James L. *Ecclesiastes* **(Old Testament Library). Philadelphia: Westminster, 1987. 192 pp.**

This is liberal, an illustration of human rationalism at work on Scripture. In many cases the Duke University scholar in Old Testament wisdom material is contributive in giving views and reasons by other writers on particular passages. Yet in many ways he is very disappointing and the work for the most part of little help. To him, Ecclesiastes has no reasoned structure but is randomly brought together (cf. p. 47). Theologically the work is of little help. Crenshaw sees a pessimistic approach in which life has no meaning (25, 34, 53 etc.), and a positive outlook is downplayed (20). He brings his own rationalization to explain away verses about fearing God (102, 184, 190). He rejects "Remember your creator" (12:1), feeling that it must be "your wife" so as to suit the context (184-85).

Delitzsch, Franz. *Ecclesiastes,* **in Keil and Delitzsch series.**

Though old, this is in many ways a productive work offering considerable help on word meaning, connections of sections, views, etc.

Eaton, Michael A. *Ecclesiastes* **(Tyndale Old Testament Commentary). Downers Grove: IVP, 1983. 159 pp.**

A carefully measured work that is usually very helpful, by an English Anglican. He holds the author is not Solomon but two persons who put themselves in Solomon's sandals to speak from his stance, so the date is unresolved. The theme is to advocate faith in a good God, who is in control and invests life with meaning and purpose, as distinguished from futility without Him. Eaton has much of benefit on introduction, word studies and problem passages.

Fredericks, Daniel C. *Qoheleth's Language. Re-evaluation of its Nature and Date.* **Lewiston, PA: Edwin Mellen Press, 1988. 301 pp.**

This examines past explanations and concludes that the Hebrew has evidences of being pre-exilic, not post-exilic as critical scholars usually hold.

Ginsburg, C. D. *The Song of Songs and Coheleth.* **NY: KTAV Publishing House, 1970rp of 1857 work.**

A famous Jewish commentary with much to offer on what the text says, what it means, etc. It is one of the better older works with help on exegesis, customs, views.

Glenn, Donald. "Ecclesiastes," in *Bible Knowledge Commentary,* **ed. John F. Walvoord and Roy B. Zuck. Volume I. Wheaton: Victor Books, 1983.**

A skilled Old Testament faculty member at Dallas Theological Seminary contributed this good brief study, giving frequent help on exegesis, connections of verses, and theology.

Goldberg, Louis. *Ecclesiastes* **(Bible Study Commentary). Grand Rapids: Zondervan, 1983.**

A conservative survey, well-organized, doing a lot to clarify meaning especially for laypeople and pastors needing a quick overview of the book or sections.

Gordis, R. Koheleth: *The Man and His World.* **NY: Schocken Books, 1968rp of 1951 ed. 396 pp.**

Here is a detailed, critical work by a liberal Jewish scholar, discussing textual and linguistic matters. Gordis uses the Hebrew substantially. He has delved into detailed research on such areas as background, style and content, and gives conclusions in concise, popular presentation.

Hengstenberg, E. W. *A Commentary on Ecclesiastes.* **Edinburgh: T. & T. Clark, 1860.**

This is one of the finest, most scholarly old works on Ecclesiastes.

Jones, Edgar. *Proverbs, Ecclesiastes* **(cf. on Proverbs).**

Kaiser, Walter C., Jr. *Ecclesiastes: Total Life.* **Chicago: Moody Press, 1979.**

An evangelical book in the Everyman's Bible Commentary series written in a very interesting fashion on the central concern Kaiser sees in Ecclesiastes: "...that basic hunger of men to see if the totality of life fits into a meaningful pattern" (p. 8). The theme is not "All is vanity" but an optimistic, "Fear God and keep His commandments." The author's "words of delight" (12:10) estimating his own work focus not on thinking like a natural man entrapped in "pessimism, skepticism, materialism, fatalism, and the like" (p. 15). The book, says Kaiser, is a divine revelation as surely as any Bible book. The real theme, as suggested in 3:11, is that "man can know how all things, men and ideas fit together..." when he "comes to know the One who built man in his own image with the capacity to understand who he is as a man, what he means, and what is the worth of things, even life itself" (17). Kaiser shows how Ecclesiastes is in tune with distinctive truths of earlier Scripture (33-38). This work is brief but outstanding in setting the message in its right perspective. It is footnoted throughout, and contains a small, select annotated bibliography. -Jan Sattem in part.

Kidner, Derek. *A Time to Mourn, and a Time to Dance.* **Downers Grove: IVP, 1976.**

In The Bible Speaks Today series, this is a lively, popular exposition of Ecclesiastes that relates the message, accurately given, to life today. Kidner feels the author is not Solomon but one very close to his spirit. For him 3:11 is a key to the book (God put eternity in man's heart), which moves toward the last two verses. All things will disappoint men; only God finally satisfies (cf. p. 98). Kidner's writing style communicates well; he (and Ecclesiastes) bring us to many fresh re-evaluations of what really counts in life, and he shows a fine grasp of the book from a scholar's perceptions and a simplicity at the same time. He even cites choice things from many sources. -Dan Phillips, in part.

Kidner, Derek. *The Wisdom,* **etc. (Cf. on Proverbs).**

Lange, J. P. "Ecclesiastes," in *Commentary on the Holy Scriptures* **(Volume 7). Reprint, 25 volumes in 12. Grand Rapids: Zondervan, 1960.**

Another of the very helpful older works, often rich in meaning on details, giving views, considering matters from different angles.

Leupold, H. C. *Exposition of Ecclesiastes.* **Grand Rapids: Baker, 1987rp of work that first came out in 1952. 301 pp.**

A thorough work, as Leupold's commentaries usually are, this is very helpful in a verse by verse older evangelical study on a scholarly level.

Longman, Tremper, III. *The Book of Ecclesiastes* **(NICOT). Grand Rapids: Eerdmans, 1998.**

The Professor of OT, Westminster Theological Seminary, argues that in 1:12—12:7 Qoheleth, not Solomon, is pessimistic, but a different writer (narrator) of the prologue (1:1-11) and epilog (12:8ff.) offers the right view of life. He uses the other material as a method to instruct his son (12:12) about the folly into which a mere human perspective can plunge one. Many readers will, however, find much in 1:12—12:7 showing a healthy outlook, as in repeating the fear of God (5:7; 7:18; 8:12-13, as well as 12:13). The fear in the three earlier places need not be seen as "fright" as Longman perceives it as fitting his theory, but can be respectful awe. Longman does not always steer readers aright, but he has a widely-researched work that stimulates scholarly minds, some of this coming in footnotes about such things as word meaning and grammar.

Murphy, Roland E. *Ecclesiastes* **(Word Biblical Commentary). Dallas: Word, 1992.**

A 170-pp. contribution by an expert in ancient wisdom literature helps teachers and students in the Hebrew, surveys earlier research, and adds new perceptions. He has much exegetical detail on verses. One feature is an opinion with which many disagree, that neither Solomon nor any Hebrew could have written the book (xx-xxi), with unconvincing reasoning. He says he finds many contradictions in the book, and mentions approaches that handle these (xxxiii-xxxiv). The book is some help when used with mature discernment.

Swindoll, Charles R. *Living on the Ragged Edge: Coming to Terms with Reality.* **Waco, TX: Word Books, 1985.**

This is a series of messages preached by one of America's most sought after speakers, a pastor in the Dallas, TX area. Swindoll writes in a creative flow that captures the imagination, leading it through what he perceives the text means. He is perceptive on human problems and principles in passages relevant to these. Devotionally and as a general exposition pulling lay readers or pastors in by clear, interesting communication, the work helps expose how the message lives. Illustrations and applications help make the book a catalyst for seeing the relevance for preaching and living.

Whybray, R. N. *Ecclesiastes.* **Grand Rapids: Eerdmans 1989. 179 pp.**

Adept in wisdom literature, the writer sees a positive outlook in the book. God bestows meaning to life; and a person's pursuits have fulfilling quality only from Him (cf. p. 27). He turns on light at many points exegetically, but conservative readers will not all think he does this in holding a third century B. C. writing. He also sees no unified flow through the book, but thirty-four unconnected subjects. At times his explanations leave matters not sufficiently clarified (cf. p. 127 on women in 7:28).

Wright, J. S. "Ecclesiastes," in *Expositor's Bible Commentary*, **Volume I. Ed. Frank Gaebelein and R. P. Polcyn. Grand Rapids: Zondervan, 1991.**

Arguing for a single writer, Qoheleth. (except possibly 12:9-12), he does not certainly think it was Solomon but sees no passages that rule out that possibility (p. 1140). He is not certain of the date (1143). His statement of the book's purpose is very good (1144-46), he has a fine one-page outline and is judicious verse by verse, showing that pessimism can be overcome and life given meaning by relating it to God and His will, with the Christian revelation in other parts of the Scripture filling out the picture, as on 3:12-14 (p. 1162). In most cases this is a very good commentary of a conservative nature.

Zuck, Roy B., ed. *Reflecting with Solomon. Selected Studies on the Book of Ecclesiastes*. **Grand Rapids: Baker, 1994.**

Here are 33 chapters by scholars on topics and views related to the book, for example authorship, themes, problems, structure, and specific passages set up to deal with all 12 chapters. Some subjects are: Ardel Caneday's "Enigmatic Pessimist or Godly Sage?", Duane Garrett's "The Theology and Purpose of Ecclesiastes," R. N. Whybray's "Qoheleth, Preacher of Joy," Zuck's "God and Man in Ecclesiastes," Derek Kidner's "The Search for Satisfaction: Ecclesiastes 1:12—2:26," and Louis Goldberg's "How Much Can We Really Know? Ecclesiastes 7:22—7:1." This is a companion vol. to Zuck's edited work *Sitting with Job: Selected Studies on the Book of Job*, which offers a comparable selection of scholarly discussions on that book.

XVII. SONG OF SOLOMON

Brooks, Richard. *Song of Songs* **(Focus on the Bible). Geanies House, Fearn, Ross-shire, Scotland: Christian Focus Publications, 1999.**

An evangelical pastor in England insists on a view opposite to that of Longman (below), certain that the main theme is Christ and the believer (7), human sexual love secondary (8). References to Solomon and the Shulamite and the places such as Sharon are vehicles to convey the chief spiritual idea (9). Attendant virgins are mature believers (21), daughters of Jerusalem believers young in the faith (32), watchmen gospel ministers (77). "I am black but lovely" in 1:5 means a Christian's dual view of self (saved but still sinful, 27), being sun-tanned in 1:6 refers to dangers, toils and snares in a hostile world (29), and later one reads scores of other ingenius allegorical imaginations boldly forced on the text. The work is one more clear example of preachers who insist on reading their opinions in arbitrarily, though they are self-convinced that they are teaching the Word.

Carr, G. Lloyd. *The Song of Solomon* **(Tyndale Old Testament Commentary). Downers Grove: IVP, 1984. 175 pp.**

This commentary is well-respected. Carr, evangelical, is very learned, using scholarly sources, yet lucid in his lengthy introduction, statement of theme (two people celebrating a literal love relationship), and verse by verse commenting, He often has something quite helpful.

Deere, Jack S. "Song of Songs," in *Bible Knowledge Commentary*, ed. John F Walvoord and Roy B. Zuck. Volume I. Wheaton: Victor Books, 1983.

A well-studied conservative treatment following the two character view, Solomon and a woman. He is clear, explains most matters that need explaining, and shows good expertise in the Hebrew word meaning and movement of the book. He develops the beauty of a love relationship as God intends it.

Fox, Michael V. *The Song of Songs and the Ancient Egyptian Love Songs*. Madison: University of Wisconsin, 1985. 454 pp.

Valuable, penetrating study of ancient love songs and certain similarities of the biblical Song to these. The work has three parts: translation and interpretation of late Egyptian songs; translation and commentary on Song of Solomon, and the literary method of discussing love in Egypt and Israel. He gives his own new translation of Song of Solomon, sensitive to meaning of idioms and usually natural in wording. He brings to the task good skill in grammar, syntax and word meanings from cognate languages. He holds to a post-exilic date. This late dating is not at all necessary to conservatives.

Ginsburg, C. D. Cf. on Ecclesiastes.

Glickman, S. Craig. *A Song for Lovers*. Downers Grove: IVP, 1976.

After he wrote his Th. M. thesis at Dallas Seminary in 1974 on "The Unity of the Song of Solomon", he wrote this. He gives his own translation, paraphrase and practical comments on the love relationship within marriage. The is generally done well.

Gordis, Robert. *The Song of Songs*. NY: Bloch, 1962.

By a Jewish scholar, this book is good in Jewish culture and contemporary history of that day. He presents the leading theories of interpretation and has good materials, but his treatment is not an exposition.

Gordis, R. *The Song of Solomon and Lamentation. A Commentary and Translation*. NY: KTAV, 1974. 108 pp.

This highly regarded effort, though so brief, packs in much worthwhile content and shows some revision of his earlier book of 1962. Gordis will many times offer the expositor good textual data, word meanings and rabbinic help. He views the Song as celebrating human love. He is disappointing in devoting so little focus to theological emphases.

Henry, Carl F. H. (Ed.). *The Biblical Expositor*. 3 volumes. Philadelphia: Holman, 1960.

The discussion holds to the two-character view of the book, which says that the Song depicts the intimacies of love between Solomon and a Shulamite maiden.

Ironside, H. A. *Song of Solomon*. NY: Loizeaux, 1950.

Many have considered this book one of the most helpful for a lighter, practical exposition.

Kinlaw, Dennis. "Songs of Songs," in *Expositor's Bible Commentary*. Volume 5. Ed. Frank Gaebelein and R. P. Polcyn. Grand Rapids: Zondervan, 1991.

Kinlaw has a good statement of views in explaining the book (pp. 1202-06), and of purpose. The latter is to describe marriage with its physical intimacies as it ought to be, in God's will, a delight to both partners (1207). Yet he believes that proper marital love is also symbolical of God and His people (1209). He approves a tenth century date and thinks that Solomon may or may not be the writer. The commentary is in many parts rather good.

Lehrman, S. M. "The Song of Songs," in *The Five Megilloth*. London: Soncino Press, 1946.

As usual in the Soncino books, this is concise but reliable explanation by Jewish scholarship.

Longman, Tremper III. *Song of Songs* (NICOT). Grand Rapids: Eerdmans, 2001.

In a work of 238 big pp. with broad study behind it, Longman says the Song may or may not be by Solomon. The story is not about him, rather the two main characters, a woman and a man, are seen in terms of a literal (natural) sexual relationship, the Song being an anthology of love poems expressing emotions, not a drama with an overall plot, and not a piece with allegorical meanings (37-37). Longman's discussion of views in history (20-47) is valuable. He sets the poetry in the world of ancient near eastern love poetry (Egyptian, Mesopotamian, northwest semitic, etc., 49-54). It affirms love, sex, and marriage in relation to God's redemptive aims for relationships, and in sync with Him (70). The commentator devotes a half page to two and a half on verses, unpacking what their meaning suggests, for instance man's admiring comparison of the woman to a mare among chariots, enhanced by ornaments (1:9). Serious users will include this, one of the top overall sources, especially in the informative introduction and effort to keep a natural sense (cf. the opposite in Brooks, among many others).

Mason, Clarence E. *Love Song. The Song of Solomon Comes Alive for Today*. Chicago: Moody, 1976.

Brief explanation, giving main views and taking the Song to be historical of Solomon and his Shulamite bride. The author taught for many years at Philadelphia College of Bible and was rather well-known as a Bible teacher.

Patterson, Paige. *Song of Solomon* (Everyman's Bible Commentary). Chicago: Moody, 1986. 124 pp.

In an Old Testament Survey course, this turns out to be very helpful, crammed as it is with statements showing awareness of problems, views, and sources, yet not going into great detail. Patterson thinks Solomon wrote the ideal of love in marriage early in his reign (p. 17), reflecting the companionship, loyalty, joy, peace, devotion, forgiveness, chastity, tenderness, and sexual union. The commentator discusses seven interpretations, preferring a literal human love but also an analogy of intimacy between the Lord and Israel, Christ and His church (22). Using a chapter to comment on each of the Song's chapters in English, Patterson is lucid and informed in verse by verse comment, often perceptive about when to be literal and when to be figurative.

Pope, M. H. *The Song of Songs* (Anchor Bible). NY: Doubleday, 1977. 743 pp.

This is liberal and highly commended by many. A very full bibliography appears, and Pope has a masterful survey of the history of interpretations. To the diligent he offers the profit of much help in textual, lexical, exegetical matters more often than in his own interpretation of the meaning. He ties the marriage relationship with rites of cults in the ancient Near East, wandering afield from a view conservatives will accept as natural. One will need to exercise much discernment, finding much help at times, much that is interpretively misleading at others, despite the high regard in which liberals hold the work.

Rowley, H. H. *The Servant of the Lord and Other Essays*. London: Blackwell, 1965.

Cf. the essay on the different approaches to the interpretation of the love relationship in the Song. Rowley, a liberal scholar, had much to offer from his vast reading in Old Testament studies. As to orientation, this work can be helpful for trained students.

Taylor, Hudson. *Union and Communion*. China Inland Mission, now Overseas Missionary Fellowship, c. 1910.

Taylor, like some writers above, saw the relationship allegorically in terms of the union between God and man, and drifts away from the real point.

Tournay, Raymond J. *Word of God, Song of Love*. NY: Paulist Press, 1988. 194 pp.

He has the Song written in the Persian era but is weak on evidence. He combines two themes, levels of meaning, one about Solomon and his Egyptian wife in lovers' intimacy and the second an allegorical idea about Messiah and the daughter of Zion with her city where she dwells. The second is a Messianic yearning to encourage Jews in the Persian era to believe in the Messianic Kingdom to come. It is as if the Messiah is asleep, delaying that new era. Here, Tournay labors at the fancy that the person sleeping in the Song is the man, not the woman. Tournay has steeped himself in rabbinics and the Hebrew language as well as scholarly literature on the Song.

XVIII. ISAIAH

Alexander, Joseph A. *Isaiah, Translated and Explained*. 2 volumes. Philadelphia: Presbyterian Board of Publication, 1851.

This is one of the best older expositions of the book from a Hebrew scholar. There are frequent word studies; he deals with syntax; he has an original translation; his commentary is more detailed than most and is often helpful verse by verse.

Allis, 0. T. *The Unity of Isaiah: A Study in Prophecy*. Philadelphia: Presbyterian and Reformed Publishing Co., 1950.

A noted conservative Old Testament scholar of a few decades back builds a carefully reasoned case for one author and unity of the book. This is his aim, and not the task of writing a commentary.

Archer, Gleason L., Jr. "Isaiah." *The Wycliffe Bible Commentary*. Chicago: Moody, 1961.

Archer has packed a lot of good material into this commentary and is very helpful in historical and cultural details as well as the interpretation of difficult phrases. He takes a premillennial covenant viewpoint, so it is nothing unusual for him to refer prophecies concerning Israel to the church.

Baron, David. *The Servant of Jehovah*. Grand Rapids: Zondervan (n. d.).

Covering chapter 53 only, this is a masterful work by a careful scholar. See also E. J. Young, *The Suffering Servant* on chapter 53, and the works by Robert Culver and F. Lindsey.

Blenkensopp, Joseph. *Isaiah 1-39* (The Anchor Bible). NY: Doubleday, 2000.

This great detail gives allegiance to views against supernatural prophecy (e. g. Isa. 13:1, he says, is "impossible to put back into the time of the prophet" (73, 277). Also, alleged editors of the prophetical material allowed fluidity and license in linking sayings to specific authors (74), a claim that undercuts truthfulness. Many other claims also malign the veracity of the book. One example of non-helpful guidance to readers is the discussion of 7:14 as probably referring to Isaiah's wife and son, and sentiment against any reference to Mary and Jesus Christ (233-34). Isaiah 11:10-16 for Blenkinsopp has no link to a divine regathering of Israel before the Messianic Kingdom. Likewise 4:2-6 only give the postexilic Jewish community's hopes [long after Isaiah's times] for restoration, and even here one meets much dense fog. One can see that Vol. 2 on Isa. 40-66, dealing with supernatural prophecy, will not explain these or perceive any coherent system for Israel's future but be time wasted for many.

Brueggemann, Walter. *Isaiah 1-39,* and *Isaiah 40-66* (Westminster Bible Companion). 2 vols. Louisville: Westminster John Knox Press, 1998.

Vols. of 314 and 263 pp. are claimed to be readable for lay people, but only accomplish this for the more advanced, and scholars will appreciate the expertise on historical/cultural setting, exegetical comments on verses (often), and theological principles showing relevance today. On many matters lay people are not served well. While the writer argues for seeing texts along canonical lines for theology that he thinks compilers sought to enhance, he inconsistently (in much Christian assessment) does not tolerate a canonical Christian link of certain details with fulfillment in Christ in Scripture's unity. For instance he does not believe in NT authority for fulfillment, as in Matthew 1 claiming a link with Isaiah 7:14. At that passage he gives no place to God's further revelation in a supernatural way. In 52:13—53:12, blinders he wears cause him to confess that he is not able to discern any clear meaning (141). Serious students do gain ideas of how a scholar can contribute much on some details but be without light on many due to self-limiting convictions.

Bullock, C. Hassell. *An Introduction to the Old Testament Prophetic Books.* Chicago: Moody, 1986. 391 pp.

A well-ordered study of introductory aspects on each prophet, showing much use of modern literature on issues. It is a conservative approach, and quite valuable.

Bultema, Harry. *Commentary on Isaiah*. Translated from Dutch by Cornelius Lambregtse. Grand Rapids: Kregel, 1981, original publication In Dutch, 1923. 630 pp.

Bultema (1884-1952), greatly nurtured for Christ by a Christian mother in the Netherlands, studied at Calvin College and Seminary and pastored Christian Reformed churches. He became persuaded of premillennial dispensationalism and left the Christian Reformed movement to found the Muskegon Berean Church. He writes a respectable commentary verse by verse, sometimes going into detail on arguments to distinguish Israel with its past and future from the church of the present (cf. pp. 51-53 and often in Chapters 40-66). He prefers the Messianic view of 7:14 but is brief and weak in discussion of such a debated verse. He argues on 11:9 that there will be literal animals in the glorified state of the new earth, that 14:12 refers not merely to the king of Babylon but to Satan, and that 26:19f refers to resurrection of believers. In introducing Chapters 40-66, he offers ten arguments that the same writer who penned 1-39 also wrote these. This is a fairly good commentary despite such a view as on 11:9.

Butler, Trent. *Isaiah* (Holman OT Commentary). Nashville: Broadman & Holman, 2002.

Butler, who did Joshua in *The Word Biblical Commentary*, holds authorship by Isaiah and gives detail about authenticity fitting the prophet's day (2-3). He has a good survey of Isaiah (9-10). The commentary is brief as in this series, helpful to a beginner or layperson needing simplicity and a quick grasp. Sometimes readers see nothing to indicate when details of Isaiah will be realized (cf. on 4:2-3; 11:10-16). Butler sees in 7:14 a near child and also a greater fulfillment in Christ, whom he also sees in 9:6-7. He leaves readers to guess who the sufferer is in such a key text as Isa. 53 (296-99). Overall readers will need to go elsewhere to find far more explaining of this biblical book, and will find mostly frustrating generality in this work.

Calvin, John. *Isaiah* (4 volumes). Grand Rapids: Eerdmans.

A lucid amillennial commentary, in this reviewer's judgment good but not as directly to the point and certainly not as recent as amillennial works by Leupold, Young, etc.

Childs, Brevard C. *Isaiah*. Louisville, KY: Westminster John Knox Press, 2001.

Childs subscribes in the main to critical approaches that claim layers of redaction and do not take the book as by Isaiah of the 8th century B. C., and a unity by him. Childs doubts seeing Isaiah as writing chapters by supernatural prophecy (3-4). But if one goes to the verse by verse explanation it is at times helpful (cf. Isa. 6, etc.). In argument that is hard to follow with confidence, Childs does appear to decide that the "writers of Isaiah" saw the child in 7:14 as the Messiah, as in 9:6-7 (68-69). Some lines of reasoning can puzzle and distress an evangelical student, for example flimsy logic by critics who late-date 11:11-16 (a prophetical section) to exilic or post-exilic times (104-05). Often, critical theories meet readers and little is done really to get to a text's point forthrightly so that one gains a clear picture (cf. on 11:11-16). One has to endure with great strain to try to sift meaning that makes sense in some discussions, such as who Isa. 53 describes. There, Childs' massive detail that is difficult to follow finally concludes by seeing the sufferer fulfilled in Jesus Christ (423). The work reflects incredible interaction with scholarly theory, and is for a smaller group of scholars of this pursuit. But it cannot rate well overall for usefulness in many sections to others, even the maturely diligent, to whom more forthright works are available.

Culver, Robert. *The Sufferings and the Glory of the Lord's Righteous Servant.* **Moline, IL: Christian Service Foundation, 1958.**

A rich, competent evangelical study of Isaiah 52:13-53:12 helpful in preaching and teaching. Culver is perhaps better known for his *Daniel and the Latter Days*. He graduated from Grace Theological Seminary and taught for many years at Trinity Evangelical Divinity School, but has pastored for a number of years. His writings reflect sound research and mature scholarly judgment.

Delitzsch, Franz. *Isaiah.* **3rd edition. 2 volumes in Keil and Delitzsch,** *Commentaries of the Old Testament.* **Grand Rapids: Eerdmans, 1964.**

Among technical works for trained students who are able to grapple with and appreciate the Hebrew, this is one of the outstanding older linguistic commentaries on Isaiah. Delitzsch put great exegetical, historical and theological learning into the work, which is highly respected. In prophecy it is amillennial.

Engnell, I. *The Call of Isaiah.* **Uppsala Universitets arsskrift, 1959.**

Those who plan a technical study of Isaiah 6 may wish to include this probing investigation into the text.

Garland, David. *Isaiah, A Study Guide.* **Grand Rapids: Zondervan, 1968.**

A handy premillennial survey of Isaiah, holding to the book's unity, using a good outline, giving a competent overall view of the book and comments on some key passages.

Goldingay, John. *Isaiah* **(New International Biblical Commentary). Peabody, MA: Hendrickson, 2001.**

An OT professor at Fuller Theological Seminary here has the opinion that not one Isaiah wrote the book, but four: Isaiah (chaps. 6, 8 etc.), a disciple (1:1; 37:2; 38:1), a poet (40:6; 50:4 etc.), and the preacher (chaps. 56-66) (pp. 2-5). If one is without solid mooring, he can be left groping for what setting a prophecy points to when Goldingay writes without orientating this (cf. Isa. 2:10– 22; 4:2-6). Many statements leave a puzzle, as Christ's coming in Jahweh's "day" (2:11), which the commentator says "will be for Christians who have resisted Christ" [?] (46). Goldingay does not see a claim of fulfillment in Jesus Christ (Matt. 1) as depending on a link with the actual meaning Isa. 7:14 has, and his remarks on 7:14 can only puzzle many evangelicals (64, 67), as also his comments on 52:13—53:12. The work time and time again leaves vagueness as to fulfillment, and he says that he does not believe that NT claims are true to what OT passages have in view (308-09). The work is an example of some misleading critical scholarship.

Gray, G. B. *A Critical and Exegetical Commentary on the Book of Isaiah* **(ICC). Edinburgh: T. & T. Clark, 1912.**

A liberally-oriented work that is an aid on many of the textual/linguistic details, which a more technical study is concerned to note.

Grogan, G. W. "Isaiah," in the *Expositor's Bible Commentary,* **Volume 6, editors Frank Gaebelein and R. P. Polcyn. Grand Rapids: Zondervan, 1986.**

Grogan was Principal of the Bible Training Institute, Glasgow, Scotland. He argues for the unity of the book, Isaiah as author, and a premillennial view. He has a good bibliography of books up to 1981 but lists only six journal articles (p. 23). He sees some prophecies fulfilled to Israel as distinct from the church in the land of Palestine during a future millennial era after the Second Advent. He regards Revelation 20:4-6 as referring to an earthly kingdom after the Second Advent (14) and thinks Isaiah 7:14 has a double fulfillment. The discussion throughout usually seems to be quite able.

Kaiser, Otto. *Isaiah 1-12, A Commentary*; also *Isaiah 13-39, A Commentary*. 2 volumes. Philadelphia: Westminster Press, 1972-74.

An example of how a liberal scholar ascribes little of even "first Isaiah" (chapters 1-39) to Isaiah, son of Amoz. This is not to say that Kaiser has no helpful commentary on many of the details in the chapters.

Kelly, William. *Lectures on the Book of Isaiah*. 4th edition. London: Hammond, 1947.

This is in some ways a useful English exposition of the book, but offers no Hebrew help. It is quite thorough and premillennial and dispensational. Kelly usually tells the reader why he takes a certain view in the debated prophetical passages. A Plymouth Brethren author, he died in 1906.

Kidner, Derek. "Isaiah," in *New Bible Commentary Revised*, ed. D. Guthrie et al. Grand Rapids: Eerdmans, 1970, pp. 588-625.

Kidner usefully sums up critical arguments in his introduction, but defends unity and authorship by Isaiah with basic arguments. He believes that 11:6-9 refers to conditions in the ultimate state, the New Heavens and New Earth. On many prophetic texts he is vague (11:11ff..; 19:23ff.; ch. 35, etc.). He does not recognize a distinct future for Israel that premillennialists see, but expects fulfillment in the church (cf. on ch. 60, p. 621).

Kissane, Edward J. *The Book of Isaiah*. 2 volumes. Dublin: Browne and Nolan, Ltd., 1952-54.

An old, conservative commentary that offers much on the verse by verse line and takes views not in accord with modern critical theories. He is often fresh and original in comments, and is still of solid value.

Leupold, H. C. *Exposition of Isaiah*. 2 volumes. Grand Rapids: Baker, 1971.

Leupold, as usual, offers much detail in explaining verses from the standpoint of the background, Hebrew word meanings, customs, and the context. It is a fine commentary and is a good recent example of amillennial understanding on prophetical sections such as Isaiah 2, 4, 9, 11, 24-27, 35, 40-66 in relation to the fulfillment of messianic and kingdom hopes.

Lindsey, F. Duane. *The Servant Songs. A Study in Isaiah*. Chicago: Moody, 1985. 170 pp.

A former professor from Dallas Theological Seminary deals in introductory fashion with special problems in the Songs, interacts with literature on them, and gives a commentary on them. He does well exegetically, and Kenneth Barker in the Foreword tabs it "one of the finest studies" on this subject. Lindsey argues for fulfillment of the Servant in Jesus Christ, taking a premillennial view. His lack of definitions for a number of terms may dishearten readers without a seminary background, i.e. "hapax legomenon," p. 84 and "hendiadys," p. 126. Lindsey often has good arguments to support his views; at times he waves aside other positions without looking at arguments for them. It is a valuable book despite some weaknesses..

MacRae, Allan A. *The Gospel of Isaiah.* **Chicago: Moody Press, 1977.**

The President and Professor of Old Testament at Biblical School of Theology in Hatfield, PA wrote this. He was one of Dr. Robert Dick Wilson's outstanding students. The work is not a commentary but a book elucidating themes in 40:1-56:8, showing the interrelation of thoughts and the development of themes, based on the original Hebrew. The section has more verses cited in the New Testament than any other Old Testament passage of its length. Several portions of Handel's *Messiah* came from here. The chapter on Cyrus as God's instrument has many good insights (cf. p. 29), as do the discussions on Isaiah 40 and the several chapters on the Servant of the Lord in Isaiah 41-53, and the thoughts on chapters 54-56.

Martin, John A. "Isaiah," in *The Bible Knowledge Commentary***, ed. John F. Walvoord and Roy B. Zuck. Volume I. Wheaton: Victor Books, 1983.**

Martin briefly defends unity by Isaiah, then provides a succinct, carefully-studied and clear commentary following a good outline. On problem passages he often offers views and reasons, but is brief due to his limitations of space. On the Servant Songs he provides logic for seeing fulfillment in Jesus Christ, and in many texts he argues for realization in a future earthly millennial era, after the Second Advent. He sees many passages fulfilled in Old Testament days and is quite specific about historical details that match these. Cf. also the related book he and his father wrote: Alfred Martin and John Martin, Isaiah: *The Glory of the Messiah* (Chicago: Moody, 1983).

Miscall, Peter D. *Isaiah.* **Sheffield, Eng.: Sheffield Academic Press, 1993.**

Miscall, in a typical liberal loyalty to critical presuppositions, thinks Isa. 1-39 "tell us much more about the fears and hopes of people of this later time [postexilic] than they do about the people and events of the later eighth century, etc. He says, in the same vein, "I regard Isaiah 40-66 as a later representation and interpretation of the return from exile and of the early days of the postexilic era" (12). In 7:14 the woman "can be any actual woman," and this characterizes the fog that one meets in the book, and with it many unhelpful comments illustrative of liberal vagueness and lack of a proper discernment, without the Spirit's interpretive light on what is actually meant by what is said.

Morgan, G. Campbell. *The Prophecy of Isaiah.* **2 volumes. London: Hodder and Stoughton, 1990.**

A thorough analytical treatment of a premillennial nature which some have regarded as one of the finest broad studies on Isaiah.

Motyer, J. Alec. *The Prophecy of Isaiah.* **Downers Grove, IL: IVP, 1993.**

Motyer in this 594-pp. pb draws on three decades of study in Isaiah to help readers by careful evangelical, exegetical work in grammar, word study, context, background, customs, and theology. He meets problems, not dodging them or putting a haze on them. He combines clarity with fresh and stimulating style and even an eye for relevancy today. He believes that 7:14 refers to "the divine son of David" (86), defending this view and connecting the child with the mighty God in 9:6-7. Characteristics of the work are discussion of issues and obvious broad adeptness in the scholarly literature about his subjects (cf. the footnotes on writings and problems). This, despite amillennial views on prophetical parts and in these showing blinders as to a true system in which God will fulfill details, has to rate as one of the top recent commentaries. Cf. also Motyer's somewhat condensed work on Isa. (408 smaller pp.).

Motyer, J. Alec. *Isaiah, An Introduction and Commentary* (Tyndale OTC). Downers Grove, IL: IVP, 1999.

This compact work retains much wording and the essence of Motyer's longer product (above). It does not have as much grammar, word study, and other detail. Some material is new. All in all, verse by verse, this is a lucid, helpful aid for teachers wanting a highly competent assist, and for pastors, students, and lay readers, except on details of prophecy. It ranks among the best medium-length expository sources, usually contributing well on verses. For prophecy, one can gain a better framework and perspective in Robert L. Thomas's comments on Isaiah, done for *The MacArthur Study Bible*, and also the comments in *The Bible Knowledge Commentary*, Vol. 2, or in W. E. Vine's work, as examples.

North, C. R. *The Suffering Servant in Deutero-Isaiah, An Historical and Critical Study*. 2nd edition, revised and enlarged. Oxford, 1956.

A helpful work from the standpoint of gaining perspective on various views and scholarly work done on the identity of the suffering servant. The book shows a wide grasp of material on the subject, and acquaints a reader with what has been done.

Oswalt, John N. *The Book of Isaiah* (NICOT). 2 vols. Grand Rapids: Eerdmans, 1986ff.

This 2-volume work replaces E. J. Young's 3-volume set, and ought to be highly regarded as a conservative work. Oswalt is Professor of Old Testament and Semitic Languages at Trinity Evangelical Divinity School, Deerfield, IL. He holds that Isaiah, son of Amoz, wrote the book, a unity. His introduction does much on the theology, taking the theme as servanthood (p. 54). He sees 7:14 having a double fulfillment, is often good on messianic texts (9:5, 6; 11:1- 10), but often takes prophetic passages as figurative, not literal. He relates sub-sections to larger sections to show how things fit. Some wish the Hebrew words were in Hebrew letters, not in English transliterations.

This and Motyer's longer work rate high among evangelical products of the past few years, offering belief in supernatural prophecy, even if amillennial on passages relating to the future kingdom and Israel's restoration. Oswalt provides a diligent fullness of comment, with readable and usually clear explanations of passages. He reasons for a single writer (Isaiah) for the entire book and says that many scholars posit different periods for different parts of the book because they are unable to accept claims the book makes, not because independent data against these is at all adequate (II. 5). The so-called "second Isaiah" claims that God can tell the future (41:23) (II, 5-6). What some commentators need among other things is a proper view of miraculous prophecy from a God who is able (6), not theirs who is too small. Oswalt reveals his amillennial perspective in saying, for instance, that in 65:25 the wolf, lion and snake will be fulfilled not literally on earth but in a figurative sense in the heavenly Jerusalem (II, 662). Some will regard this as in contrast to what a natural hermeneutic suggests. Oswalt does give profitable reasons for accepting parts such as Chaps. 40-66 as predictive and fitting adequately after earlier chapters. He also has good comments on Israel as a servant, but the Servant who does not fail as the one who makes blessing possible for Israelites and others (cf. II, 52).

Ridderbos, J. *Isaiah* (Bible Students Commentary). Grand Rapids: Zondervan, 1985. 580 pp.

This is evangelical, originally in a Dutch series in 1950-51 for lay readers without Hebrew. The NIV has been edited. The introduction is so taken up with authorship issues that it fails to deal with the aim, theology, unique characteristics and other matters that give perspective. Ridderbos sums up each section at the outset of it, and often has beneficial exegesis and theology on verses, with some freshly stimulating insights. He is amillennial on prophecy of Israel's future but gives reasons for Messianic fulfillment in such texts as the Servant Songs. It is a very good commentary on many passages, and in his amillennial stand shows how one of that persuasion reasons his view.

Scott, R. B. Y. *The Relevance of the Prophets*. NY: Macmillan, 1968.

This revised edition, like the first, assumes redaction criticism. In many respects this perspective does not seem to come into play, or appear persuasive. He does have much that helps the reader learn about prophecy as a channel of God's work with Israel, and how prophetic ministry had its effect among the people. One will receive profit here although may appreciate the overall conservative approach of Bullock, Chisholm, Wood etc. on the prophets.

Smith, W. Robertson. *The Prophets of Israel*. NY: Appleton, 1882.

A very respected work on the eighth century prophets, which still has much to offer.

Thomas, Derek. *God Delivers: Isaiah Simply Explained* (Welwyn Commentary). Grance Close, Faverdale North, Darlington, Eng.: Evangelical Press, 1991.

The Associate Professor of Systematic Theology, Reformed Theological Seminary, Jackson, Miss., is the writer. An amillennialist, he draws much from John Calvin and E. J. Young (9). Chapters receive surveys that cite verses here and there. Thomas sees many prophecies in general fuzziness and without holding that they will be literally realized, with kingdom details starting to be fulfilled from Acts 2 forward (38-39). He sees 7:14 in some clarity mixed with some confusion, yet finally fulfilled in Jesus Christ. One can gain some ideas for preaching principles, yet to a large degree would better spend time in works that far more consistently help on verses (amillennial view, Calvin, Motyer, Oswalt, Young; premillennial, Vine or notes in *MacArthur Study Bible*, or *Bible Knowledge Commentary*, or *Nelson Study Bible*).

Vine, William E. *Isaiah, Prophecies, Promises and Warnings*. London: Oliphants, 1953.

Though this helpful work of a premillennial nature is somewhat brief, it often refers to the original text and observes the syntax. It contributes to the student who has other works which get into the details more at length.

Watts, John D. W. *Isaiah.* **2 volumes (Word Biblical Commentary). Waco, TX: Word Books, 1985-87. 450 + 386 pp.**

Watts is quite liberal and given to late composition. After various writers had a hand in a long redaction history, a late author or group ca. 435 B. C. (the latest historical setting Watts sees in the book) molded traditions handed down and composed the parts into a thematic unity to speak to post-exilic needs. A conservative will gain some help from individual bibliographies of sections, comments on the Hebrew, and perception of how this liberal approach works. Watts thinks Isaiah should be divided up into twelve segments for twelve periods of time from the eighth century to Artaxerxes I's day ca. 460 B. C. His contrived scheme of connecting sections to particular generations will be an oddity to many, derived from his opinion and not from necessity in the text by convincing evidence. Sections are not seen addressing issues authentic in Isaiah's day but rather post-exilic concerns. Watts argues against a messianic significance and supernatural fulfillment of such texts as 7:14; it was fulfilled only in the wife and son of Ahaz (p. 102). The new age is not messianic times but the fifth century B. C. Throughout, readers get more of Watts' theory fudged into passages than an explanation of the text in a realistic historical setting that one more naturally gathers from the book. In 52:13-53:12 the servant is Darius and the sufferer is Zerubbabel, according to Watts, and so on.

Wood, Leon J. *The Prophets of Israel.* **Grand Rapids: Baker, 1987rp. 405 pp.**

A thoroughly conservative work, very clearly written, in two sections, prophetism and the prophets. Wood under the first division goes into the identity, meaning of "to prophesy," function, the Holy Spirit and prophecy, and other aspects. In the second, he discusses in some detail prophets before Samuel, Samuel, monarchy prophets, and the writing prophets from the ninth century to post-exilic days. This is a fine book that gives the student or pastor a much better, integrated understanding of the prophets behind the prophetic books.

Young, Edward J. *Isaiah Fifty-Three.* **Grand Rapids: Eerdmans, 1952.**

Along with works by Baron, Culver and Lindsey, this is a solid evangelical study on Isaiah 52:13-53:12. Young was an outstandingly knowledgeable evangelical Old Testament scholar and deals with the text with a great amount of expertise, even making its message meaningful to readers who are not themselves Hebrew scholars.

Young, Edward J. *Thy Servants the Prophets.* **Grand Rapids: Eerdmans, 1952.**

Young, a strong conservative with a wide breadth of reading, interacts with critical views in ways that assist evangelicals. He also contended for the unity of Isaiah in *Who Wrote Isaiah?* (Grand Rapids: Eerdmans, 1958).

Young, Edward J. *The Book of Isaiah* **(NICOT). 3 volumes. Grand Rapids: Eerdmans, 1965-72.**

This is one of the most detailed fairly recent completed commentaries from a conservative standpoint in giving an amillennial interpretation of the prophetical passages on Messiah and the kingdom over Israel and the world. It is usually exacting in its exegesis, as are other exegetical works by Young, then a member of the faculty at Westminster Theological Seminary in Philadelphia until his death in 1970. It has value as an aid in historical and cultural matters, and grapples at length with important problems like 7:14.

Youngblood, Ronald. *The Book of Isaiah. An Introduction and Commentary).* **Grand Rapids: Baker, 1993, 2nd ed.**

This evangelical gives evidence for one writer (Isaiah) and the book's unity (15-17). The 13 chapters are broad introductory surveys, crafted well; they help students and others appreciate the main aspects and themes in Isaiah. Youngblood sees 7:14 fulfilled first in the near child of 8:3, later in Jesus Christ (47-49), but 9:6-7 only in Christ (52). He views some other prophecies such as 11:11-16 pointing to the return from exile (55-56). He waffles somewhat on identifying the person in the Servant Songs, seeing several who fulfill this, but regarding Christ as the best fulfillment (149-59). The discussions are so general and areas they cover so limited that despite the quality of the book students would find more frequent, consistent help in the better commentaries.

XIX. JEREMIAH

Brueggemann, Walter. *A Commentary on Jeremiah: Exile and Homecoming.* **Grand Rapids: Eerdmans, 1998.**

This combines an earlier 2-vol. work in The International Theological Commentary. After an introduction the writer has 15 chapters, some on several chapters in Jer., done in a survey. He compacts in a lucid flow some main emphases in hit or miss fashion. An initial chapter synthesizes theories of main scholarly works in recent years (W. Holladay, R. Carroll, W. McKane, etc.). After this, an introduction furnishes more on scholarly claims that often represent quite subjective opinions, much of which firmer evangelicals would not accept. Brueggemann lacks a personal belief/assurance whether the Jeremiah in the book and his experiences are more than traditions but historically reliable, or fiction imagined by shapers of the material. Many will reject his rationalization that exposition can validly be without such certainty (12). The work generalizes a lot, and can pose the possibility that things did not happen as the text says, e. g. Jeremiah's trek to the Euphrates (Jer. 13) to bury a waistcloth perhaps is a journey only in fantasy (127). Mixed with many good statements are frequent ones that are quite vague, some evaporative as to any meaning that is literal (when, how, in a perspective of future events) in prophecy to bring Israel again to its land (32:37, p. 309) and do concrete things there. The work often suffers from a lack of completeness in explaining matters, clarity, and a forthright tie (cf. 31:38-40, p. 299). In the latter case one is left with the nebulous, problematic words that the verses refer not to a single future era of rebuilding, but to Jerusalem being at every time and circumstance under God's promise to rebuild and give well being, whatever that means. Yet this often has not been realistically the case, and is not today.

Brueggemann, Walter. *To Pluck Up, To Tear Down: A Commentary on The Book of Jeremiah 1-25* **(New ICC). Grand Rapids: Eerdmans, 1988. 222 pp.**

Much good detail will help students on the text and principles for today. But the commentary is not especially good in comparison with other works, and redactional ideas show up often. Often passages are said to have been written at a later date and redacted in, as 3:15-18 and 24:1-10. Sources in his bibliography provide help for one who wishes to do research on facets of Jeremiah, though heavily from liberal circles.

Bright, John. *Jeremiah. Introduction, Translation and Notes* **(Anchor Bible). 2nd edition. NY: Doubleday, 1978. 372 pp.**

Bright covers many key matters informatively in his introduction, but his liberal thinking rearranges the text by his arbitrary opinion. He does not offer the really good commentary on verses that can be found in such sources as Feinberg, Dyer, Thompson, or Keil.

Calvin, John. *Commentaries of Jeremiah and Lamentations* **(5 volumes). Grand Rapids: Eerdmans, 1950.**

Calvin is always worth reading, and one will find much insight at times on verses as well as the character of Jeremiah. The sheer length will keep many away, and several other works get to the point more directly. Calvin is amillennial on passages about Israel's long-range future, and premillennialists will feel that he does strange things with these.

Carroll, Robert P. *Jeremiah, A Commentary* **(Old Testament Library). Philadelphia: Westminster, 1986. 874 pp.**

In 1986 alone three massive works were published on Jeremiah (cf. Holladay and McKane as well). In Carroll's subjectivism, a Jeremiah of factual history retreats into vagueness behind redactors and layers of tradition which made up speeches and events (p. 48). We are involved here at times more with Carroll's radical wanderings in assumptions than with the Book of Jeremiah many want help on. Still, on many matters of textual, lexical, exegetical nature where his theory does not so intrude, he can be very instructive. His bibliography and interaction with views is often quite valuable.

Clements, R. E. *Jeremiah* **(Interpretation). Atlanta: John Knox Press, 1988. 276 pp.**

This series is aimed at students, teachers and preachers, using the RSV. Clements was on the faculty at King's College, University of London. This is nowhere near the best commentary, but one can glean a wealth of information even if he is not ready to accept a lot that Clements says, He assumes that the book is by unknown scribes and compilers who preserved a record of Jeremiah's prophecies (p. 3). In chapters 1-25, prose discourses are not per se Jeremiah's words but those of composers "based on words, themes and situations authentic to the prophet" (p. 11). The commentary is broad, not always verse by verse, and since Clements does not use phrases from the RSV set off, a reader finds it hard to be aware of just what part of the text Clements is commenting on at times. He thinks editors may later have named the place "the Euphrates" where Jeremiah was to bury the cloth (ch. 13), rather than the words originally being in God's speech to Jeremiah (85). He sees it as unlikely that the New Covenant in Jeremiah 31 in its words could have come from the lips or pen of Jeremiah (190). To him it was only later at Qumran and in the Christian church that the idea evolved that God meant an entirely New Covenant (191). This will be impossible for many to agree with. The commentary is quite disappointing in many ways.

Craigie, Peter C., Page H. Kelley, and Joel Drinkard, Jr. *Jeremiah 1-25;* **Gerald L. Keown, P. J. Scalise, and T. G. Smothers,** *Jeremiah 26-52* **(WBC). 2 vols. Dallas, TX: Word Books, 1991, 1995.**

Craigie died after finishing through 8:3, and others took up the task, Kelley 8:4—Chap.

16, Drinkard 17-25, etc. The usual WBC attention to form/structure/setting appears, then comment on verses, after this a synopsis explanation. Some ideas may not be necessary, for instance that in Jer. 13 of a reference to a trek to the Euphrates only being feasible at the exile, hence the verse must mean a nearby wadi early in Jeremiah's ministry (I, 190). For scholars this is another of several works that give exegetical detail, views, etc. Readers looking in material on the New Covenant (31:31ff) for correlative data on when fulfillment will come that realistically meets the details can search with disappointment about the lack of tie-in explanation. The same puzzle is left in comments on 32:37-41, or 33:15-26. The commentators seem not to have a key to a perspective of long-range prophecy fulfilled as at the Messiah's Second Coming; they handle bits and pieces well but grope in the dark instead of helping readers have an overall, proper perspective about biblical prophecy.

Curtis, A. H. W. and T. Romer, eds. *The Book of Jeremiah and its Reception.* Leuven: Leuven University Press, 1997.

Thirteen papers reflect scholarly opinions from a 1985 seminar at Lausanne. These give views on a process of alleged redaction and subsequent inclusion of Jeremiah into the Heb. Bible. The papers deal with theory of Deuteronomist influence on the prophetical books, on phrases such as "Peace, peace . . .," and "terror on every side," also reception of Jeremiah into the Qumran scrolls, and the enigmatic Matthew 16:14 reference to Jeremiah, etc. Scholars and students of this biblical book can profit more or less from the informative work.

Driver, S. R. *The Book of the Prophet Jeremiah.* London: Hodder and Stoughton, 1906.

Though liberal in its approach, this work is helpful in its detailed notes on verses. Driver was a careful scholar and aids the expositor in understanding the meanings of difficult phrases.

Dyer, Charles, "Jeremiah," in *Bible Knowledge Commentary*, ed. John F. Walvoord and Roy B. Zuck. Volume I. Wheaton: Victor Books, 1983.

A concise but carefully-researched conservative work that very often provides good help in explaining verses to preachers, students and lay people. Dyer gets to the flow of the message in Jeremiah, mingles summaries and sections on detail in a good balance, and usually has something worthwhile on key verses or problem passages.

Feinberg, Charles L *Jeremiah, A Commentary.* Grand Rapids: Zondervan, 1982.

This well-done, 335-page work eventually came to be in Volume 6 of the *Expositor's Bible Commentary*. It joins Feinberg's other works on Ezekiel, Daniel, and the Minor Prophets. A good introduction on the most notable issues climaxes with a lengthy list of commentaries and a few journal articles, a six and a half page outline, then the text of the N. I. V. (North American, 1978), and the exposition. Comments clarifying Hebrew meanings appear both in the exposition and in special notes. Feinberg gives space to different views, as on the passage of the linen belt (13:1-7) and the Branch (23:5, 6), but clearly supports his preference. He favors a premillennial view on the fulfillment of prophecies about Israel's far future, and his work is the best detailed effort by a premillennialist to date.

Guest, John. "Jeremiah, Lamentations," in *The Communicator's Commentary.* **Waco, TX: Word Books, 1988. 390 pp.**

Guest stimulates preachers by his clarity, directness about the meaning, provocative titles, and relevant applications. In much of the book his work is a catalyst for a sermon series, though he slights or obscures passages about a future for Israel (chapters 30-33 etc.).

Habel, Norman C. *Jeremiah, Lamentations* **(Concordia Commentary). Grand Rapids: Zondervan, 1981. 157 pp.**

Using the RSV, Habel gives an 8-page outline at the outset and follows it throughout. However, he does not continue the enumeration, so one can lose the relation of sections. The commentary is fairly solid in a concise, summary way in each pericope. There is discussion of some problems, others are ignored (as which river the cloth is buried in, Jeremiah 13). He cites but leaves unresolved the assumption of some scholars who theorize that points of comfort in passages were by later editors (31:7-14; 32:17-23; 33:14-26, p. 227), texts which can reasonably be from Jeremiah. On the New Covenant, Habel discusses how New Testament texts relate. He sees restoration of Jerusalem in 31:38-40 fulfilled in the New Jerusalem, not in a millennial era after the Second Advent (251). Some restoration texts are not really explained but left vague, as 33:6-19, and fulfillment is placed in the church, the new Israel to Habel. How promises that sound like literal rebuilding are realized in this spiritual fashion realistically is left unexplained (265).

Harrison, R. K. *Jeremiah & Lamentations* **(Tyndale Old Testament Commentary). Downers Grove: IVP, 1975. 240 pp.**

This famous Old Testament scholar, a conservative, concludes that we have here the basic teachings of Jeremiah under several kings. Lamentations is done by an eye-witness of Jerusalem's fall. In both books, Harrison offers a brief but well informed commentary that is usually quite helpful in getting at what the text means and not substituting redactional theory from another era.

Holladay, W. L. *Jeremiah I: A Commentary on the Book of the Prophet Jeremiah, Chapters 1-25* **(Hermeneia). Philadelphia: Fortress Press, 1986. 682 pp. Jeremiah II, Chapters 26-52, 1989. 543 pp.**

Like the works by Carroll and McKane this is highly-respected as a technical, critical commentary in the scholarly community. On text, grammar, structure, synthesis of sections and literature dealing with issues it offers much. A 95-page introduction begins Volume II, and a bibliography here updates the one in Volume I. This is the most massive of the recent detailed works, over 1,200 pages at more than 800 words a page. Holladay theorizes that 1:1 refers not to the year of Jeremiah's call but to his birth, 627 B. C., and uses this as a chronological starting point for the rest of the book. He often connects passages in Jeremiah with New Testament verses as to theme, and is skeptical about redaction that remodels the book in a Deuteronomistic pattern. Some criticize him for a highly individualistic translation in many passages, and his pleading that the original text was this way, the way of his emendations. In verse by verse commentary he explains more than Carroll or McKane, is masterful in grammar and syntax, and skillful in insights drawn from much study, so that he helps on many points, on views, etc. Still he retains a lucid flow, Many herald it as the definitive technical work on Jeremiah to date.

Huey, F. B., Jr. *Jeremiah* **(Bible Study Commentary). Grand Rapids: Zondervan, 1981. 157 pp.**

Conservative and concise, using a good outline and giving pastors, Sunday School teachers and lay people in general a quick look in a fairly able way. Dyer, Jensen, Kidner and Harrison do it better among the briefer works in overall helpfulness, though this is not to downgrade Huey.

Huey, F. B., Jr. *Jeremiah, Lamentations* **(New American Commentary). Nashville: Broadman & Holman, 1993.**

Huey was free to give more detail than in 1981, offering 512 pp. The Jeremiah introduction provides considered conclusions favoring Jeremiah as writer amid opinions, and a survey of the theology and convictions about relevant issues for today. Huey puts up front an outline of both books, then gives verse comments which usually explain vividly the details, such as the almond tree and tilted pot (Jer. 1), and artesian well (2:13). In Jer. 13, he defends the distant Euphrates area for burying the loin cloth, is frank about the prophet's emotional outbursts as in chap. 20, argues for no contradiction between Jehoiachin written as "childless" (22:28-30), yet having seven children (I Chr. 3:17), etc. On prophecy about a future for an ethnic yet spiritual Israel, Huey seems at times favorable to a premillennial expectation of literal fulfillment yet future today (283-84), yet creates doubt by seeing no distinction between millennial fulfillment, and blessings in the eternal city (289), or fuzzes this (as 32:37-44; 33:6-9). One often finds good help on Lam., as in 3:22-23, and on most passages in this often worthwhile effort.

Jensen, Irving L. *Jeremiah and Lamentations* **(Everyman's Bible Commentary). Chicago: Moody, 1974. 153 pp.**

A master at surveys does it again here for pastors, Sunday School teachers and lay persons needing a concise sketch. He has a clear outline, charts that put some material into helpful perspective (as oracles vs. the nations, chapters 46-51), and a map on Jeremiah's geography (p. 149). He sees a premillennial fulfillment of Israel's restoration as in Jeremiah 33 (p. 93 etc.), and offers brief comment on some problems, for example whether Jeremiah walked to a nearby creek or made a trek to the far off Euphrates River with the loincloth of Chapter 13.

Jensen, Irving L. *Jeremiah: Prophet of Judgment.* **Chicago: Moody, 1966.**

Jensen has written a concise evangelical commentary for those who wish for a simple survey. The work is premillennial in its orientation, and is done by a man well-known for his helpful expositional works.

Kidner, Derek. *The Message of Jeremiah* **(Bible Speaks Today). Downers Grove: IVP, 1987. 176 pp.**

This is a broad exposition of the book something akin to those by Erdman and Huey, though more refreshing than either. Kidner as usual is very readable, conservative, concise and direct on many of the issues. However, he is amillennial on the main prophetical section (Chapters 30-33), expecting spiritual but not literal realization.

King, Philip J. *Jeremiah, An Archeological Companion*. Louisville, KY: Westminster John Knox Press, 1997.

King seeks to show artifactual and inscriptional evidence related to many aspects of daily life in Judah during Jeremiah's career. He deals with archeological ideas of locations for sites mentioned, detail about recording property transfer (Jer. 32, pp. 89-90), and bread-making related to 37:21 (107-08), for example.

Laetsch, Theodore. *Jeremiah*. Saint Louis: Concordia, 1952. Also done then in paperback.

This is, in the reviewer's opinion, still one of the best single conservative amillennial commentaries available at present on Jeremiah and Lamentations. It is detailed, helpful in Hebrew word studies and historical background, and has good insight into difficult verses. Laetsch is also a lucid writer.

McConville, J. G. *Judgment and Promise. An Interpretation of the Book of Jeremiah*. Winona Lake, IND: Eisenbrauns, 1993.

Eight chapters take up issues such as repentance/hope (3:1—4:4), deferred hope (1-24), Jeremiah as a figure, etc. McConville dialogues and disagrees with theories that the book is the product of Deuteronomistic editing, believing it probable that much or all of the book derives from Jeremiah. He seeks to argue unity of the book and account for the differences of focus at different stages of Jeremiah's career as the prophet responded to varying circumstances of his people at different places in the book. He evaluates lines of argument for a Deuteronomistic conclusion on such issues as style and theology (cf. 11-26, etc.).

McKane, William. *A Critical and Exegetical Commentary on Jeremiah, Volume I. Introduction and Commentary on Jeremiah I-XXV* (ICC). Edinburgh: T. & T. Clark, 1986. 658 pp.

This provides meticulous detail in explaining verses—the text, word study, exegesis, customs, history etc.—and McKane is often helpful by giving views, though sometimes it is not easy or possible to decide what his preference is. As in much scholarship he theorizes a long history of different compositions in a haphazard, piecemeal growth that merged in what we have today. He offers copious use of words in Hebrew and Greek characters, and the Hebrew is unpointed, demanding that to follow it maximally readers need to know the languages. Overall it is quite an astute work on technical matters, views etc. It is liberal, and in much of the commentary attention is turned to source-critical issues his views exalt to importance, but which will not necessarily explain the text, at least for many. For some scholars it will offer help in its detail on versions, German sources and others, medieval Jewish comment, etc. For many it will be like a mostly dry well of water but offering plenty of content in stones, some of which can be useful as one discerningly picks what he can accept.

Nicholson, E. W. *Jeremiah* (Cambridge Bible Commentary). 2 volumes. Cambridge: U.P., 1973. 221 + 247 pp.

These volumes on Chapters 1-25 and 26-52 use the NEB, aiming at teachers and young persons, assuming no specialized knowledge of Hebrew. The writer assumes that the prose sayings and sermons were composed by a group of Deuteronomic authors, mostly based on Jeremiah's original sayings but some not on anything he said (he cites 11:1-14; 17:19-27, p. 11) to meet needs of the exile. Also, many narratives in the book are from the later authors. Nicholson is assured, for he follows what is "now shared by most scholars" (p. 12). The commentary is brief, well-worded, explaining much but at times giving arbitrary opinions that are not necessary. For example, an editor expanded on Jeremiah's original account of his call (1:8, p. 25), and we do not have in Chapter 7 Jeremiah's original speech but an editor's version (p. 75). The visit to the potter is construed to be the work of a late editor, only based on a saying by Jeremiah (p. 155). The work leaves in the vagueness of non-explanation how the restoration of Jerusalem in 31:38-40 will be fulfilled; this also applies to 32:15; 33:6 etc. This liberal work has its times of helpfulness but is not worth the time too often.

Ryken, Philip G. *Jeremiah & Lamentations* (Preaching the Word). R. Kent Hughes, gen. ed. Wheaton: Crossway Books, 2001.

Hefty at 829 pp., this is engaging exposition in terms of spiritual relevancy today, done in 66 parts by a scholar/preacher, senior pastor at Philadelphia's Tenth Presbyterian Church. One can see how an evangelical preached through on the sub-title theme, "From Sorrow to Hope," using catchy titles to messages. Ryken is ready to explain some details, such as "Perath" in Jer. 13 meaning the Euphrates, a long trek being involved. The work offers an attractive flow and simplicity as a catalyst for preaching ideas, and for students and lay readers pursuing a long devotional series. Sadly, on prophecy outright promises to Israelites of literal blessings in the land are kept vague as to when (a fad among many today), as on p. 492, or they are apparently construed as fulfilled in Christ's first coming (507-10). Natural interpretation is fuzzed away, even though many good spiritual lessons enrich, as in Jer. 32 and 33. A better way would combine literal fulfillment with spiritual principles in a straight-forward interpretation as clear as the text is, and the restoration for Israel would be as literal as Israel's judgment was within the same overall context.

Schaeffer, Francis. *Death in the City.* Downers Grove: IVP, 1969.

The famous speaker/writer shows how the message of Jeremiah and Lamentations applies to people of the modern era.

Sire, James W. *Jeremiah, Meet the 20th Century.* Downers Grove: IVP, 1975.

Twelve topical studies do not give a commentary but show the relevance of Jeremiah's message to his own generation and to 20th century readers. The book is geared for personal profit and Bible study group use. Sire often points out parallels to today – moral decay, political ills, and spiritual deadness – and tries to elicit application consistent with the lessons. Sire offers "Notes for the Leader" with extra help on larger difficulties, and he is concise and sometimes on target. References to other sources which provide more detail can be valuable to readers. The book is brief (116 pp.).

Streane, A. W. *The Book of the Prophet Jeremiah, Together with the Lamentations* (Cambridge Bible for Schools and Colleges). Cambridge: U.P., 1885.

This is one of the most painstaking and contributing among older commentaries. It offers comments on verses some works skip over, material on many of the problems, and good synopses too. It does not have refinements in chronology and material from recent discoveries such as one will find in Bright, Feinberg, Harrison, Laetsch, Holladay, Carroll, McKane, Thompson, etc. but certainly explains much of what a teacher or pastor needs.

Thompson, J. A. *The Book of Jeremiah* (New International Commentary on the Old Testament). Grand Rapids: Eerdmans, 1980. 819 pp.

This is the most detailed evangelical commentary of recent vintage, competent in its lengthy introduction (pp. 1-136) on scholarly issues and views, details of text, exegesis, history and theology. Much of the commentary is lucidly helpful for the general reader as well as teachers and church workers. It does not take up a number of questions some scholars would like or give a bibliography of the length Thompson might offer. But he is helpful on archeology and the Near Eastern treaty concept. The perspective on prophecy is amillennial, but cf. Feinberg's premillennial work.

von Orelli, Hans C. *The Prophecies of Jeremiah*. Minneapolis: Klock & Klock, 1977rp. 384 pp.

This work was originally from T. & T. Clark in Edinburgh in 1889. Cf. also his works on Isaiah and the minor prophets. He is one of the able earlier exegetes upholding the integrity of the book from meticulous study. His introduction pays high tribute to Jeremiah's character and compares him with Jesus Christ. He defends several of the sections scholars have claimed did not belong to the book (cf. list, pp. 23-24, and the individual sections). Verse by verse, essential things receive good comment. Much is readily understandable, but Hebrew words and on occasion details in Hebrew grammar will be usable only to the trained. Orelli becomes general and vague as to when and in what connection God will fulfill forecasts of. a future rebuilding of Israel's fortunes (Chapters 30-33). For the New Covenant passage in Chapter 31, he gives no discussion of New Testament texts. A compact version of his work on Jeremiah is found in "Jeremiah," the old *International Standard Bible Encyclopedia* (Grand Rapids: Eerdmans, 1939, III, 1588-91).

Wood, Fred. *Fire in My Bones*. Nashville: Broadman Press, 1959.

Discussion here is topical, helping a student or any Christian get a taste of certain streams of thought vital in the message. Wood bases the title on Jeremiah 20. This is conservative and broad in its treatment.

XX. LAMENTATIONS

Albrektson, B. *Studies in the Text and Theology of the Book of Lamentations, with a Critical Edition of the Peshitta Text* (Studia Theologica Lundensia). Lund, 1963.

This liberal, highly-regarded monograph argues that the book presents a tension between the historical event of destruction on Jerusalem and some Jewish theological thinking that Jerusalem was to be inviolable. The writer feels that the message of the book aims at steering Israelites to trust in a Person, not a place. It has much that helps supplement the use of commentaries on the book.

Calvin, John. Cf. on Jeremiah.

Dyer, Charles. "Lamentations," in _Bible Knowledge Commentary_, ed. John F. Walvoord and Roy B. Zuck. Volume I. Wheaton: Victor Books, 1983.

This is a conservative, very able work that covers most bases quite well enough to be of real help to pastors, teachers and lay people. Dyer, in addition to good help verse by verse, has a whole page chart of "Parallels Between Lamentations and Deuteronomy," and a knowledgeable introduction arguing the reasonableness of seeing Jeremiah as author.

Ellison, H. L. "Lamentations," in _Expositor's Bible Commentary_. Volume 6, ed. Frank Gaebelein and R. P. Polcyn. Grand Rapids: Zondervan, 1986.

Ellison provides a good, brief conservative introduction and terse commentary without an extensive bibliography (only ten sources, pp. 699-700). Still, he is quite capable and offers competent help on many of the most pertinent details so that the work is a worthy effort.

Gordis, Robert. Cf. on Song of Solomon.

Gottwald, N. K. _Studies in the Book of Lamentations_ (Studies in Biblical Theology). Revised edition. London, 1962. 126 pp.

A very well-respected liberal monograph which reasons that the book relates to the problem Jews felt of suffering on a national basis. It gets at the tension between the historical sting of destruction and the Deuteronomistic concept about retribution and reward. Gottwald feels that the book shows that sin is the answer to the question some asked, why supposedly godly Israel should receive punishment after reforming in Josiah's reign (2 Kings 22-23). He shows that even though the calamity occurred the book reveals hope for the future, but thinks much of the explanation is left as a mystery of God's ways. Some have faulted Gottwald for not putting _enough_ emphasis on Israel's sin as really taking the mystery out of the matter.

Guest, John. Cf. on Jeremiah.

Habel, Norman. Cf. on Jeremiah.

Harrison, R. K. Cf. on Jeremiah.

Hillers, D. R. _Lamentations: Introduction, Translation and Notes_ (Anchor Bible). Garden City, NY: Doubleday, 1972. 116 pp.

Hillers furnishes a lot of able assistance on details of the Hebrew text, word meaning, syntax, history, etc. He says he writes for the general reader and does not include much technical detail. He actually has much of this. He devotes pages xv-xlvii to introduction. His discussion of reasons for and against authorship by Jeremiah (xxi-xxii) is somewhat helpful but can leave some readers with the impression of subjectivity. His bibliography is made up of non-conservative sources and heavy on German writings. His only outline is a title to each chapter of Lamentations, though he also gives certain suggestions in his "comment" sections. The patient, advanced student, especially, can work with the Hebrew and sift out much from the "notes" methodically. "Comment" sections open things up to see a greater flow and connection; they point out form, analyze shifts in thought, and often look at views as on the issue of who the sufferer is in Chapter 3. It is, overall, a valuable work for serious students wishing such detail as the above.

Jensen, Irving. Cf. on Jeremiah.

Kaiser, Walter C. Jr. *A Biblical Approach to Personal Suffering* **[Lamentations]. Chicago: Moody, 1982.**

This is a very good and helpful examination of the lessons learned from the text of Lamentations. It should be useful to a wide audience, in that Kaiser provides an introduction which analyzes the structure of the Hebrew text and finds a personal application from Jeremiah's handling of his grief over the fate of Jerusalem. Kaiser's chief goal in this study is the determination of a biblical guide for managing grief. He interacts with a broad array of literature and reflects a study of the Hebrew text, dealing with translation difficulties when relevant. Recommended. -Dan Phillips

Kent, Dan G. *Lamentations* **(Bible Study Commentary). Grand Rapids: Zondervan, 1983. 64 pp.**

Kent thinks someone during the time of Jeremiah wrote the book, but gives arguments for and against Jeremiah (pp. 14-15). His commentary is a good, brief survey, well-informed and organized. It ought to help pastors and lay readers who need a quick, dependable short commentary that handles some of the problems in a sketchy way and keeps to the flow as well.

Provan, Iain. *Lamentations* **(New Century Bible Commentary). Grand Rapids: Eerdmans, 1991. 142 pp.**

Provan was a lecturer in Hebrew and Old Testament studies at the University of Edinburgh. He appears to be liberal. His introduction is informative and up to date on views of authorship, date and place, but he himself is unable to arrive at a view except that the book was written between the sixth and second centuries B. C. (p. 19). He has much assisting information, yet wrongly does not believe a commentary should give the text's meaning. This to many is being irresponsible. Why not let somebody else do the commentary then? Rather, he says, it should be "a catalyst for the reader's own imaginative interaction with it" (29). So usually he does not state his own view, and seems unsure the book refers to the fall of Jerusalem or what is the setting (11, 29). Still, one can find much information on verses as to the text, meaning of words, etc. He is of the opinion that Lamentations 3:21-27 focuses on humble repentance and trust in God's love, yet that Chapter 5 swings to an attitude opposed to this, reproaching God for unfairness (23). So, he feels that the theology of the book is left "ending in a question mark" (24). Many disagree with him here, as well.

Streane, A. W. Cf. on Jeremiah.

von Orelli, Hans C. Cf. on Jeremiah.

XX. EZEKIEL

Alexander, Ralph. *Ezekiel.* **Chicago: Moody Press, 1976.**

In the Everyman's Bible Commentary series, this work by the former Associate Professor of Old Testament Languages and Exegesis at Western Conservative Baptist Seminary is a very well studied, helpful survey. Alexander is keenly aware of interpretive problems and engages them discerningly even if briefly due to his limited space. His outlook is pre-millennial and dispensational. The discussion of views in Ezekiel 38-39 is one of the especially helpful sections.

Allen, Leslie C. *Ezekiel 1-19* and *Ezekiel 20-48* (WBC). 2 vols. Dallas: Word Books, 1990-1994.

One finds the expected WBC fulness of exegetical inquiry (technical notes, verse comments, general summary explanation) and a phenomenal bibliography most pertinent to scholars, as well as numerous opinions of a redactor arranging material. Passages about future blessing for Israel regathered to its land are discussed in details, yet shrouded in haze with no commitment to a clear perspective that conveys light. One is left without help on when all the aspects could convincingly be fulfilled to make good sense of prophecy (cf. 36:24ff.; 37:1-14). In the latter passage, a tiny ray of light appears in a brief reference to the Apostle Paul's belief in an eschatological consummation for the Israelite people, yet this is vaguely seen as an incorporation into the community of faith, "life from the dead" (Rom. 11:15) (II, 188). Seeing Ezekiel 40-48 realized in a future time strikes the author as "a desperate expedient that sincerely attempts to preserve belief in an inerrant prophecy" (II, 214). The WBC writer has no light on how the section can have meaningful fulfillment, and is tossed at sea, seeing the details as never implemented and yet not to be realized. In such a view, what does an expositor have to say that can allow Scripture to have a meaningful purpose, if it runs into this kind of frustration? Does God not know how to lead a prophet to make sense?

Blackwood, Andrew. *Ezekiel: Prophecy of Hope*. Grand Rapids, MI: Baker, 1965.

This is a good broad sweep of the message and is well written. But it does not involve itself enough with contextual problems to satisfy serious students. Chapters 40-48 are interpreted in a general, even vague and confused fashion involving spiritualization, rather than in a literal way including an earthly temple in the future Messianic Kingdom.

Block, Daniel I. *The Book of Ezekiel* (NICOT). 2 vols. Grand Rapids: Eerdmans, 1998.

Block's all-around attempt provides the best detailed study by an evangelical on chapters 1-24, nearly 900 pp. on the first vol. that give masterful attention to phrases, grammar, background, views, etc. In vol. 2 the expertise continues to give much light, again with great detail on some issues and only brief comment on others. Premillennialists will be disappointed, even dismayed by what they feel is a departure from natural herrmeneutics on some prophecies. Block keeps asserting a restoration of Israel to its own land (that should be Palestine), as in 36:24, 28; 37:14, 21, yet leaves readers without explanation of when in the prophetic picture. Then his comments on Ezek. 40-48 seem at times lost in a maze when he says what Ezekiel expects "lays the foundation for the Pauline spiritu-alization of the temple" fitting with the New Covenant, where Gentile communities may be transformed into the living temple of God (I Cor. 3:16-17) (II, 506). He sees fulfill-ment of Ezekiel's river of 47:1-12 in Rev. 22:1, and in distinction to a natural hermeneu-tic justifies a non-literal view on the inadequate reasoning that Ezekiel saw this in a vision. He sees details as unrealistic for a natural situation, such as a stream flowing from a temple (II, 700-01). Did literal water then not flow out of a literal rock in Israel's wilderness journey? So he sees vague generalized significance such as renewing people's relationship with God (701), as in the river in Rev. 22:1. Somehow he sees Rev. 22 as "in perfect keeping with the historical interpretation of the text," with no more curse (701), rather than recognizing a distinction between a future millennial temple with details fulfilled to Israel distinctively, and a later, eternal estate along some similar lines but then with ultimate realities. Though Block rejects such a perspective, one will find hermeneutics that is more natural and realistic in R. Alexander, Cooper, Enns, Feinberg (his commentary, plus his chapter on the temple in Prophecy in the Making, ed. Carl F. H. Henry, Carol Steam, IL., Creation House, 1982), and Ezekiel notes in The MacArthur Study Bible.

Brownlee, W. H. and Leslie C. Allen. *Ezekiel.* 2 volumes (Word Biblical Commentary). Dallas, TX: Word Books, 1986-90. 301 pp.

Brownlee prepared notes on Chapters 1-19, then died. Allen and Gerald Keown took the material, finished it, and Allen did the second volume covering the rest of the book. One will, in Chapters 1-19, find strange opinions in place of a sane explanation of the text (cf. on 1:3; 2:9-3:2; 4:4, etc.). Generally he does not manipulate texts but sometimes he does. More often he is careful and reliable on detail of the text, philology, etc. But he strains to contend for his error that Ezekiel is in Gilgal, Jordan Valley, not in Babylonia. Seeing Ezekiel 26 fulfilled by Alexander the Great, Brownlee construes matters to have references to Alexander taken as glosses, redacted later, so the passage is not miraculous prophecy (p. xxxvii). The introduction overall reveals a scholar given to radical critical theory. Allen seeks a line between older, higher critical treatment and a newer literary method. He sees most of the book as from Ezekiel but feels that others redacted the text later. At many points he shows a good amount of light on passages. He sees the King of Tyre and not Satan in 28:11-19. The dispensational approach to prophecies is untenable to him. The two sticks passage is realized in the church, he says, and he is vague about Chapters 40-48, not helpful, viewing a dispensational, futurist explanation as "desperate." The work is, overall, a disappointment.

Carley, Keith W. *The Book of the Prophet Ezekiel* (Cambridge B. C.). New York: Cambridge U. P., 1974.

Carley, lecturer in Old Testament at Rarongo Theological College, Papua, New Guinea, says some material is from followers or editors, not Ezekiel. His argumentation for this is subjectively weak. The battle of Ezekiel 38, 39 is not to be at the end of the present age but Gog and Magog are only representative of nations in chapters 34-37. Discussion of the temple (40-48) is very vague and generalized, with no effort to consider if it can be a material temple to be realized in a future day. Ezekiel, in Carley's mind, is only stressing the urgency to be vigilant against corrupting holy things (p. 321). The commentary is of small help to those looking for an awareness of issues in dealing with interpretive problems and taking a perspective that responsibly explains prophecies according to their natural, meaningful import.

Clements, Ronald E. *Ezekiel* (Westminster Bible Companion). Louisville: Westminster John Knox Press, 1996.

Even if brief (211 pp.) the book has profitable reflections for scholars while being fairly readable for others. Clements shows pastoral encouragement by God's relevance also today. He is positive about many details of introduction, such as Ezekiel authoring the work, unity, and reliability, as on the notations about dates. On prophecy, of which Ezekiel has much, statements tend to be nebulous about fulfillment, or Clements sees predictions as already realized in Ezekiel's time, for example on the temple and offerings of Chaps. 40-48. Many will be right to wonder, how so in any realistic way? One finds very different perspectives on prophecy than in books by premillennialists (R. Alexander, Cooper, Enns, Feinberg, etc.), but learns how some others look at biblical matters.

Cooke, George A. *A Critical and Exegetical Commentary on the Book of Ezekiel* (ICC). 2 volumes. London: T. & T. Clark, 1936.

A helpful work in philological detail and some problem verses because it presents material on possible interpretations. It is confused on much of the prophetical material.

Cooper, Lamar E. *Ezekiel* (New American Commentary). Nashville: Broadman & Holman, 1994.

A premillennial, dispensational conviction orientates Cooper's view of prophecy here, and guides in his attempt to show how it fits with the rest of Scripture best (49). A good chart of dates in the book and chronology of key dates in exile and restoration appear (54-55). These precede the well-organized, lucid commentary. Views of some texts are quite sketchy, or details bypassed (cf. lying on the sides, 4:4-8; those spared in relation to both righteous and wicked dying in 21:3-4; God finding no man in 22:30; generalizing the "king" in 28:11-19). Cooper deals concisely with several texts where he sees fulfillment in a future kingdom (Ezek. 36, 37). Seeing "Gog" as a symbol of a future Babylon will be odd even to many dispensationalists. Cooper gives a good, brief survey of main views on chaps. 40-48, and seeks to reason why he favors a description of future literal millennial worship in an Israel-centered situation. Yet one can wonder amid such contention for literality in details why a literal flow of a river and a symbolical flow are mingled confusingly in Ezek. 47 (409-11), and why Cooper says that Ezekiel and John (Rev. 22) describe "the same area" (410). Despite these misleading words, he later apparently sees these as different areas—Ezekiel's on earth during the millennium, and John's in the heavenly city after the millennium (413-14).

Duguid, Iain. *Ezekiel* (NIV Application Commentary). Grand Rapids: Zondervan, 1999.

An associate professor of OT, Westminster Theological Seminary (Calif.), did these 568 pp. combining explanation with application. He is amillennial on long-range prophecy. Some remarks cause more problems than they resolve, an example being in the forty days/years lying down (Ezek. 4) somehow representing the exile which was 70 years (90). Death for the disobedient in Chap. 18 seems to be "death" in exile (237), but the righteous being spared is not reconciled with the righteous marked for safety in Chap. 9, yet righteous along with wicked going down before the invader in 21:3, 4. One is left unsure how certain descriptions in Chap. 28 can reasonably fit Tyre's king, i.e. being in "Eden" and being an "anointed cherub." Seeming outright acknowledgment of "future" restoration for Israel (it sounds literal, 414-15) poses a question not answered about when/how. The commentary elsewhere puts it not in a future millennium but in the new heavens and new earth (409). What of 36:38? Duguid sees no literal future of the details in Chaps. 40-48 but symbolic ideas, "a view of heaven from halfway there" (479), Christ Himself as the new temple, the many details of sacrifice speaking only of His sacrifice (481-83). Some will herald this, but others will feel that the commentator makes claims he could not reasonably justify with a natural hermeneutic.

Dyer, Charles. "Ezekiel," in *Bible Knowledge Commentary*, ed. John F. Walvoord and Roy B. Zuck. Volume I. Wheaton: Victor Books, 1983.

Dyer surveys well, mixing synopsis with detail, hitting problem areas competently and offering considerable help on much in the book from a conservative, dispensational stance. He is often quite worthwhile in passages about a future for Israel, on history, background, and theology. Even some dispensationalists will disagree with his case for the northern invader of Ezekiel 38 coming within the tribulation period, and his reasoning which is not always well-informed about other views and how they can answer him (cf. Alexander on Ezekiel, for example). Much in Chapters 40ff. is helpful, and he has some well-done charts of the temple, altar, division of the land to portions of Israel, etc.

Eichrodt, Walther. *Ezekiel, A Commentary*. Philadelphia: Westminster Press, 1970.

Mildly liberal, this recent work has the results of a lifetime of study finished in Eichrodt's old age. In many places his discussions are very full and helpful, as in the lengthy introduction and on a verse by verse basis involving background, word meanings, and the like. Though the work does not have a system of understanding prophecy consistently with the premillennial view, it does have an excellent diagram sketch visualizing the lay-out of the temple the Lord shows Ezekiel (chapters 40-46).

Ellison, H. L. *Ezekiel: The Man and His Message*. Grand Rapids: Eerdmans, 1956.

This is a brief work of only 144 pages, but it is thought provoking. Ellison views 28:11-19 (and Isaiah 14:4-23) as not speaking of the fall of Satan as many believe. He interprets the revolt of Gog in chapters 38-39 as occurring at the end of the millennium in Revelation 20:7-11, as does Erich Sauer in *From Eternity to Eternity* (p. 134). He also takes chapters 40-48 as allegory and rejects the view of a re-establishing of a literal temple and sacrifices during the millennium. Yet he devotes only eight pages to these nine chapters. Ellison is also contributor of I and II Kings and I and II Chronicles in the *New Bible Commentary*.

Enns, Paul. *Ezekiel* (Bible Study Commentary). Grand Rapids: Zondervan, 1986. 199 pp.

As in his books in this series on Joshua, Judges and Ruth, Enns provides an excellent survey as a conservative, here developing a dispensational stance for a future for Israel in the land of Palestine. He explains many details well, provides good synopses of sections, and often supplies reasons for his views. He believes the invader in Ezekiel 38 comes in the middle of the tribulation period, as J. Dwight Pentecost argues in *Things to Come*. Good argumentation is used for seeing the temple in Ezekiel 40ff. as literal in Palestine after the Second Advent. He handles verses in an attempt to answer criticism on a dispensational view, gives good charts on temple, altar, land area, etc. and distinguishes the river in Chapter 47 from that in the New Jerusalem (p. 194).

Fairbairn, Patrick, 1838-1912. *An Exposition of Ezekiel.* **Grand Rapids: Zondervan, 1960.**

This amillennial work is quite old but shows the student how a man of that persuasion dealt with the great prophetical portions like chaps. 34-48.

Feinberg, Charles L. *The Prophecy of Ezekiel.* **Chicago: Moody Press, 1969.**

This treatment of the book is very helpful from the premillennial dispensational viewpoint. The author grapples with most of the problems and is lucid in his development of the argument. The fact that he has a consistent system of prophecy relating to the Messiah and his kingdom, whereas many commentators do not, really shows up in his insistence on a literal understanding of chaps. 40-48. In addition to this commentary, one should also read his paper delivered at the Jerusalem Conference on Biblical Prophecy, 1971, "The Rebuilding of the Temple", printed in *Prophecy in the Making*, Editor Carl F. H. Henry, published by Creation House, Carol Stream, Illinois.

Fisch, S. *Ezekiel* **(Soncino Books of the Bible). Bournemouth: Soncino, 1950.**

This is a verse by verse study based on the Hebrew which is printed at the top of each page. It shows how a Jewish scholar handles the text, and is one of the better volumes in this series.

Greenberg, Moshe. *Ezekiel 1-20 and Ezekiel 21-37* **(Anchor Bible). Garden /City, NJ: Doubleday, 1983, 1997.**

A Jewish scholar's translation and detailed exegesis done in the belief that we have Ezekiel's material. Greenberg has invested much labor to explain the text, not frequently offer his own arbitrary and unconvincing speculations of what is in view in place of the text, as Brownlee does (cf. above). The work can be quite user unfriendly in its sequence, giving bits and pieces of verses, then comments later in broader detail, not explaining the significance of a phrase in verse by verse details, then asking readers to "See Structure and Themes for a discussion," and not seeming to get to a discussion there (as on 21:8). Greenberg gives much meticulously on scraps of information, but in this mass can leave a reader groping for things put together in a broad picture. One must ransack to find clues. Greenberg takes the prince and king in Ezek. 28 to be the ruler of Tyre, and sees a future permanent restoration of Israel to the literal land in Chap. 36 based on God's honor (II, 735, 737-38), but never dispels fuzziness of when and how this realistically will come to pass. Most help, coming only now and then, is primarily for scholars and will be in delving into verses for certain details.

Hulinger, Jerry M. *A Proposed Solution to the Problem of Animal Sacrifices in Ezekiel 40-48.* **Doctoral dissertation, Dallas Theological Seminary, Dallas, TX, 1993a. UMI Diss. Service, 1994, 300 N. Zeeb Rd., Ann Arbor, MI 48106 (1-800-521-0600).**

A dispensationalist proposes that the sacrifices will resume during the future earthly millennial kingdom, simultaneously with existence of the New Covenant. He surveys views and argues that sacrifices will be necessary when the divine presence is resident among humans, this to deal with the contageous nature of uncleanness lest God withdraw and consume mankind. He reasons that this reconciles with Heb. 9-10 seeing Christ's work operating in a different sphere and for different purposes than animal sacrifices, the latter for internal cleansing of the conscience, cleansing of the heavenly sanctuary, and eternal salvation. Even many dispensationalists will not concur with some of the ideas above. Much of what is claimed as necessary seems hard to justify with compelling Scripture, and needs more convincing evidence.

Keil, C. F. *The Prophecies of Ezekiel*. 2 volumes. Grand Rapids: Eerdmans, 1950.

Valuable from the standpoint of the Hebrew text. Deals with problems verse-by-verse. Usually very helpful from an amillennial viewpoint.

Price, Randall. *The Coming Last Days Temple*. Eugene, OR: Harvest House Publishers, 1999.

One meets with a 732-pp. pb by a Ph. D in mid-East studies, University of Texas in relation to Ezekiel 40-48 (cf. also Hulinger). Price refers to sentiments to rebuild a temple, and argues for a future literal rebuilt structure in the tribulation period before Christ's Second Advent, also one in the millennium connected with an Israelite regathering to Palestine. Part of the argument focuses on the motif for such a temple, the history of the interest, problems that need to be overcome, and how animal sacrifices as in Ezek. 40-46 can be meaningful. Price does not favor the more usual dispensational view that the sacrifices are "memorial" in retrospection to Christ's cross, rather he argues that the literal offerings make an atonement related to cleansing ritual uncleanness so that sinful worshippers can approach the present, holy God (554-55). He never seems to show convincingly why Christ's sacrifice would not suffice, or prove persuasively that his theory has to be necessary under the New Covenant in which believers are freed from all things (Acts 13:38-39). His logic is that Christ's literal presence among His people requires animal sacrifices; one wonders, if so, why God's intimate presence would be approachable in the eternal state (Rev. 22:3-5) on the basis of Christ's one sacrifice, not needing animal offerings. Much of the rationale will not prove enough of what needs proving even to normal dispensationalists, as well as to others (cf. 554-57). Price also teamed with Thomas Ice to write another book, *Ready to Rebuild: The Imminent Plan to Rebuild the Last Days Temple* (Harvest House, 1992). A further work is by J. W. Schmitt and J. C. Laney, *Messiah's Coming Temple. Ezekiel's Prophetic Vision of the Future Temple* (Grand Rapids: Kregel, 1997). This latter book argues for a literal realization of details in Ezek. 40-48 in relation to a literal regathering of Israel, and defends the view in comparison with other views (a mere ideal, allegorical fulfillment today or in the New Jerusalem, etc.). Schmitt and Laney answer objections to such a view, and reason its plausibility (as do Alexander, Cooper, Enns, Feinberg, etc.).

Tatford, Frederick. *Dead Bones Live: An Exposition of the Prophecy of Ezekiel*. Eastbourne, Sussex: Prophetic Witness Publishing House, 1977.

A prolific writer (ca. 50 titles) on a lay-person's level, who has specialized in prophetic books, authored this premillennial study. He argues for connecting the Palestinian invader of chapters 38, 39 with the Gog-Magog battle (Revelation 20) at the climax of the millennium, a thousand years after the Second Advent. He sees a physical return of Jews to Palestine, and sees Ezekiel 37 as predicting both this and a spiritual revitalizing of the nation. The temple of chapters 40-46 is, to him, a literal structure of the future millennium with animal sacrifices literally offered as "visible reminders" of Christ's death for atonement (p. 258). The work is 275 pp.

Taylor, John B. *Ezekiel, An Introduction and Commentary*. Downers Grove, IL: Intervarsity Press, 1969.

This evangelical, amillennial viewpoint is often quite excellent in chapters 1-24 in explaining verses. Especially helpful are the introduction, comments on some problem verses, and sketches such as those of the altar of burnt offering and the temple lay-out (chapters 40-46). On prophecy in Ezekiel 34-48, one finds far less meaningful understanding.

Wevers, John W. *Ezekiel* (New Century B. C.). Grand Rapids: Eerdmans, 1969.

A liberal lecturer on Old Testament and Near Eastern Studies at Princeton and the University of Toronto looks at Ezekiel from the perspective of Form Criticism and Tradition-History analysis. The English text is the RSV. Works listed at the outset are by liberal writers and rather heavy on the German side. Wevers accepts a 593-71 and following dating for the prophecies and the traditional belief that originally Ezekiel wrote near Babylon, despite much attack on this. To him, however, Pelatiah's death (11:13) is not a historical occurrence but only part of a vision (p. 25). Wevers very frequently picks and chooses what in his opinion are additions to the book by later readers on subjective, arbitrary reasoning that these are somehow at variance with some statement in the original book (cf. pp. 27, 37). The smaller type in the commentary is not easy on the eyes. His continual theorizing about different layers of tradition at different dates is a feature of the work, and the subjectivism is strong, giving more his opinion than responsible commentary on the prophetic message. The lack of clarity in many places as well as the high degree of arbitrary personal theories often work against the usefulness of this book.

Zimmerli, Walther. *A Commentary on the Book of the Prophet Ezekiel*. 2 vols. (Hermeneia). Translated by Ronald E. Clements. Philadelphia: Fortress Press, 1979.

A monumental critical study of Ezekiel showing a very broad acquaintance with scholarly works ancient and modern along critical lines. The work appeared in the German in 1969. The bibliography is 27 pp. He offers many good insights into the Hebrew, and cites other scholars in support of his own convictions or for other views. Penetrating evangelical students, though perceptive of Zimmerli's naturalistic bent which shows up at many a point, can glean much that they can turn to profit (more so in chs. 1-24) in explaining the book with precision more attuned to the Hebrew. Volume I on Chapters 1-24 (1979) was followed by Volume II completing the book (1983) in the Hermeneia series. The two total to 1,115 pp. Zimmerli's is a form-critical work that takes the place of G. A. Cooke's ICC book in exhaustive probing of facets thought to be of critical and textual relevance. The student dealing with the Hebrew in detail will not want to bypass such a work on the text, exegesis, philology, problems of a technical nature and views on them. On many matters he can expect to meet with liberal thinking, but he will mine out much that is of high value if he is patient and discerning.

XXI. DANIEL

Anderson, Sir Robert. *The Coming Prince.* **London: Hodder and Stoughton, 1909.**

The premillennial author presents a detailed work on the 70 weeks of Daniel 9. In this popular treatment he reckons the chronology of the first sixty-nine weeks from the decree of Artaxerxes (Nehemiah 2) to rebuild Jerusalem to the triumphal entry of Christ (Luke 19). He figures the exact number of days involved in 483 prophetic years which he believes would contain 360 days each, not 365 as Julian years. In his reckoning, the sixty-nine weeks end in A. D. 32 which poses a problem in light of more accepted views today that Christ died in A. D. 30 or 33.

Baldwin, Joyce. *Daniel, An Introduction and Commentary* **(Tyndale Old Testament Commentary). Downers Grove: 1VP, 1978.**

The main contribution of this brief work is in the many references to literature in Baldwin's sometimes broad reading and awareness. Baldwin is also helpful in referring at times back and forth from liberal to conservative views (cf. on resurrection, 12:2), so that the reader sees the difference in interpretative systems. One is disappointed in what she does (or fails to do) with some texts, such as 7:12, "the rest of the beasts." Cf. by comparison Leon Wood. Baldwin's work seems to lack a grasp of eschatological details whereas Walvoord, Wood etc. are more clear-cut in a consistent system they can verify in a meaningful way from Scripture.

Boutflower, Charles. *In and Around the Book of Daniel.* **London. S. P. C. K., 1923.**

The author, a postmillennialist, presents more historical background and deals adequately with more critical problems than many writers on Daniel. He defends the book against various attacks. This book is valuable, though it is not a commentary per se.

Calvin, John. *Daniel* **(Geneva Series). Carlisle, PA: Banner of Truth Trust, 1986rp. 409 pp.**

This work appeared first in Latin in 1561. The reader will find much judicious comment with spiritual perception on the character of Daniel. The prophetical view Calvin advocates is amillennial, so one will see how he explains and defends that perspective on such passages as Daniel 2, 7, 9, 11, and 12.

Campbell, Donald K. *Daniel, God's Man in a Secular Society.* **Grand Rapids: Discovery House, 1988. Formerly** *Daniel, Recorder of Dreams.* **Wheaton: Victor Books, 1977.**

A popular, brief premillennial exposition of Daniel by an expositor who is a master of synthesis. Campbell taught Bible exposition at Dallas Seminary for many years. He illustrates vividly and gears the work for lay people.

Collins, John. *A Commentary on the Book of Daniel* **(Hermeneia). Minneapolis: Fortress, 1993.**

Massive in exegesis, this assumes a Maccabean date and prophecy as not foretelling but speaking of events known already to have occurred. Collins also holds that details in Dan. 1-6 are confused (26). Readers meet with many mere opinions of unbelief, such as the comment on 1:8 that vv. 8-21 originally related only to Daniel; his three friends were falsely inserted into the story by a redactor (141). Collins feels the writer of the Bible book is mistaken in conclusions, for example in Dan. 1 (145-46). The work verse by verse will at times make advanced students, also teachers, be aware of critical theory and views on points, and many details help on word meaning, grammar, etc. For most evangelical teachers and pastors, as well as for students and lay readers, positive works committed to the integrity of passages offer far better benefit along more reasonable lines.

Contesse, Peter and John Ellington. *A Handbook on the Book of Daniel.* **NY: United Bible Societies, 1993.**

Here is a verse by verse effort to render meaning into English and explain details as an aid to missionary translators for various linquistic groups. At times this results in very good information, at others the turns given to words do not convey a proper idea. For example, in 7:24 the ten horns (kings) are seen as ruling consecutively, succeeding one another rather than rightly as existing at the same time as the eleventh horn (king), the "little horn" (198). Then the work regards details of three kings falling as fulfilled in 175-164 B. C. (199), and details of the seventy sevens in 9:25-27 are all viewed as fulfilled up through ca. 167 B. C., as many liberals have held. This reviewer sees much that is reliable in the work, but also much that is misleading.

Criswell, W. A. *Expository Sermons on the Book of Daniel.* **4 volumes. Grand Rapids: Zondervan, 1972.**

The volumes in this series involve Criswell's preaching through Daniel at the First Baptist Church, Dallas, Texas. The first volume is particularly helpful on introductory issues and provides a popular yet competent answer to critics who have dated Daniel late, denied certain statements of the book, etc. Unlike many Southern Baptists, he firmly teaches a premillennial, dispensational view (cf. also his works on Matthew and Revelation). Criswell has fairly normative dispensational views on most passages but leaves the impression that "Ancient of Days" and "Son of Man" in Chapter 7 are both the preincarnate Christ, rather than God the Father and Christ the Son as evangelicals typically hold. The volumes have many practically stimulating statements, but the exposition is sweeping, not detailed.

Culver, Robert. *Daniel and the Latter Days.* **Westwood, NJ: Revell, 1954.**

In a very systematic and thorough way, the author delves into Daniel to compare the amillennial, premillennial and postmillennial interpretations. He defends the premillennial view and presents several arguments to show that it is superior. It is a penetrating work and very valuable to have. In an appendix, he gives seven arguments in support of his view that the new heavens and new earth will come at the beginning of the millennium and not at the end. Many will disagree that the Bible supports this idea.

Davies, P. R. *Daniel* **(Old Testament Guides). Sheffield, England: JS Old Testament Press, 1985. 133 pp.**

Here is typical liberal late-dating in the time of Antiochus Epiphanies. Davies does not believe the book deals with visions of Daniel in the sixth century B. C. He surveys works he esteems on important critical aspects (these are late-daters too) and makes no serious effort to discuss conservative arguments. Rather, he sees it as "trivial to deal with such protests on their logic, here."

Dougherty, R. P. Nabonidus and Belshazzar: A Study of the Closing Events of the Neo-Babylonian Empire. New Haven, CT: Yale, 1929.

This work is very helpful in relation to the problem about the reference to Belshazzar as king of Babylon in Daniel 4-5. Scholars had long denied that there was a Belshazzar and had claimed that the Bible was in error until fairly recent times when evidence was found to support the reign of a Belshazzar. Dougherty cites evidence including ancient inscriptions which have come to light, showing that there was a co-regency of Nabonidus and Belshazzar and that Nabonidus entrusted the throne at Babylon to his son Belshazzar during part of the time.

Feinberg, Charles L. *Daniel, The Man and His Visions*. Chappaqua, NY: Christian Herald Books, 1981.

A quick-moving, simple dispensational work aimed at laymen by an astute Hebrew Christian scholar who has taught more than forty years, been Dean of Talbot Seminary, and authored many books. Usually the work does not take up problem areas in verses (except some aspects of more obvious ones, at times, as "Son of Man" in 7:13, 14, = Jesus Christ, using mostly New Testament evidence, and the first sixty-nine "weeks" in 9:25, 26 come to A. D. 32, he says).

Ford, Desmond. *Daniel*. Nashville: Southern Publishing Association, 1978. Foreword by F. F. Bruce.

A leading man in new emphases within the Seventh Day Adventist circles shows how a SDA scholar who gained his Ph. D. under Bruce deals with eschatological details here. He tries to combine what he feels are the best elements in Preterism, idealism, historicalism and futurism but regards much of the prophecy as related to the ultimate consummation (69-70). He shows awareness of some problems and solutions (as 1:1, 2) but is very brief on some verses (1:17-20; 2:4; 2:36-45 verse by verse; ch. 6; 7:13, 14, sparse on proof for identity of the Son of Man as Messiah, and of the kingdom; 7:7, vague on the ten horns, etc.). On p. 151 he finds the "little horn" of ch. 7 in the system of church and state in medieval times, and relates "a time, times, and half a time" to 3 1/2 prophetic years (1260 actual years) from A. D. 537 to 1798, a year-day view, citing H. G. Guinness, *Romanism and the Reformation*, pp. 41-43. His "proof" for his little horn theory is unfortunate. The text of Daniel 7 itself puts the horn and the ten horns in the final phase of the fourth empire, that is, in the time that flows right into the future judgment (7:9-14). And Revelation 19 has the Beast of Revelation 13:1-10 on earth at the Second Coming of Christ, who is the Son of Man receiving the kingdom in Daniel 7:13-14. Ford wants the little horn to mean the Antichrist of the centuries and the end-time too, as if it did not refer to one specific person at one particular time. His identification of the "little horn" in chapter 8 as Antichrist also raises questions. Ford feels the 2,300 days of 8:14 represent years from 457 B. C. to A. D. 1844. "In 1844 began the cleansing of the sanctuary. . . " (p. 189). He regards 9:24-27 as speaking of 490 years from 457 to A. D. 33, and believes this is the first segment of 2,300 years which he sees in 8:14 (p. 207). He cites SDA writers such as Wm. Miller and Ellen White (p. 243). He has some good material on Antiochus in 11:21-35, and believes Antichrist is in view in

11:36-45. His is a good effort to look at Daniel from a SDA perspective and a year-day system.

Though the above work is now out of print, the best that was in it and some added parts are in *Daniel & The Coming King* (Newcastle, CA: Desmond Ford Publications, 7955 Bullard Dr., Newcastle, CA 95658).

Fyall, Robert. *Daniel* (Focus on the Bible Commentaries). Geanies House, Fearn, Ross-shire, Scotland, 1988.

This OT lecturer at St. John's College, Durham, Scotland, lists the biography he mainly used (9), studded with liberal and amillennial works, and no premillennial efforts. Fyall often points out valuable principles for life as on 1:8. Comments survey chapters and explain main points, often doing this well even if concisely. On prophecy, the writing gets nebulous and provides no grappling or light to explain key matters, such as the future thrust of the fourth empire in Dan. 2 (41). On 7:15ff., Fyall shows his amillennial bent by having the ten horns represent the whole of human history, and suggesting other thoughts that only work confusion (110-11). He is hit or miss on offering helps on customs, helping on the shape of a furnace (53), but silent about what a lions' den looked like (90). Daniel's praying in Chap. 9 is used for good lessons. Daniel 11:36-39 is said to be about Antiochus, with v. 39 possibly moving on to a later leader (179). The book is for the most part only worth the time for occasional principles, and has little light on a defensible far prophetical picture.

Gaebelein, Arno C. *The Prophet Daniel*. NY: Our Hope Magazine, 1911.

Dividing the book of Daniel according to the languages in the original text, the writer gives a brief yet sometimes helpful survey of a dispensational interpretation.

Gangel, Kenneth. *Daniel* (Holman OT Commentary). Nashville: Broadman & Holman, 2001.

A light, cursory exposition is along popular and premillennial lines, using a lot of long quotes and doing little more than outline prophetical matters. But it has some good principles for application. For the most part, one would derive more benefit from various works that offer so much more than the appeal of packaging.

Goldingay, John E. *Daniel* (Word Biblical Commentary). Dallas: Word Books, 1989. 351 pp.

Immense research in books and journals has gone into this. It has excellent footnote details, many word studies, and a long, learned discussion on introductory matters that is quite informative for many. It summarizes the history of interpreting Daniel from the LXX to Goldingay's work. Goldingay favors a second century date and sees much fulfillment of prophecy in Maccabean times; it is history written after things happen. He feels the author stretches history at times, and favors saying that the fourth empire in Daniel 7 is an elephant. Often numbers are symbolical. The work has much to offer on literature and views in many cases but is not of reliable value in handling prophecy, in the minds of premillennialists.

Jerome. *Jerome's Commentary on Daniel.* **Translated by Gleason L. Archer, Jr. Grand Rapids: Baker, 1977, rp of 1958 translation.**

This publisher reproduces what Wilbur Smith called in its introduction "The most important single work produced by the Church Fathers on any of the prophetic writings of the Old Testament . . . ." Jerome wrote in Latin, and Archer's English translation is done well. One value of the work is Jerome's citation of and answer to Porphyry's famous argument against the date and authorship by Daniel.

Leupold, H. C. *Exposition of Daniel.* **Columbus: Wartburg, 1949.**

This amillennial work is quite detailed and helpful in showing the amillennial type of approach to the crucial prophecies, The work by Young, however, is better.

Longman, Tremper III. *Daniel* **(NIV Application Commentary). Grand Rapids: Zondervan, 1999.**

A Westmont College professor posits sixth century B. C. material in Daniel, but his work is soft toward late-daters, even toward one who denies the possibility of supernatural prophecy in Dan. 7-12 (23). Longman seeks to resolve alleged inaccuracies as in 1:1-2 (43), difficult phrases such as "ten times better" in 1:20 (54), usually meeting them head-on in a substantial commentary of 313 pp. He is of the opinion in Dan. 7 that the four beasts represent an unspecified number of evil kingdoms that will succeed one another from the exile to Christ's future coming (190). Many principles help readers in application, but too often the comments on prophecy mislead or leave uncertainty, not help one have a sound view.

Lucas, Ernest C. *Daniel* **(Apollos Old Testament Commentary). Downers Grove, IL: IVP, 2002.**

Cf. comments on McConville (Deut.). This 359-pager reflects immensely wide reading among critical scholars of a non-evangelical world, and sees stories here as mingling what historically happened this way, and fiction (22). Much of what evangelicals normally would see as long-range prophecy is put within the second-century B. C. time of Antiochus IV, even the little horn and other kings of Dan. 7, all details even of 11:36ff. (40; 193, etc.). Lucas enters into much discussion of non-premillennial views, and those of the latter persuasion will feel that their explanations are far more natural in using hermeneutical principles and understanding long-range prophecy. For that matter, many amillennialists also will reject Lucas' second-century focus. Daniel Block's plug on the inside back cover that the series is by "the finest evangelical scholars" will, at least in this commentary, be thought an astounding misconception by many evangelicals due to a number of claims. The one like a son of man (7:13-14) is collective for the saints, Lucas says (187, 200). To him, the book of Daniel "seems devoid of any messianic hope as usually understood" (185). Lucas holds that the "anointed ones" of 9:25-26 have "nothing to suggest that either of them is the Davidic Messiah of later Judaism" (185). The concept "at that time" (12:1) refers to the period of Antiochus, seen to the very end of Chap. 11 (293-94). In the end bibliography, J. Whitcomb is the only premillennialist listed (not detailed works of S. Miller, J. Walvoord, or L. Wood). Lucas rejects premillennial views or does not mention them. He says, for example on the 1,290 and 1,335 days in 12:11-12, that he has no satisfactory explanation. The ten days of 1:12 is a round number (33). It is disconcerting to find some detail skipped, for instance "ten times smarter" (1:20), "seven times hotter" (3:19), and the nature of the fiery furnace in Chap. 3. The work will help readers see in what they may regard as anything but truly evangelical how a writer construes details that they can feel make much more defensible sense in other interpretations outside the perspective that Lucas thinks convincing.

MacArthur, John F., Jr. *The Future of Israel (Daniel 9:20-12:13).* **Chicago: Moody, 1991.**

A brief premillennial dispensational series on the verses by one of America's most able expository pastors.

McClain, Alva J. *Daniel's Prophecy of the Seventy Weeks.* **Grand Rapids: Zondervan, 1940.**

This booklet is a concise presentation of the view taken by Sir Robert Anderson. McClain systematizes the view so that it is easy to follow the line of thought.

Miller, Stephen R. *Daniel* **(New American Commentary). Nashville: Broadman & Holman, 1994.**

Miller provides a careful premillennial, dispensational explanation on details, such as on Dan. 2, 7, and 11-12. His introduction upholds Daniel in the sixth century B. C. as author, and reviews the history of criticism, answering main reasons some use for a second century date, among other things. In the commentary, he offers competent light on many problems, and shows he is aware of views, often giving copious reasons for his own. He describes what the fiery furnace looked like (115), and has good discussions on such details as the Son of Man (7:13-14), and a defense of a premillennial view in 7:15ff, and a gap before the seventieth seven in 9:27 with the seven coming right before Christ's Second Advent. Along premillennial lines it ranks close to Leon Wood's work, and on discussing critical viewpoints offers more.

Montgomery, James A. *A Critical and Exegetical Commentary on the Book of Daniel* **(ICC). Edinburgh: T. & T. Clark, 1964.**

This is a detailed study of the text from a critical standpoint, and is, in this regard, very helpful to the serious student who is dealing with problems. Often the work is in a dense fog on prophetical positions, fostering confusion.

Newell, Philip. *Daniel, The Man Greatly Beloved and His Prophecies.* **Chicago: Moody, 1962.**

A dispensational exposition based upon an expanded Bible correspondence course. It is one of the better-known older dispensational works.

Olyott, Stuart. *Dare to Stand Alone* **(Welwyn Commentary). Faverdale North, Darlington, Eng.: Evangelical Press, 1982.**

One meets a quite clear, simple evangelical book showing ready relevancy to excite lay people and students. Olyott offers many principles to apply. To a good degree he has helpful interpretation, but at times poor explanations, for instance when he sees the kingdom God sets up in Dan. 2 as already set up today (35), spiritual and not in any sense political (Daniel refers to one that is both of these in harmony, under Christ, realized at

His Second Coming). Olyott appeals to proof-texts, John 18:36 and Luke 17:21, both of which he is misusing. He denies that the ten horns in Dan. 7 refer to ten literal kings, and has almost unbelievable denial of literal details elsewhere in chap. 7. He appears uninformed about premillennial explanations that seem far more meaningful (95-96). He sees the Messiah's cutting off (Dan. 9) as during the seventieth "seven," with all fulfilled by A. D. 70 (124-25).

Pentecost, J. Dwight. *Daniel* (Bible Knowledge Commentary, I), ed. John F. Walvoord and Roy B. Zuck. Wheaton, IL: Victor Books, 1983-1985.

A premillennial dispensational survey by the long-time Professor of Bible Exposition at Dallas Theological Seminary. Pentecost discusses many of the highlights, explains quite a lot, and shows a good grasp on many of the problems, along with clear writing. Even if succinct, the work is worth expositors' consulting the attempt to show the reasonableness of a literal view relating to Israel's prophetic future, as in Dan. 7:15ff, 9:24-27, and 11:36—12:13.

Phillips, John and Jerry Vines. *Exploring the Book of Daniel*. Neptune, NJ: Loizeaux Brothers, 1990. 279 pp.

Dispensational exposition with clarity of interpretation and practical application to stimulate thought about relevance today. It is not deep in wrestling with issues. One is better off with Miller, Pentecost, Walvoord, and Wood along dispensational lines.

Porteous, Norman. *Daniel, A Commentary*. Philadelphia: Westminster, 1965.

This is a liberally-oriented work as is plain when Porteous places all the details of Daniel 2, 7 in Maccabean times. He assumes rather than proves a second-century date. His commentary is a brief example of one liberal scholar's thinking.

Pusey, Edward B. *Daniel the Prophet*. NY: Funk &Wagnalls, 1885.

The author was the Regius Professor of Hebrew at Oxford who, though trained under German critics, became a solid conservative. He was amillennial in prophecy. His greatest contribution is in historical backgrounds. On the key prophetical portions he often allegorizes.

Russell, D. S. *Daniel* (The Daily Bible Study Series). Philadelphia. Westminster, 1981.

This is by the famous author of *The Method and Message of Jewish Apocalyptic* (1964), later General Secretary of the Baptist Union of Great Britain. The series purports to have experts in their field write in a form that will appeal to the general public. Russell dates Daniel ca. 165 B. C., using arguments such as vocabulary and style. These have been answered well in favor of a 6th century date by such men as Edwin Yamauchi, *Greece and Babylon*. Yet there is much elucidation from careful scholarship even for evangelicals whose studies lead them to different conclusions. Russell in typical liberal fashion sees the parts of the image as depicting Neo-Babylon, Media, Persia and Greece. The fulfillment of God's Kingdom is not in a far off kingdom (that, says Russell, is strained and fanciful exegesis), but in the writer's own time. His hopes were not realized, for the kingdom did not come literally in the way he expected in his day (p. 54). Yet Russell does believe in the New Testament hope of the kingdom at the end of history. On

12:2, he says wrongly that the earlier Hebrews had no belief in individual life beyond the grave (p. 218). While the work often does not offer reliable help that understands the writer's expectation in the futuristic way the writer most naturally seems to mean it, there is much to open up vividly many of the verses on other details. The work is helpful if one wants to see how a liberal mind deals with what is said.

Stevens, W. C. *The Book of Daniel*. NY: Revell, 1918.

There is a good tracing of the thematic development here as Stevens covers the entire book chapter by chapter and lays out his material systematically. He points out many spiritual truths in Daniel's prayer life and non-compromise. It is a refreshing commentary. Most of what he says is good material,

Tatford, Frederick A. *The Climax of the Ages*. London: Marshall, Morgan & Scott, 1953.

As a premillennial and dispensational book, this gives a somewhat helpful discussion of several problems and goes into more detail on key passages than most dispensational works. It can take the place of several of the other dispensational works combined because it is fuller in its discussion. The higher critics, in their reviews, regard the book as "imperfectly acquainted with scholarly work" (See H. H. Rowley, *Eleven Years of Bible Bibliography*, p. 677). Tatford makes several statements in which he dismisses the beliefs of S. R. Driver and other critics as without substance, and this naturally is not popular with their group. Miller, Pentecost, Walvoord and Wood are all better.

Tregelles, Samuel P. *Remarks on the Prophetic Visions in the Book of Daniel*. London: The Sovereign Grace Advent Testimony, 1965. Reprint of work which originally appeared in 1845.

The author deals with several critical problems well and devotes fine treatment to the key chapters. He takes the view that the "little horn" of chapter 7 is the same as the "little horn" of chapter 8. He explains that while in a general way this horn can be represented as arising out of the fourth kingdom (Rome) in chapter 7, it can also be said to come more particularly out of the Grecian area in chapter 8 which was amalgamated into the fourth kingdom and became a part of it. For the view that the "little horns" must be distinguished, see E. J. Young, Appendix V.

Walvoord, John F. *Daniel, The Key to Prophetic Revelation*. Chicago: Moody, 1971.

In the opinion of the reviewer, this, Stephen Miller's effort, and Wood's 1972 work are the finest overall commentaries of a popular nature on Daniel by premillennial dispensational scholars to date. Walvoord weaves into the work an up-to-date understanding of archaeological and historical confirmations of Daniel that offset the critics and also gives a solid reasoning for a premillennial perspective of Messianic prophecy. He very capably answers the late-daters of Daniel, argues that the four kingdoms of Daniel 2 and 7 are Babylon, Media-Persia, Greece, and Rome, and deals with most problem areas in adequate detail. Still he manages to keep the great theme of the work before the reader.

Whitcomb, John C. *Daniel* (Everyman's Bible Commentary). Chicago: Moody, 1985. 176 pp.

A dispensational survey, documenting his use of scholarly literature and mingling exegesis and devotional elements. His dispensational interpretations are fairly standard. He is, around 2002, laboring on a more detailed work on Daniel not yet published.

Whitcomb, John C. *Darius the Mede: A Study in Historical Identification.* Grand Rapids: Eerdmans, 1959.

In this specialized work, which is not a commentary, a professor formerly from Grace Theological Seminary explores the problem of the identity of the Darius in Daniel 5. It is a penetrating study and is a refreshing contrast to remarks like those of H. H. Rowley in his work *Darius the Mede*. Rowley takes an extreme position, calling the Daniel 5 statement a confusion of confused traditions. Whitcomb argues that Darius was a subordinate official placed over Babylon by Cyrus. His name was Gubaru. Whitcomb gives positive arguments for this view and answers crucial objections to it (cf. review by F. F. Bruce in The *Evangelical Quarterly*, July-Sept., 1959, pp. 176-77).

Wilson, Robert Dick. *Studies In the Book of Daniel: A Discussion of the Historical Questions*. NY: Putnam's, 1917.

This is one of the outstanding conservative defenses of historical matters in Daniel. Cf. also Edwin Yamauchi, *Greece and Babylon*.

Wood, Leon J. *A Commentary on Daniel*. Grand Rapids: Zondervan, 1972.

Wood has produced after several years a detailed verse-by-verse commentary patterned much like Keil-Delitzsch, though he argues for a premillennial dispensational viewpoint. His constant reference to Hebrew and Aramaic words and sometimes a critical discussion of them will give the work appeal to some. Yet his explanations are such that less skillfully trained students may profit from using the commentary. The introduction, word studies, references to modern-day validations of Daniel, and correlation with other Scriptures building a prophetical picture make it a very worthwhile contribution done in a competent, scholarly way.

Wood, Leon J. *Daniel, A Study Guide*. Grand Rapids: Zondervan, 1975.

A 160-pp. survey in the "Study Guide" series, much briefer than his A *Commentary on Daniel*, with a list of suggestions for further study at the end of each chapter, various charts and maps, and a brief bibliography mostly by evangelical authors. This is a knowledgeably helpful brief treatment for laymen along premillennial dispensational lines of chronology on the visions.

Young, Edward J. "Daniel," in *New Bible Commentary Revised*, edited by D. Guthrie et al. Grand Rapids: Eerdmans, 1970.

The amillennial work is quite brief (pp. 688-702), a nutshell of his regular commentary. He defends Daniel as author and answers several main problems raised against historical accuracy. He also answers late-dating critical views at key points, for example against Media, Persia and Greece as the last three empires in Daniel 2 and 7. He shows briefly how an amillennialist deals with prophecies of future tribulation and kingdom.

Young, Edward J. *Daniel's Vision of the Son of Man.* London: Tyndale, 1958.

A brief but very fine study of 7:13, 14. Young defends in detail his view that the "one like a son of man" is an individual (not corporate = the people of Israel later in 7:18, 22 etc.), specifically the Messiah who turns out to be Jesus Christ in the Gospels. He offers persuasive evidence even in the context and in Old Testament usage of phrases here such as coming on the clouds of heaven.

Young, Edward J. *The Messianic Prophecies of Daniel.* Grand Rapids: Eerdmans, 1954.

This is a solid work showing how an outstanding fairly recent amillennial scholar deals with so crucial a book on eschatology. It reveals the vital points at which he attacks dispensationalism. The commentary is very good in its verse by verse exegesis but is weak in eschatology, as shown by his treatment of Daniel 9:24-27 and the "stone" in chapter 2. He fastens upon the dispensational teaching that the kingdom of the future will be a thousand years, then argues from chapter 2 that the kingdom has to be eternal. Actually, dispensationalists are misrepresented here, for they believe in both.

XXII. MINOR PROPHETS

GENERAL WORKS

Achtemeier, Elizabeth. *Minor Prophets* I (New International Biblical Commentary). Peabody, MA: Hendrickson, 1996.

Here is a brief exposition of the first six Minor Prophets, Hosea through Micah, based on the NIV. A brief introduction precedes each biblical book. Some vagueness attends discussion on a number of verses, e. g. on Hosea 1:2 how Gomer's children were "like mother, like children" (15). The authoress offers good help on many historical matters, such as Jezreel's relation to the Jehu events (1:4-5), but lacks a definite tie-in with a unified biblical prophetic picture to relieve vague generality about when God will bless Israel. One sees this often (Hosea 2:16-23; 3:5). Joel 2:21-27 seems to be fulfilled, to her mind, in Christians now (147). Joel 3:17ff apparently points, she feels, not to a millennial time but the eternal New Jerusalem (158). The river in 3:18 just pictures God's salvation as in Rev. 22:1 (160). Unable to discern a true unity, Achtemeier argues that Amos 9:11-15 represents "the work of a later hand, some later author, exilic or post-exilic" (234), and cannot be an expectation of Amos himself. Yet one can wonder why this is valid; even she admits that as the work of a later writer the words "are a witness and a confirmation" of the Lord's good will to confirm what Amos proclaimed (235). Then why would not Amos more reasonably do that, as God used him? One gets the impression that all is generalized as fulfilled today. Another problem is that the story in Jonah is not historically written in Jonah's day but much later (her theory is in the time of Malachi, 258), and has some exaggeration (257-58). Many rightly will not agree with such claims at all.

Boice, James M. *The Minor Prophets. An Expositional Commentary.* Grand Rapids: Zondervan, 1983-86. 542 pp.

Boice has a catchy title for each chapter or section of the prophets. Pages are large with two columns and he provides much good material on the relevance then and now, lessons such as God's love, repentance, sincerity (Hosea 6), etc. If a Christian took time to read these pages and dwelt on the principles over a span of weeks or months, he could grow much by applying them. Boice at times could be more definite in specifying in what framework God will bless Israel in the future, as in Hosea 14. He can be vague, as in Joel 2:1-11 where he says the invader is neither locusts nor a human army (1,107). He can be very wordy and wander on, too, as in using Joel 2:28 as a take-off into a long discussion of clericalism. He sees Joel 2:28 fulfilled at Pentecost, yet it would help if he showed some aspects were not yet fulfilled. He is more to the point on Zechariah 14.

Bullock, C. Hassell. *An Introduction to the Old Testament Prophetic Books.* Chicago: Moody Press, 1986. 391 pp.

The author of *An Introduction to the Old Testament Poetic Books* (Moody, 1979) and *An Introduction to the Old Testament Pentateuch* (Moody, 1991) covers major and minor prophets here. He places them where he judges they fit historically, not in the canonical sequence, using three periods, Neo-Assyrian, NeoBabylonian and Persian. An introduction discusses such topics as the roots of prophecy, terms for this ministry, non-literary prophets, culture, relation of prophets to kings, and priests, ministry in social oppression, devices used (oracles, visions etc.), and others. Bullock thinks Jonah is introductory to the prophets and takes up among other aspects the views on the book (parable, history etc.), structure, message etc. His vagueness on Amos 9:13-15 does not clarify when such a future boon will occur (75-76, 82). He is more helpful on Amos the man and the structure. His discussion of views about Gomer in Hosea 1-3 offer good help. In Isaiah, H. Freeman's ordering of material seems to get at issues more forthrightly and to the point, though Bullock is very aware of views and issues in a drawn out way. A fog descends on some aspects, as Zephaniah's long-range reach of the Day of the Lord, so that the best readers can glean of when that will occur is "the gospel era" (172). Even amillennialists can concur with that generality. His same hazy non-commitment about when, specifically, the long-range realization of the kingdom will come occurs on Jeremiah 30-33 (199, 201, 211) and Ezekiel 34-48 (247). To Bullock Ezekiel's temple of chapters 40-46 is fulfilled in part in temple rebuilding of 520-516 B. C., but more fully in eschatological times; he abondons this to a misty non-commitment of just what he means (249). In Daniel he deals fairly well with key matters (281-88). He is a bit more specific in Daniel 7, saying that the little horn "may represent the Antichrist" before the Second Advent (296). The final "seven" of Daniel 9 is fulfilled at the time of Christ's Death and the temple destruction in A. D. 70, but Bullock lets the seventieth go on open-ended and commits himself to a view like that of E. J. Young (297-98). He is extremely fuzzy on convictions about Daniel 11:36-45 and 12:1-3 where he is quite general.

Calvin, John. *The Minor Prophets.* 5 volumes (Geneva series). Carlisle, PA: Banner of Truth Trust, 1986rp. 2,699 pp.

This work, published first in 1563 in the French, was also published by Eerdmans as part of *Calvin's Commentaries.* Calvin wrote the works in the 1540's. He usually devotes 1-5 pages to a verse, giving much rich, lucid explanation. He gives his judgment on problems, sometimes at length, as on God's command to Hosea to marry a wife of whoredoms (he says Hosea did this not in a literal sense but in an imaginary way, a figurative sense, a parabolic representation (1, 45). The future for Israel in Hosea 1:11 is realized in the church, amillennial fashion, under Christ the one head. In Hosea 2:18-27 fulfillment is in Christians who, when they obey God, find that brute animals are at peace with them (1, 111). Israel's return in Hosea 3:5 is fulfilled today in uniting with others who worship the one head, the greater king, Jesus Christ (1, 134). Joel 3:16ff. refers to blessing on the church, the true Israelites (11, 136). Return to the land in Amos 9:11-15 is fulfilled not literally but when people come to Christ and reign spiritually with Him, finding abundant blessings (11, 413). Calvin assigns figurative meanings in Zechariah 14. Attack on Jerusalem is attack on the church (V, 409). Christ standing on the Mount of Olives means that in trials we are to set God before our eyes and He will command deliverance from the top of the mountain (V, 411-12).

Chisholm, Robert B., Jr. *Interpreting the Minor Prophets*. Grand Rapids: Zondervan, 1990. 317 pp.

This well-informed survey is by a professor of Old Testament studies, Dallas Seminary, who wrote on Hosea and Joel in the *Bible Knowledge Commentary*. Chisholm looks broadly at each prophet's structure, message, doctrinal themes, literary and rhetorical features. After a brief survey of overall themes – sin, judgment, salvation – he takes up each prophet from Hosea to Malachi successively. On long-range prophecy he is presumably premillennial, but in several texts where one would expect a commitment, he keeps things so vague that one finds no distinct word as to when the fulfillment will come (Hosea 3, 14; Joel 3:9ff.; Zechariah 14, etc.). He surveys each book section by section with much that helps, dealing briefly with main problems. At the end of each survey of a book he sums up points of theology. He views Joel 2:1-11 as meaning a human army but is not distinct on what army and when. The work is good but general. The reader who has the BKC from Dallas Seminary would already have the books covered in greater premillennial specificity in many cases.

Cohen, A., ed. *The Twelve Prophets* (Soncino Bible). Bournemouth, Hants: Soncino, 1948. 368 pp.

Jewish scholars give the Hebrew text and the Jewish Publication Society English translation, then a commentary. Different books are treated in different depth, usually concise, general, and minimal in remarks. Many details are passed over. Occasionally one finds real help on Hebrew idioms, word meanings, and views from rabbis. In certain prophetical texts the commentators take passages as teaching a glorious future for Israel (as in Joel 3:16ff; Zechariah 14:9ff.).

Feinberg, Charles L. *The Minor Prophets*. Chicago: Moody Press, 1976.

A Jewish Christian scholar in Hebrew who taught in Old Testament at Dallas Seminary and later at Talbot Seminary, where he also was Academic Dean, did this exposition of all the minor prophets. Feinberg made biblical prophecy one of his specializations and does a good survey, being aware of interpretive problems, main views, contextual factors and correlation with other Old Testament and New Testament prophetic passages in a premillennial dispensational understanding. This is a I-volume edition of what originally was issued as 5 small volumes.

Fink, Paul. "Minor Prophets," in *Liberty Bible Commentary*, ed. Jerry Falwell et al. Nashville: Thomas Nelson, 1983.

On pages 1661-1864, Fink gives what is usually a quite helpful, concise premillennial, dispensational commentary, gives good attention to expositional problems and often mentions views and arguments. His premillennial stance is clear on such texts as Hosea 1:10, 11; 2:18-27; 3:5; Joel 3:9ff,; Amos 9:11-15; Zechariah 14.

Hailey, Homer. *A Commentary on the Minor Prophets*. Grand Rapids: Baker, 1972.

A non-technical work of 428 pp. for lay people, taking an amillennial stance on the kingdom issue: in his opinion there will not be a future kingdom for Israel after the Second Advent of Christ (cf. in this work pp. 126, 200, etc.; cf. also his commentary on the Book of Revelation).

Henderson, Ebenezer. *The Book of the Twelve Minor Prophets* (Thornapple Commentaries). Grand Rapids: Baker, 1980.

This 1858 work supplies much help on matters of the text, word meaning, resolving some problems, etc. Some have found it one of the most contributive sources in getting at what a text means.

Ironside, H. A. *Notes on the Minor Prophets*. NY: Loizeaux (n. d.).

Expository addresses with practical value to the pastor-teacher along dispensational lines.

Kaiser, Walter C., Jr. *Micah – Malachi* (The Communicator's Commentary). Dallas, TX: Word Books, 1992. 494 pp.

A careful evangelical gives contemporary outlines usable to pastors. He has occasional illustrations and serious explanation of the text. He is premillennial, as on Zechariah 14, and packs in much expositional help, relating it strategically to life. In this series Lloyd Ogilvie wrote the Hosea – Jonah section, with good practical application but not as much expertise on the text as Kaiser.

Keil, C. F. and Franz Delitzsch. *The Twelve Minor Prophets*. 2 volumes. Grand Rapids: Eerdmans, 1961.

The Hebrew exegesis is helpful verse-by-verse. See earlier comments under Old Testament sets.

Laetsch, Theodore. *The Minor Prophets*. Saint Louis: Concordia, 1956.

This is a very good amillennial commentary on the minor prophets as a whole. Laetsch deals with the text verse-by-verse, grapples with difficult phrases and explains them, uses the Hebrew extensively, and presents illuminating word studies. The lucid presentation helps make it a very interesting commentary to read. In crucial prophetical sections, his strong amillennialism appears. His weakness here is offset by his helpfulness in exegesis generally plus his good background material.

Morgan, G. Campbell. *The Minor Prophets: The Men and Their Messages.* Old Tappan, NJ: Revell, 1960. 157 pp.

Morgan wrote another book on the Minor Prophets, *Voices of the Twelve Hebrew Prophets* published in England and Scotland, examining one key verse from each prophet. In the present work he goes into some detail at times. He assigns a title to each prophet, such as "Jonah – Condemnation of Exclusiveness." Unfortunately, a complete

English translation of each book is given, taking up much space. Morgan offers an outline with points that express ideas of verses, but beyond this has space only to say something of an explanatory nature now and then. He leaps over problem verses, such as Hosea 1:2, "wife of whoredoms." He does have a brief synopsis on the message in the prophet's time and in Morgan's around 1900 A. D. Overall this is far down the line in helpfulness, despite the once great name of Morgan.

Phillips, John. *Exploring the Minor Prophets. An Expository Commentary.* **Grand Rapids: Kregel, 1999.**

A respected popular expositor on a number of biblical books here has two introductory chapters, then a chapter of about 20-30 pp. on each prophet (50 on Zech.). Several charts aid readers, and a detailed outline runs before each exposition. The exposition is in general surveys of sections, at times taking a view on a main problem. In Hosea 1:2, he feels that God had Hosea marry an immoral woman but Phillips offers no help on the moral issue. Phillips is premillennial, seeing Israel's future kingdom blessings as in the millennium after Christ's Second Coming (Hosea 3:5; Joel 3:14ff; Amos 9:15; Zeph. 3:9ff; Zech 2:10-13; 14:1-21). In Mal. 2:15 he has "one" refer to God making husband and wife into one, and in 4:5 he thinks the Elijah will be fulfilled in one of the two witnesses in Rev. 11. The work helps on broad coverage, and is quite readable for preachers, church teachers, students and lay people wanting a general devotional sweep.

Pusey, Edward B. *The Minor Prophets.* **2 volumes. Grand Rapids: Baker, 1953.**

This work originally appeared in 1860. The present publication is set up in two columns to the page with the text of the Authorized Version reproduced at the top. Scripture references, Hebrew words, and other citations are relegated to the bottom of the page. The work is detailed and analytical in nature. Introduction, background and explanation of the Hebrew are quite helpful. Pusey holds to the grammatical-historical type of interpretation until he gets into sections dealing with the future of Israel, and here Israel becomes the church in the amillennial vein.

Robinson, George L. *The Twelve Minor Prophets.* **Grand Rapids: Baker, 1976. 203 pp.**

This is a reprint of the 1926 edition (New York: Harper and Brothers). He devotes a chapter to each prophet, "Hosea the Prophet of Love," etc. The studies are terse summaries. On Hosea he lists and comments on steps in Israel's downfall and has five points on the message to men today. He packs a lot of information in and organizes it well. His word portrait of Jonah is choice (pp. 74-75), and he has interesting accounts of great fish swallowing men. Though brief, the book has frequent material a preacher can use.

Smith, George A. "The Book of the Twelve Prophets," in *The Expositor's Bible,* **Volume 4. Grand Rapids: Eerdmans, 1956rp.**

Though old this is well-written and often cited, with many good statements on spiritual truths. Users will find much that is worthwhile, and sometimes may disagree, as when he sees the Jonah account as allegorical.

Taylor, John B. *The Minor Prophets* **(Scripture Union Bible Study Books). Grand Rapids: Eerdmans, 1970. 94 pp.**

This succinct effort gets directly at issues, as in giving three views on what Gomer was when Hosea married her, and views on the woman Hosea took in 3:1. He is fuzzy on what the future of Israel will be (1:10; 2:16-23 etc.) but a bit clearer on 3:5 (p. 7; cf. p. 20). Sometimes he is clear, sometimes vaguely general, as on the heavenly signs in Joel 2. He sees Amos 9:11-15 as not fulfilled literally in such aspects as agricultural prosperity, but figuratively, as if 9:13b proves his view. Reference, he feels, is to the New Jerusalem. Strangely, he also sees Zechariah 14:20-21 as in the New Jerusalem, after describing the verses before where imperfection is evident. Often, though, his work gives the lay reader a good survey without getting bogged down.

von Orelli, Hans C. *The Twelve Minor Prophets.* **Edinburgh: T. & T. Clark, 1897. 405 pp. Reprint by Klock & Klock (Minneapolis, 1977).**

This widely-read Jewish scholar of Germany defended the integrity of the Old Testament in days of Wellhausen higher critical theory. He is exegetically skilled but has a heavy technical style that makes study slow and often not easy to follow. Still, he has much good material. Gomer, he says, was a harlot before marriage. He is vague as to when blessings for Israel in Hosea will be fulfilled. Often he deals with details but provides no synthesis to allow perspective. To a large degree it is not worth the time as there are so many better works now available.

Wood, Leon J. *The Prophets of Israel.* **Grand Rapids: Baker, 1979. 405 pp.**

This quite readable work by a premillennialist covers the overall range of Old Testament prophets, various key subjects under "Prophetism" such as what "to prophesy" means, the prophets' function, early prophets, Samuel, monarchy prophets, and writing prophets both major and minor. Wood has solid sections on Elijah and Elisha (their spiritual features, episodes, miracles). The Elisha part surveys each miracle. Some sections, as on Hosea, even discuss in some detail leading problems such as whether Gomer was tainted before marriage or became unfaithful later. But sections on the books do not delve into nearly the detail Chisholm gives. Wood does sum up the message well, has an outline on each book, and organizes much on background, character qualities and work of each prophet. He deals with each prophet in relation to the reign he fitted into. Chisholm and Freeman deal more with various problems. Cf. Hobart Freeman, *Introd. to the Old Testament Prophets*, available now only in some theological libraries.

INDIVIDUAL WORKS

Hosea

Cf. some works on a given Minor Prophet combined in commentaries on other Minor Prophets, as, for example, Garrett's work embracing Joel as well as Hosea)

Andersen, F. I. and D. N. Freedman. *Hosea: A New Translation with Introduction and Commentary* **(Anchor Bible). New York: Doubleday, 1980. 701pp.**

The student, teacher or preacher finds a lengthy introduction reviewing issues important to the book, some good exegesis, copious bibliography (pp. 82-111), and some help on doctrinal aspects. One introductory section discusses the text of Hosea competing with Job for having more unintelligible passages than any other book of the Hebrew Bible (p. 66). The authors argue that Gomer's unfaithfulness came after marriage to Hosea (69, 116 etc.), and they present data from the language to support this. They also believe that the woman in 3:1 is Gomer later on. The discussion verse by verse is ponderous and at times so detailed that only the more serious, motivated student will take the time. Most verses are made clear, but not all. Hosea 3:5 is dealt with at length, yet never with a clear view really explaining a future for Israel in any definite framework. One is lost in a haze of words, and feels the authors have no theological system on eschatology. The size and price will make this formidable to some, but it is a wealth of information in many respects. The introductory section on how Hosea has been interpreted (68-76) is a good review, for example.

Beeby, H. D. Hosea: *Grace Abounding* (International Theological Commentary). F. C. Holgren and G. A. F. Knight, editors. Grand Rapids: Eerdmans, 1989. 189 pp.

Rich in helpful analysis of the text, this work also has a good bit to offer on word study, exegesis, historical background, theological comment and devotional principles. It must, however, be read with alertness to Beeby's assumptions from critical theories that lead at times to excising verses as a redactor's additions where it is subjective opinion and not based on what many will consider convincing evidence. The work is not bad in many respects but also not truly great.

Chisholm, Robert, Jr. "Hosea" and "Joel," in *Bible Knowledge Commentary*, ed. John F. Walvoord and Roy B. Zuck. Volume 1. Wheaton: Victor Books, 1983.

Premillennial dispensational commentary based on careful study, use of sources, etc. Though concise, he shows good expertise in mingling synopsis with detailed comment and dealing with problems. His discussion of views on Hosea 1:2, for example, is compact but helpful; he favors saying Gomer became unfaithful after marriage. Passages on Israel's future are usually handled without the vagueness that abounds in many commentaries, for Chisholm is definite. On Joel 2: 1-11, he has four arguments for literal locusts and four for a human army, a view he favors (pp. 1410-11). Overall the work is of a high calibre.

Cohen, Gary G. and H. R. Vandermey. *Hosea and Amos* (Everyman's Bible Commentary). Chicago: Moody, 1981. 172 pp.

Vandermey does Hosea and Cohen Amos. Both conservatives use detailed outlines and a brief introduction. The comment on Hosea 1:2 is unclear. The writers are premillennial on Israel's future (Hosea 3:5; 14:4-9; Amos 9:11-15). Both survey fairly well. The bibliography on Amos is very general, shoddy, listing only two commentaries, both very old.

Feinberg, Charles L. *Hosea: God's Love for Israel.* NY: American Board of Missions to the Jews (n. d.).

Premillennial and dispensational in its interpretation, this work is not a verse-by-verse study but deals with the text in a survey fashion. It does grapple with. most of the problems, however, and seeks to explain Jewish culture and background. See also other books in the same series: *Joel, Amos and Obadiah* (1948); *Jonah, Micah and Nahum* (1951); *Habakkuk, Zephaniah, Haggai and Malachi* (1951); and *Zechariah: Israel's Comfort and Glory* (1952). All of these are very helpful to the expositor. Cf. his *The Minor Prophets* (under General Works), which later put this material into one work.

Garland, David. *Hosea* (Bible Study Commentary). Grand Rapids: Zondervan, 1975. 81 pp.

A conservative, he keeps a reader guessing as to what his view really is on Israel's future. He is vague in the latter half of Hosea 2 and not clear on whether the bliss is in a future millennium after the Second event or in the ultimate state. On 3:5 he sounds as if he sees the ideal, ultimate future (p. 35). However, much of the book is fairly well-done. On many of the problems he at least has a brief survey. One may not be persuaded by his judgments on 1:2. The first child is Hosea's, the next two are not.

Garrett, Duane A. *Hosea, Joel* (New American Commentary). Nashville: Broadman & Holman, 1997.

A professor at Bethel Theological Seminary wrote this 426-pp. work. On prophecy, many of his statements are couched in such words about a future for Israel that they make one uncertain about what exactly is meant. Some appear to suggest a future for Israel, others seem to see this as referring to believers in general, not in a millennium but in eternity (cf. Hosea 3:5?; Joel 3:17 [4:17]; 3:18 [4:18]). In Hosea 1:2 Garrett takes the view that God commands marriage to an immoral woman (49). Verses often are illuminated, and eight excursuses give more detail on such topics as "Hosea 11:1 and Matthew 2:15." Garrett's statement that individual predictions "are actually quite rare among the writing prophets" (221) will perplex many. The overall commentary is fair, not outstanding.

Hubbard, David A. *Hosea: An Introduction and Commentary* (Tyndale Old Testament Commentary). Downers Grove: IVP, 1989. 245 pp.

A highly readable conservative effort, often refreshing in its discussion of passages. It has sections on the broad perspective and some good verse by verse comment. The introduction, among other things, is orientating on the message of Hosea. But on prophecies, he is not clear-cut as to a long-reaching millennial fulfillment where many premillennialists will feel he could be definite.

Hubbard, David A. *With Bands of Love*. Grand Rapids: Eerdmans, 1967.

A very readable and clear study of Hosea by an evangelical scholar bringing the message home to people today. A good thought-provoker for one planning a series on Hosea.

Kidner, Derek. *Love to the Loveless*. Downers Grove: IVP, 1981.

In the Bible Speaks Today series, this work on Hosea is scholarly in a readable, practical thrust. Kidner gives "A bird's-eye view of the book" in 5 1/2 pages (137-42) that helps the reader see main thoughts quickly. Though without a numbered outline, the exposition is set off under catchy headings. Kidner favors seeing Hosea 3:5 ultimately fulfilled in what Paul predicts for literal Israel at the end of the present age in Romans 11:12, 15, 25ff. (p. 44; he is unclear on what this means). This is a brief but very competent work presented in a refreshing style by an evangelical of international repute.

Knight, G. A. F. *Hosea, God's Love* **(Torch Bible Commentary). London: SCM, 1960. 127 pp.**

Knight has a so-so work. He has a Deuteronomistic view of Old Testament books. Strangely, he asserts that Hosea 3:1 is the first time in history, chronologically, where we hear of the love of God (p. 62). He does not put everything together on Hosea 1:2 when he lists views, leaving out the view that Hosea married a woman who later proved unfaithful, the children in Chapter I were literally hers and Hosea's, but they were part of a spiritually unfaithful people. Knight discerns no messianic figure in 3:5, and discusses a future for Israel (2:16ff.) without clarifying in what framework or sense it will occur, rather all is irresponsibly fuzzy.

Mays, J. L. *Hosea: A Commentary* **(Old Testament Library). Philadelphia: Westminster, 1969. 190 pp.**

This liberal work is highly-regarded by many. Mays has detailed exegesis and comments of a theological nature for pastors and students. He holds that 1:2 means God commanded Hosea to marry a woman who already was a prostitute, but does not deal with how God could command this morally. He gives much good explanation on verses, but subjectively judges that "David their King" and "at the end of days" in 3:5 are later additions that do not fit the context (p. 60).

McComiskey, Thomas, Raymond Dillard and Jeffrey Niehaus. *Hosea, Joel, Amos* **(An Exegetical and Expository Commentary). Grand Rapids: Baker, 1992. 509 pp.**

This launched a new series of volumes on the Minor Prophets, with McComiskey editing. It is evangelical and shows expertise in exegesis, background, and sensitivity to hermeneutics, plus having a good use of recent scholarship and a fine bibliography. Its format has a textual section, then an expository part. It explains many details.

Riggs, Jack R. *Hosea's Heartbreak.* **Neptune, NJ: Loizeaux, 1983. 171 pp.**

A Cedarville College (Ohio) faculty member wrote this worthy survey, using a clear outline, discussing views and reasons on problem texts such as marrying a wife of harlotries (1:2), and helping readers see the relation of truths to life now. Riggs favors the view that Gomer did not fall into the impure physical relations until after Hosea married her and the three children were born to their union. He takes "that day" in 2:14ff. to be the future period of judgment and then the Messianic Kingdom after the Second Advent as he also believes on 3:5 (pp. 62, 67, 82). The woman in 3:1 is Gomer, after the events of Hosea 1. Riggs gives practical applications at the end of each chapter, many of which are quite arresting.

Rowley, H. H. *The Marriage of Hosea.* **Manchester, England: University Press, 1956.**

This is only a 34-page discussion, but it is good. It will be helpful to the student who seeks to plunge deeply into the problem of whether Hosea married a harlot or whether Gomer became unfaithful after the marriage (cf. Hosea 1:2).

Smith, Gary V. *Hosea, Amos, Micah* (NIV Application Commentary). Grand Rapids: Zondervan, 2001.

Smith has running summaries commenting on sections, giving his views at times on problems but without much evidence, as in his persuasion that Hosea married a prostitute (Hosea 1:2). He argues well for Amos 9:11-15 fitting after details on judgment, but is satisfied to leave Israel's blessing of the last days (Hosea 3:5; Amos 9:13-15) in vague generality, not coordinated with other OT prophecy (cf. 415); he even denies that Amos can be validly correlated with a future millennial perspective that T. Finley favors (415). One finds only a partial, limited grasp of a prophetical program that God's Word in its unity conveys distinctively for Israel, but much on application, often in very helpful ways on details that do not pertain to long-range prophecy.

Stuart, Douglas. *Hosea-Micah* (Word Biblical Commentaries). Waco, TX: Word Books, 1987. 537 pp.

This is by the Professor of Old Testament at Gordon-Conwell Theological Seminary. Conservative, he believes that Hosea wrote the book and favors chronology that E. Thiele has set forth. He has impressive bibliographies on all the books, some good notes on details in the Hebrew text, summaries to give perspectives in pericopes, and full comments with much light. In Hosea 1:2 he sees a woman tainted by spiritual unfaithfulness of Israelites, who is physically legitimate at marriage to Hosea and has three children with him. He sees Israel's blessing of 2:18-27 and 3:5 fulfilled in the church today, in amillennial fashion (pp. 61, 69, 218), for the church "has inherited the restoration promises of Hosea and the rest of the Old Testament (Galatians 3:29)" (218).

Ward, J. W. *Hosea: A Theological Commentary.* New York: Harper & Row, 1966.

This is one of the better theological studies on Hosea. Yet an evangelical will want to exercise discernment in the use of a liberal work, appraising by his own perspectives at some points.

Wolff, Hans Walter. *Hosea: A Commentary on the Prophet Hosea* (Hermeneia). Translated by Gary Stansell. Philadelphia: Fortress Press, 1974.

Wolff is an Old Testament scholar at the University of Heidelberg. His well-informed exegetical comments provide considerable help usually, as do the sometimes substantial footnotes and excursuses such as on the Valley of Achor (pp. 42, 43). A bibliography appears for each section. The work, technically critical in its purpose, is for the more seriously equipped student.

Joel

Allen, Leslie C. *The Books of Joel, Obadiah, Jonah and Micah* (NICOT). Grand Rapids: Eerdmans, 1976.

The author holds that Joel is late pre-exilic or early post exilic, Obadiah is from the early postexilic times. Jonah is a tale perhaps devised by wisdom teachers of the fifth or fourth century B. C. and not by Jonah. Micah is from ca. 701 B. C. The author was lecturer in

Old Testament language and exegesis at London Bible College and now is at Fuller Theological Seminary. He has rather thorough word studies and a discussion of many issues, e. g. the relationship of Joel 2:28ff. with Acts 2 and with final times, and Joel 2:32a with Romans 10:13 (pp. 97-105). He shows good awareness of recent scholarly literature on his subjects, but many will not agree with some of his views, such as his suggestion that Jonah is simply a tale made by wisdom writers to convey a message (see p. 191).

Allen, Ronald B. *Joel* **(Bible Study Commentary). Grand Rapids: Zondervan, 1988. 120 pp.**

Allen is skilled in Hebrew and interpretation and writes attractively. He is conservative and premillennial. In his view the locusts are literal in both Chapters 1 and 2, yet supernatural in the latter case. He never seems to clear up what the supernatural locusts are in the future Armageddon time but stays general and vague. They sound like angelic hosts when Allen links them with Revelation 9:11-16. Allen has good emphases about God's grace, compassion, anger and love in 2:12-17. Apparently he sees the "northern army" of 2:20 as a human one, not identified with the locusts of 2:1-11. He has a long, helpful discussion on whether Acts 2 fulfills the outpouring of the Spirit, and sees a partial fulfillment (p. 95). In 3:9ff., he believes the blessing is in the millennium after the Second Advent, yet he identifies the fountain of verse 18 as the river in the ultimate state, the New Jerusalem (116), and is not clear on why or how he leaps from the millennium to the ultimate bliss.

Barton, John. *Joel and Obadiah. A Commentary.* **Louisville, KY: Westminster John Knox Press, 2001.**

Like Crenshaw's work on which it depends, this is another highly specialized liberal discussion of critical scholarly theory. Except for some value in seeing how certain critical scholarship works, many even diligent studying pastors and teachers will find sparse help that opens up the biblical book. Barton mentions among views the many defenders of the book's unity by one author (7, 10). But many view 2:28—3:21 as a secondary addition to Joel's words (15). Barton believes that this latter section is "a kind of Deutero-Joel" (31) tacked on later, however it is surely better to see both parts as by Joel, in meaningful unity. He dates Joel in the whole in the 400's B. C. (17). The Spirit's outpouring and prophecies after this in Joel are recognized as relating to the far future, yet the time and kind of situation left in basically irresponsible fuzziness, without light to orientate them.

Busenitz, Irvin A. *Commentary on Joel and Obadiah* **(Mentor Commentary). Geanies House, Fearn, Ross-shire, Scotland: Christian Publications, 2003.**

These 208 pages offer solid, very frequent insights on every word and phrase by a premillinnial dispensationalist with extracting skill in the Hebrew but vivid expression. Busenitz is Vice President for Academic Administration and Professor of Old Testament, The Master's Seminary. He argues for an author of Joel in the 860-50 B.C. era (cf. I Kin. 17-18) (34). The theme, "the day of the Lord", concerns, as in Joel 2-3, the future tribulation/millennial kingdom era, God's eschatological judgment and blessing (47-48). A good outline joins detailed verse by verse comments with Hebrew words tranliterated, and copious footnotes with substance from wide ranging sources (cf. also 5 1/3 pp. of bibliography at the end, from journals, commentaries, atlases, and other scholarship of various persuasions). Busenitz sees Joel 2-3 using literal locust depiction as vivid analogy for a literal human military invasion God will use in the eschatological drama. At first, some may have some confusion in reading that the creatures are "real locusts", yet on the same page (116) that they are "the nations' armies". Clarity eventuates, for example on p. 142 which sees a literal locust plague as portraying later human armies converging but meeting the Lord's judgment (3:9-15). After this judgment in "the day", Busenitz sees 3:16ff as depicting the literal blessing aspects God will bring on the godly in that same "day" (era), yet in its latter phase, in the millennium. He copiously explains each detail of both in the prophet's wording.

The work devotes 58 pp. to Obadiah, again with well-studied detail. This has to rate as one of the most explanatory, carefully researched and seasoned works on Joel, and it contributes quite well on Obadiah too.

Crenshaw, James L. *Joel* (Anchor Bible). NY: Doubleday, 1995.

Crenshaw sets forth his own translation, favors a late sixth or fifth century date (23-26), and much of the discussion is enmeshed in critical theory, Hebrew grammatical language, and specialist literature. Scholars will be main beneficiaries. The "day of the Lord" is defined vaguely, definitive statements about its future thrust missing, as in 3:9ff. (47-50, 186ff). The same blur as to prophetical perspective leaves 2:28-32 in much mystery, as if Crenshaw has no key (such as NT claims as authoritative Scripture). Readers grope in darkness. Crenshaw briefly mentions that Christians use the outpouring passage for a tie-in with Acts 2 (vii).

Finley, Thomas J. *Joel, Amos, Obadiah* (Wycliffe Exegetical Commentary). Chicago: Moody, 1990. 417 pp.

A conservative, premillennial work by the Professor of Old Testament at Talbot School of Theology. He has a good bibliography of 5 pages and a very full discussion of many issues, a rich use of other studies, help in Hebrew exegesis, and a good effort on word meaning. Hebrew words are transliterated into English. Finley sees literal locusts in chapters 1 and 2 of Joel. One wishes that he had listed and given arguments, yet he does give some when he arrives at individual verses. It sounds like he believes rich blessing will come to Israel (not the church in this case) in 2:18-27, but it also sounds like he sees it realized in past history; it is not wholly clear; he sees a partial fulfillment of Joel 2:28-32 in Acts 2ff., and details of 3:9ff. fulfilled in the future tribulation period and Messianic Kingdom after the Second Advent, not in the church or ultimate state. The treatment on Amos 9:11-15 could be stronger on reasons for a premillennial view, and the reader can feel discussion is vague about when the fulfillment will come to Israel.

Gaebelein, Arno C. *The Prophet Joel: An Exposition*. NY: Our Hope Press, 1909.

A dispensational exposition and translation. It is quite thorough.

Marsh, J. *Commentary on Amos and Micah* (Torch Bible Commentary), London: SCM Press, 1959.

A fairly good work on Micah, where Marsh's treatment is more of a contribution than his discussion on Amos.

McComiskey, Thomas. Cf. on Hosea.

Patterson, Richard. "Joel," in *Expositor's Bible Commentary*, **Volume 7, editor Frank Gaebelein. Grand Rapids: Zondervan, 1985. 725 pp.**

A skilled Old Testament scholar who is premillennial handles the text and exegesis adeptly and shows good awareness of literature and views and reasons. He takes the locust plague in Joel 1 as literal and in 2 as the human (Assyrian) army, not a far-off end-time invasion. Outpouring of the Spirit begins fulfillment in Acts 2, and the last part of Joel 3 is treated as giving events of the future tribulation period and kingdom after the Second Advent. This is a very capable work. Cf. comments about Patterson on I Kings.

Price, Walter K. *The Prophet Joel and the Day of the Lord.* **Chicago: Moody Press, 1976.**

An amillennialist turned dispensational wrote this work with a foreword by John F. Walvoord, Dallas Seminary. Price writes in a readable, inviting style. He expounds Joel section by section, seeing the "Day" as taking in not only the millennial reign after the Second Coming but the Great Tribulation up to the Coming. He believes in a pretribulation rapture of the church as he ties in the Thessalonian letters. The outpouring of the Spirit begins to be fulfilled at Pentecost, continues through the present age, and will have its ultimate fulfillment at the Second Advent. Price makes some good applications of the message to today that can help preaching and teaching.

Stuart, Douglas. Cf. on Hosea.

Thompson, J. A. and Norman F. Langford. "The Book of Joel," in the *Interpreter's Bible.* **Volume 6. New York: Abingdon, 1956.**

Thompson did the introduction and exegesis, and Langford the exposition sections. The work favors a post-exilic date based partly on 3:1-2 (seeing Israel in captivity). It is even after the return to rebuild, based on Chapter 2. Locusts are seen as literal in both chapters. Apparently the blessings for Israel in 3:16ff. are placed in the New Jerusalem, not a millennium after the Second Advent (p. 735). How they see 2:18-27 fulfilled in past history is not explained convincingly. The work is unclear on when aspects of 2:28-32 are fulfilled, as it just meshes them all in one complex. Overall this is not an outstanding commentary even if one can discern his way between the liberal parts and grasp what is being done to passages about a future Israel.

Watts, John D. W. *The Books of Joel, Obadiah, Jonah, Nahum, Habakkuk and Zephaniah* **(Cambridge Bible Commentary). New York: Cambridge University Press, 1975. 190 pp.**

Watts uses the NEB and gives brief introductions (1-3 pp.) and expositions. He late dates Joel. On problem verses he is usually succinct. Locusts are literal in both chapters, but in the latter case Watts sees them as symbolic of the Lord's "true *Mighty army*" (p. 26), whatever that means. He sees a future for Israel in Joel 2:18-27 but leaves vaguely obscure what this means. He refers to use of Joel 2 in Acts 2 but does not discuss the problem of some details not seeming to have been realistically fulfilled in Acts 2. He discusses Joel 3:9ff. in a general haze, and is mediocre among commentaries on these books.

Wolff, Hans W. *Joel and Amos: A Commentary* **(Hermeneia). Philadelphia: Fortress Press, 1977. 392 pp.**

A highly-regarded and much-cited work by a liberal using form critical methodology. He often helps on technical details and use of literature on the books. He has a detailed bibliography on Joel and Amos and copious footnote references. He uses inconclusive arguments to date Joel late. Joel 2 describes locust-like apocalyptic creatures, not ordinary locusts and not humans (p. 42), yet carried out by the nations and later (inconsistently) identified as humans after all, as Jeremiah 4:6 predicted (62). Wolff's apparent contradiction makes his position unclear, He sees Amos as finalized in post-exilic days after a long literary process (107). He discusses what he regards as six literary strata in highly speculative theorizing (107-13); 9:11-15, for example, with its comfort, could not have been in unity with the harsh judgment sections, so it must have been added by another writer (113). Even 9:11-15 is segmented into different layers of tradition (352). The eschatology of 9:11-15 is not set in a specific future, distinct situation, but generalized and fuzzed in relation to the people of God. Wolff likewise seems to see the latter part of Joel 3 as fulfilled in the church (15). The commentary evidences great learning and in this is often helpful, but it also has frequent lack of clarity. One is often unsure of where the fulfillment of things is placed and where evidence is to support many of the ideas.

Amos

Andersen, Francis I. and David N. Freedman. *Amos: A New Translation with Introduction and Commentary* **(Anchor Bible). Garden City, NY: Doubleday & Company, 1989. 979 pp.**

The work of these two scholars is ponderous here as it is on Hosea. They uphold the book's unity, often dealing rather conservatively with the text. The length allows careful explanation, sometimes in much detail. However, there ought to be, but does not appear to be, a lengthy discussion on such a vital concept as the day of the Lord. The writers regard 9:11-15 as in unity with the judgmental focus in the rest of the book. However, in considerable searching this reviewer found no clear statement telling the reader when or in what framework of eschatology the blessing for Israel will be fulfilled, despite the lengthy section. On many of the verses in Amos the student will find clearer help in the work than in comments on 9:11-15.

Cohen, Gary. Cf. on Hosea.

Cripps, Richard S. *A Critical and Exegetical Commentary on the Book of Amos.* **NY: Macmillan, 1929.**

Though this work is in the higher critical vein and, for example, argues against the unity of Amos 9:11-15 with the rest of the book (see his introduction), it is helpful on details of exegesis. One can find much aid though he does not agree with many of the conclusions of Cripps.

Finley, Thomas J. Cf. on Joel.

Garland, David. *Amos* **(Bible Study Commentary). Grand Rapids: Zondervan, 1966. 96 pp.**

This is handled much as he did Hosea in this series. He is conservative, usually clear, succinct, and aware. The outline is good. In 9:11-15, he continues to be vague on the nature of the future of Israel. But some of his wording about the future messianic age gives the impression by its detail that he means the millennium after the Second Advent, though he has no mention of Revelation 20. He does not clarify this.

Hasel, Gerhard F. *Understanding the Book of Amos.* **Grand Rapids: Baker, 1991. 171 pp.**

This is not a commentary per se but a lucid and somewhat helpful survey drawing into a rich tapestry some of the helpful lines of thought in research opinions on the book. He sees Amos as the first of the writing prophets, ca. 780-760 B. C., and as a "microcosm for the study of all prophetical writings of the Old Testament" (p. 11), so a key to all. He articulates issues in such a way as to point to the unity of the book.

Jeremias, Jorg. *The Book of Amos. A Commentary.* **Louisville, KY: Westminster John Knox Press, 1995.**

A good introduction has some elements that to many are misguided opinions, e. g. due to Amos' severe message of judgment without let-up except in 5:15 [cf. also 7:2-6], 9:11-15 with its bright encouragement for Israel's future must be conceived as a later update. Jorg reasons, unnecessarily, that it had to be written in by redactors at a later time who were seeking to resolve the severity with the comfort of coming Israelite salvation so as to encourage a post-exilic audience (5, 9). While many verses receive a fairly good elucidation, the estate in the prophetical future when 9:11-15 will be realized is blurred with no effort even to grapple with the Christian claim about the perspective given in Acts 15:13-18.

Mays, J. L. *Amos: A Commentary* **(Old Testament Library). Philadelphia: Westminster Press, 1969. 176 pp.**

A well-respected liberal work with much good information on many parts of the book. Mays, as many, lets his theories limit Amos and lead him to deny things conservatives believe can be defended reasonably. For example, Mays follows the frequent liberal line of denying that 9:11-15, with its bright hope for Israel's future, could be by the writer who spoke of harsh judgment earlier. Amos, he feels, did not speak of anything besides judgment (p. 9, 165), and 9:12 belongs after the fall of Jerusalem (165), a contention that is not necessary. Still, Mays has a lot of help in verse by verse study, and keen users can glean this out.

McComiskey, Thomas E. "Amos, Micah," in *Expositor's Bible Commentary,* **Volume 6, ed. Frank Gaebelein and R. P. Polcyn. Grand Rapids: Zondervan, 1986.**

A competent conservative introduction and commentary. It surveys sections well, explains things solidly verse by verse, and offers special notes on more technical aspects. He uses other Scripture cogently. He seems to hold a premillennial view on Amos 9:11-15. His bibliography work, though, is quite brief.

Motyer, J. A. *The Day of the Lion: The Message of Amos* **(The Bible Speaks Today). Downers Grove: IVP, 1975. 208 pp.**

A brief, competent, evangelical effort that succeeds in making the message articulate, often bringing out stimulating and refreshing lessons and applying them to people today. Expositors will find it helpful. As in many books, the description about Israel's future blessing in 9:11-15 is left in glowing language but in dim light as to the framework in which fulfillment in the land will come, millennially or in the ultimate bliss.

Paul, Shalom M. *Amos* **(Hermeneia). Minneapolis: Augsburg Fortress, 1991. 409 pp.**

A magisterial work which seems on top of many things, impressively thorough, well-written, showing awareness of issues, possibilities, and literature. Cf. the lists of sources (xix-xxvi, 299-367, nearly 80 pp.). This is a second commentary in the Hermeneia series since Hans Wolff's work was already out. Paul has a very full discussion on the situation in which Amos ministered, his kind of ministry, features of it, views about when oracles occur here, literary traits of the oracles, etc. Paul defends the authenticity of the oracles against arguments of interpolation. The commentary verse by verse is on large double-column pages. It is quite full of details of text, word meaning, geography, customs, relation to other Scripture, views on problems, etc. Footnotes steeped in further help are abundant and often long. Summary remarks at the outset of pericopes help readers see connections, overall ideas, and movement of the book. Paul defends 9:11-15 against arguments from the liberal majority who see it as unauthentic, from an exilic or post-exilic theologian-redactor. He shows how it fits well with the book. He also does much to recognize the prophecy of a future glorious state for Israel and ties it with other passages. But he does not go on to relate 9:11-15 to James's use of it in Acts 15:13-18. His bibliography does list two works on this under "Early Christian Interpretation" (pp. 316-17). In his section on Indices (364-406) where he lists literature consulted, the "New Testament" entry includes only seven passages and in Acts only 7:43 (394).

Smith, Billy K. and Frank S. Page. *Amos, Obadiah, Jonah* **(New American Commentary). Nashville: Broadman & Holman, 1995.**

Smith did the first two, Page wrote on Jonah. Verses gain reasonably full, knowledgeable explanation, with good use of a plethora of assists from scholarly literature, footnoted well, in some pertinent places, even with views, etc. Hebrew words are transliterated, and remarks about the grammar help. A fairly perceptive section appears on Amos 9:11-15, even its relation to Acts 15:13-18 in a fururistic prophetical picture. Page views Jonah as a historical account (217-19). Customs such as sea men casting lots in Jonah 1 (234) receive good illumination, and one finds frequent answers to questions readers usually ask, such as on the miraculous element in Jonah (214-15) and whether the Ninevite revival was spiritually real. This evangelical work is well-done and often firmly profitable for teachers, pastors, and other readers.

Sunukian, Donald. "Amos," in *Bible Knowledge Commentary***, ed. John F. Walvoord and Roy B. Zuck, Volume I. Wheaton: Victor Books, 1983.**

A fairly clear, diligent conservative work that concisely deals with many of the expositional issues so that a reader has something solid to explain verses. The outline is well-done. Unlike many commentaries, Sunukian's work on 9:11-15 is clear-cut, and he even has a good discussion of how James uses part of the passage in Acts 15. He is premillennial.

Smith, Gary V. Amos, *A Commentary* **(Library of Biblical Interpretation). Grand Rapids: Zondervan, 1989. 307 pp.**

A good, thorough conservative commentary leaving few key stones unturned in exposition based on the Hebrew exegesis. He is helpful on the book's unity, interpretation verse by verse, and theological relevance then and now. The work is of substantial helpfulness to expositors and lay readers.

Stuart, Douglas. Cf. on Hosea.

de Waard, J. and W. A. Smalley. *A Translator's Handbook on the Book of Amos* **(United Bible Societies' Translator's Handbooks). United Bible Societies, 1979. 274 pp.**

This offers considerable basic assistance on the text, philology, geography etc. in its detailed exegesis,

Veldkamp, Herman. *The Farmer from Tekoa (Amos).* **St. Catherine's, Ontario: Paideia Press, 1977.**

A 276-pp. work done in a fresh, readable style with 33 short chapters pulling in lay persons with intriguing captions and applications sensitive to 20th century life. Veldkamp was a minister in the Reformed Church of the Netherlands. The book makes the main aspects of Amos' prophecies come alive for the lay audience as well as pastors and teachers.

Watts, J. D. W. *Vision and Prophecy in Amos.* **Grand Rapids: Eerdmans, 1958.**

There are four chapters, dealing with the kind of prophet Amos was, the structure of the book, the hymn it preserves, and the eschatology of the book. Overall it is a stimulating study. An expanded anniversary ed. appeared in 1997 by the same title (Macon, GA: Mercer University Press). The expansion is from four chapters to eight.

Wolff, Hans W. Cf. on Joel.

Wood, Joyce Rilett. *Amos in Song and Book Culture* **(Journal of the Study of the OT Supplment Series 332). Sheffield, Eng.: Sheffield Academic Press, 2002.**

Based on a 1993 dissertation at Toronto School of Theology, this theorizes about alleged redactive compositions to comprise the present Amos, Amos' own writing included. A later author, Wood alleges, did redaction that at times debunks views of Amos. Wood suggests inconsistencies where they need not exist, as between bright statements of Israelite restoration and gloomy words about judgment, as if both cannot be true in God's moral governance and in relation to people. Also argued is the theory that parts in the book were not simply read aloud, but devised as a dramatic presentation with scenes before an audience. Wood claims this on such bases as repeated direct addresses, frequent shifts in person, various persons assumed, and characters speaking to one another, etc. (213-14). It may or may not be so.

Allen, Leslie C. Cf. on Joel.

Obadiah

Baker, D. W., Desmond Alexander and Bruce K. Waltke. *Obadiah, Jonah and Micah* **(Tyndale Old Testament Commentary). Downers Grove: 1VP, 1988. 207 pp.**

A good, concise conservative commentary, with Baker on Obadiah, Alexander on Jonah and Waltke on Micah. Overall it is quite competent and carefully thought through. Baker sees Obadiah 21 fulfilled in a king on earth after the Second Advent (p. 43) and defends the unity of verses 17-21 with the earlier part of the book. Alexander defends an early date of the Book of Jonah (8th century) against several arguments (51-63), and authorship by one writer (63-69), apparently Jonah of 2 Kings 14:25. He favors actual, historical events, not a parable or any fiction form, and capably sums up answers to problems, but appears thin on how to explain a great fish taking in Jonah, though he believes it was a miracle (110-11). Waltke provides a good verse by verse study, enriched by expertise in exegesis, history, customs, etc.

Beyer, Bryan and Walton, John H. *Obadiah/Jonah* **(Bible Study Commentary). Grand Rapids: Zondervan, 1988. 122 pp.**

Beyer was teaching Bible at Columbia Bible College, and Walton at Moody Bible Institute. Beyer dates Obadiah after 586 B. C. (Fall of Jerusalem), since verses 10-14 describe Edom's gloating at that fall. He appears to hold a premillennial view with a future millennial kingdom after the Second Advent in verses 17-21. However, he never says it is millennial, only that it is God's kingdom. But he does see a resettling of Israel in its land. Walton has packed in much good information, as on lots in Jonah 1. But since God's preparation of the great sea creature was a miracle, he sees no need to cite accounts of marine creatures taking in men (p. 29). He apparently does not view Nineveh's repentance as being a conversion to the Lord, Judaism or even monotheism (51). It was not to salvation spiritually (53). Some will not regard his explanation for why Jonah was angry (Ch. 4) as very persuasive or helpful.

Busenitz, Irven A. Cf. on Joel.

Coggins, Richard J. and Re'emi, S. Paul. *Israel Among the Nations: Nahum, Obadiah, Esther* **(International Theological Commentary), Grand Rapids: Eerdmans, 1985. 140 pp.**

Coggins does Nahum and Obadiah. He feels it is impossible to outline Nahum, yet sees a structure (p. 7), which he does not use in the commentary later. His introduction to Nahum is not very helpful, and his commentary lays out material without synthesis to pull things into perspective. A reader can laboriously sift out some things, but only the very patient will probably plod through. The theological help for the church promised in the series is not easy to find here. No outline of Obadiah appears anywhere, and no framework is given as to when verses 17-21 will be fulfilled. The work on Esther at least follows an outline and is more lively. Re'emi proposes a set of details known under Artaxerxes II that might fit the book's claims (106-07), but feels "legendary and pictorial elements" have been added (109). He gives much good comment, shows seeming contradictions between the book and history, but also details that fit history. While Coggins' work is far down the line, Re'emi's has much that is helpful.

Eaton, J. H. *Obadiah, Nahum, Habakkuk and Zephaniah* (Torch Bible Commentary). London: SCM Press, 1961.

This is a good exegesis of these books, with much help.

Finley, Thomas J. Cf. on Joel.

Raabe, Paul R. *Obadiah* (Anchor Bible). NY: Doubleday, 1996.

A very detailed exegetical work on the 21 verses (310 pp.) follows Raabe's own translation, an introduction (3-60), and 29 pp. of bibliography. This is one of the better, thorough discussions for teachers, pastors ready to grapple with comments on the overall perspective and grammatical details, and for advanced students of Hebrew.

Smith, cf. Amos.

Stuart, Douglas. Cf. on Hosea.

Watts, John D. W. Cf. on Joel.

Watts, J. D. W. *Obadiah: A Critical and Exegetical Commentary*. Grand Rapids: Eerdmans, 1967.

A worthwhile work to use in getting at the meaning of the text verse by verse, and in gaining an appreciation for its theological message.

Wolff, Hans W. *Obadiah and Jonah. A Commentary*. Minneapolis: Augsburg Publishing House, 1986. 191 pp.

A liberal redaction-critical effort that one will need to sift discerningly as regards composition, integrity of the book, theology etc. However, a great scholar offers some help in basic, thorough comments on the text, lexical details, exegesis, and bibliography. Among critical scholars Wolff is highly regarded, and his works much cited.

Jonah

Alexander, Desmond. Cf. Baker on Obadiah.

Beyer, Bryan and John H. Walton. Cf. Beyer on Obadiah.

Bolin, Thomas. *Freedom Beyond Forgiveness. The Book of Jonah Re-Examined* (Journal for the Study of the OT Supplement Series 236). Sheffield, Eng.: Sheffield Academic Press, 1997.

Bolin's overview for the history of scholarship on the issues and debates on Jonah (chap. 1) is of some help for teachers, even if he at times is quite hazy on what he means. Chapters 2-5 examine Jonah passage by passage, and the final chapter looks at Jonah and its Israelite context and theological perspective. Bolin believes that another author used the name Jonah from 2 Kings 14:25 as the main character (74), and is not clear whether the alleged author concocted fiction, but it sounds this way. Often along the way verse comments open up meaning, and the main issue is affirming Yahweh's absolute freedom, power and sovereignty beyond any of man's ideas about justice, mercy or logic; Yahweh is worthy of worship. Bolin claims that the point is summed up in two verses (1:14; 2:9). God is free to do what pleases Him, as when He delivers (184). Apparently the same God is not free to cause literal events really to occur to an authentic Jonah himself, if the account is viewed in a natural way. So the Bolin case would suggest, but one need not go that way.

Hannah, John. "Jonah," in *Bible Knowledge Commentary*, ed, John F. Walvoord and Roy B. Zuck, Volume I. Wheaton: Victor Books, 1983.

A careful conservative study that is clear, concise, and helpful on the main issues. His introduction answers several main objections to the authenticity of the book, and the commentary offers information to explain very well verse by verse, Much good material is packed in. Curiously, he says that Jonah's prayer has no petitions in it (p. 1467), then later says "his petitions rose to heaven . . ." (1468). Overall, however, this is a very fine concise commentary from one well versed on the issues and the literature.

Kennedy, James Hardee. *Studies in the Book of Jonah*. Nashville, TN: Broadman Press.

When authoring this book, Kennedy was serving as Professor of Old Testament and Hebrew at New Orleans Baptist Theological Seminary. He presents the basic teachings of the book and shows their relevance for Christian living. The exposition is careful, even introducing elements of exegesis from the Hebrew text. Though not every preacher will be able to follow him in the fine points of Hebrew grammar, he will appreciate the help he receives from the details on Jonah.

Kohlenberger, J. R. III. *Jonah and Nahum* (Everyman's Bible Commentary). Chicago: Moody, 1984. 127 pp.

This is a conservative exposition based on analysis of the Hebrew, using the NIV, following a good outline. The writer is lucidly helpful on the meanings of details, connections, and doctrinal significance. He does seem beside the point in faulting conservatives for attempting to suggest possibilities of the kind of sea creature that could swallow a man, as if such attempts slight the power of God, which they do not (cf. p. 43). God can work a miracle and use a sea creature He has made in doing it. The writer argues that the repentance of the Ninevites was done in genuine faith and was unto spiritual salvation as well as physical (61).

Limberg, James. *Jonah, A Commentary* (OT Library). Louisville, KY: Westminster John Knox Press, 1993.

Lindberg posits fiction, a made up parable using a historical name to convey lessons, a story like that of Jotham about the trees (Judg. 9:7-15), or Nathan's about a lamb (2 Sam. 12), or Jesus' parables (24). At least six theological themes (35-36) have value, and verse by verse comments are readable and usually cover main points capably and substantially. An appendix is informative about Jonah in apocryphal and other ancient literature, in literature from the first centuries A. D., in Judaism, in Islam, and among Reformers.

Martin, Hugh. *The Prophet Jonah*. London: Banner of Truth Trust, 1958, reprint.

This work was out in Spurgeon's day, and he exulted in it. The student will find here a provoking exposition that offers considerable help.

Simon, Uriel. *Jonah* (JPS Bible Commentary). Philadelphia: Jewish Publication Society, 1999.

This work of xliii (introd.) and 52 pp. (commentary) is perceptive exegetically and is a literary tool of use to scholars. Simon provides good detail on the theme of need for God's mercy as distinct from but related to Jonah's desire for justice (cf. xii). He also capably discusses the long line of ways scholars have interpreted the book, its literary genre, narrative, and other concerns such as the unity and function of the prayer in Jonah 2. Simon argues that the story is vital but whether it is history or fiction does not, to him, affect the import (xviii). It does matter very much to many, of course. He weds introductory thematic synthesis to each section, and some comment on details. In these, he furnishes some beneficial insights.

Stuart, Douglas. Cf. on Hosea.

Walton, John H. *Jonah*. Grand Rapids, MI Zondervan Publishing House, 1982.

Dr. John Walton (b. 1952) has written this 82-pp. paperback for the Bible Study Commentary series to which Leon J. Wood and John F. Walvoord are notable contributors. Walton has chosen not to write a detailed verse by verse analysis, but to deal with many problem areas of Jonah. He puts background and introductory remarks at the end and begins instead with the body of the biblical book. He addresses such issues as casting lots in 1; the great fish in 1:17; the three-day journey of 3:3 and Ninevite beliefs of 3:4ff. With respect to the three-day journey, Dr. Walton points out that the term for journey can also be understood as "project". This rendering is necessitated because of the 500-600 mile journey between Joppa and Nineveh even though other scholars have located "Nineveh" significantly closer to Joppa than Walton allows. Walton places the author (not necessarily a man named Jonah) in the reign of Jeroboam II of Israel (II Kings 14:25) and defends a date of writing somewhere within the first half of the eighth century B. C. Jonah is understood as a pre-classical prophet and thus, his mode of prophecy disclosure is a strong factor in Walton's dating schema. Conclusion: This book is helpful to those acquainted with the problems of the book of Jonah. -Jan Sattem

Watts, John D. W. Cf. on Joel.

Wolff, Hans W. Cf. on Obadiah.

Allen, Leslie C. Cf. on Joel.

Micah

Andersen, Francis, and David N. Freedman. *Micah* (Anchor Bible). NY: Doubleday, 2000.

Two eminent scholars team up. They offer a good survey of reasons why scholars have theorized that some material is by Micah and some by later editors and redactors. A consensus takes chaps. 4-7 as by later hands (17-20). In more recent years, unity of the entire book as we now have it has been a big trend (21). Overall integration of Micah is a point that these writers present (27-29). Often verses get very full comment, up to a glut of several pp., which a 637-pp. work has room to do. Discussion turns up word meaning from a wealth of sources, makes comparisons with other Scripture, gives customs (as cloak and tunic, 2:8), etc. Of the thoroughly detailed works in recent years from a critical standpoint, this is one of the most informative, despite the drawback that readers have to ransack through details to glean succinct points.

Barker, Kenneth L. and Waylon Bailey. *Micah, Nahum, Habakkuk, Zephaniah* **(New American Commentary). Nashville: Broadman & Holman, 1998.**

Barker does Micah (136 pp.), Bailey the others (137-500), both evangelical in convictions. Among other good things, Barker answers six lines of reasoning that impugn the integrity of Micah as a unit, some due to inability to accept supernatural predictive prophecy (28-29). Also, presuppositions of literary or other criticism dictate attitudes. Both writers offer much interaction to expose benefit in main body and footnotes, showing broad reading in scholarly literature. Still, they maintain a fluidity that makes the work serviceable to a wide group. Comments on verses come to grips with main facets rather fully, and reference to the Messianic age is unequivocal, in contrast to a fog by some commentators (cf. Micah 4:1). Sections on introduction spotlight major themes. These scholars handle alleged miscues well, for example Bailey in Nahum 2:2 refutes the reasoning that blessing for Israel is out of place amid judgment on Nineveh. Light appears on details such as how the Tigris River figured in the attacker's strategy in Nahum 2:6. One finds a good discussion of Habakkuk's questions, and clarity on the image of a surefooted hind in 3:19, also the meaning of purified lips in Zeph. 3:9. Evangelicals can hardly go wrong using the many helps here.

Hillers, D. R. *Micah: A Commentary on the Book of the Prophet Micah* **(Hermeneia). Philadelphia: Fortress Press, 1984. 116 pp.**

Steeped in scholarly literature of a critical type, Hillers provides a rather copious work on technical aspects of the text, syntax, exegesis, and views on problems, then goes on to exposition in a cursory way which is not outstanding. In his introduction, he is unconvinced by redactional schemes on Micah such as Wolff's, and often just seeks to interpret the text as from one situation, in unity. At times, however, he too speculates subjectively on a text he sees as having the marks of editing or modification.

Marsh, J. Cf. on Amos.

Martin, John A. "Micah," in *Bible Knowledge Commentary***, eds. John F. Walvoord and Roy B. Zuck, Volume I. Wheaton: Victor Books, 1983.**

A conservative work which handles many of the problems knowledgeably and takes a premillennial view of the kingdom in Chapter 4. Expositors gain a lot of assistance.

Mays, James L. *Micah: A Commentary.* **Philadelphia: Westminster, 1976.**

Using his own rendering from the Hebrew, Mays comments under creative captions such as "Capital Punishment for the Capital Cities" (1:2-16). The 169-pp. work is a fairly good commentary, with arresting comments in places (cf. 6:6-8, p. 142). Mays, however, believes only chapters 1-3 give us what Micah wrote ca. 701 B. C. The rest, according to his subjective opinion, comes from prophets in late exilic and post-exilic days.

McComiskey, Thomas. Cf. on Amos.

Riggs, Jack R. *Micah* **(Bible Study Commentary). Grand Rapids: Zondervan, 1987. 92 pp.**

A Dallas Seminary graduate and professor at Cedarville College in Ohio uses a clear, simple, overall outline – judgment (1:2-2:13), Messiah (Chapters 3-5), and pardon (6-7). He fills in sub-points helpfully, commenting competently on main details. His view of the kingdom is premillennial (p. 49). His work is helpful for pastors, Sunday School or Bible class teachers and lay people in general.

Smith, Ralph L. *Micah-Malachi* **(Word Biblical Commentary). Waco: Word Books, 1984. 358 pp.**

Smith is Professor of Old Testament, Southwestern Baptist Seminary, Fort Worth, TX. While he lets critical assumptions often sway him against conservative perspectives, he has much that helps in clear exposition of these seven books in some parts. He has good bibliographies, discusses views, gives a wealth of information on text, exegesis, background, etc., and often is clear. He is vague on when blessing will be fulfilled for Israel as in Micah 4. He has much good comment on Habakkuk 2:4, but inadequate discussion of the New Testament use of the passage, leaving the impression that the New Testament has misused it, being misled by the LXX (p. 107). He leaves some key verses poorly explained (Habakkuk 3:19) and deals with many in a skimpy way in general with other verses, as the whole of Habakkuk 3. Sometimes he is not easy to follow, as when Zechariah 14:6-11 depicts to him the New Jerusalem, yet 14:16-21 are handled as if they are in an imperfect situation.

Waltke, Bruce K. Cf. on Obadiah, under Baker.

Wolff, Hans W. *Micah, A Commentary.* **Minneapolis: Augsburg Fortress. 1990. 258 pp.**

A work exalted in critical circles, given to the idea that the book is written in post-exilic times, the product of centuries of composition, with only some passages stemming originally from Micah (cf. list on his pp. 8-9). His redaction segments are subjective and lacking hard evidence that they are necessary. One can glean much that does help on Micah, but he is often meeting up with Wolff's theories about composition, which are obtrusive and interruptive to the person looking at the text as a unity by one writer.

Nahum

Baker, D. W. *Nahum, Habakkuk and Zephaniah* **(Tyndale Old Testament Commentary). Downers Grove: 1VP, 1988. 121 pp.**

As Baker did in Obadiah in this series, he again presents a brief introduction and a well-studied survey of each book with a good outline, handling most things rather carefully, in a conservative stance. He sees the "Day" of Zephaniah 3 as one of wrath and also hope and help (p. 116), but is very general and vague about when and where and in what form the blessed state will be realized. He is typical of many who do not nail down things in any framework so as to clarify just where he stands.

Coggins, Richard J. Cf. on Obadiah.

Freeman, Hobart E. *Nahum, Zephaniah, Habakkuk, Minor Prophets of the Seventh Century* **(Everyman's Bible Commentary). Chicago: Moody Press, 1973.**

A helpful survey by the author of the very fine *Introduction to the Old Testament Prophets*.

Heflin, J. N. Boo. *Nahum, Habakkuk, Zephaniah, Haggai* **(Bible Study Commentary). Grand Rapids: Zondervan, 1984. 190 pp.**

Heflin is quite capable and well-informed in his introductions and commentaries, obviously having given matters adequate study. He defends Nahum against critical attacks, points out three theological themes (God is sovereign Lord, righteous judge, merciful Savior (pp. 29-31)), and helps on doctrinal themes of the other books too. He explains main details. Judicious comments appear on how Habakkuk 2:4 and Paul's concept in citing it can be correlated in the final analysis (92-93). He is quite clear on the picture from the gazelle in Habakkuk 3:19 (109). The day of the Lord in Zephaniah 3:9ff. entails both judgment and blessing (150). Heflin usually helps on ways a problem may be solved, as the meaning of purified lip in Zephaniah 3:9. He fails to specify the state in which restoration occurs in 3:9ff.; he tabs it "the New Jerusalem" (which could be identified with Revelation 21-22, the ultimate state), yet describes it in details that could be seen as millennial, before the ultimate state.

Johnson, Elliott. "Nahum," in *Bible Knowledge Commentary***, editors John F. Walvoord and Roy B. Zuck. Volume I. Wheaton: Victor Books, 1983.**

Here is a concise conservative commentary that looks carefully at verses, gives views on problems and makes good decisions often. Much of the book is explained very well even with space limitations. A chart on page 1495 lists fulfillments for twelve prophecies of Nahum, using ancient sources. Johnson is better known for his *Expository Hermeneutics* (Zondervan).

Kohlenberger, J. R. III. Cf. on Jonah.

Maier, Walter. *The Book of Nahum.* **Saint Louis: Concordia, 1959.**

The author, who was heard for years on the "Lutheran Hour," has contributed a book very rich in exegetical detail and effective in answering higher critical views. This is a very fine detailed work by a conservative and is highly desirable for the serious student. It is also lucid. The author received his Ph. D. degree in Semitics at Harvard in 1929 and served as Professor of Hebrew and Old Testament at Concordia Seminary in Saint Louis. Edward J. Young of Westminster Theological Seminary said in Christianity Today (May 25, 1959, p. 38): "This book comes to serious grips with questions of introduction and exegesis. It is solid treatment of the Hebrew text, a real commentary, the kind of work that will prove of inestimable benefit to any student who truly desires to understand the message of the prophet Nahum."

Patterson, Richard. *Nahum, Habakkuk and Zephaniah* **(Wycliffe Exegetical Commentary). Chicago: Moody, 1991. 416 pp.**

This is an outstanding conservative, detailed work backed by scholarly awareness and expertise. Comments reflect fine-tuned ability in the Hebrew text, philology, exegesis, history, and literature. Patterson has premillennial convictions in the final verses of Zephaniah. He shows the shaky reasoning of critical arguments against the unity of Nahum, and defends unity of Nahum and Habakkuk. In a long Excursus he defends New Testament uses of Habakkuk 2:4 (pp. 21-23), But some will doubt that he captures the significance of the picture of a hind in Habakkuk 3:19 when he sees only swiftness ascending and gracefully gliding (262-63). But in most details he is excellent, and the work is well worth the cost and time.

Robertson, 0. Palmer. *The Books of Nahum, Habakkuk and Zephaniah* **(New International Commentary on the Old Testament). Grand Rapids: Eerdmans, 1990, 357 pp.**

This is a very good conservative work, both perceptive on issues and in lucid style. The writer provides a good translation and commentary, often graphic. He looks at Habakkuk 2:4 from many angles (pp. 173-83), and also clearly catches the picture of living by faith in 3:19 that ties in with 2:4b. To a large extent the explanations of verses are full enough and satisfying. At times, however, questions in serious minds are not dealt with. For example, why make a sweeping statement in Zephaniah 3:12 about no deceit in the future remnant if this is in a state of imperfection and believers still have some deceit when less than absolutely perfect?

Smith, Ralph L. Cf. on Micah.

Habakkuk

Barber, Cyril J. *Habakkuk and Zephaniah* **(Everyman's Bible Commentary). Chicago: Moody, 1985. 127 pp.**

Barber, perhaps best known for his *The Minister's Library*, gives a knowledgeable introduction of Habakkuk with a clear outline of the book. Synopses at the outset of sections offer perspective, he deals with verses well and has some help on problems. He sees the gazelle in 3:19 as picturing the sure-footedness and freedom in a life of faith. He is helpful on the Day of the Lord, seeing it as both near and far and involving both judgment and blessing (pp. 79-81). He is premillennial on Zephaniah 3:9-20.

Blue, J. Ronald. "Habakkuk," in *Bible Knowledge Commentary*, **editors John F. Walvoord and Roy B. Zuck, Volume I. Wheaton: Victor Books, 1983.**

A conservative look informed by careful study and done in a clear, concise style. Blue offers some help on most issues of the book.

Gowan, Donald E. *The Triumph of Faith in Habakkuk*. **Atlanta: John Knox, 1976.**

This 94-pp. book is by the then Associate Professor of Old Testament at Pittsburgh Theological Seminary. He focuses on Habakkuk's theological thrust as it addresses deep needs of people oppressed by baffling problems such as "Why does evil prosper in a world over which a good God rules?" Gowan does not feel that Habakkuk supplies an answer to the problem of evil, but he does believe the book tells those who are just how to live by faith in God even without all the answers. And the truly just will show they are by continuing in faith even when the just do not always receive rewards now for godliness.

Heffin, J. N. Boo. Cf. on Nahum.

Lloyd-Jones, D. M. *Faith Tried and Triumphant.* **Downers Grove: IVP, 1987.**

This is a reprinting of a very good work on Habakkuk called *From Fear to Faith* (IVP, 1953). Expositors will find help on how the great English preacher brought out principles that have living force today.

Patterson, Richard. Cf. on Nahum.

Robertson, 0. Palmer. Cf. on Nahum.

Smith, Ralph. Cf. on Micah.

Szeles, Maria Eszcnyei. *Wrath and Mercy. A Commentary on the Books of Habakkuk and Zephaniah* **(International Theological Commentary). Grand Rapids: Eerdmans, 1987. 118 pp.**

This is by Professor of Old Testament, United Protestant Theological Seminary, in Cluj-Napoca, Romania. The work has many thorough and good exegetical comments on the Hebrew drawn from much study, yet some thin and cursory statements. Often the book furnishes help on theological meaning. But the authoress at times reflects higher critical loyalties as in claiming arbitrarily that certain statements must be a redactor's later insertion if the writer does not grasp them. She is flimsy or non-existent in convincing proof of her biases (cf. on Habakkuk 2:6-20 at p. 36; also cf. p. 41, etc.). A pastor or student using the work with good discernment can profit from it by exercising his own judgment.

Zephaniah

Allen, Ronald B. *A Shelter in the Fury. A Prophet's Stunning Picture of God.* **Portland, OR: Multnomah Press, 1984. 129 pp.**

Allen is a Professor at Dallas Theological Seminary. This is a very popularly-written work that shows attractively the secret in Zephaniah of finding a hiding place and a song in God to avert God's wrath and relate to His love. Allen uses several illustrations and creative writing to pull readers in, but at times drags out getting to aspects of the message. If one stays with the book patiently he eventually gets a lot of good lessons amidst all the dressing as Allen works his way through Zephaniah. The book is suggestive for teachers and preachers, and refreshing for any Christian who uses it in devotional times.

Baker, D. W. Cf. on Nahum.

Barber, Cyril J. Cf. on Habakkuk.

Berlin, Adele. *Zephaniah* (Anchor Bible). NY: Doubleday, 1994.

Berlin pays close attention to exegetical details in a flow that even helps those confined to English. Two among several features of the introduction are the choice that a prophet, Zephaniah, historically was active, or another authored or edited the book but ascribed it to him, a common critical theory (33), plus a section on differing ways readers have set up verse by verse divisions of the book during history. Prophetical details of Zeph. 3 draw terse comments on the obvious, but like many commentators committed only to a half-picture, Berlin offers no explanation but leaves in darkness the time/situation when such weal for Israel will become a reality. So the profit here is sparse to those who have a prophetical perspective embracing both testaments, and definitely favor supernatural predictive utterances.

Hannah, John D. "Zephaniah," in *Bible Knowledge Commentary*, editors John F. Walvoord and Roy B. Zuck, Volume I. Wheaton: Victor Books, 1983.

A good conservative, premillennial short study of Zephaniah by a good scholar. The work is well-informed in history, and explains verses competently within a good outline.

Heflin, J. N. Boo. Cf. on Nahum.

Motyer, J. Alec., Thomas McComiskey, and Douglas Stuart. *Zephaniah, Haggai, Zechariah, and Malachi* (vol. 3, The Minor Prophets, An Exegetical and Expository Commentary), ed. T. McComiskey. Grand Rapids: Baker Books, 1998.

Motyer, who wrote two well-regarded amillennial commentaries on Isaiah, contributes Zephaniah and Haggai in the final of 3 vols. in this series. McComiskey worked on Zechariah, later the Lord took him home, and Stuart did Malachi. The NRSV and Motyer's own translations appear, offering comparisons. Clear exposition is in one section on each set of verses, technical details in another (here the Heb. could assist some readers by transliteration). Scholars can appreciate the good quality while regretting that the latest literature listed is 1994, though for most exposition details of the message entail no essential change. Non-specialists will grasp much here to find the work worthwhile, while from a premillennial standpoint users will need to go elsewhere for better perspective on long-range prophecy related to Israel.

Patterson, Richard. Cf. on Nahum.

Robertson, 0. Palmer. Cf. on Nahum.

Smith, Ralph. Cf. on Micah.

Szeles, Maria. Cf. on Habakkuk.

Vlaardingerbroek, Johannes. *Zephaniah*. Leuven: Peeters, 1999.

The writer, although explaining many verse details fairly well, opinionizes without sturdy proof that later editorial work added things to Zephaniah's message (as 3:9-20), blessing after Zephaniah's words about judgment were fulfilled with Jerusalem's destruction (26). Some of the bright outlook (as 3:13) did not materialize, so redactive work attached aspects of a better future still to come (27), as if God's power could not help Zephaniah refer to both judgment and after this eventual blessing, and as if God could not give the future hope just as relevantly to earlier Israelites who also needed it. Interestingly, the commentator legitimizes relevancy in preaching both judgment and promise by grace, but fails to see relevancy of Zephaniah originally doing both in unity. One will get only limited help here and there, and with it some misunderstanding.

Haggai

Baldwin, J. G. *Haggai, Zechariah, Malachi* (Tyndale Old Testament Commentary). Grand Rapids: Eerdmans, 1972.

The work furnishes a detailed exegesis and rather thorough use of other writers, giving evidence of wide study.

Coggins, Richard J. *Haggai, Zechariah, Malachi* (Old Testament Guides). Sheffield, England: JSOT Press, 1987. 90 pp.

This work, available via Eisenbrauns, Winona Lake, Indiana, offers brief assistance on critical issues, historical matters and exegesis. Coggins is not a particularly interesting writer, but he offers quite a bit of expertise that can be of help as one reads and discerns carefully, choosing what is usable and bypassing other material.

Heflin, J. N. Boo. Cf. on Nahum.

Lindsey, F. Duane. "Haggai," in *Bible Knowledge Commentary*, editors John F. Walvoord and Roy B. Zuck, Volume I. Wheaton: Victor Books, 1983.

A former Dallas Seminary faculty member did this very able, brief work covering most of the vital bases to aid an expositor. He is helpful on historical background, flow of the context, meanings of verses, etc. The section on the future millennial temple in 2:6-9 and the reference to Zerubbabel in 2:20 are well done.

Mason, Rex. *The Books of Haggai, Zechariah and Malachi* (Cambridge Bible Commentary). New York: Cambridge University Press, 1977.

Using the NEB text, this series aims to bring the learning of modern scholarship to general readers, assuming no theological knowledge or grasp of Hebrew or Greek. The work is fair at times as a general, concise survey often swayed by redaction criticism. Sometimes the possible long-range Messianic reach of a prophecy is not even referred to (cf.. Haggai 2:6-9) or mentioned only barely or incidentally (2:23). Some of Mason's suggestions of a redactor will be subjectively arbitrary and bogus to some who use the work. Certain details are left vague, as for example no effort to suggest who the four "smiths" may possibly represent (Zechariah 1:20, 21). Some will not be convinced that chapters 9-14 are from later hands than 1-8, in a "continuing tradition" but "farther down-stream" (p. 79 with 80-82). The author engages in a lot of shuffling of the order of the text, a disconcerting feature to many of his "general" audience. Mason discusses 12:10 without seeing a reference to a Messiah's suffering (p. 119).

Merrill, Eugene H. *Haggai, Zechariah, Malachi*. Chicago: Moody Press, 1994.

Here is an evangelical commentary well-done in 493 pp. Introductions gather much that is most pertinent for expositors. In Hagg. 2:7, "precious things" are Gentiles' tributes (Isa. 60:5; 61:6) in the future kingdom. Merrill sees Zech. 14 as related to Christ's Second Advent and the coming of the Messianic Kingdom, in premillennial fashion. Fairly full exegetical detail meets readers verse by verse, yet Merrill's comments are readable for others than scholars, except the technical notes in special sections will be more for the latter. Problem passages usually draw careful remarks, as in seeing Zech. 12:10 as referring to the Lord, and in a future day.

Moore, T. V. *Haggai, Zechariah and Malachi*. Carlisle, PA: Banner of Truth Trust, 1979rp. 426 pp.

This work came out in 1856. It is competent in exegetical detail of a reformed nature, explaining much in the books, but disappointing to premillennialists in passages on the future kingdom. Being so old, the work will not acquaint the reader with literature of recent times.

Petersen, David L. *Haggai and Zechariah 1-8* (Old Testament Library). Philadelphia: Westminster Press, 1984. 320 pp.

A liberal work detailed in verse by verse comment, form structure, word meanings, and the like. He uses his own translation and sometimes quotations from the RSV. At times he defends verses as fitting meaningfully, not agreeing with scholars who judge them as secondary and superfluous (as Haggai 1:13, p. 57; some aspects in 2:3-9, pp. 65-66). Some verses though dealt with in detail do not seem to be explained well, as when he does not make clear when the shaking in 2:6 will occur. The glory of the future temple appears to be put in the near historical future and a future millennial temple is not even mentioned as a possibility in 2:7-9. On 2:23 he has much discussion but little light, no messianic import, and vagueness. Patience is often needed in searching for some crystallization of his interpretation in the midst of ponderous wording, for he is not soon to the point and can be nebulous about when things will be fulfilled. An example is the fuzziness about the removal of evil to Babylon in Zechariah 5:5-11.

Redditt, Paul L. *Haggai, Zechariah, Malachi* (New Century Bible). Grand Rapids: Eerdmans, 1995.

Users will receive only spotty help since the terse work leaves out so much where readers need substance. No explanation appears on "treasure" in Hagg. 2:6, no reference even to the view that in 2:23 a greater than Zerubbabel may be in view, and no attempt to help in Zech. 11:13 on Matt. 27:9 using the verse in Judas' case. One also finds no reference in Zech. 12:10 to Christ in the NT, or an eschatological time, and no offer in 14:1-3 to tie material in with Christ's feet touching the mount at His Second Coming. A list of differences appear between 12:1-9 and 14:1-21, which Redditt then leaves in the air (so why is the list relevant?), as if no reasonable harmony can be suggested. Frequent seeming unawareness of common expository concerns lowers the work to minimal profit.

Smith, Ralph. Cf. on Micah.

Verhoef, Pieter A. *The Books of Haggai and Malachi* (New International Commentary on the Old Testament). Grand Rapids: Eerdmans, 1987. 364 pp.

This is by the Professor of Old Testament, Emeritus, University of Stellenbosch, South

Africa. It is conservative and offers much on current literature, introductory matters, and verse by verse content, adeptly explaining the text and flow of thought. He takes issue with W. Rudolph who says in his commentary on Haggai that the book has no relevance at all for the Christian faith (Verhoef, p. vii), and strives to show the significance of both Haggai and Malachi to today. He has interacted with much scholarship within the text and in footnotes. He believes that someone close to Haggai in his day wrote the book with authentic material from Haggai. He upholds the unity of the book, and traces the movement through the verses carefully in relation to its background. He may or may not be premillennial, seeing the fulfillment of prophetical aspects about the temple beyond the Second Advent. He deals at length with many of the problems, giving different views and factors to weigh, as on God's love and hate (Malachi 1:2-3), "one" in 2:15, the messenger concepts of 3:1, and "Elijah" in 4:4-6.

Wolf, Herbert M. *Haggai and Malachi* (Everyman's Bible Commentary). Chicago: Moody, 1976. 128 pp.

This is clear exposition based on skill in Hebrew. On many verses he is helpful, and traces the thought through in a well-organized way. He seems vague on when the glorious temple of Haggai 2:6-9 will be realized; he says at the Second Advent in a kingdom of Christ, a generality that could fit different views, but hints at a premillennial view. In Malachi 4 he sees a fulfillment in John the Baptist as "Elijah" and a possible further fulfillment in the tribulation period before the Second Advent.

Wolff, Hans W. *Haggai, A Commentary*. Minneapolis: Augsburg, 1988. 128 pp.

This work by an expert in exegesis, history and critical study is a translation from the German Biblischer Kommentar series. Wolff supposes three layers of composition from Haggai to the final writer. The chronicler, he feels, added interpolations at 2:5, 9, 14, 17-19, 21-22. The good of the large amount of information and expertise on exegesis is disturbed by what some will consider groundless opinions about composition and rearrangement.

Wolff, Richard. *The Book of Haggai*: A Study Manual. Grand Rapids: Baker, 1967.

A soundly evangelical and careful 84-page exegetical work reflecting broad study and attention to problems historically, exegetically and theologically in careful exposition. Wolff handles difficulties well in most cases and writes clearly. He is premillennial. This is one of the better brief commentaries on Haggai.

Zechariah

Baldwin, Joyce. Cf. on Haggai.

Barker, Kenneth. "Zechariah," in *Expositor's Bible Commentary*. Volume 7, editors Frank Gaebelein and R. P. Polcyn. Grand Rapids: Zondervan, 1985.

Conservative, premillennial expertise on the text, exegesis, scholarly literature etc. The careful writer, who correlates many things in a mature study, articulates a future for ethnic Israel in such texts as 13:1 and 14:1ff. It is the best recent premillennial work.

Baron, David. *Commentary on Zechariah.* **Grand Rapids: Kregel, 1988. 555 pp.**

A converted Jew gives frequent perceptive understanding from the Hebrew text.

Coggins, Richard J. Cf. on Haggai.

Heater, Homer, Jr. *Zechariah* **(Bible Study Commentary). Grand Rapids: Zondervan, 1987. 122 pp.**

Here is a good survey by a premillennialist, well-organized, aware of main issues, contributive on most. He takes the four horns of 1:18-19 to be not the four empires of Daniel 2 and 7 or any other specific four but coming from the four quarters of the earth, a world-wide context (p. 21). The four craftsmen are likewise. He sees the future for Jerusalem in Chapter 2 as millennial, after the Second Advent. He appears to be vague on God taking evil from Israel and "setting it up among those who reject Him . . . " in Shinar (Zechariah 5, p. 43). The explanation of details in Chapter 14 as fitting in a premillennial view is helpful but brief.

Feinberg, Charles L. *God Remembers: A Study of Zechariah.* **4th edition. Portland: Multnomah Press, 1979.**

This is a reprint of one of the best premillennial expositions by the late evangelical Old Testament scholar. Feinberg taught Zechariah for many years at Dallas Seminary and Talbot Seminary in Hebrew exegesis classes. He, Barker and Unger have the best longer premillennial commentaries of a verse by verse nature on the book.

Feinberg, Charles L. *Zechariah: Israel's Comfort and Glory.* **NY: American Board of Missions to the Jews, 1952.**

Also note his commentary on Zechariah in the one-volume *Wycliffe Bible Commentary* as well as the larger volume *God Remembers*, which was first issued as a series in *Bibliotheca Sacra.*

Laney, J. Carl. *Zechariah* **(Everyman's Bible Commentary). Chicago: Moody, 1984. 143 pp.**

A lucid, well-paced premillennial exposition showing an evident keenness about explaining main issues. See, for example, pp. 24-25, and later his comments on Zechariah 14. He is Associate Professor of Biblical Literature at Western Conservative Baptist Seminary, Portland, OR.

Leupold, H. C. *Exposition of Zechariah.* **Columbus: Wartburg, 1956.**

In this commentary the student will find a good example of how an amillennial scholar of top rank deals with the crucial prophecies relating to Israel's future. As usual, Leupold is detailed and seeks to grapple with the problems.

Lindsey, F. Duane. "Zechariah," in *Bible Knowledge Commentary*, editors John F. Walvoord and Roy B. Zuck, Volume I. Wheaton: Victor Books, 1983.

Lindsey covers many of the interpretive issues fairly well, often mentioning views and sometimes bringing good reasoning to bear. He sees the eight night visions in 1:7-6:8 as God's work which "bridges the centuries from the rebuilding of the temple in Zechariah's day to the restoration of the kingdom to Israel under the Messiah ... to be fulfilled at Christ's Second Advent. . ." (p. 1549). He deals with Chapters 12-14, particularly in a premillennial framework, and makes things clear.

Moore, T. V. Cf. on Haggai.

Petersen, David I. Cf. on Haggai.

Petersen, David L. *Zechariah 9-14 and Malachi. A Commentary* (OT Library). Louisville, KY: Westminster John Knox Press, 1995.

After an introduction for the historical context of the Second Temple era, Petersen deals successively with Zech. 9-11, 12-14, and Mal. One thing he looks at is the long history of scholars who have not attributed Zech. 9-14 to Zechariah, son of Berachiah, since the early 17th century (23). A related discussion looks at redactional approaches. Petersen on Zech. 11:13 does not mention the Matt. 27:9 use of this. One finds much on 14:1-21 in relation to other OT references, but no reference to the Christian belief in the NT relation to Christ's Second Coming. He offers no prophetical perspective on how/when the details can realistically occur, as if he has no key into an integrated conception. The work, though evidencing learning, is not of immense help to evangelicals serious about grasping a meaningful prophetical picture.

Smith, Ralph. Cf. on Micah.

Unger, Merrill F. *Commentary on Zechariah*. Grand Rapids: Zondervan, 1963.

Based on the Hebrew text, this detailed work is the result of more than 15 years of lectures on Zechariah. The author was Chairman of the Department of Old Testament and Professor of Hebrew Exegesis at Dallas Seminary. He writes with lucid literary style. His interpretations are premillennial and dispensational in orientation. He uses a large variety of words, and meets the amillennial system of interpretation squarely in the key passages. An outline is given, a translation of the text is printed at the top of the page, and the commentary is set up in two columns on each page. The student will find help also in the extensive bibliography given at the end of the commentary though lacking studies of more recent years. This work and the commentaries by Barker and Feinberg are the most valuable longer premillennial studies of Zechariah.

Malachi

Baldwin, Joyce. Cf. on Haggai.

Blaising, Craig. "Malachi," in *Bible Knowledge Commentary*, **editors John F. Walvoord and Roy B. Zuck, Volume I. Wheaton: Victor Books, 1983.**

A capable conservative, premillennial study that provides considerable help, even if concise, to expositors. Blaising takes Malachi as a personal name (p. 1573), defending this against four arguments. He has good discussions of some problematic verses, as the "one" in 2:15, and details in 3:1 and 4:5-6. In the latter, he does not believe that John the Baptist fulfilled the "Elijah" expectation (1588), but Elijah is yet to come.

Coggins, Richard J. Cf. on Haggai.

Glazier-McDonald, Beth. *Malachi, The Divine Messenger.* **Atlanta, GA: Scholars Press, 1987. 288 pp.**

This 1983 dissertation at the University of Chicago does several things. It stands against the tide holding that the book is prose and contends for the poetic character of the larger part. The work explains explains the text, often in as much detail as many verse by verse commentaries, and is against emendations. It argues for every verse fitting the flow of the context and being cogent to the situation of Malachi's day ca. 450 B.C. The writer shows wide knowledge of scholarly literature, but often reasons against commonly accepted critical theory. For example, the "messenger of the covenant" in 3:1 is to her the Lord, not an addition to the text. Conservatives appreciate much of the work, but textual and redaction-critical scholars frown on her upholding the text as it is, though she has done her homework.

Hill, Andrew E. *Malachi* **(Anchor Bible). NY: Doubleday, 1998.**

Advanced, patient students of Malachi will glean much from this laborious work of 436 pp., 129 just on preliminaries such as glossary (7 pp.), thematic and rhetorical outlines, translation, and introduction. The latter has much on the place in the canon, Malachi, literary features (38-39), the main message, theology, dating and background ca. 485-480 B.C. (51), use of Mal. in the NT, and a 35-pp. bibliography. Commentary detail is meticulous on exegesis and interaction with many studies on interpretation. This is so much the case that at times it is slow and one can find it difficult "to see the forest for the trees." Transliterated Heb. words, defined, help those without facility in the Heb. In special "Notes" on each section, verses are marked out helpfully; later, "Comments" give still more information, as on problems relating to "one" in Mal. 2:15, or the "messenger" in 3:1. Hill limits 3:1 only to OT input, so a reader finds no relating of this to the NT as in Mark 1:2. But on 4:5, he discusses NT and Christian thought on 3:1 and on Elijah and concurs at last that the "messenger" in 4:5 is the one in 3:1 (383-84). He appears to see him fulfilled in John the Baptist and also possibly in one to come even later.

Hugenberger, Gordon P. *Marriage as a Covenant. Biblical Law and Ethics as Developed From Malachi.* **Grand Rapids: Baker, 1994.**

The senior pastor of the famous Park Street Church, Boston, who also is an OT teacher at Gordon-Conwell Theological Seminary, offers a hefty (414-pp.) book on Mal. 2:10-

16. He explores whether "covenant" refers to marriage, divorce in v. 16, appeal to Adam and Even, what is necessary for marriage, marriage as a covenant in other OT texts, etc. The bibliography on ancient and modern literature is massive (344-80). A study of biblical marriage can well include this widely-informed discussion of ancient Near Eastern covenants, marriage in the biblical world, and the facing of grammatical issues in a key passage.

Isbell, Charles D. *Malachi* (Bible Study Commentary). Grand Rapids: Zondervan, 1980. 80 pp.

Isbell decides Malachi is not the prophet's name but descriptive of his role, "My messenger." His explanation of God's love and hate (1:2-3) does not relate this to Romans 9 in the larger picture and show how the explanation is consistent (if so) with it. His comments on 4:4-6 do not explain much on Elijah; there is no relationship made to New Testament passages and possibilities. But earlier on 3:1 (p. 59) he offers a little on this, although it is a bigger problem than he offers help on. Overall this is a fair commentary but not high on the list.

Kaiser, Walter C., Jr. *Malachi: God's Unchanging Love*. Grand Rapids: Baker, 1984. 172 pp.

A fine work on exegesis of the text and practical import for life today. It is conservative and premillennial, and will make some contribution in an expositor's preparation to speak on the book.

Moore, T. T. Cf. on Haggai.

Morgan, G. Campbell. *Malachi's Message for Today*. Grand Rapids: Baker, 1972.

Even though Morgan's ministry was completed in the early part of this century, his exposition still has emphases relevant and timely today. He shows how Malachi's comments live. The book is provocative for a preaching series and for leading Bible studies, He excels at times in rich, stimulating word studies (cf. on 3:16, "they feared the Lord and thought on his name," showing a tie-in with other Scripture, with help for the spiritual life).

Smith, Ralph. Cf. on Micah.

Verhoef, Pieter A. Cf. on Haggai.

Wolf, Herbert M. Cf. on Haggai.

GENERAL COMMENTARIES ON THE NEW TESTAMENT

GREEK

Alford, Henry. *The Greek New Testament*. 4 vols. Chicago: Moody, 1958, Revision by Everett Harrison.

This was the great work in the life of the versatile Dean of Canterbury. An outcome of this production was the *New Testament for English Readers* (4 vols.). Alford was a Calvinist, conservative and premillennial, though not dispensational. He takes a literal interpretation of the thousand years in Rev. 20 and has a famous quote there, is strong on sovereign election as in Rom 8:29-30 and I Pet. 1:2, but, unfortunately, holds to baptismal regeneration in such texts as Titus 3:5 and John 3:5. He shows a great knowledge of the Greek text and faces problems of both a doctrinal and textual nature.

Baker Exegetical Commentary. Grand Rapids: Baker.

Any who want solid, deep discussion of NT passages, even wrestling with issues, will find frequent help here. The assists will be on grammar, word meaning, customs, and other factors to resolve what biblical statements mean, often after sifting views and utilizing the best in scholarly literature. Some examples are D. Bock's massive 2-vol. work on Luke, and T. Schreiner's hefty work on Romans. The interaction on problem texts as well as the verse by verse supply of substance to provide light will put these among the better tools for teachers in biblical institutions, pastors who study in depth, students, and laity who are ready for more detailed study.

Bengel, J. A. *Bengel's New Testament Commentary*, 2 volumes. New translation by C. T. Lewis and M. R. Vincent. Grand Rapids: Kregel, 1981rp.

This work, originally issued in 1742, has considerable comment on the Greek, flavoring the effort with judicious details about the spiritual life. It has much that helps, but has been surpassed by many other commentaries since its day.

Ellicott, Charles J. A *New Testament Commentary for English Readers*. 3 vols. New York: E. P. Dutton & Co. (n. d.).

Though concise in its statements, this old commentary reveals a thorough knowledge of the Greek and is very helpful in matters of grammar and word meanings.

Eerdman's Critical Commentary. Grand Rapids: Eerdmans.

Here is another detailed, serious work grappling with issues of exposing what the Greek text says, and what is its meaning, often among several views and arguments. Advanced Greek students and any who can stay with substantial discussion of interpretive issues will glean much from such works as Quinn/Wacker on 1, 2 Timothy.

Lenski, R. C. H. *Commentary on the New Testament*. 12 vols. Columbus: Wartburg, 1937-46.

This Lutheran scholar is careful and thorough, giving the reader much material which seriously grapples with the meaning of the text. He is evangelical and amillennial.

Marshall, I. Howard, and W. W. Gasque, eds. *New International Greek Testament Commentary*. Grand Rapids: Eerdmans, 1978ff.

This rather thorough evangelical exegetical work reveals scholarly study steeped in the literature pertinent to passages. New volumes continue to appear. Advanced students find it very helpful, and other serious readers can glean much. It interacts with modern critical discussion in books and journals. Marshall's 928-page commentary on Luke started it off (first at Exeter, England: Paternoster Press). Other authors chosen are usually well-established in New Testament scholarship. Some of the volumes published are by Paul Ellingworth (Hebrews), George W. Knight (Pastorals), F. F. Bruce (Galatians), Peter O'Brien (Philippians). C. A. Wanamaker (Thessalonian Epistles), and Peter Davids (James).

Meyer, H. A. W., ed. *A Critical and Exegetical Commentary on the New Testament*. 11 volumes. Translated from 6th edition of German of 1884. Winona Lake, IN: Alpha Publications, 1979rp.

One of the finest old works on meticulous exegesis of the Greek verse by verse, informed by much expertise and study. It provides very well-respected discussion on all but the Book of Revelation. Meyer, J. E. Huther and G. Lunemann did different parts. It is conservative in places but not in others, and helpful to trained users who know how to follow the intricacies of grammar.

Moule, C. F. D. (Ed.). *Cambridge Greek Testament Commentary*. Cambridge: University Press, 1957.

Appearance of this Cambridge University Press production began in 1955. The aim was to present a work replacing the former Cambridge Bible for Schools and Colleges and the Cambridge Greek Testament for Schools and Colleges. It is an attempt to give a theological commentary founded upon careful linguistic and historical study.

New International Biblical Commentary. Peabody, MA: Hendrickson, 1989ff.

An evangelical series by scholars who for the most part are well-known, such as Robert Mounce (Matthew), F. F. Bruce (Philippians), Gordon Fee (Pastorals), and Peter Davids (James). In cases just named they rank high, offering well-studied detail arising out of sound hermeneutics in many cases. The series began as the Good News Commentary in the early 1980's using the Good News translation (Harper and Row), but switched in the late 80's to Hendrickson and NIV. Teachers in biblical schools, pastors, and students encounter some high level dealing with details in passages, usually treating these with strong confidence in their integrity. Some examples of fairly good commentary are by Hartley (Gen.), C. Wright (Deut.), Provain (1, 2 Kings), Murphy (Prov.), and T. F. Johnson (Johan. Eps.). To some extent the quality is "a mixed bag," however, considering some derogatory statements by Bellinger on Lev. and Num., and the series introducing critical theories not accepted by many conservatives,for instance Goldingay at times on Isaiah, even amid his many good contributions.

Nicoll, W. Robertson (Ed.). *The Expositors' Greek Testament.* **5 vols. Grand Rapids: Eerdmans, 1951. Reprint.**

This is a thorough exegesis of the Greek text. It is considered to be one of the standard tools for exegetical study.

Pillar Commentary Series. Grand Rapids: Eerdmans, 1988ff.

This is an ongoing evangelical product with solid efforts so far by L. Morris (Romans), D. A. Carson (John), P. T. O'Brien (Ephesians), etc. All the vols. this reviewer has checked are solid in dealing with interpretive issues, usually not dodging opportunity to explain things forthrightly. The good scholars making the contributions are well-informed in Greek, theology, word study, customs, and views in various writings. The individual biblical book entries will say more about particular vols., where the standard is good but some writers (as those above) contribute works that are especially worthwhile overall.

Robertson, Archibald T. *Word Pictures in the New Testament.* **6 vols. Nashville: Broadman, 1931.**

Authored by one of the foremost Greek scholars in the 20th century, this work is very helpful in matters of grammar and word meanings throughout the New Testament. Robertson, a Southern Baptist, was the author of a monumental grammar of the New Testament.

Vincent, M. R. *Word Studies in the New Testament.* **4 vols. N. Y.: Scribners, 1887-1900.**

Often helpful in discerning meanings of words in a passage and thus cited frequently by some writers. It is in many places good, but not as valuable as A. T. Robertson's *Word Pictures*.

ENGLISH

Abingdon New Testament Commentary. Nashville: Abingdon Press.

Some scholarly good will help users here, although this reviewer does not rate the works high in contribution. Many works help more. One can check Smith's vol. on the Gospel of John, which is not high in assisting one's understanding. The worthwhileness will come to the patient who glean here and there, while mostly benefitting from other works.

A New Testament Commentary, **Eds. G. C. D. Howley, F. F. Bruce, and H. L. Ellisen. Grand Rapids: Zondervan, 1969. 1 vol.**

Twenty-five evangelical scholars (though most names are not well known in America) contributed. The work begins with a section of general articles on areas such as authority of the N. T., the text and canon, the language of the N. T., archaeological discoveries, environmental background, historical and political background, chronology, pagan and Jewish background, N. T. use of the O.T., etc. Bruce does the commentary on the Book of Revelation. Comments throughout are terse; there is no room for discussing issues at length. As a one-volume work it offers help at times and in a limited way.

Alford, Henry. *The New Testament for English Readers*. **4 vols. Chicago: Moody, 1955.**

This contains much that is valuable in the Greek New Testament authored by Alford, though all of the Greek New Testament words have been changed to English throughout.

Arnold, Clinton E., gen. ed. *Zondervan Bible Backgrounds Commentary*. **4 vols. Grand Rapids: Zondervan, 2002.**

Here, 2924 pp. give brief, often verse by verse comments on each NT book. Among better known writers are: Michael Wilkins (Matt.), David Garland (Mk.), Mark Strauss (Lk.), Andreas Kostenberger (Jn.), Douglas Moo (Rom., Jas., 2 Pet., Jd.), Ralph Martin (Gal.), Peter Davids (I Pet.), Robert Yarbrough (epistles of John). Many color pictures as on customs appear, also maps, and special panels. In the latter, one finds such subjects as Roman calendars and the date of Jesus' birth, Pharisees and Sadducees, and the meaning of the millennium (which never tells the meaning while briefly listing views), etc. Interpretations of verses show background customs, as on the Roman triumph in 2 Cor. 2:14, often get definite about meaning but also often leave matters vague. End notes for each book cite from broad scholarly research in ancient texts as well as recent studies. It remains to be seen how useful the vols. will be, but due to the cost of around $160 and cursory comments that often offer only sparse explanations, many will turn to works that contribute more. Vagueness or lack of definition in the brevity appears frequently, as on the meaning of "kingdom" in Matt. 13:11 and who the "restrainer" is in 2 Thess. 2:6, 8 (left undecided). Verses on Christ's coming in Matt. 24-25 refer to the church's rapture; John 15:2a, 6 deal with a professing but unsaved person; "husband of one wife" (I Tim. 3:2) means an elder should not have one or more concubines; Rev. 1:20 speaks of celestial angels; the 144,000 in Rev. 7 are Jewish believers. The vols. are beautifully produced, but represent a "mixed bag" of brief help on some matters and on many not saying much on the meaning or taking a definite stand.

Barclay, William. *Commentary on the New Testament*. **Philadelphia: Westminster, 1957-63.**

Now also available in paperback which is much more economical, this set is very rich in background, word studies and illuminating material on manners and customs. It is a good commentary to have. However, the student should realize that it sometimes is weak theologically, showing liberal bias at some points.

Erdman, Charles R. *Commentary on the New Testament*. **17 vols. Philadelphia: Westminster, 1916-36.**

Concise treatments are given to each of the N. T. books. The main value of the set lies in its clear synthesis which helps the student grasp the flow of thought as he moves through a book. Erdman possessed a lucid writing style. He was amillennial.

Gaebelein, Arno C. *Gaebelein's Concise Commentary on the New Testament*. **Chicago: Moody, 1991.**

This is a revision, in one volume, of the New Testament part of the multi-volume *Annotated Bible* by one of America's popular Bible teachers in the first half of the twentieth century. It includes diligent explanation that helps pastors and lay readers and also frequent application, somewhat akin to the broad H. A. Ironside or Warren Wiersbe expositions.

Jensen, Irving L. *Jensen's Survey of the New Testament.* **Chicago: Moody, 1981.**

A firmly evangelical work of 535 pages written on a Bible college text-book level with broad surveys of N. T. books, many charts and maps, lists of applications, study questions, selected reading lists, good organization in chapters. He takes an early date for Mt. (late 50's), says very little of substance at times in a section (cf. Mt. 13:1-53, p. 125), tends frequently to leave out some of the top-notch commentaries in reading lists (cf. Mt., Mk., Lk., Rom., etc.). But considering his objective, to furnish a book that aims to get a student into the Bible text itself, he may well go with a light survey and not give so much on key details. Outlines tend to be brief and simple, surveys at times are mere outlines (I Cor. 1-6), at times a long discussion (7 & 8) etc. All things considered, the survey is bound to be some help to those who need a light, yet well-organized overview which puts in certain key information to orientate them.

Inter-Varsity Press New Testament Commentary. **Downers Grove, IL: IVP.**

Those consulting these compact works growing out of careful, wide study will find much that is readily worth the effort. Good scholars contribute out of their wealth, and pack the vols. with details that furnish light on meaning. I. H. Marshall's lucid handling of I Peter is one example of a well-organized work that keeps the overall flow in view, yet offers pertinence verse by verse, and often a consideration of views on problem texts. For more detail, readers will need also to gain the contribution of the works that can provide even further depth.

Ironside, H. A. (addresses on individual New Testament books). N. Y.: Loizeaux, Inc. Various Dates.

He has authored works on all 27 New Testament books. These are premillennial and dispensational but of a popular strain, having grown out of messages delivered from his pulpit, the Moody Memorial Church in Chicago.

MacArthur New Testament Commentary. **Chicago: Moody Press.**

Many vols. are already out and more to come. One of the world's best-known expository preachers offers edited messages that grew out of diligent preparation and patiently worked through biblical books. MacArthur provides background, synopses of sections, light on word meanings, help on problem verses, and principles for application. His works are among the more substantial among pulpit masters in explaining the text. So far, the series includes such Scripture books as Matthew (4 vols.), Romans, Acts, I Corinthians, Galatians, Ephesians, Philippians, Colossians and Philemon, the Pastorals, and Hebrews.

New American Commentary. **Nashville, TN: Broadman Press, 1990ff.**

This new series takes the place of the old American Commentary on the New Testament, in which John Broadus on Matthew was a standout. All NAC authors "affirm the divine inspiration, inerrancy, complete truthfulness, and full authority of the Bible" (Editor's Preface). Craig Blomberg's entry on Matthew is a very good survey, marked by careful study, wide acquaintance with the literature, and perceptive handling of many problems. John Polhill's on Acts is also quite good. Some volumes, as the one on the Pastorals, are surveys that make good contributions at times but do not come up to the standard of the efforts on Matthew and Acts.

Ogilvie, Lloyd J. (Gen. Ed.) *The Communicator's Commentary* **(N. T.). Waco, Texas: Word Books, 1982-1991.**

A 12-vol. set done by 12 men selected for unusual ability to show the Bible is alive in biblical exposition, with spiritual refreshment and insight. These are Myron S. Augsburger (Mt.), David McKenna (Mk.), Bruce Larson (U.), Roger Fredrikson Gn.), Lloyd Ogilvie (Acts), D. Stuart Briscoe (Rom.), Kenneth Chafin (1, 2 Cor.), Maxie Dunham (Gal., Eph., Phil., Col., Phile.), Gary Demarest (Thess., Pastorals), Louis Evans, Jr. (Heb.), Paul Cedar James, 1, 2 Pet., Jude), Earl Palmer (1, 2, 3 Jn., Rev.) The authors seek to combine scholarship on biblical meaning, illustrations to spark applications, and outlines based on the new KJV. Frequent bold-faced headings appear over smaller sections throughout a biblical book. On many passages the sweeping comments on the main emphases are quite good and at times well-illustrated. That does not mean that readers will be able to agree on every point. See, for example, on Mt. 19:9 (Mt. 19, p. 76) where *porneia* is said to mean what Schweizer thought, "continual infidelity rather than a single act of adultery." The commentary does not always explain (but which commentary does?) how a point is consistent with some other main truth many in the audience will probably wonder about. For example, many will wonder how a person paying all to secure the pearl (Mt. 13:46) to gain the goal is consistent with God giving eternal blessing as an outright gift. Granted there is a good explanation; it would be helpful to comment on such a vital point, even if briefly. Briscoe's treatment of Romans is very well-written in the literary sense and illustrated in a very choice way. It is refreshing to see him explain such a passage as 2:7 as Cranfield and Kasemann, not as hypothetical but as actual, lived by grace consistent with justification by grace and not merit in 3:28. However, the comments on 2:11-15 do not explain much that will answer key questions people have put to me on the implications. The same is true of 3:27-31, where arousing illustration is good but basic explanation is thin (how do "we establish the law", for example?). What does 4:15 mean? (The comment on 5:13, 14 on p. 123 may help a little.) He does a fairly good job on 5:12ff., 6:6, 7:14ff., etc. The work on the Epistles of John and the Book of Revelation is too often so generalized that one can come away with little that really helps (cf. I Jn. 5:16; Rev. 2: 10, 11; 7:1-8; 9:1 -11 etc). The bibliography at the end is rather thin on better helps that make a solid attempt at interpreting the Revelation. In looking through several vols. of this commentary, the feature that has struck me as helpful is the aspect of illustrations which are often superbly refreshing and suggestive as preaching helps.

The actual verse by verse explanation as to reflecting a perceptive grasp of what really is vital to be explained and then nailing down the explanation solidly is quite good in some places but weak or non-existent on key details in others.

Ritchie New Testament Commentary Series. **10 volumes. Kilmarnock, Scotland: John Ritchie, Ltd., 1988ff, or Neptune, NJ: Loizeaux, 1988ff.**

Simple laypersons' commentaries done in a firm evangelical conviction of inerrancy and even according to a dispensational view but sometimes without a very broad effort to look at other literature that can help. For further comment, cf. John Heading, "Gospel of John," in this list.

Wesley, John. *Explanatory Notes Upon the New Testament.* **2 vols. Grand Rapids: Baker, 1981.**

Here is one good source in which to find Wesley's view of a given text most readily, even if he is brief.

Wiersbe, Warren. *The Bible Exposition Commentary.* **2 volumes. Wheaton: Victor Books, 1990.**

One of America's most appreciated staunchly evangelical Bible conference teachers gives diligent, refreshing expositions. These are all of his 23 separate, earlier books in the "Be" series on the New Testament. He strikes a particular appeal with lay people as he crystallizes sections, deals with some of the verses, handles certain problems and backgrounds and applies principles. He is premillennial.

Yeager, Randolph O. *The Renaissance New Testament.* **18 vols. Gretna, LA: Pelican Publishing Co., Inc., 1976-1985.**

Yeager, a student of the famous Julius R. Mantey in 1934, labored about 50 years to write these big vols. Amounting to more than 11,000 pp., the work is of a cost (ca. $450.00) that will turn many away and be usable in libraries. Yeager meticulously comments on the meaning of every Greek word, mode, tense, and case verse by verse, so the work is a kind of grammar, dictionary and concordance. His aim was to help students think through matters for themselves, led by the Holy Spirit (I, x-xi). The title focuses on Yeager's goal of a user being a humble child of reason, experience, and faith (I, xxiii-xxiv), patient in confidence that truth will prevail and exemplifying love as in I Corinthians 13. He explains, defines, and illustrates words at their first occurrence, but often gives overly long lists that most students will probably not use and that increase the bulk. Vol. I explains the basics of NT grammar and syntax (xxxi-lxiv). Despite the sheer detail, Yeager has some comments that are scanty and not so helpful on views and possibilities, matters on which several NT works offer more at least on more crucial issues. An example is on divorce (Matt. 19:9). Yeager sees the church's rapture in Matt. 24:40, 41 as in I Thess. 4:16. In John 8:31, he says many saved people are not disciples, do not continue in Christ's word, yet remain safe (6:192). In Matt. 13, the second and third soils represent those who remain eternally saved but do not go on in the Word, yet will receive some positive reward in eternity (6:193). John 10:28 teaches eternal security. The "restrainer" in 2 Thess. 2 is the Holy Spirit. In Revelation, Yeager favors a future for Jewish people seeing covenant land promises fulfilled as in the 144,000, and favors the 144,000 being both men and women (7:3-8). The bride in 19:7-8 is only the saved who have righteous acts, distinct from saved people who only are righteous by justification. The two witnesses of Rev. 11 are two individuals, and the "woman" in chap. 12 represents Israelites. Sections summing up different texts' meanings reflect evangelical convictions, some normative, some introducing oddities (even errors) of the author's own leaning. Evidence for some views is persuasive, for some it is not. In the latter, Yeager in Eph. 4:8 sees Christ after death going to Paradise, releasing OT saints/captives, and in His resurrection transferring these to a new location of Paradise in heaven (14:227). Overall, the work often helps, however one can in many cases learn more, faster, by going to some better-known works that more helpfully discuss possibilities. Still, Yeager is commended for his prolific effort, which will serve some of the patient.

BACKGROUND WORKS AND
SPECIAL STUDIES IN THE GOSPELS

Andrews, Samuel J. *The Life of Our Lord Upon the Earth*. Grand Rapids: Zondervan, 1954.

One of the top older works on the life of Christ, this book originally appeared in 1862. It is primarily for the advanced students, though it is helpful also to the general reader. Chronological and geographical factors are discussed carefully. However, he does not deal adequately with critical and philosophical attacks on the reliability of the gospel records.

Bruce, A. B. *The Training of the Twelve*. N. Y.: Hodder and Stoughton (n. d.).

Dr. W. H. Griffith-Thomas held this work in such regard that he rated it "one of the greatest books of the nineteenth century." It is a standard treatment of Christ's association with His disciples.

Culver, Robert D. *The Life of Christ*. Grand Rapids: Baker, 1976.

A widely-known former professor at Trinity Evangelical Divinity School and in recent years a pastor gives us a sweeping survey with photographs, diagrams and maps. Certain of the eleven special "excursus" sections on problems are helpful summaries on such matters as the length of Jesus' ministry, Jewish national responsibility for Jesus' ministry, Jesus' use of parables, some apparent discrepancies, etc. It is a fine brief work from the man who wrote *Daniel and the Latter Days* defending a premillennial perspective in Daniel's prophecies.

Edersheim, Alfred. *The Life and Times of Jesus the Messiah*. 2 vols. Grand Rapids: Eerdmans, 1953.

New Testament scholars often regard this as the top work on the life of Christ. It is extremely valuable in its information about Jewish and Hellenistic background, with many citations from primary sources in ancient literature. The author's flare for vivid description enhances the work. A recent one-volume abridged work is available, but the two-volume set is recommended. *Eternity Magazine* in 1958 wrote to several N. T. scholars to get their opinions on the best works on the life of Christ, and this work was rated best.

Enns, Paul, ed., *Moody Gospel Commentary*. Chicago: Moody Press, 1992ff.

Edited by Paul Enns who has written several books, this very readable evangelical series is designed to cover the gospels for expositors and lay readers. J. Carl Laney's 407-page volume on John began it, and other volumes are to follow. Enns and Laney are premillennial and dispensational. Cf. Laney on The Gospel of John, Ed Glasscock on Matthew, etc.

Fairweather, W. *The Background of the Gospels.* **Edinburgh: T. & T. Clark, 1920.**

The significance of Gospel events is illumined by this book which presents many helpful facets of history.

Farrar, F. W. *The Life of Christ.* **N. Y.: Dutton (n. d.).**

This is one of the most famous and most readable older works on this great subject.

Farrar, F. W. *The Life of Lives.*

This is a sequel to *The Life of Christ* dealing with the Acts and Epistles.

Foster, R. C. *Studies in the Life of Christ.* **2 vols. Grand Rapids: Baker Book House, 1962.**

A Church of Christ scholar, Prof. of N. T. at that time in the Cincinnati Bible Seminary, presents a life of Jesus with several special studies in which he interacts with liberal scholars and takes a conservative approach.

Guthrie, Donald. *Jesus the Messiah.* **Grand Rapids: Zondervan, 1972.**

A widely-recognized evangelical scholar presents a competent survey of the life of Christ. It is 386 pages with rather frequent pictures, a good index of subjects and Scriptures, a devotional flavor and yet a work careful about theological and historical aspects. He takes sayings and incidents in the ministry of Jesus and gives a comprehensive survey of salient points he feels most important to treat. Cf. also Guthrie's *A Shorter Life of Christ* (Grand Rapids: Zondervan, 1970), which concisely surveys the area and deals with problems about the historicity of Jesus.

Hastings, James. *Dictionary of Christ and the Gospels.* **2 vols. N. Y.: Scribner's, 1906-08.**

Excellent for detail on various facets of a study of the life of Christ. The student should find it helpful in good background information.

Hoehner, Harold. *Herod Antipas.* **Cambridge, Eng.: Cambridge University, 1972.**

Written by the Professor of New Testament Literature and Exegesis at Dallas Theological Seminary, this conservative work was the most thorough and up to date (to 1972) in its field. The author, who received both the Th. M. and Th. D. degrees at Dallas Seminary before writing this as a dissertation at Cambridge, seems to have dealt with all the facets and N. T. verses relating to the Herod who beheaded John and tried Jesus Christ. The bibliography shows great breadth in research.

Morgan, G. Campbell. *The Crises of the Christ.* **N. Y.: Revell, 1903.**

Dr. Wilbur Smith has said: I think this is the most important single volume that Dr. Morgan ever wrote. It is a masterpiece. It is a study of the Incarnation, the Baptism, the Temptation, the Transfiguration, the Crucifixion, the Resurrection and the Ascension" (*His*, April, 1951). Morgan's insight into these events is penetrating stimulating, and suggestive for teaching or sermonic material as well as devotionally enriching.

Pentecost, J. Dwight. *The Words and Works of Jesus Christ.* **Grand Rapids: Zondervan, 1981.**

The 629-pp. work represents the results of many years expounding his "Life of Christ" course in English Bible at Dallas Seminary, a very popular class. Pentecost's great theme is Christ presenting Himself as King, offering the Messianic Kingdom, with some receiving and some rejecting and His program with Israel as a nation postponed until the Second Advent. He handles much of the text of the gospels in a popular, expository way, explaining portions such as parables in some relation to the kingdom theme and seeking to give information on many aspects of customs, background, and dispensational place in the flow of thought. He has appendices on geography, historical setting, religious setting, social environment and chronology, and lists such as on parables and miracles, a bibliography, and documentation along the way. The intent of the work is to trace a theme expositionally, which Pentecost adheres to well. Some have faulted the work for its lack of involvement with critical issues and failure to comment on many areas debated in scholarly N. T. circles today. Well, who can cover everything? The flavor of the book is strongly conservative, with much to aid the pastor or teacher moving in a series through the life of Christ. Also available is a companion volume, *A Harmony of the Words and Works of Jesus Christ* (Zondervan, 1981, 272-pp.).

Scroggie, W. Graham. *Guide to the Gospels.* **London: Pickering & Inglis, Limited, 1952.**

This is a gold mine of carefully systematized information on many aspects in a thorough study of each Gospel. No serious student should be without it.

Shepard, J. W. *The Christ of the Gospels, An Exegetical Study.* **Grand Rapids: Eerdmans, 1939.**

This amillennial work is profitable for an exegetical study of the Gospels step by step through the life of Christ. Though it takes the Two-Document theory of Synoptic origins, it is generally solid in doctrine and helpful in shades of Greek word meanings.

Stier, Rudolph. *The Words of the Lord Jesus.* **4 vols. London: T. & T. Clark 1869.**

This is a detailed, helpful commentary on just the words spoken by Jesus. It is heavy but thorough.

Whyte, Alexander. *The Walk, Conversation, and Character of Jesus Christ Our Lord.* **N.Y.: Revell, 1905.**

The author, famed for his brilliant works on Bible characters and his great oratorical skill, has given in this work an exposition of selected texts in the Gospels. These are among the best highlight chapters ever written on certain moments in the life of our Lord on earth.

COMMENTARIES ON INDIVIDUAL NEW TESTAMENT BOOKS

I. MATTHEW

Armerding, Carl. *The Olivet Discourse of Matthew 24-25 and Other Studies.* **Findlay, Ohio: Dunham Publishing Co., 1955.**

A noted Bible teacher (Wheaton College and Bible conferences) of a past era wrote this dispensational work. He contends that "Thy coming" (24:3) is the Second Advent at the end of the future tribulation period, not Christ's coming at the rapture of the Church, which he exempts from the days to which he believes the parables of 24-25 point. An earthly regathering of Israel fulfilling Old Testament promises of a regathering is in view in 24:31, not the Church's rapture when Christ meets His own "in the air" (I Thessalonians 4:16). In 24:40, 41 those "taken" are taken off the earth to judgment. Those "left" are left on earth to enter the kingdom begun on earth. Unlike dispensationalist Gaebelein, Armerding says 24:45ff., 25:1-13 and 25:14-30 refer to the separation at the end of the age, at the Second Advent, not the separation of the church from the unsaved by the rapture.

Barbieri, Louis. "Matthew," in *Bible Knowledge Commentary***, ed. John F. Walvoord and Roy B. Zuck, Volume II. Wheaton: Victor Books, 1985.**

A fairly good dispensational survey, helpful to pastors as well as lay readers. Cf. also H. Kent's entry.

Beare, Francis W. *The Gospel According to Matthew.* **Peabody, MA: Hendrickson Publishers, 1981. 550 pp.**

A liberal work arguing for Markan priority (p. vii). Matthew is almost totally taken over from Mark. Conservatives will sift much that is good, but disagree with many of the statements, such as "Matthew has given us a grim book, singularly lacking in those notes of joy that sound through ... Luke," etc. (viii). He dates Matthew in the late first or early second century (7-8). He denies that the sermon on the mount was given at one time and place and says the "mountain" was not a particular geographical location (13). Questions the disciples ask Jesus may or may not grow out of a tradition of questions really put to Jesus; they are used to call forth answers for Christians of the later writer's day (14). Some of the scenes are "artificially constructed settings for sayings of Jesus" (14-15). We see things that happened mixed with fiction that is added, and imagination is given a large place (15). Matthew has done violence to his sources in his artificial genealogy (63). Beare seems to take Mary's conception as supernatural (66-67, 70), but denies that Isaiah 7:14 in its own right predicted a miraculous birth from a virgin centuries later (71). In gospel stories the point to Beare is not whether they have any "possible kernel of historical fact" (72), but the purpose the writer intends them to serve. Sometimes Beare has much learning on a verse and is helpful, at other times he provides little real help, as on the use of Old Testament "prophets" in 2:23. The bibliography is years out of date.

Blomberg, Craig L. *Matthew* **(New American Commentary). Nashville, TN: Broadman Press, 1992. 464 pp.**

This work using the NIV is a major contribution in the 40 volume re-doing of an old evangelical series in which John Broadus was notable on Matthew, The NAC claims inerrancy. Blomberg, Associate Professor of New Testament, Denver Seminary, has such standout works as *Interpreting the Parables* (Downers Grove: IVP, 1990). Here he has a brief, well-packed, knowledgeable introduction (21-49), favoring a date between ca. A. D. 58-69 and authorship by Matthew. He sees this gospel as historically reliable (47) as he argues in his T*he Historical Reliability of the Gospels* (IVP, 1987). He sums up sections awarely, handles problems usually in a concise but informed and pertinent way, and often offers relevant footnote material to add help from much reading. Examples are his handling of the Isaiah 7:14 problem in 1:22, 23, the Hosea 11:1 citation in 2:14, 15 and the Sermon on the Mount (eight views). He deems adultery a valid ground for divorce and remarriage in 19:9, but is sensitive to different sides of the issue. He views "great distress" in 24:21 as the period from A. D. 70 to the Second Advent (359-60), a whole era of tribulation for the saved. He sees 24:40, 41 as meaning that the *unsaved* are the ones "taken" from earth in judgment and the saved as "left" on earth with the coming of Christ, who will reign during the millennium (366). He appears to hold a post-tribulation rapture of the church (370), but with some lack of clarity as to how that would be consistent with other aspects of his views.

Boice, James M. *The Gospel of Matthew.* **2 vols. Grand Rapids: Baker, 2001.**

This prolific Philadelphia pastor/writer, now with the Lord, elucidates matters quite often in his exposition, and passes over important ones, or does not really explain them, or is unconvincing (cf. on mustard seed and leaven). Still, he can be quite helpful, as frequently in the Sermon on the Mount (he also has an entire book on that Sermon). It is unfortunate when he misrepresents many dispensationalists of today on whether the sermon applies now (most say it does), and how they can integrate details (72-73). He is sensible on many texts, for example seeing the second and third soils (Matt. 13) as depicting people not really born again. Like MacArthur's vols. on Matthew, these show how a pastor feeds his flock, and principles he draws.

Boice, James. *The Sermon on the Mount.* **Grand Rapids: Zondervan, 1972.**

This is a noted preacher and evangelical leader expounding the sermon in a practical style relevant to people today. It is one of the better, more detailed expositions of recent years especially useful for the preacher, Sunday School teacher or lay person in general. D. M. Lloyd-Jones and Stott are even better.

Broadus, John A. *Commentary on Matthew.* **Grand Rapids: Kregel, 1990 rp. 610 pp.**

In many ways it is the finest and most satisfying overall older commentary on Matthew. It helps the student on almost every verse. Broadus deals frontally with problems and gives much rich material that throws light on the text. His citations from other sources are often very helpful. From the standpoint of the Greek text, he is also sound. This 1886 work, long a part of the American Commentary on the New Testament series, is still one of the best in detailed explanation of the text where it counts.

Bruce, F. F. *Matthew*. Grand Rapids: Eerdmans, 1970. In the Scripture Union Bible Study Books series.

This concise paperback enables the reader to see the various parts of Matthew quickly as explained by an outstanding expository scholar.

Bruner, Frederick D. *The Christbook: Matthew*. 2 volumes in 1. Waco: Word Books, 1987-90. 1,127 pp.

This is a too wordy effort to teach Matthew doctrinally. Bruner arbitrarily feels that Matthew emphasizes particular doctrines chapter by chapter: chapter 1, God with us; chapter 2, man (magi, human nature under the power of sin); chapter 3, repentance; etc. He assumes Markan priority (xvii), and has artificial distinctions such as Mark being the gospel for evangelists, Matthew for teachers, Luke for deacons or social workers, John for elders or spiritual leaders (xvii). He concocts that theologically Mark is Luther, Matthew is Calvin or Thomas, Luke is Wesley or Xavier or Chrysostom, and John is Augustine or Barth (xvii). Many have difficulty seeing validity here. Often he is very instructive in detail and is steeped in the literature. Apparently liberal, he believes that Matthew erred in having only 13 names in his third series in Matthew 1 (p. 15). He feels that Jesus as a child made mistakes (15). Sometimes the detail goes rather afield from the point, and one gets more of Bruner than Matthew. But he can offer help at times. An example is 16:18 where he has sections on "the Roman Catholic position on Peter" and "The Reformation Position on Peter." He sees the church's rapture in 24:40, 41, taken away to salvation, post-tribulationally (882). He sees sexual infidelity as a ground for divorce in 19:9 and a second ground, willful desertion, in I Corinthians 7:15. He says that in 25:1 Jesus originally taught the coming bridegroom as God, but the church substituted the coming Christ for the coming God (895), yet the church is Spirit-led and we must follow this. Do we know more than Jesus?

Carson, Donald A. "Matthew," in *Expositor's Bible Commentary*, Volume 8, ed. Frank Gaebelein and R. P. Polcyn. Grand Rapids: Zondervan, 1984. 596 pp.

A conservative, 350,000-word commentary, longer than most in the EBC, up to date in sources, with a good blend of perceptive commentary that explains most verses well and has material to help readers spiritually. Many regard it as one of the top two or three by evangelicals. Its frequent helpfulness on passages seems to justify that. Some will not agree with the favoring of Markan priority.

Carson, Donald A. *The Sermon on the Mount: An Evangelical Exposition of Matthew 5-7*. Grand Rapids: Baker, 1978.

A fine verse by verse work that illumines things well for the teacher or preacher and relates to devotional life well enough to have great appeal to most readers, Quite good, it ranks close to the works of D. M. Lloyd-Jones and John R. W. Stott, although it does not contribute as much as they do and is more on a level with James Boice's work.

Carson, Donald A. *When Jesus Confronts the World: An Exposition of Matthew 8-10*. Grand Rapids: Baker, 1987. 154 pp.

Six chapters here are drawn from sermons at Eden Baptist Church, Cambridge, on Jesus' authority, authenticity, mission, trustworthiness, compassion and decisiveness. Carson has much that opens up the text for expositors, and also makes some good applications of principles for life today.

Davies, Margaret. *Matthew*. Sheffield, Eng.: Sheffield Academic Press, 1993.

The writer synthesizes sections, not treating things verse by verse, and stimulates patient readers by comments on issues of life, inviting thought. She apparently (cf. p. 33) sees in the Matthew 1 use of Isaiah 7:14 a reinterpretation of 7:14 and 8:10 and not directly what those verses meant, fabricating a non-miraculous conception of Isa. into the miraculous. She thinks the story in Matthew 2:1-12 most probably was invented as a dramatic device to claim fulfillment of OT expectations (37). She calls into question the trustworthiness of Gospel accounts (37), and often takes claims in Matthew as extremely unlikely to be historically reliable, feeling wise enough to suggest what should be said to make claims true (37-38). The work for evangelicals has its benefit mostly as an example of how unbelief can force its own creations on the pages of Scripture that one actually should be explaining.

Davies, W. D. and D. C. Allison. *A Critical and Exegetical Commentary on the Gospel According to Saint Matthew* (ICC). 3 vols. Edinburgh: T. & T. Clark, 1988ff.

This critical work replaces W. C. Allen's effort in the ICC (1912). The amount of information on issues of verses makes it outstanding, though very expensive. Despite being liberal if offers much good material even to evangelicals, giving views, arguments and sources. The 26-pp. general bibliography lists mostly liberal works, ignoring W. Hendriksen but including another evangelical, R. H. Mounce. The discussion of introductory matters runs 148-pp. The authors conclude that the Jewish favor and use of the Old Testament point to a Jewish author (33, 58). They see a "massive unity" overall in the structure, but a "structurally mixed" situation that yields no good outline (72). They hold the priority of Mark (73) and simply sum up Allen's most vital conclusions (73, etc.). They are helpful on features such as semitisms, numbers such as triads, repetition, headings, and conclusions. Various tables appear. They conclude that many statements are redactional. Their dating for Matthew is between 80-95 A. D. (138). They lean toward the gospel being put together for the church at Antioch (146-47). Among technical works this is the best, with much exegetical detail. The writers are immense in assembling views and documentation, as eight views on the structure of 1:2-17 and eight views on the Son of Man coming in 16:28. Nine reasons are given on why Mary's pregnancy can be thought due to the Holy Spirit (201-02), The authors do a lot to be fair with the book's use of Old Testament verses, such as the citation of Hosea 11:1 in Matthew 2:15 (263).

English, E. Schuyler. *Studies in the Gospel According to Matthew*. NY: Our Hope Publications, 1935.

Though a survey-type work, this book deals with dispensational problems in a helpful way in some cases. It does not grapple with the exegesis of the text, however.

Filson, Floyd. *The Gospel According to St. Matthew* (Black's New Testament Commentaries). London: Adam & Charles Black, 1975 reprint.

A professor at McCormick Theological Seminary in Chicago did this knowledgeable yet brief and to the point work. He was abreast of much scholarship on Matthew. He believes in Marcan priority and an author who was not Matthew. On 1:23 with Isaiah 7:14 he says Isaiah 7:14 meant a supernatural but not a virgin birth. He is disconcertingly brief on some key problems where many desire much more, as in writing little more than an inch of copy on who the "rock" is in 16:18. In 27:51-53, the account of saints coming out of their tombs could at first have been a figurative teaching, but the writer of this gospel takes it as a real event. There are these and many other comments where many will not agree with Filson. But he is briefly helpful at times on passages.

France, R. T. *The Gospel According to Matthew. An Introduction and Commentary* **(Tyndale New Testament Commentary). Downers Grove: IVP, 1985. 416 pp.**

This work, only a fair one, was done to replace R. V. G. Tasker's work. It handles many matters well, concisely, and usually hits the crux of interpretation, showing awareness of considerable scholarly literature and main views. France uses the NIV text. He draws up summaries of sections and shows the meaning and connection in context.

Gaebelein, A. C. *The Olivet Discourse.* **NY: Gospel Publishing House [n.d.].**

An influential Bible teacher, as in his work on Matthew 13, argues for a premillennial dispensational exposition. He rejects the view that most of the verses were fulfilled in the first century, also the view that the church will go through the tribulation period leading up to the Second Advent. He contends that Israel, not the church, is in view. He argues that the gospel of grace is relevant for the church to preach today but that the gospel of the kingdom is special before the cross and again just before the Second Coming. The unsaved are the ones "taken" in 24:40, 41, the saved are "left" on earth to enter into the kingdom, the opposite of "taken" and "left" when the church's rapture occurs. Yet Gaebelein suddenly switches and says that 24:45ff. and 25:1-13 refer to the separation between the true church and the unsaved at the church's rapture. Many even among present dispensationalists consider his view arbitrary and inconsistent here. The parable of the talents is related to the Israel/church issue in Gaebelein's treatment; he definitely does associate it with the church (p. 113).

Gaebelein, A. C. *The Seven Parables, Matthew XIII.* **20th edition. NY: Our Hope [n.d.]**

A 56-pp. dispensational work of a simple, popular nature contending that the kingdom, rejected by Israel, will be set up by Christ at His Second Advent and that in this age "mysteries" of the Kingdom outlined here are developing in Christendom, not the church. But the church is in the larger sphere, the kingdom of the heavens, he says. He contends for a pretribulation rapture of the church but believes at some verses that the developments here go to the end of the future tribulation. The mustard tree with its birds, as well as the leaven, are interpreted to refer to evil vs. the almost universal explanation of these outside dispensationalism. The treasure and pearl, likewise, are explained differently than in the common view, viz. both to Gaebelin refer to Christ having a value in men He saves, not men seeing Christ, or the kingdom, or salvation as the value above all else. Many modern dispensational thinkers disagree with Gaebelein and do not see inconsistencies between the common views and other Scripture where Gaebelein insists on irreconcilables.

Gaebelein, Arno C. *The Gospel of Matthew.* **NY. Loizeaux, 1961.**

Here is another dispensational work which is helpful on some problems but which does not get down into the exegesis of the text in a serious way. Some of the conclusions on dispensational issues are not accepted by published dispensationalists today.

Garland, David E. *Reading Matthew. A Literary and Theological Commentary.* **Macon, GA: Smyth & Helwys Publishing, Inc., 2001.**

Brief at 273 pp., this evangelical effort surveys sections and usually has knowledgeable remarks to resolve problems. Garland brings to the conciseness the use of pertinent helps from wide study, and also maintains a readable quality. All told, the work does little that several other books have not already done as well or better. At times one needs to fish in sections to locate remarks on matters of specific verses. Straight-forward verse by verse commentaries can be so much more helpful than any such broad attempt as this.

Glasscock, Ed. *Matthew* **(Moody Gospel Commentary). Chicago: Moody Press, 1997.**

The commentator is Academic Vice-President and Director of Biblical Studies, Southeastern Bible College. His is a premillennial, dispensational work of considerable detail (635 pp.), often grappling seriously to focus light on details. Still, some problems are dealt with only in part, leaving many questions, for example how Isaiah 7:14 in its own connection is suitably seen as fulfilled only in Mary and Jesus, or in a double ful-fillment, or what. The commentary handles many verses rather well (cf. an instance in "ask . . . seek . . . knock," Matt. 7:7-11). Glasscock does not see the second and third soils of Matt. 13 as picturing saved people. He believes the "rock" in 16:18 is Christ, not Peter or the confession. Prophetical verses, for example 24:40-41 ("taken . . . left") are explained in a usual dispensational way.

Green, H. Benedict. *The Gospel According to Matthew in the Revised Standard Version* **(New Clarendon Bible). Oxford: University Press, 1975.**

This work based on Marcan priority is in the series of updating the scholarship of the Old Clarendon Bible first published in 1936. Green takes a date of A. D. 90-100 (p. 33). Much of the commentary text is printed in small type that soon tires the eyes. While showing a fair grasp of pertinent aspects and often adequate though terse, it sometimes falls short of explaining enough to resolve why a statement is necessary (cf. on 3:15, p. 65). Some important details are passed over without even a comment, e. g. the promised reward in 5:12. Green at the time of writing was principal and associate lecturer in theology at the College of the Resurrection, Mirfield, at the University of Leeds.

Griffith-Thomas, W. H. *Outline Studies in the Gospel of Matthew.* **Grand Rapids: Eerdmans, 1961.**

This 476-pp. volume of 60 studies was put together from his writings as an evangelical devotional commentary by his daughter Winifred Gillespie after his death. It is a very well-outlined, concise work by the author who was a key figure in English Keswick cir-cles and in the founding of Dallas Theological Seminary in 1924. The crisp, quick-mov-ing lay-out of points makes this a good survey and a catalyst for a teacher of a Bible class of laymen. The work is dispensational in its perspective, e.g. Matthew 5-7, 13:31-33 and even pretribulational as to the rapture (p. 347), The author was unusually well-organized and knowledgeable as to pertinent biblical details and their correlation which in many places makes this a profitable synopsis of strategic points pulled into a unit.

Guelich, Robert A. *The Sermon on the Mount: A Foundation for Understanding.* **Waco, Texas: Word Books, 1982.**

Though this has elements of a critical literary nature that will please some and displease others, it is highly regarded in acquainting readers with issues and fairly recent studies. Along the line of general works on the SOM, one also will still want to consult W. D. Davies, The Setting of the Sermon on the Mount (Cambridge: U.P., 1964) and Warren S. Kissinger, The Sermon on the Mount: A History of Interpretation and Bibliography (Scarecrow Press, 1976). Davies is often helpful in showing ties with Jewish literature and Pauline thought.

Gundry, Robert. *Matthew: A Commentary on his Literary and Theological Art.* **Grand Rapids: Eerdmans, 1982. 652 pp.**

A thorough-going redaction-criticism approach by a conservative, with much that distresses many other conservatives. According to Gundry, Matthew embellishes things for Jews after the pattern of Jewish Midrash. Some of the accounts are made up, and did not happen historically. Gundry sees some texts as irreconcilable, and does not accept harmonizations some have proposed even where many believe that they are quite possible. Cf. much of an entire Journal of the Evangelical Theological Society issue taken up with scholars' arguments against Gundry and Gundry's rejoinders (26:1, March, 1983). Gundry has done a 2nd ed. (1994), correcting here and there, with a new sub-title, a new preface (detailed essay arguing his case), an appendix, and end notes. He deals with criticisms of the 1st ed. (cf. *Matthew: A Commentary on His Handbook for a Mixed Church Under Persecution,* Eerdmans, 1994).

Hagner, Donald. *Matthew* **(Word Biblical Commentary). 2 vols. Dallas, TX: Word Books, 1993.**

These 935 pp. lay out a mass of detail, often explaining exegesis and views for more advanced users. Hagner thinks the apostle Matthew wrote large portions, particularly Jesus' sayings, perhaps even more of the narrative (lxxvi). He sees such a passage as Isaiah 7:14 fulfilled once rather immediately, then again in Jesus in a deeper way that Isaiah's words entailed (20). He sees Hosea 11:1 (about Israel) as typologically foreshadowing Jesus (Matt. 2:15), in continuity (36). On many verses, explanations offer much help, examples being "perfect" in 5:48, and the mustard plant and leaven in 13:31-33, or the "rock" in 16:18. Hagner argues that divorce in 19:9 is permitted in a case of infidelity, but not remarriage, whereas Carson and many others believe that both divorce and remarriage are permitted where proper grounds exist. Those "taken" in 24:40-41 are in a post-tribulation rapture. Overall, the effort is at least among recent top evangelical works on exegetical details in this gospel.

Hare, Douglas R. A. *Matthew* **(Interpretation). Louisville, KY: Westminster John Knox Press, 1993.**

Prepared for teachers, preachers, and students, the expository series claims interpretation faithful to the text and theologically relevant to the church. One must remember that this is but a claim. The writer assumes that the author was not Matthew but a later Jewish

Christian ca. A. D. 80 (2). Strange statements appear on Mary's supernatural conception, also a fuzzing in place of clarity. Hosea 11:1 is treated as if Matthew 2:15 stamped a foreign sense on it. The Parable of the Four Soils is discussed in a way that can create doubt (153) rather than giving readers a straightforward view, free of criticizing it. Other parabolic explanation here often offers more perplexity. The work is not as consistently and reliably helpful as a number of others are, and can even frustrate more aware users at times

Hendriksen, William. *The Gospel of Matthew, in New Testament Commentary*. Grand Rapids: Baker, 1973.

This 1,015-page work is one of the best recent works of solid evangelical scholarship for teachers, preachers, and serious lay readers who desire to see views, detailed arguments at times, and explanations at length on problem passages. Yet Hendriksen as always maintains a warmth that speaks to the heart. He has many good footnotes of length documenting sources and providing further help. He is amillennial on chapters 24-25.

Hill, David. *The Gospel of Matthew (New Century Bible)*. London: Marshall Morgan Scott, 1975 reprint.

A lucid commentary by the Senior Lecturer, Professor of Biblical Studies, University of Sheffield, England. He shows a lot of reading breadth in recent scholarship at times and gives views that sometimes expand the American reader's awareness on interpretations, but shows a lack of awareness of views they are already aware of at times. He often reflects concessions to higher critical ideas that evangelicals in the more fundamental group would reject in favor of what they regard as more defensible views. All in all, it is helpful at many points but not as often helpful to expositors as Broadus, Carson, Hendriksen, etc.

Hoehner, Harold W. *Chronological Aspects of the Life of Christ*. Grand Rapids: Zondervan, 1977.

This is a fine, careful study of such aspects as the date of Jesus' birth, commencement of His ministry, duration of His ministry, day and year of His crucifixion, and the chronology of the Seventy Weeks in Daniel 9 in relation to the gospels. Hoehner holds to an A. D. 33 crucifixion and Friday as the day, presenting the different views in some detail and arguing at length for his own views.

Hultgren, Arland J. *The Parables of Jesus, A Commentary*. Grand Rapids: Eerdmans, 2000.

Though this is not on Matthew per se, it deals with much of Matthew since so many parables occur here. Hultgren's effort of 522 pp. provides the most all-around help on 38 parables in one book. He is adept at handling grammar, word study, context, customs, and other factors pertinent to explaining parables, leaving few stones unturned. He shows very broad reading perception of others' views and details about his subjects. Another standout work is by Stanley Ellisen, *Parables in the Eye of the Storm. Christ's Response in the Face of Conflict* (Grand Rapids: Kregel, 2001). The latter work is a product of Ellisen's doctoral dissertation at Dallas Theological Seminary in the 1960's, plus a long teaching career of improving the depth, breadth and perceptions. This dispensational perspective is very well-written and offers much in precision clarity on overall points, verses, context, customs, etc. A third study with broader but orientational help is Richard Longenecker, ed., *The Challenge of Jesus' Parables* (Grand Rapids: Eerdmans, 2000). Thirteen NT scholars wrote on such subjects as the history of interpreting parables, genre, parables in early Judaism, parables in relation to the kingdom in Mark 4, parables in Matthew 13, parables of love and forgiveness, and others. Despite many strengths, some parts of the book lack clarity or persuasiveness, for example some arbitrary claims by Morna Hooker on Mark 4. The overall helpfulness of the three works for evangelicals is in this order, Hultgren, Ellisen, and Longenecker. Yet another source is Peter R. Jones' *Studying the Parables of Jesus* (Macon, GA: Smith & Helwys Publishing Co., 1999). This revises but lengthens *The Teaching of the Parables* (Broadman, 1982), and deals with 12 parables on topics such as The Sure Coming of the Kingdom, Grace/Repentance, and Discipleship. Preachers and students can gain more insight into views and applications. In this work, among those unlike Ellisen's, dispensational views are set aside.

Hunter, A. M. *A Pattern For Life. An Exposition of the Sermon on the Mount.* Philadelphia: Westminster Press, 1965, revised edition (original in 1953).

This little 127-pp. book takes the sermon as Christ's "moral ideal for committed Christians" (p. 6). The former New Testament scholar of King's College, University of Aberdeen has brief chapters on "The Making of the Sermon," "The Manner of the Sermon," and "The Matter of the Sermon," then 67 pp. on the exegesis and finally 23 pp. on "The Meaning of the Sermon." He has brief but choice words about "The Doctrine of Reward" on 5:12 (pp. 41-44). This is an excellent, concise survey of the sermon verse by verse, with timely illustrations and provocative quotations usable for life and for speaking.

Jeremias, Joachim. *The Sermon on the Mount.* Translated Norman Perrin. Philadelphia: Fortress Press, 1963.

The 36-pp, work first appeared in German as *Die Bergpredigt* in 1959. Jeremias was a long time Professor of New Testament Studies at Gottingen University. He reacts against Hans Windisch's charge (*The Meaning of the Sermon on the Mount*) that Matthew 5-7 gives complete heresy, law righteousness by works and not gospel. He shows four great differences between Jesus' demands and the ethic of late Judaism in the Talmud (pp. 5, 6). He also finally turns away from the view that the sermon is an impossible ideal to drive men to God's mercy, and the view that the sermon gives an interim ethic (Albert Schweitzer, etc.). For the view Jeremias favors, he thanks literary and form criticism: the sermon, he concludes, is not a continuous sermon Jesus delivered but a collection of His sayings. The key verse is 5:20 speaking of a righteousness of theologians (scribes), another of pious laymen (Pharisees), and that of the disciples of Jesus. The instructions strung together in one place originally functioned as catechetical helps for candidates for baptism or as discipleship instruction for the newly baptized. If so, it was preceded by preaching the gospel, conversion, and empowering (p. 23). This, Jeremias argues, makes understandable Jesus' heavy demands. Lives rooted in the kingdom show the victory of that kingdom. So we have not law but gospel.

Johnson, S. Lewis. Series on highlights in the life of Christ appearing in *Bibliotheca Sacra*: **baptism, Volume 123 (July, 1966), 220-29; temptation (Oct., 1966), 342-52; transfiguration, 124 (1967), 133-43; triumphal entry, 124 (July, 1967), 218-29; agony, 124 (1967), 303-13; death, 125 (1968), 10-19.**

Here is excellent, stimulating exposition based on careful exegesis and profound insight, given with warmth. The teacher or preacher who reads a Johnson article before he ministers is bound to come away feeling he has been treated to a thought-provoking and competent study by a very competent scholar of New Testament and theology. Johnson has served on the faculties at Dallas Theological Seminary and Trinity Evangelical Divinity School.

Keener, Craig S. *A Commentary on the Gospel of Matthew.* **Grand Rapids: Eerdmans, 1999.**

In 1,040 pp., Keener submits a lengthy introduction abreast of modern scholarly thought, followed by commentary, indexes on subjects, authors and ancient sources. Details on verses mingle with what some will see as questionable critical assumptions about the gospel's sources and the contemporary Jesus research. So one can find the book a laborious test, and parts of the ponderous detail geared for quests of a few who share certain concerns. Keener does believe that the burden of proof is on those who doubt the historical authenticity of details (24). He judges it "quite likely that Jesus' disciples accurately remembered and transmitted his teachings" (26). Comments on verses provide much, as do frequent excursuses on matters such as debates about the virgin birth, dreams (1:20), magi, wealth, demons and exorcism, etc. Keener often bypasses reference to the Greek so as to appeal to those who do not know it. This hurts the quality in contributing to a lack of exegetical information and depth, as does some failure to give more than his view. Also, he does not always deal verse by verse, though he lists main ideas of a passage. Sometimes he is over the heads of many readers, as in material on source and redaction criticism, and he seems not fully confident of conservative belief that what Jesus said is fully accurate. The work still is among top recent exegetical ones, with Davies/Allison and Hagner. Cf. a condensed form of Keener's product done earlier (1997) in *Matthew* (IVP NTC). The IVP work is a good concise help.

Kent, Homer A., Jr. "Matthew," in *Wycliffe Bible Commentary*, **ed. C. F. Pfeiffer and E. F. Harrison. Chicago: Moody, 1962. 1,525 pp.**

Kent, who served several years as president of Grace Theological Seminary, Winona Lake, IN, did this dispensational study. He brought a lot of understanding to the task, and provides a reliable commentary on many matters, often giving good reasoning for views.

King, Guy H. *New Order. An Expositional Study of the Sermon on the Mount.* **London. Marshall, Morgan & Scott, Ltd., 1943.**

King was minister at Christ Church, Beckenham and a speaker at Keswick. As in his other books he writes in a freshly devotional, creative strain. He ties the truth of the sermon in with biblical truth elsewhere. He is persuaded that while Christ will set up His kingdom at His Second Coming and the principles will apply then, the truth is His mind and will for His people also apply now, just as principles in the epistles (pp. 11, 12). The life-style here is lived in dependence on the Holy Spirit through grace by those who first have been born again (12). Many apt side captions appear over sections, and the outline of the sermon runs throughout in larger headings. The print of the commentary is small. King's work is a devotionally edifying treat, served in an appetizing manner with many things suggestive for a closer walk with God, leading Bible studies, or preparing sermons. Cf. also his books on I and II Timothy, and James.

Kingsbury, J. D. *The Parables of Jesus in Matthew 13, A Study in Redaction Criticism*. Richmond, VA: John Knox Press, 1969.

This 180-page book views chapter 13 as being in a pivotal place in Matthew and a good test case for redaction-critical procedure. The detailed verse-by-verse discussion, growing out of a doctoral dissertation at Basel (1966), takes the view that this gospel presents parables here to allow Jesus as Lord to speak to circumstances in the church later but Jesus may not have said them in His day (not a position this reviewer holds).

Kissinger, W. S. *The Sermon on the Mount: A History of Interpretation and Bibliography*. American Theological Library Association, Bibliography Series, Number 3. Metuchen, NJ: Scarecrow Press and the American Theological Library Association, 1975.

Kissinger, a cataloguer of religion at the Library of Congress in Washington, D. C., surveys the history of the interpretation from the early fathers to the present, then gives a lengthy bibliography (148 pp,) of literature on the sermon and issues in Matthew 5-7. He has a similar work on parables.

Lloyd-Jones, D. Martyn. *Studies in the Sermon on the Mount*. 2 volumes. Grand Rapids: Eerdmans, 1962.

This is one of the very finest expositions of the sermon by an evangelical preacher of the modern era, a deeply perceptive man relevant to his age and a man of scholarly awareness. He is stimulating, practical, often wise in his interpretations of problem verses. It is well worth the money.

Long, Thomas G. *Matthew* (Westminster Bible Companion). Louisville, KY: Westminster John Knox Press, 1997.

A popular preacher in the Presbyterian Church (U. S. A.), who also teaches preachers, wrote to show Matthew's relevance to lay people. Long presents a survey of which there are many just as helpful or more so already on the market. He is not confident that Matthew wrote the gospel (3), and believes in such sources as Mark and Q. One is left unsure what Isaiah 7:14 meant, but wording gives the impression that Matthew 1 uses it artificially to suit its own aim (15). This suggests a rigged case and a slam at reliability. Baptism with the Holy Spirit appears to be confused with the different matter of the Spirit bestowing gifts (31), and some other texts are not made really clear, or to the point, or they offer unfortunate wording (cf. on 5:48; 7:21-23; 8:22; 12:31-32; 13:31-32; 24:31, 34, etc). Many verses are handled fairly well, but overall the work does not contribute as helpfully as several others of comparable length do (331 pp.). If one does use it, he will find some ideas for preaching, though this is also the case in many better works.

MacArthur, John, Jr. *Kingdom Living Here and Now.* **Chicago: Moody Press, 1980.**

Exposition of the Beatitudes (Matthew 5:1-12) is the thrust. A good evangelical study in detail that shows the relevance today. MacArthur believes that the beatitudes give features in the life-style of the truly saved person, all in some measure present in his composite experience as fruit of the Spirit, wrought through grace. He cannot tolerate "easy-believism" that allows the gift nature of salvation but does not balance this with a call to manifest the fruit of authentic life.

MacArthur, John, Jr. *Matthew.* **4 volumes (The MacArthur New Testament Commentary). Chicago: Moody, 1985-90.**

Conservative, premillennial exposition which often deals in some detail with problem verses and shows the vital lessons of Jesus' teachings in a very readable manner. The author often explains customs, gives views and reasons. In Matthew 13, he sees the fourth soil only as representing a genuinely saved person, and the leaven in a good sense. In Matthew 24, he views verses 15ff. as related to tribulation and Second Advent, not A. D. 70, the one taken as removed in judgment and the one left as preserved on earth safely to enter the earthly kingdom promised in Old Testament prophecy.

McNeile, Alan H. *The Gospel According to Matthew.* **Grand Rapids: Baker, 1980rp, formerly NY: St. Martin's Press, 1915.**

The work is still respected in exegesis but is far out of date as to interaction with literature. Liberal in its approach, this book is still helpful in tracing the argument. It assists on many details and thus is one of the better serious commentaries, though it often leaves the student wishing it would say more about a problem.

Morris, Leon. *The Gospel According to Matthew* **(Pillar Commentary). Grand Rapids: Eerdmans, 1992.**

One of the world's best-known evangelical, amillennial NT scholars provides a thorough, clear, well-studied and mature tool based on the Greek but highly readable even for those who do not know Greek. Morris usually surges quickly to the crux, and gives main views, reasons for his choices, word meaning, contextual factors, background, and customs. His work here is right up with the No. 1 commentaries in all-around contribution. In prophetical passages such as Matthew 24-25, one will see an amillennial perspective near its best. Footnotes that often are substantial, and various indexes, provide more help.

Mounce, Robert H. *Matthew* **(New International Bible Commentary). Peabody, MA: Hendrickson, 1991. 228 pp.**

This was formerly the Good News Commentary (San Francisco: Harper and Row, 1985). It switched from the Good News translation to the NIV. Mounce is President of Whitworth College, Spokane, WA, and author of several New Testament commentaries (cf. on Book of Revelation, etc.). He gives a mere 5 page introduction and a fairly conservative, amillennial study of Matthew.

Plummer, Alfred. *An Exegetical Commentary on the Gospel According to Matthew* **(Thornapple Commentaries). Grand Rapids: Baker, 1982. 451 pp. Formerly Grand Rapids: Eerdmans, 1953, from 1915 ed.**

Any work by Plummer is helpful, for he possessed a keen ability to write with clarity and deep scholarship. He is good in the Greek and historical background, and does not dodge problems, though he at times takes a liberal view. He was amillennial in eschatology. He held a position which the liberals of his day considered too conservative and which the conservatives reckoned too liberal. This commentary is valuable. He holds to a non-Matthean authorship of the book.

Ridderbos, Herman N. *Matthew* **(Bible Students Commentary). Grand Rapids: Zondervan, 1987. 556 pp.**

This is from the famous Dutch series (cf. Aalders on Genesis, etc.), originally from 1950-51. It offers expositors quite a lot of help in explaining verses, looking at views, giving reasons in a competent fashion, etc. In prophecy Ridderbos is amillennial, and he does not concern himself much with critical issues that some scholars want. Due to the dating, the product cannot show awareness of work done in Matthew since the 1940's.

Robertson, Arthur. *Matthew* **(Everyman's Bible Commentary). Chicago: Moody, 1983. 168 pp.**

An evangelical work of a concise nature with a brief introduction looking at the importance, uniqueness, theme (King), purpose, relationship to the other gospels, author, date (A.D. 50-60), Jesus' teaching methods, relevance to today, etc. The commentary follows a clear outline, has apt comments usually, and is right to the point on problem verses. Robertson is only rarely unclear, as on mystery (ch. 13), third soil (13), etc. He interprets 24:40-41 to mean taken in deliverance and left to face judgment, yet sees chapters 24-25 overall in a premillennial, dispensational way.

Robinson, Haddon W. *What Jesus Said About Successful Living. Principles from the Sermon on the Mount for Today.* **Grand Rapids: Discovery House, 1989. 298 pp.**

An outstanding preacher, former Dallas Theological Seminary faculty member, President of Denver Theological Seminary and now teacher at Gordon Conwell Theological Seminary has done this conservative book. The reader will soon see the popularly written, devotionally enriched nature of the work and will be able to draw out material for life or sermons. Like James Boice, Don Carson, Guy King, D. M. Lloyd Jones, J. D. Pentecost, and John R. W. Stott, Robinson exposes the meaning for today in graphic style.

Ryken, Philip G. *When You Pray: Making the Lord's Prayer Your Own.* **Wheaton, IL: Crossway, 2000.**

Ryken has 206 pp. on the prayer Jesus taught His disciples (Matt. 6:9-12; Lk. 11:2-4). The book is warm, stimulating, practical, expounding the verses helpfully for preachers, church teachers, and Christians in general, with principles to apply. Intriguing chapter titles meet readers, also many illustrations of the various spiritual life facets here. End notes on chapters reflect diligent research in good writers (Spurgeon, Jonathan Edwards,

D. A. Carson, etc.). One will find much stimulation to prayer from creative, rich writing and spiritual insight. Ryken's work joins many that help on the guide for prayer, e. g. by J. MacArthur, R. K. Hughes, etc.

Shepard, Thomas. *The Ten Virgins*. Macdill AFB, Florida: Tyndale Bible Society [n.d.].

This recent paperback is a reprint of the Boston printing of 1852, dating back to the first published work in 1659. Shepard, a Puritan, preached the messages between 1636-40. Here we have 243 pp., whereas the 1842 ed. had 630! There is very detailed explanation and a thorough application of each point to believers. Shepard develops two great lessons for the religious community: (1) he shows the relation between assurance of salvation and the growth of fruit in the life-style, which are evidences of God's gracious salvation; (2) he holds that the inward response of the "hypocrite" is distinct from that of a truly saved person. He expounds these in the contrast between the wise and foolish virgins. About ten percent of the book expounds the parable. Shepard correlates with this such subjects as: the true nature of a saving response; the character of mere profession; the power in expecting Christ's future coming to arouse devotion in believers and disturb the false security of the mere professor; the nature of repentance, etc. Shepard tries to deal with every excuse a lost person might make to Christ's appeal, so as to awaken him to his need. Yet he seeks to buttress and encourage real Christians.

Stott, John R. W. *Christian Counter-Culture. Studies in the Sermon on the Mount*. Downers Grove: IVP, 1978.

This is a flowing, articulate exposition by one of the world's masters. Stott as usual is well-organized, sharply perceptive of the points that need to be expounded, and sensitively relevant in practical principles. This is one of the very best, most clear books on the sermon in capturing cogently what Jesus said and meant.

Thomas, Robert L. *Charts on the Gospels and the Life of Christ.* Grand Rapids: Zondervan, 2000.

This valuable 167-pp. source in an 8 fi by 11 layout has 41 charts to help in study of the gospels. Among these are periods of Jesus's life, a harmonistic overview of the four gospels, sections found in only one gospel (or two, or three, or four), OT citations in the gospels, the Herod family, the Lord's discourses, major events of Passion Week, chronology of that week, the theme of each gospel, seven lessons of Jesus on discipleship, the kingdom, six phases of Jesus's trial, and others. Cf. also Thomas's *The NIV Harmony of the Gospels*.

Walvoord, John F. *Matthew: Thy Kingdom Come*. Chicago: Moody Press, 1974.

An effort by a leading dispensational scholar to trace the theme of the Messianic Kingdom step by step through the first gospel. The work is written clearly and seeks to survey the main ideas of each section without becoming involved in minute detail or a verse-by-verse study. It is often quite brief and general.

Watson, Thomas. *The Beatitudes. An Exposition of Matthew 5:1-12*. London: Banner of Truth Trust, 1971.

This is a reprint of a Puritan study. Watson explains the text well, with much food for thought for those preparing Bible studies or sermons.

Zodhiates, Spiros. *The Pursuit of Happiness.* Grand Rapids: Eerdmans, 1966.

The author, a faithful witness for Christ among the Greek-speaking world and writer of several other fine books, discusses in rich detail the meaning of the beatitudes. His thorough treatments on word meanings, backgrounds, and spiritual truths flowing from them are often refreshing and rewarding.

II. MARK

Anderson, Hugh. *The Gospel of Mark* (New Century Bible Commentary). Grand Rapids: Eerdmans, 1981. 366 pp.

The Professor of New Testament and Theology at the University of Edinburgh has done a thorough-going redaction criticism of Mark. He favors Marcan priority and a date shortly after A. D. 65 by a writer other than John Mark. He brings vast awareness of literature to his work, and helpfully discusses possibilities on many problems: John's baptism had its closest similarities to Qumran ceremonials yet is in contrast to them (70-71); "The Kingdom of God is at hand" means just that, not "has come (arrived)," and Anderson sees both present and future aspects; as a prelude to the Sower and the Seed (4:1-9), he gives two pages of general survey on the history of interpreting the parables; later he thinks he has strong reasons for saying the explanation of this parable comes not from Jesus but from the church (132), and feels there are inconsistencies in the details (133). He is not sure to what extent sayings in Mark 13 go back to Jesus himself or to redaction (290). Sometimes he makes no effort to explain how a view may be compatible with theological factors, e.g. on 13:13, how enduring to the end and being saved may integrate with the gift aspect of salvation (295). On the whole, this is a work of high quality that usually helps if one is discerning where the writer's assumptions on redaction are subjective and arbitrary. Much has to be sifted to get what is worthwhile and leave the chaff.

Beasley-Murray, G. R. *A Commentary on Mark Thirteen*. NY: Macmillan & Co. Ltd., 1957.

The reader can also consult the author's work on criticism and theology of Mark 13, Jesus and the Future, an Examination of the Criticism of the Eschatological Discourse, Mark 13, with Special Reference to the Little Apocalypse Theory (London: Macmillan, 1954). Beasley-Murray does an exposition based on his earlier work, and also summarizes critical issues in Mark 13 as he sees them. Still, Jesus and the Future discusses these more in detail than this 124-pp. book. He believes that details of Mark 13 have a high claim to authenticity as representing the words Jesus Himself spoke to His disciples. He inclines to the opinion that "the abomination that causes horror" (13:14) is purely historical, not a reference to the Antichrist, not to be elucidated by II Thessalonians 2:4 (pp. 682-690). Greater light on what happened in A. D. 70 and what was yet future to that would serve many of the readers better. Yet the work has a wealth of competent material that serious students will find valuable.

Brooks, James A. *Mark* (New American Commentary), Volume 23, ed. David Dockery. Nashville: Broadman Press, 1991. 288 pp.

The NAC is an evangelical Southern Baptist effort of 40 volumes based on the NIV, new in distinction to the American commentary edited by Alvah Hovey, in which John Broadus on Matthew was one of the standouts. Brooks' commentary is fair but not high on a list of fine works. He is readable and upholds full trustworthiness (inerrancy), shows how the text applies to life, stresses the unity, but fails at a number of points to be convincing. He assumes Marcan priority, and fails to explain what "baptized with the Holy Spirit" means in 1:7-8, sees the Kingdom in Mark as God's kingly rule in hearts (p. 47) with the possible exception of 14:25 and 15:43, sometimes is extremely brief, and almost skips over some verses, as 4:13-20, making but the barest comment. Sometimes he deals with a verse in more adequate detail, as "abomination of desolation" (13:14) and the Son not knowing.

Burdick, Donald W. "Mark," in *Wycliffe Bible Commentary*, ed. C. F. Pfeiffer and E. F. Harrison. Chicago: Moody, 1962. 1,525 pp.

A careful New Testament scholar from Conservative Baptist Seminary, Denver, is the author. He has provided a solid, well-organized and knowledgeable study from a conservative, premillennial viewpoint. Though brief it is worth the time.

Cole, R. Alan. *The Gospel According to St. Mark. An Introduction and Commentary* (Tyndale New Testament). Grand Rapids. Eerdmans, 1961.

A minister in the Church of Southeast Asia wrote this evangelical study, concluding for Markan priority (p. 47) yet not for any direct literary dependence but Matthean, Markan and Lukan "use of the same, or similar tradition blocks" (p. 48). The commentary itself is provided with a 4-pp. outline set down at the outset and is terse but knowledgeable. Cole sees the Olivet Discourse as referring directly to the destruction of Jerusalem in A. D. 70, though he acknowledges that the meaning reaches on to later fulfillment also (p. 203), a double fulfillment of the same words.

Cranfield, C. E. B. *The Gospel According to St. Mark* (Cambridge Greek Testament Commentary). New York: Cambridge University Press, 1966. 496 pp.

One of the finer commentaries on Mark by the famous exegetical scholar from The University of Durham in Scotland. Cranfield is quite helpful on the Greek text, word meanings, customs etc., and is clear, insightful, and refreshing to those who believe in the historical veracity of words and events in Jesus' ministry.

Earle, Ralph. *Mark, The Gospel of Action* (Everyman's Bible Commentary). Chicago: Moody, 1970. 127 pp.

Here is a brief conservative survey by a professor (then) at the Nazarene Theological Seminary, Kansas City, MO. Earle is usually helpful. At times he is overly general, not nailing things down as on the identity of the second and third soils in Mark 4; at other times he commits himself, as in expecting a yet future, final fulfillment of the "abomination of desolation" in Mark 13.

Edwards, James R. *The Gospel according to Mark* (Pillar NTC). Grand Rapids: Eerdmans, 2002.

This lucid and quite worthy 552-pp. product sees Mark as the writer (6) and applauds his skill as a writer and theologian (3), reliable in what he says. Edwards almost always handles issues in verses well, and contributes still more by eight excursuses that deal with such subjects as "The Secrecy Motif and Jesus' Messianic Self-Consciousness" (1:34), "Son of Man" (2:12), "How Should the Transfiguration Be Understood?" (9:8), "Women in the Gospel of Mark" (14:9), etc. Illumination of details is often a help, e. g. baptism (1:4), "mystery" (4:11). Edwards does have questionable remarks here and there, as in saying that the "seed" meaning the word (gospel) in 4:14 becomes the hearers in vv. 15ff (136). The text does not require equating the word planted in people with the people in whom it is planted. Edwards clarifies the significance of the transfiguration, while showing various views that are inadequate to explain it (269-71).

English, E. Schuyler. *Studies in the Gospel According to Mark.* NY: Our Hope Publications, 1943.

A layman who was converted under the ministry of Dr. Donald G. Barnhouse, English has demonstrated what can be done by a serious-minded Christian though he may not have had the benefits of special seminary training. His work shows diligence. This is one of the best older dispensational commentaries on the English text.

France, R. T. *The Gospel of Mark. A Commentary on the Greek Text.* Grand Rapids: Eerdmans, 2002.

A noted scholar has an apt comment beginning his Introduction, that a commentary should be on the biblical book, not about commentaries on Mark (1), issues in Mark and not all the issues scholars can raise. Still, his footnotes cite many where he can draw help. He assumes that Mark wrote this gospel (6-9). He packs in much learning to shine light on verses, but with all due respect his ideas have misguided him to have Christ's enthronement to have kingly, universal and eternal dominion here and now be the meaning of texts that are about Christ's coming at the Second Advent (8:38; 13:26; 14:62, cf. pp. 32, 342-43, 534-35, 610-13). France has a good summary of textual evidence for excluding Mark 16:9ff. (685-88).

Geddert, Timothy J. *Mark* (Believers Church BC). Scottsdale, PA: Herald Press, 2001.

I. Howard Marshall commends the "outstanding scholarship" and "utter simplicity and clarity" (back cover). Geddert had done his dissertation on Mark 13, and teaches at Mennonite Brethren Biblical Seminary, Fresno, CA. Using for the most part the NRSV and NIV, he comments verse by verse with commitment to a mixture of critical loyalties that he recommends (22). Pastors and students will find well-organized remarks, frankly some good, some needing better information. In the latter category, his comment that the bountiful harvest of the fourth soil (Mark 4) is unrealistic in first-century conditions (93) needs the input of Philip Payne and others who have written journal articles documenting astounding Palestinian yields. Geddert is right, at least, in saying that God makes the harvest great spiritually (94). Some problems are passed over, as on how to view the second and third soils. Comments on prophecy in Mark 13 show misconceptions about a premillennial, dispensational explanation, and uncertainty on how to interpret details. Overall, the book is brief on much, offering less than a number of longer or shorter commentaries for one's time and money.

Grassmick, John D. "Mark," in the *Bible Knowledge Commentary*, ed. John F. Walvoord and Roy B. Zuck, Volume II. Wheaton: Victor Books, 1985.

A rather careful, diligent contribution from a conservative and premillennialist. He holds Markan priority (p. 98) after giving arguments for views. One will find the priority of Matthew favored in the Matthew introduction of the same commentary. Grassmick seems informed by good use of the Greek and scholarly literature, and sometimes goes into some detail summing up arguments for views, as on the disputed ending in 16:9ff.

Guelich, R. A. *Mark 1:1-8:26* (Word Biblical Commentary). 2 Volumes. Dallas: Word Books, 1989ff.

A much-praised moderately conservative work (some will not feel it is conservative) showing a lot of expertise in linguistic details, giving of views and arguments, and listing or citing many more modern scholarly sources. It will be quite helpful to scholars, including pastors who grapple with interpretive issues.

Gundry, Robert H. *Mark, A Commentary on His Apology for the Cross.* Grand Rapids: Eerdmans, 1993.

Cf. Gundry on Matthew for his view about midrash. Here, again, he offers prolific bibliography (32 pp.) and commentary so prolonged that details at times are user unfriendly for many, and it can be hard to locate individual verses in the pages of "Notes." Gundry presents Jesus in His success yet in His self-denial and suffering unto the cross, a perspective so different from today's health-and-wealth idea of discipleship (cf. 2-3). Explanation of details is ponderous, giving the patient much to consider. Frequent statements may be grasped only by an inner circle of scholars (cf. the first note on 39), and some will recoil at misleading claims such as one that Mark's not mentioning disciples receiving the Spirit shows that Mark is "not interested in" this (38). A writer does not have to include every detail in which he has an interest! Gundry shows the future Second Advent context of certain predictions in Mark 13, but one must read with great alertness and sometimes re-reading to follow him. Overall, teachers, more studious pastors, and advanced students will find much stimulation in the thorough comments, as on issues in 4:26-29.

Hendriksen, William. *The Gospel of Mark.* Grand Rapids: Baker, 1975.

All of Hendriksen's commentaries offer very helpful material that shows awareness of issues in the interpretation and deals well with most of the problems. This is no exception and is one of the better works of a less technical nature. Hendriksen seriously attempts to resolve problems and sometimes has good footnotes. He has, however, been faulted on some counts, as when his 858 footnotes have only 17 references to books and articles from the previous 15 years of scholarship (Peter R. Jones, review, WTJ 39 (Fall, 1976), p. 140).

Hiebert, D. Edmond. *Mark: A Portrait of the Servant.* Chicago: Moody Press, 1974. Cf. rev. ed., *The Gospel of Mark, An Expositional Commentary* (Greenville, SC: Bob Jones University Press, 1994).

A detailed and competent work by a soundly evangelical scholar, formerly of the Mennonite Seminary in Fresno. It usually offers good help on a passage because Hiebert shows awareness and discussion of problems. Readers will face some difficulty at times finding a verse or section quickly because the Table of Contents does not identify which part of Mark is being treated. However, there is a very detailed outline at the outset and then sections are marked off by headings throughout the commentary. It will be particularly helpful to pulpiteers, serious lay students, and Bible College students, among others.

Hughes, R. Kent. *Mark: Jesus, Servant and Savior.* **2 volumes (Preaching the Word Commentary). Westchester, IL: Crossway Books, Good News Publishers, 1989.**

A good expositor who pastors Wheaton College Church and has done several commentaries in this series (cf. Joshua, etc.) gives broad, flowing studies that can be provocative for sermons and a spiritual enrichment in day by day lay reading. He is conservative, premillennial, and draws material from many sources to illustrate the passages.

Hurtado, L. W. *Mark* **(New International Bible Commentary). 2nd ed. Peabody, MA: Hendrickson, 1989. 306 pp.**

This was originally in the Good News Commentary (1983), and has changed to the NIV. It is a mild redaction-critical work by the Professor of Religion at the University of Manitoba. Discerning evangelicals will, if well-trained, sift much that is good here as they use this with other works that see some things quite differently. It is at times fairly good but not among the better commentaries.

Lane, William L. *The Gospel According to Mark* **(NIC). Grand Rapids: Eerdmans, 1974.**

The author writes from the standpoint that "redaction criticism is a valid hermeneutical approach to understanding the text of Mark and the intention of the evangelist", though he does not believe this necessarily "should lead to the dehistoricizing of the New Testament Gospel" (p. 7). His commentary and copious notes reflect a good awareness of scholarly sources and acquaint one quickly with problem areas, views, and recent literature on various issues. Lane often defends the text against criticism that impugns its authenticity.

Mann, C. S. *Mark* **(Anchor Bible). Garden City, NY: Doubleday, 1986. 716 pp.**

Basically a liberal work but often profitable in technical aspects and thoroughness. He surveys scholarly thinking on Mark and reviews approaches of recent years. His bibliographies are valuable, and he frequently has good input on Greek grammar, words, customs in Jesus' day, etc. In his mind, Mark is the third gospel to be written, and all three synoptics date before A. D. 70.

Martin, Ralph P. *Where The Action Is.* **Glendale, CA: Gospel Light Publications, 1977.**

This paperback provides a very concise and an easier commentary for laymen. One will not necessarily always agree with Martin's concepts, as when he argues that Jesus did not in His triumphal entry ride in as king (Mark 11:1-19, pp. 98-99).

Plummer, Alfred. *The Gospel According to St. Mark.* **In the Cambridge Greek Testament. Cambridge: University Press, 1938.**

This is an excellent liberal study of the book from the standpoint of the Greek. There are excellent cross-references on key words, and usually serious efforts to explain the meaning.

Schneck, Richard. *Isaiah in the Gospel of Mark, I-VIII.* **Vallejo, CA: Bibal Press, 1994.**

A doctoral dissertation in the Universidad Javeriana, Bogota, Colombia, this 339-pp. study by a Jesuit discusses references from Isaiah (1:2-3, etc.). Schneck concludes with respect for Markan proper use of OT citations (246).

Scroggie, W. Graham. *The Gospel of Mark.* **Grand Rapids: Zondervan, 1976 edition.**

The author (1877-1958) first published this through Marshall, Morgan & Scott in London as part of "The Study Hour Series". Scroggie was perhaps best known for his *Guide to the Gospels*. He ultimately succeeded Charles Haddon Spurgeon as pastor of the Metropolitan Tabernacle in London. This volume is a 285-page verse-by-verse exposition with its main attention paid to the English text. Scroggie assumes Marcan priority, as did many of his day, and concurs with A. T. Robertson on an A. D. 50 date. Scroggie's writing style is well-organized and clear, and the work is peppered with valuable illustrations for the Bible student and Sunday School teacher. -Jan Sattem

Such, W. A. *The Abomination of Desolation in the Gospel of Mark. Its Historical Reference in Mark 13:14 and its Impact in the Gospel.* **Lanham, MD: University Press of America, 1999.**

This is a revision of Such's dissertation at the University of St. Andrews, Scotland. It is one of the most comprehensive examinations on the issue yet, and presents both clarity and puzzling statements. Such argues that the evangelist displays knowledge here of the Roman commander Titus laying final siege to Jerusalem in the Jewish-Roman War 66-74 A. D., and tries to show the impact of the warning and Titus' activity on the gospel as a whole. In view of supernatural prophecy, and Jesus speaking the words and Mark accurately reporting what He said, some will prefer to give credit to Jesus, and also see a greater reference to the final Antichrist at the end of the age, as in Matt. 24. Such admits a problem that his claim raises "where the line is between Markan creation of material dealing with his post-70 C. E. situation and Mark as preserver of tradition about Jesus" (208).

Swete, Henry B. *Commentary on Mark.* **Grand Rapids: Kregel, 1977. Reprint of 1913 work.**

Swete's work is one of the best older conservative commentaries on the Greek text. Swete was an Anglican minister and a scholar in Latin, Greek, and theology, and taught at Cambridge. He does a fairly good job on the Messianic character of the suffering Servant.

Taylor, Vincent. *The Gospel According to St. Mark.* **Grand Rapids: Baker, 1966. 696 pp. 2d rev. ed.**

Though liberal in viewpoint, this is a work very helpful in the Greek grammar. The introduction is valuable and the commentary is rated by some as the best on Mark up to its time.

Telford, William R., ed. *The Interpretation of Mark.* **2nd ed. Edinburgh: T. & T. Clark, 1995. 1st ed. Philadelphia: Fortress Press, 1985.**

Advanced students meet with 13 journal articles on different topics by eminent scholars such as Ernest Best and Andrew Lincoln. Telford's own introduction looks at the literary explosion of Markan studies within the previous 30 years and shows developments. An index of Markan texts and an index of topics aids in locating specific items.

Witherington, Ben, III. *The Gospel of Mark. A Socio-Rhetorical Commentary.* **Grand Rapids: Eerdmans, 2001.**

This is billed (back cover) as the first overall effort to read Mark as an ancient biography and a form of ancient rhetoric. An Asbury Theological Seminary NT professor gives a fresh translation and a detailed and often insightful, but sometimes too wordy, commentary. The work is 463 big pp. Many statements are reasonable, providing light, some issues need better resolution, e. g. the "rocky" ground in Mark 4 pictures Jesus' disciples who deserted Him later, yet the thorny soil represents those like the rich ruler who are not able to become genuine disciples (168-69). One can puzzle over how this particular view of the two cases is probable. The commentator believes that in Mark 13 only vv. 24-27, 32-37 refer to Second Advent matters, other verses to events climaxing in A. D. 70 (340). Rather often, comments are more assertions than pointers to evidence. Verse comments end at Mark 16:8. The work does help as a supplement to other commentaries, but is not of high contribution compared with many that are better.

Wolff, Richard. *The Gospel of Mark.* **Wheaton: Tyndale House, 1971.**

Though brief, this commentary helps the reader to see the movement and meaning in Mark quite well. Wolff became known a few years ago for his competent writings that have a lot to offer (See *The General Epistles of James and Jude*, etc.).

Wuest, Kenneth S. *Mark in the Greek New Testament.* **Grand Rapids: Eerdmans, 1957.**

This is a verse-by-verse evangelical, expository work which deals with the Greek text but does so in a way which the English reader can follow though he does not know Greek. It is a good book to give to a layman who is serious about studying Mark, and also helpful to the pastor or teacher.

III. LUKE

Arndt, William. *The Gospel According to Luke.* **St. Louis: Concordia, 1956.**

This conservative commentary is a detailed work in the Greek and is well-written. The author did the famous Greek-English lexicon and two books on alleged contradictions.

Bailey, Kenneth E. *Poet and Peasant.* **Grand Rapids: Eerdmans, 1960. Also** *Through Peasant Eyes: More Lucan Parables, Their Culture and State.* **Eerdmans, 1981.**

Bailey discusses four Lukan parables at length in the first book, making a great contribution as to cultural data that opens up the parables. His data is based on studies while teaching for many years in the mid-East, also on extensive travels, correspondence, and scholarly probing into the literature. Particularly insightful are his remarks on Luke 15 (the triad of parables) and Luke 11 (Friend at Midnight). The second book continues to be rich in peasant cultural background, with data not available to many who study the parables. But the second book treats ten further parables (7:36-50 and others in 9:51-19:48, Luke's travel narrative). These are well-done but not treated in as much detail. Both books are excellent in making parables "come alive" and making readers think. In more recent years both volumes have been put into one book. Cf. Hultgren in the Matthew section.

Benware, Paul N. *Luke* (Everyman's Bible Commentary). Chicago: Moody, 147 pp.

A conservative, premillennial survey by a diligent young scholar. Often the book is helpful on problem areas, though brief. At other points the brevity of the series and length of Luke are among the reasons for over-generality that adds nothing to the understanding.

Bock, Darrell. *Luke 1:1-9:50* and *Luke 9:51-24:*53 (Baker Exegetical Commentary on the NT). Grand Rapids: Baker, 1994, 1996.

This evangelical work of 2,148 pp. begins with 48 pp. on introductory issues. It has an overview, a conviction that Luke was the writer and a careful one to give material not fabricated but as a first class historian (13). There is a summary of each section, also the theology (27-43), a 5-pp. outline, etc. Bock has, after each section's synopsis, exegetical detail on each verse, weighing views, giving reasons, explaining customs, offering many interactions with vast scholarly opinion. Some details are that he concludes that Matt. 5-7 and Luke 6 present summaries of the same sermon (553), in 7:47 he shows why forgiveness preceded the woman's acts of love, and in 2:36-38 he deals with views on Anna's 84 years, yet has nothing about whether she lodged in a temple room or was just at the temple daily. All in all, those needing thorough discussion find it in these vols. with massive bibliography, indexes of subjects, authors, Greek words, Scripture, and ancient writings. This is one of the top evangelical works on Luke all-around.

Bock, Darrell. *Luke* (IVP NTC). Downers Grove: IVP, 1994.

One meets with a far shorter work than the 2-vol. effort. Bock says (12) that the larger work has focused on accuracy and rationale for views, this one on relevancy and relational matters of faith. Evangelical comments run quickly to their points, yet the generality causes skipping some key details (cf. on Anna, 2:36-38), or seem to argue around a more likely view with unconvincing reasoning (3:16). In other cases, Bock seems to select the most probable view, an instance being in seeing the sermon (Luke 6) as a condensed version of the same sermon in Matt. 5-7 (119). One can also find the second and third soils of Luke 8 taken to represent people not actually saved (148-49). One can wonder in 14:34-35 how inability to be worthy disciples is in harmony with salvation as a gift, for the work passes by this. Bock in most verses touches clearly on key issues, and an author lacks space to deal with every important matter, whether in a short or massive attempt. For a work with much application, cf. Darrell Bock, *Luke* (NIV Application Commentary. Grand Rapids: Zondervan, 1996, 640 pp.).

Creed, J. M. *The Gospel According to St Luke.* London, 1965.

A detailed, technical work on the Greek text. It is, with the commentary by Plummer and the works by Fitzmyer and Marshall, among the best along these lines.

Ellis, E. Earle. *The Gospel of Luke* **(New Century Bible). London: Oliphants, 1966.**

One of the better commentaries of more recent years from the standpoint of explaining the text even where there are problems, though briefly. The author is an evangelical and well-versed in critical scholarship today.

Evans, Craig A. *Luke* **(New International Bible Commentary). Peabody, MA: Hendrickson, 1991. 416 pp.**

A lucid study, often of help on problem texts but cursory at times. Evans gives authorship by Luke "provisional acceptance" and feels that this issue is not vital to how this gospel is interpreted (3). After a brief introduction (1-16), general summaries of each section are followed by added notes on a few key details, with bypassing of many, such as Anna's 84 years in 2:36-38, and problems of interpretation in 11:5-7. While Evans shows high expertise even when terse, one will find other works explaining far more to make their time fruitful.

Fitzmyer, Joseph A. *The Gospel According to Luke* **(Anchor Bible). 2 volumes. Garden City, NY: Doubleday, 1981-85. 1,642 pp.**

An internationally known Catholic scholar presents an excellent appraisal of "The Current State of Lukan Studies" (3-34) and has "A Sketch of Lukan Theology" (143-270). In explaining the gospel text, Fitzmyer has often helpful sources on various points. This will rank as one of the best-regarded commentaries at this time from the standpoint of awareness of critical literature and comments reflecting current learning. He gives his own translation and a fairly lucid, detailed exposition that is abreast of language, background, and views. It is a mixed bag with Fitzmyer, though. He often takes views that evangelicals appreciate, such as Jesus' resurrection body being able to eat food. At other times he stumbles where there are possible solutions, as when he feels that there is no way to harmonize the accounts of Jesus' resurrection. Indices to both volumes help find material.

Geldenhuys, T. N. *Commentary on the Gospel of Luke* **(NIC). Grand Rapids: Eerdmans, 1952.**

Amillennial in its interpretation of the kingdom program, this work is solid and explains many verses rather well but is not the best.

Godet, Franz L. *A Commentary on the Gospel of St. Luke.* **2 volumes. Edinburgh: T. & T. Clark, 1982; available from Philadelphia: Fortress Press; also 1-volume ed. available from Grand Rapids: Kregel. Originally issued in 1870.**

Though old, this work is almost exhaustive in dealing with interpretive problems and shows a wide acquaintance with commentators of all ages up to his day. He is regarded by Greek authorities as weak on textual criticism but strong on exegesis. Zondervan in 1959 also issued a reprint of the 1881 edition.

Gooding, David. *According to Luke. A New Exposition of the Third Gospel.* **Grand Rapids: Eerdmans, 1987.**

Gooding was formerly Prof. of Greek, Queen's University, Belfast, and well known in many countries for biblical exposition. His writing of a simplified, flowing explanation is in 362 pp., moving section by section. He often refers to I. H. Marshall's large work on the Greek text for more detail, as in giving six lines on the Luke 3 genealogy and referring to nine pp. in Marshall (78). He avoids other discussions also, as whether Luke 6 has the same sermon as Matt. 5-7, but says that Jesus, as many preachers, could vary material on different occasions (117-18). He generalizes "mysteries of the kingdom" in Luke 8:4-21 to refer only to "God's way of salvation is a plan . . which no one would ever have known anything about if God had not revealed it" (140). The commentary seems fair in a number of places checked, but is not as consistently profitable as several others are. Gooding has a similar (440-pp.) work on Acts, *True to the Faith* (London: Hodder & Stoughton, 1990), which is helpful to a pastor in terms of summing up spiritual emphases in passages.

Green, Joel B. *The Gospel of Luke* **(NICNT). Grand Rapids: Eerdmans, 1997.**

This work with pp. i-xcii plus 928 replaced Norval Geldenhuys' effort of 1951. Green puts more focus on literary criticism, narrative criticism, and social-scientific analysis than on earlier issues about historical critical matters, redaction and source criticism, etc. One sees topics such as family allegiances, friendship, purity, and status. He seeks to show OT background for this gospel, and not Mark, or Matthew, or oral tradition. Green sets up a misleading opinion that Luke and those using his work were "not so much concerned with the issue, Did it happen? as with the queries What happened? and what does it all mean? (36). It surely is both. However, he does appear to believe that the details are fact in Luke's perspective, but thinks Luke is more burdened with how to understand things (20). One can say that Luke saw the two in a necessary balance and need not have any thought of ranking them.

Griffith-Thomas, W. H. *Outline Studies in Luke. A Devotional Commentary.* **Grand Rapids: Kregel, 1984. 410 pp.**

This outlines sections, arranges ideas homiletically, gives practical insights, and has crisp simplicity in wording. The author (1861-1924), Welch by birth, was a professor of Systematic Theology at Wycliffe College, Toronto, also a pastor, world conference speaker, writer of many books and a co-founder of Dallas Seminary. He died before he was to become the first professor of Systematic Theology, Dallas Seminary. Here as in Matthew, Romans and Hebrews he offers considerable help for pastors and the gist of things pulled together devotionally for lay people. He is well-known for his devotional work on Genesis.

Kistemaker, Simon. *The Parables of Jesus.* **Grand Rapids: Baker, 1980.**

A past national president of Evangelical Theological Society deals with all of Jesus' parables and shows a lucid style, warmth, and broad acquaintance with scholarly writings on his material which is obvious in footnotes. He uses the NIV text. The contribution is very good on background, the main thrust of parables, key expository details, and the practical contribution for life. This is one of the best fairly recent evangelical works on the parables in general (cf. Bailey, Ellisen, Hultgren, Longenecker, etc, under Matthew and Luke).

Liefeld, Walter L. "Luke" in *Expositor's Bible Commentary*, Volume 8, ed. Frank Gaebelein and J. D. Douglas. Grand Rapids: Zondervan, 1984, pp. 797-1,059.

Liefeld has a generally good introduction with a fine discussion of themes and theology (13 points). He is disappointing in his discussion of distinctive features (p. 798). He can be vague and not nail things down as on baptism with fire (857) and what 16:8b-9, 17:7-10 and 19:11-27 are getting at. Still, in many passages he is helpful on main aspects and clear, giving the expositor aid, mingling informative comment with practical material. He is conservative and premillennial.

Marshall, 1. Howard. *The Gospel of Luke*. London: Paternoster, 1977.

One of the leading evangelicals of the British Isles has written this. It was my privilege to read a section before Dr. Marshall sent it to Paternoster. It is a serious attempt to explain verses in detail, with a keen perception of problems and different recent views, and an attempt to take a stand on most issues. The form is somewhat like the ICC, and the author has sought to provide for serious evangelical scholars a technically and exegetically-based answer to Bultmannian-type theories that are destructive to the Gospel's real authority.

Martin, John A. "Luke," in *Bible Knowledge Commentary*, ed. John F. Walvoord and Roy B. Zuck, Volume II. Wheaton: Victor Books, 1985.

Conservative, premillennial work of a concise yet clear and well-informed nature. Despite the brevity to which he is held, Martin frequently gives views and an assessment, as in mentioning two views on the parables of Luke 15: restoration of a saved person to fellowship or bringing of unsaved people to salvation, the latter of which he favors (p. 244). Usually he has something helpful to say on problem verses.

Morgan, G. Campbell. *The Gospel According to Luke*. NY: Revell, 1931.

This is a valuable commentary to have on the English text. It is one of Morgan's better works in detailed exposition.

Morris, Leon. *Luke*. Grand Rapids: Eerdmans, 1974.

Morris has written a good conservative commentary of some detail. It is lucid and not technical in nature.

Pate, C. Marvin. *Luke* (Moody Gospel Commentary). Chicago: Moody, 1995.

Pate devotes 521 pp. to explaining some of the pressing issues in verses, while passing by others with no comment or very general remarks that cover little. He uses transliteration for Greek words. In a dispensational effort, he reasons where relevant for a future restoration of Israel, and often supports Luke's factual reliability. On certain problems he goes into more detail about views, for example on how the genealogies of Luke 3 and Matthew 1 relate (leaving this unresolved). He takes Matthew 5-7 and Luke 6 as giving versions of the same sermon, with variations explainable. Overall, the book is a fair medium-range survey exposition for those wanting brevity with attention to some of the leading issues.

Plummer, Alfred. *A Critical and Exegetical Commentary on the Gospel According to St. Luke* **(ICC). NY: Scribners, 1910.**

This used to be often considered the best older commentary on the Greek.

Spencer, W. D. and Spencer, A. B. *The Prayer Life of Jesus: Shout of Agony. Revelation of Love, a Commentary.* **NY: University Press of America, 1990. 296 pp.**

A comprehensive work dealing with Matthew 6:9-13; Luke 11:2-4 as well as with parables on prayer, Jesus' emphasis on prayer in His busy life, New Testament words for prayer, Jesus' positions while in prayer, John 17, Gethsemane, and the cross. It has a lot of good comment and ought to be refreshment amidst other studies. The authors teach at Gordon-Conwell Theological Seminary, South Hampton, MA.

Tenney, Merrill C. "Luke," in *Wycliffe Bible Commentary***, ed. C. F. Pfeiffer and E. F. Harrison. Chicago: Moody, 1962.**

Tenney is limited in his space, but usually makes good use of it to explain verses so as to provide help. He is conservative and premillennial. Sometimes he is quite clear, other times one can only guess what he means when he is vague, as when he says that "the kingdom of God is nigh at hand" (21:29) are words complementary to 17:21, "The kingdom of God is within you" (p. 1063). Overall he offers a fairly good commentary for those wanting a brief study with considerable competence behind it.

Wilcock, Michael. *Saviour of the World: The Message of Luke's Gospel.* **Downers Grove, IL: IVP. 1979.**

In the Bible Speaks Today series, It is a clear, homiletically well-organized 215-pp. exposition of the main thrust in passages, not an attempt at a phrase by phrase commentary. He often shows a refreshingly high view of the gospels, as when he takes the talents (Matthew 25:14-30) and pounds (Luke 19:11-27) to be different though similar parables with complimentary emphases.

IV. JOHN

Ashton, John, ed. *The Interpretation of John.* **2nd ed. Edinburgh: T. & T. Clark, 1997. 1st ed. Fortress Press, 1986.**

Ashton furnishes an introduction on "The Problem of John," and 14 chapters by German scholars with various critical views from Bultmann on. The work can help advanced users see much about opinions when specialists theorize on this gospel. Only a few devoted to probing critical channels will stay at the work and be able to follow it and find varing degrees on benefit.

Barrett, C. K. *The Gospel According to John.* **NY: Macmillan, 1955.**

Though liberal, this is probably the best critical commentary on the Greek text, especially on the grammar, where he is superior to Westcott, Godet and others.

Beasley-Murray, G. R. *John* **(Word Biblical Commentary). Waco, TX: Word Books, 1987. 441 pp.**

An evangelical of a somewhat critical leaning has done this competent, usually detailed work on text, grammar, movement of passages, and bibliography. He provides a fairly good survey on the relationship between the fourth gospel and the synoptics (xxxv-xxxvii). He argues for leaving the text in its present order rather than rearranging it a la Bultmann and others (xliii). Still, he sometimes allows his eye for critical theories to see this as more important than explaining the text. He remains subjective at times as when citing with seeming acceptance the idea that John the Baptist said "Look, the Lamb of God" (1:36) and verse 29 gives the evangelist's addition, "who takes away the sin of the world" (lii). Yet he states his conviction for a high view of the reliability of the material as of God (liii). The fourth gospel was written, he supposes, by one of a circle associated with the beloved disciple whom he feels was not one of the twelve (lxxiv). On some problems he helps in a cursory manner, as on "born of water and of the Spirit" (3:5), on others he is thinner, as on 3:14-15. More should be done with the relation between verses, as the description in 10:27 of the people God keeps safe in 10:28-29. His explanation of 15:2 pitifully leaps over details without meaningful comments; he generalizes what "abide" means in a rather meaningless way. On 20:22 he is confusing. The work is good at times, fair at others and weak in some.

Bernard, J. A. *Gospel According to St. John* (International Critical Commentary). Edinburgh: T. & T. Clark, 1928.

A liberal work, now outdated as to literature but long held in high esteem on critical and exegetical matters.

Blomberg, Craig L. *The Historical Reliability of John's Gospel. Issues & Commentary*. Downer's Grove: IVP, 2001.

Blomberg provides a brief commentary on successive sections of the Fourth Gospel (more than 200 pp.), and draws the conclusion that a good case can be built for the historicity and reliability. He responds to claims of inaccuracy. On individual passages, he offers views, for example the unfruitful branches in John 15 picture people not really born again (206). The introduction of ca. 50 pp. argues for and against authorship by the Apostle John, concluding that he was the writer. It also looks at differences between this gospel and the other three, and provides some perspective on these.

Blum, Edwin. "John," in *Bible Knowledge Commentary*, ed. John F. Walvoord and Roy B. Zuck, Volume II. Wheaton: Victor Books, 1985.

Though limited to conciseness, Blum poured much expertise into this, so it is a good survey, often helpful on problems, connections, and exegetical points. Blum on such texts as 15:2a takes what has come to be called a lordship salvation perspective.

Boice, James M. *The Gospel of John: An Evangelical Commentary*. 5 Volumes. Grand Rapids: Zondervan, 1975-79.

A keen scholar and good evangelical Bible pastor-teacher contributed this work based on his thorough messages. Boice often presents various possible interpretations and shows his reasons for the view he prefers. His good illustrations and frequent outstanding evangelistic content add value to the work. At times he becomes more topical than expositional in the sense of following the text verse by verse as he seeks to draw in so many truths in relation to John's Gospel. Boice is not afraid to disagree with the majority of commentators. For example, on 15:2 most say that "takes away" (*airo*) refers to the

Father's removal of unfruitful people. Boice takes the view that airo here means God "lifts up" the unfruitful among the saved so that they may begin to bear fruit.

Borchert, Gerald. *John* **(New American Commentary). 2 vols. Nashville: Broadman & Holman, 1996ff.**

The evangelical introduction of more than 90 pp. concludes that John the Apostle provided the material and a loving scribe wrote it (90) in the A. D. 90's (93). Vol. 2 deals with Johannine themes and theology. Borchert uses word meaning and grammar to conclude that 1:1 refers to Jesus being God. Usually he explains verses well, but at other times he falls short and disappoints (cf. on 3:5-8; 10:28-29). His wide reading allows him to illumine points. The commentary is often helpful, yet several other works explain more to help teachers, preachers, students and lay people.

Bowman, Robert M., Jr. *Jehovah's Witnesses, Jesus Christ and the Gospel of John.* **Grand Rapids: Baker, 1989. 171 pp.**

He puts his focus on John 1:1, answering Jehovah's Witnesses who have changed their line of argument from a few years ago. Bowman also deals with 8:58 and 20:28. For years Bowman has shown skill in refuting cultic error as associate editor of *Christian Research Journal* and in other capacities.

Brown, R. E. *The Gospel According to John* **(Anchor Bible). 2 volumes. Garden City, NY: Doubleday, 1966, 1970.**

A Catholic work of much learning, which rates among the top fairly recent studies especially for serious students or for teaching the book in-depth and being made aware of scholarly study done on this Gospel. Brown brings immense learning to the task, and leaves few stones unturned. At 1,208 pages this is one of the most detailed fairly recent works in English on the Gospel of John. He analyzes views and issues, reasons, the current status of studies, etc. Notes and comments explain verses very fully as he uses the translation of the New American Bible (Patterson, NJ: St. Anthony Guild Press, 1970). Many regard as arbitrary his five stage theory of composition. He also has a shorter work, *The Gospel and Epistles of John: A Concise Commentary.*

Bruce, F. F. *The Gospel of John: Introduction, Exposition and Notes.* **Grand Rapids: Eerdmans, 1983. 425 pp.**

Bruce gives a fresh translation of the Greek, much good commentary, a copious use of current literature, and application. Clarity prevails as he offers help for pastors, seminarians and lay people. At times, however, his vocabulary will mystify those not trained in languages, e. g. "sotto voce," p. 174; "ingressive sense of the aorist," p. 246, etc. Overall it is a very fine commentary by one of the leading evangelicals of recent decades.

Bultmann, Rudolf. T*he Gospel of John, A Commentary.* **Translated G. R. Beasley-Murray. Philadelphia: Westminster, 1971. Translated from** *Das Evangelium des Johannes.* **Gottingen: Vandenhoeck and Ruprecht, 1964.**

A 744-pp. work late in Bultmann's life. Walter Schmithals wrote the introduction for this English edition, since Bultmann had not done an introduction. Form-critical and redaction-critical theories stand behind introduction and commentary. Schmithals says the author of the gospel is unknown but that the composition and redaction lay in the period

A. D. 80-120. There is much of value for mature, discerning evangelicals, but they must always be able to sift the worthwhile from among many liberal conclusions.

Burge, Gary. "John," in *Evangelical Commentary on the Bible*, ed. Walter A. Elwell. Grand Rapids: Baker, 1989.

Although brief, Burge shows awareness of issues and often uses his space well to provide help.

Burge, Gary M. *John* (NIV Application Commentary). Grand Rapids: Zondervan, 2000.

A Wheaton College professor seeks to interpret John in its Jewish flavor, i.e. with sensitivity to the OT rooting and Palestinian Judaism of Jesus' day. He uses such materials to see the Messianic aspects. Burge offers different views on some of the problems, such as "water and Spirit" in 3:6, and Peter's responses in 21:15-17. He gives background custom as for the events of the festival when Jesus invited drinking from Him (7:37-39), and footwashing in chap. 13. This does not mean that in all verses comments are adequate (cf. 15:2, 6, for example) to nail details down distinctly, or look at views. Since this series often just sums up passages, remarks on some verses can be difficult and slow to be located, or at times not be there due to the generalities. Some key verses are handled too quickly, or only partially (cf. 10:28, 29). The comments are sufficient at times, but not consistently enough to put the work among the more dependable.

Carson, Donald A. *The Gospel According to John*. Grand Rapids: Eerdmans, 1991. 715 pp.

An excellent commentary out of an evangelical's breadth of scholarly study and keen awareness of recent literature. He aims the work for teachers and preachers but it is readable for lay-people too. The introduction is 84 pages, giving characteristics of this gospel, how it has been interpreted, its genuineness, purpose, doctrinal distinctives and other matters. He has technical notes and comments, but his focus is more on seeing the flow of the text and drawing out doctrinal principles. Some rate it at the top of evangelical works, or a close run with the work by Leon Morris.

Carson, Donald A. *The Farewell Discourse and Final Prayer of Jesus* [John 14-17]. Grand Rapids: Baker, 1980.

One of the better expositions of John 14-17 in some detail with frequent meaningful articulation of principles for daily life. This study is meant to distill the fruits of scholarly labors and research for the church at large, and it succeeds at that. Carson's style is fairly vivid, and easily grasped, with an excellent foreward dramatically setting the stage for the discourse. Many of the problems are faced rather squarely and are fairly satisfactory. The book's appeal as one of the better evangelical expositions in recent years is expanded by the presence of several personal illustrations (e. g. p. 109ff.) and a frank style. -Dan Phillips.

Godet, F. *Commentary on the Gospel of John*. 2 volumes. Grand Rapids: Zondervan (n. d.). Reprint of 3rd edition of 1893.

A good scholar is at his best here. He is exhaustive and excellent, though this work is old.

Harrison, Everett F. *John, The Gospel of Faith*. Chicago: Moody, 1962.

This work is contained in *The Everyman's Bible Commentary Series* and is concise as it provides a well-written, easy-to-read survey and overview. Along this line it is helpful. See also Harrison's work on John in *Wycliffe Bible Commentary*, ed. Pfeiffer and Harrison.

Haenchen, Ernst. *A Commentary on the Gospel of John* (Hermeneia). 2 Volumes. Philadelphia: Fortress Press, 1984-86. 674 pp.

This is a translation from a German work of 1980, *Das Johannes Evangelium: Ein Kommentar* (Mingen: J. C. B. Mohr). Liberal in orientation, he holds to three authors, one for the gospel of miracles, one an evangelist, and one an ecclesiastical supplementer. So, he sees some of the account as added from church tradition by a redactor (3:20-21; 6:51-58, etc.). Much critical theory appears, picking and choosing on subjective bases. Since Haenchen worked on the manuscript from 1954 until around 1975, the year he died, his use of other scholarly literature often does not bring things up to date to 1975. However, lengthy bibliographies added after his death draw things into the 1980's and have value for earnest researchers as they read with due awareness of the liberal slants. Haenchen's work on Acts also is respected.

Heading, John. *What the Bible Teaches: John* (Ritchie New Testament Commentaries), Volume 6. Kilmarnock, Scotland: John Ritchie Ltd., 1988. 349 pp.

This work and others in the Ritchie series are distributed in the States by Loizeaux Brothers, Neptune, NJ. The series is ten volumes, taking a stand on inerrancy and pre-millennial dispensational interpretation, even a pre-tribulational rapture. It is very simple, geared for some lay readers, and does not reflect a breadth of study though it has many helpful comments. The bibliography (pp. 15-16) is heavily evangelical and quite turned to older works such as by David Brown, E. W. Bullinger, J. N. Darby, F. Godet, Matthew Henry, William Kelly, F. B. Meyer, J. C. Ryle, etc. It overlooks some key details, such as "born of water and of the Spirit" (3:5), and reads in some fanciful things that are not the point, as having the lifted brazen serpent "retaining the purity and metallic perfection of brass that remained uncontaminated," so that it might speak of Jesus' "infinite divine perfection" (p. 62). It neglects aspects that are important, as in being silent about looking to be healed in Numbers 21, and believing in John 3. In 15:2, the branch not bearing fruit represents a saved person who needs to be "lifted up by exhortation ... to rise to spiritual heights (Colossians 3:1-4) . . ." (254). Yet 15:6 refers to a mere professor (255).

Hendriksen, William. *Exposition of the Gospel According to John*. 2 Volumes in one. Grand Rapids: Baker, 1961.

Trained in the Christian Reformed tradition, Hendriksen is thoroughly conservative and believes in plenary verbal inspiration. He served for ten years as Professor of New Testament Literature in Calvin Seminary. His introductions are quite extended and carefully written. In his commentary, which is very usable, he first presents a brief synthetic outline of a section, follows up with a detailed discussion verse-by-verse, then gives a survey of the argument in that section. His footnote discussions show a wide breadth of reading. He is usually quite helpful on problems, Greek word meanings, and matters of history, culture or geography. There are many stimulating sermon hints and devotional thoughts. He is good in presenting several different views to a question and documenting them thoroughly. He is amillennial in matters pertaining to the kingdom (cf. his comment on 10:16 as well as his book *More Than Conquerors*, pp. 222ff.). Though the author is very helpful in the Greek, the manner of discussion can be extremely valuable to the layman.

Hengstenberg, E. W. *Commentary on the Gospel of St. John.* 2 Volumes. Edinburgh: T. & T. Clark, 1865.

This work, recently reprinted, has much judicious material tying the thought to Old Testament background theology. At times it is very provocative (cf. on Jn. 1:15, 30, "He is preferred before me," italics mine). Hengstenberg is one of the towering older names, well-known for Christology of the Old Testament, for example.

Kent, Homer A., Jr. *Light in the Darkness. Studies in the Gospel of John.* Grand Rapids: Baker, 1974.

Kent's paragraph-by-paragraph survey of John's Gospel deals with some of the main problem areas in exposition. It is geared to be a guide for personal or group study. Kent utilizes photographs, maps, and diagrams. It is a good expositional survey by an evangelical (former President, Grace Theological Seminary, Winona Lake, IN).

Laney, J. Carl. *John* (Moody Gospel Commentary). Chicago: Moody, 1992. 407 pp.

This initiated a new, conservative paperback series under general editor Paul Enns, who has written in the Bible Study Commentary (Joshua, Judges, Ruth, Ezekiel). Laney, Professor of Biblical Literature at Western Conservative Baptist Seminary, Portland, OR, shows keen awareness of textual and critical matters, also historical and cultural aspects, and theme (belief and unbelief, with 20:30-31 on the purpose). He writes clearly, verse by verse, explaining the main issues and applying lessons in well-organized homiletical sections, aiming primarily to help teachers and preachers. He meets many of the problems head on and discusses them clearly. He sees 15:2a as referring to a nominal, so-called Christian who is not saved and is cut off, and 15:6 to this kind of person also. Jesus breathing on the disciples in 20:22 is a temporary giving of the Spirit to enable until Pentecost. Overall this is a good survey, competently done.

Lloyd-Jones, D. M. *John 17.* 4 volumes: *Saved in Eternity* (17:1-5); *Safe in the World* (17:6-19); *Sanctified Through the Truth* (17:17-19); and *Growing in the Spirit* (17:17-24). Westchester, IL: Crossway Books, 1988-89.

These expositions, which overlap on verses, are from 1952-53 messages. Lloyd-Jones, Westminster Chapel's minister for around thirty years in London, helps other pastors and lay readers find much devotional stimulation for spiritual triumph by dwelling on their position in God's grace. Cf. other works on John 17 under Rainsford in this section. Lloyd-Jones is best, Rainsford next, then Wiersbe and Brown.

Macduff, J. R. *Noontide at Sychar. The Story of Jacob's Well.* London: James Nisbet & Co., 1877.

Detailed, stimulating facets for a preacher preparing a message on this area in John 4.

Meyer, F. B. *The Gospel of John, The Life and Light of Men.* **London: Marshall, Morgan & Scott, 1950.**

A well-organized, suggestively rich lighter, devotional commentary by the famous preacher and writer of a well-known series on Bible characters (Abraham, Moses, Elijah, etc.) and several other insightful devotional books. Here is a commentary by a bright light that can refresh personally, stimulate messages and help illustrate them.

Michaels, J. R. *John* **(New International Biblical Commentary). Peabody, MA: Hendrickson, 1989. 386 pp.**

This was in the Good News Commentary (San Francisco: Harper & Row, 1984), but switched to the NIV. Michaels has also done I Peter (Word Biblical Commentary, 1988). The work on John is evangelical, shows marks of good scholarship, helps on many of the verses, and is fairly good overall though not outstanding.

Milne, Bruce. *The Message of John. Here is Your King!* **Downers Grove, IL: IVP, 1993.**

A reader finds a general, brief exposition that starts with sensible reasoning that the Apostle John is the author (cf. Carson for a fuller case). The verse by verse comments are well-organized and to the point, packing in much for preachers, students, and lay readers. Milne often shows relevance for current times. Problem verses draw concise but knowledgeable remarks (cf. 3:5; 7:53—8:11; 10:34), but one finds in 15:2, 6 a quick rush to an opinion without showing sensitivity to views. Overall, the commentary is quite useful for those needing brevity wedded with awareness, but far short of the helpfulness in several longer yet readable works.

Mitchell, John G. *An Everlasting Love. A Devotional Study of The Gospel of John.* **Portland: Multnomah Press, 1982.**

At the age of 90, the founder of Multnomah School of the Bible gives his readers some of the heartwarming fragrance of Christ he has long taught at Bible conferences, in the classroom, and as pastor of the Central Bible Church, Portland. The book is written as the man from England's Tyneside district spoke, simply and to the heart, moving verse by verse. There is much for the lay reader and refreshment from a lighter source for the pastor or teacher who also spends time in heavy, detailed analyses. Mitchell frequently makes pointed applications, offers illustrations, and ties things of Scripture together helpfully. He does not always nail down the meanings of verses specifically (cf. 17:15; 20:22 etc.).

Morgan, G. Campbell. *The Gospel According to John.* **NY: Revell, 1933.**

This is another of Morgan's better works and is good on the English text, though expositionally not as helpful as Hendriksen, Laney, Phillips and Pink.

Morris, Leon. *The Gospel According to John* **(NICNT). Grand Rapids: Eerdmans, 1995, rev. ed.**

This very detailed work of 936 pages, abreast of modern scholarship on John, has much to offer in the introduction and in the verse by verse insights. It now ranks as one of the finest on this gospel by an evangelical. It is based on the Greek. The new ed. (old one 1971) is done in light of more recent writings, with many minor modifications and some additions.

Phillips, John. *Exploring the Gospel of John.* **Neptune, NJ: Loizeaux, 1988. 425 pp.**

An articulate exposition that relates well to life, done by one of the fine Bible conference leaders of today, a prolific writer. Phillips, an evangelical, is well organized throughout as he follows his outline step by step. One can wonder why the 23-page outline is placed at the end rather than at the outset. Phillips helps the pastor or lay reader follow the flow of thought through John and touches lightly on some problems. It might serve best in a series of daily readings.

Pink, Arthur W. *The Gospel of John.* **3 volumes in 1. Grand Rapids: Zondervan, 1975rp. Formerly Swengel, PA: Bible Truth Depot, 1945.**

Before his death in 1952, Pink was a voluminous writer for the magazine, *Studies in the Scriptures*, which was published for 31 years. His expositions are non-technical and clearly intended for lay readers. Textual problems are for the most part untreated, but Pink does grapple seriously with doctrinal difficulties. He is conservative, Calvinistic, and switched from dispensationalism to amillennialism in his later years (compare his book The *Redeemer's Return* with his later *Exposition of Hebrews* and *Exposition of the Sermon on the Mount*. Ralph Keiper has written in *Eternity* (April, 1955, p. 32): "His works show hours of study; each line is filled with information and blessing. His books are not shallow. His studies fill the soul with 'strong meat' which needs to be well digested." His work on John has sometimes been called the best among older more detailed books on the English text.

Rainsford, Marcus. *Our Lord Prays for His Own.* **Chicago: Moody, 1950. 476 pp.**

This highly-esteemed older work of 1895 is by one of the finest expositors of the nineteenth century, sought after by men such as D. L. Moody. Rainsford, from Ireland, pastored St. John's Church (Belgrave Chapel) in London from 1886 to 1897, the year he died. Verse by verse he has a gold mine here, giving insight on most of the details of the great prayer. One pastor told this writer that Rainsford's book was the best on prayer he had read and that he made it a point to go through it afresh every year, finding himself often in tears as he identified with Jesus praying. Another fine work on John 17 is that of Lloyd-Jones (cf. above, this section). Still another is that of Warren Wiersbe (*Prayer: Basic Training*. Wheaton: Tyndale House, 1988. 144 pp.). Here are twelve chapters in which one of America's most beloved expositors digs out truths and lucidly articulates them in a way relevant for life today. Wiersbe's work was originally entitled *Listen! Our Lord is Praying*. Yet a further is by John Brown (*An Exposition of Our Lord's Intercessory Prayer*. Grand Rapids: Baker, 1980rp). Brown's work first came out in 1850 (Edinburgh: Oliphant & Sons. 255 pp.). He mentions several other expositions of John 17 before his book. He sets forth much of the basic meaning in the prayer in detail that will help a preacher and also edify any Christian who reads him.

Ridderbos, Herman. *The Gospel of John. A Theological Commentary.* **Grand Rapids: Eerdmans, 1997.**

Originally 2 vols. in the Netherlands in 1987 and 1992, this offers 721 pp. explaining and upholding John's gospel as reliable, answering the question "Who is Jesus?" Ridderbos devotes most of his attention to elucidating verses, not rehearsing contemporary scholarly opinions. The work is detailed and at times of substantial help to preaching. On some verses he has good help, and others do not contribute much due to many vague statements (cf. 6:37; 15:2, 6; 18:36). An asset in places, the commentary is not one of the top, clear helps this reviewer would use with confidence of getting frequent assists.

Schnackenburg, R. *Das Johnannes-evangelium*. 3 volumes in Herder's theologischer Kommentar zum Neuen Testament. Freiburg/Basel/ Vienna: Herder, 1975.

This Catholic scholar's work is widely regarded to be outstanding as a detailed critical, liberal study of John's Gospel in German circles. This work has also come out in English translation in Herder's Theological Commentary on the New Testament. This is the new German ICC, in effect, and was published in 1980-1982.

Scroggle, W. G. *The Gospel of John*. Grand Rapids: Zondervan, 1976, reprint, paperback.

A concise, well-organized tracing of the exposition by an evangelical master of synthesis, primarily helpful to pastors and laymen seriously inclined to study but not ready for something technical or detailed.

Smith, D. Moody. *John* (Abingdon NT Commentary). Nashville: Abingdon Press, 1999.

In fairly detailed work, Smith often states his own view, with or without support (for the latter, cf. on 3:5, "born of water and spirit"), at times with nebulous remarks (15:2a, 6). Instead of going verse by verse, discussions are general and may or may not touch on specific issues in verses. The work too often is below average and cannot compare favorably with many other commentaries.

Stott, John R. W. *Christ the Liberator*. Downers Grove, IL: InterVarsity, 1971.

This book has other messages at Urbana, 1970, but Stott's expositions on John 13-17 fill the first 89 pages. In the opinion of the reviewer, they are some of the best ever published with respect to coming right to grips with the message for Christians in a concise focus. Stott is well-organized in elucidating the passage, and he brings key issues out clearly in their application to spiritual living and representing Christ in the world.

Swete, Henry B. *The Last Discourse and Prayer of Our Lord. A Study of John XIV-XVII*. London: Macmillan and Co., 1913.

Swete has much good content, but usually only his own view (e.g. 14:6, "truth" and "life" are but other aspects of "the way" to bring out its meaning more clearly; 15:2, the unfruitful branch is in Christ "by the communion of the Sacraments" and can lose his part in Christ, with no elucidation on what that means exactly, how it comports with 6:37-41, 10:28, 29 etc.). Swete, known for fine older commentaries on Mark and Revelation, was Regius Professor of Divinity in the University of Cambridge and Honorable Chaplain to the King.

Tenney, Merrill C. *John, The Gospel of Belief*. Grand Rapids: Eerdmans, 1976rp, originally in 1948.

This is an analytic survey of John which traces the flow of argument with an alliterated outline. It is very good in helping the student to see the movement in the book though it should not be expected to get down into exegetical detail as the verse-by-verse studies can. Cf. also Tenney's "John," in the *Expositor's Bible Commentary*, Volume 9, ed. Frank Gaebelein and J. D. Douglas (Grand Rapids: Zondervan, 1981). The latter is a verse by verse commentary by the noted New Testament scholar, and it offers considerable help on the flow of thought as well as some of the problems, though he is vague on some as well (as 15:2a, 6).

Wenham, John. *Easter Enigma: Are the Resurrection Accounts in Conflict?* Grand Rapids: Zondervan, 1984.

An evangelical seeks to fit the gospel accounts of the resurrection together, whereas some have seen them as contradictory.

Westcott, B. F. *The Gospel According to St. John*. Grand Rapids: Eerdmans, 1973.

This is a reprint of a 1908 work which used to be generally regarded as the classic commentary on John. Westcott, born in England in 1825, studied at Dublin and was called "in learning a second Origen, in piety a second Augustine." He teamed with F. J. A. Hort to labor 28 years in producing the famous Greek New Testament. He was conservative and Calvinistic. His knowledge of Greek was extensive, and he uses Greek and Latin in his comments. This plus his involved thinking at times makes it rather difficult for many to follow him. This is a good work to consult in any thorough study of John, and the student who wants to build his library with the best will not pass it by.

Witherington, Ben, III. *John's Wisdom. A Commentary on the Fourth Gospel*. Louisville, KY: Westminster John Knox Press, 1995.

This pb of 411 pp. discusses features of ancient biographies and views John, comparatively, as a biography in a dramatic mode for Christian use in evangelism (4). The writer feels that John uses familiar elements and techniques from the Greco-Roman theater to reveal Jesus' deity (5). He believes that the fourth evangelist used material that the beloved disciple, apparently not the Apostle, had brought into a unit (6-16). Much of the introduction narrows to usefulness mostly to scholars as it assesses theories about sources and engages in much subjective conjecture. One gains the impression that this commentator feels that the gospel writer gave some material for his own purpose and not because it is historically accurate and factual where he puts it (37). One who tries to see verse by verse help can become frustrated in the ponderous general discussions that bounce around, and with the vagueness (cf. for example on 15:6). Many will lay it aside to use works that in more instances get specific about expounding verses.

V. ACTS

Alexander, J. A. *Acts*. Carlisle, PA: Banner of Truth Trust, 1991rp.

This work, originally out in 1857, has proved helpful to many, though it is now far out of date as to literature commenting on Acts. For many basic details verse by verse, it still is of good value and often will help on word meaning and special problems. The fact that it was reprinted is indicative of its respected place in Acts studies.

Arrington, F. L. *The Acts of the Apostles. An Introduction and Commentary.* **Peabody, MA: Hendrickson, 1988. 298 pp.**

This is a fairly good work done by Professor of New Testament Greek and Exegesis, Church of God School of Theology, Cleveland, TN. It helps on many of the basic points in passages in an evangelical vein, though it does not rank high.

Barrett, C. K. *A Critical and Exegetical Commentary on the Acts of the Apostles* **(ICC). 2 vols. Edinburgh: T. & T. Clark, 1994, 1998.**

A renowned NT scholar of the University of Durham in Scotland adds this 1272-pp. work to his careful books such as on John, Romans, the Corinthian Epistles, and the Pastorals. The Acts effort can be handled adeptly only by those advanced in Greek due to considerable explanation verse by verse along exegetical lines, and such matters as Barrett's theories about sources. Barrett discerns no unifying theme or plan (but many do), and offers no outline (cf. an opposite perspective in Bruce Winter and Andrew Clarke, eds., *The Book of Acts in its Ancient Setting*, Eerdmans, 1993). Barrett's bibliographies before units of verse by verse comments point out scholarly literature. He posits ties with other passages, or contradictions, and he claims the Acts makes mistakes. He rejects harmonizations that some have regarded adequate, and discredits reliability. One needs to be cautious in the face of such opinionated claims, with which many excellent scholars do not agree. But one finds in such a source how some learned writers think, and that is part of a true education.

Blaiklock, E. M. *Acts, The Birth of the Church.* **Old Tappan, NJ: Fleming H. Revell, 1980.**

This is done by an Emeritus Professor of Classics at the University of Auckland, New Zealand. It is a cursory, light treatment that discusses sections of verses with a fleeting glimpse that is written well but says little that solidly explains problem areas beyond generalizations. Most of the help found here is also given in other commentaries that offer a lot more besides on a more consistent basis.

Boice, James M. *Acts, An Expositional Commentary.* **Grand Rapids: Baker, 1997.**

Fifty messages work the way through Acts. One gets some good exposition, but also sees much peripheral, even if entertaining (to some) comment, and at times must search for actual, direct comment that comes to grips with Acts verses. At times but not often misleading teaching appears, as on 1:6-7, which sees the kingdom Jesus taught as only spiritual, citing Luke 17:21 as if the kingdom cannot be both literal on earth and spiritual (23). Boice can stress ideas, such as "fire" in Acts 2, yet not explain other details, such as what is meant by tongues-speaking, or 2:38? Though much enriching comment appears in the entirety, one would more profitably spend time in any or several other commentaries which stay with passages and expose more of their teaching more often, without a surplus of other remarks.

Bruce, F. F. *The Acts of the Apostles. The Greek Text with Introduction and Commentary.* **3rd ed., revised and enlarged. Grand Rapids: Eerdmans, 1990. 569 pp.**

This is an effort to be a bit more technical, using Greek grammar more than in his work on Acts in the NICNT. It is briefer, but good. The larger work explains more. The author, one of the foremost New Testament scholars of recent years, has been editor of *The Evangelical Quarterly*. All of his works are exacting in their scholarship. This is a revision and enlargement since the 1951 first edition and the 1952 second edition. Bruce weaves into it comments in light of scholarly study since those years. The 96-page introduction has a new section on the theology of Acts.

Bruce, F. F. *The Book of the Acts* (New International Commentary on the New Testament). Grand Rapids: Eerdmans, 1988. 541 pp.

This work, first issued in 1954, is now revised not long before Bruce died, with a new translation of the Greek text in place of the ASV. The bibliographical lists are extensively updated in footnotes, Bruce has interacted with later studies, arranged comments on fewer verses, and achieved a more lucid style in places. However, the basic verse-by-verse commentary remains substantially the same. It remains the finest commentary on Acts as to exposition in detail. Bruce points to I. H. Marshall's commentary for detail on Luke's theology. He shows a fine grasp of pertinent history, a sound explanation of most passages, and insights on many of the problems.

Bruce, F. F. "The Acts of the Apostles," in *New Bible Commentary*. Revised ed. J. D. Douglas. Grand Rapids: Eerdmans, 1970.

A boiled down version of Bruce's expertise, quite helpful in itself.

Carter, C. W. and Ralph Earle. *The Acts of the Apostles*. Grand Rapids: Zondervan, 1973.

The introduction and exegesis are by Earle, and the outlines, expositions, and special notes are by Carter. It is a fairly good commentary by these Nazarene scholars and will be of help more especially for preparing church sermons, Sunday School lessons, and Bible studies.

Couch, Mal, ed. *A Bible Handbook to the Acts of the Apostles*. Grand Rapids: Kregel, 1999.

Eight contributors and four other researchers and writers, most of them not widely known (yet these can convey truth too), are listed (8-9). But names are not supplied later to indicate who wrote which parts. The dispensational guide looks at introductory issues, then at such topics as tongues viewed as known human dialects unknown to the speakers in Acts 2, also earthly languages in I Corinthians 12-14 (38-39). Among other discussions are elders, how "Israel" is used, also signs, wonders, miracles and healings, the Davidic Covenant, the New Covenant, demons, the Holy Spirit in key Acts passages (2:38; 8:4-25; 9:1-19; 10:44—11:17; 19:1-7), how the Spirit's outpouring in Acts 2 relates to prophecy in Joel 2, etc. Pages 177-399 give time-lines for Acts 1-9, 10-12, and 13-28, and detailed sections on laying on of hands, sign gifts, and arguments against progressive dispensationalism. Chapter by chapter end notes conclude the handbook. Those of dispensational perspective will find help here, and those who have not taken dispensational views can see, as well, reasons for various interpretations.

Conzelmann, Hans. *Acts of the Apostles* (Hermeneia). Philadelphia: Fortress Press, 1987. 287 pp.

Using the RSV, the author furnishes frequent help on texts, commenting on syntax, background, customs, etc. He is liberal and features copious use of redaction criticism for suppositions on parts of Acts. He considers many things, such as miracles, as untrustworthy. As a much-studied scholar immersed in the book and the literature, he does have much to assist the pastor or student who knows how to draw out what is worthwhile and leave what is not, as in any commentary.

Dunn, James D. G. *The Acts of the Apostles.* **Valley Forge, PA: Trinity Press International, 1996.**

Dunn is uncertain who wrote Acts, and favors dating it in the A. D. 80's (xi). A stretching discussion of commentaries on Acts is helpful (xxii—xxvi). Dunn sometimes raises more questions than he seeks to resolve where he might do so, as on possible ways in which Judas' death in Acts 1 may relate to the material in Matthew 27 (4-5). He sees tongues in Acts as human languages, but those in I Corinthians as unknown, probably angelic utterance (25), without proof. In the overall picture, many passages are explained thoroughly enough to form a fairly good commentary.

Fernando, Ajith. *Acts* **(NIV Application Commentary). Grand Rapids: Zondervan, 1998.**

Fernando, national director of Youth for Christ in Sri Lanka and a Bible expositor, devotes 651 pp. He is aggressive against criticisms of Luke on historical details, showing alert use of a wide range of scholarly studies. He has much on application, and at times is right to the point present in verses, though a verse by verse attention to Acts sometimes disappears in much, even if good discussion that hinders knowing where one is in a passage. He also deals with some problems, has an overdose of application which if even shortened some would allow for more on what the Word of God itself says. He believes that the tongues (Acts 2) are for today (97). All in all, the work has much light on meaning at times and relevance now, but the long discussions that have difficulty getting to the point may too often blunt the effectiveness for some, while being welcomed by others.

Fitzmyer, Joseph A. *The Acts of the Apostles* **(Anchor Bible). NY: Doubleday, 1997.**

An 830-pp. probe, this often profitable effort devotes ca. 100 pp. to introduction, then the rest to lengthy bibliographies and commentary (bibliographies appear in the sections throughout). The commentator chooses a middle road on historical reliability between skeptics (Conzelmann, Dibelius, Haenchen, etc.;) and advocates (Bruce, Gasque, Marshall, Ramsay, etc.). He thinks that statements in Acts at times are erroneous and confused, though the majority is reliable, and he feels capable of deciding these (124-25). Some of his problems are with speeches, which he regards as giving some things not exactly as they happened, also miracles, and heavenly interventions such as the Spirit coming in Acts 2, 10 etc. The several lists of sources are, in many items, pertinent only for scholars having access. Introductory comments to each set of verses, then notes on verses, often cover most essentials well. Fitzmyer meets differing views, as on whether tongues (2:4) are ecstatic or foreign languages/dialects. Some explanations will not be approved by all grammatically or otherwise, as is the case in all commentaries. An example is saying in 2:38 that sins are remitted by water baptism and "one is enabled thereby to call upon the name of the Lord and so find salvation . . ." (265).

Gaebelein, Arno C. *The Acts of the Apostles*. NY: Loizeaux, 1961.

This is one of the best older dispensational works on Acts and is at times helpful in study-ing the transitional problems. It does not involve itself with exegetical details as do the works of Bruce.

Gasque, W. W. *A History of the Interpretation of the Acts of the Apostles*. Peabody, MA: Hendrickson, 1989. 359 pp.

Gasque's work was originally a doctoral dissertation at Manchester under F. F. Bruce (1969). He has taught at Regent College. He surveys 19th and 20th century work in Acts, and reveals the methodology of scholarship with its conclusions and biases about critical problems. Gasque is evangelical, Fourteen years after his first edition in 1975 (*A History of the Criticism of the Acts of the Apostles*. Grand Rapids: Eerdmans), Gasque has a paperback edition that adds a 15-page supplement on work in Acts since his doctoral studies. The research has been republished under the first title above by Wipf and Stock Publishers, Eugene, OR, 2000. One of Gasque's conclusions is that "it would seem that there is no reason to doubt the essential [meaning what?] reliability of the narrative in Acts" (309).

Griffith-Thomas, W. H. *Outline Studies in the Acts of the Apostles*. Grand Rapids: Eerdmans, 1956.

An extremely carefully-outlined study of the key facets chapter by chapter. It is helpful for quick overviews where many of the most pertinent aspects are pulled together, as also in his volume on Matthew (cf. on Matthew).

Haenchen, Ernest. *The Acts of the Apostles: A Commentary*, Translated by B. Noble et al. Philadelphia: Westminster Press, 1971.

This is a standard work of well-read scholarship on Acts in detail, but is quite liberal. It does offer much help on many of the passages, and can be of service for more serious study if balanced with Bruce's evangelical commentary, which is better. Haenchen's work is from the Meyer Kommentar in German (14th ed.). The lengthy introduction has, among other things, a helpful survey on scholarly work done on Acts. The commentary is accompanied by bibliographies on each area of Acts.

Harrison, Everett F. *Interpreting Acts: The Expanding Church*. Grand Rapids: Zondervan, 1986. Originally in 1975. Chicago: Moody.

A well-organized and non-technical commentary by a fine evangelical scholar with a clear outline and a brief but broad, discerning discussion of vital issues in some problem passages (e.g., 1:23-26; 9:7 with 22:9; 15:15-18; 21:10-11; 23:5 etc.). Some classic prob-lems receive too little comment. The commentary reads easily and comes directly to the point.

Hemer, Colin J. *The Book of Acts in the Setting of Hellenistic History*. Tubingen: Mohr-Siebeck, 1989. 482 pp.

A noted author seeks to establish a case for the historical accuracy of Acts on the ground of Luke's correctness in aspects of detail not essential to the spiritual message, as sup-ported by external historical data (p. 104). In his method he will be viewed as supporting himself well in places and building on suppositions in others. Cf. also his work *The*

Letters to the Seven Churches of Asia (section on Revelation). One will also find much help on the kinds of matters Hemer takes up in such works as those by Sir William Ramsay, Merrill F. Unger (*The Archaeology of the New Testament*), commentaries on Acts by F. F. Bruce, R. L. Longnecker, etc.

Hughes, R. Kent. *Acts, The Church Afire* (Preaching the Word). Wheaton, IL: Crossway Books, 1996.

In 42 chapters this articulate pastor gives sermons he preached in a relational way. Sometimes the basic meaning of the passage is explained, at other times the focus is mostly on other things than making clear the idea. For example, one finds no explanations of tongues in Acts 2, or what such a crucial verse as 2:38 means. Main values seem to be in making spiritual applications of some ideas and giving engaging illustrations, both of which will be a catalyst for preachers as well as edifying to lay people. An instance is on the prayer meeting of Acts 12, another is Paul's leadership in the ship crisis of Acts 27.

Ironside, H. A. *Lectures on the Book of Acts*. NY: Loizeaux, 1943.

Good expository messages with a practical vein and illustrations. The interpretation is dispensational. Trained as well as lay readers find Ironside's books helpful for edification and for preparing Bible class lessons.

Kent, Homer A. *Jerusalem to Rome, Studies in Acts.* Grand Rapids: Baker, 1977.

This paperback is a good brief survey of Acts by the former president at Grace Theological Seminary in Winona Lake, Indiana. He is helpful on the general progression of thought and on selected problem areas.

Kistemaker, Simon J. *Exposition of the Acts of the Apostles.* Grand Rapids: Baker, 1990. 1,010 pp.

A 40-page introduction is followed by a detailed commentary on each pericope, giving notes on the Greek text, exposition, and doctrinal and practical remarks. Kistemaker has much that contributes as an evangelical as he elucidates the flow of the book, gets underneath problems, and shows the relevance. It is one of the better conservative works, and is in the Hendriksen NT Commentary series.

Ladd, George E. "Acts" in *Wycliffe Bible Commentary*, ed. E. F. Harrison and Charles Pfeiffer. Chicago: Moody, 1962.

This is a good, brief commentary by a knowledgeable scholar. The work handles many of the problems well, even if briefly.

Larkin, William. *Acts* (IVP NTC). Downers Grove, IL: IVP, 1995.

Users will meet with a very capable medium-length exposition conversant with many of the leading issues evangelicals take up. The writer first shows the relevance of Acts today, then acceptance of Luke as author in the early 60's, and a belief that details are trustworthy. He gives a good survey of 15 aspects under "Theology." Verse by verse information is to the point, at times overly brief even if forthright (cf. 1:6-7). Larkin is usually alert to perceive and cover problems, or attempt to do this (cf. 1:26, Matthias a proper choice; also 7:4, 6, 16), but sometimes blurred (2:38; 22:16). He has a fine bibliography (394-422) at the end.

Levinskaya, Irena. *The Book of Acts in Its Diaspora Setting.* **Vol. 5 in The Book of Acts in the First Century Setting. Grand Rapids: Eerdmans, 1996.**

The authoress has technical discussion on how Jews related to societies during dispersion, as in fostering good rapport with Gentiles and Roman leaders. She gives chapters on scattered Jews in Acts, proselytes, God-fearers, Jews in Syrian Antioch, Asia Minor, Macedonia, Rome, etc. Her study at times attests Luke's accuracy as she contributes much especially for teachers, pastors and serious other inquirers about enriching factors in the background.

Longenecker, Richard N. "The Acts of the Apostles," in *Expositor's Bible Commentary,* **Volume 9, ed. Frank Gaebelein and J. D. Douglas. Grand Rapids: Zondervan, 1981.**

Allowed pages 207-573 for a substantial commentary, Longenecker provides a high-ranking evangelical work. He views Luke as the author and has good sections on criticism of Acts by scholars, Luke's purposes, the narrative of Acts (taking up criticisms versus the historical accuracy), speeches (taking up criticisms versus them), a lengthy bibliography, and a commentary that does not evade problems (cf. on 1:26; 2:4; 7:2-8; 15:13-18; 19:11-12 etc.) and is only at times vague (2:38, *eis* in relation to baptism and forgiveness, etc.). The work rates well with Bruce, Marshall, Polhill etc.

MacArthur, John. *Acts 1-12* **and** *Acts 13-28* **(MacArthur NTC). Chicago: Moody Press, 1994ff.**

Traditional evangelical convictions about author, date, and purpose lead in to earnest verse by verse exposition that shows an alert grasp of what texts say and mean (cf. 1:6-7; 2:4; 2:38 with 10:44-48 and 11:14-17, etc.). Solid attention to explaining details to feed believers involves, at times here, grappling to give light on problems, draw lessons, and provide illustrations. Among expository preachers, MacArthur stays with the text more than many, and pastors, students, and lay readers receive much instruction to help growth.

Marshall, I. Howard. *The Acts of the Apostles* **(Tyndale NTC). Grand Rapids: Eerdmans, 1980.**

Marshall has written a good commentary to replace E. M. Blaiklock's work. He reflects a wide awareness of current viewpoints on introductory matters and takes the stance that Luke completed the composition toward A. D. 70, leaving the place open. He provides a three-page outline right before the commentary and it appears throughout as well. Marshall usually offers reasonable evidence for views on problem verses, even if at times briefly, as in the selection of Matthias in 1:23-26. In 2:2, 3 some will feel that he confuses the Spirit's filling of believers with baptism in the Spirit. Sometimes he puts forth views but takes no clear stand, e.g. whether tongues in Acts and I Corinthians were always human languages or sometimes non-human or some other view (cf. 2:4). Sometimes, as in 7:4, he does not refer to a view often held that might resolve an apparent tension with another biblical text, e. g. the possibility that Abram is mentioned first in Genesis 11:26 not because he was born when Sarah was 70 but because he was the most prominent of the three sons in regard to God's purposes. All in all, the handling of problems and the verse-by-verse comments are well-done. This, with Bruce's NIC work, is one of the finer, more often helpful evangelical commentaries on Acts in recent times.

Marshall, I. Howard and David Peterson, eds. *Witness to the Gospel. The Theology of Acts*. Grand Rapids: Eerdmans, 1998.

More than 20 scholars contribute chapters in a very orientating book on such topics as Marshall's rationale for a book on theology, Darrell Bock's on Scripture and the realization of God's promises, John Nolland's part on the kingdom, Joel Green on salvation, and Craig Blomberg on the Christian's relation to the law of Moses, etc. Teachers, pastors, students and the laity can gather much about possible meanings linked with various themes in Acts.

Morgan, G. Campbell. *The Acts of the Apostles*. London: Pickering and Inglis, 1947.

This is another good English exposition but it sometimes is not helpful on tough problems (cf. 2:38; 15:14-17, etc.), though it is one of Morgan's better commentaries and one which the student can profitably consult.

Morgan, G. Campbell. *The Birth of the Church*. Old Tappan, NJ: Revell, 1968.

Here are detailed expositions treating various aspects of Acts 2. Morgan originally delivered them as Bible studies moving through the narrative of the Day of Pentecost.

Phillips, John. *Exploring Acts*. Neptune, NJ: Loizeaux, 1986. 528 pp.

An evangelical Bible teacher's articulate, flowing exposition that is helpful as a survey for students, preachers and Sunday School teachers, who ought to use some of the more masterful, works as well (Bruce, Harrison, Longenecker, Marshall, Polhill, etc.).

Polhill, John B. *Acts* (New American Commentary), Volume 26. Nashville: Broadman Press, 1992. 574 pp.

This is a very good, well-studied work by a Southern Baptist scholar who shows keen awareness of a wide range of literature and does the new series proud. The series is new in distinction to the old American Commentary works such as that of John Broadus on Matthew. It is evangelical, upholds inerrancy, and Polhill is amillennial. Polhill argues for historical reliability of details in the book, usually has perceptive comments, is helpful on problem verses, cites good sources, and uses the Greek competently. He believes Christians are "the true or 'restored' Israel" (p. 67; cf. for this view also Jervell, *Luke and the People of God*. Minneapolis: Augsburg, 1972; and H. C. Kee, *Good News to the Ends of the Earth: The Theology of Acts*. Philadelphia: Trinity, 1990). He is almost always clear on a difficult text. One exception is on 8:14-17 where he seems weak on why the Spirit was delayed after baptism. Another is 15:13-18, where he sees Amos 9:11-15 as fulfilled in the church (p. 330) in amillennial fashion but does not say a word about the land aspects for Israel in Amos 9:13-15. He is not distinct on 19:1-7 on whether the twelve disciples were saved already in the Old Testament sense or unsaved until they responded to Paul's more complete message.

Rackham, Richard B. *The Acts of the Apostles.* **Grand Rapids: Baker, 1978, rp of 1964rp of work dating back to 1901.**

This is a very good though at times terse commentary from the standpoint of Greek and, historical background. Rackham was conservative but amillennial. Verse by verse he often offers good help, and he has addenda on topics such as breaking of bread, Sadducees and Pharisees, etc.

Ryrie, Charles C. *The Acts of the Apostles.* **Chicago:. Moody, 1960.**

Though brief, this paperback is often clear from the dispensational viewpoint and handles transitional problem passages in a helpful way (cf. 8:14-17; 19:1-6, etc.). The author used to be Dean of the Graduate School and Chairman of the Department of Systematic Theology, Dallas Theological Seminary, and is also author of *Dispensationalism Today* (Moody Press, 1965), a definitive work on classic dispensationalism which also helps in understanding Acts.

Scroggie, W. G. *The Acts of the Apostles.* **Grand Rapids: Zondervan, 1976 reprint, paperback.**

A homiletically suggestive organization and exposition by an evangelical who knew how to articulate the main points that are pertinent.

Stott, John R. W. *The Message of Acts: The Spirit, The Church and the World* **(Bible Speaks Today series). Downers Grove: IVP, 1990. 405 pp.**

This evangelical exposition is verse by verse, and it also takes up key questions such as charismatic gifts, signs and wonders, baptism in the spirit, etc. After his introduction, Stott has four divisions: Jews (1:6-6:7); foundations for world mission (6:8-12:24); the apostle to the Gentiles (12:25-21:17); and on the way to Rome (21:18-28:31). As he usually is, Stott is very articulate in capturing the message, showing the flow, and letting the text come alive. This and the works by Phillips, Kistemaker, McClain, Ryrie, Scroggie and Toussaint are lucid for lay people and also helpful many times for pastors.

Walker, Thomas. *The Acts of the Apostles.* **Chicago: Moody, 1965.**

This work, originally in the Indian Commentary series (1910), was written for missionary workers, It is excellent on problems and detailed in general (586 pages). Wilbur Smith, who searched for years to obtain a second-hand copy while it was long out of print, describes the work as in his day (mid-century) "without question the greatest commentary on the Book of Acts from a missionary standpoint that has been written in our language" (cf. preface written by Smith). It is a very helpful commentary.

Williams, D. J. *Acts* **(Good News Commentary). San Francisco: Harper and Row, 1985. 478 pp.**

For the most part this is a good commentary in its exegesis and information on historical setting. Williams is thorough, immersed in literature on Acts but often using information well. In some things he sounds evangelical, in others he will astound many evangelicals by his rationalizing. For example in the reference to angels in 1:11 when Jesus ascended, Williams offers, "perhaps all he wanted to say was that there was an overwhelming sense of the divine in what happened" (p. 9).

Witherington, Ben, III. *The Acts of the Apostles. A Socio-Rhetorical Commentary.* **Grand Rapids: Eerdmans, 1998.**

An Asbury Theological Seminary NT scholar did this work of xlviii + 875 pp. He wants to offer strength where he feels many do not contribute by focusing on rhetorical values, as on the speeches (cf. 39-49), and on Acts fitting in a pattern, he says, of Hellenistic historiographic writings (x). The thorough introduction, more than 100 pp. (most of what he gives is quite protracted) shows Luke in a pattern of historians careful about facts (49). In the background, he posits two imprisonments of Paul in Rome, and fits the Pastorals by Paul within the time between the two. Used with other works that help one integrate even more on a verse by verse explanation (Barrett, Bruce, Longenecker, Marshall, Polhill, Toussaint, etc.), the author provides substantial input.

VI. ROMANS

Anderson, Norman. *Freedom Under Law.* **Eastbourne: Kingsway, 1988.**

A professor emeritus of legal studies and biblical scholar shows how law relates to true freedom. Various types of freedoms flourish under protection by laws. Later, Anderson takes up law in the spiritual life according to the Scripture. He argues in Matthew 5:17-20 for fulfillment of the law in an appropriate sense that God has designed for it to have (p. 121). God purposed that Mosaic rules and regulations on ceremonial cleanness have their place in Old Testament times but also look forward to moral cleanness such as was realized in Jesus' spiritual life teaching and spiritual power. The Mosaic law was not aimed to be a way to merit salvation by obeying, but revealed ways God willed for saved people to live for their well-being (p. 155). The law could inform of the need for life, but could not impart life; God gives the life in grace through Christ in the gospel. And in the gospel way God gives power to obey God's will shown in moral principles of the law, etc.

Barnhouse, Donald Grey. *Expositions of Bible Doctrines.* **12 volumes. Grand Rapids: Eerdmans, 1952-64.**

The late editor of *Eternity Magazine* authored this excellent set which uses Romans as a point of departure for thorough studies on crucial themes and whole Bible orientation. He handles Romans in an expository manner which is very rich. His many striking illustrations help make the series especially valuable to the pastor as well as the teacher. One must have special tenacity to stay with the vast detail.

Barrett, C. K. *A Commentary on the Epistle to the Romans* **(Harper's NTC). San Francisco: Harper and Row, 1991. 2nd ed., revised from 1st ed. of 1957, reprinted in 1971.**

Barrett deals briefly but perceptively with much of the book, but many including this reviewer cannot take seriously certain statements such as his belief, however popular in liberal circles, that Paul in Romans 5:12 did not necessarily view Genesis 1-3 as "a straightforward narrative of events that really happened" (p. 111). Yet on many parts of Romans Barrett does grapple helpfully with interpretive issues.

Black, Matthew. *Romans* **(New Century B. C.). Grand Rapids: Eerdmans, 1973.**

This work by a scholar at the University of St. Andrews was done before the commentaries by Cranfield, Kasemann, etc. and so does not list them as bibliography. And many older works certain U. S. readers might miss are Godet, Hodge, Shedd, etc. However, Black is a widely-read scholar using good footnotes showing conversance with much modern literature and frequently furnishing lists of sources on key points along the way. He argues for the integrity of Chapter 16 as originally a part of the epistle. This is at the most a good brief commentary. Now and then Black makes odd statements - e.g. on 1:3 Jesus seems to have "found difficulty with this popular belief" of his being of Davidic descent and "to have taken exception to it" in Mark 12:35ff. (p. 35), even in a context where Black apparently accepts His Davidic descent. His treatment of "from faith to faith" (1:17) is not compelling (p. 46), or his assumption that only Gentiles are indicated in 1:19-32 and Jews in 2:1-29, though he has a brief footnote acknowledging recent challenges to this sharp categorizing (p. 54). One wonders why he handles 2:13 in less than a full line on the page or why he does not do more with 3:31, or why he does not explain how the physical body is annulled in 6:6, or why he flies through 6:22, 7:9 and 8:13 so quickly and does not grapple more with views on 7:14-25 (cf. p. 101). Still, he is very helpful in many places, such as on robbing temples (pp. 59-60), Christ as a propitiatory sacrifice in 3:25 (p. 69). Many on 5:12 will be more satisfied reading Murray or S. L. Johnson, Jr. ("Romans 5:12 – an Exercise in Exegesis and Theology," *New Dimensions in New Testament Study,* ed. R. N. Longenecker and M. C. Tenney. Grand Rapids: Zondervan, pp. 298-316).

Blaiklock, E. M. *The Way of Excellence.* **Grand Rapids: Zondervan, 1968.**

This 78-pp. book does an exposition of I Corinthians 13, then of Romans 12 as examples of vital chapters illustrating Paul's view of ethics, their standards and power. The title is derived from the last verse of I Corinthians 12. Blaiklock has been a long-time Professor of Classics, University of Auckland. He writes simply, introducing interesting quotes, bits of relevant history, and other thought-provoking material that is devotionally easy and refreshing to read as he explains verse by verse. Captivating captions stand over the verses, but a meaningful expository outline would pull the good thoughts into greater cohesiveness. Much here is provocative to flavor sermons.

Boice, James M. *Romans, An Expositional Commentary, Volume I. Justification by Faith, Romans 1-4.* **Grand Rapids: Baker, 1991.**

The Philadelphia preacher gives expositions highlighting doctrinal points and their application to human life. This is only the first commentary of several volumes. It has a lot to teach and build up a believer. Briefer works that bring the doctrinal truth home to believers in general are those by R. Kent Hughes and Alan Johnson, or even John Stott.

Bruce, F. F. *The Letter of Paul to the Romans: An Introduction and Commentary* **(Tyndale NTC). 2nd ed. Grand Rapids: Eerdmans, 1985. 274 pp.**

This is a very solid exegetical work abreast of good scholarship in the Greek and in the backgrounds of the New Testament epistles. But it is brief in spots. It was revised before

Bruce's death so the research is updated in a few footnotes. It also now uses the RSV instead of the AV.

Calvin, Jean. *The Epistles of Paul the Apostle to the Romans and to the Thessalonians* **(Calvin's Commentaries). Translated by Ross Mackenzie, edited by David W. and Thomas F. Torrance. Grand Rapids: Eerdmans, 1961.**

Calvin sees the theme of Romans as righteousness for men by God's mercy in Christ, offered in the gospel and received by faith (p. 5). He takes six pages to survey the epistle chapter by chapter, then begins verse by verse comments, without giving an outline. He has many perceptive discussions that are deeply enriching. He takes 2:7 as the life pattern of the truly saved through grace; 3:28 as meaning justification by faith without any merit by works but James 2 as speaking of works out of faith that prove the reality of justification practically; 7:14ff. as depicting a regenerate person, etc. As a clear, engrossing commentary that explains most points with a keen grasp of how things relate, this is one of the finer, old evangelical works from a theological standpoint.

Cranfield, C. E. B. *A Critical and Exegetical Commentary on the Epistle to the Romans* **(New ICC). 2 volumes. Edinburgh: T. & T. Clark, 1975-79.**

An exceptionally good commentary in meeting the exegetical issues in a perceptive and well-organized way. Cranfield often presents various views from very wide reading, and gives specific reasons for his own as well as reasons why the others are not as good (cf. on 2:6ff.; 7:14ff., etc.). I personally regard this as the best work on Romans so far to help the scholar who is knowledgeable in the Greek. Even others who are willing and able to study where technical matters are discussed can find much that they can follow in getting at the basic thrust of things on a passage.

Cranfield, C. E. B. *On Romans and Other New Testament Essays.* **Edinburgh: T. & T. Clark, 1998.**

Thirteen chapters give Cranfield's remarks in journals about key topics. Among these are the works of the law in Romans, 6:1-14, sanctification as freedom, the question of the OT law's place in the Christian life, the identity of Jesus' brothers (Matt. 25:40), Christ's resurrection, and the virgin birth. Near the end one finds a list of this discerning exegete/theologian's publications, excluding reviews (177-87), which is a catalyst for investments during reading times.

Cranfield, C. E. B. *Romans, A Shorter Commentary.* **Grand Rapids: Eerdmans, 1985.**

This is a single volume that condenses the two volumes but retains lists of arguments on crucial matters, also lists of main views, etc. It gets to the point faster, and saves those who want the shorter version a lot of money. The person with the longer work need not buy the shorter.

Dunn, James D. G. *Romans.* **2 volumes (Word Biblical Commentaries). Dallas, TX: Word Books, 1988. 976 pp.**

This is the Professor of Divinity, University of Durham, Scotland. He has bought into critical theories more than will please many conservatives, but certainly brings massive study to the task and will contribute much on views, reasons, word meaning, grammar, and bibliography on each pericope. In interaction with other scholarship this is one of the best on Romans.

Fitzmyer, Joseph A. *Romans* (Anchor Bible). NY: Doubleday, 1992.

The studious find one of the several highly regarded and more detailed exegetical probes in these 793 pp. The writer explains verse by verse matters rather at length (269ff), after introductory issues and long bibliographic lists that interest mostly scholars. Fitzmyer deals with such subjects as Rome and Roman Christians, authorship (Paul), how chaps. 15-16 and Tertius relate to the unity and integrity, and Pauline teaching on subjects. He tackles problems in verses, and mounts reasons for his stances, using general comment syntheses and then a look at particulars in verses. Sometimes details that he does cover never get to clarification about theological issues, e. g. how works relate to the gift of life in 2:7-10 (cf. by contrast Cranfield's exegesis). Though Fitzmyer gives five views of the "I" in 7:7-25, his own conclusion is vague, and not on an individual and psychological level but a historical, corporate one dealing with all humanity (465). Some statements leave one unsure, suggesting that the passage deals with both Christians and the unsaved (465), later just the unsaved (476), with more opinion than persuasive proof. Still, he handles many texts clearly, such as 8:26-27, and some passages without taking a stand among views while at least stating the overall point (12:20).

Gifford, E. H. *The Epistle to the Romans*. London: John Murray, 1886.

A careful work which traces the argument closely and states it well, this commentary is also helpful in most of the details of exegesis. It does lack in word studies in depth and does not comment upon the text as much as some would prefer at times. But it is one of the top older commentaries.

Godet, F. *Commentary on St. Paul's Epistle to the Romans*. Grand Rapids: Kregel, 1977rp. 542 pp.

This famous work was translated from the French in 1864, and has gone through several printings in English. Godet, also known for other fine commentaries as on Luke (2 volumes), gives good detail on what verses mean, providing much that evangelicals easily identify with. Of course such an older work cannot be up on current studies as newer works can be.

Govett, Robert. *Govett on Romans*. Miami Springs, FL: Conley & Schoettle Publishing Co., 1981, rp. of The Righteousness of God, The Salvation of the Believer. London, 1891.

This 556-pp. evangelical work treats some aspects in detail but it is not always easy to find Govett's comments on a given verse quickly since not all verses are marked off. Govett brings other passages to bear on a verse (cf. 2:7). He does not always explain how his view is in harmony with other statements in Romans (cf. 2:7, which poses tensions for some with 3:28; 4:4, 5 etc.). He is sweepingly brief or almost nil on some long sections (cf. 2:17ff., pp. 34-35; 3:10-18, pp. 43-44, etc.). But Govett is helpful in some ways (3:31; 4:4; he even writes many pages, 94-124, on Genesis 15 and 17 in relation to Romans 4). Some of Govett's ideas are not easy to harmonize with Scripture, e. g. his statement that "if you have accepted by faith the eternal righteousness of God, yours is eternal life. If you are beside that a worker of righteousness through faith, a walker in newness of life, you are on the way to the first resurrection of blessedness" (p. 143). He distinguishes eternal life from "the reign in life" for the worthy. To him, those by "mercy justified" will not necessarily obey Christ's commands, do His will, and enter the kingdom of heaven, which he apparently equates with the millennial era after the Second Advent. Eternal life is by faith without works, but special reward – the millennial kingdom blessings, to him – is obtained according to works. So, men may be eternally saved, yet shut out of the millennial kingdom but participate in the eternal blessings after that. Along the same lines Govett distinguishes between the "gift" (eternal life) and the "prize" or "crown" of I Corinthians 9:24-27, Philippians 3:14 etc., the crown referring to the special reward in the millennium before the eternal state, special reward only for the so-called obedient among the justified (cf. pp. 153-154, 158-178; cf. also his remarks on 6:22, 23 at pp. 229-235; and on 8:13-14, pp. 301-313, etc.). As we might expect from this line of things, we are told on 8:16 that "not all children are sons" (p. 317), for we become "children" by His grace, "sons" by obedience (318). And he sees two inheritances in 8:17: all the saved are "heirs indeed of God," but only some of the saved suffer with Christ and are "joint-heirs with Christ" (pp. 319-321). To a considerable degree Govett's concepts are also in Zane Hodges' books (cf. as on Hebrews, James, I John).

Haldane, Robert. *Exposition of the Epistle to the Romans, with Remarks on the Commentaries of Dr. MacKnight. Professor Moses Stuart, and Professor Tholuck.* **NY: Robert Carter, 1847.**

This is a much-respected 746-pp. work (668 pp. through Romans 16:27, then several appendices on subjects relating to Romans. Though hampered by lack of any outline to relate things, the work has much gold if one has time and is willing to read voluminously to dig out the many nuggets. Whether or not one agrees with Haldane on a verse, his awareness of (or reviews of) many aspects of truth brought together is bound to prosper. Unlike most English expositors of which he is aware, Haldane sees 2:7 as hypothetical, law and not gospel. We may sample other verses: 5:14, "even over them," infants who did not personally sin but sinned in Adam's act as the representative head of the race; 7:14ff. refers to Paul even as a mature believer representative of all Christians (cf. p. 297); 8:5, 13 contrast the unsaved and the saved; God finally works all things absolutely to the good of His children, 8:28; the section in 8:28-39 has much to help a believer grow in assurance of God's preserving grace; in 9:22, vessels of wrath are "fitted for destruction" by their sins, whereas vessels of glory are fitted by God; 11:26 speaks of literal and spiritually saved Israel, as distinct from Gentiles, being joined to Christ, along with saved Gentiles. Israel will be restored to its own land (p. 556). This is one of the greatest of the older commentaries, almost always offering solid help and much to stimulate the heart.

Hamilton, Floyd E. *The Epistle to the Romans. An Exegetical and Devotional Commentary.* **Grand Rapids: Baker, 1958.**

Hamilton has a brief introduction affirming conservative views, even the belief that the original autograph manuscripts of the Bible were without error. He provides a clear outline of Romans sprinkled throughout. The commentary is competent in explaining the sense, though does not always give the reader the precise idea of a Greek phrase (cf. "obedience of faith," 1:5) as one finds Cranfield attempting to do. He often gives different main views (cf. on 2:7), but does not necessarily resolve a problem due to the brevity of attempted proof (again 2:7). He favors the representative, federal view in 5:12. Hamilton often seeks helpfully to explain for general readers various aspects theologically, so answering some lead questions (5:12; 7:14-25 in general). In 8:5 he basically sees the patterns of unsaved and saved. Each chapter closes with a list of questions on the chapter. This is a fairly good commentary for the general reader who seeks things explained briefly and with some correlation of theological aspects.

Harrison, Everett F. "Romans," in *Expositor's Bible Commentary*, Volume 10, ed. Frank Gaebelein. Grand Rapids: Zondervan, 1976.

This substantial work (pp. 1-171) is in many places one of the more excellent commentaries. Harrison was a skilled, meticulous exegete (cf. on 5:12). But on 7:14ff. he presents arguments well for two main views, then is disappointing to this reviewer when he selects another view that does not seem to be defended well and is only hypothetical. Still, by and large Harrison's work makes a solid contribution.

Hodge, Charles. *A Commentary on Romans* (The Geneva Series of Commentaries). London: Banner of Truth Trust, 1972.

This is a reprint of an 1864 work by Hodge, who lectured at Princeton Theological Seminary for many years. He deals with the epistle verse-by-verse with good theological perspective and use of the Greek. It is a good, solid evangelical commentary helpful to a teacher, preacher, or layman on the problems because it delves into them with a zest.

Hughes, R. Kent. *Righteousness from Heaven* (Preaching the Word). Westchester, IL: Crossway Books/Good News Publishers, 1991. 339 pp.

Very readable expositions that explain sections of Romans and bring in frequent items from broad reading to stimulate the user. Hughes, a studious pastor, works hard at communicating winsomely with punch and representing what the text says, then making applications to show how the truth can be real in daily life. His studies are broad, and will be of more use to lay-people wanting a quick, interestingly-related escort through Romans.

Johnson, Alan F. *The Freedom Letter (Romans)*. Chicago: Moody Press, 1974.

One of the finer, more readable surveys of recent decades which explains the passages carefully and competently based on much study and grasp of things. Johnson even comments briefly on many of the expositional problems and stays in touch with the reader by way of illustrations and practical comments. For the general reader, who desires to follow the main flow and see how to deal with some of the main problems in interpretation without descending into the depths of complications, this is a fine work. The author is a professor at Wheaton College and a recent past national president of the Evangelical Theological Society. He earned his Th. D. from Dallas Seminary.

Kasemann, Ernst. *Commentary on Romans*. Translated from the 4th ed. of *An Die Romer*. J. C. Mohr (Paul Siebeck): Tubingen, 1980. Grand Rapids: Eerdmans, 1980.

A thorough, 428-pp. work of big pages without an introduction but with the attempt to interpret verse by verse. Kasemann's discussions are carried on within an orbit of higher critical scholars for the most part. He shows very wide awareness of literature within this range, his students supplying detailed bibliographies loaded with German studies for each set of verses. Many of the discussions are ponderous, introducing at times so many big points and side points that it is a problem seeing the forest for the trees, keeping to the thread of thought in Romans, and seeing an explanation of exegetical phrases converging with clarity as so often in Cranfield. Certainly Kasemann tries not to leave many stones unturned. More paragraphs summarizing synthesis would pull his heavy details into greater effectiveness, as would having interpretations of verses within a section marked off distinctly. The reference in 7:14-25 is to the results of sins in the pre-Christian experience. All in all, this is one of the more contributing recent works of technical theology and word usage by a liberal scholar of international stature. There is much of value for those willing and able to do very patient, probing study and to come to deeply thought-out convictions, whether or not they finally agree at every point with Kasemann. Kasemann does not always make clear what he means by a point. Sometimes familiarity with terminology and ideas in Bultmann and after him helps to follow Kasemann's lines of thought.

Kaye, Bruce N. *The Thought Structure of Romans with Special Reference to Chapter 6.* **Austin, TX: Schola Press, 1979.**

This 202-page work was originally presented to the theology faculty of the University of Basel in Switzerland as a dissertation. Written under the tutelage of Dr. Bo Reicke, it should prove invaluable to the seminarian and pastor who desire precise knowledge of Romans 6. Dr. Kaye deals in the five basic areas of sin, relationship with Christ, law and grace, baptism, and slavery and freedom as they grow out of the text. Heavy reference is made to the original Greek when deciphering Pauline writing style and logic. The volume is thorough in its approach and quite conservative. The footnotes and bibliography alone are worth the price of the book. -Jan Sattem

King, John Phillip. *Death, Burial and Baptism in Romans 6:1-14.* **Ph. D. dissertation, Emory University, 1977.**

A detailed study (559 pp.) presenting baptism in Romans 6 as an initiatory rite of passage in the church. Looks at various views of baptism here, ancient attitudes toward the meaning and the significance of death, etc.

Leenhardt, Franz. *The Epistle to the Romans. A Commentary.* **Translated by H. Knight. Cleveland, New York. World Publishing Co., 1965.**

This is a work widely held in good regard. It has insightful things to say on some of the key passages such as Romans 7:14ff. but sometimes lacks in comment one would appreciate on specific verses. It has a lot to contribute at some points if one uses it at various times in working on a series of studies, but I would not rate it at the very top as being as helpful as often as works by Cranfield, Hendriksen, Moo, Murray, and Schreiner. And it is not one of the better general works that will most profit laymen, for it does not rate as well as Hughes, Johnson, McClain, Newell, Stott, etc.

Liddon, H. P. *Explanatory Analysis of St. Paul's Epistle to the Romans.* **Minneapolis: Klock & Klock, 1977, rp of 1899 work.**

Though Liddon lays out immense detail, he does it in a point-by-point, systematic order that analyzes the text verse by verse as to grammar, logic, and doctrine. Serious readers can follow his clear outline and trace the argument of Paul's epistle. Liddon treats Greek words, views on problems, and pertinent details of syntax, history, and connection with other Scripture, This meticulous effort and Stifler's briefer work are models to help an expositor pursue the chain of argument.

Lightfoot, J. B. *Notes on Epistles of Paul: 1-11 Thessalonians, I Corinthians 1-7, Romans 1-7, Ephesians 1:1-1-4.* **Grand Rapids: Baker, 1980.**

A brilliant New Testament exegetical scholar well-known for masterful commentaries on such books as Galatians, Philippians, and Colossians makes comments here on each phrase of the verses he covers.

Lloyd-Jones, D. Martyn. *Romans.* **6 volumes. Grand Rapids: Zondervan, 1971-76.**

An outstanding preacher of Westminster Chapel, London, gave this series of sermons on Friday evenings. He covered 1:1-14:17 during the period October, 1955 to March, 1968. He begins here at 3:20 because he wants to start the published volumes at what he calls the "heart" of Romans. The content is very perceptive of how the great doctrines relate to life as he reasons things out in a readable way, talking directly to people (for these are edited sermons left pretty much as he delivered them). The material has much gold, but the detail will probably leave its impact primarily on preachers doing an extended series and scheduling the great blocks of time to read the section on the verses they plan to cover in a given sermon. The studies are bound to leave their impact on the reader, broadening, deepening, enriching. Lloyd-Jones sometimes devotes entire sermons (chapters) to other passages related to a Romans text, e.g. on 8:17-39 he gives five chapters on problem passages such as II Peter 2:1, Matthew 25:1-13 (danger of false profession) and Hebrews 6:4-8; 10:26-29. He argues that 7:14-25 refers to pre-salvation experience.

Martin, Ralph P. "Romans," in *New Bible Commentary Revised.* **ed. D. Guthrie et al. Grand Rapids: Eerdmans, 1970.**

This survey by an outstanding New Testament scholar should not be overlooked due to the wealth of commentaries on Romans. Here and there he will make good contributions in a diligent study.

Mauro, Philip. *The "Wretched Man" and His Deliverance, Romans VII.* **Williamsport, PA: Bible Truth Depot [n.d.].**

Mauro argues that Romans 7 describes "a conscientious, unconverted Jew, fully instructed in the Law, and seeking zealously to accomplish a righteousness of his own by "works of law" (p. 22). In his mind he sees the spirituality of the law but is utterly unable to do it because of indwelling sin. The final two chapters deal with "Sickness among the children of God" and "The 'Cause' of Sickness among Saints" (emphasizing sin, as I Corinthians 11:27-32, but not contending that every illness in a saint is a chastening for some sin, p. 119; Mauro recognizes other purposes of illness). He argues for a view that the saved, when ill, should look to God only and use the means the Great Physician has prescribed, not resort to physicians. He and his family committed illness only to the Lord's hands, claiming Psalm 37:4 and being restored. This, he reasons, is God's way even in the face of problems such as people sometimes die who do not accept medical help, etc. (p. 123). Such a view appears also in health-wealth circles, etc.

McClain , Alva J. *Romans, The Gospel of God's Grace.* **Chicago: Moody, 1973.**

A non-technical commentary but often perceptive in explaining what is crucial in a passage. McClain, better known for his premillennial work *The Greatness of the Kingdom*, is easy to read but has depth. In his thinking, 7:14ff. presents Paul as a saved man and 8:4-9 is a contrast not of two kinds of Christians but of Christians and non-Christians. The section in Chapters 9-11 is perceptive regarding Israel's role in God's plan for the future as distinguished from the church.

Mickelsen, A. B. **"Romans" in** *Wycliffe Bible Commentary,* **ed. Charles Pfeiffer and E. F. Harrison. Chicago: Moody, 1962.**

In the field of brief works this is one of the more contributing scholarly commentaries by an evangelical scholar of high competence. It is helpful to scholars, pastors and laymen alike, showing good awareness of issues and good hermeneutics.

Moo, Douglas. *Romans 1-8* **and** *Romans 9-16* **(Baker Exegetical Commentary). 2 vols. Grand Rapids, MI: Baker, 1991ff. Formerly Wycliffe Exegetical Commentary, Moody Press.**

Moo's detailed evangelical exegesis thrusts his work among the top recent thorough efforts (Cranfield, Schreiner). He carefully analyzes each passage, interacting with views and arguments and sifting out, usually with clarity, his own views with support. He has a long bibliography and copious, frequently lengthy footnotes on considerations. He writes so cautiously at times that one finds his view only after a search. The work is meticulously abreast of scholarly learning, and offers patient teachers, studious pastors, and advanced Greek students much to consider in deciding the meaning and import.

Mounce, Robert. *Romans* **(New American Commentary). Nashville: Broadman & Holman, 1995.**

Mounce gives a fairly good overview (summary) of Romans section by section (30-57), but one can wonder why he leaves out some parts from his outline (Rom. 2; 3:1-20, 27-32; 5:12-21; 7; parts of Rom. 12; 15:14ff). Some problems get scanty comment, e. g. "spirit" in 1:4, how doing good in 2:7-10 fits with grace in a salvation that is a gift not of works, the valid purpose of circumcision in light of 2:25-29, etc. Discussion in 6:1-10, like many, needs more to make practical how the ideal of death/resurrection with Christ is workable in light of sin's reality daily, causing defeat. But at times this commentary is better at specific reasons, as in showing evidence that 7:14ff is Paul's experience as a Christian, or that 11:25-27 conveys a future beyond the present age for Israelite believers. For the most part, texts are illumined even if concisely, and Mounce is lucid, helpful for pastors, students and lay people in a medium-length effort.

Morris, Leon. *The Epistle to the Romans.* **Grand Rapids: Eerdmans, 578 pp.**

The noted scholar completed this at 74 years of age in his retirement, providing a work that is quite thorough in many places. He is evangelical and on Romans 11 amillennial, and demonstrates a mature, profound grasp of issues that need to be explained and a broad knowledge of literature looking at Romans from various angles. He makes perceptive judgments on problems. Additional excursuses are included on God's righteousness, truth, the law, justification, judgment and sin. He is Reformed in his theology, and most of his statements are quite good or at least adequate. All in all, the commentary is worthy a place on the shelf alongside works by Cranfield, Hendriksen, Moo, Murray, and Schreiner.

Murray, John. *The Epistle to the Romans* **(NIC). 2 volumes. Grand Rapids: Eerdmans, 1959-65.**

This is an outstanding work on Romans from the standpoint of exegesis and doctrinal discussion. Murray deals with problem verses with careful scholarship and good insight, leaving few stones unturned. It is one of the most helpful works on the epistle for the teacher or pastor who is serious about his Bible study.

Murray, John. *The Imputation Of Adam's Sin.* **Grand Rapids: Eerdmans, 1959.**

An excellent little book surveying the main views on Romans 5:12ff. and looking at the chief arguments for them. Much of the essence is in his fine commentary on Romans. Murray's book is the best book by an evangelical on theological facets of the text, and grew out of a series in the *Westminster Theological Journal.*

Newell, William. *Romans Verse by Verse.* **Chicago: Moody, 1948.**

Dr. Chafer, president of Dallas Theological Seminary until 1952, used to say that Newell knew more about the book of Romans than any other man he knew. Newell has written here a detailed English commentary which is very helpful to laymen and easy to read.

Nygren, Anders. *Commentary on Romans.* **Translated by Carl C. Rasmussen. London: SCM Press, 1958.**

A very helpful treatment of Romans from the standpoint of its stimulating discussion of issues in Romans. It is not a verse-by-verse study, however.

Piper, John. *The Justification of God. An Exegetical and Theological Study of Romans 9:1-23.* **Grand Rapids: Baker, 1983.**

A competent, scholarly standard exegetical work of much research which reacts with major studies of today both in America and Europe. Piper seeks in this 316-page study to show how the passage reflects God acting in honor and in display of His glory even in unconditional election. Unlike many, he holds that election here reaches to individuals and pertains to eternal salvation. He sees double predestination in the chapter (cf. p. 194: *Katertismena* means that God fitted vessels of wrath for destruction). Piper has taught at Bethel College for several years and been pastor of Bethlehem Baptist Church, Minneapolis. He received his Doctor of Theology degree from the University of Munich.

Sanday, William and Arthur C. Headlam. *A Critical and Exegetical Commentary on the Epistle to the Romans* **(ICC). Edinburgh: T. & T. Clark, 1950.**

Because of its thoroughness in matters of the Greek text, some have regarded this as the best of the older Greek works on Romans. It is good, but not as lucid and normally workable as commentaries by Bruce, Cranfield, Gifford, Murray, and Schreiner. These other works do not go into the minutia as Sanday and Headlam, but get to the point much better. However, the ICC work should be obtained by the serious student who can use his Greek. Cranfield's new ICC work on Romans is better overall, as is Moo.

Schreiner, Thomas R. *Romans* (Baker Exegetical Commentary). Grand Rapids: Baker, 1998.

These 919 pp. put this close to the best among recent and all-time thorough works for scholars and more seriously capable lay people. For those without direct Greek knowledge, the many Greek terms receive both transliteration and translation. Still, some words are beyond many readers. Schreiner details views, reasons, and evaluations. He is vigorous for unity of the entire epistle, all sent to Rome (5-23). In exegesis and exposition, one searches to find discussion of individual verses, which are not always marked out obviously. On some problems, the writer is copious with much help, as on "spirit of holiness" (1:4) or on 2:7-10, or on circumcision in 2:25-29 by the Spirit's power, etc. He takes 7:14ff as relating both to Christians and non-Christians, and 11:25-26 as meaning that God will save a fullness of Israelites at the end of the age, but never relates this to a millennial kingdom then, and regathering of spiritually saved ethnic Israelites fitting OT promises. One will need to go to clear-cut premillenial works for this. Schreiner takes coals of fire in 12:20 as related to judgment, not any view that sees mercy and repentance for the unsaved.

Sproule, R. C. *The Gospel of God. Expositions of Paul's Letter to the Romans.* Geanies House, Fearn, Ross-shire, Scotland: Christian Focus Publications, 1999.

One sees how a prolific writer-theologian in the Reformed tradition deals with the book. He offers a 5-pp. outline, then a flowing commentary which at most points stays with the text and directly illumines it, though sometimes expanding on themes. He is clear often, but falls short of really clear explanation in some cases (4:15 and 5:13; 6:2, etc.). Phrases from verses helpfully show up in bold face. Sproule may give specific proof on a point, or just his opinion as in 1:4 referring to the Holy Spirit. He seems unclear in 2:7-10 on how judgment by works harmonizes with justification by faith. Some items are not helpful, e. g. the attempt to be provocative about two ways to get into heaven (51). Other sections are rather profitable, as 7:14ff. On Romans 11, he acknowledges a future restoration of Israel and their possession of their land, if his words mean what they appear to say, yet his amillennial convictions render this improbable, and one finds that often what writers appear to say is not what they actually mean.

Stier, Rudolf. *The Words of the Apostles.* Edinburgh: T. &T. Clark, 1869.

Stier wrote in great and helpful detail *The Words of the Lord Jesus* and also this volume on the apostles. Though old, the works are often quite insightful in solid commentary style that delves competently into meaning and implications.

Stifler, James M. *The Epistle to the Romans.* NY: Revell, 1897.

The author, who taught Romans from the Greek for many years, has produced this work which is accurate from the standpoint of the Greek, but geared for English readers. He traces the argument of the epistle very well so that the reader receives help in a nutshell form in thinking his way through Paul's profound reasoning. Stifler is dispensational (cf. 16:25ff),

Stott, John R. W. *Men Made New*. Chicago: IVP, 1966.

Excellent brief evangelical survey of Romans 5-8 with much articulate perception into the meaning and a very fine ability to marshal material in a well-organized and lucid way. Particularly helpful for laymen in general, teachers in church Bible classes, collegians, etc. Stott is always well-read, competent, and adept in clarifying in his commentaries.

Stott, John R. W. *Romans, God's Good News for the World* (Bible Speaks Today). Downers Grove, IL: IVP, 1994.

This is typical Stott lucidity in exposition for one of the best medium-detail explanations for pastors, students and lay people. Verse comments are fairly full and to the point. Main and sub–headings throughout keep the flow of logic obvious. Stott handles most verses well, but could clarify more at times (4:15, "where there is no law"). On Rom. 5 he dates Adam ca. 10,000 years ago, but strangely holds that a kind of homo sapiens goes back two million years, yet he believes these pre-Adamic humanoids were not authentically human, God-like, bearing God's image (164). He thinks animal death was before the death coming by Adam in 5:12 (166). It is not easy to grasp Stott's idea that 7:14-25 refers to Jewish Christians, regenerate but not enjoying freedom in Christ, under the law but not yet in or under the Spirit (210). Romans 8 goes on to the ideal. He does not explain how this links with his comments on 8:14 where those led by the Spirit are sons and daughters. In 11:25-26, he believes the church is "the Israel of God" in Gal. 6:16, by viewing "all Israel" finally as saved Israelites flowing into the church (305). He appears to leave no room for a future millennium with a future for saved, ethnic Israelites distinct from the church.

Talbot, Louis T. *Addresses on Romans*. Los Angeles: Church of the Open Door [n. d.].

A popular series of radio expositions by a dynamic former pastor of The Church of the Open Door (Los Angeles) and key figure in the success of the Bible Institute of Los Angeles, now developed into Biola University, one of the leading Christian liberal arts institutions in the world. His wife, Carol Talbot, has written his colorful life in *For This I Was Born*. The work on Romans is basic exposition alive with frequent potent illustrations drawn mostly from Talbot's ministry. The material is an example of how one very effective channel of God's gospel communicated it, and has much that is helpful for personal reading by laymen and ministers alike. Many aspects will prime a preacher or Bible study leader. Many, however, will not agree with Talbot that 7:14-24 refers to the defeated Christian life, but will hold that even the mature Christian life will experience in some degree daily the down pull of sin and yet the uplift of the Spirit described in chapter 8.

Thomas, W. H. Griffith. *St. Paul's Epistle to the Romans*. Grand Rapids: Eerdmans, 1953.

This is a devotional commentary based upon the English text and providing many homiletical suggestions which pastors will find helpful. It cannot rank with the detailed exegetical works on the Greek text, but in its class it is usable along with Barnhouse, Bruce, Johnson, McClain, Morris, Murray, Newell, Stott, etc.

Watson, Thomas. *A Divine Cordial: Exposition of Romans 8:28.* **Wilmington, DE: Sov. Grace Publishers, 1972.**

This 94-pp. paperback is excellent in looking in tremendous detail at 8:28 to see if all things do work together for good to those who love God, who are called according to His purpose, and in what senses they do. There is much solid and rich food for thought and much to make one think through. If a preacher or teacher is preparing to speak on Romans 8:28 this is a good book to expand his thinking on various facets of the matter.

Wilson, Geoffrey B. Romans. *A Digest of Reformed Comment.* **London: Banner of Truth Trust, 1969.**

Wilson in many places in the 255-pp. verse by verse study attempts to provide a citation of what he regards as choice statements by reformed writers. So we often see names such as David Brown, R. Haldane, C. Hodge, J. Murray, and M. Poole. Disconcerting factors are the lack of an outline and absence of comprehensive surveys before plunging into a set of verses. There is much very fine explanation from a standpoint that many reformed writers favor (cf. 7:14-25), but sometimes vagueness as to what, exactly, is meant that relates to a larger picture (cf. 11:25, 26).

Witmer, John. "Romans," in *Bible Knowledge Commentary,* **ed. John F. Walvoord and Roy B. Zuck, Volume II. Wheaton. Victor Books, 1985.**

A careful theologian at Dallas Theological Seminary wrote this, a concise yet well-supported commentary. Expositors will find here pertinent, well-phrased comments on most verses and a capable handling of many of the problems. He sees 7:15ff. as Paul's experience as a believer. In 11:25-27, he is clearly premillennial and dispensational.

VII. FIRST CORINTHIANS

Barrett, C. K. *The First Epistle to the Corinthians.* **London: Adam & Charles Black, 1971.**

This is a fine scholarly explanation of First Corinthians. It is briefer on some problems than the serious student would like, but is nevertheless usually helpful. The work is also in Harper's NTC published in America.

Bartchy, S. S. Mallan Chresai. *First-Century Slavery and the Interpretation of I Corinthians 7:21,* **Society of Biblical Literature Dissertation Series No. 11. Cambridge, MA: SBL, 1973.**

This results from a 1971 doctoral work at Harvard University. It surveys the history of interpreting 7:21, also slavery in the first century A. D. The author discusses I Corinthians 7 as a whole, also verses 17-24, and v. 21 within its context. From the standpoint of increasing a reader's awareness of what Paul could mean, and insights on slavery, it is quite helpful.

Bieringer, R., ed. *The Corinthian Correspondence.* **Leuven: Leuven University Press, 1996.**

An 800-pp. work prints 42 papers by scholars on 1 and 2 Corinthians. Some are: Paul's argument in I Cor. 1:10—3:4, those claiming no resurrection, dangerous boasting in 2

Cor. 10-12, Paul's journey to Paradise (2 Cor. 12:2-4), and a theological profile on the sexual ascetics in I Cor. 7. One meets here with various perspectives from specialists.

Blomberg, Craig. *1 Corinthians* (NIV Application Commentary). Grand Rapids: Zondervan, 1994.

An articulate scholar contributes this. One of the good features is an annotated list of commentaries (31-34), though he claims John MacArthur's "dispensationalism at times overwhelms sane exegesis" (33). He sees the "perfect" in 2:6 as all the saved, with some not experientially consistent with this, and the "spiritual" person in v. 15 as anyone with the Spirit, baptized into Christ (12:13). That the spiritual person discerns all means that all Christians "have the ability to bring God's perspective to bear on every aspect of life" (65). In 3:1-4, the contrast shifts, he says, to only Christians who make right decisions and Christians not in this way controlled (72). Blomberg sees both divorce and remarriage in 7:15, and in chaps. 12-14 views "tongues" as ecstatic utterances distinct from human languages in Acts 2. Most main problem verses get some attention, and many things are explained, while applications gain much space to fit the series.

Boyer, James L. *For A World Like Ours: Studies in I Corinthians*. Grand Rapids: Baker, 1971.

Boyer was Professor of New Testament and Greek at Grace Theological Seminary, Winona Lake, IN. This 153-pp. paperback is a study guide based on the Greek, giving maps, charts, pictures and comments of a brief nature plus a list of questions ending each chapter. It is geared for the popular audience as a thumbnail sketch.

Bruce, F. F. *1 and 2 Corinthians*. Grand Rapids: Eerdmans, 1980.

This is a knowledgeable, brief explanation of the books that is often helpful but at times too sparse. Bruce always, however, has a lot to offer on a number of areas and brings much expertise to his commentary from a grasp of the New Testament world. However, this does not rank with his outstanding works on Acts and Hebrews (NICNT).

Carson, Donald A. *Showing the Spirit: A Theological Exposition of I Corinthians 12-14*. Grand Rapids: Baker, 1987. 229 pp.

An evangelical exposition offering good insight at times on the ways issues can be treated through Chapters 12-14. Then Carson has a section discussing theology of spiritual gifts, drawing from the texts in Acts and I Corinthians. Chapter 5 evaluates charismatic claims and experience today. Carson concludes that charismatics should guard against pride in having gifts and saying that tongues are a sign of "the second blessing." Noncharismatics ought to guard against saying that the gifts ceased. Carson believes that "that which is perfect" (I Corinthians 13:10) relates to Christ's parousia. He feels that tongues can be valid privately and publicly today if proper conditions are met. He defends women's right to prophesy.

Clark, Gordon H. *First Corinthians. A Contemporary Commentary*. Jefferson, MD: Trinity Foundation, 1991rp. 349 pp. Originally in 1975 (Nutley, NJ: Presbyterian and Reformed Publishing Co.)

A worthy evangelical commentary of a Reformed nature that briefly discusses many of the main issues of interpretation and is aware of the Greek, yet readable and lucid. It is not among the top works on Corinthians.

Conzelmann, Hans. *A Commentary on the First Epistle to the Corinthians* **(Hermeneia). Philadelphia: Fortress Press, 1975.**

A lengthy bibliography, interaction with critical views, often long footnotes on additional help, and an awareness of relevant literature in New Testament times as well as recently unite in this technical, liberal work that is very well-respected. Subjective opinions that some sections show they do not fit their context and could not be of the same date as others are unconvincing (cf. 10:1-22, which Conzelmann thinks "fits badly into its context," p. 3). Read discerningly by evangelicals who are aware of basic exegetical issues, the subjectivism is immediately recognizable. Often the commentary shows good, discerning help on the meaning of a text and guards against misconceptions (cf. on 1:17, not depreciating baptism). But sometimes it is rather jumbled and muddies the waters in part (3:15, loss of salvation is a danger, he thinks) or very incomplete toward meeting the issues in very big problem verses or giving an adequate defense of his view or making a reasonably serious effort to explain or give other views (5:5; 7:15; 9:27; 13:8, 13; 15:2, 29, etc.). The commentary is primarily and occasionally helpful to serious students, not so much for satisfying comments to resolve verses but for certain insights, references to early sources, and copious footnotes which can frequently contribute solidly.

Fee, Gordon H. *The First Epistle to the Corinthians* **(New International Commentary on the NT). Grand Rapids: Eerdmans, 1987. 880 pp.**

This is the all-around best evangelical commentary on the epistle at this time. Fee is well-organized, clear, and perceptive on issues. His work replaces the Grosheide commentary in this series in 1953. He is thorough verse by verse, skilled in Greek details, and keeps the argument of the epistle in view. His grasp of literature on I Corinthians is masterful, and he takes up more matters than other commentaries on the letter, looking at various views and reasons, supporting his views, applying truth to the church and the Christian life. He will meet with disagreement on some issues, of course. In a 10-page discussion he sees 14:34-35 as a textual gloss, thus having no bearing on women's role in the church. This is a curious conviction since such a gloss does not have a proper attestation. Fee devotes 40 pages just to 11:2-16, taking "head" to denote source, not authority. He is affiliated with the Assemblies of God and is sure all the gifts are for today, yet argues his position well, even if one disagrees with him.

Godet, Franz. *Commentary on the First Epistle to the Corinthians.* **Grand Rapids: Kregel, 1977. Reprint of 1886 work.**

Godet, a Swiss Protestant Reformed scholar, was Professor of New Testament in the Free Evangelical Theological School, Neuchatel. He deals seriously with the text in the Greek, usually giving solid comments in a serious effort to explain a passage and showing connections between sections. His is one of the finer works among the older commentaries, well-worth consulting for its scholarship and its warm strain. A 1957 printing was issued by Zondervan.

Gromacki, Robert G. *Called To Be Saints. An Exposition of I Corinthians.* **Grand Rapids: Baker, 1977.**

This Cedarville College (Ohio) New Testament professor has been prolific as a writer of commentaries. Skilled in the Greek, he does a survey that sums up sections, comments on many verses, and meets problem texts often with good insight. He has a high view of the text's integrity.

Grosheide, F. W. *Commentary on First Corinthians* (NIC). Grand Rapids: Eerdmans, 1954.

This is a lucid evangelical work of capable scholarship which ranks among the top commentaries from the standpoint of the Greek and dealing with problems.

Hering, Jean. *The First Epistle of Saint Paul to the Corinthians*. Translated by A. W. Heathcote and P. J. Allcock. London: Epworth, 1962.

Brief on many of the texts but often with fresh insights and a good grasp of issues. Evangelical and helpful on a hit or miss basis.

Hodge, Charles. *Corinthians 1 and 2*. Carlisle, PA: Banner of Truth Trust, 1978rp.

The famous theologian's work, originally in 1857, is very worthy of reprint and much used by pastors, students and lay people in general. As on Romans, he explains each verse in a careful manner, informed by much study, and is particularly adept and helpful in bringing out the doctrinal truth. Those who use his works find much assistance in thinking through issues consistently with Scripture, seen from a Reformed perspective.

Hughes, Robert B. *First Corinthians*. Chicago: Moody, 1985. 157 pp.

Clear, concise, conservative, competent survey. Those needing a simple discussion of some of the issues in a readable style will find this well-organized evangelical study suitable.

Ironside, H. A. *Addresses on the First Epistle to the Corinthians*. 3rd edition. NY: Lolzeaux, 1952.

A popular work of a survey nature, this is helpful because of its insight into the problems of the Corinthians and the practical applications today. The illustrations are good.

Johnson, S. Lewis. "First Corinthians." *The Wycliffe Bible Commentary*. Chicago: Moody, 1962.

This work in the English, based upon a careful study of the Greek text, is helpful because it gets right to the crux of problems. However, by necessity, it is brief.

Lowery, David. "I and II Corinthians," in *Bible Knowledge Commentary*, ed. John F. Walvoord and Roy B. Zuck, Volume II. Wheaton: Victor Books, 1985.

Lowery, teaching in the New Testament Department at Dallas Theological Seminary, did these surveys well, showing awareness of issues that need to be explained and getting to the point. In such a concise work he is sometimes quite helpful and sometimes general. His handling of problem verses often seems quite well-informed.

Luck, G. Coleman. *First Corinthians*. Chicago: Moody, 1958.

Like Ironside's work this is in a simple, evangelical popular style which gets right to the point in many of the problem passages. It is only for light reading, not for deeper study.

It is in the Everyman's series.

MacArthur, John F., Jr. *Spiritual Gifts (I Corinthians 12)*. Chicago: Moody, 1991.

An exposition on a key, much-discussed section and subject from a viewpoint that some gifts were intended to be permanent in the church age and some temporary, in the early church. Cf. also his *Charismatic Chaos* (1991).

Mare, W. Harold. "I Corinthians," in *Expositor's Bible Commentary*, ed. Frank Gaebelein and J. D. Douglas. Grand Rapids: Zondervan, 1976.

Another good survey invested with awareness of issues and literature, usually providing adequate reasoning. Evangelical. One will find considerable help here for preparing messages or Bible class sessions or Sunday School lessons, or just for informed Christian reading.

Martin, Ralph P. *The Spirit and the Congregation. Studies in I Corinthians 12-15*. Grand Rapids: Eerdmans, 1984. 168 pp.

This is a work helpful to those with a wide reading skill in Greek and seeking perception of different views Martin interacts with. It is a very contributing work on this part of Corinthians, whether one agrees with Martin or not. It is evangelical. Martin stimulates thinking on spiritual gifts, the nature of prophecy, and the nature of resurrection. He shows awareness of theological literature and aspects of history and Greek that may help in interpreting verses.

Morris, Leon. *The First Epistle of Paul to the Corinthians. An Introduction and Commentary* (Tyndale NTC). Grand Rapids: Eerdmans, 1984, updated since 1958.

Though the works in the Tyndale Series are concise, this is a good commentary and is recent. Morris is adequate a good part of the time in his comments on passages, but weak in detail on historical background, evidently because of the brevity to which he was held.

Naylor, Peter. *1 Corinthians* (Welwyn Commentary). Auburn, WA: Evangelical Press, 1996.

Like others in the series, this is practical exposition, rather substantial here (432 pp.). A lot of good discernment will stimulate some pastors and students as well as lay users. Yet some statements are puzzling, such as "If we are committed to the Lord we are mature, perfect, or complete (Col. 2:10)" (66). Many infant Christians are committed in some degree, but not mature yet. Much, however, is more helpful, at least on what the author means (cf. on 7:15). Some is not as clear as he apparently thinks (cf. 5:5), and on some texts one must keep re-reading to figure out which view is favored. Overall the work is about medium in contribution among simpler expositions.

Orr, William F. and James A. Walther. *I Corinthians* (Anchor Bible). New York: Doubleday, 1976.

Orr was Professor of New Testament, Pittsburgh Theological Seminary. Walther was an Associate Professor in that department. They first give a study on the life of Paul (124 pp.), later the commentary. One sometimes can be disconcerted to have to keep switching from the brief sections verse by verse (finding some verses passed over) to the comments in the sweeping sections. Comments in both sections often tend to be sparse in explaining texts sufficiently, sometimes raising more questions than they answer (cf. 3:15; 7:15; 9:24-27) or not going on to tie things together. Sometimes comments focus on some odd view rather than on more likely views that might help the reader (5:5, p. 186). Still there are many helpful comments throughout based on study (6:4, etc.). This is a good work to consult in scholarly research, but not consistently as helpful in putting things together and in focus as some other works are, old and recent.

Prior, David. *The Message of I Corinthians: Life in the Local Church* (Bible Speaks Today). Downers Grove: 1VP, 1985. 285 pp.

This expounds the broad message of paragraphs, and is not a verse by verse study. Footnotes cite reputed names (Barrett, Bruce, Conzelmann etc.), but there is a lack of reference to recent journal literature. Prior's exposition is practical, applied, often fresh with stimulating comment. Many will appreciate his insightful strokes that are relevant today on areas such as divorce, remarriage, and tongues. He has a fair discussion of tongues, yet some will not be convinced by his notion that tongues are ecstatic languages and will opt for earthly languages here and in Acts. Yet he has much to provoke thinking.

Robertson, A. T. and Alfred Plummer. *A Critical and Exegetical Commentary on the First Epistle to the Corinthians* (lCC). New York: Charles Scribner's Sons, 1911.

This, after Fee, is the most detailed and the best critical commentary on the epistle. Though not as readable as works by Godet, Grosheide, Johnson and Morris, it is more detailed in discussing possibilities for a given passage.

Thomas, Robert L. *Understanding Spiritual Gifts. A Verse-by-Verse Study of I Corinthians 12-14.* Grand Rapids: Kregel, 1999.

This careful exegetical discussion appeared first in 1978. Thomas offers fine-tuned reasoning through sets of verses. The introduction previews the entire passage, giving a detailed outline and literary framework. Six appendices, all substantial, say more on 13:11, review W. Grudem's book *The Gift of Prophecy in the New Testament and Today*, the spiritual gift of prophecy in Rev. 22:18, correlation of revelatory spiritual gifts and NT canonicity, details on 18 spiritual gifts, and how a Christian can discover and use his gifts. In addition to sections in the book dealing with sets of verses, special end notes (215-76) take up exegetical issues such as evaluating views in a well-organized way. Thomas holds that some gifts were temporary, others permanent.

Witherington, Ben, III. *Conflict & Community in Corinth. A Socio-Rhetorical Commentary on 1 and 2 Corinthians.* Grand Rapids: Eerdmans, 1995.

A 492-pp. product seeks energetically to explain social conditions, and assumes use of Greco-Roman features of rhetoric. It also deals with ancient customs where they occur. The author offers much to make one think, yet at times loses clarity about what he means or how it ties all facets together, which can frustrate. General discussion at points (as on I Cor. 2) can leave one groping to decide how parts of a text fit what it is being held to say; if all believers are spiritual, how do some who appear to have minimal discernment and tolerate ungodly lives discern all things in 2:15? And where is comment to aid practically on this? One fears that the work will be of use in many parts only to the very patient and advanced. Several other works are a better possibility overall.

Zodhiates, Spiros. *A Richer Life For You in Christ. An Exposition of I Corinthians 1 Based on the Greek Text.* **Ridgefield, NJ: AMG Press, 1972.**

Born on Cyprus of Greek parents, Zodhiates was president of American Mission to the Greeks, Inc., later headquartered in Chattanooga. His works on *The Pursuit of Happiness* (Beatitudes) and *The Epistle of James and The Life of Faith* (3 volumes) are known to many. In this paperback, as in his other works, he uses the Greek, and writes in great detail, with often choice illustrations as he expounds the passage in a simple, popular devotional way. Sometimes he has several chapters on a single verse as he does an evangelical study of different facets. The book is furnished with indices of subjects, English words, and Greek words.

Zodhiates, Spiros. *A Revolutionary Mystery. An Exposition of I Corinthians 2:1-16.* **Ridgefield: AMG, 1974.**

Zodhiates expounds and illustrates with interesting chapter titles, e.g. "God's Strength in Your Weakness," "Why So Many Mysteries in the Christian Faith?," "How to Enjoy God Without Fully Understanding Him," "How You Can Be Spiritual Yet Human," etc. For a devotional refresher, this in an interesting, often stimulating book for young believers, and has many good reminders or further lessons to edify the more mature as well. Zodhiates is a master of illustration, and in this respect provides help even in bringing together material to enhance a sermon or Bible study.

Zodhiates, Spiros. *Getting the Most Out of Life. An Exposition of I Corinthians 3.* **Ridgefield: AMG, 1976.**

1 have seen few books written on I Corinthians 3 but enjoyed reading, from the archives of King's College, University of Aberdeen, Anthony Burgess's exposition of the entire chapter. It was *The Scriptural Directory For Church Officers and Peoples, A Practical Commentary Upon the whole 3rd Chapter of the 1st Epistle of St. Paul to the Corinthians* (London, 1659). Done in a reformed viewpoint with often choice statements to awaken believers to servanthood in church life and vital preparation for the judgment seat and reward, it gripped my heart at many a point. N. A. Woychuk wrote *For All Eternity* (NY: Books, Inc., 1955), a devotional on 3:10-15 with considerable arbitrary symbolism on "gold ... straw" etc. Zodhiates, like Burgess, has done the entire chapter, using his customary explanations of Greek words, illustrating, exhorting along instructive but devotional lines. Again he has intriguing titles to sections, such as "Are You Still in the First Grade, Spiritually Speaking?," "The Sin of Idolizing a Preacher," "The Only Thing You Can Do to Save Yourself," "What Kind of Reward Has God Promised to Believers?," etc. This paperback is 379 pages, with indices of English words, Greek words, and subjects. Zodhiates says that the reward is not so much what Christians will have as what they will be in enjoying God and other believers; the "crown" concept does not necessarily refer to a material reward but is symbolic of spiritual values (p. 215).

Zodhiates, Spiros. *You and Public Opinion (I Corinthians 4:1-5): also Formula for Happiness (I Corinthians 4:6-21).* **Chattanooga, TN: AMG, 1983.**

Note Zodhiates' change of address from Ridgefield, NJ to Chattanooga, TN. These 2 volumes are along the same lines as the other volumes on I Corinthians, very detailed and illustrated.

Zodhiates, Spiros. *Tongues (I Corinthians 12-14).* **Chattanooga, TN: AMGT 1981.**

An exposition of the 3 chapters with creative titles and illustrations and an effort to use the Greek as in the author's other books.

Zodhiates, Spiros. *To Love is to Live.* **Chattanooga, TN: AMG, 1983 reprint.**

A detailed exposition of I Corinthians 13 with illustrations, done in the usual Zodhiates style which is very helpful, especially on love in 13:1-7. Preachers and Bible class teachers can find much usable material on a rich set of verses.

Zodhiates, Spiros. *Conquering the Fear of Death. An Exposition of I Corinthians 15, Based Upon the Original Greek Text.* **Grand Rapids: Eerdmans, 1970.**

An 869-pp. hardback for popular reading, with 164 studies expounding verse by verse and illustrating. Again the titles are often very inviting. This, as his other books, can be helpful not only for a general reader but for speakers looking for illustrations and refreshment amidst technical studies. It can be invigorating to read the book, or parts of it, over several weeks before Easter, and letting the truth of the resurrection get more into the spiritual bloodstream. He sees 15:29 as referring to believers being "baptized for the dead," i.e., undergoing baptism that "destined them for and allied them with the dead" (p. 502), in other words identified them with the saved who had died, many as martyrs (501). He frequently seeks to explain the rich meaning in a Greek word.

VIII. SECOND CORINTHIANS

Barnett, Paul. *The Message of 2 Corinthians* **(Bible Speaks Today). Downers Grove: IVP, 1988. 188 pp.**

A flowing, competent, broad commentary on the message of sections and on Paul as a minister and human being with weaknesses facing problems and criticisms but experiencing God's power in his weakness. Barnett often has good application to concerns today. He devotes more detail to chapters 1-6 (100 pp.), and is cursory on such problems as "thorn" (Chapter 12). The book is a refreshment for a series of devotional times and often a catalyst for grasping and ministering the Word.

Barnett, Paul. *The Second Epistle to the Corinthians* **(NICNT). Grand Rapids: Eerdmans, 1997.**

This vol. replaces the famous and good one by Philip E. Hughes in the NICNT. The 662 pp. are by the Bishop of N. Sydney, Australia. He also did 2 Cor. in the Bible Speaks

Today series. The work joins careful exegetical efforts by Martin, Furnish, Hughes, etc. Barnett ably considers views and reasons that partition 2 Cor. into several separate letters, and himself favors one unified letter by Paul (24). He sees the "false apostles" as Greek-speaking Jews from Judaea (Judaizers) claiming righteousness based on the law (35; cf. 33-40). Like Hafemann and many in recent years, Barnett construes Paul's "triumph" imagery (2:14-16) to denote Christ leading the *saved* captive as prisoners moving to execution, rather than seeing, in accord with the Roman custom, the general's own soldiers as linked with him in a triumphant way, and enemies (the unsaved) on their way to the death here (150). He sees 5:1-5 as referring to hope of a new body at the future resurrection, and leaves undecided what Paul's "thorn" was (12:9), though with helpful remarks. Some will wonder about certain assumptions on 13:5, where Barnett thinks that all the Corinthians were saved for sure, or so his words convey. Overall the work is among the best, but not as lucid as Hughes which it replaces, though with plenty that is substantial, and quite useful.

Barrett, C. K. *The Second Epistle to the Corinthians* **(Black's NTC). London: Adam & Charles Black, 1973.**

Along with works by Danker, Furnish, Garland, Harris, Hughes, Kistemaker, Martin, and Plummer this is one of the top commentaries in usually getting at key issues and bringing quality comments on these based on broad research and awareness. In America this is in Harper's NTC.

Belleville, Linda L. *2 Corinthians* **(IVP NTC). Downers Grove, IL: IVP, 1996.**

Fascinating vividness meets one here in a 357-pager. The introduction reviews some themes, as on Christian suffering and God's power, the Spirit's work, authority, discipline, and pastoral ministry (cf. 11:28-29) with its role in nurturing, correction, and strategy. Usually the work has logic easy to follow, staying with 2 Corinthians. It is one of the better medium-length survey expositions as it explains and applies without bringing in extra sermonic anecdotes, which sometimes interferes with conveying Scripture light itself. Another, equally illumining book often helpful on background is James M. Scott, *2 Corinthians* (New International Biblical Commentary, Peabody, MA: Hendrickson, 1998, 289 pp.).

Bruce, F. F. Cf. on I Corinthians.

Carson, Donald A. *From Triumphalism to Maturity. An Exposition of 2 Corinthians 10-13.* **Grand Rapids: Baker, 1984. 186 pp.**

False triumphalism is, to Carson, the selfish spirit of serving for what one can get out of it, whatever the form. Talk of success can be sinful; we need to be humble, not boastful in a wrong sense. The way to live is the way of self-sacrifice, depending on God's power to win over our weaknesses. Maturity flowing from Christ's death and resurrection exults in His power in servant living. Carson shows a competent awareness of the argument and issues in the passage and current scholarship, and applies principles to touch people now. Sometimes he is too quick and brief and general.

Danker, Frederick W. *II Corinthians* **(Augsburg Commentary on the New Testament). Minneapolis: Augsburg, 1989. 223 pp.**

An evangelical work that ranks high among commentaries conversant with much scholarly study into the setting of that day and offering a lot of information. It is by the author of *Multipurpose Tools for Bible Study* (Saint Louis: Concordia, 1970, 3rd ed., 295 pp.). Danker's background study of "Benefactor" helps him illumine chapters 8-9. See also his benefactor *Epigraphic Study of a Graeco-Roman and New Testament Semantic Field* (Saint Louis: Clayton, 1982). Benefactors might give out of wealth with a noble spirit of obligation, while also having a right to see those to whom they shared respond in a noble way according to their means. Danker is, overall, quite good in a number of ways, and will contribute to one's study in this book.

Furnish, Victor Paul. *II Corinthians. Translated, with Introduction, Notes and Commentary* (Anchor Bible). Garden City, NY: Doubleday, 1984. 621 pp.

Some scholars regard this as the best on the epistle due to its copious comment, expertise and adeptness in current literature. It is by the Professor of New Testament, Perkins School of Theology, Dallas, and is liberal. Furnish has much to offer serious students. He writes clearly, discussing each section with its structure and themes, gives detail on text, word study, grammar, geography, history etc. He includes 38 pages of select bibliography, and interacts with primary and secondary sources. He thinks with certain others (Barrett, Bruce, etc.) that chapters 1-9 and 10-13 represent two separate letters originally, though they are coherent. He likewise does not grasp the meaningful way in which 6:14-7:1 fits in the epistle. But his richness in many aspects such as grammar provides much for mature users trained to discern, and for translators.

Garland, David. *2 Corinthians* (New American Commentary). Nashville: Broadman & Holman, 1999.

A substantial (587-pp.) exegetical effort with brief introductory data on background and the letter's unity versus any theory of fragmenting it (cf. 44) helps readers. Garland has achieved one of the better recent studies by delving into views and reasons. One meets on 2 Cor. 5 the interpretation that Paul sees Christians getting resurrection bodies at *death* (251). There, various views are held on Paul's meaning. Garland does not decide a view on Paul's "thorn" (2 Cor. 12).

Grogan, Geoffrey. *2 Corinthians* (Focus on the Bible). Geanies House, Fearn, Ross-shire, Scotland: Christian Focus Publications, 1996.

This is one more of the almost too numerous to count popular expositions. It has some help for Christians in general (cf. also ***Derek Prime, Let's Study 2 Corinthians.*** Carlisle, PA: Banner of Truth Trust, 2000). A broad flow of teaching directed at key issues in texts leads to questions after each section, inviting leaders to apply details. The triumph in 2:14-16 is partly explained well, then confusingly turned to a picture inconsistent with customs of a Roman triumph, arguing that Roman captives [enemies, headed to punishment] portray Christ's people as captives, on the general's side. However, this is a popular scholarly misconception today. The discussion of 5:1-5 seems to state favoring one view, then wind up choosing the other, a new body. One value of the refreshing survey is in putting great truths before believers quickly and simply.

Gromacki, Robert G. *Stand Firm in the Faith. An Exposition of 2 Corinthians*. Grand Rapids: Baker, 1978.

This is a good evangelical commentary along the lines of his I Corinthians work, perceptive in Greek, upholding unity of the book, dealing well with problems in frequent cases, and showing connections in the flow as well as pointing out principles for life today.

Hafemann, Scott J. *2 Corinthians* (NIV Application Commentary). Grand Rapids: Zondervan, 2000.

The writer concludes for unity (32) and sees opponents of Jewish heritage (34). The theme is suffering in the Spirit's power (34). Readers encounter much good comment about suffering, for instance in 2 Cor. 1. Hafemann shows adept grasp in many passages, and as the series calls for much on application, making this quite rich for church teachers and Christians in general. Some will not agree with his view, yet a popular one, that has the triumph in 2:14-16 feature believers as captives led to death (some see the Roman custom as more consistently having a general's enemies, still enemies but captives, headed for their death, and in Col. 2:15 Christ triumphed over enemies, etc.).

Hafemann, Scott J. *Suffering and Ministry in the Spirit. Paul's Defense of His Ministry in II Corinthians 2:14-3:3*. Grand Rapids: Eerdmans.

This is an exhaustive effort to shed light on the text in an abridgement of a 1985 dissertation at Tubingen. The author argues that 3:6ff. is grasped only if we profoundly see the context in 2:14-3:3. In his argument we have here a brief on Paul's self-concept as an apostle and a potent apologetic on the authority and authenticity of his apostolic ministry (p. 1). On 2:14 he decides that *thriambeuein* ("to triumph") deals with the person conquered and led in procession, not the conqueror (33). Paul is a conquered slave of Christ being led to death so as to show forth the power of God, the conqueror. Paul fulfills his ministry through his weakness/death, through which the Spirit in power shows others the meaning of Christ's death. Hafemann also has much rich detail on the sacrificial language (2:14-16a) and Paul's suffering, as well as the significance of 3:1-3. On the idea of Paul's weakness and triumph, also cf. David A. Black, *Paul, Apostle of Weakness* (New York: Lang, 1984). Black is a graduate of Talbot School of Theology and has taught there as well as at Grace Theological Seminary, West.

Harris, Murray. "Second Corinthians," In *Expositor's Bible Commentary*, ed. Frank Gaebelein. Grand Rapids: Zondervan, 1981.

Harris, who wrote his Ph. D. dissertation at Manchester University on II Corinthians 5:1-10 and has taught at Trinity Evangelical Divinity School for many years, has contributed a fine commentary showing breadth of scholarly reading and often a good grasp of issues. One is bound to learn much and receive good help here on some passages.

Harvey, A. E. *Renewal Through Suffering. A Study of 2 Corinthians*. Edinburgh: T. & T. Clark, 1996.

Harvey in 143 pages seeks to develop his theme that some light on suffering language in chaps. 4-5 is found in Paul's traumatic ordeal in chap. 1 not long before the writing. His own first and last chapters show his main idea. Paul's own suffering greatly shaped him in his walk with Christ and ability to share with other Christian sufferers.

Hering, Jean. *The Second Epistle of Saint Paul to the Corinthians*. Translated by A. W. Heathcote and P. J. Allcock. London: Epworth, 1967.

As his work on I Corinthians, this is concisely written with many good insights. It is helpful for those who desire a briefer study but it cannot measure up to the more thorough works such as those by Barrett, Danker, Furnish, Garland, Hughes, Kistemaker, Martin and Plummer.

Hodge, Charles. *An Exposition of the Second Epistle to the Corinthians.* **Grand Rapids: Eerdmans, 1953.**

This is a solid work with good insight in following the reasoning of Paul, and helpful in most matters of exposition, including problems. Hodge, as usual, is helpful theologically.

Hughes, Philip E. *Commentary on the Second Epistle to the Corinthians* **(NICNT). Grand Rapids: Eerdmans, 1962.**

This is detailed (508 pages), uses the Greek carefully, discusses technical details in the footnotes, deals carefully and sometimes at length with problems, and shows acquaintance with a great number of other works. It is one of the finer earlier contributions to the NIC series.

Kent, Homer A., Jr. *A Heart Opened Wide: Studies in II Corinthians* **(NTS). Grand Rapids. Baker, 1982.**

This book will be helpful for individual Bible study or preaching. The style is fairly popular, but most of the major phrases receive comment, even extending to some transliterated interaction with the Greek text (at times treating textual difficulties as well). Kent applies the text frequently to modern life and pastoral work. He includes questions for discussion purposes. Kent, well-known for other evangelical expositions on several New Testament books, outlines clearly and surveys well for those looking for a brief work on the progressing message of the epistle and the main expository problems.

Kistemaker, Simon J. *Exposition of the Second Epistle to the Corinthians* **(New Testament Commentary). Grand Rapids: Baker, 1997.**

As usual in his continuing NT commentaries after W. Hendriksen's death, Kistemaker explains many things with good Greek expertise and a fair amount of fulness. Footnotes show wide awareness of and drawing from the richness of writings. Expositors will profit from his six theological themes (20-25), and focus on the theme, "proclaiming God's glory." Unity and integrity of the epistle is a conviction. Cf. my longer review in *The Master's Seminary Journal*, 9:2, Fall, 1998. In short, this is among the best evangelical efforts to devote detail on 2 Cor. (here 495 pp.), often showing richness as on customs (as 4:7, treasure), or as in laying out principles of giving in Chaps. 8-9.

Kruse, C. G. *The Second Epistle of Paul to the Corinthians* **(Tyndale NTC). Grand Rapids: Eerdmans, 1987. 224 pp.**

R. V. G. Tasker's work served well for years, but Kruse's replaces it with stronger exegesis. It is a fairly concise evangelical effort that brings together much that is of help in following the thought through and dealing with problems in a well written flow, using the NIV.

Lewis, J. P., ed. *Interpreting 2 Corinthians 5:14-21.* **An Exercise in Hermeneutics (Studies in the Bible and Early Christianity, 17). Lewiston, NY: Mellen, 1989. 194 pp.**

This expensive book is written by four writers and deals penetratingly with interpretive history, exegesis, problems and theology.

Lowery, David. Cf. on I Corinthians.

Martin, Ralph P. *2 Corinthians* **(Word Biblical Commentary). Waco, TX: Word Books, 1986. 527 pp.**

A well-regarded evangelical scholar writes clearly, keeping account of the flow, connections and verse by verse detail, offering frequent help on the Greek, the setting, the doctrine, etc. By and large he makes a good contribution, weighing matters carefully in many cases but being questionable in others. He displays mastery of a great amount of current literature so as to cite views and reasons, and is sometimes lengthy on possibilities, as on Paul's thorn (pp. 411-16), though he concludes with uncertainty what the thorn was.

McCant, Jerry W. *2 Corinthians.* **Sheffield, Eng.: Sheffield Academic Press, 1999.**

Readers encounter a brief (196-pp.) but well-informed summary on each part, done in 18 steps. McCant's introduction sums up views on Paul defending himself yet disclaiming that he does in 12:19, also his opponents, his taking the part of a fool, his parody of "boasting in weakness," and Hellenistic rhetorical self advertisement, or Hebrew, not Greek conventions. McCant subscribes to Paul as author. The work seeks to show the parodic sense in which Paul boasted, for example in his being God's aroma contrasting himself with "hawkers" of wares, and his self-commendation as in 2:14-17. One learns much through features Paul utilizes in what the author terms a "defense speech" as an apostle, with a conclusion to the letter in a loving pastoral blessing.

Naylor, Peter. *2 Corinthians,* **Vol. I, Chaps. 1-7 (EP Student Commentary). Darlington, Eng.: Evangelical Press, 2002.**

Naylor, a retired pastor who studied semitics and has a Ph. D. in Baptist history, did 370 pp., often with clarity. He is against editorial redaction, and sees unity with sections fitting reasonably. He traces the excellency of ministry related to the New Covenant. Commentary as well as end notes (337-68) cite top works and get involved in Greek words and grammar, interacting much on the text's meaning. Commentary on each section ends with a paragraph about how to apply the truth. What Naylor says on each verse usually throws light on main details. He fits 2:5-11 with the offender in I Cor. 5 (99), sees 2:14-16 as Paul and other believers compared with a Roman triumph as victors in Christ's train, distinct from the lost headed for death and like enemy captives in that custom (114). Naylor is not so helpful on "from death to death" in 2:16. He is vivid on some customs, e.g. treasure in jars (4:7). So far in 2 Cor. he has one of the most useable medium-range expositions for pastors, students and Christians in general.

Plummer, Alfred. *A Critical and Exegetical Commentary on the Second Epistle to the Corinthians* **(ICC). NY: Scribners, 1915.**

This is one of the best older commentaries on the epistle from the standpoint of the Greek text and critical study.

Robertson, A. T. *The Glory of the Ministry.* **NY: Revell, 1911.**

Over against an attitude of having wrong motives in the ministry and giving it up as too demanding, Robertson writes to expose from 2 Corinthians the glory of being in the ministry and living in the will of God. The book had a shaping effect on this writer's life when he was young and contemplating the rigors of public ministry. Robertson, a great Southern Baptist grammarian, is well-known for his large grammar, and his *Word Pictures in the New Testament* (6 Volumes) commenting on most verses of the New Testament, etc.

Spencer, A. B. and W. D. Spencer. *2 Corinthians* **(Bible Study Commentary). Grand Rapids: Zondervan, 1989. 144 pp.**

The Spencers were faculty members at Gordon-Conwell Theological Seminary, South Hamilton, MA. They believe that Paul defends the leadership style that he and his associates model to help readers follow the right example, not be led astray. Their work is a survey but furnishes a clear flushing out of principles that can assist Christian workers.

Tasker, R. V. G. *Second Epistle to the Corinthians* **(Tyndale Series). London: Tyndale Press, 1978. Published In U. S. by Eerdmans.**

This is a good brief conservative work which, among other things, argues for the unity of the epistle. Kruse's study has replaced it.

IX. GALATIANS

Betz, Hans D. *A Commentary on Paul's Letter to the Churches of Galatia* **(Hermeneia). Philadelphia: Fortress Press, 1979.**

Betz has taught New Testament at the Claremont School of Theology and Claremont Graduate School, also the University of Chicago Divinity School. Serious students looking for vigorous critical comments on interpretation of the Greek with heavy awareness and use of critical studies will gain much help here. Betz favors the North Galatia theory (p. 5) and authorship by Paul within A. D. 50-55. He lays out a formal analysis (outline) of 8 pp., also develops a detailed 6 page conception of Paul's logic of theological argument to answer opponents. There is often much help on main possibilities in the grammar, problems and views critical scholars debate, and possible similarities with other ancient sources. The fact that the analysis (outline) printed in the introduction is not included throughout makes it very difficult to keep any overall threads of thought in mind as one gets enmeshed in ponderous verse by verse detail. Unless one can get inside the thinking of Betz, he will have frustrations trying to grasp how certain discussions really help him adequately resolve theological problems in some verses if they do (5:4, 21). On other verses clarity is more apparent (6:11). The copious, often lengthy footnotes are very instructive for examples of word usage, other textual readings, distinctions in interpretation, references to other literature, etc. Also, Betz' bibliography is very extensive at the end, and he provides excellent indices on references in the Old Testament and Apocrypha, Old Testament Pseudepigrapha, other Jewish literature, New Testament, early Christian writings, Greek and Latin authors, Greek words, subjects, and names of commentators and other authors of ancient and modern times.

Bruce, F. F. *The Epistle to the Galatians. A Commentary on the Greek Text* **(The New International Greek Testament Commentary). Grand Rapids: Eerdmans, 1983.**

The late Emeritus Professor of New Testament at the University of Manchester, whom some rated the foremost evangelical New Testament scholar of our day, has provided a work of first rank treating technical questions. He favors the South Galatian theory after a fair and lengthy review that shows a grasp of the breadth of literature, a grasp evident throughout the work. Bruce on a verse by verse progression shows good perception of which problems need comment and explains matters with a sharp insight usually (cf. 1:6, 7; 2:20; 3:16; 5:22, 23, 25, etc.). This takes its place as one of the truly great commentaries on Galatians on the technical, thorough side for students intense about their study.

Burton, Ernest D. *A Critical and Exegetical Commentary on St. Paul's Epistle to the Galatians* **(ICC). London: T. & T. Clark, 1921. Reprint 1962.**

This is one of the most detailed critical works available and is very helpful in the Greek text, though liberal. Many regard it as the best technical commentary on the book, others say Betz.

Campbell, Donald. "Galatians," in *Bible Knowledge Commentary,* **ed, John F. Walvoord and Roy B. Zuck, Volume II. Wheaton: Victor Books, 1985.**

Campbell, third president at Dallas Theological Seminary and a long-time, excellent Bible teacher there, gives a very helpful brief survey, using his space well. He sometimes is contributive on problems, as on 3:17, the 430 years, and on 6:2, 5 on bearing one another's load and yet bearing one's own, etc. He concludes in 6:16 that "the Israel of God" means believers who are Jewish, not the church.

Cole, R. A. *The Letter of Paul to the Galatians: An Introduction and Commentary* **(Tyndale NTC). Grand Rapids: Eerdmans, 1989. 240 pp.**

This is a revision of a work of twenty years before, interacting with scholarly studies since then. It is a good evangelical commentary, well-informed, solid, clear with good help at times on problem verses.

Dunn, James D. G. *The Theology of Paul's Letter to the Galatians* **(NT Theology). Cambridge: Cambridge University Press, 1993.**

Dunn posits that Galatians gives the living heart of Paul's gospel. Examples from his topics are the significance of Paul's conversion, also of the Antioch incident (2:11-14), sufficiency of faith, the law's role, the believer's relation to Israel (3:8-16, 26-29 etc.), and how heirs of Abraham ought to live, led by the Spirit with Christ as the pattern, and Paul's use of the OT.

Dunn, James D. G. *The Epistle to the Galatians* **(Black's NTC). Peabody, MA: Hendrickson, 1993.**

This 395-pp. writing joins Dunn's work above on Galatians, and his 1988 commentary on Romans. His commentary here is in small print, not a help to some. It is quite capable and studiously informed, varying between fairly concise and thorough. Sometimes one meets arbitrary, unnecessary opinion, such as the claim that Paul's lack of personal greeting is linked with clauses of rebuke (34). However, Dunn regularly offers light on problems. He sees greater weight in matching Gal. 2 with Acts 11 than to Acts 15 (cf. 2:1). Some discussions give much (5:16-18). In 6:16, he sees "Israel of God" as including ethnic Israelites and also Gentiles who believe, all who are spiritual "seed" in Gal. 3. One can have problems with some wording, such as Paul exaggerates in 2:20 (145), or 4:24ff deals not with two covenants but with one aim of God through Abraham and his seed (249: cf. Witherington, *Galatians*, 330: "It is the argument of the agitators, not Paul, that the Mosaic covenant is an extension of the Abrahamic covenant"). With strengths and weaknesses, Dunn's work helps on most issues, even if not one of the best.

Eadie, John. *Commentary on the Epistle of Paul to the Galatians*. Grand Rapids: Zondervan (n.d.). Reprint of 1894 edition published by T. & T. Clark.

Based on the Greek text, this commentary grapples with problems in an energetic fashion, presenting various views and coming to conclusions. It is voluminous (480 pages).

Fung, Ronald Y. K. *The Epistle to the Galatians* (New International Commentary on the New Testament). Grand Rapids: Eerdmans, 1988. 342 pp.

This takes the place of Hermann Ridderbos's work. It is thorough, usually with traditional conservative views and with many satisfactory explanations, some even excellent. On verses he is lucid, frequently with some detail, though he skips past some real problems such as having fallen from grace (5:4), not really explaining. The same thing happens on "crucified with Christ". He holds the South Galatia theory, takes an A. D. 48 date, has a fairly good introduction overall in which he updates scholarly discussion, and relates 2:1-10 to the famine visit in Acts 11:27-30.

George, Timothy. *Galatians* (New American Commentary). Nashville: Broadman & Holman, 1994.

A well-written product weds exegesis and theological exposition to help preaching. George attends to problems with help on word study, exegesis, background, and sensitivity to other Scripture. In 1:6-7, for instance, he covers many bases on views and reasons about "another," and throughout he keeps a readable flow for users in general. Some lengthy footnotes add insight or interaction with notable exegetical works. This knowledgeable exposition is among the best medium-length studies.

Gromacki, Robert G. *Stand Fast in Liberty. An Exposition of Galatians*. Grand Rapids: Baker, 1979.

This is an evangelical work along the lines of his commentaries on both Corinthian letters, competent in Greek, keeping the flow of Galatians in view, getting to the point on most verses well but usually with brevity.

Harrison, Everett F. "Galatians," in *Wycliffe Bible Commentary*, ed. C. F. Pfeiffer and E. F. Harrison. Chicago: Moody, 1962.

The author, a famous New Testament scholar at Fuller Theological Seminary for many years and a leading evangelical in his field, offers a concise, well-pondered work explaining many issues satisfactorily. His thoughts are carefully weighed, and he often provides good though brief reasons for views.

Hendriksen, William. *New Testament Commentary: Galatians.* **Grand Rapids: Baker, 1968. 260 pp.**

Staunch reformed commentary is competent in the Greek and the background, offering rich detail on verses, documented views, reasons, and a warmth of practical comment, all of this helpful to expositors. Hendriksen's many New Testament commentaries are well-respected and widely-used by pastors, Bible class teachers and many lay people. Often his discussions are quite full and illuminating. Due to the date the work cannot be current in discussing scholarly contributions, but it does carry quite a weight of explaining the verses up to its day.

Hubbard, David A. *Galatians, Gospel of Freedom.* **Waco: Word Books, Publisher, 1977.**

A 118-pp. paperback written by the then President of Fuller Theological Seminary (Pasadena, California) along popular lines with intriguing chapter titles: "How Good is the Good News?", "Will My Faith Cost Me My Freedom?", etc. Hubbard delivered the messages orally at a Mt. Hermon (California) conference, to the Christian Endeavor of Australia, and to listeners of the radio program "The Joyful Sound." Vivid illustrations scattered throughout add to the enjoyment of reading devotionally. Chapter 8, "Will My Faith Cost Me My Freedom?" alone is worth the price of the book.

Kent, Homer A., Jr. *Freedom of God's Sons. Studies in Galatians.* **Grand Rapids: Baker.**

This paperback is a well-outlined, brief evangelical exposition of competent quality, with a short introduction favoring Paul as author ca. A. D. 49 (linking 2:1-10 with Acts 11:27-30), a South Galatian view, etc. Kent shows good awareness of main possibilities in some problem areas (cf. on 1:6, 7; 6:11), treats others rather briefly where there are difficulties and widely varying views (5:4; 6:16).

Lightfoot, J. B. *Commentaries on Galatians, Philippians, Colossians and Philemon.* **3 volumes in 1. Peabody, MA: Hendrickson, 1981rp of 1890-97 works. 1,208 pp.**

Lightfoot is highly-regarded for his work on the Greek text, top notch exegesis verse by verse, special notes on key problems, giving of views and reasons, etc. He was rarely gifted, and his commentaries rich with assistance to pastors and students.

Longenecker, Richard N. *Galatians* **(Word Biblical Commentary). Dallas: Word Books, 1990. 323 pp.**

A noted evangelical scholar, who also wrote a fine commentary on Acts, has a long introduction that surveys scholarly issues and study, then a commentary verse by verse with each pericope carrying its own bibliography, translation, notes and literary analysis. Longenecker leaves few stones unturned, at least the more crucial ones, and is helpful on views, reasons, and summation as well as detail on individual issues. He is Professor of New Testament, Wycliffe College, University of Toronto. One of his early steps to fame was his good book *Paul, Apostle of Liberty* (NY: Harper and Row, 1964, 310 pp.).

Luther, Martin. *Commentary on Galatians*. Translated by Erasmus Middleton, ed. John P. Fallowes. Grand Rapids: Kregel, 1979, rp of 1850 work.

A fuller version of Luther on Galatians can be found in *Luther's Works* (volumes 26, 27) published by Concordia Publishing House. Varying sets of lecture notes by Luther on Galatians have led to more than 30 English editions. This Kregel edition abridges Luther. Much of the heart-pulse of Luther's stand for justification by faith appears here, as he distinguishes between the rigors of keeping the law in a false bid to gain standing and the freedom God gives through grace, leading to a new life-style of fruit in grace.

MacArthur, John. *Galatians* (MacArthur New Testament Commentary). Chicago: Moody, 1987. 221 pp.

A fairly thorough evangelical work explaining in a lucid way the meaning of sections and verses, with sensitivity to grammar and word meaning. MacArthur places Galatians after Paul's first journey, before the Jerusalem Council in Acts 15 (p. xii). He sees "the Israel of God" in 6:16 as literal Jews who have become saved, not as people of the church per se including Gentiles. As in many commentaries, a discrepancy can occur, as when it is said that Paul finished a second journey to Galatia previous to writing Galatians (p. 118). In most respects the commentary is articulate in helping pastors and lay people grasp matters of the gospel of grace and freedom of the Christian life.

Machen, J. Gresham. *Machen's Notes on Galatians*, ed. by J. H. Skilton, in An International Library of Philosophy and Theology, Biblical and Theological Studies. Philadelphia: Presbyterian and Reformed, 1972.

Skilton combines Machen's comments on 1:1-3:14, added references to Galatians from Machen's other works, and gives a lengthy list of questions on the Greek, two synopses of Galatians, sections such as a discussion relating Galatians to Acts 15 and a discussion on faith and works.

Martyn, J. Louis. *Galatians* (Anchor Bible). NY: Doubleday, 1997.

One finds 614 pp. with exacting detail but often wordiness, done in 52 "Comment" sections, each dealing with issues such as the nature of Paul's apostleship, redemption, defection (1:6), Christ's gospel and its counterfeit (1:6-8), crucifixion with Christ (2:20), etc. Martyn gives his graphic translation, then painstaking explanation verse by verse, achieving one of the best efforts to expose the text for teachers, and pastors and students more adept in Greek. Even at strenuous lengths to take up issues, Martyn does not appear to identify what covenant contrasts with that of Sinai (4:24), and does not mention all options about "Israel" (6:16), which to him is the spiritual plural seed of 3:29, the church in which all distinctions vanish (574-77). One of his contributions is in showing how Paul's doctrine differed from others in his time.

McKnight, Scot. *Galatians* (NIV Application Commentary). Grand Rapids: Zondervan, 1995.

A more popular 320-pager, true to series intent, sums up salient points in verses, then has much on fleshing it into life-style. McKnight discusses legalism with illustrations to identify its forms in life today, sometimes helpfully, at other times needing further qualification (35-45). Commentary on verses moves right to the point, as on "another" gospel. This series, though helpful as it aims for applying, is set up in general sections that can delay one while he hunts for discussion on a specific verse. All in all, working with series intent, the writer provides good grasps of things in many cases to achieve one of the best devotional works.

Morris, Leon. *Galatians. Paul's Charter of Christian Freedom*. Downers Grove, IL: IVP, 1996.

This concise product often says a lot that shoots to the crux in a well-organized form. Morris has readable print and flowing style. Teachers, preachers, students and laity will profit by following through verses and getting some careful help on some of the problems, though at times space does not allow posing considerations (3:17; 6:16), contributing to some generality. It is a rather good survey by a discerning scholar, it simply vies with many works that provide far more, at least for teachers and diligent studying pastors.

Ramsay, William. *A Historical Commentary on Galatians*. Grand Rapids: Baker, 1965.

Here is a helpful commentary on the historical background of the epistle. Ramsay has been called an outstanding authority on the background of Paul's travels.

Perkins, William. *A Commentary on Galatians*, ed. G. T. Sheppard (Pilgrim Classic Commentary). NY: Pilgrim, 1989. 615 pp.

This is a reprint of the 1617 edition with some grammatical changes and modernizing of spelling. Perkins was a Puritan scholar (1558-1602) of the Reformed Church of England. This is his last work before death, a good verse by verse study that elucidates much of the epistle. Presaging it are introductory chapters by Sheppard, B. S. Childs and J. H. Augustine.

Ridderbos, H. N. *The Epistle of Paul to the Churches of Galatia* (NIC). Grand Rapids: Eerdmans, 1953.

This is a work more lucid than the more technical commentaries like Betz, Burton, Eadie and Lightfoot. It is good on the English text, with accurate knowledge of the Greek, but Betz, Burton, Dunn, Eadie and Lightfoot are more valuable as are Bruce, Fung, Hendriksen, Longenecker, and MacArthur. Fung has replaced it.

Silva, Moises. *Explorations in Exegetical Method. Galatians as a Test Case*. Grand Rapids: Baker, 1996.

This book, dedicated to the faculty at Westminster Theological Seminary, aims to guide in developing exegetical method. Silva says that he is at work on Galatians for the Baker Exegetical Commentary, and this book is a sort of prolegomena for the larger one (10). It is not for beginners, but advanced students, with firm Greek skill and some awareness of present-day NT study. Silva discusses text, vocabulary, syntax, use of such things as conjunctions, currents in historical study on Galatians (also Acts as it relates), the issue of dating the epistle, and Paul's theological distinctives (use of Hab. 2:4, eschatology in Galatians, and function of the law as in 3:12, 18, 21 (v. 12 last). An epilogue looks at the relation between interpreting a passage and applying it today, how exegesis relates to systematic theology, and the role of the Holy Spirit in the task. The book's 2nd ed. (2001) changed the title to *Interpreting Galatians, Explorations in Exegetical Method*, adding an appendix, "Paul's Use of Scripture."

Stott, John. *The Message of Galatians.* **London: InterVarsity, 1968.**

Here is a short but provocative expository treatment of the text. It is well-suited for the preacher/teacher or the interested layman and highly readable. It is in The Bible Speaks Today series.

Strauss, Lehman. *Galatians and Ephesians,* **NY: Loizeaux, 1957.**

The contribution of this work is mainly in its popular and simple expository method. Strauss, an outstanding Bible conference speaker, expounds the books somewhat like Ironside, but in more detail and with careful homiletical points.

Tenney, Merrill C. *Galatians: Charter of Christian Liberty.* **Grand Rapids: Eerdmans, 1950.**

The author presents a study of the epistle by using different methods of Bible study. It is difficult to find help on any given problem or passage.

Witherington, Ben, III. *Grace in Galatia. A Commentary on Paul's Letter to the Galatians.* **Grand Rapids: Eerdmans, 1998.**

In line with his constant assumption in various NT commentaries that writers use conventions of ancient rhetoric, the author's present outline does this. His vigorous exegetical detail offers much, but is more for scholars and advanced students, whereas many will think it is at times too wordy, not soon enough to the point, and heavy. He explains many of the verses persuasively, on others his brevity leaves questions (1:6-7; 3:17 on chronology), or he looks at only one view (2:1-10 related to Acts 11:27-30, whereas cf. Dunn, for example). But by and large one finds a thorough, competent work that gives rich benefit to more skilled users.

X. EPHESIANS

Abbott, T. K. *A Critical and Exegetical Commentary on the Epistles to the Ephesians and to the Colossians* **(ICC). Edinburgh: T. & T. Clark, 1897.**

From the grammatical and philological standpoint, this is a desirable commentary. However, some of the material is not particularly helpful in unfolding meaning which the expositor can give in a normal presentation. On problems it is generally one of the most helpful for the careful and trained expositor who wants to view different sides to a question.

Arnold, Clinton E. *Power and Magic: The Concept of Power in Ephesians.* **Grand Rapids: Baker, 1992.**

A former student I had the privilege of teaching wrote this, formerly published by Cambridge University Press as Vol. 63 in The Society for New Testament Society, Monograph Series (1991), using the title, *Ephesians: Power and Magic.* The work grew out of a dissertation at the University of Aberdeen (1986). Arnold brings wide research to bear on references and terminology on God's power and the powers of evil in Ephesians (6:12, etc.). His chapters after an introduction are the religious climate of western Asia Minor in the first century A. D., with a power background, then powers in Ephesians (1:15-23; 4:8-10; 3:14, etc.), God's power for believers as in 1:15-23 and 3:14-

21, the warfare with the powers, Ephesians theology in light of such background and implications of proper power for believers. Arhold also wrote Powers of Darkness, Principalities & Powers in Paul's Letters (Downers Grove, IL: IVP, 1992), with much on spiritual warfare, for example points of counsel about dealing with demonic influence (210-17).

Barth, Marcus. *Ephesians*. 2 volumes (Anchor Bible). Garden City, NY: Doubleday, 1974.

Ephesians is held to be by Paul, written from prison in Rome to Gentile Christians of the church at Ephesus. Barth, Professor of New Testament at Basel, has provided a detailed and very highly contributing commentary with footnotes and also bibliographies on each section of the epistle, acquainting the serious student with scholarly work up to 1974.

Bruce, F. F. *The Epistle to the Ephesians*. Old Tappan, NJ: Fleming H. Revell, 1974rp.

A frequently helpful brief commentary that touches on most main issues. One of the better brief works by an evangelical of scholarly stature.

Bruce, F. F. *The Epistles to the Colossians, to Philemon and to the Ephesians* (New International Commentary on the New Testament). Grand Rapids: Eerdmans, 1984. 442 pp.

This is a revision of his work on Colossians when he teamed in 1957 with E. K. Simpson (Ephesians) in the NICNT. It is also a replacement for J. Jac Muller's Philippians and Philemon in the NICNT, the Philemon part of it. Here, Bruce gives a longer introduction to Colossians and often more detail on views, along with footnote additions updating the work. Ephesians is given 170 pages and problems usually dealt with well, certainly with more help than Simpson's effort that was mostly eloquence and little solid content. The Ephesians part differs from Bruce's Revell publication of 1961, 1974. He feels that there is no solid proof that Onesimus was a runaway slave; he may have gone on business and not returned promptly enough (p. 197). Bruce is incisive and careful on many of the problems, furnishing a first-class commentary.

Eadie, John. *Commentary on the Epistle to the Ephesians*. Grand Rapids: Zondervan (n. d.). Reprint of 1883 edition by T. & T. Clark.

Eadie though outdated is good on the Greek text, often deals with problems quite extensively, and has a warm devotional spirit.

Gnilka, J. *Der Epheserbrief*, in Herder's Theologischer Kommentar zum Neuen Testament, Band (Vol. X, No. 2). Freiburg/Vienna: Herder 1971.

Gnilka, in this detailed commentary, views Ephesians as a pseudonymous epistle. His work is one example of higher critical handling of Ephesians. Gnilka's conclusion is by no means necessary. Cf. A. van Roon's *The Authenticity of Ephesians* (Leiden: E. J. Brill, 1974), translated from a theological dissertation at Leiden University under Dr. G. Sevenster in 1969. The conclusion of van Roon (p. 440), after considering various factors in great detail, is: "that it is not only plausible but even probable that Paul was the author of Ephesians." Cf. also Hoehner, below.

Harris, W. Hall III. *The Descent of Christ: Ephesians 4:7-11 and Traditional Hebrew Imagery.* **(Arbeiten zur Geschichte des Antiken Judentums und des Urchristentums), ed. Martin Hengel et al, Vol. 32. Leiden: E. J. Brill, 1996.**

This publishes a Ph. D work at England's University of Sheffield. Background chapters deal with Christ's descent and Moses' ascent to heaven as related to rabbinic and other sources on Ps. 68, then a chapter looks at the Eph. 4 passage. Harris sees Christ's descent as between death and resurrection and offers a history of interpretations favoring some version of such a view until the 20th century when more have seen a first advent descent to the earth, or else a descent in the sense of providing gifts to the church, the second of which he favors. He sees "lower parts of the earth" as lower parts, that is the earth, and Christ as coming later to distribute gifts when He poured out the Spirit as in Acts 2:33. He seeks to relate a descent of Christ in Eph. 4 with Ps. 68:19. Those seeking thorough consideration of the Eph. 4 text in relation to Ps. 68 will find much to weigh.

Hendriksen, William. *Epistle to the Ephesians.* **Grand Rapids: Baker, 1966.**

The works of Hendriksen on Bible books are all worth having. Here, as always, he is scholarly, detailed, and warm in his comments.

Hoehner, Harold W. *Ephesians, An Exegetical Commentary.* **Grand Rapids: Baker, 2002.**

This 930-pp. work costing $54.99 is the most detailed single-volume work on the epistle up to Dec., 2002, when it was issued. Hoehner, Distinguished Professor of NT Studies at Dallas Theological Seminary, also authored *Herod Antipas*, *Chronological Aspects of the Life of Chirst*, and the shorter work on Ephesians in the *Bible Knowledge Commentary*. He defends Paul as author, and the recipients as the Ephesians, both at length and with awareness of different arguments. He grapples with grammar, word study, context, customs, and other hermeneutical factors in thorough discussion of problems. He shows adept awareness of recent, top scholarly works. All in all, this is, as many believe, the fullest serious effort to shine light on the meanings as Hoehner guides readers to wrestle with and think through details to follow Paul's thought.

Hoehner, Harold. "Ephesians," in *Bible Knowledge Commentary***, ed. John F. Walvoord and Roy B. Zuck, Volume II. Wheaton: Victor Books, 1985.**

An outstanding New Testament scholar from Dallas Theological Seminary who gained his Ph. D. at Cambridge University has done this very fine, brief study, packing in much judicious explanation that helps the user. Hoehner is perceptive on problem phrases, as when he interprets "this" (touto) in 2:8 as referring back to the entire phrase involving salvation (p. 624), and when he discusses the "mystery" not being made known to men in Old Testament times "as" it has now been revealed, and gives five arguments for his view (629). He meets other problems head on (cf., for example, "one baptism," 4:5; "lower parts," 4:11; etc.). The section on the armor seems quite well-done. Overall, this is one of the more helpful commentaries if one wants careful explanation even in brevity (pp. 613-45 in double columns), as he ties together things that relate exegetically and doctrinally.

Hughes, R. Kent. *Ephesians: The Mystery of the Body of Christ* **(Preaching the Word). Westchester, IL: Crossway Books/Good News Publishers, 1990. 304 pp.**

Cf. comment under Gospel of Mark. Hughes has a highly readable, practical exposition that is refreshing for any Christian's series of devotions. He not only explains Ephesians competently in a broad, sweeping fashion, but relates it winsomely and vitally to the Christian's life today. It is like an alpine breeze in its spiritually invigorating tone, while keeping true to the text.

Kent, Homer A., Jr. *Ephesians, The Glory of the Church.* **Chicago: Moody, 1971.**

A well-organized, evangelical survey that is good to have laymen read during a series on the book. Kent is aware of main views. and issues in popular exposition of the meaning in an interesting fashion.

Lincoln, Andrew. *Ephesians* **(Word Bible Commentary). Waco, TX: Word Books, 1990.**

This detailed evangelical effort ranks at the top or near the best with Peter O'Brien and H. Hoehner's longer work in overall exegetical explanation. Lincoln shows immense reading, views, reasons, turning of details, summary, and often judicious decisions.

Loane, Marcus L. *Three Letters From Prison. Studies in Ephesians, Colossians and Philemon.* **Waco, TX: Word, 1972.**

The archbishop of Sydney, known also for his work *The Hope of Glory* on Romans 8, comments only on a key passage from each chapter (but does all of Philemon): Ephesians 1:13-14; 2:4-9; 3:14-21; 4:29-32; 5:15-21; 6:10-18; Colossians 1:9, 12-18; 2:8-15; 3:5-11; 4:1-6. What he says is suggestive for popular speaking but covers too little, and will not rank with the better commentaries on the passages.

Lloyd-Jones, D. Martyn. *Expositions on Ephesians.* **8 volumes under their various individual titles. Grand Rapids: Baker, 1972-82.**

These are sermons by the reputed evangelical preacher of London's Westminster Chapel, who died in 1981. They are very choice popular material, competent, perceptive, highly edifying and provocative on key points of faith, as well as helpful in planning sermons or Bible studies. Lloyd-Jones stood staunchly for fundamentals of the Christian faith, and also knew how to help people see the relation of verses to practical living. His volumes cover chapters 1, 2, 3, 4:1-16, 4:17-5:17, 5:18-6:9, 6:10-13, 6:10-20 (this volume goes back and covers vv. 10-13 again but the sermons are new). There are many rich, helpful comments on the husband-wife relationship in 5:21-33. The volume on 6:10-20 is quite instructive on being a good soldier and warring a good warfare.

MacArthur, John. *Ephesians* **(MacArthur New Testament Commentary). Chicago: Moody, 1986. 402 pp.**

The expository focus in the 29 sections is on laying hold of resources in Christ. MacArthur is at his best when explaining details of spiritual life, as he richly does here. Salvation is of grace, without merit of any kind (pp. 11, 23, 61-62). Redemption is seen more clearly in its aspects in 1:7. Comments on the Christian life (3:14-21; chapters 4-6) are instructive and refreshing. The author makes word meanings clear, as "worthy" (*axios* in 4:1), prefers seeing "one baptism" as water baptism, has a good section on gifts and gifted people (4:7-11) and on each believer functioning in his or her role (4:12-16). He points out seven questions to ask in principle in deciding whether to drink wine (pp. 237-44). He develops the Spirit-filled life in much detail (5:18-21), as in a husband's love for his wife and her submission to him (5:21ff.). The section on the armor and prayer are edifying too. It is a lucid exposition, quite full at many points on essential matters, often helpful on problems, though not in great detail.

Martin, Alfred. "Ephesians," in *Wycliffe Bible Commentary*, ed. C. F. Pfeiffer and E. F. Harrison. Chicago: Moody, 1962.

The Dean of the Faculty and Professor of Old Testament Synthesis at Moody Bible Institute prepared this worthy commentary surveying Ephesians. While Martin has meaningful comments on verses usually, he is helpful on problem texts concisely (time of the Spirit sealing, 1:13; etc.). At points he states his view but leaves readers unclear as to his proof (2:8, "this"; 4:4, "one baptism," etc.). Hoehner's shorter work is much better in giving substance to his views in a brief commentary.

Martin, Ralph P. "Ephesians," in *New Bible Commentary Revised*, ed. D. Guthrie et al. Grand Rapids: Eerdmans, 1970.

A concise evangelical summary showing awareness of issues and reasons but not as useful as often as Hoehner's similar brief work.

O'Brien, Peter T. *The Letter to the Ephesians* (Pillar NTC). Grand Rapids: Eerdmans, 1999.

Here is the second best (cf. Hoehner) all-around exegetical work of recent times, and so far, on Ephesians. O'Brien writes clearly, exposes word meaning and grammar, looks carefully at views, gives reasons, argues well, and is helpful on background. Usually his verse-by-verse comments take up the issues rather thoroughly and cover points in the 536 pp. If this writer could choose but two works to do the job, this would be the second work, having the best blend of things, Hoehner's big work being the most contributive, being ponderous and exhaustive.

Paxson, Ruth. *Ephesians: The Wealth, Walk and Warfare of the Christian*. NY: Revell, 1939.

This is one of the richest simple devotional works on the English text. There is much spiritual insight, good outlines suggestive for preaching, and very colorful and refreshing phrases which leave the reader blessed with his unfathomable wealth in Christ. The comments are sprinkled with illustrations which are choice. For the most part it follows the epistle fairly closely, though not verse-by-verse, but the authoress also uses Ephesians as a springboard into lengthy but rich discussions of vital subjects. For example, there is a systematic study of the different aspects of Satanic attack upon the believer in connection with 6:10ff. This work is edifying on the English text and is excellent for laypeople.

Robinson, J. Armitage. *St. Paul's Epistle to the Ephesians: A Revised Text and Translation with Exposition and Notes*. 2nd ed. Grand Rapids: Kregel, 1979rp of 1904 revision. 314 pp.

Some rated this or Westcott as the best older commentary on the Greek text. It is valuable. It has been regarded well since 1904 for its sometimes valuable use of grammar and its exegesis. Other works have replaced its great usefulness by fuller discussions and awareness of later scholarly study on the issues.

Snodgrass, Klyne. *Ephesians* **(NIV Application Commentary). Grand Rapids: Zondervan, 1996.**

One encounters a well-informed survey exposition with, of course, copious help for relevant application. Customs and meaning are articulate as on the Spirit as "seal" and "deposit" in 1:13-14. Snodgrass usually deals, even if briefly, with issues and makes distinct his views among the possibilities, giving some reasoning. Overall the work is among the better medium-range practical expositions, and is high on devotional application.

Sproule, R. C. *Ephesians* **(Focus on the Bible). Geanies House, Fearn, Ross-shire, Scotland: Christian Focus Publications, 1994.**

A brief survey exposition by a well-known Reformation thinker consists of ten chapters, giving a view on some key details, skipping others. Some he does cover are the Holy Spirit (1:17), faith as God's gift (2:8, "that"), prophets in 2:20 are OT prophets, "captives" are Christ's people freed from sin (4:9), etc. Lay people wanting quick, light simplicity will benefit (and profit more in a number of other works), while expositors will also seek works of more discussion.

Stoeckhardt, George. *Commentary on St. Paul's Letter to the Ephesians.* **Translated Martin S. Sommer. St. Louis: Concordia, 1952.**

The author lived in 1842-1913. The introduction of 32 pp. is soundly evangelical and shows a good awareness of critical views up to 1908, the arguments of which he discusses at some length and competently. He defends in detail the Ephesian destination (cf. p. 29). Constantly using Greek phrases, he explains in detail which helps general readers grasp much of the picture. However, some Greek grammar and Latin phrases are not explained for the uninitiated. The author often mentions differing views (cf. "in one body," 2:15, p. 149; "foundation of the apostles ...," 2:20, pp. 152-53 etc.) but supports his own from the context. Sometimes he does not give a second view (cf. "one baptism," 4:4-6, p. 180). But in most verses he offers rather detailed comments that cover the main points with competent awareness theologically and exegetically.

Stott, John R. W. *One People.* **Downers Grove, IL: InterVarsity, 1968.**

Discusses the clergy and the laity according to the New Testament metaphors for the church, the training and service of the laity, and fellowship in the church. It is helpful in relation to Ephesians 4:1-16.

Westcott, B. F. *The Epistle to the Ephesians.* **Grand Rapids: Eerdmans, reprint, 1950.**

Detailed and scholarly, this much respected old work is helpful in grammar and problems on the more technical side. Several commentaries now offer even more help.

XI. PHILIPPIANS

Abbott, T. K. Cf. on Ephesians.

Beare, F. W. *A Commentary on the Epistle to the Philippians* **(Harper's New Testament Commentary). NY: Harper & Row, 1959.**

While this is a liberal work, it has much to offer on explanation of the text because the author wrestles with issues on hard verses.

Bockmuehl, Markus. *The Epistle to the Philippians* **(Black's NTC). Peabody, MA: Hendrickson, 1998.**

This series claims to bring the latest scholarship to a broader readership, students and expositors. The present work is by a lecturer in divinity at Cambridge University. A 46-pp. introduction covers, among its topics, what latest research reflects about religion at Philippi, pagan and Judaism, also a decision favoring the letter's unity versus theories of partition (20-25). Bockmuehl also provides reasons for Rome as the most convincing place of writing. Some of what is said in interaction with top scholars may render the introduction outside a realistic grasp or interest of non-scholars. Comments verse by verse pack in much that clarifies (e. g. faulty preachers in 1:15; 1:19; 2:5-11 with views on the hymn much of which non-scholars may think unnecessary; "perfect" in 3:12, 15; also 4:5; financial terms in 4:15-17, etc.). As a whole this is a very profitable 327-pp. work, even if not among the very best.

Boice, James. *Exposition of Philippians.* **Grand Rapids: Zondervan, 1971. Since then Baker in 2000 republished the book under the title,** *Philippians, An Expositional Commentary.*

A lucid and very readable simple exposition that is helpful and competent on many of the issues. The work is geared more to simple study. The exposition is practical and sermonic, with sometimes good background and comparison with relevant passages from other Scripture. He illustrates heavily from literature, history, and contemporary life.

Bruce, F. F. *Philippians* **(New International Biblical Commentary). Peabody, MA: Hendrickson, 1989. 208 pp.**

This concise but direct and well-informed work by an evangelical giant among commentators was formerly in the *Good News Commentary* (San Francisco: Harper and Row, 1983). It has switched to the NIV, and Bruce before his death brought the citations of literature up to date. It has frequent comments that help, but the pastor or student will no doubt wish to use more detailed works too.

Carson, Donald A. *Basics for Believers. An Exposition of Philippians.* **Grand Rapids: Baker, 1996.**

One finds an articulate, brief pb that gets to the point well on most verses but has to bypass a lot too. It shows Carson's usual good grasp, and is particularly usable for those wanting a reliable but lighter survey—pastors, Bible class teachers, college students, and lay users.

Collange, Jean-Francois. *The Epistle of Saint Paul to the Philippians.* **London: Epworth Press, 1979.**

A highly-praised French work which has seen much use among scholars for its interaction with literature up to its time, also views, and often incisive comments on passages. Its liberal leanings at too many points limit its usefulness among staunch conservatives, yet employed by a mature and discerning student it yields substantial help at points.

Fee, Gordon D. *Paul's Letter to the Philippians* **(NICNT). Grand Rapids: Eerdmans, 1995.**

This effort of 543 pp. with 497 on commentary replaces in the series J. J. Muller's 1955 work which also has Philemon. Fee's study is careful phrase by phrase, usually helpful, yet not as much an assist as O'Brien or Hawthorne, for example. Cf. Fee's shorter 204-pp. *Philippians* in the IVP NTC series, 1999. This longer attempt has a 26-pp. bibliography, and Fee reflects keen awareness of views, as in his careful assessment of efforts to divide the letter into three epistles, and Fee's reasons for unity (21-23). Another help is in giving five theological emphases (46-53). Hermeneutical factors receive attention, matters such as words, grammar, context, setting, customs.

Ferguson, Sinclair. *Let's Study Philippians.* **Carlisle, PA: Banner of Truth Trust, 1997.**

A professor of systematic theology at Philadelphia's Westminster Theological Seminary contributed this 136-pager. It is a catalyst for personal or group Bible study, done in 27 chapters. Study guide material with tips appears on pp. 119-35 for a 13-time series.

Getz, Gene. *A Profile of Christian Maturity. A Study of Philippians with 20th Century Lessons for Your Church.* **Grand Rapids: Zondervan, 1976.**

A provocative catalyst for personal study, application and growth, or group or family use, this is a well-organized little book. Each chapter has several parts: Something to Think About, A Look at Paul's Letters, What Did Paul Say?, What Did Paul Mean?, Application, Life Response, and A Project. Each of the fourteen chapters takes a few verses, dealing briefly and simply with them.

Gnilka, J. *Der Philipper Brief,* **in Herder's Theologischer Kommentar zum Neuen Testament, Band X, Faszikel 3. Freiburg/Vienna: Herder, 1968.**

If one wishes to see a thorough-going redaction-critical approach to Philippians, this 226-page study by a Catholic will be relevant. Gnilka believes that the epistle joins two original letters that were later redacted (1:1-31a, 4:2-7, 10-23, and 3:1b-4:1, 8-9, cf. his introduction). Gnilka. thinks that the epistle originated in Ephesus while Paul was on his third journey. He also includes excursuses on *episkopos* and *diakonos*, "to be with Christ," the hymn in 2:6-11 which he believes to be pre-Pauline and the heresies related to the letter. The commentary is somewhat helpful in acquainting readers with discussions of research by those Gnilka regards as scholarly on various issues in Philippians, but one will not find an awareness of evangelical works here.

Gromacki, Robert G. *Stand United in Joy.* **Grand Rapids, MI: Baker Book House, 1980.**

Gromacki, long the Professor of Bible and Greek and Chairman of Biblical Education at

Cedarville College in Ohio, has written this 197-pp. exposition for the New Testament Studies Commentary. The volume is divided into thirteen chapters and is an ideal tool for adult Bible study or Sunday School curricula. The author has included discussion questions of a relevant nature at the conclusion of each chapter. Gromacki's grasp of Philippians is evident from his thorough treatment of several difficult passages. He devotes an appropriate amount of space to the more difficult issues (e.g., Kenosis in 2:6-8) while not allowing less controversial areas to suffer. He is careful to include all lexical and syntactical information in a transliterated Greek form so that the layman can benefit. Gromacki places Philippians within Paul's first Roman imprisonment (59-61 A. D.). In his introduction, Gromacki also includes a helpful graphic relating Epaphroditus to Philippians and harmonizing other Biblical accounts. A brief work suitable for the layman, pastor or seminary student. - Jan Sattem

Gwyn-Thomas, John. *Rejoice ... Always! Studies in Philippians 4.* **Carlisle, PA: Banner of Truth Trust, 1989. 159 pp.**

A pastor in Cambridge, England, gives messages on the one chapter, explaining verses perceptively and sensitively and relating how they apply today. J. I. Packer commends the book and the author in the introduction, saying that Gwyn-Thomas is a good spiritual shepherd. This reviewer found the book often provocative in an extended series of devotional readings while teaching in Philippians 4.

Hawthorne, Gerald F. *Philippians* **(Word Biblical Commentary). Waco, TX: Word Books, 1983. 232 pp.**

Some rank this as the top commentary on Philippians due to the wide reading and masterfully good survey on introductory questions and its carefulness on grammar, philology, capture of the epistle's flow and handling of difficult passages such as 2:5-11, plus its frequent bibliographical lists that are so current. Cf. Hawthorne's shorter book of 1987 which sums up the detail here (*Philippians*, also Word Books, 118 pp.). In the summation work, he focuses on topics of theology, aiming to help pastors, Sunday school teachers and lay persons in general, Knowledge of Greek will help a reader follow quite a lot of the more thorough work. Hawthorne has indeed provided a wealth of help. He feels that Paul's opponents were Jewish missionaries rather than Judaizing "Christians" as Lightfoot held. He is evangelical, a faculty member at Wheaton College.

Hendriksen, William. *Exposition of Philippians.* **Grand Rapids: Baker, 1961.**

This work is based upon the Greek text but is not technical. It is rich devotionally and has a wealth of good commentary material. It is very helpful on problem passages (example, 3:1-2; 4:1-3), giving different views and coming to a conclusion, often with good reasoning.

Kent, Homer A. Jr. "Philippians," in *Expositor's Bible Commentary*, **Volume II, ed. Frank Gaebelein and J. D. Douglas. Grand Rapids: Zondervan, 1978.**

A writer of many commentaries and a professor and past president at Grace Theological Seminary furnishes a substantial work that comes to grips with most of the issues in a clear evangelical competency. This one ranks high in its frequency of usefulness on views, reasons, etc.

King, Guy. *The Joy Way.* **London: Marshall, Morgan & Scott, 1952.**

This devotional commentary is rich in illustrations and sermonic material. Its style is vivid and interesting. It is a very good book to recommend to a layman and will do the preacher's heart much good! It is so old it may only be available at some school libraries.

Lightfoot, John B. *Commentary on the Epistle of St. Paul to the Philippians.* **Grand Rapids: Zondervan, 1953.**

This 1879 work is outstanding in Greek exegesis and thus is valuable to have. Other commentaries like Carson, Hendriksen, King, Lloyd-Jones, MacArthur, Meyer, Pentecost, Robertson and Rees will have to supply the devotional aspect.

Lightner, Robert. "Philippians," in *Bible Knowledge Commentary*, **ed. John F. Walvoord and Roy B. Zuck, Volume II. Wheaton: Victor Books, 1985.**

An author of many books, this Professor of Systematic Theology at Dallas Theological Seminary contributes a worthy survey that touches contributively on many of the problem verses, taking a stand and giving reasons concisely.

Lloyd-Jones, D. Martyn. *The Life of Joy and The Life of Peace.* **2 volumes on Philippians. Grand Rapids: Baker, 1989. The 2 vols. now are in 1 vol.,** *The Life of Joy and Peace*, **Baker, 1999.**

Typical rich pastoral comments from a master preacher well-known for his *Studies in the Sermon on the Mount* and expositions such as on Romans, Ephesians and 2 Peter. This work has been republished from the British edition of 1989, and gives messages preached at Westminster Chapel in 1947-48. Devotionally it ranks as one of the more capable and refreshing efforts to stimulate pastors and lay readers.

MacArthur, John, Jr. *Philippians* **(MacArthur NTC). Chicago: Moody Press, 2001.**

One discovers a sensitive, adept expositional tracing of joy with pastoral alertness to giving light by which believers can make applications. MacArthur seeks to clarify each phrase. Highlights differ for various readers. Some here are the detailed expositions of 2:13, 3:4-11, 3:12-16, 4:5 (Christ is "near" in sufficiency to help, Ps. 34:18); 4:13; 4:14-19. The work is of special use to pastors, Bible class leaders, students and lay Christians committed to patient absorbing and applying that fosters growth. This is one of the better expositions.

Martin, Ralph P. *Carmen Christi* **(Philippians 2:5-11). Cambridge: University Press, 1967.**

An exhaustive work on various views and thought on the verses based on immensely wide, thorough study. The work will acquaint the reader with various facets of this early Christian hymn and concepts of how it fits into its passage.

Martin, Ralph P. *The Epistle to the Philippians: An Introduction and Commentary* **(Tyndale New Testament Commentary). Grand Rapids: Eerdmans, 1987.**

This is a revision and updating after the 1959 edition by one of America's foremost evangelical New Testament scholars. It is usually insightful on meanings of verses in view of

Greek grammar and exegesis and shows a fairly frequent use of other scholarly literature, critical positions, etc.

Martin, Ralph P. *Commentary on Philippians* (New Century Bible Commentary). Grand Rapids: Eerdmans, 1980.

Here Martin shows more use of critical sources and must be studied with discernment since he has been inclined away from some of his older, some will feel more defensible positions. Conservatives will probably prefer his Tyndale effort for its theological convictions.

Melick, Richard R., Jr. *Philippians, Colossians, Philemon* (New American Commentary). Nashville: Broadman & Holman, 1991.

An evangelical survey exposition, this is usually adequate, but sometimes lacking in giving reasons on introductory and verse by verse issues. At times Melick mentions views, but often does not identify who holds them, as on the problem of how Phil. 2:5-11 relates to the flow of the letter (97-98). In some cases his preference between views is not supported enough, as in deciding that the "perfect" in Phil. 3:15 is used in irony of some who wrongly felt that they were perfect (140). Some issues receive greatly generalized, faint explanations, for example what "the Lord is near" (Phil. 4:5) means, and dealing with prayer so briefly in 4:6-7, or barely noting and fuzzing the string of financial terms in 4:15-17. Overall, the work provides only a fair amount of solid help for serious expositors, and it is a mediocre readable survey for general Christian use.

Meyer, F. B. *Devotional Commentary on Philippians*. Grand Rapids: Kregel, 1979.

One of the famous English devotional writers and spiritual life speakers during the late 19th century and early 20th authored this perceptive and easy-flowing book. Lay persons as well as pastors and Bible teachers looking for a work that speaks to the heart and offers many insights into a deeper maturity in commitments of faith will find this a fresh breath. Meyer is known well for his series on Bible characters – Abraham, Moses, Elijah, etc.

Motyer, J. Alec. *Philippian Studies: The Richness of Christ*. Chicago: InterVarsity, 1966.

A committed British evangelical Christian scholar has done this series of carefully-considered studies on the whole of the book. He deals with problems briefly, but with awareness (those who preach with envy, 1:15; 3:11, etc.), and also says many things that are enriching and highly readable for growing Christians and also stimulating for preachers, teachers, and anyone who speaks on the book. Cf. also his two works on Isaiah.

Motyer, J. Alec. *The Message of Philippians* (Bible Speaks Today). Downers Grove: IVP, 1984. 234 pp.

This work, distinct from his 1966 *Philippian Studies*, is a lucid exposition of twenty-four sections, using the RSV text and a clear outline. Motyer (pronounced Mo-teer) gives good synopses of sections, keeps connections in the flow of thought in view, and deals with verses in an engaging style. He seems sound exegetically, theologically and applicationally. He defines many key Greek words such as those for "citizenship" (p. 93), "walk" (p. 181), etc. and offers an articulate discussion on many of the problems. Many references are footnoted, helping the readability. The work is stimulating for expositors but also for any lay person who wants to use a book with an attractive, simple flow without delving into technical points other works handle.

Muller, Jac. J. *The Epistles of Paul to the Philippians and to Philemon* **(NIC). Grand Rapids: Eerdmans, 1955.**

This is one of the more detailed commentaries that grapples with interpretations of problem verses. It ranks close to Bruce, Hendriksen, Lightfoot, Martin (Tyndale) and Robertson along this line but is not close to Hawthorne, O'Brien, Fee, or Silva.

Mounce, Robert H. "Philippians," in *Wycliffe Bible Commentary***, ed. C. F. Pfeiffer and E. H. Harrison. Chicago: Moody, 1962.**

Another competent, concise study by an evangelical, about as helpful as Lightner's entry, usually substantial on the issues verse by verse. He has had the space to write more at length in his works on Matthew and Revelation.

O'Brien, Peter T. *The Epistle to the Philippians. A Commentary on the Greek Text* **(New International Greek Testament Commentary). Grand Rapids: Eerdmans, 1991.**

O'Brien has the best exegetical work on the letter. He argues well for unity of Philippians, by Paul (9-18), writing from Rome, not Caesarea (19-26). Verse comments show careful grasp and argument reflecting the Greek, and alert immersion in the context and other factors to explain with knowledgeable aptness. A typical example comes in weighing six views to identify the troubling preachers (1:15-17) (102-05). The commentator is thorough and clear on key problem verses (2:6-7; 2:13, etc.), and one comes away confident of seeing a masterful sifting.

Pentecost, J. Dwight. *The Joy of Living***. Grand Rapids: Zondervan, 1974.**

A simple and practical exposition by a fine Bible teacher on the Dallas Seminary faculty. Pentecost explains the book verse by verse and richly relates and illustrates how the truths can apply to daily Christian lives of joy.

Peterman, G. W. *Paul's Gift From Philippi. Conventions of Gift-exchange and Christian Giving***. Cambridge, Eng.: Press Syndicate, University of Cambridge, 1997.**

These 245 pages deal with ancient social reciprocity, giving/receiving in the OT and exra-biblical Jewish writings, also data in Greco-Roman life, partnership, the "thank-you" in Phil. 4:10-20, giving/receiving in other Pauline writings, etc. An appendix, one of three, deals with support of traveling preachers and philosophers. The study revises a doctoral dissertation at King's College, London, 1992, and both text and copious foot-notes show use of much literature.

Rees, Paul S. *The Adequate Man: Studies in Philippians***. London: Marshall, Morgan & Scott, 1958.**

A lucid devotional work, this book follows the thought of the epistle closely and deals with it in a rich sermonic way. There are many choice phrases and fitting illustrations which illumine the text, plus suggestive outlines. The author's central purpose is to show that the believer can live a wholly adequate life, like Paul, by divine resource. This is another recommended book which will be especially enjoyed by laymen in the church. It is usually sound from the standpoint of the Greek.

Rees, Paul S. *The Epistles to the Philippians, Colossians, and Philemon* **(Proclaiming the New Testament). Grand Rapids: Baker, 1964.**

A good attempt at bringing out homiletic points sometimes richly suggestive for preaching.

Robertson, Archibald T. *Paul's Joy in Christ.* **NY: Revell, 1917.**

Though he discusses Philippians in his *Word Pictures*, Robertson here devotes an entire detailed book on the epistle. He is rich in word studies and in the explanation of the text.

Silva, Moises. *Philippians* **(Wycliffe Exegetical Commentary). Chicago: Moody, 1988. 255 pp.**

A high-quality evangelical production, usually with good insights into the Greek and handling of different views in the current literature. Silva's is the first in this conservative, scholarly series that was switched to Baker Book House. On many of the verses Silva is top-notch in perceiving and addressing issues in a clear wording. He sees two groups against Paul, true Jewish Christians holding that grace ideas led Paul too far in freedom from the law (Philippians 1) and Judaizers within the Christian circle (Philippians 3). The theme to Silva is not joy as many say but a steadfast continuance in sanctification, victorious over difficulties. Silva is saturated with a wide sweep of writings and carefully weighs interpretations.

Strauss, Lehman. *Studies in Philippians.* **NY: Loizeaux, 1959.**

A homiletical and lucid exposition with a wealth of helpful practical comments mingled into the explanation.

Thielman, Frank. *Philippians* **(NIV Application Commentary). Grand Rapids: Zondervan, 1995.**

At substantial length (256 pp.), the author offers one more of many works that combine well-studied explanatory details and much to help readers grasp meaningful applications at each stage. Some verses and issues get skipped in general discussions. If part of the great space given to material on relational matters and application were devoted to elucidating the text itself more, space would still remain for much applying. Users would have a more balanced profit.

Walvoord, John F. *Philippians, Triumph in Christ.* **Chicago: Moody, 1971.**

A simple exposition of the book which is readable for the average lay person.

Witherington, Ben, III. *Friendship and Finances in Philippi. The Letter of Paul to the Philippians.* **Valley Forge, PA: Trinity Press International, 1994.**

A scholar and minister continues his prolific output of NT commentaries, one of the better among shorter (here 180 pp.) works. He writes articulately for a general audience — pastors, students, and educated lay users (6), explaining verses briefly with a good thrust toward resolving issues. This bypasses much of the exegesis in longer works, yet comes to the point quickly for quite a readable survey. End notes (139-71) often add key details such as further arguments.

Wuest, Kenneth S. *Philippians in the Greek New Testament*. Grand Rapids: Eerdmans, 1942.

This is one of Wuest's better expositions of a book. He is often sound though simple in the Greek, explaining the text verse by verse and giving helpful word studies. Though he uses the Greek, he does not reproduce it in his book and so his commentary is very helpful even to the Christian who does not know Greek. Again, this is a good book to recommend to laymen as well as useful often for preaching and teaching.

XII. COLOSSIANS

Cf. other Colossians commentaries sometimes combined with epistles above.

Abbott, T. K. Cf. on Ephesians.

Bruce, F. F. Cf. on Ephesians.

Gannett, Alden A. *Christ Preeminent. A Commentary on Colossians.* Grand Rapids: Kregel, 1998.

Here is a warm exposition of 109 pp. on Christ's centrality and relevance for vital living. A long-time Bible college president offers provocative insights for practical applications, using rather frequent illustrations helpful to teachers, pastors, students and others. Gannett was a highly stimulating teacher and godly model in spiritual life at Dallas Theological Seminary, now graduated to heavenly glory. The book is a refreshing survey and a catalyst for a richer walk, as a simple exposition on many key truths.

Garland, David. *Colossians and Philemon* (NIV Application Commentary). Grand Rapids: Zondervan, 1998.

Garland is customarily carefully studied and perceptive about pertinent issues to cover the picture. Here he is sometimes helpful, sometimes not in explaining verses, interacting with views (cf. especially the footnotes), in only some cases giving quite a bit to the expositor or other readers, though much on how the truths apply. A long discussion results in his view that the opponents at Colosse are rival Jews (28-32). He offers fairly brief but firm help on some of the problem verses, as 1:15, and is fuzzy on others (1:23; 2:6, etc.); it also can be hard at times to locate where he deals with specific verses, or to see how little he gives on them. On Philemon, Garland has a brief survey of four views about Onesimus, choosing the runaway slave view. The main help is the application.

Griffith-Thomas, W. H. *Christ Pre-eminent*. Chicago: Moody, 1923.

A former noted Bible teacher, author of many books, did this refreshing focus on Christ in Colossians. He is articulate, sometimes provocative, and usually helpful for edification.

Gromacki, Robert G. *Stand Perfect in Wisdom: An Exposition of Colossians and Philemon*. Grand Rapids: Baker, 1981.

A sound survey that keeps the flow of the books in mind, explains verses fairly well, and deals with some of the problems with insight. This work will be most helpful for lay reading and for Sunday School and Bible class teachers who need a simple, competent study to guide them.

Harris, Murray J. *Colossians and Philemon* **(Exegetical Guide to the Greek New Testament). Grand Rapids: Eerdmans, 1991.**

This is the first of twenty commentaries predicted in this series. Harris, who has the fine commentary on the second letter to the Corinthians and has taught New Testament at Trinity Evangelical Divinity School, helps a person who is beginning to review his Greek to see, paragraph by paragraph, a structural analysis of every phrase and every word and virtually every feature of the message the Greek text conveys. One learns much in the Greek about the two epistles and also gets some homiletical suggestions from a meticulous scholar.

Hendriksen, Wm. *Epistles to Colossians and Philemon.* **Grand Rapids: Baker, 1964.**

See comments on John, Philippians. The same applies here.

Johnson, S. Lewis. "Studies In the Epistle to the Colossians," *Bib. Sac.,* **118 (July-Sept., 1961) to 121 (Oct.-Dec., 1964).**

One of the most contributive discussions of Colossians verse by verse, with help on difficulties and evaluation of different interpretations, written by a former professor at Dallas Seminary who is outstanding as an exegete, expositor, and theologian. Johnson also has taught at Trinity Evangelical Divinity School.

Hughes R. Kent. *Colossians and Philemon: The Supremacy of Christ* **(Preaching the Word). Westchester, IL: Crossway Books/Good News Publishers, 1989. 183 pp.**

The evaluation here is much along the lines of his works on Mark and Ephesians. In vivid strokes he causes the vital message for Christians to be seen, and gives ideas to expositors as well as refreshing any Christians who read it in a devotional series.

Kent, Homer A., Jr. *Treasures of Wisdom: Studies in Colossians & Philemon.* **Grand Rapids: Baker, 1978.**

A clear, brief commentary that is very aware of problem verses such as 1:15 and even provides knowledge from Greek words, context, etc. to resolve them competently. Excellent footnotes from good sources help. The author served several years as President of Grace Theological Seminary and Professor of New Testament.

Lightfoot, John B. *Commentary of the Epistles of St. Paul to the Colossians and Philemon.* **Grand Rapids: Zondervan, 1959. One can find this now in** *Commentaries on Galatians, Philippians, Colossians and Philemon* **Peabody, MA: Hendrickson, 1981.**

Lightfoot is excellent in this 1865 work revised in 1879. His work on Colossians 1:15 ("first-born of every creature") is especially helpful on a problem text. Many regard the commentary as the best older work on the Greek text.

Lohse, Eduard. *Colossians and Philemon* (Hermeneia). Philadelphia: Fortress Press, 1971.

Though expensive, this is a very fine commentary for the teacher who wants an exacting inquiry into the text and possible background, and the benefit of Lohse's wide acquaintance with literature on or related to Colossians. Good use of Jewish and Hellenistic backgrounds, references to Qumran material that Lohse feels relates to thoughts in these epistles, and fine acquaintance with much scholarly work.

Lucas, R. C. *Fullness & Freedom: The Message of Colossians & Philemon* (The Bible Speaks Today series). Downers Grove, IL: IVP, 1980.

The rector of St. Helen's Church, Bishopsgate in London, wrote this work which is not a "commentary" but an accurate, readable exposition keyed to practical life. His fresh style is akin to John R. W. Stott's in the same series (*Only One Way* on Galatians; *God's New Society* on Ephesians, etc.). Lucas is aware of some problems and draws from Lightfoot, E. Lohse and others. While comments on many areas are good, brevity that the series necessitates makes some discussions disappointing, as on 1:15. The introduction to Philemon is good on slavery, yet one is astonished to find less that a page verse by verse. The main message of fullness and freedom beams brightly.

Martin, Ralph P. *Colossians and Philemon* (New Century Bible). Revised ed. Greenwood, SC: Attic Press, 1978. 174 pp.

A work of good competence by a recognized New Testament scholar, one of whose concentrations has been Colossians. He shows awareness of scholarly knowledge about backgrounds, views on problems and defense of his exegesis verse by verse.

Martin, Ralph P. *Colossians. The Church's Lord and the Christian's Liberty. An Expository Commentary with a Present-Day Application*. Grand Rapids: Zondervan, 1973.

Using the RSV text, Martin comments section by section in simple exposition backed by careful study on issues. This is a fine brief work.

O'Brien, Peter T. *Colossians, Philemon* (Word Biblical Commentary). Waco, TX: Word, 1987.

A close and careful study of the Greek text, reflecting familiarity with journal articles, doctrinally satisfying from an evangelical perspective. O'Brien defends Pauline authorship for the letters, notes the existence of 44 different suggestions for the identity of the Colossian heresy before making a cautious and sound suggestion (which offers some help). Faces doctrinally difficult passages and phrases (1:15, 19; 2:11f.) squarely and with generally satisfying results (i.e. affirming Paul's teaching on male headship in the home [3:18] as against modern predilections to the contrary). - Dan Phillips

Patzia, A. G. Cf. on Ephesians.

Peake, A. S. "The Epistle to the Colossians," in *The Expositor's Greek Testament*, Volume 3. Grand Rapids: Eerdmans, 1951.

One of the older, much-used commentaries, which offers considerable help on Greek words, grammar, background etc. and will prove rather contributive, consulted along with newer and longer studies.

Rees, Paul S. Cf. on Philippians.

Robertson, A. T. *Paul and the Intellectuals*. NY: Doubleday, 1928.

This exposition of the epistle comes from the Stone Lectures at Princeton Seminary in 1926. This great grammarian is helpful in the Greek and on the background.

Schweizer, E. *The Letter to the Colossians: A Commentary*. Minneapolis: Augsburg, 1982. 230 pp.

A highly-regarded work translated from the German. It is profitable often in exegesis, setting and discussion of many of the problems with awareness of views and reasons. It is liberal, technical to some degree, and will contribute well to serious students here and there.

Simpson, E. K and F. F. Bruce. *Commentary on the Epistles to the Ephesians and the Colossians* (NIC). Grand Rapids: Eerdmans, 1957.

In the opinion of the reviewer, while the portion on Ephesians is not of great help, the work on Colossians by Bruce is excellent. It is worth the time on almost every verse.

Vaughn, Curtis. "Colossians," in *Expositor's Bible Commentary*, ed. Frank Gaebelein and J. D. Douglas. Grand Rapids: Zondervan, 1978.

Author of several commentaries, Vaughn writes clearly but concisely, giving the reader help on most verses and sometimes good insights on problems. It often is substantial, but compared to longer evangelical works it is not as valuable.

Wright, N. T. *The Epistles of Paul to the Colossians and to Philemon* (Tyndale New Testament Commentary). Grand Rapids: Eerdmans, 1988.

As is typical of this evangelical series, readers are given concise but well thought out comments on verses, some aid on difficult texts with reasons, and clarity.

XIII. FIRST AND SECOND THESSALONIANS

Best, Ernest. *The First and Second Epistles to the Thessalonians* (Harper's New Testament Commentaries). NY: Harper & Row, 1973.

A work with various liberal ideas, yet with much that a more serious and discerning student can find helpful on the detail of the Greek. Among more thorough technical studies this is widely acclaimed to be high on the list. Best acquaints readers with much in scholarly literature of recent years.

Bruce, F. F. *1 and 2 Thessalonians* (Word Biblical Commentary). Waco, TX: Word Books, 1982. 228 pp.

Exegesis of the Greek text. Disappointingly brief and vague in some respects for a series as ambitious as this one. Though taking <u>orge</u> in I Thessalonians 1:10 and 5:9 to mean divine wrath at the end-time, Bruce does not seriously interact with any recent dispensational literature in examining I Thessalonians 4 or 5. In analyzing II Thessalonians 2, the only dispensationalist cited is Kelly (1903), with an allusion to Darby and a dismissal of the school of thought; citation of Walvoord's *Blessed Hope and the Tribulation* in the bibliography, but no interaction. He seems to see I Thessalonians 2:15-16 as a later insertion, presumably by a later anti-Semitic Gentile (pp. 48-51). Bruce is highly-regarded on exegesis and also on his skillful use of current literature. Those with training in Greek will be able to follow technical aspects in the notes and comments. He sees no distinction between "day of the Lord" and "day of Christ" etc., and disagrees with dispensational thinking that the rapture occurs before the "day of the Lord." This was the first work out in the 52-volume series. Also cf. Bruce, "1 and 2 Thessalonians," *New Bible Commentary Revised*, ed. D. Guthrie et al. Grand Rapids: Eerdmans, 1970.- Dan Phillips

Collins, Raymond F., ed. *The Thessalonian Correspondence* (Bibliotheca ephemeridum Theologicarium lovaniensium). Leuven: Leuven University Press and Peeters, 1990.

Collins collected scholarly writings in several languages on many topics pertinent to these two epistles. For inquiry into matters in which teachers in advanced classes tend to be more interested, the contributions vary in their helpfulness.

Constable, Thomas. "I and II Thessalonians," in *Bible Knowledge Commentary*, ed. John F. Walvoord and Roy B. Zuck, Volume II. Wheaton: Victor Books, 1985.

A diligently prepared brief work by an evangelical, who explains profitably verse by verse and comments well on many of the difficult passages. He deals with passages about the rapture and "Day of the Lord" (I Thessalonians 4-5; II Thessalonians 2) in a premillennial, dispensational way. A similar but more detailed effort of this nature is in the commentary by Robert L. Thomas. Constable is quite helpful in giving views, for example in regard to problems in II Thessalonians 2:1-12. He takes the restrainer to be the Holy Spirit.

Hendriksen, William. *First and Second Thessalonians*. Grand Rapids: Baker, 1953.

As usual, the author is detailed, careful in word meanings and background, lucid and warm in application. He always has considerable usefulness for an expositor. '

Hiebert, D. Edmond. *The Thessalonian Epistles*. Chicago: Moody, 1971.

This work by the late Dr. Hiebert, Professor of New Testament, Biblical Seminary, Fresno, California, takes its place among the best on Paul's two eschatological epistles. The author, taking the premillennial, pretribulational view, is not unaware of major interpretive problems, and he fairly presents different sides and then draws his conclusions. Many features make this volume valuable: background information, extensive bibliography up to its day, numerous footnotes, and a rich use of the original Greek.

Hogg, C. F. and W. E. Vine. *The Epistles of Paul the Apostle to the Thessalonians*. London: Alfred Holness, 1914.

A premillennial and dispensational work, this commentary is rich in word meanings and details in the Greek.

Holmes, Michael V. *1 and 2 Thessalonians* **(NIV Application Commentary). Grand Rapids: Zondervan, 1998.**

One finds a capable, brief explanation on many of the main points, often with well-informed exegetical input, plus the series' usual extra focus on ways to apply principles. Sometimes Holmes deals with different views on a problem, as on a man acquiring a wife or else controlling his sexual impulses (I Thess. 4:4), where he argues for the latter (126). He opts out of deciding what the "restrainer" in 2 Thess. 2:7 means, among seven views that he lists (233-34), where it would be better to take a stand. The work rates well among medium-length practical expositions, and will benefit pastors, students, and lay readers, especially on showing the relevancy of points.

Malherbe, Abraham. *The Letters to the Thessalonians* **(Anchor Bible). NY: Doubleday, 2000.**

One comes to one of the best contributive products of detailed exegesis, about 500 pp. of it. The author delves helpfully into most issues and gives much to shine light on meaning in many verses. For teachers, pastors who study deeply, and students this is among the quite worthwhile catalysts for thought.

Marshall, I. Howard. *1 and 2 Thessalonians.* **Grand Rapids, MI: Eerdmans, 1983.**

Marshall, former Professor in New Testament Exegesis at the University of Aberdeen, Scotland, wrote this 240-page volume to update the earlier commentary in this "New Century Bible" series by A. L Moore. The author deals with much of the post-1972 critical literature bearing on these epistles. He builds upon E. Best's work in the Harper's New Testament Commentaries (1973). Marshall's introductory remarks reflect much awareness and are valuable. His conclusions for Pauline authorship and an early date for both epistles meet with the general consensus of conservative scholars. His verse by verse treatment is regrettably brief. Comments on the Greek abound, as do references to recent scholarly works. A tremendous help to the seminarian and pastor. -Jan Sattem

Martyn, D. Michael. *1, 2 Thessalonians* **(New American Commentary). Nashville: Broadman & Holman, 1995.**

In many cases this is capable among briefer exegetical studies verse by verse, with weakness at times on points about prophecy (he sees a post-tribulational rapture, 154-55). The work also is occasionally imbalanced as in assessing I Thessalonians 4:13-18 as "not . . . about the parousia but . . . about grieving for the dead" (143). It is both, together. One will gain frequent, well-studied help in most cases, even some good evaluation of views, and notes with substance from wide investigation. But some will wish for a better habit of reaching a decision, as in Martyn's finally coming to no leaning on the restrainer's identity (2 Thess. 2).

Mayhue, Richard. *First and Second Thessalonians. Triumphs and Trials of a Consecrated Church* **(Focus on the Bible). Geanies House, Fearn, Ross-shire, Scotland: Christian Focus Publications, 1999.**

A one-page outline on each letter and fifteen-page introduction leads into a vigorous, well-studied exposition running to 220 pp. After this, the author attaches study questions. Mayhue uses 33 "overview" sections to offer exegetical, thematic, or theological summaries, fitting facets within Scripture. For example, on the resurrection comments at I Thess. 1:10 sum up 14 points in the Bible about the subject. Among good features in the introduction are summaries of the major themes and the theological importance. Several reasons may support a chosen view (as "possess his own body" by self-controlling sexual purity, I Thess. 4:4). At other times, Mayhue is distinct even if brief on the meaning. In terms of the work's many helps for pastors, students or lay readers, it rates among the best assists among medium-length writings. Cf. also Mayhue's work on Revelation 2-3, etc.

Milligan, George. *The Epistles of Paul to the Thessalonians.* **NY: Macmillan, 1908.**

Some regarded this in its day as the best work on the Greek text. However, it is old, and the works by Best, Bruce, Hendriksen, Hiebert, Hogg and Vine, Marshall, Morris, Thomas and Wanamaker have been more helpful to some.

Morris, Leon. *The Epistles of Paul to the Thessalonians* **(Tyndale New Testament Commentary). Grand Rapids: Eerdmans, 1984. 152 pp. Revision of 1956 and 1959 edition.**

This commentary is abreast of recent scholarship and grapples with most of the issues in a helpful way. It is on the English text but based on study of the Greek text, and is more complete than his shorter work done in the Tyndale Series. The revision is mainly along lines of updating with scholarly literature since the 1950's and a change to the NIV rather than the KJV. He argues for a post-tribulational rapture view in I Thessalonians 4-5, in distinction to Constable, Ryrie, Thomas and Walvoord. It is a good commentary in most respects, helpful to pastors, students and lay people.

Ryrie, Charles C. *The Epistles to the Thessalonians.* **Chicago: Moody, 1959.**

This paperback study is brief but expounds the epistles from the premillennial dispensational viewpoint in a quite clear way. The brevity does not allow the author to grapple in a thorough way with the text so as to support his conclusions solidly on debated matters (examples: I Thessalonians 5:1ff and 2 Thessalonians 1 and 2).

Stott, John R. W. *The Gospel and the End of Time. The Message of 1 and 2 Thessalonians.* **Downers Grove: IVP, 1991. 220 pp.**

Stott is evangelical and has unusual ability to write lucidly and sum up things, informed by good scholarly thinking. As in other expositions (Sermon on the Mount, Romans 5-8, Acts, Galatians, Ephesians, etc.) he has good comments. He is too brief on introductory matters (5 pp. on I Thessalonians and 3 on II Thessalonians), but his commentary is well-organized and articulate. He tends to be general quite often here, without detail on verses. One will be refreshed by the flow of the letters, at least. Stott stops at times to deal with problems, as how Satan hindered Paul's return (2:18), and what "vessel" means in 4:4. He favors the state as God's agent for punishing evil (p. 170). This is not a top commentary, but will serve lay people in a series of readable devotional segments.

Thomas, Robert. "The Thessalonian Epistles," in *Expositor's Bible Commentary*, **ed. Frank Gaebelein. Grand Rapids: Zondervan, 1976-1992.**

Though held to brevity in this series, the Professor of New Testament Literature and

Exegesis at The Master's Seminary offers a careful exegetical study rich in many aspects of the Greek and discussion of main views on problems. From the standpoint of a dispensational perspective on verses related to the Lord's coming this is the best exegetically-based work. As with other works in the above series, Zondervan has put out a pb ed. (*1, 2 Thessalonians, 1, 2 Timothy, and Titus*. Grand Rapids: 1996). The paperbacks make these commentaries available for less cost.

Walvoord, John F. *The Thessalonian Epistles*. Findlay, OH: Dunham, 1955.

Written by the former President of Dallas Theological Seminary, this expository work represents the premillennial dispensational approach in the crucial passages on future things. It is along the popular line and is not exegetically detailed.

Wanamaker, Charles A. *The Epistles to the Thessalonians* (New Testament Greek Text Commentary). Grand Rapids: Eerdmans, 1991. 316 pp.

A fairly recent series offering considerable expertise on details of the Greek, views on interpretive issues, lines of argumentation, and interaction with other scholars. It is evangelical. Wanamaker's effort now has to rate among the top works.

Wolff, Richard. *General Epistles of First and Second Thessalonians*. Wheaton: Tyndale House, 1970.

For a study briefer than many, yet competent, this will be helpful.

XIV. PASTORAL EPISTLES

Barrett, C. K *The Pastoral Epistles in the New English Bible* (New Clarendon Bible). Oxford: The Clarendon Press, 1963.

A worthwhile scholarly study that deals well with many of the verses, although sometimes only briefly. Barrett shows, as usual, a good knowledge of scholarly work in recent years on different views.

Bernard, J. H. *The Pastoral Epistles*. Grand Rapids: Baker, 1980.

Earlier this was published in *The Cambridge Greek Testament* (Cambridge: University, 1922). It is one of the finest older works which grapples seriously with the Greek. Bernard was a fine scholar in his day.

Blaiklock, E. M. *The Pastoral Epistles: A Study Guide Commentary*. Grand Rapids: Zondervan, 1972.

Blaiklock believes in Pauline authorship (cf. also his entry on "Pastoral Epistles," *Zondervan Pictorial Bible Dictionary*). This is a good brief discussion for a quick survey, by a good scholar. He handles some of the problem verses even if very concisely (I Timothy 2:15, etc.), and skips over others (Titus 3:5, etc.). Stimulating questions for discussion are given at the end of each chapter.

Calvin, John. *1, 2 Timothy and Titus* (Crossway Classic Commentaries). Wheaton, IL: Crossway, 1998.

Publishers shortened and brought older writing up to date. One will not go wrong here, but find considerable insight on what verses mean. He will, however, be wise to go to several commentaries which offer even more on exegetical concerns, views, reasons, etc. while being enriched by this perceptive mind.

Dibelius, Martin, and Hans Conzelmann. *The Pastoral Epistles* **(Hermeneia). Translated by Philip Buttolph and Adela Yarbro. Philadelphia: Fortress Press, 1972.**

A technical, critical commentary referring the more advanced student to a plethora of scholarly literature and leading him through various form-critical positions. The writers say the Pastorals are not by Paul. Copious footnotes, as in other Hermeneia volumes, refer to recent literature, and the commentary frequently quotes ancient extra-biblical writings that might relate to the language and ideas in the epistles. For slow technical study the work offers some help, but very little along the line of spiritual stimulation from the emphases of the epistles.

Draper, James T., Jr. *Titus: Patterns for Church Living.* **Wheaton, IL: Tyndale, 1978.**

A 119-pp. evangelical work with popular expositions of a practical character. Draper was pastor of First Baptist, Euless, Texas at the time he wrote this.

Ellicott, Charles J. *A Critical and Grammatical Commentary on the Pastoral Epistles* **with a revised translation. Andover: Warren F. Draper, 1865.**

Though brief, Ellicott is outstanding in the Greek and very helpful.

Fee, Gordon D. *1 and 2 Timothy and Titus* **(New International Biblical Commentary). Peabody, MA: Hendrickson, 1988.**

This is a reworking of his 1984 work in the *Good News Commentary* (San Francisco: Harper and Row). As in his work on I Corinthians, Fee is clear in most cases (not easy to follow when he gets too terse), capable on Greek grammar and local setting, unity and integrity of the books. Each section has a summary. He aims to be of help to teachers, preachers and students. His belief is that Paul authored the books and wrote to meet specific situations in the churches, not to give a manual for the church as some have held. The work has switched from the GNT to the NIV. Fee is evangelical.

Getz, Gene A. *A Profile for a Christian Life-Style. A Study of Titus.* **Grand Rapids: Zondervan, 1978.**

Getz has authored several books on character studies and life-style principles in biblical books. Here again he has much practical helpfulness as he points out traits that believers today can emulate in the enabling of the Spirit. The book is simple, well-organized, and contributive for a leader or any Christian in a devotional series day by day.

Guthrie, Donald. *The Pastoral Epistles* **(Tyndale New Testament Commentary). Grand Rapids: Eerdmans, 1990. Revised edition.**

A recent work, this has a good introduction, but the commentary lacks detail. The author is better known for his three-volume work on New Testament introduction. This book is helpful, especially for an up-to-date conservative answer to critical views concerning introductory matters. The revisions are not extensive since the 1957 edition.

Hendriksen, William. *I and II Timothy and Titus.* **Grand Rapids: Baker, 1957.**

As usual, Hendriksen is detailed and offers much aid in word meanings, possible views which he documents, and full discussion of the passages. His commentary is one of the finer works for serious students.

Hiebert, D. Edmond. *First Timothy, Second Timothy, Titus and Philemon.* **Chicago: Moody Press, 1957, 1958, 1957 respectively.**

These three works in the *Everyman's Bible Commentary* series are fine brief commentaries by a careful conservative scholar. They are helpful on most verses and on certain problems, showing clarity in most cases.

Hughes, R. Kent and Bryan Chapell. *1 and 2 Timothy and Titus* **(Preaching the Word). Wheaton: Crossway Books, 2000.**

Hughes does the Timothys, Chapell Titus, both giving frequently refreshing survey expositions along homiletically useful, applicational lines for pastors, teachers, students, and laity. Illustrations occur often, and solid explanation in between is not always present (cf. I Tim. 2:1-2; and v. 8, the significance of raised hands). On some texts basic explanation is quite good (2:11-15), yet on v. 15 the light hint at a meaning does not give much to go on (cf. also on 4:10, 16, or 2 Tim. 4:8, in the latter a vagueness on the NT "crown" concept). Overall, the treatments help mostly on often choice illustrations and pastoral applications, and this is well worth the time.

Huther, J. E. *Critical and Exegetical Commentary on the Pastoral Epistles.* **H. A. W. Meyer's Commentary on the New Testament. Edinburgh: T. & T. Clark, 1873-85.**

This work, with that of Bernard among older efforts, deals with the Greek text in a thorough manner and offers the student much help. It is one of the more valuable commentaries on the Greek.

Johnson, Luke T. *The First and Second Letters to Timothy* **(Anchor Bible). NY: Doubleday, 2001.**

A highly regarded scholar provides clear results of great industry in older and newer thought. One gains access to much on word study, exegetical details, ways of grasping Paul's meaning, and literature that probes issues. Johnson is confident that Paul was the author. The work is quite worthwhile in opening up many parts of the books.

Kelly, J. N. D. *A Commentary on the Pastoral Epistles* **(Harper's New Testament Commentary). Grand Rapids: Baker, 1981rp. 264pp.**

A thorough explanation which usually deals with problems perceptively and mentions differing views. This is one of the better commentaries of recent decades. Held in high respect by scholars, the effort concludes for authenticity of the epistles and carries on a judicious exegesis while often being quite instructive in reasoning.

Kent, Homer A., Jr. *The Pastoral Epistles.* **Revised edition. Chicago: Moody Press, 1982.**

This is a fairly detailed exposition that usually gives various views on many of the larger interpretive problems and provides reasons for the view favored. Kent uses his own translation. The outline is very clear, and the evangelical exposition is geared for Bible college students, pastors desiring a brief, knowledgeable survey that comes right to the point without being technical, and laymen wanting a commentary that will satisfy them without losing them.

King, Guy. *A Leader Led*. London: Marshall, Morgan & Scott, 1953.

___. *To My Son*. Fort Washington, PA: Christian Literature Crusade, 1944. 1958 reprint.

The two books above are expositional studies of I and II Timothy respectively. They are based on the English text and are outstanding popular treatments with many thoughts provocative for the preacher and the teacher. The very interesting writing style makes them ideal to recommend to laymen. King, a noted spiritual life speaker in his day, has given much rich food for thought here, presenting it simply yet in provocative words.

Kostenberger, Andreas J., T. R. Schreiner, and H. S. Baldwin, eds. *Women in the Church: a Fresh Analysis of I Timothy 2:9-15*. Grand Rapids: Baker, 1995.

Eleven chapters plus two long appendices show scholars probing this text in a thorough, balanced effort to explain it the traditional way and show where they feel other views are not as feasible. The contributors clarify problems, appraise arguments, analyze the verses, and make applications. One appendix deals with the history of interpreting the passage. The writers are the three editors, plus S. M. Bauch, T. David Gordon, Robert Yarbrough, Harold O. J. Brown, and Daniel Doriani. Baldwin's Appendix 2 looks in great detail at *authenteo* ("to teach") in ancient Greek literature. Pages 307-21 list bibliography. Two other works for a traditional view of male headship are: James E. Wordwine, *The Pauline Doctrine of Male Headship, The Apostle vs. Biblical Feminists* (Vancouver, WA: Westminster Institute, 1996), foreword by Geo. W. Knight, III; and Richard Hove, *Equality in Christ. Galatians 3:28 and the Gender Dispute* (Wheaton, IL: Crossway Books, 1999).

Knight, George W., III. *The Pastoral Epistles* (New International Greek Testament Commentary). Grand Rapids: Eerdmans, 1992.

This has to rate near the top in terms of the most frequently helpful evangelical exegetical works that grapple with the meaning at length. It is also quite worthwhile theologically. Knight provides judicious material illumining issues, views, reasons for choices, etc. He is often well-balanced in use of various channels to decide what is taught, and able to weigh matters before the readers. He looks alertly at near context, overall context, grammar, word study, Pauline and other thought in Scripture's unity, and offers much insight. Those seriously studying these letters need to give this work much attention.

Lea, Thomas and Griffin, Hayne Jr. *I, II Timothy, Titus* (New American Commentary). Nashville: Broadman, 1992. 352 pp.

Lea who does the epistles by Timothy is Professor of New Testament, Southwestern Baptist Seminary, Fort Worth. Griffin, writing on Titus, has a Ph. D. in New Testament from King's College, University of Aberdeen, Scotland. The authors give seven arguments for Paul as author of the epistles (23-49). They have good discussions on doctrinal themes, significance of the Pastorals and surveys of each. They follow clear outlines, devote good space to verses, deal with problems in a survey fashion without depth, etc. Sometimes explanations do not go very far to satisfy, as on the law not being made for the righteous in I Timothy 1:9, and on the spiritual status of the two in 1:20. "Husband of one wife" is resolved to mean a one woman man, free of sexual promiscuity and laxity (110), but discussion covers only about two-thirds of a page. The work has a fairly adept survey of views and some of the vital arguments on some texts, such as women being saved through child bearing (2:15), and is disappointingly vague and brief on some, such as Timothy saving himself and others (4:16), the status of the unfaithful in 2 Timothy 2:20, etc. Sometimes it states bare views but does not give arguments to grapple with matters, such as on what "crown of righteousness" means in 2 Timothy 4:8. Excursuses appear at times, as on biblical evidence and Baptist practice on ordination (141-44). Some good explanations and sources in footnotes add to the value.

Litfin, A. Duane. "I and II Timothy and Titus," in *Bible Knowledge Commentary*, ed. John F. Walvoord and Roy B. Zuck. Volume II. Wheaton: Victor Books, 1985.

An evangelical survey championing authorship by Paul and dealing with much of the material in a concisely helpful fashion, assisting at times on problem texts, following a good outline, etc.

MacArthur, John, Jr. *1 Timothy, 2 Timothy, and Titus* (MacArthur NTC). 3 vols. Chicago: Moody Press, 1995-1996.

One of the world's most widely-known pastors gives articulate and rather detailed, basic expositions of verses with arresting illustrations. He deals with word meaning, flow of context, background, and sometimes mentions other views. The works are especially profitable for pastors, students, and lay readers aroused to read about main expositional issues and to grow.

Marshall, I. Howard. *Pastoral Epistles* (ICC). Edinburgh: T. & T. Clark, 1999.

This may be the best technical exegetical work of recent years. Mounce is close, and Knight explains many points with rich diligence. Marshall is much like Cranfield on Romans (also ICC) in looking with clarity at issues, views, and reasons, and sifting things with insight. The work's vigorous effort to understand the meaning is not hindered by Marshall's hedging about Paul being the author, yet even there he covers a lot of bases to help readers be more informed on arguments. The well-organized comments offer much on most verses (cf. on I Tim. 2:1-2, 15; 3:1-12; 4:16; 2 Tim. 1:7, 16-18; 2:1-2; 3:5-6, for examples). Marshall has great skill in pulling together a broad library of learning to furnish insight, yet retain lucidity and come to the point.

Mounce, William D. *Pastoral Epistles* (Word Biblical Commentary). Nashville: Thomas Nelson, 2000.

Here is one of the best three exegetical works in recent years for advanced students and teachers wanting detail (cf. also Marshall and Knight). The 641 big pages, in typical WBC form, provide much detailed grappling with grammar, word study, context, background, customs, etc., while showing helpful sources from voluminous awareness on issues. Mounce is open to Pauline authorship, and usually puts forth solid help by carefully explaining data.

Plummer, Alfred. *The Pastoral Epistles in the Greek New Testament.* **Grand Rapids: Eerdmans, 1964.**

The author is lucid in his statements and has written a fair commentary based upon the Greek. Among older works it is not as helpful as Bernard and Huther, however.

Quinn, Jerome and William C. Wacker. *The First and Second Letters to Timothy* **(Eerdman's Critical Commentary). Grand Rapids: Eerdmans, 2000.**

Massive at 918 pp., this work in its overall help to the advanced may reasonably rate closely behind Marshall, Mounce, and Knight among the efforts of recent exegetical detail. Quinn did the Anchor Bible vol. on Titus (1990), also quite detailed and valuable. Remarks on verses show meticulous attempts to resolve issues and still usually maintain clarity. At times the crux of things is not made obvious, for example the great detail on "endless genealogies" (I Tim. 1) that has no clear composite focus to a point. In some cases users must hunt down the essential thrust of a passage. One finds rich, informative assists on word meaning, issues, and views, and can hardly go wrong consulting this.

Quinn, Jerome D. *The Letter to Titus* **(Anchor Bible). NY: Doubleday, 1990.**

As in 1 and 2 Timothy, published later (cf. above), Quinn ransacks evidence in a 382-pp. effort to deal patiently with exegesis and bring out verse meanings. The work is a benefit in acquainting users with pertinent factors to stir their thinking, or to remind them.

Stott, John R. W. *Guard the Gospel.* **Downers Grove: IVP, 1973.**

An articulate and well-organized exposition of Second Timothy that is very suggestive for messages on the epistle. Though brief, Stott has quite good insight into the meaning of verses and has a rare ability to state truth succinctly.

Towner, Philip H. *1-2 Timothy & Titus* **(IVP NTC). Downers Grove, IL: IVP. 1994.**

Favoring authorship by Paul (30-32), Towner provides a succinct, lucid commentary that sometimes explains verses or parts of them, sometimes ignores things (as "especially those who believe," 4:10; "save both yourself and your hearers," 4:16; or 2 Tim. 4:8, where the words do not really resolve Towner's idea that a faithful life is necessary for receiving a crown, final righteousness, with this being of grace and not earned). Overall, the work seems below average, a mixture of being of some help and of little help, this depending on which verse. It will be of mediocre benefit only to those wanting a cursory, yet easily flowing guide. It grew out of Towner's Ph. D. dissertation under I. Howard Marshall at the University of Aberdeen, Scotland, but does not approach Marshall's usual kind of serious explanation.

Wuest, Kenneth S. *The Pastoral Epistles in the Greek New Testament.* **Grand Rapids: Eerdmans, 1964.**

This work is helpful to the serious student because of its Greek word studies and verse by verse clarity in exposition and frequent application.

XV. PHILEMON

Barth, Markus and Helmut Blanke. *The Letter to Philemon* **(Eerdman's Critical Commentary). Grand Rapids: Eerdmans, 2000.**

A 561-pp. contribution ranks as the best on Philemon in detailed verse by verse information of an exegetical nature going into detail on problems for serious study. Pages 1-103 deal with slavery in NT times in its various facets, 104-142 on literary, biographical and contextual issues. The slavery section of 37 sections has one on "Fugitive Slaves." The user can wish in all the detail for a section on a Christian attitude toward slavery. Comments are quite thorough, for example 11 pp. on v. 1, more than 10 on v. 2, nearly 12 on v. 12, almost 15 on v. 13, etc. Further help is in 23 excursuses on such topics as "House Churches," "Love, Faith, and Faithfulness," and "Legal Options for One's Future." Many will disagree with the view on v. 22 that Paul writes not from Roman imprisonment, but from Ephesus. The writers draw from an awesome panorama of writings enriching their remarks.

Bruce, F. F. Cf. on Ephesians.

Ellis, E. Earle. Cf. on Colossians.

Fitzmyer, Joseph A. *The Letter to Philemon* **(Anchor Bible). NY: Doubleday, 2000.**

As in his pattern of top-level scholarship, the author offers careful exegesis and illuminating research on background as well as probing many of the most relevant issues that students of this epistle need to think about.

Gaebelein, Frank. *Philemon: The Gospel of Emancipation.* **NY: Loizeaux, 1960.**

This is an expository work on Philemon and is good on the English text.

Hendriksen, William. *Epistles to Colossians and Philemon.* **Grand Rapids: Baker, 1964.**

See comments on John, Philippians, etc., on Hendriksen.

Gromacki, Robert G. Cf. on Colossians.

Ironside, H. A. *Charge That to My Account.* **Chicago: Moody, 1931.**

A good practical discussion of the book, with Ironside's usual illustrative richness.

Kent, Homer A., Jr. Cf. on Colossians.

Lightfoot, John B. *St. Paul's Epistles to the Colossians and Philemon.* **Grand Rapids: Zondervan, 1965. Reprint of 1879 work.**

As earlier stated, this work is excellent on Colossians and is also helpful on Philemon in the Greek text.

Lohse, E. Cf. on Colossians.

Lucas, R. C. Cf. on Colossians.

Martin, Ralph P. Cf. on Colossians.

Muller, Jac. J. *The Epistles of Paul to the Philippians and to Philemon* (NIC). Grand Rapids: Zondervan, 1955.

This used to be one of the finer works on Philippians and is also very helpful in Philemon. It is highly desirable.

O'Brien, Peter T. Cf. on Colossians.

Vincent, M. R. *A Critical and Exegetical Commentary on Paul's Epistles to the Philippians and Philemon* (ICC). Edinburgh: T. & T. Clark, 1902.

Obtain this work for a detailed examination of the Greek text with good word studies.

Rees, Paul S. Cf. on Philippians.

XVI. HEBREWS

Altridge, Harold. *The Epistle to the Hebrews* (Hermeneia). Philadelphia: Fortress Press, 1989.

Technical detail abounds, with many informative points made about pertinent scholarship on syntax or background. All in all, this is behind Bruce and, with Lane's 2 vols., near the top in exegetical coverage. Altridge has 14 excursuses scattered in the 437 pp.. In addition to detail in the main body, substantial footnote detail delves into various issues, such as cross-references, commentary literature, writers in church history, etc. Sometimes Altridge is ambiguous, as in stating that those in 6:4-6 are apostates whose rejection leaves them with no hope of repentance, yet describing them in words that seem to denote their past salvation. So he does not clarify whether they have lost salvation once held, or never were genuinely saved. He does say that the writer hopes for better things from his readers. Generalities in the excursus on "rest" (126-28) keep elusive what the "rest" means.

Archer, Gleason L, Jr. *The Epistle to the Hebrews. A Study Manual.* Grand Rapids: Baker, 1957.

Archer aims to provide a well-organized, "handy guide" (p. 1) as a systematic exposition to help a pastor, Bible teacher or English Bible instructor in a college. Taking the central theme, Christ's superiority and its implications for victorious living, Archer follows the progression of the developing theme. He gives a 5-pp. outline at the outset, then writes the book in the form of his detailed outline, filling in verse by verse with key word meanings, related Old Testament passages, and brief help on problem passages such as 6:4-6 and 10:26-39 (he holds that those in view are professors though never genuinely saved). This is a very good brief survey compactly arranged.

Brown, Raymond. *Christ Above All. The Message of Hebrews.* Downers Grove: IVP, 1982.

A principal of Spurgeon's College, London (not the Catholic R. E. Brown who wrote on the Gospel of John) did this in the refreshing *Bible Speaks Today* series, drawing on such greats as Bruce, Hughes and Westcott but keeping the exposition very readable and practical. Possibly Apollos wrote Hebrews in the early eighties. "Rest" in chapter 4 is a future reality on which we need to concentrate, yet is not attained by works but is God's gift (p. 90). Hebrews 6:4-6 and 10:26-31 are taken to refer to those who once had outward signs of being Christians but never were "genuinely born again by God's Spirit" (114). The penitent offender and weak backslider are not in view (cf. 189), yet Brown speaks confusingly of the ones described as if once they really trusted in Christ. This is a stimulating, inviting exposition for laymen or Christian workers who want a book competent but easy to read.

Bruce, F. F. *The Epistle to the Hebrews* (New International Commentary on the New Testament). Grand Rapids: Eerdmans, 1990.

Before his death Bruce updated this outstanding evangelical work since it first appeared in 1964. The introduction does much to bring a reader abreast of the main facets related to the book, Bruce offers good discussion of how the epistle uses the Old Testament Scripture and the harmony with the gospel witness about Jesus (pp. 25-34). The commentary is excellent on detail about most verses, competent in Greek grammar, word study, background, etc. and lucid. It remains the best evangelical work on Hebrews.

Delitzsch, Franz. *Commentary on the Epistle to the Hebrews*. Edinburgh; T. & T. Clark, 1868-1870. 2 volumes.

Though somewhat technical, this work grapples seriously with the Greek text and stimulates thinking on the problems of the epistle. It is good on the Greek.

Demarest, Bruce. *A History of Interpretation of Hebrews 7:1-10 from the Reformation to the Present*. Tubingen: J. C. B. Mohr, 1976.

A 1973 University of Manchester dissertation which, as its title suggests, offers the reader interested in detail a competent account of how the Melchizedekian verses have been explained.

Ellingworth, Paul. *Commentary on Hebrews* (NIGTC). Grand Rapids: Eerdmans, 1993.

For scholars and advanced students, he packs much into this 764-pp. work of complex, almost encyclopedic detail verse by verse. Many pastors and students will become frustrated trying to plod through a maze of comments on verses where Ellingworth leaps into laborious detail without giving a prior adequate synthesis to show the overall progression. One must search to locate where he discusses some verses, and can be bogged down by the hodge-podge piling of comments without clarity to orientate things. Even on problems, the author often seems generalized, not coming right to clear grips with meaning in such texts as 6:4-6, and obscures rather than shining light. For the extremely patient, the work often has a mass of discussion from which many benefits can be sifted, and in listing scholars' sources for studying Hebrews this prolific book rates with Altridge and Lane. It is unfortunate here that so fine a mind has not been too widely user friendly, as works that get more to the point along the way, doing this even with their much detail (Bruce, P. Hughes, etc.).

Greenlee, J. Harold. *An Exegetical Summary of Hebrews*. Dallas, TX: Summer Institute of Linguistics [Wycliffe], 1998.

A 616-pp. work that is somewhat of an encyclopedia word by word/phrase by phrase in defining Greek terms and giving grammar to aid in proper translation of the sense. It is a gold mine for translators, teachers, students, and lay readers (who can glean much due to explanations that are forthright). Greenlee on each verse asks a series of key, probing questions, and his meticulous step by step exegesis elicits answers. On some problems, his answers give more than one view, as on "fall away" (6:6), where options are real Christians (he cites commentators by abbreviations), or those who were not truly Christians (197). The work exhibits painstaking but well-organized analysis, and diligent notations on views that respected scholars take on the various issues.

Gromacki, Robert G. *Stand Bold in Grace. An Exposition of Hebrews.* Woodlands, TX: Kress Christian Publications, 2002.

This is a re-publication of a former Baker Book House effort. Gromacki, Distinguished Prof. of Greek at Cedarville College, now retired, takes the view that "fall away" in 6:4-6 involves the saved who remain saved but live poorly, and the one who draws back to perdition in Chap. 10 never truly had eternal life but faces eternal punishment. Much in the 278 pp. is good exposition informed by keen awareness of what the Greek is saying.

Guthrie, Donald. Hebrews. *An Introduction and Commentary* (Tyndale New Testament Commentary). Grand Rapids: Eerdmans, 1983.

This volume replaces Hewitt's in the series to meet new needs. Though vague, Guthrie apparently favors a date shortly before or after A. D. 70, leaving authorship open. The "rest" in chapter 4 is both present after conversion and future. The discussions of 6:4-6 and 10:26-31 do not appear to arrive at an unequivocal explanation of whether the really saved can actually lose salvation. A clearer taking of some stand would help. However, on many verses Guthrie is clear enough, though this is a concise commentary. I would not rate it near the top but about in the middle.

Guthrie, George H. *Hebrews* (NIV Application Commentary). Grand Rapids: Zondervan, 1998.

One finds a work sensitively informed in Greek and theology, one that rather often explains matters with perception. Guthrie believes that the genuinely saved will persevere, not fall away. Some vagueness attaches to his effort on what "rest" means as his words go all around it yet fall short of clarifying just what it is as "something" and "the whole soteriological process" and "the process of entry into God's presence" (152), whatever that means. Frequent illustrations and application material are a big concern, for example on drawing near to God (4:14-16). The work offers fairly good light on main pertinent issues, usually, and gives remarks to stimulate vital practical living.

Guthrie, George H. *The Structure of Hebrews. A Text-Linguistic Analysis.* Leiden: E. J. Brill, 1994.

Scholars wrestling with the structure find much information in this work that grew out of a Master's thesis at Trinity Evangelical Divinity School and a doctoral dissertation at Southwestern Seminary. Chapter 1 traces the history of views on the structure, 2 categorizes and appraises approaches, 3 Guthrie's method of analysis, etc. Chapter 7 finally offers his own proposal. An expositional outline on p. 117 goes only through 10:25.

Hagner, Donald A. *Hebrews.* 2nd edition. (New International Biblical Commentary). Peabody, MA: Hendrickson, 1990. 296 pp.

This work was originally in the *Good News Commentary* (San Francisco: Harper and

Row, 1983). It is by a professor at Fuller Theological Seminary, evangelical, and fairly helpful at times, but not nearly in the range of Bruce, Ellingworth, Lane, Morris, etc. for explanitory detail.

Hodges, Zane C. "Hebrews," in *Bible Knowledge Commentary*, ed. John F. Walvoord and Roy B. Zuck, Volume II. Wheaton: Victor Books, 1985.

A substantial commentary explaining Hebrews from the non-Lordship salvation viewpoint. Hodges takes passages such as the warnings in chapters 6 and 10 to relate to the saved guarding against failure to gain special reward, not the possibility of mere professors ending up unsaved. As in his commentary on the epistles of John in the BKC, he makes the distinction that the saved who are carnal will be in the kingdom but not possess it, will enter but not inherit, will be there but not be sons, etc. His views are further expounded in four of his books: *The Hungry Inherit* (Portland, OR: Multnomah Press, 1980, 143 pp.), *The Gospel Under Siege* (Dallas: Redencion Viva, 1985, 120 pp.), *Grace in Eclipse* (Dallas: Redencion Viva, 1985, 120 pp.) and *Absolutely Free!* (Grand Rapids: Zondervan, 1989, 238 pp.). Another view, that salvation is entirely of God's grace, a free gift without any works or merit in any way, but manifests its reality in God-enabled fruit of obedience to God, is set forth in John MacArthur, *The Gospel According to Jesus* (Grand Rapids: Zondervan, 1988, 253 pp.). Cf. also an evaluation of the views and a favoring of the latter explanation in Richard P. Belcher, *A Layman's Guide to the Lordship Controversy* (Southbridge, MA: Crowne Publications, Inc., 1990, 123 pp.).

Hughes, Philip E. *A Commentary on the Epistle to the Hebrews*. Grand Rapids: Eerdmans, 1977.

A 623-page evangelical work by visiting Professor of New Testament at Westminster Theological Seminary. This, as his NICNT work on II Corinthians, is very good. He has a lengthy section on authorship, showing good awareness of scholarly discussion, finally leaning slightly to Barnabus over Apollos. He dates Hebrews before A. D. 70. The commentary is very readable and handles verses usually at length, with fine use of Greek (sometimes in lengthy notes). The special notes on problem areas are a help, as are the several Excursus sections on such subjects as Melchizedek, the blood of Jesus and his heavenly priesthood, etc. In a lengthy discussion of 6:4-6, he takes the view that some may prove never to have been truly saved to begin with despite their profession, benefit from contact with blessings, and witness as so-called Christians (pp. 206-22). The commentary is quite full and able to discuss ramifications where many even of the good commentaries are too general for some eager readers.

Hughes, R. Kent. *Hebrews, An Anchor for the Soul* (Preaching the Word). 2 vols. Wheaton, IL: Crossway Books, 1993.

These vols. (557 pp.) are devoted to Charles L. Feinberg, the late Academic Dean of Talbot School of Theology and Prof. of OT. Hughes, once a student there, has 48 messages he preached at College Church, Wheaton, and gives engaging introductions to each, frequent choice quotes and illustrations (both vols. end with long indexes to illustrations), and well-studied exposition. End notes reflect use of exegetical and other sources. Hughes sees those who "fall away" (Heb. 6) as unregenerated, having been Christians in name only. Unlike Gromacki, he refers those who shrink back in chap. 10

to the same ones. The ten messages on faith in Heb. 11 are a vital catalyst to help believers make vital surges forward.

Kent, Homer A., Jr. *The Epistle to the Hebrews: A Commentary*. Grand Rapids: Baker, 1972.

A helpful evangelical commentary especially from the standpoint of clarity on the Greek where this is crucial to the interpretation, without being technical. It is also often helpful in discussing different main views and their support on problem passages (6:4-6, those who fall away; chapter 8, the new covenant, etc.). Dr. Kent served as Dean of the Seminary and also Professor of New Testament and Greek at Grace Theological Seminary.

Kistemaker, Simon J. *Hebrews* (Hendriksen New Testament Commentary). Grand Rapids: Baker, 1984.

The author has been going on with commentaries in the series William Hendriksen began. He writes from an evangelical, reformed perspective, providing diligently studied comments competent in aspects of the Greek, giving views and reasons, writing clearly, explaining most matters well.

Koester, Craig. *Hebrews* (Anchor Bible). New York: Doubleday, 2001.

This is a detailed, 604-pp. exegetical explanation for each section of verses. It gathers many of the factors that can assist in deciding the meaning, but often does not draw a clear, overall picture. In many places, details are highly informative, in others overall resolution is lacking. One can read what "rest" is (268, 278-80), yet be left groping to grasp what it is, and the same in various details about problematic verses in 6:4-6 where clarity is obscured. For example one can have had blessings so fully ("receiving the Spirit into oneself," 6:4), and become apostate, so has such a person lost salvation once possessed? The same attention to bits and pieces, but obtuseness on an overall doctrinal perception pervades the discussion of 10:26-39. Along with much information about certain details, a good survey appears on how Hebrews has been interpreted (19ff), another on the theology of the epistle (96-129), yet leaving a lot unclear.

Lane, William L. *Hebrews. A Call to Commitment* (New International Biblical Commentary). Peabody, MA: Hendrickson, 1988. 184 pp.

Lane, known among other things for his excellent work on Mark (NICNT), has written a fairly good briefer commentary on Hebrews, informed by scholarly awareness of the literature, views and arguments and skill in the Greek text and background. The work uses the NIV and is evangelical.

Lane, William L. *Hebrews*, 2 vols. (Word Biblical Commentary). Waco, TX: Word Books, 1987-1991.

A work that has much to offer in details of the Greek text, exegesis, setting and bibliography. It will help readers be aware of a wealth of scholarly opinion and especially be helpful to teachers, preachers who study deeply, and Bible class leaders who are serious about their preparation. In bibliography it is of a high rating, in commentary not as good as the work by Bruce.

Lightfoot, Neil R. *Jesus Christ Today, A Commentary on the Book of Hebrews.* **Grand Rapids: Baker, 1976.**

An evangelical professor at Abilene Christian College (Texas) wrote this very readable, knowledgeable work, admittedly indebted much to A. B. Bruce, F. F. Bruce, and James Moffatt but also using a long list of other commentaries and literature in reference works and journals. Footnotes are frequent and often of helpful substance, drawn from sources. He concludes as Origen that only God knows who wrote Hebrews, ca. A. D. 65. He leans to the view that the "rest" in Hebrews 4 is future for Christians, that 6:4-6 refers to losing salvation at one time truly possessed, and that baptismal regeneration is correct (p. 122). On most verses he explains very well what most non-specialists but serious readers need to have explained. He uses the RSV.

MacArthur, John F., Jr. *Hebrews* **(MacArthur New Testament Commentary). Chicago: Moody, 1983. 466 pp.**

The forty studies centralize "The Preeminence of Jesus Christ." MacArthur wisely declines to guess the author but dates the book ca. A. D. 65 (p. x), He sees three groups: Hebrews who are truly saved, unsaved Hebrews who are intellectually persuaded but have not genuinely received Christ (2:1-3a; 6:4-6; 10:26ff.), and unsaved Hebrews who are not even convinced (9:14-15, 27-28). He is richly edifying on many passages, such as Christ's priesthood that encourages believers to come to him (4:15-5: 10). The commentary flows lucidly and can stimulate pastors, Bible class teachers and any Christians. The sections on Hebrews 11 (aspects of faith) and 12 (disciplined living) are well-done.

MacDonald, Wm. *The Epistle to the Hebrews: From Ritual to Reality.* **Neptune, NJ: Loizeaux Brothers, 1971.**

A conservative exposition by a recent president of Emmaus Bible School (Plymouth Brethren). MacDonald gives fine-point outlines and explains verse by verse, understanding that the epistle is aimed at true Christians and professing Christians mingled among them. Hebrews 6:4-6 refers to professors who had not really been born again. Comments are brief.

Moffatt, James. *A Critical and Exegetical Commentary on the Epistle to the Hebrews* **(ICC). Edinburgh: T. & T. Clark, 1924.**

Some regard this work rather highly for its exegetical excellence at times in the Greek.

Morgan, G. Campbell. *The Triumphs of Faith: Expositions of Hebrews 11.* **Grand Rapids: Baker, 1973, reprint of 1934 ed.**

Preached expositions with good practical applications running through Hebrews 11. Some errors can agitate readers, e. g. having Moses' birth 64 years after Joseph's death, and the rejection of total depravity (p. 151). However, there is much to edify and to stimulate Christians, even to be suggestive for messages in a great chapter.

Morris, Leon. "Hebrews," in *Expositor's Bible Commentary*, **Volume 12, ed. Frank Gaebelein and J. D. Douglas. Grand Rapids: Zondervan, 1981.**

This is a substantial work (pp. 1-158) by a highly competent and prolific New Testament scholar in the evangelical realm. He is brief, aware of issues and arguments, sums things up well in several cases, and clear. For a shorter commentary this is a worthy effort which will be of service to teachers, preachers, Sunday School teachers and serious lay persons.

Morris, Leon. *Hebrews* **(Bible Study Commentary). Grand Rapids: Zondervan, 1983. 137 pp.**

A well-organized, lucid survey that gives synopses of sections and usually broad comment but dips into many of the verses for serious explanation, views on problems, and reasons. It is primarily of help to lay persons and pastors needing a concise but competent study. Longer, more detailed works ought to be used with it.

Murray, Andrew. *The Holiest of All.* **Westwood, NJ: Revell, 1960.**

One will find rich devotional reading here by an author with keen insight into spiritual truths. Such a work, though it does not deal with textual problems as exegetical books do, has value in that it stimulates the student along many rich lines of spiritual meditation.

Newell, William. *Hebrews Verse by Verse.* **Chicago: Moody, 1947.**

The student will find this a helpful volume on the English text much like Newell's valuable works on Romans and Revelation. Newell was premillennial and dispensational. On Hebrew 6, Newell takes the stance that professors are in view.

Owen, John. *An Exposition of the Epistle to the Hebrews.* **7 Volumes. Grand Rapids: Baker, n. d.**

Kregel in Grand Rapids has a 1-volume abridgement that makes the comments more manageable. Owen, a Puritan scholar, was voluminous on just about everything he wrote, and he did many masterful works. Here, the patient will meet with ponderous discussion of connections between New Testament fulfillments in Christ and Old Testament preparation for Him. Much is rich and worthwhile if one has time to sort through the laborious discussions to follow through to what he can use. Theologically Owen has a lot to contribute. He has many points and sees things from various sides, reasons through views and arguments, and often is very helpful to the person who begins his study early enough to devote the time it takes. In Hebrews 6 and 10, Owen decides reference is to mere professors who fall away or shrink back, never having been actually born again.

Owen, John. *Hebrews: The Epistle of Warning.* **One volume abridgement of his multi-volume set on the book. Grand Rapids: Kregel, 1985. 283 pp.**

Anytime one can get a book by Owen amounting only to 283 pages, he has made an unusual find. M. J. Tyron condensed the commentary yet retained the essence verse by verse. Owen wrestles well with such problem texts as 6:4-6, and on several passages such as this is worth the time. His was one of the great theological minds of the Puritan tradition.

Pentecost, J. Dwight. *Faith that Endures. A Practical Commentary on the Book of Hebrews.* **Grand Rapids: Kregel, 2000. Rev. ed. 1st ed. 1992.**

A beloved teacher, faithful pastor, Bible conference speaker, and writer did these 224 pp. on exposition. Many of the parts help pastors, students and lay people. The writer favors Paul as author (14-20). His perspective is that even in passages about stiff warnings, the saved always are in view (chaps. 6, 10, etc.). Those who draw back to "peridition" (destruction), a word normally of what the unsaved will face, are saved individuals; they remain saved, though they have not endured by a successful faith. They will experience the saving of their souls in an unusual, for some not an acceptable sense, finally, that of being delivered (saved) from the consequences of their wasteful lives (174). Their earlier faith had been validated by their works in the context, but they wind up not finishing well, still saved through grace. The book is lucid and profitable to help Christians see the value of going forward.

Pink, Arthur W. *An Exposition of Hebrews*. 2 volumes. Grand Rapids: Baker, 1963.

This is a rich study of the English text with many suggestive channels of thought which help the student in preparing messages or lessons. Though Pink's earlier writings reveal a dispensational belief, his later works such as this and *An Exposition of the Sermon on the Mount* show a switchover to an amillennial system.

Saphir, Adolph. *Lectures on Hebrews*. 2 volumes. NY: Gospel Publishing House (n.d.).

Careful insight into the text and fine articulation of the meaning by a Hebrew Christian.

Sauer, Erich. *In the Arena of Faith*. Grand Rapids: Eerdmans, 1955.

A fine study of Hebrews 12 with special value for its rich, detailed background behind the athletic terminology ("Let us run . . . ") here and in other New Testament passages. The well-organized material, written in a warming, heart-touching style, is helpful in preparing messages or Bible studies on passages dealing with athletic imagery. It grips the life.

Stibbs, Alan M. *So Great Salvation*. London: Paternoster, 1970.

This is a good book on Hebrews from the standpoint of a capable brief survey that is well-organized and helpful in following the line of thought more quickly (than in Bruce, Delitzsch, etc.)

Thomas, W. H. Griffith. *Let Us Go On*. Grand Rapids: Eerdmans, 1961.

Expositional in nature, this book is often helpful to a degree on the English text. It is devotional in nature.

Trotter, Andrew H., Jr. *Interpreting the Epistle to the Hebrews*. Grand Rapids: Baker, 1997.

Trotter has two sections, background issues and exegesis (vocabulary, grammar, style, and theology). The work is in a series on "Guides to NT Exegesis" for religion majors, seminarians and pastors (many pastors, however, will soon go elsewhere). Trotter offers his own methods and principles as a handbook for interpreting the epistle in ways, he says, sensitive to its genre (diatribe, rhythm, and other rhetorical elements, cf. a list of 15, p. 67). One is exposed to much value with which he can grapple to grasp the Greek. The last chapter, 9, discusses theology such as the doctrine and use of OT scripture (features of this), Christ, eschatology, and sanctification and perseverance as in the warning passages. Some will feel that things Trotter thinks irrelevant do matter, for example whether those who fall away (6:4-6) were genuinely saved or not (219), since if they were saved his remarks about them make it appear they became lost again, and such a matter is very important in one's doctrine, and it is misleading advice to say that such a matter is irrelevant.

Turner, George Allen. *The New and Living Way: An Exposition of the Epistle to the Hebrews*. **Minneapolis: Bethany Fellowship, 1975.**

This work, by a conservative scholar from Asbury Theological Seminary who is Arminian in his theology, offers a good example of a serious effort to explain relevant texts in Hebrews in accordance with the belief that the truly saved can fall away and lose salvation (cf. his comments on such passages as Hebrews 3, 4, 6; cf. N. Lightfoot for similiar thinking). Even if one is not of this conviction, it may be very helpful to see how Turner sets forth his case (cf. also the *Beacon Bible Commentary* for Arminian views).

Westcott, B. F. *The Epistle to the Hebrews*. **London: Macmillan and Company, 1889. Eerdmans reprint, 1950.**

This famous work discusses the Greek text and presents valuable studies on subjects related to it. Many have rated it as the best older commentary from the standpoint of dealing seriously with the Greek, so it offers substantial help.

XVII. JAMES

Adamson, James. *The Epistle of James* **(NICNT). Grand Rapids: Eerdmans, 1976.**

This is one of the very best commentaries because it seriously tackles the issues verse by verse with a good use of the Greek and backgrounds and added detail on certain problems by the use of special excursuses (cf., for example, on anointing with oil and the prayer of a righteous man).

Blue, Ronald. "James," in *Bible Knowledge Commentary*, **ed. John F. Walvoord and Roy B. Zuck. Volume II. Wheaton, IL: Victor Books, 1985.**

Blue offers a clear, concise study, well-organized, with attention given to some of the problem verses. He will not convince many with interpretations such as seeing the "crown" of 1:12 as relating to fullness of life now (p. 821). He does mention the view that reference is to eternal life for all believers, all of them loving God, and cites I John 4:8. He mentions two views on 2:14ff., and is somewhat confusing. In James 5:14-15, he takes the unusual view that reference is to one who has grown weary (weak) morally and spiritually, not to a person with physical illness (834). He seems to see 5:20 as dealing with a saved person who needs restoration, not a professing believer who needs evangelism, yet curiously takes his view despite an admission that the Greek *planethe* ("should wander") "suggests one who has missed his path and is hopelessly lost" (835). Despite some ambiguity, he apparently really holds the former idea. Some will want clarity about what he finally favors. If a saved person (his view), has he "lost" salvation?

Davids, Peter. *Commentary on "James"* **(NIGTC). Grand Rapids: Eerdmans, 1982.**

Davids is former Associate Professor of Biblical Studies at Trinity Episcopal School for Ministry in Ambridge, PA. He has done one of the finest recent critical works on James geared to be helpful to those who study the Greek text, showing a good grasp of technical points, critical matters, and old and new literature in English, German and French (a very long list). Davids writes in a style that often refreshes, and not only provides a verse by verse commentary that shows great awareness of literature and facets important to explain the text but in a special section develops seven themes of theology. These are suffering or testing, eschatology, Christ, poverty/piety, the law-grace-faith relationship ("Grace which has no outward result is not grace at all," p. 50), wisdom, and prayer. He did his Ph.D. thesis in 1974, "Themes in the Epistle of James that are Judaistic in Character" at Manchester. Davids favors an early date (between A. D. 40 and the Jerusalem Council) by James the Just, brother of Jesus. Paul and James are essentially consistent with one another even if they have different emphases (pp. 50-51, 119-134).

Dibelius, M. and Greven, H. *James: A Commentary on the Epistle of James* (Hermeneia). 11th revised edition. Philadelphia: Fortress Press, 1976. 285 pp.

This is the English production of the German edition, *Der Brief des Jakobus* (1964). Abreast of much liberal scholarly thought, it is informative here as well as on research that elucidates the text. Dibelius was for thirty-two years Professor of the University of Heidelberg, Germany. Greven has updated the exhaustive bibliography and revised the commentary for the English. A long introduction (1-61) shows very instructive use of scholarly literature, with many notes. Dibelius reasons that the letter is pseudonymous, having attached the claim that James wrote it (1:1). He defends this as involving no fraudulent effort to deceive, saying it was a literary custom of that day (cf. 18-20, 65). Many will not be able to justify such reasoning. The date, as he sees it, is around A. D. 80-130 (45). He construes "twelve tribes" (1:1) as metaphorical, not denoting Jewish people per se but "the true Israel", in his mind Christians whatever their racial tie, who are scattered away from their true home, heaven (66). He says that 1:12 (crown of life, etc.) is an isolated saying separated from what precedes it in the text (71). That may persuade some but will not satisfy others. His discussion of 2:14-26 is too often reasoned in such a manner that it is not easy to follow the logic, and perhaps only the extremely serious and skilled or patient will stay with it.

Greenlee, J. Harold. *An Exegetical Summary of James*. Dallas, TX: Summer Institute of Linguistics, Inc., 1993.

Greenlee uses about 20 commentaries plus lexical aids and translations (7-9) to compile a verse by verse study of word meaning, grammatical relationship, and the answering of key questions. This process results in exposing most main points. Greenlee also gives views on problems, citing which scholars favor each. As seen in 2:14-26, this provides much analysis for translators, while being useful to pastors, church teachers, and students. But it does not conclude on all the meanings or applications that expositors should responsibly make.

Hiebert, D. E. *The Epistle of James: Tests of a Living Faith*. Chicago: Moody, 1979. 354 pp.

A lucid evangelical work that looks at every verse, discussing exegetical matters, views, supports, and the relevance to a practical spiritual life. The work delves into many of the issues in a knowledgeable manner and will be of value to teachers to some extent and to expositors, students and lay persons who want a fairly detailed but readable commentary.

Hodges, Zane C. *The Epistle of James. Proven Character Through Testing.* Irving, TX: Grace Evangelical Society, 1994.

Hodges' 128-pp. pb has a brief introduction (7-16), then six chapters explaining James verse by verse, each chapter entitled by an exhortation, such as "Respond to Trials Properly" (1:1-18). To him the threefold admonition in 1:19 is the structural key for 1:21—3:6. He takes what has been called a "non-Lordship" view that those who have eternal life by grace may lose faith and not persevere in good works, but the eternal salvation remains intact; lack of works do not reflect on professing believers possibly not having genuinely received life as a gift. In 1:12, "crown" is probably a present enrichment of life experience as Job had in Job 42. In 2:14-26, only the saved are in view, so the faith that is dead without works is an "ineffectual, unproductive faith" of the saved (63). Many good comments mingle with views on some key texts that many interpreters will not accept as exegetically or theologically the most defensible. One can see more of Hodges' viewpoints in commentaries on Hebrews and the Johannine Epistles in the *Bible Knowledge Commentary*, Vol. II, as well as in his books *The Hungry Inherit, The Gospel Under Siege, Grace in Eclipse*, and *Absolutely Free*!

Johnson, L. T. *The Letter of James* (Anchor Bible). New York: Doubleday, 1995.

This is a thorough introduction and exegetical investigation. It deals with some matters in detail, for instance 2:14-26 and 5:12-20 (he sees physical sickness in v. 14), and is briefly general on others, e. g. "crown" in 1:12 and how the necessity of faithfulness to gain this eternal life is in harmony with life as God's gift in grace. The commentary rates as one among several earnest works on detail, and furnishes users with more studious knowledge of Greek good help at a number of points.

Kent, Homer A., Jr. *Faith that Works, Studies in the Epistle of James.* Grand Rapids: Baker, 1986. 203 pp.

A writer of many commentaries and long-time faculty member at Grace Theological Seminary did this evangelical survey. Kent keeps summaries of the argument in view, shows connections between sections, deals helpfully with most verses, and is forthright in dealing with problems and stating reasons. This is a good, clear exposition that will assist preachers in places, and help Bible class teachers, Sunday School teachers and lay persons in general as in a series of Bible readings.

King, Guy. *A Belief that Behaves.* 6th edition. London: Marshall, Morgan & Scott, 1941. Distributed in United States by Christian Literature Crusade, Fort Washington, PA.

This is a practical, expository development of James with creative chapter titles, illustrations and many other sermonic hints. King was a lucid writer and has given the reader much to think about in this provocative book based on the English. It is one of the more simple and stimulating works to recommend to the layman and is good for the preacher or teacher's heart.

Kistemaker, Simon J. *James and I-III John* (Hendriksen New Testament Commentary). Grand Rapids: Baker, 1986. 425 pp.

This continues the Hendriksen commentary began in 1953. Hendriksen died in the early

1980's. Using the NIV text, Kistemaker explains passages in scholarly competence and makes practical comments that are also usable to a pastor or any Christian. He makes things fairly clear in many cases but not with a constant citation of Greek or technical matters that some commentaries take up. He also does not show the relationship between sections as some do. Cf. also in I Peter. In 1995, Baker combined two separate works, James-III John (1986) and Peter and Jude (1987) in *Exposition of James, Epistles of John, Peter, and Jude* in one thick vol. containing 425 and 443 pp.

Laws, Sophie. *The Epistle of James* (Harper's NTC). New York: Harper, 1980. 273 pp.

A lecturer in New Testament at King's College, University of London, gives a 43 page introduction, then about 200-page translation and commentary. She decides that the epistle was not by James of Jerusalem but one using the honored name as a pseudonym after the death of James in A. D. 62 (41-42). She puts 1:12 (trial and crown) with verses 13-18 rather than with verses 2-11 on trials. The crown is eternal life itself (68). Many verses are explained rather fully and capably, out of a wide grasp of things. Some will feel that she fails to set things in a totally fair balance in making unnecessary leaps from supposed differences between Paul in Romans 4 and James 2:14-26 (131-134). She has much of value, however, as in saying that what James means to contrast "is 'faith without works' and 'works inseparable from faith'" (13). On many matters the pertinent, clear and extended comments make this one of the most contributive commentaries on the epistle.

MacArthur, John, Jr. *James* (MacArthur NTC). Chicago: Moody Press, 1998.

Twenty-two messages represent pastoral exposition, feeding a flock. MacArthur sees tests of genuine, saving faith. With most interpreters, he takes "crown" (1:12) as eternal life for every true believer, given through grace and shown real in a grace-enabled life that perseveres (42). Similarly in 2:14-26 he sees the gift of genuine, saving faith as issuing in good works, but a pseudo and merely professed faith as that of a person not really saved. He compares this with Matt. 7:21-23. Often illustrations join the exposition. MacArthur views "sick" in 5:14 as not physical illness, which he does not regard as fitting the context, but being emotionally/spiritually ill, down due to suffering evil treatment. Yet he acknowledges that the anointing oil may be for physical wounds from persecution, yet also metaphorical for elders' refreshing stimulation (278).

Martin, Ralph P. *James* (Word Biblical Commentary). Waco, TX: Word Books, 1988. 240 pp.

This work by a moderate evangelical shows broad awareness of scholarly opinions and lines of argument. This is true in the introduction and in the verse by verse commentary. Martin shows expertise in Greek details, relationships to other Scripture, and bibliography. Douglas Stuart may not be overrating it by calling it "the best longer work on James" (*A Guide to Selecting and Using Bible Commentaries*. Dallas: Word, 1990, p. 126). Adams, Davids, Hiebert, Johnson, Mayor, Mitton, and Laws also appear often helpful in a straight-forward way.

Mayor, Joseph B. *The Epistle of James*. 3rd edition. Grand Rapids: Kregel, 1990rp. 621 pp.

First issued in 1892, this commentary of more than 600 pages gives the reader almost 300 pages in introductory explorations about the identity of the writer James, the date (he says near the end of the A. D. 40's), the relations to other New Testament books, grammar and style, etc. It is a work of towering scholarship and exhaustive detail. From the standpoint of the Greek text it is the best older and one of the best at any time on James.

This is a reprint of the 1910 edition with a 2-page Foreword by Cyril J. Barber, who wrote *The Minister's Library*. The massive 291-page introduction is a gold mine on facets in the study of the book. One learns much from Mayor's skillful assembling of relevant data on issues and verses, and he is rich in Scripture. Highly-regarded, it stands as one of the most helpful works on exegesis, views, arguments etc. even though not up to date today on scholarly works. Mayor died in 1916. Baker also has a 1978 reprint (460 pp.), and Zondervan had a 1954 publication (291 + 264 pp.).

Mitton, C. Leslie. *The Epistle of James*. Grand Rapids: Eerdmans, 1966.

This work by a more fairly English scholar is in the Evangelical Bible Commentary series. The author is lucid, thorough, helpful on problems, and lists different viewpoints on debated matters.

Moo, Douglas J. *The Letter of James* (Pillar NTC). Grand Rapids: Eerdmans, 2000.

Moo in this exegetical study is longer (271 pp.) than his earlier effort in this list. He argues for authorship by James, the Lord's brother (20-22), discusses seven areas of theology (27-43), and argues that in James faith of those God has freely justified expresses its reality in obeying God (38, etc.), as Paul held in "faith working through love" (Gal. 5:6). Clear exposition is thought out well, and sometimes Moo grapples with views and problems (not all, cf. "crown," 1:12, and Hodges). In 2:14 he distinctly counters Hodges (123-24), and again at 2:18, 26 (128-29, 143). His detail on 2:14-26 is fairly helpful; he also is diligent with "spirit" in 4:5, and "sick" in 5:14. Among medium-length works, this is one of the best in recent years.

Moo, Douglas J. *The Letter of James: An Introduction and Commentary* (Tyndale New Testament Commentary). Downers Grove: IVP, 1985. 191 pp.

Eerdmans published the same commentary in 1989. It is a concise, conservative, clear work adept in exegetical details from careful research by a member of the New Testament faculty at Trinity Evangelical Divinity School. It is helpful especially for teachers and preachers. Moo, who did the massive 2-volume work on Romans, also wrote "James" in *The Evangelical Commentary on the Bible*, ed. W. A. Elwell (Grand Rapids: Baker, 1989).

Motyer, J. Alec. *The Tests of Faith. The Message of James* (Bible Speaks Today). Downers Grove: IVP, 1985. 214 pp.

Motyer (pronounced Mo-teer) attempts, with much lucid, unifying helpfulness, to show a tie-in between sections of James. He sees three keys in 1:26, 27: a controlled tongue, a compassion for those in need and helpless, and purity from worldly defilement. He sees the compassion developed in chapter 2, the tongue in chapter 3, and the purity in 4:1-5:6. James commences and ends with perseverance and prayer. The book is an asset on suggestive aspects of unity in carrying out themes.

Nystrom, David P. *James* (NIV Application Commentary). Grand Rapids: Zondervan, 1997.

Nystrom shows wide conversance with the literature (cf. footnotes), a good annotated bibliography, usually adequate survey comments on sections, and, as the series designs, a plethora of ways to put the teaching into "shoe leather." He has good judgment as in taking "the crown of life" in 1:12 as the crown that is eternal life, the inheritance all Christians will receive (72). In 2:14-26, he argues with most in seeing a genuine faith when spiritually saved; such reality issues in proper works, reflects that eternal life is present, and also leads on to it in its final blessedness. "Deeds are not something extra to be added to faith; they are a necessary constituent part of the faith" (149-50). Nystrom concludes bodily illness in 5:14. Overall, this exposition usually is reliable to offer good light on verses.

Reicke, Bo. *The Epistles of James, Peter and Jude* (The Anchor Bible). NY: Doubleday, 1964.

A reputed scholar from the University of Basel did this work favoring dating I Peter in the 60's, and the other three epistles in the 90's. James, brother of Jesus, did not actually write "James", he feels. He sees expressions in the epistles which remind him of Qumran ideas, and in James sayings very close to Jesus' sayings as preserved in the Gospels. The actual verse by verse commentary often is quite helpful as to perspective but frequently very sparse and generalized on verses so that the reader looking for detail on word meanings or views has to go to Adamson, Davids, Martin, Mayor, Mitton, and others to find help. Some sections (e. g. James 1:19-27) are treated in a somewhat general discussion, though individual verses are worked in briefly. Only 4 pages are devoted to James 2, about 4 1/2 to chapter 3, etc. Commentary on the other epistles likewise is brief (this is unfortunate), though at times offering quite helpful comments.

Richardson, Kurt A. *James* (New American Commentary). Nashville: Broadman & Holman, 1997.

A good introduction is followed by clarity about most verses in a fair exposition. Some Greek words are dealt with, even if lightly, for example "trials" in 1:2, but others are not, as in "many kinds" of trials in 1:2. The author devotes good discussion to some verses, others lack reasonable coverage. Overall, the work is often a fair survey, and too often does not explain things much beyond this. This reviewer feels that the book misses a proper balance at times, as in saying on 2:14ff that James comments on "The nature of faith, not on the question of salvation in the end" (127). Why not acknowledge both as related as they are?

Robertson, A. T. *Studies in the Epistle of James*. Nashville: Broadman, 1959.

Here is another work helpful in the Greek text, not outstanding on detail.

Ropes, J. H. *A Critical and Exegetical Commentary on the Epistle of St. James* (ICC). Edinburgh: T. & T. Clark, 1916. 319 pp.

In this liberal technical work, Ropes decides that the author was not James the Lord's brother but a teacher in Palestine between A. D. 75 and 125 (49). He devotes pp. 1-115 to introduction. His work is one of the better older ones on details of the Greek text and at times has fairly good input on what a phrase means, such as "the crown of life" in 1:12

(150-52). But Ropes fails to explain how reward as a crown, eternal life, is consistent with eternal life being entirely God's gift, not by works. At a number of points he is rather flat when he might be clearer.

Strauss, Lehman. *James Your Brother*. NY: Loizeaux, 1956.

Good on preaching material, evangelical and expositional.

Stulac, George M. *James* (IVP NTC). Downers Grove, IL: IVP, 1993.

A Presbyterian pastor provides a clear, refreshing survey that shows often how to apply truth. This is one of the top three or four popular expositions, though teachers, pastors and students can need more grappling with details to bolster discussions, as in R. Martin, J. B. Mayor, P. Davids, J. Adamson, R. C. H. Lenski, etc. At times, Stulac's work gets fairly detailed on views and arguments, as in 4:5. In 5:14-16 physical illness may also involve sin.

Wolff, Richard. *The General Epistles of James and Jude*. Wheaton: Tyndale House, 1969.

The author explains the books very well in a brief way. Often he is quite helpful on citations from Jewish sources or other early channels. For concise discussion that is usually to the mark, this is one of the best shorter commentaries on the books in recent times.

Zodhiates, Spiros. *The Epistle of James and the Life of Faith*. 3 volumes. Grand Rapids: Eerdmans, 1959-60.

Valuable mainly for good illustrations and its other choice sermonic material, this work is authored by a Greek who has been greatly used in soul-winning in Greece. It combines a thorough study of the text with a warmth in presentation, including many practical questions. It is one of the most enjoyable detailed works to read on James, and is of great value to the pastor.

XVIII. FIRST PETER

Abernathy, C. David. *An Exegetical Summary of I Peter*. Dallas, TX: Summer Institute of Linguistics, Inc., 1998.

As Greenlee has done on Hebrews, this is a laying out of exegetical details verse by verse. So it offers much on word meaning, grammatical relationship to help in proper translation, and sometimes different views possible on interpretive problems. It has value for teachers, pastors, students, and any Christian reader seriously prepared to go into some study depth.

Achtemeier, Paul J. *I Peter* (Hermeneia). Philadelphia: Fortress Press, 1996.

The commentary provides much on exegetical details such as grammar, word meaning, views, reasons, and selected points from very wide reading in the history of interpreting the epistle (these often in footnotes which are copious and at times rather lengthy). Among specialists, and especially in the field of NT scholarly inquiry, the work is regarded as one of the best of a technical nature. Many expositors may want to use it to some degree, but consult the many works that come to points helpful for exposition with a better flow without the minute detail, often on challenges of great interest only to those in an elite circle. Many will think misguided Achtemeier's reasons against the Apostle Peter being the writer, and also his seeking to make it appear good for a student long ago to ascribe a writing to a respected figure. If biblical books are to be credited with integrity in claims to giving truth, why not be truthful on a basic, the claim of authorship also? (cf. his pp. 39-43).

Barbieri, Louis. *First and Second Peter.* Chicago: Moody, 1977.

A 126-pp., brief exposition by a former professor of Bible at Dallas Seminary. Barbieri surveys with some reference to historical setting and awareness of Greek, dealing concisely with certain of the problem passages. The work is geared for devotional reading or a quick summation for lay Bible studies.

Beare, F. W. *The First Epistle of Peter. The Greek Text.* Oxford: Blackwell, 1969.

This is a liberal scholarly work offering some help for more skilled in-depth users. It mingles some contributions along practical lines. Beare shows broad awareness of issues and views gained by laborious study. He is against authorship by Peter, and argues for a late date.

Best, Ernest. *I Peter* (New Century Bible Commentary). Grand Rapids: Eerdmans, 1982rp of 1971 ed. 188 pp.

Best taught at the universities of St. Andrews and Glasgow, retiring in 1982. He concludes that Peter did not write the letter but that it came from pseudonymous authorship in the Petrine school (p. 63) between A. D. 80-100 (64) from Rome (65). Best has stimulating remarks on many verses, e. g. 1:5; 2:2, 3. His systematic and somewhat detailed comments on 3:19 conclude that Christ went prior to His resurrection to preach to angelic spirits in their prison a message of salvation which they possibly rejected (or else the passage is not clear as to the result), linking the text with bound angels in II Peter 2:4; Jude 6 and I Enoch. 10ff. This is at many points a good commentary even though rather brief in many instances. Many will not be able to follow his preferred view and defense of it on 4:6: Christ offered the Gospel to those after their deaths who had physically died prior to His death, who never had the opportunity to hear it when they were alive. For that adds up to a "second chance," and Best's answers to objections appear to be rather lame.

Bigg, Charles. *A Critical and Exegetical Commentary on the Epistles of St. Peter and St. Jude* (ICC). London: T. & T. Clark, 1901. Reprint 1961.

This is probably the second best older study on I Peter from the standpoint of the Greek text. Selwyn is the other. As other ICC works, it deals with details of philology, grammar and possible views on problems.

Blum, Edwin. "I and II Peter," in *Expositor's Bible Commentary*, Volume 12, ed. Frank Gaebelein. Grand Rapids: Zondervan, 1981.

A perceptive evangelical work by a good scholar who offers help on problem verses and explains much of the material in a worthy way.

Cranfield, C. E. B. *First Epistle of Peter.* London: SCM Press, 1950.

Cranfield is an outstanding exegete and offers comments of a critical, exegetical nature that are concise but helpful. One could wish so great a master had said more detail, as he does on Romans.

Davids, Peter H. *The First Epistle of Peter* (NICNT). Grand Rapids: Eerdmans, 1990.

Davids is known for his fine commentary on James. Here he has a 42-page introduction that reviews issues in an evangelical manner and discusses scholarly literature. A 266-page commentary follows, in which he capably handles the Greek and deals with the different views on problem passages.

Elliott, John H. *I Peter* (Anchor Bible). New York: Doubleday, 2000.

A massive production of 956 large pp., this has the typical AB minute detail on introductory issues (much of its 150 pp. on questions a smaller group, some scholars, pursue), then a book length on a vast bibliography (155-304), a translation, a commentary, and indexes of subjects and ancient writings. Elliott in 1966 published *The Elect and the Holy* (E. J. Brill) on the temple analogies in I Peter 2, later other books (cf. xiii). In detailed study for teaching the advanced, readers will glean much and often, but they must devote much time for sifting since a lot of seemingly superfluous matter slows the process. On I Peter 3:18-22 alone, pp. 637-710 are devoted, even with a long layout of views in history variously interpreting when and what Christ preached. Elliott says that Christ's going was in the course of His ascension, at which time He confirmed the condemnation of those who disobeyed prior to the Noahic flood (cf. 650-51, etc.). Grudem and others have a good discussion of views and issues on this as well.

Grudem, Wayne A. *I Peter* (Tyndale New Testament Commentary). Grand Rapids: Eerdmans, 1988. 239 pp.

An evangelical work which is at many points a good one, informative about views and helpful in the Greek. He holds to double predestination in 2:8, and says that God destined the stumbling and disobedience of the unsaved (p. 106). At 3:19-20, he believes the spirits in prison are unsaved humans of Noah's day, who are now in prison. He has a special appendix going into the "spirits" passage at some length. His work replaces the former contribution by A. M. Stibbs and Andrew Walls. He favors traditional conservative views or, in the "spirits" case, his 36-page discussion takes one of the conservative options.

Hiebert, D. E. *First Peter*. Chicago: Moody, 1984. 329 pp.

This book prints expositions from his series in *Bibliotheca Sacra* and *Studia Missionalia*. As in James, Heibert is vigorous in seeking to explain verses and sections, discuss views with an awareness of scholarly work, and use the Greek competently. It is a fairly good evangelical product.

Kelly, J. N. D. *A Commentary on the Epistles of Peter and of Jude* (Harper's New Testament Commentary). NY: Harper and Row, 1969. Grand Rapids: Baker, 1981rp. 387 pp.

This is one of the better commentaries for the serious student. Kelly shows good scholarship and insight, and usually is helpful on problems. He has taught at Oxford University. He posits a date of A. D. 64 for I Peter but is not firm on authorship by Peter. He feels that Peter did not author II Peter, but that it was written later (ca. 100-110). But he is excellent in exegesis of the text and grappling with issues and views. On many verses he has a lot to contribute.

Kistemaker, Simon J. *Peter and Jude* **(Hendriksen New Testament Commentary). Grand Rapids: Baker, 1987. 441 pp.**

A careful evangelical scholar in the reformed tradition carries on the Hendriksen series with good attention to exegesis, views, arguments and some practical application. It is quite readable for preacher or lay person.

Leighton, Robert. *Commentary Upon First Peter.* **London: The Religious Tract Society (n. d.).**

A thorough discussion of the text with an exceptionally warm devotional spirit. Among older works it is easily one of the most helpful.

Luther, Martin. *Commentary on Peter and Jude.* **Grand Rapids: Kregel, 1990. 303 pp.**

The reader wanting to see how the great reformer handles these epistles will find a readable work with many judicious comments but one weak on some of the problems such as how to interpret the spirits in prison (3:19-21). Many commentaries are better overall.

Marshall, I. Howard. *I Peter* **(The IVP New Testament Commentary). Downers Grove: IVP, 1991. 184 pp.**

This launched a new series under the general editorship of Grant R. Osborne of Trinity Evangelical Divinity School. It aims to be brief, capture the message competently, and be practical for the church. Some of those who contribute to it are Darrell Bock (Luke), William Lane (Romans), Alan Johnson (I Corinthians), Gordon Fee (Philippians), Ray Stedman (Hebrews), and J. R. Michaels (Revelation). Marshall writes lucidly, refreshingly; he is aware of views on problems, reasons well usually, and crystallizes things helpfully. He has a five-point defense of authorship by Peter (pp. 22-23), and a good list of nine points in Peter's theology. He has excellent remarks about trial in 1:6-7, a very instructive section on "Purity and Growth" (2:1-3), and a good list of views on 3:19-21, though some will wonder about his preference that Christ went to a prison in the heavens as He ascended and proclaimed His victory over evil supernatural beings. All in all, it is a very fine concise work which is bound to assist students who need a quick, well-informed review, and any Christian who uses it in a plan of daily readings.

Meyer, F. B. *Tried By Fire.* **NY: Revell (n. d.).**

The famous devotional writer of England has here dealt with I Peter in an expository way. He is very good on the subject of suffering. This is a very valuable devotional work to have.

Michaels, J. Ramsay. *I Peter* **(Word Biblical Commentary). Waco, TX: Word Books, 1988. 337 pp.**

Some view this as the current best basic evangelical work in English. Michaels deals well with Greek details, is abreast of scholarly writings and gives helpful lists, wrestles with views and supports and often defends his view well. Differing from much thought, he thinks that Peter lived through persecution under Nero and authored the epistle in the A. D. 70's along with help from the church at Rome, despite evidence for death under Nero.

Mounce, Robert H. *A Living Hope [1 and 2 Peter]*. **Grand Rapids: Eerdmans, 1982.**

Evidently meant to be a personal study guide, the book is really not very helpful. Mounce's comments are very brief and generally superficial. He begs many questions, calls the church the new Israel, and does not answer most "why?" or "how?" questions. His commentary on the Book of Revelation is at many points quite good. -Dan Phillips

A solid evangelical argues for authorship by Peter in the 60's and uses the NIV clause by clause, giving the rich Greek meaning and generously applying the points to today. The work is more useful for aggressive students, pastors and lay workers. Mounce could do far better to tie things together with synopses but he makes occasional good contributions, at times verse by verse, meeting some issues fairly well.

Raymer, Roger. **"I Peter," in** *Bible Knowledge Commentary*, **ed. John F. Walvoord and Roy B. Zuck, Volume II. Wheaton: Victor Books, 1985.**

A concise evangelical entry that is backed by solid study and provides a lot of assistance on many of the problems as well as a capable job on the flow of thought and matters verse by verse.

Reicke, Bo. *The Epistles of James, Peter and Jude* **(Anchor Bible). NY: Doubleday, 1964.**

A competent treatment of the Greek text by a widely read liberal scholar. It is especially valuable on I Peter, the book in which the Basel scholar did his doctoral dissertation, "The Disobedient Spirits and Christian Baptism" (on 3:18ff.). Reicke dates I Peter in the 60's, James and II Peter and Jude in the 90's. The commentary would be better if it discussed other views more often on difficult passages. Historical and social aspects are one of the stronger contributions.

Selwyn, E.G. *The First Epistle of St. Peter*. **Grand Rapids: Baker, 1981, reprint.**

This is one of the finest of all English scholarly liberal works on the Greek text. Selwyn gives detailed introduction material and exegesis plus 230 pages of further special notes. Though not up to date on scholarly literature and discussion, it still makes a great contribution.

Stibbs, A. M. *The First Epistle General of Peter*. **Grand Rapids: Eerdmans, 1959.**

Stibbs has done a fairly thorough and discerning work. This is a very good commentary on the English but based on a careful study of the Greek.

Waltner, Erland, and J. D. Charles. *1-2 Peter, Jude* **(Believers Church BC). Scottsdale, PA: Herald Press, 1999.**

The writers fit this series by giving brief introductions and fairly good, simple exposition, quite readable for pastors and lay people. Waltner does I Peter, Charles the other two. The work often cites Anabaptist (mostly), Brethren, and Wesleyan writings and experiences. Waltner sees believers in the "holy nation" (2:9-10) as "the true Israel of God" (77). Sometimes he favors a view without much support or good grasp or fairness to some other views (as on I Pet. 3:19, Christ preached between death and resurrection, or on the very brief comments about "crown" in 5:4). Much lack of clarity attends discussion on whether the corrupt teachers in 2 Peter 2 were once saved, and lost salvation, or not ever really saved. The work at best is far down the line, and expositors find more steady help in several other efforts.

Wuest, Kenneth S. *First Peter in the Greek New Testament*. Grand Rapids: Eerdmans, 1956.

Later available in paperback, this is one of Wuest's better works on a New Testament book. It is based on the Greek text though presented so that the English reader can have a lucid exposition. The word studies are sometimes good even if brief and aimed for simple use.

XIX. SECOND PETER

Bauckham, Richard J. *Jude, 2 Peter* (Word Biblical Commentary). Waco, TX: Word Books, 1983. 357 pp.

Some will not think the work evangelical. It has discussion looking at the Greek exegesis in some detail and with competence and showing a high familiarity with literature on the epistles as well as extra-biblical sources he feels pertains. In some cases he offers a spread of possibilities on views and arguments on problems. His bibliography is extensive. He will disturb many readers with his denial of authorship by Peter (he says the church at Rome produced it), and his view that the early readers would not disrespect it for being pseudonymous but take its message to heart as "a faithful mediator of the apostolic message" (pp. 161–62). Bauckham's view of inspiration is hazy, and he leaves students unsure whether he feels that any of the predictions or statements in the two epistles are objectively, actually true. In his thinking II Peter is dependent on Jude. The work is flawed in some of its doctrinal content but impressive in its help on exegesis and highly regarded in the academic community.

Barbieri, Louis. Cf. on I Peter.

Bigg, Charles. Cf. on I Peter.

Blum, Edwin. Cf. on I Peter.

Brown, John. *2 Peter 1: Parting Counsels* (Geneva series). Carlisle, PA: Banner of Truth Trust, 1980rp of 1856 work. 329 pp.

Brown was minister of Broughton Place, Edinburgh (1829-58), at which post he died. He gives rich, solid comments verse by verse and can refresh any Christian in his devotional times or help a preacher pull together facets of truth and how they relate to life. To Brown, making the calling and election sure refers not to seeing to their existence but to the evidence of them (p. 53). Some, however, feel that they are saved when they are far from it (54). He is helpful on furnishing the virtues in verses 5-8. After 225 pages the rest of the book is given to other discourses on how Christians may have proper assurance of salvation, pray for the preacher (Ephesians 6:19), etc.

Charles, J. Daryl. *Virtue and Vice* [on 2 Pet. 1:5-7] (Journal for the Study of the NT Supplement Series 150). Sheffield, Eng.: Sheffield Academic Press, 1997.

Charles probes to ascertain the literary strategy in 2 Peter, looks at ethics and virtue, and investigates word for word in 2 Peter 1:5-7, for example, virtue lists in Jewish literature and elsewhere in the NT (as Gal. 5:22-23), also at 13 vice lists in the NT (cf. 122). Chapter 6 is wholly devoted to 2 Pet. 1, 1:1-4 (basis of virtue), the catalog (1:5-7), and the necessity of virtue (1:8-11). The final or 7th chapter concludes on the function of the virtues in 1:5-7. An appendix then discusses perseverance and apostasy, seeing 2 Peter 1 as introducing the virtue motif, 2 Peter 2 as illustrating it (and its opposite), and 2 Peter 3 as defending it. Charles relates a life of virtue to perseverance and sees the faith's supplying of every kind of virtue as confirming divine calling and election (174). One can find at the end of the book a list of 152 published monographs in the Supplement Series, dealing with topics that relate at different parts of Scripture.

Clark, Gordon H. *II Peter: A Short Commentary*. Nutley, NJ: Presbyterian and Reformed Publishing Co., 1972.

This is a 78-page evangelical work that attempts to answer objections to the authenticity of II Peter (i.e., he believes that it was written indeed by the Apostle Peter) and to interpret the text according to the Greek grammar and textual evidence. There is a pronounced Calvinistic strain. It is a worthwhile book, and offers fresh help on such details as "daystar arise in your hearts" (1:19), "denying the Lord that bought them" (2:1), and "not willing that any should perish" (3:9).

Gangel, Kenneth. "2 Peter," in *Bible Knowledge Commentary*, ed. John F. Walvoord and Roy B. Zuck, Volume II. Wheaton: Victor Books, 1985.

A brief but often substantial tracing of the message verse by verse, dealing with problems fairly well or at least giving views. Gangel uses Greek word study (1:5, *epichoregeo*), feels the blind in 1:9 are carnal but saved, apparently favors saying that "they" in 2:20 refers to unstable, unsaved people who were "listeners" in verse 18, but gives four views, etc. He is premillennial in his "day of the Lord" concept in 3:10-13.

Gardner, Paul. *2 Peter and Jude* (Focus on the Bible). Geanies House, Fearn, Ross-shire, Scotland: Christian Focus Publications, 1998.

One can be impressed with this, among brief efforts, for some sensible, flowing exposition after convictions that the Apostle Peter wrote 2 Peter and Jude, the half brother of Jesus, wrote the letter of Jude. The work can be frequently clear (2 Pet. 1:20-21), or nebulous (as on the status of those who need to make sure, 2 Pet. 1:9-10, or how or when the angels sinned in 2:4). Overall the commentary is mediocre in covering issues. But stimulating thoughts appear on how Jude, much neglected, is relevant today for preaching (145-46).

Green, Michael E. *The Second Epistle General of Peter and the General Epistle of Jude* (Tyndale New Testament Commentary). Grand Rapids: Eerdmans, 1968.

An articulate evangelical commentary, upholding the Petrine authorship after a careful weighing of evidence, then explaining the text carefully though concisely. It rates as one of the best overall brief works.

Hiebert, D. E. *Second Peter and Jude*. Greenville, SC: Unusual Publications, 1989. 324 pp.

He takes conservative positions, even seeing Jude as following Peter's second epistle. He usually has something clarifying on a verse and displays considerable awareness of views and issues. Preachers and lay readers will find his present work worth the time.

Kelly, J. N. D. Cf. on I Peter.

Lloyd-Jones, D. M. *Expository Sermons on Peter*. Carlisle, PA: Banner of Truth Trust, 1983. 263 pp. Trust, 1983. 263 pp. Rp 1999.

The book gives 25 sermons preached in 1946-47, the preacher's first series through a book of Scripture. He delivered the messages at Westminster Chapel, London. He usually includes 1-4 verses in a sermon and moves through the epistle. One is soon aware that Lloyd-Jones has much insight, explaining the essentials of the text adeptly and developing how these have vital force for living in this world. The book is a primer for expositors and refreshing for Christians in general.

Lucas, Dick, and Christopher Green. *The Message of 2 Peter & Jude* (The Bible Speaks Today). Downers Grove, IL: IVP. 1995.

Lucas, a fine expository preacher, did the two introductions, Green the verse by verse comments. Little is done before 2 Peter to define in any substantial way who the false teachers are, but their characteristics are made clear both in 2 Peter and Jude. The Apostle Peter is assumed as the author (2 Pet.) and Jude the half brother of Jesus (Jude). The commentary expounds details in an eminently lucid way, clearly setting forth points and giving content that can foster growth along lines of productive godliness (2 Pet. 1:5-7 is worth the read, as are remarks about unorthodox teaching and life-style in 2 Pet. 2). Green does not view the corrupt teachers of 2:20-22 as ever having been truly saved (122), but only as having known in public confession, or claim. He gives six points of counsel on how to deal with such cases in the church (120-21). For both books, the practical exposition is quite well-done, useful for pastors, students, and lay people.

Mayor, J. B. *The Epistles of Jude and Second Peter: The Greek Text with Introduction, Notes and Comments*. Grand Rapids: Baker, 1979.

This is quite a good older work on the Greek exegesis by the man who did an outstanding commentary on James. Mayor is more for serious students who know the Greek and are ready to read more technical detail on verses without being overcome.

Mayor, Joseph. *The Second Epistle of St. Peter and the Epistle of St. Jude*. NY: Macmillan, (n. d.).

Along with Bigg, this is an old, detailed study of the Greek text which the student will want to have.

Mounce, Robert H. Cf. on I Peter.

Reicke, Bo. Cf. on James.

Wuest, Kenneth S. *In These Last Days: Studies in the Greek Text of II Peter, John and Jude For the English Reader*. Grand Rapids: Eerdmans, 1957.

This work is recommended as a very good simple book to give to a layman to stimulate his study. It is also good for the pastor and Sunday school teacher because it deals with the Greek word meanings verse-by-verse and has a warm devotional strain.

XX. THE JOHANNINE EPISTLES

Akin, Daniel L. *1, 2, 3 John* **(New American Commentary). Nashville: Broadman & Holman, 2001.**

One encounters a fairly good exegetical study favoring authorship by the Apostle John, 5:13 as stating the main purpose (giving avenues for assurance of having eternal life). Akin offers insightful argument on some problem texts (5:13; partially in 5:16), generalizes others though stating his view (3:6), and is nebulous on nailing down some (2:12-14; 2:28; 3:9). Good excursuses appear, as on "light" in 1:5, but generally verse by verse material is brief (as 1:7, pp. 72-73). Akin does not discuss the views and issues in limited or unlimited atonement in 2:2. So the commentary is only sometimes up.

Barclay, William. *Letters of John and Jude.* **Philadelphia: Westminster, 1961.**

This is a lucid and well-organized exposition of the epistles with many helpful lists on different facets of truth John can have in mind at different points as on "light" and "darkness" in I John 1:5 (Cf. also Stott on this.). There is stimulating background material and warm application.

Brooke, A. H. *The Johannine Epistles* **(ICC). Edinburgh: T. & T. Clark.**

This ICC work rates with Westcott as one of the top two detailed older commentaries of a technical nature based on the Greek text.

Brown, Raymond. *The Epistles of John* **(Anchor Bible). Garden City, NY: Doubleday, 1982. 840 pp.**

Many rate this as the best work on these epistles in view of its extensive discussion of issues and the skill in which the famous Roman Catholic scholar handles so many aspects. He is highly-informed exegetically, full in consideration of views and lines of reasoning, and has a tone of respect for the truthfulness and relevance of the message. If the expositor, teacher or lay person wants a commentary that looks at just about every side of a matter in a readable manner and with authoritative grasp of the literature, he will consult this work. The same is true of Brown's detailed commentary on the Gospel of John. Brown, however, will not always agree with a reader's convictions, as when he favors John the Presbyter as the author. The sheer length will not please some, but the diligent and serious will find the source very useful.

Bruce, F. F. *The Epistles of John.* **Grand Rapids: Eerdmans, 1970.**

A verse-by-verse evangelical commentary of 160 pp. intended for the general reader and using the R.V. Bruce, as usual, has much to offer, even though briefly here. The brevity removes it from being among the better commentaries to explain the text, which has problems requiring at times more than he gives. Footnotes, sometimes substantial, go into some points for readers who wish to pursue things a bit.

Bultmann, Rudolf. *The Johannine Epistles* **(Hermeneia series). Translated by R. P. O'Hara with L. C. McGaughy and R. W. Funk, ed. by R. W. Funk. Philadelphia: Fortress Press, 1973.**

A detailed commentary with Bultmann's use of the RSV, which he alters according to his radical view of the text. Included in the work is a list of best-known commentaries and other literature relating to these letters issued in this century, combined with the main scholarly studies during the last century, provided by E. J. Epp and J. W. Dunky. These are only the works these scholars consider to be scholarly, from their liberal perspective and circle of learning.

Burdick, Donald W. *The Epistles of John*, **Chicago: Moody Press, 1970.**

A part of the Everyman's Bible Commentary series, this work by a careful evangelical New Testament scholar from Denver Seminary is quite perceptive on problems and good as a brief commentary.

Burdick, Donald W. *The Letters of John the Apostle. An In-Depth Commentary.* **Chicago: Moody, 1985. 488 pp.**

This is far more detailed in getting at issues than his Everyman's Commentary effort of 1970. It is a diligent conservative product on Greek syntax, word meaning and theology, and follows the line of thought through the epistles well. The introduction (pp. 3-92) takes up the background, authorship, date, place, recipients, occasion, purpose, character and content of I John. Later, he also has introductions to II and III John. He believes that I John gives grounds for assurance, tests of practice that can provide valid assurance (cf. pp. 81-82). Though copious in aspects of grammar that open up the books, Burdick is more lucid than Westcott's helpful exegetical work of the past, and certainly one of the best now on the Greek. At some points one ought to go to longer discussions of views and issues in Brown, and also consult Brooke, Marshall, Plummer, Smalley, and Strecker etc. on technical matters, Marshall and Smalley also for more on studies of recent years.

Burge, Gary. *Letters of John* **(NIV Application Commentary). Grand Rapids: Zondervan, 1996.**

This is of mediocre helpfulness overall, an assist only here and there. The introduction would be more help if Burge had a section distinctly on the theme of each epistle and why he says this. He does ask provocative questions about five areas that I John suggests, which users need to consider carefully in implementing the truth today (19-20). Ambiguity prevails at times, as in calling those with false claims in 1:6 "Christians," yet describing them elsewhere as hostile and lacking genuineness (68-69), later finally saying they may not be Christians (82). One does not find the clarity he finds, for example, in Stott, as in 1:6—2:2 and in some other problem texts, though the exposition is fairly good. Some views seem unconvincing or not supported well (2:12-14; 5:16-17), or leave a matter without giving confidence, where far more could be made clear (3:9)

Eaton, Michael. *1, 2, 3 John* **(Focus on the Bible). Geanies House, Fearn, Ross-shire, Scotland: Christian Focus Publications, 1996.**

This 232-pp. light exposition which skips a lot of issues is useful primarily, and in a lesser way than many commentaries, for general readers. It grew out of a doctoral dissertation at the University of South Africa in 1989. Eaton stands for the Apostle John writing these epistles as well as the Gospel of John. Some definitions are too vaguely general, for example the attempt to say what "knowing God" means in I John (21-25). Lay people would be farther ahead by using works by such men as Bruce, Burdick (his simpler of two commentaries), Hiebert, Kistemaker, Ryrie, Stott, or Vine, or the survey by M.Thompson.

Findlay, George. G. *Fellowship in the Life Eternal.* **London: Hodder and Stoughton, 1909. Eerdmans reprint.**

Based on the Greek text, this work is one of the great commentaries on the three epistles from more than three quarters of a century ago.

Findlay, George G. *Studies in John's Epistles.* **Grand Rapids: Kregel, 1989rp of 1925 edition from lectures in 1909. 477 pp.**

This is another production of Findlay's above work.

Hiebert, D. Edmond. *The Epistles of John. An Expositional Commentary.* **Greenville, SC: Bob Jones University Press, 1991.**

This is one of the best medium-length (here 371-pp.) explanations that is serious and clear to deal with most key matters, not pass them by. Hiebert sees ways to have assurance of real salvation, and I John 5:13 as a key for the whole epistle, not confining its focus to details in 5:1-12 or 5:11-12 (251-52). He views 5:16 as a case of a saved person praying for another saved person who receives "life" in the sense of restoration and promotion of his spiritual welfare (260). He usually takes a stand on what a phrase means, gives reasons, and is plain. His comments in the main body, his extensive bibliography (351-60), and frequent footnote references to good sources all exemplify his earnest attempt to give readers light.

Hodges, Zane C. "I, II and III John," in *Bible Knowledge Commentary***, ed. John F. Walvoord and Roy B. Zuck, Volume II. Wheaton: Victor Books, 1985.**

Cf. the comment on Hodges' work in the Hebrews section. The same non-Lordship salvation view is championed here in a lucid and capable way. Passages given Hodges' turns will surprise and dismay many from an exegetical standpoint (cf. 3:4-10; 3:15; 4:7, 8; 5:13 etc.).

Hodges, Zane C. *The Epistles of John. Walking in the Light of God's Love.* **Irving, TX: Grace Evangelical Society, 1999.**

In 312 pp., Hodges, who also dealt with these epistles in the *Bible Knowledge Commentary*, Vol. 2, gives a "non-Lordship" explanation. He opposes the view that I John aims to lead readers to see how to be assured of salvation, as some say in 5:13, and sees "fellowship" in 1:3 as the theme. Only the saved are in view in most cases. To "know" Christ in 2:3 means, to him, knowing Him in intimate fellowship (75-76). The person who "abides in death" (3:14) is saved, not having fellowship with God, but will be safe forever, though missing out in terms of special reward. Hodges has expressed his concept on several Johannine texts and many other NT passages in books such as *The Hungry Inherit, The Gospel Under Siege, Grace in Eclipse*, and *Absolutely Free*! Cf. also his work on James and on Hebrews, and other writings listed on the latter.

Johnson, T. F. *1, 2, and 3 John* **(New International Biblical Commentary). Peabody, MA: Hendrickson, 1993.**

Johnson identifies the writer of the Gospel of John as "The disciple whom Jesus loved" (20:20, 24), but sees these epistles as by an "elder," a different man (2). The concise verse comments are usually clear and well-reasoned, showing the idea of the Greek with Greek words transliterated, and with explanations of word meaning and grammar. Sections of added notes in smaller print take up some details. Some problems receive discussion, some are bypassed, in the latter category limited or unlimited atonement in I John 2:2, or interpretations of 2:12-14, or 5:16 (where much is not explained or not explained well). True, the commentary quite often is helpful, but uneven, and not one of the better all-around works one can more consistently count on.

King, Guy. *The Fellowship.* Fort Washington, PA: Christian Literature Crusade, 1963.

Only 127 pages long, this book is like King's other expositions in that it is rich in phraseology, sermonic ideas and illustrations. It is a good, brief work to recommend to laymen and also good for the preacher or teacher's heart.

Kistemaker, Simon J. Cf. on James.

Kruse, Colin G. *The Letters of John* (Pillar NTC). Grand Rapids: Eerdmans, 2000.

Kruse contributes 255 pp. He concludes authorship of all three by the Apostle John (7-8), and has a good discussion on the nature and grounds for the secessionists' teachings as in I John (15-27). He also helps on themes, such as assurance in I John (33-36), and unpacks meanings of details often, as in I John 1:9, yet passes over big issues such as "sins of the whole world" (2:2), or whether those who know God in 2:3 are the genuinely saved and those who do not are mere professors, or what 2:9 means by "still in darkness," or what is a fitting, consistent view in 2:12-14 between "children" as all the saved (he says), yet his view that "fathers" are older ones in the fellowship. Among other blurred verses are 2:28 and 5:16. Yet Kruse is forthright on some points, at least with his view, as "seed" means the Holy Spirit (3:9, p. 125) and the meaning of 4:4. The work overall is fair; it just comes short too often in covering problems.

Marshall, I. Howard. *The Epistles of John* (NICNT). Grand Rapids: Eerdmans, 1978.

Like Ryrie and Stott, Marshall has keen ability to follow the thought of a book and articulate it with clarity. He often is helpful on stating views gleaned from the literature and is up-to-date. His use of the Greek, good footnotes, and detail on many of the problem verses make this a very good evangelical commentary by one of the best New Testament scholars in the British Isles (ca. 2001 he retired from being head of the New Testament Department at King's College, University of Aberdeen, Scotland).

Morris, Leon. "1, 2, 3 John" in *New Bible Commentary Revised,* ed. D. Guthrie et al. Grand Rapids: Eerdmans, 1970.

This is a brief study (pp. 1259-73) by a top evangelical exegete. Some of the passages are dealt with rather well despite the terseness, and the expositor or any Christian can receive help at certain points.

Plummer, Alfred. *The Epistles of John* (Cambridge Bible). Cambridge: University Press, 1906.

Though old, this is a good study from the Greek text which will be helpful in any more advanced study of the epistles. There are other works more highly recommended, however.

Ryrie, Charles C. "I, II and III John." *The Wycliffe Bible Commentary.* **Chicago: Moody, 1962.**

This is a brief study based on the English text. The author's rare ability to state truth precisely and concisely enables him to say a lot in these verse-by-verse studies. His work is recommended as a good survey discussion, and it includes unusually lucid homiletical outlines of the epistles.

Smalley, Stephen S. *1, 2, 3 John* **(Word Biblical Commentary). Waco, TX: Word Books, 1984. 420 pp.**

This ranks high with Brown, Burdick and Marshall in recent years. Smalley is excellent in helping the reader be up on views and arguments from recent years, drawn from massive research, and is second only to Brown in this regard. He is usually quite full in discussing issues so that he offers much help on verses, and does so with clarity, directness and confidence. He delves into changes in tense, many of the syntactical aspects, and doctrine. He sees the author of II and III John as John the presbyter, a Christian in the Johannine circle, and this same man may also have written I John, all in the A. D. 90's. Smalley often makes good choices on views, and tends to give definite reasons for them. He sees *charisma* (2:20, 27) as both the Spirit and the Word; 3:4-10 relates to a potential state without sin, but in practice Christians do sin (1:8-2:2). Sin in 5:16-17 is apostasy, willful disobedience, etc. He is not clear on whether the saved can lose salvation.

Stott, John R. W. *The Epistles of John* **(Tyndale NTC). 2nd edition. Grand Rapids: Eerdmans, 1988. 234 pp.**

Here is a recent lucid, stimulating work by a gifted writer who has served as rector of the All Souls (Anglican) Church, Langham Place, London. Several New Testament scholars have hailed it as an outstanding commentary from the standpoint of exegesis, exposition and warm application. It was listed among 22 "Choice Evangelical Books of 1964" in *Christianity Today* (February 12, 1965, p. 16). Stott displays a vast breadth of reading in the best conservative works on the Johannine epistles. This 1988 version updates the 1964 original.

Strecker, Gregg. *The Johannine-Epistles. A Commentary on 1, 2, and 3 John.* **Philadelphia: Fortress Press, 1996.**

Done in 317 large pp., the work, usable for scholars and advanced Greek students as is customary in this Hermeneia series, argues that John the Presbyter wrote 2 and 3 John, and a Johannine school produced I John and the Gospel of John in the first half of the second century (xli-xlii). One finds meticulous grappling with exegesis, ponderous technical analysis, long and often very informative footnotes, etc. A synopsis at the outset of all sections would help orientate users and clear the haze of being in a labyrinth of detail, needing perspective. One often wishes to see a plain mentioning of views on problems and discussion reasoning through these, as Cranfield does on Romans or Marshall on the Pastorals. If one wants to glean out bits and pieces with perseverance he will mine some rich ore, though a great lack of clarity about progression will often be noticeable to many.

Thompson, Marianne M. *1-3 John* **(IVP NTC). Downers Grove, IL: IVP, 1992.**

A lucid 168-pp., crisp exposition with some application in a flow for popular, general use. In a number of verses the book helps, at others it frustrates due to passing by views and reasons, or lacks sufficient comments. Much generalizing leaves an impression that in order to be seen as saved one must live an ideally perfect life (cf. 43), yet at other points one reads that Christians sin (45). The work has a healthy clarity that real grace, distinct from cheap so-called (but not genuine) grace (51) elicits confession of sin and seeking obedience to God. Such a life with God helps one's assurance to be a properly experienced reality, as in 2:3 (51), even this by grace. Some statements are quite helpful, as "righteous conduct does not make us God's children. Rather, such conduct is the consequence or expression of a relationship that already exists" after rebirth (87). Many issues are left in a blur, for instance "God's seed remains" (3:9).

Vine, W. E. *Epistles of John.* **Grand Rapids: Zondervan, 1965.**

This is a concise but carefully stated work very helpful in getting at the interpretation. There is often a reference to Greek tenses which is helpful.

Westcott, B. F. *The Epistles of John.* **Cambridge and London: Macmillan, 1883.**

This work has long been ranked by many as the best older effort on the Greek text. It is detailed, thorough, and very useful for its incisive, definitive statements on problem areas as well as grammatical matters.

White, R. E. O. *An Open Letter to Evangelicals.* **Grand Rapids: Eerdmans, 1964.**

A Baptist minister presents both a commentary with occasional deep insight and some penetrating applications to spiritual life, ethics, and other particulars. It is a verse-by-verse devotional and homiletical exposition which sometimes deals with problems including the difficult passage in 3:4-10.

Wuest, Kenneth S. Cf. on II Peter.

XXI. JUDE

Cf. several commentators on 2 Peter, and some on 1 Peter for works also on Jude. Remember also that various general commentaries have a section on Jude, such as those of multiple vols., or 1 vol. works, or study Bibles, to name a few.

Barclay, William. Cf. Johannine Epistles.

Bauckham, Richard J. *Jude, 2 Peter* **(Word Bible Commentary). Waco: Word, 1983.**

Provides a rich source of exegetical material, closely examining the Greek text and displaying thorough familiarity with the literature, as well as with extra-biblical material. Sure to become a standard; unsatisfactory, however, from an evangelical viewpoint, in that the author denies Petrine authorship of 2 Peter and sees a great deal of use of apocryphal and apocalyptic sources. The author's understanding of inspiration is very foggy, and one is not certain whether he believes that any of the predictions or statements in the two epistles are objectively and actually true. Thus, little direct help for some doctrinal concerns, but great help in the detailed work of exegesis; theologically disappointing but academically extremely impressive. -Dan Phillips.

Bigg, Charles. Cf. on I Peter.

Blum, Edwin. "Jude," in *Expositor's Bible Commentary*, Volume 12, ed. Frank Gaebelein. Grand Rapids: Zondervan, 1981.

A worthy evangelical work which, though brief, argues well and knowledgeably, helping on the verses.

Green, Michael E. Cf. on II Peter.

Hiebert, D. E. Cf. on II Peter.

Jenkyns, William. *An Exposition Upon The Epistle of Jude*. Minneapolis: James & Klock, 1976. Reprint of 1863 work.

An exceptionally thorough analysis of the Greek text and its theological and practical import. A student looking for detail laying out the progression of thought will certainly find it here, and frequent valuable input to help his study.

Kelly, J. N. D. Cf. under I Peter.

Kistemaker, Simon J. Cf. on I Peter.

Lawlor, George L. *The Epistle of Jude*. Nutley, NJ: Presbyterian and Reformed Publishing Co., 1972.

The author, a graduate of Grace Theological Seminary where he studied under Alva J. McClain, Herman A. Hoyt and Homer A. Kent, Sr., was Professor of Greek and New Testament at Cedarville College in Ohio when he wrote this commentary. The interpretation verse by verse is detailed, lucid, handles the Greek well, discusses problems at length, and uses good scholarly sources which he documents carefully. This is one of the most helpful works on Jude in recent decades.

Luther, Martin. Cf. on I Peter.

MacArthur, John F., Jr. *Beware the Pretenders*. Wheaton: Scripture Press/Victor Books, 1980.

One of the earlier MacArthur expositions, following the verses of Jude and pointing out the relevance of the truths to being on guard against error today.

Manton, Thomas. *Commentary on Jude*. London: 1655, reprinted by The Sovereign Grace Publishers. Also cf. *Jude* (Crossway Classic Commentary). Wheaton, IL: Crossway Books, 1999.

Though a very old work, it is good. It is a sermonic composition by a Puritan whom C. H. Spurgeon and J. C. Ryle saw as the best Puritan expositor (cf. p. ix of Crossway ed.). Manton, a London pastor in the 1650's, deals with every word of every verse, exposing meaning and often using this as a take-off point to draw in aspects that relate for believers, e. g. "to those . . . called" (v. 1) leads on to how people respond to God's call, how they can have assurance of being called, etc. After each section of detailed exposition, Manton adds a section of special notes on each verse (v. 1 involves pp. 15-40, v. 2 entails 41-56, but several vv. receive far shorter treatments, as v. 10 has but 2 fi pp.). The angels' sin in v. 6 is seen as soon after creation, not in Gen. 6. Many parts offer a rich larder, for example "faith" and "praying in the Spirit" (v. 20). Here, as in other verses, good application is made obvious, and devotional reading can be enhanced.

Mayor, Joseph. *The Second Epistle of St. Peter and the Epistle of St. Jude.* **NY: Macmillan (n. d.).**

Cf. on II Peter.

Plummer, Alfred. *The General Epistles of St. James and St. Jude* **(Expositor's Bible). NY: Hodder & Stoughton (n. d.).**

This is a good study in the Greek text.

Reicke, Bo. Cf. on James.

Wolff, Richard. *A Commentary on the Epistle of Jude.* **Grand Rapids: Zondervan, 1960.**

This is a thorough and scholarly verse-by-verse exposition which shows a good breadth of reading. It is conservative and recommended.

Wuest, Kenneth S. Cf. on II Peter.

XXII. REVELATION

Alford's Greek Testament **(premillennial) is fairly good on The Revelation. In addition:**

Aune, David. *Revelation 1-5,* **and** *Revelation 6-16,* **and** *Revelation 17-22* **(Word Biblical Commentary). 3 vols. Nashville: Thomas Nelson, 1997-1998.**

This magisterial work has nearly 300 pp. on introduction, massive bibliographies, indexes, thirty excursuses, with 1,354 pp. just on commentary. Aune is an amillennial preterist or historicist, which shows in seeing the "beast" as Nero (957-60), the ten kings of Chap. 17 as successive in history rather than at the same time and approaching the Second Advent (950). He seems unaware about the confusion in his seeing the ten as successive, yet allied in destroying Rome (957). One finds rather extensive sections about views on problems, as 4 pp. on "angels" in 1:20 and detail similarly on "Nicolaitans," "eating food sacrificed to idols," "the twenty-four elders," "666 and Gematria," etc. Along with works by Beale, Hendriksen, and Kistemaker, for examples, one can see how scholars differing from a futurist, premillennial perspective construe details such as "woman" in Rev. 12, the two witnesses in 11, and the thousand years. Much detail does not at all points reflect a proper discernment of meaning.

Barclay, William. *Letters to the Seven Churches.* **London: S. C. M. Press Ltd., 1957.**

He is good on the seven churches from the standpoint of philology and explaining historical customs which illumine many statements found here. A major weakness is that he does not document his sources so that it becomes difficult to check up on him.

Barnhouse, Donald Grey. *Revelation.* **Grand Rapids: Zondervan, 1971.**

Devotional, popular-level commentary incorporating illustrations, word studies, and broad scriptural comparison. He is premillennial. and pretribulational, using a fairly literal interpretation. He was a great preacher and Bible teacher in the latter first half and middle of this century.

Bauckham, Richard. *The Theology of the Book of Revelation.* **Cambridge: Cambridge University Press, 1993.**

This is a 169-pp. pb with seven chapters on topics such as the Lamb and His followers' victory, the New Jerusalem as place, people, and presence of God, and the relevance today as the author sees it. Descriptions of the Revelation, he feels, are not to be taken literally; seals, trumpets, and bowls do not convey a sequence of events, rather they only depict God's impending judgment (20). He says that if one sees a literal earthquake related to Babylon's fall (16:17-21) this contradicts later images of the way Babylon falls (17:16; 18:8), as if both cannot give facets that can be resolved in the overall picture (cf. 20-21). This reviewer found the book helpful only occasionally. A much more profitable work was by Merrill Tenney, *Interpreting Revelation*, some decades back, available at some seminary or theological college libraries. The work edited by Mal Couch (in this list) is also of help, and cf. those edited by Gregg and Pace.

Beale, G. K. *The Book of Revelation* **(New International Greek Testament Commentary). Grand Rapids: Eerdmans, 1999.**

A Wheaton College professor did this monumental 1,245-pp. probe that has to be one of the best recent works along amillennial lines. Beale brings incredible research, as Aune does, with an awareness of Jewish and Christian literature giving opinions on verses. The work is for scholars such as exegetes, advanced students (some of it will be readily grasped by other students), studious pastors, etc. Some of many discussions that put much data to consider before the reader are those on the locust-like beings, and the harlot. Beale interacts much with views and arguments and gives more than most writers to stimulate reflection. Excellent indexes cover authors and biblical and other ancient writings. On a given verse, he brings much to bear when one is seeking possibilities.

Beasley-Murray, G. R. *The Book of Revelation* **(New Century Bible). Greenwood, SC: Attic Press, 1974.**

A well-outlined, competent work that explains many facets rather well verse by verse but shows no use of certain great commentators as Beckwith, a total absence of dispensational works such as by Walter Scott, J. B. Smith, and John Walvoord. He is unable to reach a conclusion as to which man by the name of John wrote the book, but favors the traditional date around A. D. 95. His willingness to devote lengthy or at least pertinent discussion on some problem verses makes his work often helpful, e. g. 1:4, seven spirits; 1:10, Lord's day; 1:20, seven stars; 6:2, white horse rider; 7:4-8, the 144,000; 11:3, 4, the two witnesses (but do they represent the church as he says?); 12:4, the dragon stood before the woman to devour the child as soon as he was born; 13:18, the 666; 19:7-9, the bride and the guests, etc. One may need to read him several times on Revelation 20 to decide where he really believes the "thousand years" fit into the scheme of things.

Beckwith, Isbon T. *The Apocalypse of John*. NY: Macmillan, 1919.

This is often a highly-rated commentary. There is an excellent introduction, detail, and the fact that Beckwith does justice to the Jewish flavor of the book. Generally one gains much verse by verse. Beckwith is amillennial.

Beckwith, Roger T. and Wilfred Stott. *This is The Day, The Biblical Doctrine of the Christian Sabbath in its Jewish and Early Christian Setting*. Greenwood, SC: Attic Press, 1978.

The "Lord's Day" is Sunday in Revelation 1:10 in the early church, not Easter Day, Day of the Lord, etc. A competent, well-researched and argued book with many good footnotes arranged by chapters at the end.

Bratcher, Robert G. and Howard A. Hatton, *A Handbook on the Revelation of John*. New York: United Bible Sociieties, 1993.

Often verse by verse comments on key phrases are generalized rather than going far enough really to give adequate light on problems (2:4, 7, 17; 3:5, 10; 6:2, etc.). The 144,000 in 7:4-8 are seen as "the totality of God's people," and the number as not literal. The book is often of little or no help on interpretive issues, having a purpose to focus on exegetical details only to help translation (cf. vii). For the latter it is useful, but it does not furnish Greek grammatical details as some works in the Summer Institute of Linguistics, Inc. do (cf. Greenlee on Hebrews, etc.).

Bruce, F. F. "The Revelation," in *The International Bible Commentary*, ed. F. F. Bruce. 1 volume.

A brief survey by one of the foremost New Testament scholars of the past half century. Most of Bruce's works have been in books in which he did not need to show much of his viewpoint about eschatological matters. Here one can see how he deals with the Revelation.

Caird, G. B. A Commentary on The Revelation of St. John the Divine. NY: Harper & Row, 1966.

He is not sure whether the Apostle John wrote it though he leaves this open and dates the book ca. A. D. 95. As a brief commentary this does a fair job, but skipping verses (as 1:10) is disconcerting to some as is covering some key sections so fast (as 1:12ff.). The 144,000 are the whole band of the saved, and he also equates them with the great throng of 7:9ff. He holds, curiously, that the birth of the child in 12:2-5 is not the Nativity but the Cross; fleeing of the woman (he says she is the church) is handled with exceeding vagueness, but apparently related to the entire present age. One has difficulty respecting his awareness of things when on p. 235 he sweepingly claims that until Daniel the Jewish people had no expectation of an afterlife, a liberal notion widely held but often ably refuted by evangelicals. To him "All the evidence we have is against ... a literal interpretation" of resurrection in 20:5" (p. 254). This simply is not true. Though at times vague in regard to the millennium, he appears to see it as a state before the eternal state, with many questions left hanging. He is often quite helpful in bringing in possible background from Jewish apocalyptic literature. It is a fair commentary, quite good in many places but mystifying in some.

Campbell, Donald K. and Jeffrey L. Townsend, eds. *The Coming Millennial Kingdom.* **Grand Rapids: Kregel, 1997.**

Fourteen scholars wrote chapters reasoning out how the view makes the best hermeneutical sense in different parts of the Bible. Some of these are: Genesis (Robert Chisholm), Psalm 89 (Ron Allen), Jeremiah (Walt Kaiser), Daniel (Ken Barker), Matthew (David Lowery), Acts (Darrell Bock), Revelation (Harold Hoehner). The substance of this book has been much discussed and has been of substantial help to many pastors, Bible teachers, and lay people.

Couch, Mal, ed. *A Bible Handbook to Revelation.* **Grand Rapids: Kregel, 2001.**

Several writers give a dispensational perspective. Five chapters are introductory on such matters as differing systems that interpret the Revelation. Eleven chapters look at aspects of theology. Then ca. 100 pp. survey sections. Writers seek to dispel the idea that the Revelation is too mysterious to grasp. Various charts compare views, such as rapture positions. Authors argue for literal interpretation mingled with recognizing figurative language where they feel this meets sane criteria, as in the seven lamps before the throne, or the lamb (cf. 48). They endeavor to show that their concepts are the most natural hermeneutically. Many discussions offer clear reasons, but some are hazy and ineffective, or not thought through well enough.

Charles, R. H. *The Revelation of St. John* **(ICC). 2 volumes. Naperville, IL: Allenson, 1959.**

This is a voluminous work on critical and exegetical matters. The serious student who is laboring in the Greek will want to use this commentary even though he may not agree with various liberal conclusions.

Chilton, David. *The Days of Vengeance. An Exposition of the Book of Revelation.* **Fort Worth, TX: Dominion Press, 1987. 721 pp.**

A learned advocacy of a postmillennial view. Cf. also Chilton's first book on eschatology, *Paradise Restored: A Biblical Theology of Dominion* (Fort Worth: Dominion Press, 1985). Gary North in the "Publisher's Preface" (p. xv) says that what Chilton generalized in the first book, "is now supported with chapter and verse – indeed, lots and lots of chapters and verses." He asserts that Chilton has, at long last among commentators, found the secret key that unlocks the code of the Book of Revelation (xvi). Many will disagree on that.

Clark, David S. *The Message from Patmos: A Postmillennial Commentary on the Book of Revelation.* **Grand Rapids: Baker, 1989. 148 pp.**

A more succinct effort than Chilton's to support the postmillennial interpretation.

Colclasure, Chuck. *The Overcomers.* **Nashville: Thomas Nelson, 1981.**

This 206-pp. book develops the view that all Christians are overcomers by faith, and pulls together from all of the Apocalypse spiritual lessons pertaining to salvation and spiritual victory, hope, comfort, and encouragement. It is more topical than expository, and shows how to take an amillennial perspective in various key passages.

Coleman, Robert E. *Songs of Heaven.* **Old Tappan, NJ: Revell, 1980.**

Fourteen meditations on songs in the Apocalypse, using exposition, illustration, reference to hymns we know today, and a devotional thrust that warms and refreshes.

Easley, Kendell H. *Revelation* **(Holman NTC). Nashville: Broadman & Holman, 1998.**

Easley has an introduction with an apt illustration before each of Revelation's 22 chapters, then commentary, application, and further data on details of history, geography, or grammar. He gives a teaching outline, and four to seven subjects to discuss in a group. In keeping with the series, preachers and others find charts and boxes highlighting main thoughts or bolstering points. Easley in interpretation often will disappoint dispensational readers, an instance being in seeing the woman of Rev. 12 and the two witnesses of chap. 11 as the whole body of Christ, or the 42 months of 11:2-3 not literal but figurative for a time Christians suffer, and the thousand years as not literal (there will be no future thousand year reign of Christ on earth). One of the disappointing things in the work is Easley's vagueness. He chooses to combine different views, sometimes faulting a view on uninformed grounds, e. g. saying that dispensationalists have no adequate reasoning for how a millennial era of peace can end in a war (p. 7). Problem verses often receive only a light brush (love, 2:4; overcome, 2:7; crown, 2:10, manna, 2:17, etc.). Or views are taken with very light discussion, as elders mean angels in 4:4, and the white horse rider depicts generals at various times in history in 6:2, and the thousand years in 20:1-6 represent no specific chronological program for the future, just a "promillennialism" which is left vague and hanging (368). The confused work overall is of little consistent help for those who are seriously wrestling with hermeneutics and the Revelation.

Ellul, Jacques. *Apocalypse: The Book of Revelation.* **Translated by G. W. Schreiner. NY: Seabury Press, 1977.**

Ellul is a famous theologian of the Reformed Church of France and Professor of Law and History, University of Bordeaux. He sees apocalyptic as not allowing a literal interpretation of prophecy, and writes so much in a philosophical train of thought that the reader is often dumbfounded as to what is going on or what is being really explained in any definite sense. Rather than rescuing the Apocalypse from improper treatment (and indeed it has had plenty of that!), Ellul only plunges it again into a fog for many readers.

Epp, Theodore. *Practical Studies in the Revelation.* **2 volumes. Lincoln, NE: Back to the Bible Broadcast, 1969.**

This includes several simple studies with a clear perspective on the pattern of events to take place according to a more literal understanding of biblical prophecy. The chapters are quite readable for laymen and less advanced students of Scripture. At many points Epp includes spiritual lessons and challenges that show the practicality of the Book of Revelation to experience today, in a premillennial perspective.

Feinberg, Charles L. "The Book of Revelation," in the *Liberty Bible Commentary***, ed. Jerry Falwell et al. Nashville, TN: Thomas Nelson Publishers, 1983. 2,721 pp.**

The late Dr. Feinberg, an outstanding voice for premillennialism in the dispensational pattern and a Jewish Christian, was allowed pp. 2,652-2,721 for a work of brevity. He has a detailed outline, treats many of the problems, giving views of his own and reasons. He believes that 1:19 is the key verse; 1:20 refers to ministers of local churches, not celestial beings; there are five crowns for believers and they may win one or more of these as special reward (cf. on 2:10); 4:4 supports a pre-tribulational rapture since the elders represent the church in heaven after chapters 1-3 (even many dispensationalists do not agree with his view or the seven reasons); the 144,000 in chapter 7 are Israelites, not the church saints; the locusts are literal but supernatural beings; etc. One also can see Feinberg comments in *A Commentary on Revelation; The Grand Finale* (Winona Lake, IND: BMH Books, 1985).

Fiorenza, Elizabeth S. *Invitation to the Book of Revelation: A Commentary on the Apocalypse with Complete Text From the Jerusalem Bible.* **Garden City, NY: Doubleday, 1981.**

This 223-page work is by a professor of Biblical Theology at the University of Notre Dame. Two other Catholic women have written recognized commentaries on the Revelation (Josephine M. Ford, Anchor Bible, 1975, also on Notre Dame faculty; and Adela Yarbro Collins, 1979). Fiorenza was also scheduled to come out with a more definitive commentary on Revelation in the Hermeneia series (Fortress Press). She is against source-critical theories on the composition and takes a futurist scheme of interpretation, but she is very different from the futurist views of premillennialists. She does not take the Apostle John as author. The "Five who have fallen" (chapter 17) are emperors in the first century, Caesar, Caligula, Nero and Domitian (p. 166) (she does not mention a fifth!). The first seal deals with the conquest by the Roman Empire (Babylon); the 144,000 are the Church; the thousand years refer to an earthly Messianic Kingdom as Jesus hoped for, not the "spiritual" interpretation common in Roman Catholic circles and among many Protestants (amillennialism).

Ford, Josephine. *Revelation* **(Anchor Bible). Garden. City, NY: Doubleday, 1975.**

The very liberal author was Professor of New Testament Studies at Notre Dame University. Her viewpoint is that Revelation is by multiple authors in the mid-first century. Chapters 4-11 are by John the Baptist or his disciples, chapters 12-22 by unknown writers. Ford gives a new translation but comments in general on sections, not verse by verse. The bibliography is helpful if one wishes to consult liberal authors and have an extensive list, but evangelical writers are missing. There is little help exegetically to put the book together in a meaningful way for conservative readers. One can waste much time here; it only takes a willingness to fritter it away.

Gregg, Steve, ed. *Revelation, Four Views. A Parallel Commentary.* **Nashville: Thomas Nelson, 1997.**

This combines four major ways to interpret the book, comparing verse by verse how these explain points. First, Gregg looks at postmillennial, amillennial, and premillennial views, then devotes most of the commentary to laying out four perspectives—preterist (fulfilled mostly in the first century), historicist (all through church history), futurist (much yet future), and idealist (principles of righteousness and evil apply at any time [giving the wrong impression, since even a futurist view applies principles to help believers even today]. Some bad misrepresentations, though, occur by generalities as on p. 2

where "Futurist interpreters usually apply everything after chapter four to a relatively brief period before the return of Christ." If so, what of references to the first advent in Rev. 12 (birth of the man child), the battle after Christ returns (Chap. 19), the thousand years, and the eternal New Jerusalem, or many lessons of godliness in the other chapters? In premillennial belief, all of these can help believers in very real ways as they live looking for Christ's appearing. Saints learn much from worship in chap. 4, gratitude for the lamb in 5, comfort in future blessings as at the end of Rev. 7, lessons on facing trials, comfort of blessing rather than punishment in 14, and the bride's future in 19, to name a few. Strengths and weaknesses occur, the latter as in using weaker arguments to support the 24 elders being human or angelic, and a watered down version and thus misrepresentation of how pre-tribulation rapturists can reason for their view on 3:10.

Hailey, Homer. *Revelation: An Introduction and Commentary.* **Grand Rapids: Baker, 1977.**

Hailey, amillennial like William Hendriksen (*More Than Conquerors*), goes so far as to contend that all of Revelation 1-19 was fulfilled in pre-Constantine times, before ca. 235. Even the "thousand years" are symbolic of the period from Constantine until Satan is released. Only 20:7ff. is clearly yet future. Armageddon took place in the subduing of the Roman Empire. The four horsemen of Chapter 6 are Christ going with the gospel, persecution of saints, problems in the economic situation, and judgments on Christ-rejecters (186-93). The great tribulation is the 240 years of Roman-Christian struggle; the two witnesses the church; the woman of chapter 12 the people of God; the coming of the warrior in 19:1ff. is not Jesus' Second Advent but a picture of victory over the world's sinful forces; Gog and Magog denote trends such as atheism, materialism, humanism, communism (397). The work is a clear presentation of one amillennialist's handling of the Revelation, with much that is baffling for hermeneutics.

Hemer, Colin J. *The Letters to the Seven Churches of Asia in Their Local Setting.* **Sheffield, England: Department of Biblical Studies, University of Sheffield/Journal for Study of the Old Testament Press, 1986. 338 pp.**

This is based on Hemer's Ph. D. thesis under F. F. Bruce at the University of Manchester. It is an exegetical study of the seven letters with much research into the local setting (manners and customs as on the white stone) that helps readers grasp what was meant in that culture. The work is very helpful for one teaching or preaching in one or all of the letters, and well-documented in ancient sources.

Hendriksen, William. *More Than Conquerors.* **Grand Rapids: Baker, 1982rp of 1940 edition (Tyndale Press). 216 pp.**

An evangelical but amillennial approach to the Apocalypse. Some will doubt that this is one of Hendriksen's better works, but premillennial readers will profit from following how an amillennialist can explain his view. The work is quite readable, and Hendriksen often provides several arguments to support his view, which he has thought through carefully.

Hoeksema, Herman. *Behold, He Cometh!* **Grand Rapids: Reformed Free Publishing Association, 1969.**

A 726-page work, result of a lifetime of study, posthumously published from a preached series given in the magazine *The Standard Bearer*. It is done with warmth and simple amillennial explanation on a popular basis by a noted writer on *Reformed Dogmatics*. The seven seals depict "the main aspects and larger currents of the history of this dispensation . . . " (p. 186). The woman of Chapter 12 is the Church; the millennium is the whole present age, etc.

Hoyt, Herman A. *Studies in Revelation*. Winona Lake, IND: BMH Books, 1985.

This dispensational book of 148 pp. has clear, simple exposition in a well-organized way that gives pastors, college students and lay people main ideas. Hoyt outlines in advance each chapter or segment. Even many dispensationalists will not see validity in his view that the churches of Rev. 2-3 depict seven distinct eras in the history of the church, an old view (34). Usual dispensational views appear on the 144,000 and the woman (chap. 12), but one of the two witnesses is taken to be Elijah, with Moses possibly the other. Babylon of chap. 17 is a literal, rebuilt city on the Euphrates, and 21:1—22:5 describes not the millennial time but the eternal state. The work is not nearly as helpful to dispensationalists as efforts by R. Thomas and J. Walvoord.

Hughes, Philip E. *The Book of the Revelation*. Grand Rapids: Eerdmans, 1990. 242 pp.

A renowned New Testament scholar and Anglican clergyman provides an amillennial work (cf. p. 211, the thousand years are today). He is clear and lucid, but not outstanding in exegesis. He has a very good commentary on the second epistle to the Corinthians and a fairly good one on Hebrews.

Johnson, Alan F. "Revelation," in *Expositor's Bible Commentary*, Volume 12, ed. Frank Gaebelein. Grand Rapids: Zondervan, 1981.

A faculty member of Wheaton College did this fairly-well documented study in a premillennial manner, grappling with views on issues, displaying wide reading and awareness.

Johnson, Alan F. *Revelation* (Bible Study Commentary). Grand Rapids: Zondervan, 1983. 220 pp.

This is a less-documented work articulating the essence of Johnson's views. Even here he often mentions different views and concisely states some reasons, and is usually clear, often thought-provoking. He is not always convincing as when he sees the 144,000 of chapter 7 as the whole elect people of God. He distinguishes a millennial kingdom in chapter 20 from the eternal state after this (21:1ff.), surveys views, and gives his reasoning. Pages 218-20 list commentaries under four basic views on the Revelation.

Karleen, Paul S. *The Pre-Wrath Rapture of the Church – Is It Biblical?* Langhorne, PA: BF Press, 1991. 102 pp.

A graduate of Yale University, Dallas Seminary and University of Pennsylvania (Ph. D. in Linguistics of Ancient Greek) has a well organized and penetrating evaluation of Marvin Rosenthal's *The Pre-Wrath Rapture of the Church* (cf. in this section). He takes up several issues Rosenthal raised and devotes a chapter to each, pointing out what he regards as flaws in the Rosenthal case. In essence Karleen defends a pre-tribulational rapture. A boiled down version of his book appears in "Evaluating the Pre-wrath Rapture of the Church," *Voice, An Independent Church Journal* (IFCA), Volume 70, No. 1, Grandville, MI: January/February, 1991, pp. 9-13. An even longer work arguing for a Rosenthal-type view is Robert Van Kampen, *The Sign* (Wheaton: Crossway Books, 1992, 538 pp., with fold-out map; 2nd ed., 1993, and Van Kampen's later title, *The Prewrath Position Explained Plain and Simple*, Gd. Haven, MI: Sola Scriptura, 1999, pb). Cf., against the Rosenthal/Van Kampen view, Renald Showers, *The Pre-Wrath Rapture View, an Examination and Critique* (Grand Rapids: Kregel, 2001).

Keener, Craig S. *Revelation* (NIV Application Commentary). Grand Rapids: Zondervan, 2000.

As in his work on Matthew, Keener is detailed (here 576 pp.), aware about exegetical literature as for teachers and yet readable for others, even giving pastoral perceptions. While he relates such passages as Rev. 19-20 to the Second Advent, his comments on chaps. 4-18 alternate between historicist and futurist ideas. In line with series aims, many comments suggest ways to apply points, which is the main usefulness, except that readers must be very discerning to realize where he puts in history what belongs in the future, at least in his primary sense. This reviewer does not rate it as highly helpful on getting a true perspective.

Kistemaker, Simon J. *Exposition of the Book of Revelation*. Grand Rapids: Baker, 2001.

Amillennial views are made clear on such matters as seals, trumpets, bowls, the 144,000, the woman in chap. 12, the two witnesses, and the thousand years. Many fine things help in the introduction, such as arguing for John the Apostle as author. But Kistemaker is typical of his symbolism on numbers when he says that seven in the seven churches is not literal, but a symbol of completeness, using arbitrary reasons (4). He misrepresents a futurist view in saying that it makes all but Chaps. 1-3 irrelevant to the church today (41). Similarly, his reasons against a future millennium show blind spots and logic that futurists can easily answer, which he should have realized. However, the work is one amillennialist's valuable record of beliefs, and much that he says about verses offers good help. He, with Aune, Beale, Hendriksen, Metzger and Polythress, etc., as well as Colclasure, help readers see how amillennialist thinking can be articulated.

Kuyper, Abraham. *The Revelation of St. John*. Translated by J. H. de Vries. Grand Rapids: Eerdmans, 1963.

This is the larger part of the fourth volume in Dr. Kuyper's Dutch work on "The Consummation of the World," his last work, begun at age 76 seven years before his death. He takes what he thinks best in Augustine's view and in an idealist position. In history and on the current scene the things the visions depict repeat themselves. Numbers here, to Kuyper, are not literal. The work is not verse by verse but set up in general chapters: "The Mysticism of Numbers," "The Seven Churches," "The Transition to the Prophetical Part" (at 4:1), "The Seven Seals," etc. Kuyper divides the Revelation into Chapters 1, 2-3, 4:1-22:6, and 22:7ff. The twenty-four elders are believers in Christ who will dwell on the new earth, including even Old Testament believers who join those before Pentecost (p. 61). Kuyper wonders if the fourth seal events have already come (p. 76). The trumpets come from the last seal and the vials from the last trumpet (p. 84). The trumpet and vial judgments are God's acts upon a world after the day of grace ends. The judgments, as in 8:7ff., are taken apparently as actual physical calamities on the earth, on nature and on people (p. 90). The blood mingled with hail and fire is a material substance especially prepared by God in heaven. The great star that falls is a meteor shower (94, 95). The locust-like hosts picture military invaders. He understands the "thousand years" (chapter 20) as symbolic of the abundant fullness of God's action in bringing judgment on Satan to consummation (277), and much vagueness attaches to Kuyper's work here and in many places. Cf. this work also in the 1998 reprint of Eugene, OR: Wipf and Stock Publishers. There, see a summary of the 4 vols. in the "Foreword" by the translator. The lack of clarity, too often, and lack of a well-defined system grasping prophecy in a unity makes the work of questionable help, actually very confusing.

Ladd, George. *A Commentary on the Revelation of John*. Grand Rapids: Eerdmans, 1972.

A premillennial but not pretribulational effort to interpret the apocalypse. Ladd shows keen awareness of issues and is competent in his comments, though sometimes too brief. It is a very fine evangelical work in general.

Landels, William. *The Victor's Sevenfold Reward: Being Discourses on the Promises of Our Lord to the Seven Churches*. London: James Nisbet & Co., 1878.

Very good, well-organized, perceptive discussion on aspects of reward, quite picturesque, eloquent, and suggestive with word pictures. Quite stimulating when one is preparing a series or wants a book that speaks in some detail on an aspect of reward.

Loane, Marcus. *They Overcame. An Exposition of Revelation 1-3*. Grand Rapids: Baker, 1971.

A well-written evangelical book more in the stimulating practical line that helps a reader see points of relevance to churches today. Along with the works by Mayhue and Stott this is one of the better popular-style books on the seven churches in recent years.

MacArthur, John, Jr. *Revelation 1-11*, and *Revelation 12-22* (MacArthur NTC). 2 vols. Chicago: Moody Press, 1999-2000.

Here 677 pp. explain and apply the Revelation in a dispensational way. After a 10-pp. introduction contending for the Apostle John as author ca. A. D. 95, material that was originally in sermons expounds each verse. The "angels" (messengers) in 2:1 are seen as human leaders, overcomers are all the saved, believers' names will not be erased from the heavenly roll as citizens' names are blotted from an earthly city record, the 24 elders are the whole raptured church (dispensationalists and non-dispensationalists differ on this), judgments in chaps. 6-19 are literal, the 144,000 are physical but saved Israelites with their very tribes listed, the locust-like creatures are vile demons that take on a visible form resembling locusts, the woman in chap. 12 is Israel which brought forth the child, Christ, etc. MacArthur makes points of truth applicable in various parts of the Revelation to guide believers to live godly lives.

Mauro, Philip. *Things Which Soon Must Come to Pass*. Swengel, PA: Reiner Publications, 1974.

A 623-page amillennial work reprinted. Along with works by Aune, Beale, Hendriksen,

Kistemaker, Hoeksema, etc., one can see how an interpreter develops an amillennial view in the Revelation. Beckwith, Lenski and Mounce also do, and Colclasure, Erdman, Metzger, Morris, Poythress, and Wilcock have brief treatments.

Mayhue, Richard. *What Would Jesus Say About Your Church?* Geanies House, Fearn, Ross-shire, Scotland: Christian Focus Publications, rp, 2002.

This 224-pp. pb done along popular lines can help lay people, pastors, and students, even those who take different views on certain interpretive issues (2:4; 3:5, etc.). A chapter deals with each church in Rev. 2-3, and beyond these Thessalonica, Philippi, Corinth, Antioch, and Jerusalem. An introductory chapter explores Jesus' expectation, "I will build My church" (Matt. 16:18). The chapters, 10-15 pp. long, are titled according to particular needs, e. g. "Ephesus: The Lost Love Church," and "Pergamum: The Compromising Church." A study guide near the end can assist individual and group Bible study. Mayhue is articulate and provocative for those sensitive to learn relevancy for church life today, based on Scripture.

Metzger, Bruce. *Breaking the Code. Understanding the Book of Revelation.* Nashville: Abingdon Press, 1993.

A small pb (111 pp.) sees the book as, to most church members, "a closed book" and explains it in a way that closes it even more in many parts, having no good key to unlock it. Metzger does help at times, whether one agrees with him or not, in his favoring angels in 1:20 and 2:1. He is not distinct rather often, as in leaving vague the first love (2:4), who the overcomer is (2:7), who is not blotted out (3:5), etc. The white horse rider in 6:2 symbolizes for him a Parthian invasion, and the riders overall depict God's judgments in history at various times. The measured temple in 11:1 is not at Jerusalem, but a symbol of God's people; many will question his supporting this with I Cor. 3:16, 2 Cor. 6:16, and Eph. 2:21. The woman in Rev. 12 means all of God's people; Metzger seems to take no stand on what the thousand years represent. The description of the New Jerusalem as a cube is "architecturally preposterous," and unable to be literal. [Is God not able?] Many will feel that quite often Metzger, though a great scholar, is not "Breaking the Code."

Michaels, J. Ramsey. *Revelation* (IVP NTC). Downers Grove, IL: IVP. 1997.

Michaels takes no stand on authorship by the Apostle John, using arbitrary reasoning against it (18-19). He also is flimsy and misrepresenting in remarks against a futurist approach, as if simply not properly informed of how better futurist thinkers explain details, and unfair to them (23). His bibliography does not even list Robert L. Thomas' detailed exegetical 2-vol. work taking a futurist position. Somehow Michaels is able to discuss possible views for the "woman" (Rev. 12) without being aware of the common premillennial view that she represents Israel for various reasons (148), which Michaels does not forthrightly mention or answer. The same seeming lack of awareness shows in discussing the 144,000 who, to Michaels, are saints out of all nations in 7:9, and the view of the two witnesses in Rev. 11. One would almost think that he author did this amillennial work without checking many interpreters who argue the hermeneutical naturalness of taking literal views in Rev. 6-20. So he often is out of touch, and limits his readers where he might have provided more representative, informed discussions.

Morgan, G. Campbell. *The Letters of Our Lord.* **London: Pickering and Inglis, 1945. This also carries the title** *First Century Messages to Twentieth Century Believers.*

A 112-page study, this book deals with expositions on the seven churches in chapters 2-3. When one is studying this portion of the Apocalypse he will find Morgan helpful, along with Barclay, Hemer, Landels, Loane, Mayhue, Ramsay, Seiss, Stott, Trench, and Yamauchi.

Morris, Leon. *The Book of Revelation. An Introduction and Commentary* **(Tyndale NTC). Grand Rapids: Eerdmans, 1987, revised, updated. 256 pp.**

Morris concisely comments on verses in an amillennial vein, as on Revelation 20. He is frequently helpful on views and information from his wide reading. Noteworthy here and there, the work does not rank high as do his commentaries on John, Matthew, Romans and the Thessalonian Epistles.

Morris, Henry M. *The Revelation Record.* **Wheaton: Tyndale; and San Diego: Creation-Life, 1983.**

A 521–pp. premillennial, pretribulational work by a writer who has specialized in hydrology and geology and desires to help with the many references to natural phenomena. His perspective is full verbal inspiration, and a literal interpretation in the futuristic vein. At times things are rather artificially blocked off: chapters 4-11 cover the first half of the seven-year tribulation period, chapters 12-19 the second half (p. 27). Morris holds that the 24 elders are men, the locust-like beings of chapter 9 are demonic spirits, the two witnesses of chapter 11 are Enoch and Elijah who have waited in heaven in their natural bodies [?] since departing this earth. Babylon in chapters 17-18 is the literal, rebuilt city of Babylon on the Euphrates as a world center of trade, communications, education, etc. (pp. 348-49), the rider on the white horse of 6:2 is Christ who is on the white horse in 19:11, etc. Morris is fairly thorough in taking things literally and gives his reasons, but allows for symbolism, e. g. the woman (12:1), the white horse (6:2; 19:11), the two-edged sword, etc. There is sometimes an indefiniteness (lack of clarity) in who the "overcomer" is, at times sounding like some more faithful among the saved (p. 59) but sometimes every redeemed person (pp. 227, 443).

Mounce, Robert. *The Book of Revelation* **(NICNT). Grand Rapids: Eerdmans, 1977.**

This is a very well-written, fine commentary based on exceptional awareness of views and literature. Tentatively Mounce accepts authorship by John the Apostle, son of Zebedee, and a date of ca. A. D. 95-96. Mounce holds that there can be elements of various views – preterist, historicist, futurist, idealist – but that John's predictions, stated in forms from his own culture, will receive a final, total realization in the last days of history. He furnishes a clear, detailed outline (pp. 47-49), an excellent bibliography of commentaries, journal articles, and other works (49-60), and very knowledgeable comments verse by verse showing awareness of main views on problems and giving good detail to many issues, whatever view he finally favors. He holds that the 144,000 are the new Israel, the church, and the number is symbolic of completeness (168-69). The references to other Jewish literature with similar-sounding descriptions is often evident, but one is not always sure a verse in the Revelation has been really explained after all the sincere effort, as the great mountain burning with fire, 8:8, 9 (pp. 186-87). His conviction about the thousand years seems to be finally influenced by Beckwith's amillennial concept. John taught a literal millennium – gave it in that form – but the realization may be not in an actual era of political social history but in a different form, a life of highest union with God in a non-temporal sense (p. 359). His discussion of the millennium in general has a number of turns many premillennialists cannot easily figure. He gathers choice citations in ancient Jewish writings about the length of a temporary reign.

Newell, William R. *The Book of Revelation*. Chicago: Moody, 1935.

This is a premillennial, dispensational study which takes a thorough-going literal approach to the book. It is good on the English text and will have its main usefulness in some points for lay people. Read Ironside and Ryrie to maintain a balance in a lighter dispensational work.

Pate, C. Marvin, ed. *Four Views on the Book of Revelation*. Grand Rapids: Zondervan, 1998.

After an introduction, Pate, Prof. of Bible at Moody Bible Institute, contributes a chapter favoring a progressive dispensational approach. Then follow Kenneth Gentry, Jr. (preterist perspective), Sam Hamstra, Jr. (idealist), and Robert L. Thomas (classical dispensationalist). Each contributor argues for and defends his orientation in a survey of how he believes it is borne out in the Revelation. Those studying the book gain orientating benefits of comparing as they weigh very different lines of interpreting the Bible's last book.

Phillips, John. *Exploring Revelation. An Expository Commentary* (The John Phillips Commentary Series). Grand Rapids: Kregel, 1974, rp 2001.

Here is a very light dispensational work, often alliterative, picturesque, with frequent illustrations (some quite good), but scant in supporting interpretation. Often Phillips shows no real attempt to grapple with meaning, as on leaving the first love (2:4), being blotted out (3:5), identifying the seven stars, giving more than opinion on being kept in 3:10, who the overcomer is in 2:7, what 4:1 means, etc. He does take the 24 elders as angels (86) and the 144,000 as Israelites, both with shallow support. The work as a whole offers minimal light to help any but elemental readers grasp some points, and for others is pretty much a waste of time unless certain illustrations help.

Poythress, Vern S. *The Returning King. A Guide to the Book of Revelation*. Phillipsburg, NJ: Presbyterian & Reformed Publishing, 2000.

A 213-pp. amillennial pb, this includes an introduction of normal matters such as four schools of interpretation (very general and thin). Poythress, without much except opinion, prefers a combination of elements from the views, and a repeated pattern of events in the first century, now, and in the final crisis (37). He opts for angels in 2:1 with little evidence, is ambiguous about who the overcomer is (2:7, "faithful saints"?), has no mention of leaving the first love (2:4), gives no help on the book of life (3:5), generalizes on those kept in 3:10, and thinks the horsemen in Rev. 6 "correspond to" the four living creatures (?) and the four horsemen of Zech. 1:8 (meaning what?). He views the first four seal trends as realized in Roman Empire tumults, occurring also now, and again to occur just before Christ's Second Coming. The 144,000 are all of God's people, the multitude in 7:9 the same, the woman in Chap. 12 this same group, the millennium is today, etc. One finds in very brief opinion generally what he finds in Aune, Beale, Colclasure, Hendriksen, Kistemaker, Metzger, etc.

Ramsay, William. *The Letters to the Seven Churches of Asia*. Grand Rapids: Baker, 1985rp of 1905 ed. and reprint in 1963. 446 pp.

This is the outstanding older work on the historical background of the churches in chapters 2-3. The student will obtain much rich detail here to lend colorful vividness to his preaching and teaching. Ramsay takes the preterist point of view on the book. Colin Hemer's 1986 work now surpasses this in updating on scholarly discussion and discovery and in comments on some details. Until Hemer and Yamauchi, this was the outstanding work.

Rosenthal, Marvin. *The Pre-Wrath Rapture of the Church*. Nashville: Thomas Nelson, 1990. 319 pp.

A frequent speaker at Bible conferences on prophecy, Rosenthal was for thirty years a firm pre-tribulationalist but here shows in detail his arguments for turning to a new view. He reasons that the church will not escape all of the oppression in the future tribulation period by being raptured to heaven, but will be taken out of the earth when the wrath begins sometime well into the second half of the seven years. His view requires re-defining many aspects of prophecy and 20 chapters to expound. Cf. Karleen (this list) for other works for the Rosenthal kind of view, or Karleen's and Showers' arguing that it is not correct.

Ryrie, Charles C. *Revelation*. Chicago: Moody, 1968.

This work is included because it offers a quick yet lucid and competent study of Revelation in a well-organized way. It lays out the various parts of the book in a simple fashion and the comments are brief and to the point, yet briefly offer solutions to many of the difficult problems of exposition. It would help the average church member gain a perspective of prophecy as taught in the final book of Scripture, and then he could go on to more detailed study such as by Walvoord or greater detail in Thomas. Ryrie is dispensational. Other shorter dispensational works are by Feinberg, W. Smith, and Walvoord in the briefer of his two studies.

Scott, Walter. *Exposition of the Revelation of Jesus Christ*. Westwood, NJ: Revell (n. d.).

A helpful older premillennial work that is at some points lucid in expounding the meaning.

Seiss, J. A. *Lectures on the Apocalypse*, 3 volumes. Grand Rapids: Zondervan, 1957. Reprint in one volume.

An expository older premillennial work of great detail on units of the book.

Thomas, Robert L. *Revelation 1-7; Revelation 8-22: An Exegetical Commentary* (Wycliffe Exegetical Commentary). Chicago: Moody Press, 1992.

Thomas did 2 volumes in this most exegetically detailed yet premillennial effort. The field is one of his specialties since his Th. D. dissertation, "The Argument of The Book of Revelation." He brings more than thirty years of Greek teaching expertise to the task. He argues for authorship by the Apostle John (pp. 2-19) and a date of ca. A. D. 95 (20-23). His wide interaction looks at issues fairly and carefully. A good section explores hermeneutics for interpreting the Apocalypse (29-39). He employs his own translation verse by verse. He deals in considerable detail with many interpretive issues, gives reasons for views, is clear, and follows a detailed outline. He favors seeing the Lord's day (1:10) as Sunday, sees in 1:19 a three-fold division of the book due to grammar, opts for human messengers in 1:20, and sees a mixed group in the churches (some genuinely saved, others only professors). He looks penetratingly at views on Nicolaitans (2:6), sees "the overcomer" as applicable to all genuinely saved persons, reasoning this out with awareness of relevant factors, and prefers taking "crown of life" in 2:10 as a genitive of apposition, "crown which is (eternal) life," understood as received through grace and not merit. Thomas favors a pre-tribulational removal of the church in 3:10, devoting six pages to an appraisal of arguments for views. The twenty-four elders are exalted celestial beings. The white horse rider of 6:2 is decided, after a long evaluation of views, to personify a movement or force working against the Messiah's interests in the future tribulation period. He defends the view that the 144,000 in chapter 7 are distinctively certain men of Israel, not the church, etc. Thomas devotes much detail to defending a premillennial view on such issues as the two witnesses, seals, trumpets and bowls, the thousand years after the Second Event, etc.

Tickle, J. *The Book of Revelation. A Catholic Interpretation of the Apocalypse.* Liguori, MO: Liguori Publications, 1983. 143 pp.

The Rector of the Immaculate Heart of Mary Cathedral, Los Cruces, New Mexico gives a Roman Catholic interpretation of the symbols and the message.

Trench, R. C. *Commentary on the Epistles to the Seven Churches.* NY: Macmillan, 1861.

This is another work which will be profitable at times in a study of chapters 2-3. Trench is helpful in the Greek, and also on customs and detail about older views, many of which are still held today.

Walvoord, John F. *The Revelation of Jesus Christ.* Chicago: Moody, 1966.

Written by one of the foremost modern-day articulators of premillennial dispensationalism, this book is a lucid exposition of the Revelation which combines textual exposition with theological orientation. Walvoord shows awareness of wide reading, gives various views, is fair, and deals with problems as they arise. It is the best broad dispensational work to appear in recent years, and Robert Thomas has the best detailed technical work so far.

Wainwright, Arthur W. *Mysterious Apocalypse: Interpreting the Book of Revelation.* Nashville: Abingdon Press, 1993.

One meets with a broad, detailed examination of the history of how writers have interpreted the Book of Revelation. Of course this also appears in a number of the more detailed commentaries, in their introductions, and to some degree in works (in this list) by Couch, Gregg, Pate, etc.

Walvoord, John F. "Revelation," in *Bible Knowledge Commentary*, **ed. John F. Walvoord and Roy B. Zuck, Volume II. Wheaton: Victor Books, 1985.**

This is a condensed statement of views Walvoord develops in his larger work, *The Revelation of Jesus Christ*. It is, then, premillennial and dispensational.

Wilcock, Michael. *I Saw Heaven Opened: The Message of Revelation* **(Bible Speaks Today). Downers Grove: IVP, 1975. 223 pp.**

A work that lucidly explains symbolism here and favors an amillennial view.

Yamauchi, Edwin M. *The Archaeology of the New Testament Cities in Western Asia Minor.* **Grand Rapids: Baker, 1980.**

A respected evangelical scholar has researched at length on historical background and customs in Ephesus, Pergamus, Sardis and Laodicea. The expositor planning a message or series in this part of Scripture will find substantial background help here, as on all the seven churches in Ramsay and Hemer.

Also available from Kress Christian Publications

The Gromacki Expository Series, by Dr. Robert Gromacki
- *Called to Be Saints: An Exposition of 1 Corinthians*
- *Stand Firm in the Faith: An Exposition of 2 Corinthians*
- *Stand Fast in Liberty: An Exposition of Galatians*
- *Stand United in Joy: An Exposition of Philippians*
- *Stand Perfect in Wisdom: An Exposition of Colossians & Philemon*
- *Stand True to the Charge: An Exposition of 1 Timothy*
- *Stand Bold in Grace: An Exposition of Hebrews*

Notes for the Study and Exposition of 1 John, by Eric Kress
"I have found this treatment of 1 John very helpful in my own preparation. It is concise, well outlined, and detailed enough in the text to get at the right interpretation.", Dr. John MacArthur, Pastor and Teacher, Grace Community Church, Sun Valley, CA.

For more information and other titles, visit www.kresschristianpublications.com